The New Testament

BIBLICAL COMMENTARY

ON

THE NEW TESTAMENT,

BY

DR. HERMANN OLSHAUSEN,

PROFESSOR OF THEOLOGY IN THE UNIVERSITY OF ERLANGEN.

TRANSLATED FROM THE GERMAN

FOR CLARK'S FOREIGN AND THEOLOGICAL LIBRARY.

FIRST AMERICAN EDITION.

REVISED AFTER THE FOURTH GERMAN EDITION,

BY

A. C. KENDRICK, D.D.,

PROFESSOR OF GREEK IN THE UNIVERSITY OF ROCHESTER.

TO WHICH IS PREFIXED OLSHAUSEN'S

PROOF OF THE GENUINENESS OF THE WRITINGS OF THE NEW TESTAMENT.

TRANSLATED BY DAVID FOSDICK, JR.

VOL. III

NEW YORK:

SHELDON & COMPANY, PUBLISHERS,

498 & 500 BROADWAY.

1866.

STEREOTYPED BY
THOMAS B. SMITH,
82 & 84 Beekman-street, N. Y.

PRINTED BY
PUDNEY & RUSSELL,
79 John-street.

TABLE OF CONTENTS.

FIRST PART.

OF THE SUFFERINGS AND DEATH OF JESUS CHRIST.

[CONTINUED FROM VOLUME II.]

SECOND PART.

OF THE RESURRECTION OF JESUS CHRIST.

COMMENTARY ON THE ACTS OF THE APOSTLES.

FIRST PART.

FROM THE ASCENSION OF CHRIST TO THE CONVERSION OF PAUL.

SECOND PART.

FROM PAUL'S CONVERSION TILL HIS SECOND MISSIONARY JOURNEY.

THIRD PART.

FROM PAUL'S THIRD MISSIONARY JOURNEY TILL THE FIRST CAPTIVITY AT ROME.

GENERAL INTRODUCTION TO THE EPISTLES OF ST. PAUL.

THE EPISTLE TO THE ROMANS—INTRODUCTION.

FIRST PART.

THE INTRODUCTION.

(i. 1-17.)

SECOND PART.

THE DOCTRINAL EXPOSITION.

(i. 18—xi. 36.)

A. SECTION I.

On the Sinfulness of the Human Race.—(i. 18—iii. 20.)

B. SECTION II.

The Description of the New Way of Salvation in Christ.—(iii. 21—v. 11.)

C. SECTION III.

Of the Vicarious Office of Christ.—(v. 12—vii. 6.)

ORDER OF THE SECTIONS OF THE GOSPELS IN VOLUME III.

ARRANGED AFTER EACH GOSPEL.

ST MATTHEW.

ST. MARK.

ST. LUKE.

ST. JOHN.

ACTS OF THE APOSTLES.

ROMANS.

COMMENTARY

ON

THE GOSPELS.

---

§ 1. The Last Meal of Jesus with his Disciples, Continued.

Ver. 29.—As his true disciples, and children of the Spirit, the Saviour bequeaths the kingdom to them as an inheritance. The strict signification of διατίθεμαι (whence διαθήκη, Testament) must be retained, and can in no way (as Kuinoel, Henneberg, and others would have it) be resolved into the general signification "to promise." It is precisely the analogy of the transmission of earthly dominion from Father to Son, that leads to the idea of an inheritance which the Lord again at his departure leaves to his disciples as a sacred legacy. (Comp. remarks on John xvii. 22.)

Ver. 30.—The manner in which the kingdom is described evidently forbids the supposition, as was previously remarked, that the apostles were completely involved in the Jewish notions of the Messiah, for if such were the case, the Saviour would not assuredly have confirmed them in their errors. (Comp. the observations upon the ἐσθίειν καὶ πίνειν in Matth. viii. 11, xxvi. 29; Luke xiv. 15. Upon the καθίζειν ἐπὶ θρόνων, κ. τ. λ. Matth. xix. 28 in the Commentary.) The words ἐν τῇ βασιλείᾳ μου are wanting in very good codices. Perhaps to many transcribers they seemed superfluous, after the ἐπὶ τῆς τραπέζης μου. The reading καθίσησθε, and the usual one καθίσεσθε, in respect of authorities are about equal. But the origin of the former is more simply explained than that of the latter; for the preceding ἐσθίητε καὶ πίνητε easily accounts for καθίσησθε being written. It is not inconceivable, that the words which follow, addressed to Peter, as related by Luke, were spoken immediately after. But as was observed in our general survey of the sequence of events in the Lord's supper, the parallel passages in John xii. 31–38 render this supposition improbable. For as John preserves the order of sequence very accurately, whilst Luke, in this part of his history, evidently neglects it, and it is incredible that the Lord would have uttered the same or entirely similar words twice in reference to the same event; we must, with John, transfer the passages in Luke xxii. 31–38, more towards the end of the repast, to which their import is perfectly suited. Luke has here merely delivered in an abridged form the elements of the discourse in which finally very interesting thoughts are preserved to us.

In accordance with the sequence of the individual events in the supper as above ascertained, the next incident of the feast which claims our attention is the complaint of the Lord concerning the betrayer, which was followed by his withdrawal (Matth. xxvi. 21, seq.; Mark xiv. 18, seq.; John xiii. 21, seq.; Luke xxii. 21–23). This connects itself most fitly and suitably with the Saviour's previous promise to his faithful disciples; his joy on their account must, by contrast, have awakened his sorrow for the conduct of the traitor.

With regard to the less suitable position of the words which belong to this event in Luke, the necessary explanation has been already given. The narrative of John, however, as was elsewhere remarked, comes under discussion here: for the variations in the accounts which become comprehensible only through John's narration, require a special synoptical treatment. For instance Luke not only places the words concerning the traitor too late—since he represents them as having been uttered after the supper—but also merely gives them by allusion. Matthew and Mark, indeed, give them more expressly, but their account might lead to the supposition that Jesus had openly and aloud uttered the words *ὁ ἐμβάψας μετ' ἐμοῦ, οὗτός με παραδώσει, he that hath dipped with me*, etc. John alone makes the whole proceeding plain by his statement. But in Matth. xxvi. 25, one fact appears to have been supplied which is wanting in John; our attention will now be turned to the manner in which this fact may be annexed to the history.

Ver. 21, 22.—During the meal (*ἐσθιόντων αὐτῶν*) the Lord was powerfully affected with sorrow and depression of mind, at the reflection that one of his disciples would betray him. (John xiii. 21, *ἐταράχθη τῷ πνεύματι.*) From design, however, he now expressed these thoughts openly, partly perhaps in the hope that the power of his sorrowing love might yet affect the heart of the ill-fated disciple—(compare on this the particulars at Luke xxii. 22)—and in the event of the contrary happening, to occasion his withdrawal, by informing him that his black design was discovered. But even here the Saviour exercised the highest forbearance; for he did not complain of Judas's conduct to the other disciples, much less did he express indignation against the traitor himself, or upbraid him for his iniquity, but allowed him to depart under a convenient pretext (John xiii. 27, seq.)

Ver. 23.—The disciples, dismayed at this disclosure of their master, and in their innocence rather seeking the guilt in themselves* than charging it on any one else, though they might have in some measure anticipated the behaviour of Judas, ask Jesus (*ἀπορούμενοι περὶ τίνος λέγει*, John xiii. 22), "Is it I?"

According to the account of Matthew and Mark, the Lord appears to have given a thoroughly explicit answer to this question, since he says, "He who dippeth with me in the dish, he it is." But, in the first place, the question of Judas, "Whether it was he?" Matth. xxvi. 25, appears on this supposition altogether superfluous; and, secondly, this open answer is in contradiction to the forbearing manner in which John represents the Saviour to have acted.

We must, therefore, without doubt, complete the narratives of Matthew and Mark from that of John. To the question of John, which Peter suggested, Jesus replied, *in a low voice*, "He it is for whom I shall sop a morsel." Even thus, a discrepancy still remains, but really an unessential one. According to Matthew and Mark, Judas at that instant dipped in the dish with Jesus. According to John, Jesus dipped a morsel and handed it to Judas. But to this unessential difference no importance whatever can be attached. It is sufficiently explained by supposing, that in order to avoid mentioning Judas by name, Jesus gave John a sign by which he might know the betrayer. At all events, however, we must say that John has certainly given the correct account of the occurrence; the other two Evangelists have narrated it in a somewhat modified manner. The view defended by Henneberg, according to which the *ὁ ἐμβάψας μετ' ἐμοῦ* in Matthew and Mark merely signifies, "One of my household companions, who daily eats and drinks with me," is altogether erroneous; for that applied to each of the disciples, and would therefore have been no answer whatever to the question, "Is it I?"

Finally, the dipping of the sop took place, as related by John, in entire accordance with the customs of the feast. The head of the family took from the passover cake a piece (*ψωμίον*), dipped it in the bitter liquor (חֲרוֹסֶת) and gave it to the persons at table in turn. Hence if we suppose that at the question of John, "who is it?" the turn of Judas was just come, then the selection of this particular sign is simply explained from the occasion. (*Τρύβλιον* or *τρυβλίον*, is explained by Suidas through *πινάκιον*, patina, paropsis. In the LXX. for קְעָרָה, Exodus xxv. 29.)

The discourse of Christ now connects the destiny of the Son of Man with a higher necessity, Luke xxii. 22—*κατὰ τὸ ὡρισμένον*, scil. *ὑπὸ τοῦ θεοῦ*. This necessity is the will and ordination of God which

* But John and Peter, who were most developed in character amongst the disciples, were clear to themselves, that, in them, the possibility of such a deed could not be supposed. They appear to have asked, not "Is it I?" but merely, "Who is it?"

are made known in the prophecies of Scripture. Matthew and Mark have "as it is written concerning him" (*καθὼς γέγραπται περὶ αὐτοῦ*). Compare upon the prophecies here meant, Luke xxiv. 26, 27; 1 Cor. xv. 4. The *ὑπάγειν* in Matthew and Mark, like *πορεύεσθαι* in Luke, agrees with the Hebrew הָלַךְ in the signification, "to die." (Compare Genesis xv. 2.) But the necessity of the Lord's will being accomplished in its purely objective aspect, does not destroy the man's subjective free agency. Compare observations on Matth. xxvi. 54. There is no predestination of evil; compare Commentary, Part I. on Matth. x. 1, xiii. 10, seq., xxiv. 1. Hence, therefore, the curse of the Lord comes upon "him through whom the Son of Man goeth." The form of execration: "it were good for him," etc., is an expression of the deepest abandonment, of utter perdition. It is so strong, that it intimates the exclusion of *every hope.* For the winning, no matter how late, of eternal life, must assuredly render it a blessing to be born. The declaration "It were better for him that he had never been born," may be regarded as the strongest among all the expressions of Scripture in support of the doctrine of eternal perdition. (Compare John xvii. 12; *υἱὸς τῆς ἀπωλείας*. In the Old Testament, Job iii. 11; Jeremiah xv. 10, xx. 14. (Upon the development of evil in Judas, and upon his condemnation in general, compare the particulars at Matth. xxvii. 9.) John further subjoins a remarkable statement, xiii. 27, in the parallel passage "after the sop then Satan entered into him" (*μετὰ τὸ ψωμίον τότε εἰσῆλθεν εἰς ἐκεῖνον ὁ Σατανᾶς*). These words refer back to John xiii. 2, and at Luke xxii. 3, have a real parallel. From the comparison of these passages, we may infer that the expression *entered* is not to be strained, for Luke speaks of the entrance of the Devil into the heart of Judas, in the same connexion in which John first uses the expression, "he put the thought into his heart," *i. e.*, exercised upon him a more subtle, less immediate influence. The meaning of the statement then is clear and intelligible; it expresses the lowest depth of moral debasement. But I cannot assent to the observations of Lücke (Part II. p. 482), where he terms the expression a *figurative* one. With the same propriety we might designate the operation of the Holy Ghost a figurative expression, which Lücke, however, will not acknowledge.*

* Lücke, on this subject, in his second edition, remarks, that "He does not call the agency of the Devil a figurative expression; but the particular words *εἰσῆλθεν εἰς ἐκεῖνον ὁ Σατανᾶς*." This certainly is an important distinction. I acknowledge that I previously understood his words as Schleiermacher interprets them; that, every mention of the Devil and his agency was explainable from a tropical usus loquendi. Yet, even of the *εἰσῆλθεν εἰς*, I cannot concede that it is a mere figure, *i. e.*, a figure without a real truth corresponding to it.

Certainly we must not conceive the workings of the Devil *materially*; by this I mean, that they must not be reduced from a purely spiritual influence to a material one more or

If the existence of a kingdom of darkness is certain, its agency must also be admitted, and that an altogether real though not a material agency. Perhaps it was to guard against gross material views of the operations of the world of evil, that the aforesaid scholar selected the above expression. But such passages are important, especially in John, for they shew that in the gospel he teaches the same doctrine concerning the Devil which he expresses in the Revelation, and which all the writers of the New Testament support.

According to John's observation, the accomplishment of the dark deed of Judas followed immediately upon his receiving the sop from the Redeemer (μετὰ τὸ ψωμίον). It is not improbable that he either understood the question put by the Evangelist to Christ, or suspected its import, when taken in connexion with the subsequent action of Jesus; and that this inflamed his malignity. But it must ever remain worthy of consideration, that this presenting of the bread to Judas proved to him *a curse*, as immediately after, in the supper the bread was to the faithful disciples the medium of *blessing*.

Ver. 25.—In conclusion, Matthew remarks that Judas also asked the Lord "Is it I?" and that the Lord answered plainly σὺ εἶπας (precisely similar in the Latin, "tu dixti;" compare Plaut. Mercat. 1, 2, 52.) This statement seems to stand in contradiction to John xiii. 28, according to which passage the design of Judas remained unknown to all the disciples. The simplest explanation of this, is the supposition that Judas, agitated with shame and wrath at seeing himself detected, probably stammered out also the same question as the other disciples; but either they did not observe it, or else both it and the answer of Jesus were uttered briefly and in a low voice, so as not to fix the attention of the disciples.

John and Peter however knew him to be the traitor, but they might not have thought that the moment for executing his design was so near. According to John's account, which on this point is very careful, the Redeemer himself called upon Judas to hasten the prosecution of his purpose (ὃ ποιεῖς, ποίησον τάχιον). In these words, it is self-evident, there is no incitement to the deed, but only a summons to withdraw from the circle of his disciples, and hasten the accomplishment of that upon which he had already determined. The disciples might easily misunderstand the meaning of these words; and John himself, who knew that Judas was

less subtil. But, as the operations of the Devil are to be deemed real generally, so also is the *entering* (εἰσέρχεσθαι). As the sacred influences of the Spirit of God gradually take possession of a man, until God himself makes his abode in the man, so also the evil powers of darkness. As God, although he must be regarded as the supreme personality, enters and makes his abode in *created* personalities; so also the Prince of Darkness enters into the souls of those who lay themselves open to his influence.

the traitor, might not have thought, as has been remarked, that the completion of the treason was so near. Hence they formed different surmises concerning his withdrawal, but by no means probable ones; for, as it was already night, purchases could not be made, nor even alms distributed conveniently. (Upon γλωσσόκομον, consult the remarks on John xii. 6.) John concludes his account with the picturesque words "and it was night" (ἦν δὲ νύξ), which along with the chronological reference to the closing day, suggest also the idea that it was the season in which darkness had power. (Luke xxii. 53.) Upon the retirement of the representative of darkness from the Lord's presence, his love, like a long-restrained stream, broke forth in the words, "Now is the Son of Man glorified," etc., the exposition of which we have already given at John xiii. 31, et seq.

To the following words in John (and other passages), the elements of a discourse which Luke alone gives, xxii. 31–38, bear a great resemblance. Only that the former for the most part omits what is personal, up to the passage John xiii. 36–38, and gives rather what is general; whilst Luke, on the other hand, narrates more in detail what had direct reference to Peter; on this account, both narratives may be easily explained independently of each other.

This conversation of the Lord with Peter follows very appropriately upon the complaint concerning the betrayer. The latter entirely succumbed under the temptation. Peter, on the contrary—although by his natural diposition exposed to the assaults of the enemy, and though he fell, yet, in the radical and essential integrity of his soul, he had power, through faith and repentance, to rise once more from his fall; nay, that very event was to work for his highest good by thoroughly subduing his old nature, and thus preparing him to become an efficient labourer in the kingdom of God. The admonition on the part of the Saviour, of his approaching fall must also have produced a beneficent humiliation in the Apostle's mind, and restrained him from all exultation over the unhappy Judas.

This conversation must also have occurred before the institution of the supper, for according to Matth. xxvi. 30, the hymn with which the supper concluded immediately preceded the departure to the Mount of Olives, and the extended discourses recorded by John chaps. xiv.—xvii., in which these words cannot be included, had been pronounced previously.

But, above all, the question still arises, how are the words (Matth. xxvi. 30–35; Mark xiv. 26–31) to be connected with the preceding passage of Luke? Both the Evangelists, Matth. xxvi. 30, and Mark xiv. 26, place the words after the conclusion of the supper, so that they might have been spoken, perhaps, on the way to the Mount of Olives. It is very possible indeed that the Redeemer reverted again to the same circumstance, and John xvi. 31, 32, seems to indicate something of the kind. I must, however, confess, that in consequence of the demonstrably close connexion with the passage in Luke, it appears to me more probable that the whole was delivered in one connected discourse. It will be at least convenient in our exposition to consider the account of Matthew and Mark at the same time with that of Luke, for in all essential particulars they are identical.

The discourse of Jesus, when Judas had left the room, might well commence with the general observation "*all* ye shall be offended" (π ά ν τ ε ς ὑμεῖς σκανδαλισθήσεσθε), Matth. xxvi. 31, which forms an antithesis with the above "*one* of you" etc. (ε ἷ ς ἐξ ὑμῶν παραδώσει με). (Matth. xxvi. 21.) The discourse is evidently intended to damp every self-approving emotion. (Upon σκανδαλίζεσθαι, compare the Commentary, Part I. on Matth. xviii. 6.) The necessity of this phenomenon, the Lord refers to a prophecy in the Old Testament, Zech. xiii. 7. The passage is, in its connexion, like the last chapters of Zechariah generally, very difficult. It contains, however, unmistakeable references to the Messiah, as Christ's employment of it in the passage under discussion clearly shews. The accounts of Matthew and Mark accord exactly in the citation; (Matthew merely subjoins τῆς ποίμνης). This agreement again is a hint which directs to some sort of use which, according to this citation, Mark might have made of Matthew; for the LXX. read: πατάξατε τοὺς ποιμένας καὶ ἐκσπάσατε τὰ πρόβατα. (The Alexandrine MS. reads πάταξον and διασκορπισθήσονται. But this, perhaps, is a correction after the citation in the New Testament.) The Hebrew text has the imperative of the singular הַךְ. But the hypothesis which has been put forth, of a proverbial usage of the words, is evidently forbidden by the γέγραπται γάρ, *for it is written.* The thought implies, finally, the uniting, connecting, sustaining work of Christ. He is the living, power-diffusing centre of his church, as it were the heart of the body. If he suffer, all suffer with him. The incidental intimation that the Lord would, after the resurrection, go into Galilee (Matth. xxvi. 32), will be touched upon at the passages, Matth. xxviii. 7; Mark xvi. 7. Here the only question is, "How are we to understand the connexion of these words in Matthew and Mark?" They manifestly indicate to the dispersed disciples a general place of rendezvous. "There, in Galilee," Jesus means to say, "you shall again see me after the dispersion."

From the general words of Christ, "*all* ye," etc. (πάντες ὑμεῖς σκανδαλισθήσεσθε), the reply of Peter ("though all be offended yet will not I,") forms a natural transition to the special address to him (Luke xxii. 31). "It is precisely *thou*," answers Jesus, "who art destined to the sorest conflict." The expression "Satan hath sought you that he may sift you as wheat" (ὁ σατανᾶς ἐξῃτήσατο ὑμᾶς τοῦ σινιάσαι ὡς τὸν σῖτον) expresses the following idea: "There are in the course of our moral development moments in which man is assailed by the whole power of evil, with all its temptations. In such moments, whatever is really good in the man survives the test; but what is impure becomes also manifest. This discriminating agency is referred to the Representative of evil (Satan), for the reason that sin in all its forms is regarded as subject to him; the Divine agency assumes the merely negative form of yielding to the world of sin, of holding back the powers of grace. (Comp. the extended representation in the prologue to Job, which corresponds entirely with this idea.) The object of such sifting is, first, the establishing and perfecting of goodness in its elements; and, secondly, the ripening of the germs of evil, in order that they may be finally separated.

The reference of Satan to human personages, whether to Sanhedrists, or to Judas himself, who might have sought to lead the other disciples astray, is to be rejected here, as also in the account of the Lord's temptation, as without either historical or exegetical support. Compare Matth. xvi. 23. (Σινιάσαι, occurs only here. It comes from σίνιον, *Vannus*, a winnowing-machine. Compare Matth. iii. 12. In sense it is equivalent to πειράζειν, but denotes the strongest forms of temptation.)

Ver. 32.—In this sifting, Judas proved like chaff. Peter was made to fall, but in faith he raised himself again. Of this the Lord admonished him prophetically, and refers the victory of his faith to his own prayer in his behalf. This remarkable reflection leads to the subject of intercession. For we cannot here prevent the question arising, did the Saviour pray for Judas also? On this the Scripture gives no decided statements. But from the idea of intercession the question may be answered in the following manner.

Intercession, even that of the Saviour himself, must be regarded as not intended to destroy the free agency of those for whom it is made. It is well calculated therefore to sustain the resolution of a mind determined toward goodness, but it cannot *constrain* to good, the resisting disposition in the mind. Hence it is a rational hypothesis that whilst Judas yet hesitated within himself whether or not he should yield himself up to the black purposes of his heart, so long may the Lord have followed him with prayer that the victory might incline to the better side. But, after he had wholly resigned himself in will to those purposes, the act was already virtually performed; and, in that case, the power of the Spirit could only prove detrimental by aggravating the guilt of Judas, who was now desperately determined in opposition to its impulse. (Compare on this subject the direct reference in 1 John v. 16, where prayer for him who has committed a sin unto death is represented as unnecessary.)

When this surrender on the part of Judas took place, cannot be decisively determined. According to John xiii. 11, Jesus knew absolutely that Judas was to be his betrayer; and, according to vi. 64, knew it even from the beginning, that is, from the calling. Now the prayer for Peter had for its object his perseverance in the faith, not his fidelity nor his preservation from the fall. The fall, like a salutary crisis in a perilous disease, seems to have been necessary for Peter, in order thoroughly to destroy the old man in him, and to achieve a permanent victory for the new. To raise himself immediately again from his fall, it was only necessary that Peter should firmly maintain his faith in the Lord's forgiving love. On his recovery from the fall, through faith and repentance (compare remarks at Matth. xxvi. 75), therefore depended his efficiency. He, the rock of faith, after his conversion, was to strengthen the weak in faith. These words of Christ, "I have prayed for thee," etc., are also, in so far, very important, as they shew that faith is not the work of man, but the work of God in him. Man's work is merely not to strive against the faith-producing power of God. (The "brethren" (ἀδελφοί) are all Christians generally, the Apostles and immediate friends of the Lord not excluded. "The Acts of the Apostles," shew that it was Peter who strengthened the wavering faith of the other disciples. 'Επιστρέφειν, = שׁוּב, is here to be understood as meaning μετάνοια, that is, spiritual conversion. Kuinoel's observation that the first mention of the fall of Peter occurs at verse 34, is very easily explained when we reflect that the ἵνα μὴ ἐκλείπῃ ἡ πίστις σου presupposes the fall. The MSS. D.K, and many others, have the reading ἐκλίπῃ, but ἐκλείπῃ is better ascertained.)

Ver. 33, 34.—The natural security of Peter, and his confidence in his own power and good intentions, were so great that he did not attend even to this premonition of the Saviour. Yet Jesus forewarned him of his denial most unequivocally. Here we are not at all to conjecture any insincerity in the mind of Peter. He meant ingenuously what he professed. But in his inexperience he knew not how often, with the permission of God, all inward power fails to man, and how, in such a state of inward nakedness and destitution, an humble faith in the power of God alone can accomplish the victory. In the momentary feeling of his power, and in proud self-confidence, he believed himself invincible, even in the most severe conflict. (Mark, in the passage parallel to this, xiv. 30, writes, ἢ δὶς ἀλέκτορα φωνῆσαι, *before the cock crows twice*. This expression goes upon the supposition that the cock crows about midnight, and then again towards morning. [Φωνεῖν, = קָרָא.] On this account the morning watch was named *ἀλεκτοροφωνία*, *cock-crowing*, Mark xiii. 35.) According to Matthew xxvi. 35, Peter, conscious of his own sincerity, did not receive in quiet this distinct announcement of his fall, but boasted once more that he would accompany Jesus even to death. Such self-will, bordering upon obstinacy, entirely accords with the character of Peter; there is therefore nothing improbable in this statement of Matthew.

Ver. 35-38.—The following passage, which is peculiar to Luke, is involved in much obscurity. Christ evidently means to represent his approaching passion as the profoundest depth of his humiliation. To that conclusion we are led by ver. 37, in which the *καὶ μετὰ ἀνόμων ἐλογίσθη*, *and he was reckoned among transgressors*, from Isaiah liii. 12, adds to the general idea of the suffering and death of the Lord, still further the particular one (*ἔτι τοῦτο*) that he should die, not as a righteous person, but with the appearance of unrighteousness, and amongst malefactors. (The LXX. read here: *ἐν τοῖς ἀνόμοις*. We must, further, not lose sight of the fact that our Lord himself explains this passage from Isaiah liii. as referring to himself, which, for the general view of that important chapter, is of the utmost consequence. Τελεσθῆναι has here a like signification with *πληρωθῆναι*; as has *τέλος ἔχειν* with *πληροῦσθαι*. But it is remarkable that the fulfilment of all the prophecies referring to the Lord (*τὰ περὶ ἐμοῦ*) should be associated with this point of time, even previous to the arrest. For the Scriptures prophesy, also, of the Lord's coming in his glory; and even of particular incidents in the sufferings of the Lord, *e. g.*, "*I thirst*," and "*A bone of him shall not be broken*," John xix. 28–36, which were fulfilled subsequently. The simplest explanation is, that the Saviour probably comprehended the prospective sufferings which should end his earthly being as one continued act. The expression *τὰ περὶ ἐμοῦ τέλος ἔχει* should then be rendered in the following manner, "What stands written of me, as regards this earthly life, with all which it involves, is being fulfilled." Thus the events, apparently still future, are included in the present.) The Saviour now contrasts this last disastrous time, in which darkness had power (Luke xxii. 53) with the former times of blessing. The description of that time of blessing is expressed in words taken from the instructions given to the Apostles, Matth. x. 9, 10. (Compare the Commentary, Part I. on this passage.) All external things were then supplied to them without care, and this external abundance was a type of the power of the Spirit abounding within them. But with this time of blessing now stands in contrast the time of conflict and necessity, in which they must carefully provide all that they are able to procure.

So far, then, the connexion is clear, and the meaning of the figurative discourse easily intelligible.* But the subjoined ὁ μὴ ἔχων πωλησάτω τὸ ἱμάτιον αὐτοῦ καὶ ἀγορασάτω μάχαιραν, *let him that hath not*, etc., together with the remark of the disciples, and the answer of Jesus, present a difficulty. First: as regards the μὴ ἔχων, it evidently stands in contrast with the ἔχων, but the object of this antithesis does not appear. This difficulty has led some to the explanation of ἀράτω, "to make away with, to sell." So that the meaning would be, "he who has scrip or purse, let him sell them; he who has them not, let him sell his mantle, and buy a sword." But then the important contrast with verse 35 falls quite away!—not to dwell upon the perversion of language, that αἴρειν should be rendered, "to sell." It is obvious that the Lord means to say, "then might every one leave scrip and purse at home; but now must he who has them take both with him." Hence the passage is better to be understood thus: he who has anything, let him take with him what he can, and also a sword; but he who has nothing, let him seek to supply himself at least with a sword, even at the greatest sacrifices—ἱμάτιον, a symbol of what is most necessary. The μὴ ἔχων may then be taken as equivalent to οὐδὲν ἔχων = אֲשֶׁר אֵין לוֹ.

The second difficulty lies in the mentioning of a sword. It naturally excites surprise that the Saviour, the King of Peace, should wish to incite his friends to external resistance! But, with this, were it at all conceivable, the ἱκανόν ἐστι, *it is enough*, verse 38, would not accord, for there were only two swords, and just as little the words of Christ to Peter, "put up thy sword into the sheath," Matth. xxvi. 52, when he was about to make use of it. Those interpretations of the passage, which assume an error in the translation, or which take μάχαιρα for a butcher's knife, so that it is parallel with βαλάντιον and πήρα, as articles requisite for a journey, are the mere resorts of despair as to the passage. The only correct explanation is that which takes μάχαιρα like βαλάντιον and πήρα, in a figurative sense. The expressions cannot here have reference to journeying, for no journey was contemplated; they merely intimate to them, to hold themselves in a state of preparation, to make ready. In just the same way, μάχαιρα, *sword*, relates to defence, not, however, to bodily, but to spiritual defence. It is therefore the sword of the Spirit that is meant (Eph. vi. 17), with which they should provide themselves.

* Cf. diss. Winterbergii in Velthusen syll., vol. v. p. 104, seq. Here the knot is cut asunder. In this a misunderstanding of Christ's words on the part of the disciples is assumed. De Wette appears altogether obscure and confused in his explication of this passage. He complains that I understand the passage as "figurative, or even in a double sense," and yet his explanation comes out to be nearly the same. At the conclusion ἱκανόν ἐστι is, in the most open manner, explained as it was by me: "In a twofold sense; two swords are enough, and there is enough on this subject. You surely do not understand me." Where, then, is the exegetical consistency?

The meaning of the whole passage, then, is this: "Formerly in the days of blessing, the Lord cared and struggled for you, ye needed not to provide anything; all flowed to you; but henceforth, in the evil days, you must employ all your cares and efforts in order to collect whatever suitable means you possess for subserving the purposes of spiritual life: but especially you need the sword of the Spirit, that you may be able to resist in the evil day, and to maintain the field. Possess yourselves of that sword, therefore, though it cost you the most intense efforts, renounce everything earthly, even that which is most necessary, that you may belong only to that which is imperishable, and to him alone, who is from everlasting, and may receive his power."

(Compare, on the distinction of good and evil days, the remarks on Luke xxii. 53.) Now the disciples misunderstood this concealed meaning of the words of Jesus; they were thinking of iron swords, and replied that they already had some. The Redeemer felt that it would be useless, at such a moment, to enter into extended details which might simplify his meaning; for the disciples were too widely mistaken to allow a hope of bringing them to the right position for forming a proper judgment; he therefore uttered his *ἱκανόν ἐστι, it is enough*, as we give an evasive answer to children, when we feel the impossibility of making ourselves intelligible to them.

The phrase *ἱκανόν ἐστι* includes a kind of double meaning, since it may be taken in reference to the two swords, in the sense "two swords suffice," as well as in reference to the whole dialogue, in the signification, "there is enough on this subject, I see you do not yet understand me." The suggestion of *irony* in the meaning, "Yes, your two swords will do, that will be a fine protection," seems to me unsuited to the solemn earnestness of the Lord. (In the Hebrew, the word רַב corresponds with *ἱκανόν*, in the formulæ; רַב לָכֶם, רַב עַתָּה; or רַב לָךְ compare Gesenius' lexicon, under רַב.)

Finally, The history of the institution of the holy supper, forms the conclusion of the account of the Lord's last meal. (Matth. xxvi. 26–29; Mark xiv. 22–25; Luke xxii. 19, 20—compare with these passages 1 Cor. xi. 23–26.) The immediately preceding exhortations to repentance, and the several admonitions of Jesus, constitute, as it were, the confession sermon, which should lead the disciples to strict self-examination. (1 Cor. xi. 28.) After Judas had withdrawn, and when all that was necessary had been spoken, the Saviour proceeded to the institution of a sacred ordinance, which he left to his church, as an ever-enduring remembrancer, until his second coming.

In the profound and secluded quiet of this little circle of disciples, the Redeemer performed the unostentatious act which was to become of world-wide interest.* But alas! even that repast of love has, up to the present day, been an object of the most violent and long-continued controversies that the history of the church and its doctrines records.† The simple words of the institution have hence been forced to bear meanings the most various and contradictory. Exegesis, however, would utterly mistake its purpose, should it enter into the detail of interpretations which have been invented in support of the views of one party or another; this is the business of dogmatic history. Exegesis ought to seek immediately to transport the reader into that train of ideas which the Saviour must have had in speaking the words, and the disciples in hearing them. True, the interpreter must present openly his individual view in connexion with the prevailing opinions.

First, however, it should not be overlooked that the view entertained by the disciples concerning the Sacrament of the altar, cannot be considered as perfect at the institution of the sacred feast itself. On the contrary, it is most probable that they by no means apprehended the *fulness* of the ideas which the Saviour associated with it. We find them, before the outpouring of the Holy Ghost, still so undeveloped and crude in all their notions, that it is probable they would not, until after that event, fully understand the profound import of the transaction, especially as we have no reason whatever to suppose that Christ connected with the act any explanation of

* The supper has not, as many seem to think, its extraordinary interest in the mere historical fact, that in the course of centuries it has furnished occasion to so much disputation and conjecture, and that millions have regarded, and still regard it, as a precious jewel of the church: but it has its prominent significance purely in itself. One of the profoundest metaphysical problems—the question of the relation of spirit to matter—comes under discussion, as in the doctrines of the resurrection and glorification of the flesh generally, so particularly in that of the holy Supper. From the various fundamental views on this problem developed themselves also the various theories regarding the supper. *Idealism* appears in the Roman Catholic doctrine of transubstantiation, in which matter is volatalized into spirit. *Dualism* is expressed in the view of Zuinglius, in which spirit and matter are rigidly and absolutely dissevered. *Realism* distinguishes, on the contrary, the Luthero-Calvinistic interpretation which neither confounds nor separates spirit and matter, but conceives both as existing in their true connexion and mutual dependence. The doctrine of the two natures in Christ, is, accordingly, the ante-type for the doctrine of the relation of the *higher* and *lower* in the supper. As in Christ divinity and humanity are united, without the one being deprived of its identical nature by the other; so also in the supper, the word of God unites itself with matter and consecrates it to the sacrament. "Accedit verbum ad elementum et fit sacramentum." In these words of Augustine rests the only true canon for the doctrine of the sacraments.

† The latest treatises upon the supper, are by Scheibel—Breslau, 1823; by Schultz—Leipzig, 1824; by Schulthess—Leipzig, 1824; by Lindner—Leipzig, 1831; Sartorius has given a review upon the latest treatises on the doctrine of the supper in the Evang. R. Zeitung, 1832, Maiheft. Compare, also, Eisenlohr in "Klaiber's Stud.," B. i. h. i. s. i., ff. Upon the question, "In his last meal held with the Apostles, had Jesus an intention to found a religious ordinance?" compare further, "Upon the substance of the holy supper," by Moser: examine the latter, with reference to Steudel's essays in the Tübinger Zeitschrift Jahrg. 1832-1833.

its nature. This consideration is comforting, in so far as it warrants the inference, that the blessing of participating in the supper depends not on *the degree of purity in our apprehension* of its nature, but on the sincerity of the desire after power and assistance from above—always supposing that the mind's eye is not wilfully closed to correct conceptions. Hence members of all ecclesiastical organizations, however various their conceptions of the supper, may partake in its blessings, provided they only have faith, that is, spiritual susceptibility to the powers of life, which Christ tenders in this ordinance.

But again, exegesis, in order to call up in our minds the train of ideas which the Lord himself, and the Apostles, after their illumination by the Holy Ghost, had severally as to the institution and observance of the sacred supper, should not separate the ordinance from ecclesiastical practice, from the authentic declarations of the Scriptures concerning the nature of the supper, or from the general connexion of the Christian doctrines. Such a separation would equally betray us into error.

First. As regards the ecclesiastical practice, it must have its influence upon our views, since the discussion concerns a service which was to be repeated. Were an expositor unfolding the narratives of Matthew and Mark only, and on mere grammatical principles, he might infer that Christ had only intended to take a final leave of his disciples, by means of a symbolic service, representing his death, and that he had not thought at all of ordaining its repetition.* On the other hand he might infer from John xiii. 14–17, that

* It appears difficult, concerning the first supper, to retain the full significance of the Sacrament; inasmuch as the work of Christ was not yet completed, his body not yet thoroughly glorified, the Holy Ghost not yet shed forth. We might believe that this first participation possessed only a typical character; that it was after the resurrection that the entire power of the ordinance was first to be recognized. A remembrance of the Lord's death could not, in fact, have place in the first supper. For this event was still prospective. The breaking of the bread and the distributing of the cup possessed rather a prophetic character. It was, in the first instance, an ante-type, and, after death, became an after-type. Kniewel, in his book "of the Christian religion," Danzig, 1835, p. 218, expresses himself to the effect that, in the first supper, the disciples as yet enjoyed but the sacrament of the old covenant. But, according to that view, the founding of the sacrament of the new covenant would certainly be altogether wanting! Besides, the disciples, even before the supper, ate the paschal lamb. Much rather must we believe that "the first supper was the event which fulfilled the Old Testament type; the elevation of the shadow into the substance." Zinzendorf advances the preposterous opinion, that, in the first supper before the passion, it was only the bloody death-sweat of Jesus that was partaken of. But, besides the repulsiveness of this theory, the struggle of Gethsemane took place posterior to the instituting of the supper. Compare Acta hist. Eccl. vol. xx. p. 806. To those who hold that the glorification of Christ's humanity commenced only with the resurrection or ascension to heaven, it is really incomprehensible how Jesus, before his passion, could have dispensed his flesh and blood. To them nothing remains but to say "that Christ created his own flesh and blood from nothing." According to our view of the glorified humanity—a view which appears to grow essentially clearer upon closer examina-

the intention of Jesus was that the feet-washing should be repeated. But the ecclesiastical practice of the primitive church, which was established by the Apostles, whom we must regard as the authentic interpreters of the meaning of the Lord, exhibits the direct contrary to both inferences. And since the accounts of Luke and Paul furnish the positive command for repeating it in the institutory words of the ordinance, it is clear that Matthew and Mark took it for granted as known to their readers from ecclesiastical practice.

Secondly. As regards the authentic declarations of Scripture, amongst these are to be especially reckoned the passages in 1 Cor. x. 16, 17, xi. 23–29, and in a certain sense also, John vi., (on which consult the particulars in the commentary). In these passages a specific spiritual character is ascribed to the supper. Self-examination is enjoined previous to its reception, and a *blessing* or *curse* annexed as its sanctions. These considerations overturn the Zuinglian notion, "that the supper was merely a commemorative meal;" a view which makes no specific character conceivable in the supper.

Finally. As to the question, "How does the specifically higher quality in the supper stand related to the elements?" The answer to this question requires that we should regard *the connexion* in which this doctrine stands with the whole remaining cycle of gospel doctrines, according to that fundamental principle of interpretation, the analogy of the faith. The chief point for consideration in the doctrine of the supper, is the teaching of the Scriptures as to the relations of *flesh* and *spirit* generally, and the glorification of the body in particular. Now, where the biblical doctrine of the Resurrection, and of the spiritual body (σῶμα πνευματικόν), 1 Cor. xv. 44, seq., which believers obtain in it, are denied; and where the *Spirit* and *Body* are held to exist in rigid *Dualism*, without any approximation ever occurring, there must naturally be an attenuation of whatever is specific in the supper into a general spiritual influence such as is experienced in prayer. In like manner, the Catholic theory of Transubstantiation is proved erroneous, when tested by the analogy of the faith. For as the Word on becoming flesh (John i. 14) did not transform flesh into its own substance, nor itself into that of flesh, but as always, even in the glorification of the body of Christ, humanity and Deity were *united* in him, so also in the supper. Hence according to the monophysite doctrine of Transubstantiation held by the Catholics, the supper appears as a repeated *sacrifice;* a view at once opposed by the circumstance, that

tion, from whatever point we proceed—the full efficacy of this first supper becomes completely obvious. The Saviour already bore the glorified body within himself. The mortal body enveloped it as the shell does the kernel. Therefore the influence of his glorified corporeity might even then have proceeded from him.

Christ in that case must have sacrificed himself, *prior* to the true sacrifice which he offered on Golgotha; for he instituted the supper before his death. We may, however, as we have said, regard the original institution of the supper, like the Old Testament sacrifices as typical of the coming sacrificial death of Christ, and in like manner we may look upon the constantly-renewed repetition of the supper, as a representation of it.* This, however, is only one and not the most essential of the many references which meet and blend in the last supper, like flowers in a garland.

In accordance with what has been said, I hold that Luther's notion of the holy supper is that which coincides most completely, in all essentials, with ecclesiastical practice, with the authentic declarations of the institutory words, and with the harmony of the Scripture doctrines. According to my conviction, the Scripture teaches that in and under the elements of the holy supper, the Redeemer who now sits in his glorified humanity at the right hand of God, *dispensed his glorified bodily nature* (which certainly can never be dissevered from a spiritual and Divine existence) his spiritualized flesh and blood, to the faithful, to be a φάρμακον τῆς ἀθανασίας, *medicine of immortality*, as Ignatius terms it; a germ of new life even for their bodies, yet to be awakened. (Compare the remarks on John vi. 54, seq.) My view, however, deviates in this from that of Luther, first, that I do not consider it included in the idea of the supper, that *all* who partake of it receive the Lord's body. For although the Lord's body is received, yet it is surely not received *through the mouth* (as Luther says—compare the passage in Scheibel on the supper, p. 344) since it is a spiritual body. This, at the least, is a mode of expression, which, even though it may be correctly explained, would still be foreign to the Scriptures, and which, on account of its liability to misconception, is better avoided. Where the organ of the spiritual body is deficient, that is *the mouth of faith*, especially where no new spiritual man requiring spiritual nourishment has been born through baptism, there the body of the Lord cannot be received. But where there are in one who has been born again gross faithlessness, and consequent apostacy from the faith, in that case the power of the supper thrusts the man away from itself; just as the Holy Ghost departs from, and does not enter into such an one. (Upon 1 Cor. xi. 29, from which passage

* Scheibel probably intends merely to promulgate this representative character of the supper, when he would have it thought to be a sacrificial repast. This expression would seem at the same time to suggest the idea, that as men used to bind themselves together for the attainment of some common object, by a sacrificial meal; in like manner, the supper is to be the partly spiritual, partly material bond of union to believers. Paul, 1 Cor. x. 17, gives prominence expressly to this relation, in regarding the faithful many as one body—(as many bread corns form one loaf)—because they are partakers of the same bread.

some persons seek to prove the contrary, compare the Commentary.)

Secondly, according to my persuasion, the *whole* Christ is not received in the supper, but an *influence* from him, and specifically as *glorified*. The notion that the *entire* Christ is received in the supper, led to the doctrine of the ubiquity of the body of Christ, and of the right hand of God. This, regarded as personal ubiquity, is certainly not biblical. The only truth contained in this representation is as follows. The Lord, by virtue of his union of natures, can *operate* even with his humanity on behalf of all. As the sun sends forth its beams over all, so the Saviour breathes from himself a vivifying power. This power, being alike Divine and human, is able to transform man in spirit, soul, and body, and is received wherever there exist the moral capacities for receiving it. But every operation of Christ contains the power of producing him complete in the mind,* as the spark begets the flame from which it sprang. (Compare John iv. 14.)

As in the person of the Saviour are united the Divine and the human natures distinct yet inseparable, so also in the supper the power of Christ is associated with the bread and wine, without the one destroying, or even altering, the essential nature of the other.

If we regard in this light the individual accounts concerning the supper, it is clear, in the first place, that 1 Cor. xi. 23, seq.

* This thought should not be overlooked, since without it my views might be misunderstood, when I say that "not the whole Christ, but an influence of him, is present in the supper." In Luther's doctrine of the ubiquity of the body of Christ, there lies, on the one hand, something bordering on the views of the Docetic Monophysites—(which comes out particularly in the conclusion, that the right hand of God is everywhere; which is undoubtedly contrary to the meaning of the sacred writers)—and so far it is erroneous. But, on the other hand, Luther was perfectly correct in stating it as a necessary condition of the presence of the flesh and blood of Christ in the supper, that the glorified humanity of Christ should be able to accompany the omnipresent agency of the Son of God.

We may, however, hold this latter opinion without admitting the Lutheran doctrine of the ubiquity of Christ and of the right hand of God, if we discriminate between the individual *personality* of the God-man, and the *influence* proceeding from him. True, however, this influence cannot be considered as absolutely distinct from Christ, nor so understood, for otherwise, it would follow that it is not Christ that is in the supper, but something else, to wit, his *influence*. Rather should we maintain, that everything which is in Christ, and which proceeds from him, even his Divinely human efficiency, *partakes of his nature*. For example, in this efficacy he himself is present, viz., in the germ, or in the ability of producing himself, as in the spark rests the capacity to produce the greatest flame, in susceptible materials. Similarly, the soul which participates in the real efficiency of Christ, receives therewith the power to become like him. In him the Divine implanted seed calls forth a new spiritual production, which transforms first the soul and then the body also, and which, without that efficiency of the Saviour, never could have been produced. Sartorius, in the spirited essay in the "Evang. R. Zeitung, Jahrg. 1833, Feb.," on the communicatio idiomatum, has defended to the last point the strictly Lutheran view of the ubiquity. (Concerning the ubiquity of the right hand of God, compare the particulars in Matth. xxvi. 62, et seq.).

must be considered as the chief passage. For Matthew and Mark relate but briefly, presuming on their readers' knowledge from the practice of the church, whilst in John the history of the institution is entirely wanting, as the passage in John vi. merely alludes to the supper (compare upon the grounds of this omission the remarks on John xiii. 1) and even Luke, although on the whole following Paul, particularly in the *τοῦτο ποιεῖτε εἰς τὴν ἐμὴν ἀνάμνησιν, do this in remembrance of me* (Luke xxii. 19), still but follows him ; and above all, the apostle declares, 1 Cor. xi. 23, that he had received instructions immediately from the Lord concerning what should be the practice of the church in respect to this ordinance. It may be said therefore that the Redeemer has in this passage explained his intent in founding the supper (upon the *παρέλαβον ἀπὸ τοῦ κυρίου* compare the Comm. on 1 Cor. xi. 23) ; and therefore the passage cannot be unregarded in interpreting the Gospels. As regards further the *form* of the service, it was observed in the introduction to this paragraph, that a dividing of bread and a sending round of several cups of wine, during the singing of psalms, was customary in every paschal feast. To this custom the Saviour gave a profounder import, since he viewed the breaking of the bread and the distribution of the wine as symbols of his vicarious death upon the cross. The doctrine of Transubstantiation, when carried out to its complete consequences, the regarding of the supper as an actual repetition of the sacrifice itself, is a view in absolute contradiction to the practice of the ancient church, as well as to the uniform tenor of Scripture doctrine. It was, as we have already observed, merely to represent *in figure* the one offering by which he perfected all who are sanctified, Hebrews x. 14. The *essence* of the holy supper consists in the *word* accompanying the external rite, which, as the word of God, is *spirit* and *life* (John vi. 63), and operates accordingly. In the next place, we have to notice the expressions "*take, eat, drink*" (*λάβετε, φάγετε, πίετε*), which are preserved by Matthew and Mark only ; and in Mark the two latter words are wanting. (Several codices, it is true, have the reading *φάγετε*, but it has been merely received into their text from Matthew.) These words express the receptive position of the disciples, who represent the church ; Christ is the dispenser, satisfying with himself their spiritual hunger and thirst. Through him the church is nourished. From this relation it follows that the Lord himself could not have partaken of the bread and wine with the disciples. We have here no allusion to a parting feast in which *all*, as co-ordinate, enjoy the same food, in token of internal union, but *nourishment* received, as by the infant at the mother's breast. The idea of reciprocity therefore is excluded.*

* This was erroneously believed by Chrysostom, who in his exposition of Matthew, Homily 73, says—*τὸ ἑαυτοῦ αἷμα, καὶ αὐτὸς ἔπιε.*

We are warranted, therefore, in the inference, that according to the intent of the sacred ordinance, no self-communion of the clergy, such as is usual not only in the Catholic church, but also here and there in the Evangelical church, ought to be practised. The officiating clergyman occupies, so to speak, the place of Christ. They who partake of the sacred supper form the church. In self-communion, the clergyman unites in himself both characters, which seems to be contradictory. (Compare Russwurm upon the self-communion of the Evangelical churches. Hanover, 1829.) Where, however, the custom is already established, and men cannot be persuaded that it is inappropriate, the Lord will grant his blessing even upon such a form of the solemnity. The next point for discussion is the words designating the element to be partaken: "this is my body," etc. (*τοῦτό ἐστι τὸ σῶμά μου, τὸ αἷμά μου*). In the Aramaic language, which Jesus no doubt spoke in the immediate circle of his disciples, the words uttered were probably הוּא בִסְרִי הוּא דְמִי, or, perhaps, more correctly, according to Scheibel (in a passage quoted elsewhere, 135), דֵּן הוּא גּוּפִי, דֵּן—הוּא—דְמִי. At least גּוּף is in any case more correct than בְּסַר, which corresponds to the Greek *σάρξ*, since assuredly, in regard to these significant words, the greatest precision of expression was observed by the Evangelists, and *all the four* Evangelists have *σῶμα*, *body*, which is the more striking, as the following *αἷμα* should rather lead to *σάρξ*, which latter expression, moreover, occurs in John vi. The reason why *body* (*σῶμα*) is here selected, may be understood from the statements of Luke* and Paul. The subjoined expression "given, broken for you" (*ὑπὲρ ὑμῶν διδόμενον, κλώμενον*), imperatively requires it. Since, for instance, *σῶμα*, *body*, indicates the physical organism as a whole (whether dead or living), of which organism the living substance is called *σάρξ*, its lifeless substance *κρέας*; hence to the idea of its being destroyed by death (which the *κλώμενον*, referring to the breaking of the sacrificial cakes, signified)—only *σῶμα* could refer. (Compare upon the *ὑπὲρ ὑμῶν διδόμενον, ἐκχυνόμενον*, in reference to the atoning vicarious death of Christ, and also concerning *περὶ πολλῶν*, the detailed explanation in Comm. Part I. on Matth. xx. 28.)

Thus, the Saviour compared the *whole* cake (פִּתָּא), which he broke, to his body. Yet he did not give to each the whole body, but as he did a part of the cake, so he gave to each a part of the body, that is *σάρξ*, *flesh*.† According to the intent of the ordinance, *σάρξ*

* The dependence of Luke upon Paul—compare Introduction Part I., s. 17, seq.—appears unmistakably in the words of the institution of the supper.

† This view concerning the breaking of bread in the supper, as typical of the destruction of what is inferior, in order to the calling forth of what is superior, appears also in "Oschelaleddin"—in Tholuck's Bluthensammel, s. 104—who sings—

When blossoms fall superior fruits arise,
When bodies die, then spirits mount the skies;

might just as properly have been used; only that, on account of the symbolical reference to his death, Jesus chose *σῶμα*, *body*, equivalent to גוּף. In *αἷμα*, *blood*, there was no difficulty whatever, since the whole quantity of it could be expressed only by the same term as *a part*. But as each person did not receive the entire *body*, neither did each receive the whole of the *blood;* that is, each did not drink the entire cup-full, signifying all the blood, but all partook of the one cup; thus the one Christ dispensed himself amongst them all, in order that he might live in them, and they in him. *Αἷμα*, *blood*, then, as conjoined with *σάρξ*, *flesh* (for which expression *σῶμα* is to be taken in the institutory words), constitutes the other half of our physical being. Whilst *flesh* is the more material part, *blood* is conceived as that which *animates* the flesh, the bearer of the *ψυχή*—Genesis ix. 4; Deut. xii. 23. The two, therefore, with the Spirit (*πνεῦμα*), complete our human nature.*

So is destruction destined to disclose,
Else from its womb the immortal ne'er had rose.
Hence, thus in parts must broken be the bread,
That man thereon be nourishingly fed.

* Lücke, in an interesting programme for Christmas, 1837, has brought afresh under discussion the question, "How ought the twofold form of communion, by means of bread and wine, to be regarded?" I cannot, however, agree with his conclusion, which leads altogether to the Zuinglian view of the supper. The chief idea of the supper he makes the founding of the new covenant, through the sacrifice of Christ, which is symbolically represented in the supper. This idea then would first be brought home to the consciousness of the disciples by their partaking of the bread, but in the reception of the cup alone would it be truly and perfectly expressed. But the idea of Christ's presence in the supper, Lücke fails to find. The sentence, *τοῦτο ποιεῖτε εἰς τὴν ἐμὴν ἀνάμνησιν*, "*this do in remembrance of me*" (p. 8) he regards as showing clearly, on the contrary, mortis meditationem esse primariam, quin potius unicam in sacra cœna. Such a conclusion as this may be deduced from the institutory words regarded simply as such. These, however, as containing the mystery, in order to be perfectly understood, necessarily require illustration from the important doctrinal discourse of Jesus, John vi., and the Pauline explanations, 1 Cor. x. 11. From them we infer that the supper was unquestionably intended as a symbolical representation of the sacrifice of Christ: that the *ἀνάμνησις*, *remembering*, was to refer to the historical event of Christ's death; and that the rite symbolizes a sealing of the covenant; but that besides, and even above all this, there is in this pregnant ordinance an actual distribution of his real existence itself. (Compare on this subject the explanations in the Commentary on the passages quoted.) Now, the reason why this participation was made in a twofold form, might be the following. First, the form of the festival, which was one of eating and drinking, required it. At the paschal meal they ate the lamb, and drank of the cup: Christ adopted this usage, and this custom, and filled it with higher powers. Secondly: the symbolical representation of the death required a distinction between the blood and the body, in order to bring before the mind the idea of the shedding of the blood. Lastly: *body* and *blood* (*σῶμα* and *αἷμα*) denote the totality of humanity. *Body* alone would represent only its material part. The *blood* as the bearer of the psychical element should also be embraced. It is on this account, probably, that *σῶμα* not *σάρξ*, was employed in the institutory words; because the latter forms the antithesis with *πνεῦμα*, but *σῶμα* with *ψυχή*. The immediate question, however, is not concerning *spiritual* communication in the supper, but of the communication of *humanity*; which is constituted of soul and body. And further, the choice of the expression *body*, in the institutory words, may be accounted

The question, it is now self-evident, is not now of the agency of the Spirit, it is *flesh* and *blood* (σάρξ, αἷμα), which the Redeemer distributes in the supper to his believing followers. The annexed pronoun has naturally a peculiar force, "*my* flesh," etc. (σῶμά μου, αἷμά μου). In themselves *flesh* and *blood* are powerless, John vi. 63; Rom. vii. 18. They cannot even inherit, much less bestow, the kingdom of God, 1 Cor. xv. 50. But the flesh and blood of Christ, which are imperishable and glorious, possess the power of eternal life. He who eats and drinks of them shall have life in himself, and will be raised up at the last day. (John vi. 53, seq.)

With this heavenly flesh and blood the Lord feeds his disciples, as a mother from her bosom nourishes her infant child with her own blood. Schultz (loc. cit. p. 93, seq.) thinks that we may speak of earthly and heavenly bodies (σώματα ἐπίγεια, ἐπουράνια), but not of spiritual flesh (σὰρξ πνευματική), or the like. By mere accident this expression certainly does not occur in the New Testament; but still a body consists necessarily of flesh, whether of a merely earthly, or glorified nature. We see therefore no intrinsic impropriety in applying the epithet to *flesh*. In strict consistency with his *Dualism*, which makes an absolute separation between matter and spirit, Schultz was forced to assert, that there could not be a spiritual body (σῶμα πνευματίκον),* since for ever, according to his system, spirit and body are *beside*, not *in* each other—a doctrine which is certainly unknown to the holy Scriptures.

But according to this conception of body and blood, the query now occurs, how could Jesus, in instituting the sacred ordinance, have spoken of his glorified body, when he yet bore the mortal body? The expressions in Luke and Paul, "given, shed for you," seem to favour the opinion, that the body which the Lord intended to distribute, was not the glorified one, but that which was natural, capable of suffering, and of being nailed to the cross.

Yet even the most zealous defenders of this view admit that the body of the Lord communicates the energies of eternal life; it cannot therefore resemble the perishable sinful human body. The sentiment that it was the body which was afterwards nailed to the cross, is important to them only as enabling them to combat the notion of

for from the fact that it signifies our physical nature as a whole, our collective organism; with which, also, the idea of breaking better agrees. Still, as dwelt upon above, when regarded alone and in itself, we may speak of the *flesh* of Christ in the supper.

* Σῶμα, *body*, must be taken as equivalent to οὐσία, *substance*, as Tertullian uses corpus (= substantia); and hence says of spirit "est corpus sui generis." Schultz seems to unite with the conception of σῶμα, only the abstract idea of something entire and distinctly individualized. But accordingly to this, what is a spiritual body? What in fact individualizes the spirit except the body? No one would wish to revive the Gnostic doctrine of an ὅρος, that is, of a principle individualizing and limiting spirits: and still it is a powerful proof how difficult it is, without the hypothesis of a glorified corporeity, to fix the individuality of spirits.

an ideal, ætherial docetic body, in order to maintain the reality of the body of Christ. And in this relation the assertion is entirely correct; though it might with propriety be differently expressed, so as to assert most emphatically the reality and identity of the body of Christ *before* and *after* the resurrection, in opposition to all the docetic errors; and yet distinguish perfectly between Christ's body as glorified, and as not glorified. But the communicating of the flesh and blood of Christ could never proceed naturally except from the former. If we now suppose that the glorification of the Lord's body was gradually perfected (on this subject, compare the Commentary, Part I. on Matth. xvii. 1, and the remarks in the history of the resurrection), then will its efficaciousness, prior to its return from the dead, contain nothing whatever surprising, any more than the fact that the Saviour could by breathing impart the Holy Spirit (John xx. 22), although the spirit was not fully poured out till a later period, John vii. 39. In the mortal body the immortal one already rested; as in the regenerated, the new man lives, though enveloped by the old. The resurrection was merely the breaking forth of the butterfly from the chrysalis, within which it had long since been fully matured.

Τοῦτό ἐστι, this is, therefore, are the only words which remain for examination; words which were long regarded as the key to an understanding of the whole passage. Schultz, however (p. 116, seq.), is certainly right when he remarks that nothing can be proved from this formula in favour of either the one or the other view of the supper. Were the Catholic view intended to be sustained by the word of Scripture, then *μετεμορφώθη*, or something similar, would be necessary.*

But regarded under a strictly grammatical view *τοῦτό ἐστι*, will bear the meaning of "this signifies" just as well as of "this is, actually." So that from these words *merely*, we cannot decide between the views of Luther and Zuinglius. (Of the numerous examples quoted by Schultz, concerning *τοῦτό ἐστι*, compare the following: 1 Peter i. 25; Philemon, ver. 12; Luke xii. 1; Hebrews x. 20; and on the tropical use of *εἶναι*, generally consult John xv. 1–5, xiv. 6, x. 7–9 and elsewhere).

The phrase *may*, however, have the other signification, viz., "it is in deed, and in truth." In the passage itself there is no decisive

* If, however, the doctrine of transubstantiation had been so stated that we might regard the transformation of elements *only as occurring at the moment of consecration and participation*, there could be little biblical opposition to it. But the passages (1 Cor. x. 16, xi. 26) speak of the bread, even after consecration, and whilst being partaken of, in a way that, by *forced* construction only, can be made to harmonize with the Catholic view. In conclusion, it is much to be regretted that this method of comprehending the dogma does not obtain as the prevailing one in the Greek and Latin churches; for by means of it a great part of their corrupt practice would fall away of itself.

ground for the one view rather than the other; but the authentic declarations of Scripture, and the general scope of its doctrines, combined with the practice of the most ancient churches, lead to a decision in favour of the strict acceptation of the words. (Compare my remarks in the "Evang. Kirchen-Zeit. Jahrg. 1834, N. 48. The institutory words of the ordinance contain the mystery, but not its elucidation.)

Ver. 27, 28.—We must still notice the expression "blood of the new covenant" (*αἷμα τῆς καινῆς διαθήκης*), which occurs in Matthew and Mark, and for which Luke and Paul use, "the new covenant in my blood" (*ἡ καινὴ διαθήκη ἐν τῷ ἐμῷ αἵματι*). The two formulæ are not essentially distinguishable. Both comprehend the relation of the Redeemer's shed blood, to the new life established according to the New Testament. The only question that arises is, "What is the proper foundation of this relation?" Evidently, the remission of sins, for without shedding of blood there is no remission (compare upon this thought the comment upon Hebrews ix. 22). In the New Testament, sin is no longer borne with by the Divine patience, as under the economy of the Old Testament, Rom. iii. 25; but, through the reconciliation perfected by Christ's vicarious death it was done away (Coloss. ii. 14), since he became a curse for us, Gal. iii. 13. Hence, both the above modes of expression might be chosen, in so far as the new relation of men to God was established by the shedding of the blood of the Lord.*

The assertion that in the supper the Lord represented his death not as an expiatory but as a covenant sacrifice, which is made by Dr. Paulus in his edition of Usteri's Paul, Lehrbegriff, in the Heidelb. Jahrbücher, 1831, September, p. 844, is completely contradicted by the expressive clause in Matth. xxvi. 28, *ἐκχυνόμενον εἰς ἄφεσιν ἁμαρτιῶν, shed for the remission of sins.* But Luke and Paul have merely the definite injunction: *τοῦτο ποιεῖτε εἰς τὴν ἐμὴν ἀνάμνησιν, this do*, etc. The passage in 1 Cor. xi. 26 determines accurately both the nature of the remembrance, and its limit in time.

* Lindner, in his treatise on the Lord's Supper, Leipzig, 1831, has deduced from the latter passage the view, that "the very thing which Christ dispensed in the supper was the forgiveness of sins." But this representation is surely incorrect. True, wherever Christ is present there is forgiveness of sins, and, since he is present in the supper, it cannot be received without remission of sins. But the *specific character* of the supper consists not in that fact; it rather assumes the forgiveness of sins as its negative side, and completes it by a positive element, to wit, the imparting of new and higher life. The *general* forgiveness of sins is so far assumed that only the baptized and faithful can partake of the supper. The *continued daily* remission of sins is symbolized by the feet-washing which occurred *before* the institution of the supper, of which remission, confession and absolution constitute the subsequent representation; moreover, the Christian comes as one who has already received the forgiveness of sins; in whom the germ of the new life already rests; but who in this new life must now be nourished and strengthened with heavenly food.

The former refers especially to the death of Christ, as that in which his atoning and pontifical work was concentrated. The latter extends to the Parousia (ἄχρις οὗ ἔλθῃ).

The solemnization of the holy supper was therefore to be a perpetual symbolical repetition of the great act accomplished on Golgotha, by which the world was reconciled to God, and thus to announce to the world (καταγγέλετε τὸν θάνατον τοῦ κυρίου) its reconciliation; just as, under the economy of the Old Testament, every sacrifice preached that Adam had fallen, and that a restoration of human nature was necessary. But whilst the Jewish sacrifice only awakened a desire for the forgiveness of sins, the holy supper actually and energetically nourishes men with the bread that came from heaven to give life to the world. The supper therefore necessarily presupposes baptism, but baptism does not conversely presuppose the supper.

Only they who are born after the flesh can partake of material food; and in like manner only those who are born after the Spirit can enjoy spiritual food. And as the act of birth can take place but once, whilst the using of food must be frequently repeated, so also *baptism* is to be performed but once, whilst *the supper* must be often solemnized.

This analogy is apparently overturned by the facts, that the supper appears to have been instituted prior to the institution of baptism, and even before the glorification of Christ. (Compare Matth. xxviii. 18.) But if we reflect that baptism had long before been practised by John the Baptist, and by the apostles (compare John iv. 1, *et seq.*), and that in Matthew (xxviii. 19) the Lord merely enjoins the ordinance as a perpetual and universal observance for *all nations*, this apparent contradiction will be removed. Had the Saviour instituted the supper as the glorified Redeemer after his resurrection, it might easily have led to an entirely ideal view of the sacrament. But the more imminent was the danger of this error, as the history of the first centuries shews, the more carefully was it to be here avoided.

Ver. 29.—But the object of thus representing, under the aspect of the supper, the Lord's death for the sins of the world, could possess a significancy only so long as the Lord was separated from his church below. After his glorious return, the supper will assume a different form. To this points the conclusion of the Lord's discourse, according to Matthew and Mark, in which he declares that he will not drink again of the fruit of the vine until he does it in the kingdom of his heavenly Father. (On the right position of these words, compare Luke xxii. 16.) It must not be overlooked that Luke has the words three times (chap. xxii. 16, 18, and 30), from which it seems highly probable that the Lord uttered them several times, during the last supper. From these words we might think ourselves warranted to infer, that surely the Lord himself partook of the supper with the disciples. The words, "my body, my blood" (σῶμά σου, αἷμά μου), however, contradict this supposition too completely. It is much simpler to assume that the drinking of the fruit of the vine (πιεῖν ἐκ τοῦ γεννήματος τῆς ἀμπέλου)* refers to the cup of wine used previously, Luke xxii. 17, from which the Lord also drank. We are also specially led to this conclusion, by the passage in Luke xxii. 16, where it is said of the paschal lamb, "I will no longer eat of it" etc. (οὐκέτι οὐ μὴ φάγω ἐξ αὐτοῦ ἕως ὅτου, κ. τ. λ.) Here it is clear, that the discourse could not have referred to the bread in the supper, but to the passover. So that the meaning of the words is as follows "in the kingdom of God I will hold a new paschal feast with you."

As to the import of the particular idea (compare the observations relative to this subject, in the first part of the Commentary Luke xxii. 30), many persons, influenced by the prevailing Idealism, have accustomed themselves, in contempt of the resurrection and glorification of the flesh, to regard it as involving merely the general idea of joy. "There shall we enjoy ourselves more intimately, more spiritually with one another, than here." Were this notion correct, we should be justified in asserting that the thought was conveyed in words exceedingly liable to mistake, especially by the disciples, who were involved doubtless in gross material views of the Messiah. Without doubt those† are nearer to the grammatical truth—(looking particularly to the ὅταν αὐτὸ πίνω καινόν)—who confess, "that this passage clearly expresses the Jewish idea of a banquet that should take place in the kingdom of the Messiah; where what was physical would also be glorified." But the opinion most conformable to the doctrine of Scripture, is that this very idea of the marriage supper of the lamb (δεῖπνον τοῦ γάμου τοῦ ἀρνίου, Revelation xix. 9), has an independent truth. All anxiety about materialism in this view, is sufficiently removed by the observation that in the world of the glorified, everything will be glorified. Accordingly, the idea of a covenant feast with the Lord, must be conceived under a spiritualized and glorified form in the world of the resurrection

Thus understood then, this thought furnishes an admirable conclusion to the feast. Glancing away beyond the period of the gradual development of that kingdom of God, which like a grain

* It should be carefully noted that Jesus does not say, "ἐκ τουτου τοῦ ποτηρίου," but "ἐκ τούτου τοῦ γεννήματος." The οὗτος evidently forms the antithesis with καινός, and therefore the discourse in these words refers to the festival in general.

† The explanation of this passage, from the association of Christ with his disciples after his resurrection, is altogether untenable; for this time alone is never called βασιλεία τοῦ Θεοῦ.

of mustard seed, is in the world growing and maturing amidst many conflicts, the Lord transports himself with his disciples into that consummated harmony of existence in which even the material world appears correspondent with the spiritual (Rom. viii. 8, 18, seq.), and Paradise is restored.

Hence as in paradise the only food made use of was that afforded by plants, so also the Saviour, instead of the bloody passover, instituted a bloodless festival of the most simple means of nourishment, from which the higher elements of life were infused into man, as he once, by eating of the fruit, became subject to the power of death. Comforted then by this glance into the recovered paradise, the Lord advances against the Cherub's sword which must pierce the heart of every one who enters there, but over whose terrors Jesus has triumphed on behalf of all who by faith appropriate his merits to themselves.

§ 2. JESUS' STRUGGLE IN GETHSEMANE, AND HIS ARREST.

(Matth. xxvi. 36–56; Mark xiv. 32–52; Luke xxii. 40–53; John xviii. 1–11.)

After the conclusion of the supper,* followed immediately, as we have already remarked, by the discourses recorded by John, chs. xiv.—xvii. (which without doubt were delivered in the festival chamber); the Saviour with his disciples hastened out of the city, from which his gracious presence was now withdrawn.

Jesus went over the mountain stream Cedron to the Mount of Olives. Κεδρών = קִדְרוֹן from קָדַר to be dark, black. Perhaps the name is derived from the depth of the densely-grown forest valley through which the brook flowed. The reading τῶν κεδρῶν, arose certainly from the ignorance of transcribers, who thought they ought to regard the name as a plural form. The brook flowed between the city and the Mount of Olives, and poured itself into the Dead Sea. It is often named in the Old Testament. (Comp. 2 Sam. xv. 23; 1 Kings ii. 37, xv. 13; 2 Kings xxiii. 4–6. Upon ὄρος τῶν ἐλαιῶν comp. in the Commentary Part I. on Matth. xxi. 1.) Here, either upon or near the Mount of Olives, was a country-seat —χωρίον, Matth. xxvi. 36; Mark xiv. 32, with a garden, κῆπος = גַּן John xviii. 1, 2, which Jesus had often visited with his disciples, and which was well-known to Judas; thither the Lord proceeded.

Γεθσημανῆ or Γεθσημανεί is the name given by Matthew and Mark to the estate, that is גַּת שְׁמָנָא oil-press, or olive-press. Scarcely had

* Matth. xxvi. 30, applies ὑμνήσαντες to the psalms which were wont to be sung at the conclusion of the feast. They are called "the great hallelujah." Compare the foregoing description of the proceedings in solemnizing the Jewish passover.

he arrived, when he retired into the deep solitude of the garden. The rest of the disciples may have remained in the house with the friendly owner of the garden; only three ventured to accompany him, and beheld the mighty struggle of his soul. These were they who were also present at the transfiguration (compare Matth. xvii. 1, seq.) Hence they were able to estimate alike the exaltation and the humiliation of the Lord's life. (Ἀδημονέω from ἀδήμων, sorrowful, distressed; it is a strong expression for agony, trembling or fainting of soul. Symmachus uses it for עָטַף, Psalm lxi. 3, and for חָפַז Psalm cxvi. 11.)

We have now arrived at the event, which may be regarded as the beginning of the passion of Christ, in the narrower sense of the word, and it is but meet to make a pause in our consideration of particulars, and to review the general course of development in the Saviour's life.*

That suffering without measure, should burst in upon the holy one of God, seems to be the less surprising, that the noblest of the human race have been exposed to great privations and bitter conflicts; and the sufferings of Jesus only now became visible; they had long burdened him invisibly.† The sinfulness of the world, the unbelief, want of love, and ignorance, of men, had been long causes of acute suffering to the heart of the Son of God. But in the latter moments of his earthly pilgrimage, they were concentrated into greater intensity. To the observer, however, it appears wonderful, that the Saviour in such suffering, did not stand altogether unmoved, like the rock in a tempest, but that he trembled, moaned, and implored his heavenly Father to avert the agonizing hour! If we compare the demeanor of Jesus with the conduct of other sages, even such as lived before his time, of Socrates for example, or of noble Christian martyrs, as Huss, Polycarp, and others, these persons appear to have displayed more steadfastness and courage, than we discover in the bearing of Christ. The following observations may help to render this phenomenon comprehensible.

First, It must not be overlooked, that the Gospel reveals a view of life, in which, stoical indifference, hardihood, and inflexibility in reference to pain and suffering of every kind, do not appear as the

* (Compare on this subject my essay in Knapps' Christoterpe Jahrg. 1832, p. 182, seq.) which contains a further detail of the thoughts here intimated. Here, however, I would observe: that the symbolic character of the names Cedron, Gethsemane, Golgotha, is not to be overlooked. Throughout the whole of the sacred Scriptures, runs the conception of names as a very significant index to the characters of persons or relations. The essay of Dettinger in the "Tübinger Zeitschrift," 1837, p. 4, 1838, p. 1, contains a defence of the historical character of this narrative concerning the agony of Christ, against the attack of Strauss, which is eminently worthy of being studied.

† Clem. Alex. quis dives salvetur, c. 8, Segaars' edition, p. 22, πάσχει δι' ἡμᾶς ὁ σωτὴρ ἀπὸ γενέσεως μέχρι τοῦ σημείου. Id est:—usque ad crucem. The pilgrimage of a sinful world was, to the holy one of God, necessarily a continuous suffering and sympathy.

most exalted virtues. On the contrary, it honours and carefully fosters the tender susceptibilities of meekness, of compassion, of sympathy, and is not ashamed of tears, nor of the true, natural expression of anguish, or of terror. However, it should be well observed, that the Lord did not tremble before the rude populace, who would have misunderstood the true expression of his sorrows, but only in presence of his most confidential friends. The former would have been contrary to decorum, the latter was not.

Secondly, The faintness of Jesus did not arise from the fear of visible enemies, or under physical pain.* His struggle was an invisible agony of the soul; a sense of being forsaken of God (compare remarks on Matth. xxvii. 46); a contest against the power of darkness (compare Luke xxii. 53); for as, in the beginning of his ministry, the Saviour was tempted by the enemy though the medium of *desire*, so now at its end was he assailed through the medium of *fear*. Compare in the Comm., Vol. I. p. 275.

Finally, the suffering of the Lord was not something that affected merely his own individual life (Heb. ii. 10); it stood in connexion with the development of humanity at large. (Compare the particulars at Matthew xxvii. 45, seq.) Christ suffered and endured as the representative of mankind collectively. He bore their guilt. Hence his sufferings have a special character, and cannot be compared with any other sufferings. But it is not the fainting alone that is surprising in the following statement concerning the Lord, but also the fluctuation in his inward resolution. If we compare the confident faith and victorious courage which breathe through the intercession of Christ as high priest, John xvii., it will appear truly astonishing that, after a few hours the Saviour could appear involved in such an inward struggle as that in which he is represented in the passage about to be considered. We can hence conceive how some, as particularly Usteri and Goldhorn,† have from this circumstance come to the opinion that the narrative of the Synoptical Evangelists, concerning the struggle of Jesus in Gethsemane, is probably erroneous, since, in the minute narrative of John, who alone of the Evangelists was an eye-witness of the occurrence, there is no mention of it. (Luke contains the account, abridged certainly, but still essentially similar to those of Matthew and Mark.) But the supposition that the Saviour could not have endured any such inward struggle of the soul cannot be sustained against the abun-

* The view, that prospective extreme bodily suffering called forth the Redeemer's struggles, altogether obscures, and even annihilates the very essence of his messianic character. Were it correct, Christ would in truth have exhibited much less firmness of soul, not only than many martyrs, but even than many unregenerate and immoral men who have borne far greater tortures without blenching.

† The former in the celebrated critical essay concerning John, the latter in a distinct treatise in Tzschirner's Magazine, vol. I. Part 2.

dant proofs of the fact; for in the first place, John himself speaks of such a struggle in other passages of his Gospel. (Compare John xii. 20, seq.) And, in the next place, the other writers of the New Testament (Heb. v. 7, seq.), also the prophecies of the Old (Psalm xxii. 19; Isaiah liii.), have all included the idea of yielding and fainting in their portraiture of the Messiah. A milder mode of representing the matter, has therefore been chosen by those who say that "the struggle in Gethsemane certainly occurred; and that the first three Evangelists have merely assigned to it the *wrong place;* that it belongs in fact to an antecedent time, that to which John xii. 20, seq. transfers it."

Such a transposition might certainly be possible; but the event mentioned by John xii. 20, occurred under totally different circumstances, and therefore if the silence of John be deemed so decisive, we must assume not only a chronological inversion, but also an actual misrepresentation of the event on the part of the Synoptical writers. But his silence cannot justify such an assumption, for in John there occur frequent omissions of matters which the others have carefully recorded.*

The fact is easily explained if we can only assign a cause which would account for such sudden fluctuations in the inner life of Jesus; but such a cause presents itself to us in the phenomenon which frequently occurs in the experience of believers (as in the case of the Apostle Paul, according to 2 Cor. xii.), and may at least be employed by way of analogy, to show that a sudden withdrawal takes place, of those higher powers of the spirit which determine the tone and feeling of the soul.

That such a forsaking occurred on the cross, the evangelical history expressly asserts, Matth. xxvii. 46. In the history of the temptation we found ourselves obliged to assume it. (Comp. Comm., Part I. on Matth. iv. 1.)—Nothing is therefore more natural, than here also to suppose something similar. By this assumption alone, does the greatness of the struggle of Jesus on the one hand, and of his victory on the other, appear in its full significance. Whilst a Socrates can conquer, only so long as he remains in the full possession of his spirit's undiminished energy, the Redeemer triumphed over the whole power of darkness, even when forsaken by God, and by the fulness of his own Spirit.—The further expansion of this thought is given in the treatise published in "the Christoterpe."

* I hold it impossible to assign for this omission any other causes than those which have been mentioned. We might suppose that John had his Gnostic readers in view, in omitting an account which might have given offence by shewing weakness in Christ. But the same reason ought to have prevented John from making any allusion whatever to the event. This supposition would therefore prove too much, and consequently prove nothing, even granting we were disposed to assign it any force whatever.

The apprehensions expressed by Dettinger on this subject (in the work quoted before, p. 108) are entirely unfounded. He asks whether "spirit" here signifies the Divine nature, or only the spiritual principle of human nature? I answer, both. A contest, whilst in full possession of the Divine nature, is a nonentity. Hence the Scripture teaches us, Philip. ii. 7, that God, in becoming man, emptied himself of the fulness of Divine power. This abnegation reached its maximum point when (as in Gethsemane, and on the cross), the Saviour was totally forsaken by the Father. The mode of conceiving this abnegation and abandonment is a matter ot peculiar difficulty, but this difficulty rests in the subject itself, not in my representation; nor is it at all greater than that involved in the doctrine of the incarnation, and in other doctrines. Meanwhile, nothing can be more perverse than to say, with De Wette, that the withdrawal of God is a doctrine alike unphilosophical and immoral, since it destroys the omnipresence of God. This by no means follows, if we regard the withdrawal of God only as ACTUAL, not as ESSENTIAL. An omnipresence of God thus *actually* distinct, must at all events be assumed, otherwise everything is involved in chaos. The Omnipresent is present in various ways, in heaven, in hell, in the heart of the righteous, and in the heart of the godless, respectively. God, in his absolute freedom, possesses also the free exercise of his attributes. As (according to Rom. iii. 25) he suspended, in the ages before Christ, the full exercise of his justice, so, in like manner, God may restrain the gracious operation of his nature. Viewed in this light, the oneness of the person of the God-man is not destroyed by the Divine withdrawal. God is thus revealed in him, not as the gracious, but as the *just* God, that is, he sustains, as representative of mankind, the wrath of God. The objections ct Dettinger and De Wette proceed from an incorrect view of the relation of the Divine attributes to his *Being*. God is not constrained, through any innate necessity, to render the collective attributes of his nature always and on all occasions operative. His freedom dictates the form of their display. Finally, the supposition, that, in Gethsemane, a like withdrawal of God from Christ took place, as on the cross, does not sufficiently explain the fainting of the garden. Also in his humanity as such, we must believe that there was, agreeably to the ordinance of God, a state of helpless destitution, of complete exposure to the assaults of the power of darkness, which state, assuming the distinction between *soul* (ψυχή) and *spirit* (πνεῦμα), we can conceive as a limitation of the power of the latter. What thus occurs in sinful man, as a consequence of sin (viz., the weakening of the energy of the spirit, and a separation of the soul from the body in death), he, as the representative of mankind, became liable to of his own free will. In his sinless soul he achieved the complete victory; became obedient unto death, even the death of the cross; and learnt perfect obedience in that he himself suffered: Philip. ii. 8; Heb. ii. 17, 18, iv. 15. According to this interpretation, we need not at all suppose, as Dettinger, agreeing with Strauss, does in a passage quoted—that the soul resembles a lake, which ebbs and flows according as its conducting canals are closed, or its sluices opened. Rather should we abandon the unbiblical view of the identity of soul and spirit. As a man may lose his body without annihilation of his personality, so also may he lose the spirit. The soul is the sustainer of both.

Ver. 38, 39.—The confession of his profound sorrow, and the imploring request to his disciples to strengthen him, by their proximity and their watching, form a wonderfully impressive contrast with the mission of Christ, and with the very object of these sufferings. He, the helper of the whole world, confesses to those to whom he brings help his own need of assistance, and seeks from these very persons the aid which they are unable to render! (Περίλυπος occurs in Mark vi. 26, and in Luke xviii. 23, 24. It is formed after the analogy of *περιχαρής*.*) The *ἡ ψυχή μου* does not stand merely for *ἐγώ*: it is different from *τὸ πνεῦμά μου*. The former signifies rather what is purely human, that which moves the feeling; the latter means the spiritual consciousness. Compare John xiii. 21, where the personal feeling is less intended, hence *ἐταράχθη τῷ πνεύματι* is employed. Compare John xi. 33. When about to pray, Jesus removed to some distance from his disciples, and fell upon his face on the ground. (Luke subjoins, with more exact statement, *ὡσεὶ λίθου βολήν*, xxii. 41. The phrase *ἀπεσπάσθη ἀπ' αὐτῶν*, expresses the suddenness and violence of the Saviour's movements.) Mark gives the prayer itself in the most detailed manner; for, besides the "passing away of the cup" (compare Matth. xx. 22) he also mentions the passing by of the hour of suffering. Remarkable in this supplication of the Saviour, is the prayer of the Son, based upon the omnipotence of the Father (*πάντα δυνατά σοι*), to remove from him the hour of suffering. With a definite knowledge of the will of the Father, there seems to be expressed a contrary will on the part of the Son. But, first, this supplication must on no account be taken as isolated or dissevered from the appended words, *πλὴν οὐχ ὡς ἐγὼ θέλω, ἀλλ' ὡς σύ*, *yet not as I will, but as thou wilt.* In the first petition, the weakness of the flesh (2 Cor. xiii. 4), alone finds utterance, which the Saviour must necessarily have partaken of, for otherwise his agonies would have been merely the semblance of suffering. In the second prayer there is the expression of the victorious spirit. Again, it must not be overlooked, that the wish to be exempted from death,

* The words are from the passages of the Psalms xli. 5–11, xlii. 5, which probably recurred to the memory of the Saviour in the heavy hour of his sufferings.

and from the bitter path of suffering, is not a sinful one, but rather a pure and holy wish. For death is the reward of sin, and, as such, bitter even to sinful creatures, to whom, in some respects, it may be regarded as a release from distress and misery. How much more, then, must it have excited a shuddering horror in the pure unspotted soul of Jesus! It would have argued a false and beggarly spirit, at once stupid and unfeeling, if, with no living, genuine, soul-thrilling utterance of the terror inspired in his holy human soul by the dark valley of death, he could have descended into it.* This feature, so far from impairing the sacred picture of Christ, is essential to its complete perfection.

A higher necessity required, however, that this feeling, in itself entirely legitimate, should now be subdued. It was not the irresistible will of the Father which urged the Son on to this bitter death, for the Divine will of the Son was one with that of the Father. But the conflict of absolute justice with mercy, in a word, the mystery in the work of redemption for the race of man, demanded a complete sacrifice; and a voluntary yielding to this higher necessity, which was impossible without a severe struggle against human sensibility, we find intimated in this sublime and sacred moment. With the victory in Gethsemane, therefore, everything was already virtually completed; the Father's will itself was fully apprehended by the soul of Jesus. And as in human conflicts the mind becomes tranquil when the resolution has been unalterably formed, so also we discover it here, in the life of the Redeemer. Hence the struggle in Gethsemane was even more fearful than that on Golgotha—(compare Heb. v. 7); as ordinarily with excitable minds the prospect of danger is more painful than the danger itself with all its terrors.

Ver. 40, 41.—After this, his first victory over the assaults of darkness, Jesus returned to the three disciples, and found them sleeping, heedless of his admonition. The comment of Luke xxii. 45—"ἀπὸ τῆς λύπης"—that they were sleeping for sorrow, may be explained thus: their trouble, by reason of the violent mental excitement it called forth, is to be understood as the cause of their exhaustion and sleepiness. In accordance with this view, εἰς λύπην stands in the LXX. for דָּוֶה, faint, sick Addressing Peter, as their speaker, the Lord again exhorted them to watchfulness and prayer,

* Luther calls attention also to the perfection of Christ's bodily organization, and the acuteness of suffering it must have occasioned. "We men," he writes, "conceived and born in sin, have an impure, hard flesh, which does not soon feel. The fresher and sounder the man is, the finer the skin, and the purer the blood, so much the more does he feel, and is susceptible of what befalls him. Now, since Christ's body is pure and sinless, whilst ours is impure, we therefore scarcely feel the terrors of death in one fifth of the degree in which Christ felt them, since he was to be the greatest martyr, and had to suffer death's extremest terrors."—Compare the Sermon on Christ's Passion in the Garden, Leipzig edition, Part XVI. 187.

with the warning that both lessen the danger of temptation. Here the train of ideas is manifestly as follows. "An abandonment to sorrow, and its consequent emotions, diminishes the dominant energy of the spirit, and thus facilitates the victory of indwelling sin; whilst resistance to the besetting disposition, and prayer, which supplies man with fresh energy from the spiritual world, secure us against temptation." Hence, also, Christ refers us to the weakness of human nature (ἡ σὰρξ ἀσθενής), which hinders the execution of that which man's nobler part (πνεῦμα, in Paul, νοῦς) would prefer. Compare particulars on the words in Romans vii. 22, 23.

Ver. 42-44.—A second and a third time does the Redeemer retire to pray; and as often as he returns does he find the disciples sleeping, entirely subdued by the power of darkness. Luke does not record this threefold struggle, but mentions it compendiously, as if only one prayer had taken place; but beyond doubt the more exact description of Matthew and Mark is the more correct. The three assaults through the medium of fear, stand parallel to the three stages in the history of the temptation. In Luke xxii. 43, 44, some incidents are adduced which have escaped the other two Evangelists. These two verses are wanting in the manuscripts A.B. 13, 69, 124, and others. Some MSS., as E.S. 24, 36, attach asterisks to them. Nevertheless they are authentic. The omissions and signs originated perhaps in the apprehension that the strengthening of Jesus by an angel would have made him appear too deeply humbled, and the words might favour Arianism. (This passage further belongs to those in which, under the term ἄγγελος, *angel*, no external appearance,* no visible personage should be understood. The angel certainly appeared to *Christ* alone (ὤφθη αὐτῷ), and probably inwardly, in his spirit. The strengthening by the angel is,

* It is surprising that a man like Dettinger (in the passage quoted elsewhere, 1835) could take offence at this conclusion, imagining that through this hypothesis the historical truth of the account might be damaged. "It is better," he says, "to state openly, with Strauss, that it is a mythical decoration." I thought the words, "There is here under the ἄγγελος, no appearance to be understood, as of a visible personality," indicated my meaning plainly enough, to make such misconceptions impossible; but since they are not so considered, I shall explain myself more particularly. I distinguish two sorts of angelic appearances; first, those where the appearing angel personally comes in view to him to whom the vision is imparted; and secondly, purely spiritual appearances. Of the first kind was the angelic vision which, according to Luke i. appeared in the temple to Zacharias; of the second was the one here mentioned. In this hypothesis I am decided, by the relation of angelic visions to the other forms of revelation from the superior world. They belong to the inferior class of revelations; and hence are not suited to him upon whom all the angels of God ascend and descend, John i. 51. Add to this that the angel was here to reveal nothing, but merely strengthen Christ in his human nature. Here, therefore, the personality of the angel disappears, and his appearance, in fact, is but equivalent to the expression "there flowed in upon him power from on high." This view of the angels as powers, with the personality dismissed, is particularly revealed in the Old Testament, in the doctrine of the cherubim. But this is not the place to enter into its details.

therefore, to be understood as an afflux of spiritual power to the Redeemer, in his extremest agony of abandonment.) How an angel could strengthen Christ—in whom the eternal word of the Father had become flesh (John i. 1–14), may be conceived, by assuming that in the season of temptation and of struggle, the fulness of his Divine life withdrew itself, so that the human soul of Christ was that which struggled, and which was strengthened. Without doubt we must conclude that this strengthening followed the threefold prayer, of which Luke alone makes no mention; it is then parallel to Mark i. 13, where it said, after the temptation was ended, "the angels ministered to him" (οἱ ἄγγελοι διηκόνουν αὐτῷ). The following καὶ γενόμενος κ. τ. λ., is then to be understood as the pluperfect, and signifies that the aid was given at the very height and crisis of the struggle. Although this inference is grammatically admissible (compare Winer's Gr. s. 251), yet still, the καὶ γενόμενος, when taken in connexion with the following ἐγένετο δέ, seems to contradict it. Hence we can only say that Luke in this place has not recorded with precision the sequence of the events. (Ἀγωνία is often equivalent to ἀγών, struggle, strife. Then it means agony, faintness, death-struggle. In the New Testament it occurs in this passage only. Ἐκτενέστερον is from ἐκτενής, used also of prayer, Acts xii. 5.)

As a physical expression of the Saviour's fearful struggle, Luke mentions further that he "sweat as it were great drops of blood" (ἱδρὼς ὡσεὶ θρόμβοι αἵματος). Although, on the authority of medical statements, we can believe that in the highest state of mental agony, a blood exudation may take place (compare the passages in Kuinoel, vol. ii. p. 654), still we must acknowledge that in those words of Luke, only a *comparison* of the sweat with drops of blood is directly expressed. In relation to real drops of blood, ὡσεί, *as if*, would be altogether out of place. But the point of comparison is twofold; first, that the sweat of Christ assumed the form of drops, which supposes a high degree of agony; and then, that these drops, through their largeness and weight, loosened themselves and fell to the earth. Possibly, as a third point of comparison, the red color was superadded, which would lead to the notion of an exudation from the veins. Still this is not decidedly expressed in the words; but neither are the words directly contradictory of this hypothesis; and since in the church it has become the general acceptation, there is no reason to deviate from, and still less to contend against it.

Ver. 47, seq. contains an account of Christ's capture. After Jesus had wrestled through the heavy struggle, tranquillity and full self-possession were again restored to him; so that to Judas and the company that attended him he appeared in striking majesty. Mark and Luke record the occurrence in an abridged form; but Matthew and John narrate it in detail, and mutually complete each other's accounts. Concerning the preparations for the seizure of Jesus, John informs us xviii. 3. The high priests, uncertain whether the disciples of Christ would not defend him, had taken with them not only some of those who guarded the Temple (ἐκ τῶν ἀρχιερέων ὑπηρέτας), but also a company of Roman soldiers. ('Η σπεῖρα means properly a cohort, compare Acts x. 1, xxvii. 1. A cohort at the time of Augustus was 555 men strong. In this passage there is naturally meant only a division of the cohort stationed in Jerusalem.) The soldiers had not only furnished themselves with weapons, but also with torches (φανοί), of pitch or wax, and with lanterns (λαμπάδες), in which oil was burned.

These torches—since (as it was the passover), it must necessarily have been moonlight—were required, either from the heavens being overcast, or from the apprehension that Jesus had concealed himself in the house, or in the garden. Now according to Matthew and Mark, Judas, who conducted the troop, had preconcerted a sign with the soldiers (Mark xiv. 44 has the expression σύσσημον, which occurs but this once in the New Testament; it signifies a sign agreed upon by several persons), whereby they might easily recognize Jesus, viz., that he would kiss him.

The contrast presented in this selection of the natural expression of affection as a signal of the most detestable treachery, is disclosed in the words of Christ at Luke xxii. 48 : 'Ιούδα, φιλήματι τὸν υἱὸν τοῦ ἀνθρώπου παραδίδως; *Judas, betrayest thou*, etc. But John xviii. 4, et seq., gives a still more particular account concerning the incidents of Judas's approach with the soldiers. The Lord, in the fullest consciousness as to the significance of the moment (εἰδὼς πάντα τὰ ἐρχόμενα ἐπ' αὐτόν), went to meet them, enquired whom they sought, and surrendered himself to them, saying: "I am he." Here John (xviii. 6) mentions that they went backwards and fell to the ground (ἀπῆλθον εἰς τὰ ὀπίσω καὶ ἔπεσον χαμαί).

We need not postulate a particular miracle to account for this action ; the person of Jesus himself is the miracle, and the majesty which beamed forth from him might easily have affected, in the profoundest manner, men who knew of him, and in part might have heard him (John vii. 46). Indeed, similar incidents have occurred in the lives of men, as in that of Marius, for example, whose mere rude energy of aspect exercised a commanding influence. Besides, it is self-evident that the act of falling down ought not to be considered strictly as having extended to all without exception, nor as a lightning-like and complete prostration. But spiritual impression was powerful enough to make itself physically observable in their timorous retreat, during which one or more fell to the earth. The account of Judas's kiss, by Matthew, as Lücke part

II. p. 599, observes, corresponds with the account of John, if we suppose that Judas advanced alone before the others. When the Lord saw Judas and was kissed by him, he accompanied him to meet the approaching troop, in order to defend his disciples, and on this occasion the armed men fell down, overwhelmed by the power of his spirit. In the protection which the Saviour thus visibly afforded to his disciples, John discovers a fulfilment of the word of Christ xvii. 12, the proper intention of which, however, refers unquestionably to the eternal preservation of their souls. This shews how the disciples of the Lord themselves discerned in his pregnant words manifold meanings, a fact, which, as Tholuck justly remarks, is not unimportant to the understanding of the Old Testament prophecies.

The proposal of one disciple to defend themselves with the two swords in their possession, Luke xxii. 38, is minutely recounted by John; he even mentions Peter as the disciple (from whose character, such a daring attempt might have been anticipated), and also the servant of the high priest, whose name was Malchus. Since John was known in the house of the high priest (John xviii. 15), this circumstance is easily explained. According to John xviii. 26, he also knew the relatives of this Malchus. Moreover, both John and Luke remark particularly, that it was the right ear which was cut off. But Luke alone recounts the sudden healing of the wound, Luke xxii. 51. This best explains why Peter withdrew unharmed; astonishment at the cure absorbed general attention. According to John xviii. 11, the Lord after commanding Peter to put up his sword into his sheath, uttered merely these words so full of import: *τὸ ποτήριον ὃ δέδωκέ μοι ὁ πατὴρ, οὐ μὴ πίω αὐτό, the cup which my Father*, etc.; Matth. xxvi. 52, 53, gives the address more in detail.

Our surprise that a somewhat long discourse was delivered to Peter, under the existing circumstances, vanishes when we assume that the words were uttered during the healing. The attention of all was directed to this event, and that rendered it possible for Christ to impart the necessary hint to Peter.

First, the words of Jesus: "they that take the sword shall perish by the sword" (*οἱ λαβόντες μάχαιραν, ἐν μαχαίρᾳ ἀπολοῦνται*), doubtless refer to Peter, according to Gen. ix. 6, Rev. xiii. 10. An arbitrary self-defence against magisterial ordinances is placed in the same category with murder. The reference of the words to the Jews as maintained by Euthymius Zigabenus, viz., "these my murderers shall yet be destroyed," is altogether untenable. The choice of the word *μάχαιρα*, was evidently suggested by the preceding, *ἀπόστρεψόν σου τὴν μάχαιραν*. And what follows places the help of God in contrast with the self-sufficiency of Peter. Parallel with this is the expression: *ἐᾶτε ἕως τούτου, suffer thus far*,

Luke xxii. 51, which some refer to the officers thus, Suffer me to delay so long, to wit, until Malchus' ear shall be healed. It is better to take the words as an injunction to the disciples—"Stay! thus far and no further!"

Again, the thought concerning the twelve legions of angels, is very remarkable. The number twelve might have been selected with reference to the number of the disciples, and the term, *legion* (λεγεών) alludes evidently to the *heavenly host* (στρατία οὐράνιος, Luke ii. 13, corresponding to the צְבָא יְהוָה). Thus the general idea is: "think you that I need earthly aid from you, so few as you are, when the heavenly assistance of the hosts of God stands at my bidding?" Παραστήσει, by Hebrew idiom, for παραστῆσαι, comp. Gesenius' Lehrgeb., p. 771. The striking feature however in the words is the ἢ δοκεῖς ὅτι οὐ δύναμαι ἄρτι; *or thinkest that I cannot now?* —that is, even now, though it has proceeded so far—παρακαλέσαι, κ. τ. λ. From these words the Lord would seem to affirm the *possibility* that he needed not to proceed to his death; of which yet the words immediately following (ver. 54, ὅτι οὕτω δεῖ γενέσθαι), emphatically express the *necessity*. At the passage in Matth. xxvi. 24, we discussed the relation of necessity and freedom. There, however, the necessity of Christ's death was compared with the freedom of action in Judas, who betrayed him. Here, on the contrary, the possibility of evading death seems to have rested in Christ himself. But even here we can understand this possibility as subjective only. In Christ's humanity, there existed ever the possibilitas peccandi, and therefore the possibility of his not entering freely into the higher necessity; but since in the person of the Lord humanity appeared not isolated, but in union with his divinity, a union becoming gradually more intimate, and in his approaching glorification, presupposing already a total penetration of the humanity by the divinity, there was also in Christ an *objective* impossibility to will otherwise than in accordance with God's eternal counsel. In this relation, therefore, we meet in Christ the same union of opposites as in other respects. Jesus, in his human soul, with unconstrained resignation, yielded himself to the eternal counsel of the Father; "no man took his life from him, he laid it down of himself." John x. 18 (comp. in the Commentary, Part I., Matth. iv. 1.—Compare upon the πῶς οὖν πληρωθῶσιν αἱ γραφαί; a thought which is repeated in ver. 56, our observations on Matth. xxvi. 24).

The Scripture is the revealed will of God, and so far the record of necessity. Its prophecies are independent of the truth or infidelity of man: they are fulfilled unconditionally; yet without destroying this freedom of will. In the concluding verses, Matth. xxvi. 55, 56, however, the Saviour further rebukes the officers, that they had come with weapons, as against a robber. He reminds them of his free open teaching in the Temple, and thus exposes their depravity, in that they were afraid of the people. But this also must have happened (τοῦτο δὲ ὅλον γέγονεν) in order that the prophecy (Luke xxii. 37, Isaiah liii. 12) might be fulfilled. According to Luke xxii. 53, there follows here a sentence full of significance: This is your hour and the power of darkness (αὕτη ὑμῶν ἐστιν ἡ ὥρα, καὶ ἡ ἐξουσία τοῦ σκότους). Irony here, in the sense of, "You, bad men, prefer the night for the accomplishment of your deeds," is out of the question; partly, because it would be unbecoming in the Saviour on such an occasion, and partly because the expression "power of darkness" is unsuited to such a meaning. The interpretation defended by Kuinoel, "this is the time given you of God for the prosecution of your design, and the power of your sin," is, in the first member of the sentence, doubtless correct; but as regards the second, the expression "power of darkness" does not refer fittingly to the sin of the officers themselves. Darkness (σκότος) does not signify sin in one or another individual; this is always called ἁμαρτία; but the sinful element, generally; the antithesis of Light (φῶς). Hence these remarkable words express the thought, that even what is sinful can attain to reality only in accordance with the will of God (which we conceive, in reference to *evil*, as working negatively, quoad formale actionis, *i. e.*, as permitting), and in certain times God permits the Light to prevail, and at other times the darkness, according to his own wisdom. (Compare John ix. 4, and Luke xxii. 55.) The moment in which the Holy One of God could, by the sin of men, be brought to the cross, was the culminating point of evil generally. But in reaching that it destroyed itself, and thus revealed its own nothingness, since the murder of the Just One expiated the sins of the whole world.

According to the prophecy of the Lord, Matth. xxvi. 31, the disciples of the Saviour were now scattered, Matth. xxvi. 56. Mark xiv. 51 relates further the particular incident of a young man, lightly clothed, who was apprehended, but escaped, leaving his linen garment in the soldier's grasp. This incident becomes significant only on the assumption that the person of whom it is related is in some way remarkable. To me it appears most probable, that here Mark writes concerning himself. (The pleonastic union of εἷς τις occurs in the New Testament at John xi. 49. Compare Winer's Grammar, 4th edit. p. 105, where εἷς stands for the indefinite article, John vi. 9.—Τις or εἷς would have been sufficient. Σινδών, either from Sidon, or perhaps from the Hebrew סָדִין (compare Gesenius' Lexicon under this word), is equivalent to λέντιον, linen garment. The νεανίσκοι, *youths*, who apprehended the young man were the ὑπηρέται ἀρχιερέων, *servants of the chief priests*, John xviii. 3.)

§ 8. EXAMINATION OF JESUS BEFORE CAIAPHAS AND THE SANHEDRIM. PETER'S DENIAL.

(Matth. xxvi. 57–75; Mark xiv. 53–72; Luke xxii. 54–71; John xviii. 12–27.)

John xviii. 12–14 = (Matth. xxvi. 57; Mark xiv. 53; Luke xxii. 54.)

A correct apprehension of the scene, which reveals itself to our view in what follows, requires a description of the judicial institutions of the Jews at the time of Christ. It was already observed at Matth. v. 21, x. 17, that the Jews in all considerable towns (indeed, according to the Talmud, in all towns of a population exceeding 120) had lesser tribunals, entitled, "*little* Sanhedrim." There were two of these in Jerusalem. As the highest tribunal, however, there existed in Jerusalem the great Sanhedrim = (סַנְהֶדְרִין), which consisted of 71 persons. The origin of this tribunal they derived from Moses himself, who named 70 elders (Numbers xi. 16), who, with him as president, made out the 71. But the Greek name points to a much more recent time, and comes evidently from the word* *συνέδριον*. Ezra, perhaps, founded the tribunal; but certainly the name first arose during the Greco-Syrian dynasty.

The composition of the tribunal was as follows. The officiating high priest (*ἀρχιερεύς*), was the president for the time: he bore the name נָשִׂיא, that is prince, princeps. Secondly, to it belonged the discharged high priests; the twenty-four presidents of the classes of priests—Matth. ii. 24—who also were called *ἀρχιερεῖς*; the rulers of the synagogues (*πρεσβύτεροι*), and other persons of consideration who were acquainted with the law (*γραμματεῖς*). For their meetings they had a particular locality. In cases of emergency, the meetings were held also in the dwelling of the high priest, and such was the case in the examination of Christ. To the cognizance of this court belonged all important cases, but peculiarly all spiritual affairs. Now, since they had denounced Jesus as a false Messiah, they naturally drew his case before their tribunal. Meanwhile, if their malice had not subsequently determined them to put Christ to death, they might have entirely completed his prosecution. Forty years, however, before the destruction of Jerusalem, and three before the death of the Lord, the Romans took from the Sanhedrim the jurisdiction concerning life and death, and hence the judgment was transferred to Pilate. (Comp. J. D. Michaelis' "Mos. Recht." Part I. p. 50, seq.—Winer's "Reallex," p. 677, seq.—Buxtorf. Lex. p. 1513, seq.) It is remarkable, that (according to John xviii. 13)

* Twice only in the New Testament is the Sanhedrim called Πρεσβυτέριον, namely, in Luke xxii. 66, and in Acts xxii. 5.

Christ was not conducted by the guard directly to the officiating high priest, Caiaphas, but to his father-in-law, Annas,* who had been high priest prievously (Josephus. Antiq. xviii. 2) but was deposed, under Tiberius, by the Roman procurator, Valerius Gratus. In his stead, Ismael was appointed, then Eleazer, the son of Annas, next Simon, the son of Camithus; and, lastly, in the year A. D. 26, Joseph or Caiaphas, the son-in-law of Annas.

It is probable that this Annas, having been formerly high priest himself, and being the father of one high priest, and the father-in law of two, thus possessed much influence.† Perhaps also he was even vicar (סְגָן) of the officiating high priest, and on that account they would probably first request his advice concerning the difficult question before them. Finally, the palace of Annas may have been so situated, that it was first reached by the guard with Jesus under arrest. Accordingly, it appears that Jesus was detained here until the Sanhedrim was assembled in the palace of Caiaphas. The latter supposition seems the more worthy of adoption, as it is uncertain whether Annas sustained that office; and since no proper examination occurred in his palace, we may conjecture that he admitted Jesus to his presence chiefly through curiosity, and only incidentally directed a few questions to him. But John, in mentioning the name of Caiaphas, calls attention to his previous statement that this Caiaphas had first counselled the execution of one on behalf of all (comp. John xi. 49, 50), by way of intimating the certain issue of the present trial.

The most difficult circumstance in this section is the synoptical relation of the four Evangelists. For whilst John states expressly that Jesus was conducted first to Annas, and only mentions subsequently his being sent to Caiaphas (xviii. 24), the Synoptical writers relate only the examination in Caiaphas' palace. There also they place the denial by Peter, whilst John leaves it doubtful whether it occurred in the palace of Annas or in that of Caiaphas; for he mentions that incident before (xviii. 15–18), as well as after (xviii. 25–27), the sending of Christ to Caiaphas. In ancient times it was attempted to solve this difficulty by very violent means; ver. 24 was transferred to ver. 13, after the *πρῶτον*. One MS. has this

* As regards the form of the names, in the New Testament, of the two officiating high priests, 'Αννας is derived either from חָנַן or עָנָן. Dr. Paulus, in his Exegotical Manual, Part I. § 1, p. 346, declares for the latter. Caiaphas is properly the name Joseph, as is observed by Josephus, Antiq. xviii. 8, 2. Καιάφας is synonymous with Πέτρος, and is formed from כֵּיפָא, *Cephas* — rock. Caiaphas should have been the true rock of the Church of God, but he was its caricature; and Simon Peter came, as the rock of the new church, into his place. Compare the succession of high priests at the time of Christ, together with the passages quoted as proofs, in Schraders' "Leben Pauli," s. 1, ff.

† In determining who were eligible to the high priesthood, a sort of nepotism must have arisen. They were chosen generally from those influential families which were called *γένος ἀρχιερατικόν*, Acts iv. 6.

reading still, and in the Philoxenian translation, ver. 24 is marked on the margin as interpolated. But the difficulty is more easily removed by taking the ἀπέστειλε in ver. 24 as the pluperfect tense. Thus everything related concerning the trial of Christ and the denial of Peter would be referred to the palace of Caiaphas. Lücke and Meyer declare themselves entirely in favour of this hypothesis, and the *enallage* thus assumed certainly involves no essential difficulty. Compare Winer's Grammar, p. 251, where many passages quoted from profane writers prove that the aorist may be employed for the pluperfect. But the absence of any particle of transition, as well as the position of ver. 24, seem wholly adverse to the hypothesis. Had the words stood after ver. 18, such an assumption would have been more tenable: as it is, it would involve at least extreme negligence in John as a writer. If we confine ourselves to John, it seems clearly his intention to inform us that a trial took place in the palace of Annas, and that Peter was present in that palace. Without the Synoptical narratives, no one could have understood his account differently. For these reasons I declare myself with Euthymius, Grotius, and others, favourable to the supposition that John intended to correct and complete the Synoptical accounts, and therefore he supplies the notice of the examination in the palace of Annas. That there can be an error in the account of John we cannot imagine, for he was an eye-witness, and has narrated the circumstances with care and minuteness; so minute is he indeed in this part of his history, that he has given even the kinship of the high priest's servant (xviii. 26): what he has added concerning the examination by the high priest (ver. 19–23), has no resemblance to that held before Caiaphas, and therefore cannot possibly be identified with the latter.

Add to this, that the Synoptical writers, who were not present at the scene, and who therefore had everything from report, might easily have misapprehended the place, especially since both Annas and Caiaphas were called high priests. When informed that such or such an incident occurred in the palace of the high priest, they would immediately think of Caiaphas, the officiating one, and transfer everything to him. This John easily corrects, but what they had fully and exactly recorded, viz., the decisive examination in the palace of Caiaphas,* this he passes over entirely.

The course of events would accordingly be as follows: When the guard conducted Jesus into the city, they brought him at once

* In his last edition, Tholuck comes to the conclusion that ver. 24 may be merely a gloss, which some reader of the gospel subjoined, to meet the misconception that the events recorded should be referred to the palace of Annas. But such a hypothesis could be justified only if our critical authorities indicated the spuriousness of the passage, verse 24. But such is by no means the case.

to the house of Annas, which they arrived at first; partly, as we have remarked, that he might be detained there till the Sanhedrim were summoned; and partly perhaps that Annas might gratify a desire to see and speak with him. Annas commenced a conversation with Christ, but in consequence of his reply, one of the servants smote the Redeemer; and whilst Annas, who had satisfied his curiosity, and saw that from Christ's answers he could extract nothing, withdrew himself, the multitude practised their outrages upon the holy person of Christ. Peter, under the protection of John, had pressed into the outer court, but he denied that he knew the Lord, when urged to confess that he knew him. One of these denials occurred just at the moment—ver. 24, 25—in which Christ was being led away to Caiaphas, whence Jesus could regard him with a glance full of meaning. On reaching the palace of Caiaphas, the Saviour was immediately brought to trial; and the judgment, and transference to Pilate, succeeded without interval. In this place, therefore, there was no conceivable opportunity in which the rude ill-treatment of Christ could have occurred. According to Matth. xxvi. 67, 68, Mark xiv. 65, it would seem to have taken place in the presence of the Sanhedrim; but this is at all events incompatible with the dignity of the highest tribunal of the land, a dignity which would be at least externally preserved. Luke xxii. 64–71, gives the whole examination as a supplement merely, and therefore there is nothing to be inferred from his allocation of these events. But how natural everything appears, if we regard the rudeness which a menial ventured to practise against Jesus, in the very presence of Annas, as a signal which, after his withdrawal, called forth still more numerous expressions of insolence. Left alone with the prisoner, the common crowds of soldiery and guards of the Temple could dare to mock him; but at the palace of Caiaphas the guards were not thus left in company with Christ. The only objection to this interpretation is the fact, that, according to the general assumption, John was acquainted with Caiaphas, not with Annas. If, however, we reflect that both the high priests were nearly related, it will be plain that an acquaintance with the one almost implies an acquaintance with the other. As regards the title *ἀρχιερεύς*, it is well known that it was bestowed not only upon the officiating, but also upon the retired or superseded high priests.

John xviii. 15–18, 24–27.—According to the sequence of events laid down, we shall now consider Peter's denial,* and the examination of Christ before Annas. Both events took place nearly simultaneously. Crowds of soldiers and guards of the Temple, together with the servants of the high priest, filled the fore-court. In a hall

* Compare the treatise by Rudolph upon the denial of Peter, in Winer's "Zeitschr. f. Wissensch Theol. h. 1, s. 109, ff."

which ran out to the fore-court, Annas probably spoke with the Saviour, during which Peter was questioned without, and the question was repeated as they led away Christ to Caiaphas. As regards the "other disciple," ver. 15, there can be no doubt that, by this expression, John signifies himself. The objections to this view are altogether without weight. The most plausible is that John being the son of a Galilean fisherman, could scarcely have had a personal acquaintance with the high priest; but as we have frequently remarked, we are by no means to think the circumstances of Zebedee contemptible. We might suppose that John was acquainted with the domestics only of the high priest; but the expression γνωστὸς τῷ ἀρχιερεῖ, *known to the high priest*, renders this improbable; and we must not forget that extraordinary complications often bring together persons whose positions in society are most dissimilar. Further, in the particulars of the denial of Peter, John deviates again from the Synoptical writers. These mention three acts of denial, John speaks of but two. It may indeed be said that in the second denial John distinguishes two separate acts (ver. 25, 26), in the first of which several persons inquire of Peter, μὴ καὶ σὺ ἐκ τῶν μαθητῶν αὐτοῦ εἶ; *art thou also*, etc.; in the second, only one, a servant (δοῦλος), makes the inquiry. This will not, however, reconcile the two accounts, for, according to Matth. xxvi. 71, and Mark xiv. 69, the second question, as well as the first, proceeded from a damsel. Besides, Luke does not agree with Matthew and Mark, since he, xxii. 58, speaks of a δοῦλος, where those two name a damsel; and where they speak of the whole surrounding concourse, Matthew xxvi. 73, Mark xiv. 70, he mentions a second individual (male) servant.

Attempts to reconcile such slight differences are altogether unprofitable; we must take them as they are given. They are a security for the independence of the evangelical narrative, and therefore only help to promote the object of the Scriptures. In accordance with Christ's antecedent prophecy, however (Matth. xxvi. 75) the threefold denial must have, without a doubt, actually occurred. John's purpose is here not to give a complete report of the event, but merely to determine correctly its locality. To the threefold denial, the thrice-repeated question, John xxi. 1, et seq. also adverts. The palace of the high priest was, without doubt, a large and magnificent building. It enclosed a court (αὐλή) in which were stationed the soldiers, who, in consequence of the coldness of the night, had kindled a fire. This court lay deeper than the principal building, to which they ascended probably by a staircase (Mark xiv. 66). A colonnade, which was usually covered in, extended to the street (προαύλιον, Mark xiv. 68, πυλῶν in Matth. xxvi. 71); through this colonnade lay the passage into the court. Here a damsel was stationed as doorkeeper, John xviii. 17. (The Romans and Greeks had men for doorkeepers; the Jews, women, generally. Compare 2 Samuel iv. 6; Acts xii. 13.) This portress seems to have recognized Peter, who at the beginning fled with the other disciples, but soon followed Christ at a distance (*μακρόθεν*), and, by the influence of John, was admitted immediately to the house; she probably recognized him by his appearance, and by his terror, which must have been excessive to have attracted such general notice. He had followed the Lord to see what would be the issue (*ἰδεῖν τὸ τέλος*, Matth. xxvi. 58), and already evidently feared the worst. The damsel keeping the door fixed a piercing glance on him (*ἐμβλέψασα αὐτῷ*, Mark xiv. 67, *ἀτενίσασα αὐτῷ*, Luke xxii. 56), and asked him about his connexion with the "Nazarene." Here Peter made one denial. And now, to remove himself from the place of danger, he hastened to the Pylon (Matth. xxvi. 71; Mark xiv. 68), in which was the door that led to the street. But here another damsel questioned him, and again the weak disciple, with an oath, denied his Master.

This fresh question prevented Peter from leaving the court. He drew near the blazing watch fire, and, with affected boldness, seated himself amongst the servants of the Temple, who were keeping guard. John xviii. 18–25. For an hour (Luke xxii. 59), Peter kept himself quiet here, and remained unnoticed. This occasioned him probably to make some enquiries concerning Jesus; and now all knew him from his accent to be a Galilean. (Matth. xxvi. 73; Mark xiv. 70. The pronunciation of the Galileans was broader and flatter than that of the inhabitants of Judea. Compare Buxt. Lex. page 434.) One in particular, a relative of Malchus, whose ear Peter smote off, and who himself was present at the capture of Jesus (John xviii. 26), declared that he knew him. But again Peter denied his Lord. On this occasion the cock crowed. This predicted sign recalled the warning of Christ to the disciple's memory, and a penitent feeling gained predominance in his soul. Luke, xxii. 61, significantly observes that the Lord turned around, and that his glance pierced Peter's heart. This fully corresponds with John xviii. 24, et seq. according to which Jesus was just being led to Caiaphas, when the last denial of Peter occurred. Hence, as he must have passed through the court and the Pylon, he could have glanced at the disciple. Upon his master disappearing, the disciple too hastened out, and wept bitterly, Mark xiv. 72. (The import of *ἐπιβαλὼν ἔκλαιε*,* is doubtful. Fritzsche, however, defends very thoroughly the ancient explanation of Theophylact, in which *ἐπιβαλών* is explained by *ἐπικαλυψάμενος τὴν κεφαλήν*. The act of

* Com. Ver. "When he thought thereon he wept." Ἐπιβαλών, *casting upon*, scil. his mind — throwing his mind upon, *thinking upon*: or, with Theoph., "casting (scil. his garment) upon" — *covering his head*. The former meaning seems preferable.—[K.

veiling is confessedly a natural expression of humiliated sorrow, and accordingly this meaning very well corresponds with the circumstances. Fritzsche, indeed, thinks that Peter, by this act, sought to conceal himself; but I cannot concur in this view, for the very reason that the sudden veiling would have made him recognizable rather than the contrary. General usage sufficiently corroborates this acceptation of the term, which is not at all the case with other interpretations, as for example that which supplies τοὺς ὀφθαλμούς, *the eyes,* and translates, "directing to Jesus *the eyes*, or τὸν νοῦν, *the mind*," and understands the words thus, viz., "*giving heed*, he wept." Perhaps, however, it would be best to regard the participle ἐπιβαλών as in parallelism with πικρῶς, and to understand it as intimating the violence of the weeping. Ἐπιβαλών, like ὁρμᾶν, is frequently used to signify violent emotion.)

This narrative concerning Peter, presents us the first significant figure, representing all the weak and timorous amongst the faithful, in that grand picture which the history of the Lord's sufferings unfolds. The most energetic, the most zealous amongst the disciples, appears utterly feeble, utterly wretched! "The Spirit was willing, but, alas! the flesh was weak." How touching the simplicity with which the Evangelists relate this deep fall of the chief amongst them. They do not soften down its harshness: they plainly state that *a damsel* asked him. But, as they do not excuse Peter, neither do they criminate him, nor express wonder at his conduct. Without any comment whatever, they state the simple fact. We, however, cannot and must not exclude reflection, and we are compelled to ask ourselves the question: "how was it possible that *Peter*, this resolute disciple, to whom Christ had expressly foretold his fall, could, even when no danger threatened him, deny his Lord so decidedly?"* The denial would be more conceivable if he had had death in prospect as the alternative. But the *examination* had in truth no reference to the followers of Christ: Peter was thus terrified at the question of a maiden. According to a merely superficial interpretation of the narrative, there appears here a psychological enigma. But, if we penetrate more deeply into the scene, then, in order to an explanation in the case of Peter, precisely as in the case of Christ's struggle in Gethsemane, we shall be forced to recognize internal causes.

It was the hour of the power of darkness (Luke xxii. 53) which had in so inconceivable a way impaired and obscured the spiritual

* Dr. Paulus, indeed, undertakes to defend the denying Apostle. He is of opinion that Peter did not tell a lie, because no one possessed the right of asking him. "Nothing is less to be objected against him," he says, than "the Saviour's language in respect to 'confessing him before men.'"—*Exposition of the Gospels*, Bk. iii. p. 649. This astounding assertion, however, needs no further confutation. We merely mention it here as a psychological curiosity

energy of the disciple, that he could not only deny Christ, but also remain exposed to the danger of repeating his crime after he had once denied him. There befel Peter, on this occasion, a more than merely human temptation (compare 1 Cor. x. 13), which was necessary to cure him of his self-approving delusion, and to make him a mirror for others; a temptation from which our Lord hath taught us to pray for deliverance in the Lord's prayer, and from which Peter would have escaped if he had previously humbled himself, in obedience to the word of his Master. Thus the Lord practises towards his people the most various kinds of discipline, for the perfecting of their spiritual life. As Peter's *fall* tended ultimately to his salvation, so to the others did their *preservation* from it. As his fall led the proud Peter to humility, so their preservation in the same peril under which Peter succumbed, confirmed the rest of the disciples immoveably in their confidence in that Divine grace which had preserved them.

Ver. 19–23.—Here commences the discourse of Annas with Christ. It was evidently the offspring of mere inquisitiveness rather than a formal examination. As afterwards Herod, so on this occasion the high priest, desired to look upon the extraordinary man, and to see something wonderful effected by him. Hence, also, the form of Christ's answer. It would, in fact, not have been suitable for a judicial examination. The party accused, whether rightly or wrongfully, and even when interrogated in an illegal manner, ought both to hear and to answer the language of official authority. This submission to the magistracy we find observed by the Saviour, in the most delicate manner. He replied decorously even to the unjust, wicked judges, or where all defence would have been in vain, he kept silence (Matth. xxvi. 63). Here, however, there was no judicial relation whatever, for Annas was no longer high priest. On this account the Lord could censure the impertinent and perhaps malignant curiosity of the priest. The demeanour of Christ, under his rude maltreatment by the servant, is also worthy of notice. We have here an authentic practical exposition of the command, Matth. v. 39. As was observed in the Commentary, Part I. on Matth. v. 43, it would have been an encouragement to further insolence, if the Saviour had not asserted his right to legal protection, since the injury was done him in the presence of the servant's master, whose *duty* it was to reprimand him.

When he was afterwards abandoned, a solitary prey to the rude caprice of the soldiery, there remained to the Redeemer no other weapon than that of silence; for an appeal to justice made in the midst of outrage, is merely a provocative of further outrage. This one act of violence finally became (probably after Annas had retired), a signal to several others (Matth. xxvi. 67, 68; Mark xiv.

65; Luke xxii. 63–65). It is wonderful that the spirit of prophecy considered it not unsuitable to its dignity, to predict this maltreatment minutely, Isaiah l. 6, Micah v. 1, and at the same time to sketch the state of mind which the Holy One of God opposed to the wicked multitude. "The Lord helpeth me," says the Messiah in Isaiah l. 7, "therefore am I not put to shame: therefore have I set my face like a flint." Here is expressed unwavering faith in God's eternal love, even in the deepest abandonment. In like manner, the prophet, in another passage, depicts that inexpressible meekness and patient resignation which no mockery could disturb, when he says: "He was oppressed and he was afflicted, yet he opened not his mouth, as a lamb that is brought to the slaughter, and as a sheep that is dumb before her shearers." (Isaiah liii. 7.) To estimate the entire greatness of this conduct, we should constantly remember that the *mocked* One was the Eternal Word of the Father, that for our sakes had become flesh, and endured all this for us!!

Matthew xxvi. 59–61; Mark xiv. 55–59; Luke xxii. 66–71.

After the Lord had been led away to Caiaphas (John xviiii. 24) immediately followed the formal trial before the collected Sanhedrim. In the interim, according to Luke xxii. 66, ere the Sanhedrim had assembled, the morning dawned. Matth. (xxvii. 1) and Mark (xv. 1) transfer the judgment to the morning, and John xviii. 28 the leading away of Jesus to the judgment hall of Pilate. If, however, we consider that the first gray of dawn may be called morning, there will be no discrepancy between the two accounts. Besides, the summoning of the whole Sanhedrim might well have occupied so much time that the chief part of the night would have elapsed.

As respects now the position held by this high council, the examination of the cause of Christ was not in itself irregular. This tribunal was not merely permitted, but was expressly bound to test, according to the word of God, the pretensions of every one laying claim to be a prophet, or the Messiah (compare Matth. xxi. 23, in the Commentary, Part I). But it was, first, a false proceeding of the Sanhedrim to arrest Jesus, since they had already received, in reply to their inquiries, the most open declarations of his dignity as the Messiah: and again to seek, contrary to their better knowledge, false witnesses against the Holy One of God. It is manifest that they had prepared these pretended witnesses against him beforehand, for otherwise they could not have procured them during the night. In this proceeding their ill-will towards Christ is expressly manifested, and therefore he preferred keeping silence during their accusations. It was in the further inquiry only, that, true to the obligations of the subject, he expressed himself before his unjust judges. There appeared first against Christ several false witnesses, according to prophecy, Ps. xxvii. 12. But, as Mark observes

(xiv. 56), their statements did not coincide; they contradicted one another in their depositions. (The reading is uncertain in the text of Matth. xxvi. 60. The usual text reads: *καὶ οὐχ εὗρον, καὶ πολλῶν ψευδομαρτύρων προσελθόντων οὐχ εὗρον*. According to the best authorities, this reading contains the thought to be expressed, only somewhat amplified by transcribers. Griesbach and Schulz have restored the text as follows: *καὶ οὐχ εὗρον πολλῶν ψευδομαρτύρων προσελθόντων*.) At last, however, there came two witnesses who impeached the words of Christ relative to the destruction of the Temple. We have already, John ii. 19, 20, discussed the question, to what extent these latter persons could be styled *false* witnesses, since Christ in fact did utter this language.*

Matth. xxvi. 62–66; Mark xiv. 60–40.—When, now, Caiaphas, who presided over the assembly, perceived that by these means nothing was to be gained in favour of their design, he sought to neutralize the silent, yet eloquent, testimony of Christ against the false witnesses. He summoned him to defend himself, and, as Jesus still kept silence, he adjured him to declare if he was Christ, the Son of God, to which question the Saviour then answered with a direct affirmative. Immediately before this decisive question and answer should probably be placed that language in Luke xxii. 67, 68, which declares the Saviour's motive for keeping silence. The latter Evangelist precedes it, it is true, with the question, *εἰ σὺ εἶ ὁ Χριστὸς, εἰπὲ ἡμῖν, if thou art the Christ, tell us*; yet this may be classed with those slight inaccuracies of arrangement, of which several instances occur in the last chapters of Luke; for, in verse 69, the declaration of Christ's sitting at the right hand of God does not concur happily with his alleged motive for silence. But it stands very appropriately before the question of the high priest, and softens down what would otherwise seem harsh in Christ's utter silence at the high priest's question. It is probable, therefore, that the Lord only delayed his answer in order to give them the impression that he knew how useless would be any defence, since his death was already resolved upon. Thus he preserved decorum before the magistracy, which, even in its degeneracy, is God's ministry, and yet, by his conduct, bore witness against the iniquity with which they desecrated their sacred office.

In the question of the high priest, "Christ" (Χριστός), and "Son of God" (υἱὸς τοῦ Θεοῦ), are again placed together. But since the name "Son of God" here stands last, nothing can be more simple than to regard it as a further determination of the first expression. But, because the high priest uses the name "Son of God," it does

* How such an assertion offended the Jews, who were so attached to the sensible Temple, is shewn in Acts vi. 13, 14, where they accused Stephen of having said something similar.

not follow that it was then generally recognized. We must rather (in accordance with John x. 33), understand the question thus: "Art thou THE Son of God, whom thou professest thyself to be?" The sequel shews that the high priest—as previously the people—regarded this pretension as blasphemy,* which would not have been the case, had he only declared that he was the Messiah. The accusation, "he has declared himself to be the Son of God," was, in itself, a charge involving life and death; for it was, as the passages in John v. 18, x. 33, prove, held to be blasphemy. On the other hand, the accusation, "he hath declared himself to be the Messiah," would have required proof before the Sanhedrim that he was not the Messiah; but nowhere in the trial of Christ is there any reference to such proof. It is, moreover, evident that the Pharisees could not allow the adducing of proofs of this Messiahship, for Jesus had performed too many miracles to fail in witnesses to his Messiahship. This passage serves as a decisive proof that "Son of God" at the time of Christ, was not a usual title of the Messiah. (Compare upon υἱὸς τοῦ Θεοῦ, Luke i. 35, and Matth. xvi. 16. Ἐξορκίζω = ὁρκίζω = הִשְׁבִּיעַ, Mark v. 7; Genesis xxiv. 3. The name "Living God" (Θεὸς ζῶν) in this connexion, seems to signify God as the omnipresent punisher of falsehood.)

Now the open and solemn affirmation of Christ that "he was the Son of God," and the direct statement of his future manifestation in the glory of the Father, is very important, because it enables us to perceive how the commands of the Sermon on the Mount (Matth. v. 34) are to be understood; namely, that they should not bind believers in their relations to the world. Again, it is important, because in it Jesus officially expresses, before the highest theocratic authority, that which hitherto he had but privately taught. Thus Christ at once confirmed the idea of Messiah's character, and the certainty that in him this idea was perfectly realized. At the same time this address of Christ brought before the consciousness of the Sanhedrists, in all its force, the significance of that moment. They were compelled to recognize that they were then pronouncing judgment on the king of their people, on him of whom all the prophets had prophesied. This open declaration of the Saviour thus determined essentially the character of their guilt. At this sublime moment the discourse of Christ assumes a character of kingly dignity. He speaks as the Lord of heaven, not as a helpless prisoner; and the confession of his Messiahship is followed by the threatening of his second advent.

As so often in the Gospel history, there is presented here also a grand and profoundly affecting contrast. The judge of the living

* Compare on this subject the comment on John xix. 7, where the charge against Christ before Pilate was, "He hath called himself God's Son."

and the dead stands as an accused prisoner before a human judge, and is by him condemned! yet in this humiliation the Saviour gives a glimpse of that glory in which he shall yet appear as judge of all the world, even of his judges. (Πλήν is used adversatively, but, in the beginning of the discourse = אֲבָל, as imo, utique.) For ἀπ' ἄρτι Luke xxii. 69 has ἀπὸ τοῦ νῦν: it is best referred merely to the sitting at the right hand of God, which revealed itself immediately in the spiritual agency of Christ; for then we entirely avoid the difficulty as to how Christ can represent himself, *even now*, as coming. And, again, the idea of "coming" (ἔρχεσθαι), would properly be associated with ἄρτι, *now*, but not with ἀπ' ἄρτι, *henceforth;* which latter expression would represent Christ's coming as *continuous*, whereas it is assuredly but a single event. If, however, we wish to retain the connexion, then the thought must be explained of the *speedy* coming in glory, according to Matth. x. 23, xvi. 28, xxiv. 30. The idea of the coming in glory is, according to Matth. xxiv. 30, to be assumed as known; but the καθῆσθαι ἐκ δεξιῶν, *sitting at the right hand*, requires here a particular discussion. Instead of this expression, there occurs in one place, with a slight modification of the meaning, ἑστὼς ἐκ δεξιῶν, *standing at the right hand* (Acts vii. 55, 56), and in a few places, εἶναι ἐν δεξιᾷ, *being at the right hand* (Rom. viii. 34; 1 Peter iii. 22; Heb. i. 3, viii. 1). The formula does not occur in any of John's writings, not even in Revelation. Yet the Apocalypse describes Christ as sitting on the throne of the Father. (Rev. iii. 21, xxii. 1, 3.) To understand the force of this form of expression, it is of the utmost importance to observe, that it is *never* said of Christ, before his incarnation, that "he sat at the right hand of God." Thus, doubtless, the expression refers to the exaltation of his glorified humanity, in which the Lord is represented as partaker in the Divine sovereignty of the universe.* But the reasons of the writers of the New Testament for selecting this particular designation are doubtful.

J. D. Michaelis understands it to imply a reference to the Ark

* From this fundamental idea Luther's theory of the "ubiquity of the right hand of God" is to be estimated; a theory which he surely could never have sanctioned had not the Reformers objected to his doctrine of the "ubiquity of the body of Christ," the sitting at the right hand of God. For if it be said that the right hand of God is omnipresent, the reality of Christ's glorified body is manifestly annihilated. The anxiety, lest in this restricting of the right hand of God, the omnipresence should be involved, is just as unfounded as the notion that, supposing the soul dwells in a man's head, the filling of his whole organism by the soul's being may be considered as destroyed. God, as is self-evident, is everywhere present, yet, as we formerly observed, he reveals himself variously in the hearts of the righteous and the godless, in heaven and upon earth respectively. The being of God in heaven—the highest concentration of his power—is that which is meant by the right hand of God, and Christ's sitting on the right hand of God, accordingly means nothing more than his being associated in the most intimate communion with the Father, and in the exercise of all the Divine attributes, and his participation in the Divine universal sovereignty.

of the Covenant, which is represented as the throne of God; but it is not evident how with the Ark of the Covenant the precise idea of the right hand can acquire significancy. Better, therefore, to regard the position on the right hand as a place of honour, as is done by Knapp (scr. var. arg. p. 39, seq.), who refers to the general custom of all nations. (Comp. Just. Lipsius quis locus honestior priscis, dexter, an sinister? opp. i. p. 759, seq. Callimachi hymn. in Apoll. v. 30, says of Apollo: δύναται γὰρ, ἐπεὶ Διὶ δεξιὸς ἧσται.*) The expression implies therefore the most exalted honour, a participation in God's universal sovereignty. Accordingly, Christ was convinced of this, even in the depth of his humiliation, and ventured to urge it upon his unjust judges. When we consider the solemn earnestness and energy of spirit with which the Lord must have uttered these words, we may conjecture that a dark foreboding, that he might have spoken truly, must have sent a thrill of terror through the priests. But they had proceeded too far to retreat. In hypocritical sorrow the high priest (though inwardly he must have rejoiced at having thus entrapped Christ through his own confession) rent his garment, (compare Joshua vii. 6; Judges xi. 35; 2 Samuel i. 11), declared Jesus a blasphemer† (John x. 33), and the Sanhedrim condemned the Lord of Glory! They hated even unto death him who loved them even unto death! They certainly had not a thoroughly clear knowledge that he was the Lord of Glory (1 Cor. ii. 8; Acts iii. 17; Luke xix. 42). The very fact of his being made prisoner they may have regarded as a proof that he was not the Messiah, still less the Son of God. Yet their depraved hearts were still affected by the splendour of his Divine nature; and it was only because they had closed up the eyes of their spirit through fear of learning too much, and being forced to abandon their sinful courses, that they did not attain to a perfectly clear understanding. Hence their very ignorance was their guilt, and the fearful curse of this guilt was, that they became in their blindness the murderers of the Holy One of God.

§ 4. PROCEEDINGS BEFORE HEROD AND PILATE.

(Matth. xxvii. 1-31; Mark xv. 1-20; Luke xxiii. 1-25; John xviii. 28 et seq. xix. to v. 16.)

Matth. xxvii. 1, 2. The sitting of the Sanhedrim was held on the night of Jesus' arrest. Now when morning approached, the

* "For he is able, since he sits at the right hand of Jove." —[K.

† Here we ought to give prominence to the fact, that if the Lord were not indeed and in truth the being whom he professed himself to be, then must he rightly have been so denominated. Hence, every hypothesis which disputes the heavenly dignity of Christ is liable to the danger of damaging his moral character.

council sentenced him to death, and led him away to Pilate; for the Jews themselves had been deprived of the jurisdiction concerning life and death. Compare Joseph. Antiq. xx. 6. (On the remark of John, "that the Jews went not into Pilate's hall of judgment," that they might be able to eat the passover, we have already given the necessary explanation, Matth. xxvi. 17. Under the word passover, the *Chagigah* must be understood, for it was eaten on the same day, and they would have been debarred from partaking of this feast by the defilement contracted by entering a heathen house. It would not have excluded them from partaking of the paschal lamb, because this was not slaughtered and eaten until the following day, when they would be again clean according to law.) In this place Matthew completes the history of the unhappy Judas, who becomes the second figure in the sublime picture of Christ's passion. The history of Judas is impressed with a peculiar and unique character; we shall therefore collect here all the particulars referring to him and to the condition of his spirit.

Ver. 3-10.—We shall first consider the statements made concerning his external fortunes. Judas, when he perceives the issue of his treachery, terrified, and seized with remorse, cast down the pieces of silver* before the high priests. (*Μεταμέλομαι* is also used to express true repentance [*μετάνοια*]. Compare Matth. xxi. 29, 32. But here it signifies remorse for the consequences of sin merely, not for the sin itself.) That feeling of remorse proceeded from a lively consciousness of his having betrayed an innocent person, for as such he had known Christ. (Compare upon *αἷμα ἀθῶον* Matth. xxiii. 35, where *αἷμα δίκαιον* is employed.) With icy coldness the hypocritical Pharisees repel † the ill-fated wretch: they lay on him the burden of the guilt, and persuade themselves that they are free from it; whilst they were in all respects like him, culpable in the highest degree. (Σὺ *ὄψει*, Attic for *ὄψῃ*,‡ is parallel with the Hebrew דְּעִי וְעַתָּה, וּרְאִי, 1 Samuel xxv. 17. The LXX. give: *νῦν γνῶθι καὶ ἴδε σὺ τί ποιήσεις.*) Reduced to despair by this cheerless reply, he threw the money from him and hanged himself. The *ἐν τῷ ναῷ*, *in the temple*, in this passage causes a considerable difficulty; since the *ναός*, the temple proper, might be entered by the priests only. If we suppose that the money was thrown in through the opened veil into

* The expression: *τριάκοντα ἀργύρια*, is after the Hebrew כֶּסֶף, which is often connected with שֶׁקֶל. Here, doubtless, 30 shekels—about 15 dollars—are meant. There is something contemptuous in the fact that this was the lowest price of a slave. Compare Exodus xxi. 32. Zechariah xi. 12.

† The Pharisees expressed that shameful exultation, which often arises in the human heart, when one sees a brother fallen into sin. Yet in this emotion, hateful as it is, there is also expressed, from the greater depth of the mind, the wish to be free from sin. In so far, therefore, it is a corrupted expression of what is the nobler elements in man.

‡ Compare similar forms in Winer's Grammar, s. 72.

the holy place, then of necessity *εἰς* should be used, and besides, this would be an extraordinary act. Hence, it is better to assume that *ναός* in this passage is employed somewhat loosely, like *ἱερόν*, and that the scene occurred in some outer hall.) Luke, however, in the Acts of the Apostles, seems to come into opposition with the *ἀπήγξατο*, *hung himself*, of Matthew. In Luke's history, for instance, it is mentioned that Judas fell headlong downwards (*πρηνὴς γενόμενος*), and burst asunder (*ἐλάκησε μέσος· λακέω* signifies primarily to sound, to crash—then, to tear asunder with a crashing noise, *ἐλάκησε* = *διεῤῥάγη*), so that his bowels gushed out. To reconcile this disagreement, very violent and altogether untenable hypotheses have been framed. Some would have *ἀπήγξατο* refer to his trouble of mind, "he was benumbed with agony and remorse." Others would understand *πρηνὴς γενόμενος* like *ἀπήγξατο*, "he hanged himself." Rather than give assent to these forced interpretations, we would prefer the supposition that a twofold tradition obtained concerning the fate of Judas, since in such secondary matters, variations elsewhere occur. Yet we must confess that the accounts may be so connected as to permit the conjecture that Judas hanged himself, and, falling down, was so injured that his bowels gushed out. We may then translate the *πρηνὴς γενόμενος*, "as he fell down prone," *i. e.*, upon his belly.*

After Judas had got rid of the money, a new trait of hypocrisy displayed itself in the high priests. As it was blood-money, they would not place the thirty pieces of silver in the treasury of the Temple, lest they should defile it; but they had no consciousness of their own sin in condemning the innocent! (*Κορβανᾶς*, קָרְבָּן is the sacred treasure of the Temple, which was kept in seven chests called trumpets שׁוֹפָרוֹת. Comp. Mark vii. 11.† *Τιμὴ αἵματος*, the reward of blood, money paid for the betrayal of one who was innocent. They therefore applied the thirty pieces of silver to the purchase of a place of burial for pilgrims (*ξένοι*). Matthew designates this field definitely as the "potter's field" (*ὁ ἀγρὸς τοῦ κεραμέως*). The article intimates that there was a spot which bore the name of the potter's field; either because it belonged to a potter, or because potters' clay abounded there. The field was now called *ἀγρὸς αἵματος*, *field of blood* = *ἀκελδαμά*, Acts i. 19, after the Hebrew חֲקַל דְּמָא. According to Acts i. 18, Judas would seem to have acquired possession of the place himself. But *ἐκτήσατο χωρίον ἐκ μισθοῦ* is easily explained so as to obviate such an impression; the purchase, to wit, is

* Papias seems to have held another tradition concerning the end of Judas, judging from Œcumenius on Acts i. 18, and from Theophylact on the same passage and on Matth. xxvii. 5. It was, that Judas was crushed to death by a carriage, by which therefore his suicide would entirely be done away with. Comp. Schleiermacher's essay concerning the evidence of Papias, in "Ullmann's Studien," year 1832, heft. 4, s. 743.

† See on the treasury at Mark xii. 41–44.—K.

attributed to Judas himself, because it took place in consequence of his deed of treachery.) Matthew discovers the fulfilment of a prophecy in this occurrence. But, first, it is very remarkable that the prophecy mentioned does not occur in Jeremiah.* Several manuscripts read, instead, Zechariah and Isaiah. The latter name has nothing whatever to do with the quotation, and has been introduced into this passage merely through the neglect of transcribers, for there does not occur in Isaiah anything at all resembling the passage before us. But in Zechariah there is in fact a passage bearing an affinity to Matthew's quotation, Zechariah xi. 13, 14. The simplest solution of the difficulty is therefore to suppose that the Evangelist mistook the name of the prophet, or the earliest transcribers might have read some contraction of the name falsely ; or perhaps there was no name at all there first, and some transcriber supplied it erroneously. Yet this hypothesis seems contradicted by the relation of the passage in Matthew to that in Zechariah. Between the two passages, there is but a distant resemblance. On the one hand allusions in Zechariah which must have appeared important to Matthew, are entirely wanting in the citation (*e. g.* the throwing down of the money in the Temple, which Matthew particularly mentions, ver. 5) ; whilst on the other hand Matthew adds circumstances wholly unknown to Zechariah. Some have thought therefore that this citation (of Matthew) must be traceable to an apocryphal writing, and consequently to an apocrypha of Jeremiah. This view has been deemed particularly plausible from the circumstance, that Jerome declares he had seen such an apocrypha.† (So specially Kuinoel.) But this apocrypha, which is in the Hebrew language, like others under the name of Jeremiah in the Arabic and Sahidic languages, was not written till *after* the birth of Christ. We have no trace whatever of such apocryphas existing prior to that event. They sprung rather from the great religious excitement which characterized the first centuries after Christ. Then probably the originators of such writings made use of this particular passage, in order to foist upon Jeremiah a book of which this passage formed the basis. (So Fritzsche rightly at the passage.) Hence even Jerome declares himself favourable to the hypothesis, that the quotation was from Zechariah. Whether then the Evangelist confounded the names, or in after times the name of Jeremiah crept in falsely, matters but little. If we but compare the passage more closely with the original text, we shall see that everything which Matthew gives is contained also in Zechariah.

* The reference of the quotation to Jeremiah xxxii. 6, et seq., is so uncertain that it deserves no regard.

† Compare my History of the Gospels, p. 57.

There fails only the one reference in Matthew, which the prophet plainly predicted,* viz., that of throwing down the money.

But the order of thought is different, and also Matthew does not follow the LXX., hence the discrepancy appears greater. As regards the appended statement of Matthew, *τὴν τιμὴν τοῦ τετιμημένου, ὃν ἐτιμήσαντο ἀπὸ υἱῶν Ἰσραήλ*, it is clearly referable to Zechariah xi. 12, 13, where the LXX. for *τιμή* read *μισθός*, and have *δοκιμάζεσθαι* for *τιμᾶσθαι*. (In the Hebrew שְׂכָרִי is put for *μισθός μου*.) The Hebrew אֶל־הַיּוֹצֵר which the LXX. give by *εἰς τὸ χωνευτήριον*, *i. e.* into the smelting furnace, is by Matthew, conformably to his object, more precisely determined by the subjoined *ἀγρός*. Finally, the words *καθὰ συνέταξέ μοι κύριος* in Matthew correspond to the *εἶπε κύριος πρός με* in the LXX. The *καθά*, = *καθ' ἅ*, which is identical with *καθώς*, occurs only in this passage of the New Testament. Hence the only question to be considered is, whether this passage (Zechar. xi. 12, 13) is really to be understood as referring to the Messiah. Now, as regards its exposition, the second half of Zechariah is one of the most difficult parts of the Old Testament. (Compare on its authenticity, Hengstenberg's treatise upon Daniel, Berlin, 1831, Appendix.) But, however we may conceive this part of the oracle of Zechariah as a connected whole, we shall be obliged to acknowledge that it is full of remarkable allusions to the Messiah. (Compare especially Zech. ix. 9; x. 11; xii. 10; xiii. 1, 6, 7; xiv. 7.) Although, therefore, as it seems to me, the immediate reference of this passage is not to the Messiah, yet, without doubt, the people of Israel are regarded as a type of the future Saviour, and their fortunes as prophecies are therefore typical of his.

After this discussion of the historical statements concerning the end of Judas, let us now proceed to an estimate of his personal character.† On this subject the question immediately suggests

* Comp. Hengstenberg's Christology, vol. ii., s.s. 258, 465, seq. This scholar thinks that the difficulty can be solved by this means, viz., he, as in Mark i. 2, 3, supposes that the prophet Zechariah, in the passage Zech. xi. 12, 13, has had reference to the antecedent prophecies of Jeremiah: particularly Jeremiah chs. xviii. xix. Now since Matthew quoted the passage from Zechariah, he would, if this view hold good, have attributed the prophecy to its first source, namely, Jeremiah, whence it was drawn by Zechariah himself.

But the correctness of the assumption, that Zechariah drew from Jeremiah, seems to me to have been left unproved by Hengstenberg. In the two chapters of Jeremiah, the 18th and 19th, the discourse refers to the potter only, as in Romans ix. 21, seq., to wit, in so far as he is a symbol of creative agency. The cruse purchased from the potter, which Jeremiah dashes to pieces before the ancients of the people, symbolizes the Divine retributive justice. On the contrary, Zechariah's train of thought refers to the ingratitude of Israel, which blinded that people to the inestimable grace of Jehovah. How this thought can have been borrowed from these chapters of Jeremiah, I confess I cannot perceive.

† It is remarkable how the most opposite extremes combined in the character of the people of Israel. That which was holiest, just as that which was most unholy in its nature, issued from them; the most exalted fidelity, and the blackest treachery! In Genesis

itself: from what motive could the Lord have called him into proximity with himself? Certainly the fearful sin into which he fell became possible only through that calling. The easy answer, "Christ made a mistake in the selection," must be rejected, partly because it tends to impugn the character of the Saviour, and partly because it stands in manifest opposition to John vi. 64-70. As Jesus knew perfectly what was in man (John ii. 25), he knew what was in Judas, and therefore that he would betray him. We must therefore penetrate deeper into this difficult question.*

It is no true benefit to a man if the evil germ which lies within him does not advance directly to maturity. Hence, if Judas had not actually betrayed Christ, yet that would not have changed his nature, and, therefore, have profited him nothing. Again, his proximity to Christ might and ought to have been to him a means of facilitating the annihilation of the germ of iniquity within him. Judas, accordingly, was in this respect like all persons to whom abundant means of spiritual support have been vouchsafed, but who neglect to profit by them. We may say, "it were better for him that this privilege had not been extended to him," but in that case, all possibility of help would have been removed. The case of Judas, however, assumes a peculiarity of character by the fact that a necessity of effecting the deed seems to have been imposed on him. According to the prophecies of the Old Testament, Christ was to die. His death was to become the foundation of the world's redemption. It seems, therefore, that there must have been some one who should betray him, and hence that Judas only had the *misfortune* to be obliged to play his part, but was a stranger to its *guilt*. This remark leads us back to what has been already frequently touched upon, the relation of free will to necessity; on this subject consult the observations on Matthew xxvi. 24. There the Saviour expresses the necessity for his own death, yet declares, that notwithstanding this, the whole burden of the guilt rested upon Judas; that is, that he had acted freely. To sit brooding over this abyss leads to nothing. The human mind must ever come to the conclusion already expressed, that in God everything is necessary, in man everything is free; that, consequently, the Divine knowledge

xlix. 17, the treachery of Judas is perhaps prophetically intimated. If so, we may thence conclude that he was descended from the tribe of Dan.

* Compare Doctor Schollmeyer's treatise, "Jesus and Judas," Lüneberg, 1836. He is of opinion that the sinfulness of Judas was not developed until after his entrance into the company of the Apostles, and thus that the Lord did not err when he chose him. But, still the question remains to be answered: for what reason did Jesus retain him amongst his followers, till he had an opportunity of carrying out his wicked intention? Thus the difficulty is by this view not solved, but removed further off; the more so, since Jesus must have foreknown that the germ of sinfulness, hereafter to be developed, was already existing in the heart of Judas.

of man's moral development and action is necessarily the knowledge of them as free. The same difficulty which is here presented to us, is involved also in every sinful development of life; it by no means belongs peculiarly to the history of Judas. We ought to remember, in respect to Judas, that his selection was not accidental, but that Jesus, from his profound knowledge of man's inmost nature, had chosen the twelve; then it will be evident that he *could* not exclude Judas. For this high calling brought Judas into this position; this alone gave a *possibility* of his salvation, though certainly with this possibility was associated the alternative, which, through Judas's free self-determination, became the *actual* consequence, namely, that he might despise the offered grace, and plunge himself into the abyss of perdition.

If we now glance at the gradual development of his sinful nature, we find that the Scriptures specify covetousness as his master passion, John xii. 6. This vice is called in 1 Timothy vi. 10, *ῥίζα πάντων τῶν κακῶν, the root of all evil.* The meaning of which we may easily comprehend, if we reflect that the essence of covetousness is nothing else than absolute self-seeking, self-appropriation.* In the accumulating of external wealth, this passion appears in its rudest form only. Spiritually, it is the sinful tendency to an absolute appropriation of everything to its individual self. All the efforts of Judas for the promotion of the kingdom of God, proceeded without doubt from the expectation of becoming some great personage. Vain wishes of the kind may have shewed themselves in the *minds* of the other disciples also, but their hearts were filled with a different love from that of self. The design of Judas developed itself but gradually. The petty dishonesties on which he ventured, and after which he yet could bear the presence of the Holy One, without repenting and confessing his sin, gradually hardened his heart, and subjected him to the influence of the power of darkness. And now, when the hour came that it had full authority, and when it infused hellish thoughts into his heart, all power of resistance failed him. The pieces of money which the priests offered to him blinded his perverted judgment. (Matth. xxvi. 14.) His better nature may have struggled long against the Satanic thought, but the fetters of darkness had now bound him: he yielded himself captive. The tragic fate of the unhappy disciple, together with the remorse that arose in him, upon beholding the consequences of his act, have in modern times given occasion to many divines to extenuate his guilt, and to attribute to him this and the other less guilty motive for his deed. Viewed in one aspect, such attempts certainly are evidences of a charitable judgment,

* Meanwhile this lust, because it is like the sinfulness which rejects God, is the reason why, in Ephesians v. 5, the covetous man is called *εἰδωλολάτρης*.

which loves to view the sin of a brother in the mildest light. But in another point of view they are conversely not unfrequently evidence of a want of moral earnestness and decision, and of secret horror of beholding the whole extent of that sin's development, whose germs we trace in our own breast.

It is in the faithful disciple only, who acknowledges the sin within himself in all its magnitude, and who has learned by the power of the Saviour to control and subdue it—that lenity of judgment appears associated with that full power of truth, which in reference to sin expresses itself by calling what is evil, "evil." If genuine repentance had been awakened in Judas, he would have expressed sentence of condemnation against himself; and in accordance with truth, have entitled his sin a fearful, a devilish act; a sin, of such deep premeditation, that it could only result from the full development of a completely wicked life. But his weak remorse was merely horror at the consequences of his deed, and therefore could lead to nothing but despair. But although this morally strict view of the conduct of Judas must be maintained, yet we can by no means ascribe to him an ordinary character. The remorse he felt for his deed, although a fearful evidence of his unbelief—for had he any feeling of the love that was in Christ, he would have sunk into his arms—nevertheless clearly proves, that his better self was capable of shuddering at the fruits of his crime, whilst his suicide, the new sin, offspring of the first, still removes him from the rude ordinary character, that would enjoy quietly the fruits of its treason. But even the sublime spiritual calling, which had introduced him into the circle of the apostles, only plunged him into the deeper perdition, upon his so entirely missing its object. Common men become petty villains, if they yield themselves to the power of darkness; great characters become greatly wicked, when once they allow sin to dominate within them. Granting, then, that Judas presented to himself every possible kind of exculpation for his treachery; that his vanity had been wounded by the reprimand of Jesus (John xii. 7); that his ambition desired a speedier revelation of the Messiah's kingdom, and that he hoped to hasten it, by delivering Jesus into the hands of his enemies, convinced that Jesus could at any time free himself by a miracle; still his deed is not essentially altered by such considerations. His traitorous act acquires its fearful character, not from the external circumstances of the perpetration, but from the radical feeling out of which it grew. This was alienation from God, the absence of faith and love; attachment to the creature, and to his own mere self; hence his first sin became in turn parent to another, and his end was that he went to his own place. Acts i. 26.

We might imagine, that in his fiery self-willed nature, Peter would have conceived the thought, that if he were only to deliver Christ into the hands of his enemies, he must *of necessity* reveal his glory; but supposing anything of the kind, we shall be obliged to admit, that however similar in external respects, there would yet be a specific internal difference between his act and that of Judas. For assuming that it was actually done by Peter, and that the Saviour was condemned, as happened after the treason of Judas, how would Peter then have demeaned himself? Sorrow indescribable would have seized him: but because in Peter such perverseness would at least have been uprightly meant, he would not have relinquished his faith in Christ's pardoning love. His sin would therefore have led him, not to a sorrow that has no hope, but to the true repentance of faith—and thus his deed would have become, not the parent of fresh disobedience, but a source of thorough regeneration. (Upon the literature of the question just treated, compare Hase's Leben Jesu. s. 163, ff.)

Ver. 11–14.—In all the following section the Evangelists mutually supply each other's omissions very admirably. Matthew and Mark give only brief notices of the trial of Christ before Pilate. Matthew, however, introduces the interesting incident concerning the dream of Pilate's wife, xxvii. 19. Luke communicates the proceedings before Herod, xxiii. 4–12. But John narrates the most important circumstance, that is, the conversation of the Lord with the Roman statesman. By these communications we are placed in a proper position to take a deep glance into the heart of Pilate, and to regard him as the third significant figure in the picture of Christ's last moments. Thus whilst Peter represents the weak in faith, and Judas those who apostatise and go over to the ranks of the Lord's declared enemies, Pilate stands before us in the character of a natural worldly-minded man; of one who indeed is not void of susceptibility to Divine influences (nothing of which shews itself in the Pharisees), but who is immersed in the scepticism of the then fashionable world; and who, bound by worldly regards of every kind, sacrifices his conscience to circumstances, for circumstances are his god. Pontius Pilate was the fifth procurator of Judea, and the successor of Valerius Gratus. Compare the first chronological table following the introduction to the Acts of the Apostles.

In the thirteenth year of the reign of Tiberias, he entered upon his office, Joseph. Antiq. xviii. 2. He bears here the name *ἡγεμών*, but his proper official title was *ἐπίτροπος*. The former title was specially given to the independent administrators of the Roman provinces, viz., to proconsuls (*ἀνθυπάτοις*), and propraetors (*ἀντιστρατήγοις*). But the title was also frequently given to the procurators (*ἐπιτρόποις*) who yet were properly subject to those former officers; a practice resembling the custom, which prevails at present, of placing each officer by courtesy a step higher in rank than that to which he is actually entitled. Compare Acts xxiii. 24, xxiv. 1, xxvi. 30. The procurator of Judea was subject to the proconsul of Syria, who resided in Cæsarea. According to the account of Josephus, Pilate was guilty of much oppression, and practised many cruelties against the Jews. To these, however, he may have been excited, partly by their frequent insurrections and his dread of Tiberias, and partly because it was customary with all the Roman officers of state, in the provinces, to practise extortions of every kind. John's accurate portraiture is decisive in regard to his real character. He was susceptible to Divine influences; he believed against his will, in Christ. But the scepticism, which at that time influenced so many of the nobility, and his fear of man, caused him also to fall. According to the account of John xviii. 29–32, Pilate enquired into the grounds of the accusation brought against Jesus. He might have already heard much concerning Jesus—which conjecture is sustained by the dream of his wife—and have known that it was on account of spiritual matters the Jews persecuted him.* Hence he requested that they would take him before the forum of the Sanhedrim, and punish him according to their own law. But this they refused to do, observing that he was adjudged worthy of death, but that the execution of the sentence was not permitted to them by law.

It has been noticed above, that—according to Josephus (Antiq. xx. 6), with which the accounts of the Rabbis coincide—the Jews lost the authority to decree punishment of death forty years before the destruction of Jerusalem. Accordingly, the passage is to be taken entirely simply as implying that the Jews require Pilate to acknowledge and approve of the sentence of death they had passed. But, because of the stoning of Stephen (Acts vii), several scholars have supposed that it must be inferred, that the high council retained the capital jurisdiction in affairs of religion, and therefore, that in this case the appeal to the Roman jurisdiction was adopted only because they wished to put Jesus to death from political motives, as an usurper of the kingdom. But it is in no wise to be discovered on what ground the high priests could have sentenced him as a political criminal. We must say that the evangelical history at least contains no trace of an indication leading to any special purpose therein. We see rather, from John's careful description, that the sole cause of the political charge was their hope by that

* Compare Matthew xxvii. 18, from which passage we may see that Pilate judged quite correctly as to the position of the Pharisees, relatively to Jesus. If not previously, yet from the fact of their arresting Jesus, he must have learned it, since he was obliged to issue orders to the Roman soldiers for that purpose. But it is probable that the fame of Jesus had already reached him.

allegation to conquer the obstinacy of Pilate. To this it must be added, that the stoning of Stephen was not the legal punishment of a criminal, but the tumultuous vengeance of the mob. In short, every other explanation of our passage bears a forced character. For example, in the words "It is not lawful for us to put any one to death" (ἡμῖν οικ ἔξεστιν ἀποκτεῖναι οὐδένα), we must supply "on account of political offences," or "on the Sabbath day," as Augustin thinks, who is followed by Kuinoel; but for these changes of the text, there manifestly is no ground whatever. It was, however, by no means an indifferent circumstance, that, according to the ordinance of God, the Saviour was to be delivered over to the jurisdiction of the Romans; for, since the Jews did not inflict the punishment of crucifixion, which, for heavy offences, the Romans decreed to such persons as were not Roman citizens; therefore this manner of punishment was the consequence of the transference of Christ to the Roman authorities. Nay, even if Pilate had been pliant, and sentenced Christ immediately upon the religious accusations, he would probably have delivered him to the Jews to be stoned. But, when the Jews saw themselves compelled to charge him with political offences, then Pilate was obliged, through his soldiers, to execute him according to the Roman law.

This fact appeared important to John, xviii. 32, who considered it to be a fulfilment of one of Christ's prophecies concerning the manner of his death. (Compare John viii. 28, xii. 32, 33, with Matth. xx. 19, and the comments on the latter passage.) But this prophecy was full of significance, not merely as foretelling an accidental circumstance, but also because crucifixion is conceived as a symbol replete with manifold allusions (on which we shall subsequently enlarge), and then, because the crucifixion connects itself essentially with the resurrection. Cruel as was this mode of execution, yet it did not destroy the bodily organization, nor deform it, like stoning, and other death-punishments. Hence, Divine wisdom ordained that the Son of God should be executed in this way, that his sacred body might be preserved from any species of mutilation.

Now the following dialogue of Christ with Pilate (John xviii. 33, et seq.), clearly proves that, at first, there was no mention made of political accusations. The conversation turns upon the notion of the Messiah's kingdom, whence it is evident that the Jews at first accused him as a false Messiah only. The same appears from Matt. xxvii. 11, and Mark xv. 2. Luke xxiii. 2, on the contrary, has, at the very beginning of the trial, given prominence to the political element, which, however, must be assigned to a later stage of the examination. Now, when Pilate saw that, during all these accusations, the Lord maintained a calm and dignified silence, he marvelled at the extraordinary phenomenon (Matth. xxvii. 12, 13;

Mark xv. 3–5). He therefore ordered Jesus, who was hitherto standing before the multitude of people, to be led into the Prætorium, and there held with him a private conversation.

John xviii. 33–38.—In order to a distinct apprehension of the proceedings of Pilate with Christ, we must endeavour to realize to ourselves the scene. The Procurator occupied the palace which in former days was the palace of Herod, in Jerusalem, an extensive and stately edifice. (Joseph. Antiq. xv. 9, 3, B. J. I. 21, 1.) In front of this building stood the judgment-seat (Βῆμα, John xix. 13), on which Pilate sat when he adjudicated amongst the Jews. But, in order to speak with Christ in private, he several times entered the palace. (John xviii. 33, xix. 9.) This palace, like the residence of Annas, had a vestibule or court (αὐλή), in which was stationed a cohort of Roman soldiers (Matth. xxvii. 27 ; Mark xv. 16), and which was enclosed towards the street by a Pylon through which a door conducted. The Jews would not enter through this lest they should be defiled, John xviii. 28. They therefore remained outside, standing around the judgment-seat. The edifice itself, together with the court, is called by the Evangelists πραιτώριον, as is seen in Mark xv. 16, where it is said : οἱ στρατιῶται ἀπήγαγον αὐτὸν ἔσω τῆς αὐλῆς, ὅ ἐστι πραιτώριον. Hence, when it occurs in the history of Christ's sufferings, no different sense of the word need be supposed. The meaning is different in Acts xxiii, 35, where it is used—not for the official residence of the Roman magistrates—but merely for "Palace." (So also in Sueton. August. 63, 72. Calig. 37, Titus 8.) In like manner it occurs in Philippians i. 13, in a different sense.

Pilate having retired into the Prætorium (probably merely to the court), immediately ordered Jesus to be brought before him (ἐφώνησε τὸν Ἰησοῦν), and asked him *if he was the King of the Jews*. The Lord's reply as to whether Pilate made this inquiry merely of himself, leads to the conclusion that, in the public accusation which had been brought against him at the commencement of the trial, the expression *King of the Jews* (ὁ βασιλεὺς τῶν Ἰουδαίων) had not occurred. It was therefore important to Christ, as helping to inform him of Pilate's disposition towards him, to know in what sense he took the expression, whether as a Roman, in a merely external sense, referring to a *political* ruler, or in the Jewish sense of the *theocratic* king, Messiah. Pilate, in reply, declared publicly that he was no Jew, and therefore that he was incapable of judging concerning questions of the Jewish religion, but that the high priest had brought Christ before his tribunal, as one who ought to be punished.

When the Saviour perceived that Pilate rightly understood the state of the case, and that no misapprehension was to be apprehended, he openly declared that he was a sovereign, and had a kingdom, ver. 36.* The nature of this kingdom, however, he described but negatively, "It is *not* of this world." The proof of this was given by the Saviour, in a way strikingly calculated to impress the Roman procurator; viz., Jesus had suffered himself to be arrested without making any resistance to the orders of the magistrates, thus giving it to be understood that he wished to undertake nothing of a hostile character.

These words of the Lord, "My kingdom is not of this world" (ἡ βασιλεία ἡ ἐμὴ οὐκ ἔστιν ἐκ τοῦ κόσμου τούτου), have been employed by many to prove that the kingdom of Christ should be understood as confined to the internal or moral world. But, in this instance, the discussion merely concerns the relation of Christ's kingdom to the kingdoms of the world: (ἐκ points to the origin of the kingdom of God as not from the κόσμος, like the kingdoms of the earth); but in no way whatever does it limit the extent of the kingdom of God itself. Like the kingdom of truth, it has a necessary tendency to become universal and all-prevalent, and to transform not only the spiritual, but ultimately also the material world.

From the idea of a *kingdom*, Pilate now gives prominence to the idea of the *king*, and repeats the question whether he considered himself a king, to which Christ simply gives an affirmative reply. Very many interpreters, and particularly Tholuck,† perceive mockery and contempt in this question of Pilate. But to me the gravity of the Redeemer's answer seems not at all consistent with such a view. Besides, the subsequent portraiture of the process which was going on in Pilate, testifies that his mind was affected. The demeanour of Christ had made an impression upon him; he imagined at least something noble and dignified in the Redeemer. But the more precise explanation which the Lord added to his declaration, embraces the idea of *king* in its profoundest essence.

For, first, he states his origin to be above this world, by which he also designates his kingdom itself as not of this world. (In γεγέννημαι, the act of his birth is signified, in ἐλήλυθα εἰς τὸν κόσμον, abiding existence in the world; the two forms of expression are

* The Lord confessed his regal dignity in presence of the highest political authority, and his sonship to God before the highest theocratic council.

† In the last edition of his commentary, Tholuck, however, declares himself favourable to the opinion that, in the exclamation of Pilate, there may be perceived an expression of sorrowful complaint that the truth should be veiled from mortals. With justice he recalls attention to the scepticism which at the time of Christ had taken possession of many distinguished Romans and Greeks, who regarded as vain every more profound inquiry after truth. In this sense, Pliny the elder, in the preface to his natural history, penned the words: "Solum certum est, nihil certi esse, nec miserius quidquam homine, nec superbius." The fearful laxity of morals at that time, must doubtless, to a great degree, be traced to this profound scepticism. The revelation of eternal truth alone was able to breathe new life into human nature, thus ruined and in progress towards utter dissolution.

therefore not equivalent.) Here, however, he appears as a conqueror for that truth, which constitutes his true kingdom; or rather as a sovereign, who, having been absent from his kingdom, comes to resume its possession (Luke xix. 12). Every one who springs from his kingdom (bears the truth in him, and is born of it), hearkens to its call, and rallies beneath its banner. This announcement ought evidently to have been an incentive to Pilate to acknowledge himself as a friend of truth, a subject of him who was truth itself; but unbelief was too deeply rooted in his heart. The summons of Christ thrilled his spirit, but worldly fetters restrained him from obeying it. And here the question arises: "Who then, in this sinful world, can be said *to be of the truth?*" If, however, we compare John x. 14, we shall see that this expression cannot signify perfect sinlessness, but only a *susceptibility* to the truth; for the Apostles hearkened to the voice of Christ, but that they were not sinless is sufficiently shewn by the denial of Peter. There are unsusceptible dead souls in which the voice of truth awakens no echo; but there are other spirits whose inmost nature vibrates when a sound of the eternal truth reaches them: for they feel that it alone has power to still their secret yearnings. The Redeemer, the Lord and king of truth, calls all such to himself, and his will strives to rule without limit in their hearts. Pilate, therefore, trained in the Hellenic philosophy, knew very well that the Lord had used the term *truth* in its most absolute sense (John i. 14), but the possibility of attaining to a knowledge of absolute truth was to him doubtful.

Like so many of the noblest men of that singularly stirring time, Pilate had fallen a prey to scepticism. He had passed through the circle of philosophical systems without having discovered the truth, and the question, "What is truth?" (*τί ἐστιν ἀλήθεια*) only expresses his despair of finding the truth: instead of mockery or scorn, therefore, these words seem rather a sad utterance of utter despondency.*

The Roman, deeply affected, breaks up the dialogue; and, heathen though he was, defends the king Messiah against the Jews, against the people of the theocracy, Christ's own heritage (John i. 11), who were breathing nothing but vengeance against the Holy One of God! He proposes to them, that according to the custom of releasing a prisoner at the feast, he should grant them the imprisoned Jesus, the Christ. But here the question arises, whether —according to the account of Luke xxiii. 7–17, seq.—this proposal of Pilate to set Jesus at liberty ought not to be placed after his

* As the answer to the question "What is truth?" the only correct Biblical answer is, "Christ is truth." For absolute eternal truth is not a mere representation nor a relation of any kind, it is both Essence and Being. Now the Spirit is the true being, but the Spirit is Person, and Christ is the most exalted personality.

transmission to Herod? Any formal discrepancy between Luke and John is in no way involved in this question, for the latter does not mention the sending of Christ to Herod at all; but the verses 39–40 of John xviii., connect themselves so immediately with the foregoing transaction, that everything favours the conclusion, that John meant the events to be regarded as having transpired in this order. If we consider that John has here narrated with uncommon precision, whilst, in this part of the evangelical history, Luke appears to be much less careful; and, further, if we take into consideration, that it was the first refusal of Pilate to pronounce judgment upon Christ which gave occasion to the political accusations before mentioned (Luke xxiii. 5), which, in turn, occasioned the sending of Christ to Herod; it will appear highly probable that the whole scene, in which the people desired the liberation of Barabbas, ought to be referred to the period previous to the sending of Christ to Herod. As regards the custom of releasing a prisoner at the feast, it is uncertain whether it was of Roman or Jewish origin. According to Livy, Book V. 13, during the Lectisternia, of the Romans, all prisoners were freed from their fetters. Here, however, there appears to be only one spoken of who was to be set at liberty; hence it may be the more probable conclusion that it was a Jewish custom. There is something so very natural in it, that even at the present day it prevails in many states, especially in the East, and even in the West something similar takes place upon the accession of a new king to the throne.

According to Matth. xxvii. 15, seq.; Mark xv. 6, seq.; Luke xxiii. 18, seq., besides the Saviour, there was proposed to them another prisoner for liberation; one who in an insurrection had committed a murder. (Mark xv. 7; Luke xxiii. 19.) This man, of whom nothing else is known, was called Βαραββᾶς = בר אבא. But it is remarkable that three manuscripts, besides the Armenian and a Syrian translation, give him in addition the name Jesus (Ἰησοῦς). That this reading is very ancient, is shewn by Origen in his exposition of this passage in Matthew. He observes that "many manuscripts also had not the name Ἰησοῦς" (consequently the greater number must have had it), and that it might have been added by heretics. Griesbach has sought to deprive these words of Origen of all their significance, by remarking that Origen's declaration was contained only in the Latin translation, in which much was corrupted, and therefore it might not have emanated from Origen at all. But this conjecture is utterly improbable, for no doctrinal interest could be subserved by the interpolation. If the passage is actually from Origen, it is in the highest degree probable, that Ἰησοῦς Βαραββᾶς is the correct reading. This father, for instance, indicates how Ἰησοῦς might have disappeared from the text. It was thought unseemly that a murderer should have also borne the sacred name of Jesus, and hence *Barabbas* only was retained in the text.

It is a most striking circumstance that two Jesuses should have thus met, as that Pilate's question should take the form, "whether do you wish that I should release *that* Jesus, who is named Christ, or *that one* who is called Barabbas?" How applicable the words: "ludit in humanis Divina potentia rebus" to this transaction!

We find more than once, particularly in the history of Christ's suffering, similar marvellous instances of providential control in matters apparently unessential. But even the other name, *Barabbas*, is specially significant; it means "Son of the Father." All therefore, which in the Redeemer existed in *essence*, appeared in the murderer in *caricature*. It is not improbable even that his whole enterprise had been a caricature of the Most Holy; that probably he had pretended to the plenipotential character of the Messiah.* But the blinded multitude, in their phrenzy, chose the hellish caricature, in preference to the heavenly original.† All the endeavours of Pilate, who well knew the secret motive of the high priests for their hatred against the Saviour (namely, *envy*, for they feared that through him they should lose the favour of the people, Matth. xxvii. 18; Mark xv. 10), were fruitless. The high priests demanded the release of Barabbas, and desired that Jesus might be crucified.

As the procurator from the judgment seat thus strove to save Christ from the hands of the blood-thirsty priests, he received a message from his wife directing his attention to the righteous character of the person whom he was called upon to judge, Matth. xxvii. 19. She was named, according to tradition, Claudia Procula,‡ and

* It is quite in the order of things, that, in giving prominence to such allusions, unbelief and estrangement from God will see only a reprehensible play of the fancy. But if unbelief were to express itself without reserve, it would say precisely the same of similar allusions, which are stated by the writers of the holy Scriptures themselves; for instance, that preserving the limbs of Christ from being broken, and the streaming forth of water and blood from his wounded side, should be significant. But he, to whom the Bible is the true word of God, and who believes that Christ is indeed the Son of the living God, will know how both this and similar references are to be estimated.

† The ideas which stir within the soul, and strive to take form and utterance in action, always appear caricatured in the impure minded. They are affected by them without being able to grasp their true form and import. At the time of Christ, the striving after freedom was, as in our time, universal; the idea in this struggle was correct, but the manner in which its realization was sought was false, for it referred merely to externals, and by that means did injury in all its relations. Whom the Son maketh free, he alone is truly free, John viii. 36.

‡ So Nicephorus names her, in his Church History, i. 30. Of late days some persons have regarded the account of Procula's dream as an interpolation in the text of Matthew of a subsequent period; but without a trace of probability. It is a prurience peculiar to modern critics to desire, by the charge "*Interpolation*," or otherwise, to remove every peculiarly interesting feature of the evangelists' history, that everything may be thoroughly commonplace.

had accompanied her husband into the province. According to Tacitus, Ann. iii. 33, it was forbidden to the officers of the Roman government to take their wives into their respective provinces in company with them; but the mandate was not rigorously enforced. She had probably heard a great deal concerning Christ, and knew therefore the danger to which her husband was exposed of perpetrating an awful act of guilt, by passing on him sentence of condemnation.

The strange conceits that the vision of Procula was a piece of sorcery on the part of Christ, in order to save himself! or even of the devil to hinder Christ's atoning death, require no refutation. Yet, in considering this remarkable event, we cannot avoid inquiring after the purpose for which an overruling Providence permitted this intimation. For since the death of Christ was pre-ordained, the effect of this dream could be injurious only; for it must have augmented the responsibility of Pilate, who already knew too much to be innocent, and yet was too firmly bound by worldly lust to venture boldly to defend the right. It may be said, however, first, that the dream might have been advantageous to Procula herself, and it is not impossible that by its silent agency she was converted to faith in Christ. But again, above all, we must guard ourselves, as has been frequently remarked, against so conceiving the idea of necessity as if it circumscribed individual freedom. Looking at the *man subjectively*, there remained at any moment the perfect possibility to Pilate of releasing Christ, and even of confessing him; just as it was possible that those members of the Sanhedrim favourable to Christ, Nicodemus and Joseph of Arimathea, might openly confess their faith, and effect a reversal of the sentence of the council. True, if anything of the kind had happened, the world's history would have been entirely different; and this leads us back to that higher *objective* necessity, which still rests only in God, not in human individuals, whose actions, though *free*, carry into perfect effect the Divine necessity. Thus it consisted with the councils of God, since Christ's death was not merely an apparent but a veritable result of human sin, that to Pilate everything should be brought home that could give him certainty concerning the innocence of Christ. If Pilate's own guilt was aggravated by this, it was only the curse of his want of truth, which made even his susceptibility for what was godly, and all the offered means for its discovery, tend to his destruction, since they could not bring him to a decision for that which was good.

Luke xxiii. 4–12.—In order to recall Pilate from his exertions on behalf of the Saviour, the priests brought an accusation against Jesus which, with Pilate, was more serious; they accused him of political offences. Jesus was charged with having excited an insurrection of the people (Luke xxiii. has at ver. 2 διαστρέφειν, at ver. 5 ἀνασείειν, and at ver. 14 ἀποστρέφειν), and with having dissuaded them from paying the tribute, Luke xxiii. 2. The power of darkness had so completely blinded them, that they did not see the contradiction involved in their desiring the actual insurrectionist to be released, and falsely charging with insurrection him who had delivered the precept, "render to Cæsar the things that are Cæsar's." (Matth. xxii. 21.) But whilst, to the anxious Pilate, they repeated these dangerous accusations, with the most virulent emphasis (ver. 5 ἐπίσχυον, ver. 23 κατίσχυον), they also mentioned that he had commenced his operations in Galilee. Luke xxiii. 5.

This statement is eagerly seized upon by the unhappy Pilate, who hoped he might thus free himself from the burden of the responsibility, by devolving it upon some one else, whilst at the same time he was evidently placing in jeopardy the life of the Righteous One, which he should have shielded with his own, since Herod could have taken the resolution to surrender him, as his own subject, to death. Here then we find him already toppling to his fall. The transfer of Christ to the jurisdiction of Herod was but a brief respite for his smitten conscience. Herod Antipas, who was then ruler of Galilee (compare the first chronological table after the introduction to Acts) was in Jerusalem at the time of the solemnization of the feast. Pilate therefore ordered that Christ should be conducted to him. Here, however, it must have appeared that Jesus was not born in Galilee, but in Judea. Herod on this account sent him back, without having brought the case to a hearing. From this condition of things, then, the conduct of Christ towards him is to be explained. Though Herod was in so far the ruler of Christ's district, as Christ had lived a long time in his territory, yet he was not born under him, nor did he, as an accused person, stand before him as his official judge. Here, therefore, Jesus gave as little satisfaction to the reprehensible curiosity of the wonder-seeking prince as to that of Annas, in his former conversation. (In ver. 8, 9, ἱκανός is employed = πολύς, ἐξ ἱκανοῦ scil. χρόνου.) The desire of Herod here mentioned, proves that the fame of Christ, and of his works, had been generally spread abroad. The vindictive priests finally had accompanied the Lord to Herod. They surrounded him, and accused him violently. (Ver. 10, εὐτόνως only once again in the New Testament, Acts xviii. 28.) But when Herod saw no miracle performed, he ascribed it to the want of power in Jesus, with his body-guard made sport of Jesus, and sent him back again to Pilate, clothed, in mockery, in an (old) purple mantle.

(Ver. 11.—The στρατεύματα here mentioned were the followers in the suite of Herod who had attended him to Jerusalem. The word elsewhere, in the New Testament, signifies invariably an army.

Kuinoel cites erroneously, Acts xxiii. 10, for the meaning of body guard. The λαμπρός, which indicates the colour of the garment Christ wore, expresses the brightness of the colour, and may just as well signify a white colour as any other. According to John xix. 5, and Matth. xxvii. 28, however, it is most probable that the robe was of a purple colour, and therefore must have been a scoff at the kingly dignity of the Lord.) In conclusion, Luke notices further, that on this day Pilate and Herod were reconciled to each other, for formerly they were at variance. It cannot now be shewn, whether it was the cruelty of Pilate to some of Herod's subjects (Luke xiii. 1) that had excited this enmity. Nor is it said that the sending of Christ to Herod was the occasion of their reconciliation. We are informed merely that both events occurred on the same day. This observation would be entirely superfluous, had not Luke meant something more profound. This deeper idea of Luke was the significant fact, that it frequently happens, when anything more noble is to be opposed, that the interests of worldly men, previously hostile to one another, unite to smother in its birth the foreign element; and this arises, though not always consciously, from the correct apprehension, that the unrestrained development of this adverse element would annihilate all their interests together. Hence, individual considerations are merged in the preservation of the whole. The persecutions of the church exhibit the same drama at large. Psalm ii. 2.

John xix. 1-16.—With what feelings must Pilate have observed the tumultuous concourse again wending towards his palace! He had hoped that he had freed himself from the responsibility, and it is again devolved upon him! He repeats that he finds no fault in Jesus, and reminds them that Herod also had found none. (Luke xxiii. 13-16.) Still, to give some satisfaction to their wild hatred, he commands Jesus to be scourged. In his view, this must have been an act of lenity; for he meant by it, if possible, to save the life of Jesus (Luke xxiii. 16, 22; John xix. 1). Whilst the soldiers scourged Jesus in the court of Pilate, he probably retired into the interior of his dwelling.* In his absence, the soldiery indulged their ungoverned passion, in mockery of the sublime prisoner.† But without knowing what they did, they were bodying forth a profoundly significant symbol, which awakens a multitude of most strikingly contrasted thoughts. They crown with a coronet of

* Tholuck thinks, with others, that the mockery was enacted in the presence of Pilate. This view is incredible, if but for the reason that the dignity of his magistracy could not suffer it.

† Both Matthew xxvii. 26, et. seq., and Mark xv. 15, et seq., place somewhat inexactly the scourging and the mockery of Christ subsequently to his being sentenced. The mockery of Christ may have been repeated after Pilate had withdrawn, but certainly not the scourging.

thorns the king of heaven and earth, as if to intimate how painful to him was the sovereignty he exercised over the souls of millions. When they had thus invested the Redeemer, Pilate again led him forth from the court,* in his attire of sorrow, and exhibited to the people their king, in his crown of thorns, exclaiming, "behold the man!" (Ἴδε ὁ ἄνθρωπος). The only true interpretation of this expression is that which regards it as the overflow of the Roman's deepest sympathy with the fate of the being who had exercised on him so mighty an influence. Those views are wholly unsatisfactory which derive from the words scorn or mockery, or the purpose of presenting to the Jews their king, as an insignificant, not a formidable personage. To conceive Pilate as a thoroughly superficial man of the world, destroys the profound character of the scenes between him and Christ. He appears to have felt but too much of the greatness of the Lord, and yet to have rendered himself thereby infinitely more culpable than he would have been otherwise.

The view we have here taken of Pilate is corroborated, first, by his scepticism, to which thoroughly superficial minds are never attracted; and again by his subsequent conversations with the Lord, which disclose, in a striking manner, the inward struggle of the unhappy Roman, and reveal the germ of belief which would fain unfold itself in his heart.

But while the rude Roman who had grown up amid the din of battle, and had familiarized himself with cruelty and sternness, was thus seized with a feeling of tender sympathy upon beholding in his crown of thorns, the king in whom were so wondrously commingled heavenly majesty and the deepest humiliation—the attendants of the sanctuary, who all their life-long had been employed about the sacred law and its prophecies, vociferated their merciless "Crucify him, crucify him!" Once more did Pilate desire to deliver him over to them for punishment, which, in that case, could not have been the punishment of death; but they longed for his blood. They therefore brought forward a new accusation, which was punishable with death according to the law, viz., "that he was a blasphemer, because he made himself out to be the Son of God," verse 7. This passage proves clearly that the Jews did not employ "Son of God" as = "Christ" or "King of the Jews," because they had previously charged Jesus with having assumed the latter title, whilst the other appears to have been perfectly new to Pilate. Moreover, in this name alone did they perceive a blasphemy, which, by the law, demanded death. Compare on John x. 34, et seq., and also Leviticus xxiv. 16. This new statement terrified still more the al-

* Verse 5 is a parenthetical sentence, which interrupts the discourse of Pilate. He went forth, verse 4, addressed the people, and during his address, the Redeemer came forth through the door, from the court, and shewed himself to the people.

ready frightened Pilate (μᾶλλον ἐφοβήθη). He descended once more from his judgment seat, ordered Jesus to be led into the Prætorium, and began to enquire more particularly concerning his origin. As the earthly origin of Christ was already manifest, by his having been sent to Herod, the enquiry "whence art thou" (πόθεν εἶ σύ) could refer to the name "Son of God," only.* Pilate thus wished to know if he actually was of higher origin: a son of God. His notion of "a son of God," like that of the centurion (Matth. xxvii. 54), may in some respects have been very obscure; but in any case, he must, if only in the most indefinite and general manner, have conceived it as denoting a heavenly being. The fact that such a conception could be, though but remotely, suggested to this sceptic, decidedly contradicts the idea that he was superficial. By the presence of the *essence*, his empty *system* of scepticism was overturned. The reality of Divinity affected him by its indwelling power, whilst he, in theory, denied its actuality. The deep and hidden necessities of his nature, which from misunderstood speculation had conducted him to scepticism, now made themselves felt with all their power. The eye of his mind saw light, and he could no longer persuade himself that the light was not. What glory and dignity must therefore have shone forth from the being of Christ, that, in his lowest humiliation, under a Jewish form, so hateful to the heathen, and in his raiment of mockery, it could thus triumph over the mind of Pilate! But now the Saviour answered no further to the question of Pilate. He perceived that Pilate would not be able to fight through the battle, therefore he wished not to lead him into greater temptation. This silence, however, impressed the Roman at once with amazement and anxiety; he sought to compel Christ to answer, by reminding him of his own authority. But the Lord employs this allusion to Pilate's power, in order to admonish the magistrate of a superior power, which was above even *him*. By this remark, he once more awakens the feeling of dependence in his judge, but at the same time intimates by his language, with holy self-reliance, that he knows himself to be controlled by the superior power of God, and not by *his*. Yet with deep sympathy for the condition of the unhappy man, the merciful Redeemer added—foreseeing the issue of Pilate's moral struggle—that those hard-hearted priests, who not only thirsted for his own blood, but had also brought Pilate into so heavy a temptation, had sinned more heavily than he. Thus the accused, the deeply humbled, here again appears, as he appeared before the Sanhedrim, the judge and commander of the Roman governor, whilst he computes the amount of his sin, and suffers a ray of hope for pardon to shine in upon him. If those priests *perhaps* sinned against the Holy Ghost, or at least bordered upon that

* Compare concerning the πόθεν in this sense, the passage, John vii. 27, 28.

sin, Pilate doubtless sinned only against the Father or against the Son of Man, and that in proportion to the lesser degree of his moral or religious consciousness, therefore, if not here, at least above, there might be forgiveness for him. (Compare upon Matthew xii. 31.)

With lofty dignity must the Saviour have thus spoken to Pilate! And yet Pilate, instead of feeling offended at him, began now to strive for his deliverance with earnestness, as if he had not done so from the beginning. His exertions, however, were powerless. The secret ties of this world's love held his feeble moral nature in fetters. At the popular exclamation, "thou art not Cæsar's friend," (*οὐκ εἶ φίλος τοῦ Καίσαρος*), he was a fallen man. The name "friend of Cæsar," is not to be apprehended in the sense of the honorary title, amicus Cæsaris; but must be understood of loyal adherence —fidelity towards the emperor. The meaning then is, "If you liberate this man, you prove that you are not faithful to the emperor." Now, to a Tiberius,* a mere suspicion was as bad as an actual offence. Therefore Pilate hastily commanded Jesus to be led forth, seated himself upon the judgment seat, and after he had again cried out, "Behold your king!" (*ἴδε ὁ βασιλεὺς ὑμῶν*, verse 15), now perhaps, less in order to excite compassion, than to shew his scorn of the people, who had so cruelly urged him to act in opposition to his conscience—he delivered the Saviour over to them to be crucified. (Ver. 13.—The place where the *βῆμα* stood was named *λιθόστρωτον*, equivalent to גַּבְּתָא. The Hebrew name indicates the elevation of the place, from גָּבַהּ to be high; the Greek for a Mosaic paving which formed the floor beneath the *βῆμα*. The Roman magistrates and generals carried similar pavimenta tessalata with them on their journeys into the provinces. [Compare Sueton. Cæs. 46.] Upon the *παρασκευὴ τοῦ πάσχα* compare the comm. on Matt. xxvi. 17. The expression must be understood as relating to the usual day of preparation, that is Friday, which was called the preparation day of the passover, because it occurred during the feast. This conclusion is supported in an especial manner by the fact, that the Synoptical writers distinctly name the *παρασκευή* as the day of the Saviour's death. (Matth. xxvii. 62; Mark xv. 42; Luke xxiii. 54.) Mark indeed subjoins the further explanation *ὅ ἐστι προσάββατον*. And besides, John writes *παρασκευὴ τῶν Ἰουδαίων*, for the same day, which can in no case be understood as relating to the preparation day of the Paschal Festival, and indeed this expression is never used in that sense in any other connexion.)

There remains a chronological difficulty in determining the hour at which the passing of the sentence took place. John, in this passage, names the sixth hour as that of the sentence, whilst, according-

* Tacitus, writing of the reign of Tiberius Cæsar, says, "Majestatis crimen omnium accusationum complementum erat."

ing to Mark xv. 25, the third hour was that of the crucifixion. If this passage of Mark were the only one under discussion, we should certainly prefer the account of John; but according to Matthew xxvii. 45; Mark xv. 33; and Luke xxiii. 44, when the sixth hour arrived, the Saviour had already hung a long time on the cross. I declare myself favourable, with Theophylact, Beza, Bengel, and Lücke, to the reading *τρίτῃ* in the text of John, for the following reasons: Several MSS. (as D.L.) read *τρίτῃ* in John; the numeral signs of 3 and 6 may be easily mistaken one for the other; and besides it might easily have happened that some transcribers transposed the events, and, as in John, no further specification of the hour occurs, they might, on the authority of Matthew xxvii. 45, and the parallel passages, have transferred the number 6 from the crucifixion to the time of the sentence.

Should it be thought necessary, however, to defend the *ἕκτῃ*, as Tholuck does, who thinks it improbable that any discrepancy could have crept into the MSS., if the correct number stood in them originally, we must suppose that the variation in the statements of the hour arose probably from that division of the day which divided it into four sections of three hours each. Hence, the second section of the day included the time from the third to the sixth hours. Of this section, then, Mark mentions the beginning, John the end. But even according to this view, there will yet remain a discrepancy on the part of John; since the passages Matth. xxvii. 45, and parallels, shew that at the sixth hour the Saviour had already hung a long time on the cross. Perhaps, therefore, we should prefer to this the hypothesis of Rettig, who here, and at John i. 39, iv. 6, applies the mode of computing the hours from midnight to midnight; which Aulius Gellius, Noct. Att. iii. 2, and Pliny, Nat. Hist. ii. 77, shew to have been the practice of the Romans. The fact that John wrote for the people of Asia Minor accords well with this hypothesis; but *less* so the circumstance, that according to John xviii. 28, it was already *morning* when they led Jesus away to Pilate. The proceedings before Pilate and Herod, must, however, have consumed considerable time. Compare Ullman's Stud. Jahrg. 1830, h. 1. s. 101, ff.

Finally, it is recorded by Matthew alone, xxvii. 24, 25, that Pilate, by a symbolical act, in the view of the multitude excused himself from guilt in the murder of the Lord. But his having pronounced the sentence, as well as his declaration, that he whom he delivered to them to be crucified was a righteous person, must naturally render that but an empty ceremony. (Compare upon the symbolical act, Deut. xxi. 6. Ἀθῷος ἀπό = נָקִי מִן.) But the blinded multitude cried out, *τὸ αἷμα αὐτοῦ ἐφ' ἡμᾶς καὶ ἐπὶ τὰ τέκνα ἡμῶν*, *his blood be*, etc., with which imprecation they were unwittingly invoking the greatest blessing, because, whilst the blood of Abel cries for vengeance, the blood of Christ calls only for forgiveness (Heb. xii. 24). After the departure of Pilate, who had now released Barabbas to the people, the barbarous soldiery may, as was observed above, have further mocked the Saviour, who still wore the purple robe and the crown of thorns. When they were about to lead him to the place of execution, however, they again clothed him with his own raiment (Matth. xxvii. 31; Mark xv. 20), and then laid upon him the cross.

In this place, upon concluding the examination of Christ before Pilate, some notice concerning the fate of the unhappy Roman will not be inappropriate. No account is given us of the effect produced upon Pilate by the tidings of the resurrection. According to Josephus, he afterwards indulged in such gross oppressions and malversations, in his province, that, in the last year of the reign of Tiberius, the Proconsul of Syria deposed him from his government, and exiled him into Gaul. (Compare Joseph. Antiq. xviii. 5; Tacitus' Annals, xv. 44.) As to what the ecclesiastical fathers recount concerning the *Actis* of Pilate, which he is said to have sent to the Emperor Tiberius, in relation to the death of Christ, and which occasioned him, as asserted by tradition, to procure Christ's admission amongst the number of the gods, the story is doubtless tricked out with legendary ornaments. But, according to the evangelical history, it is in the highest degree probable that Pilate did actually write to Tiberius on the subject; for, since the affair had reference to political relations, Pilate would not have wished that any information whatever concerning the king of the Jews should reach Rome before his own report. But, now that he had sentenced Jesus to death, he had no longer any motive to conceal his favourable opinion concerning the Saviour.

Hence, from the favorable opinions of Pilate concerning Christ, a legend might have originated in after days, that Tiberius had ordered that Christ should be admitted by the Senate into the number of gods. Justin Mart. Apol., i. 76–84; Tertullian's Apol. v. 21; Eusebius. Eccles. Hist. ii. 2; Epiph. hær. L. 1. Compare Winer's Bibl. Realwörterb. under this word.

§ 5. CRUCIFIXION AND DEATH OF JESUS.

(Matth. xxvii. 32–56; Mark xv. 21–41; Luke xxiii. 26–49; John xix. 17–30.)

In the following description of the Saviour's crucifixion and death, the narrative of John falls far short of completeness. On the other hand, however, Luke supplies several particulars which render the awful scene remarkably vivid, and which are peculiar to him. Of these, for example, are the address of Jesus to the women of Jerusalem who were lamenting over the Lord (Luke xxiii. 27, et seq.), and the transaction with the two malefactors (Luke xxiii. 39, et seq). Some few particulars, also, are peculiar to Matthew, chiefly the description of the astonishing phenomena that occurred at the death of the Redeemer (Matth. xxvii. 51, et seq.)

In wild haste the high priests now, contrary to all usage, caused the scarcely sentenced prisoner to be conducted to the place of execution. Guarded by Roman soldiers (of the German legion, which was stationed in Palestine), the guiltless Jesus,* the Lamb of God that beareth the sins of the world, goes forth bearing his cross (John xix. 17).

The symbolical expression, " take his cross" (λαμβάνειν τὸν σταυρὸν αὐτοῦ) (Matth. x. 38, xvi. 24), is sublimely consecrated by this affecting incident. But the Redeemer was probably so exhausted from the severe conflicts of both his body and soul, that he sank beneath the heavy burden. They were therefore obliged to compel another, a certain Simon of Cyrene, to bear the cross for him who was the helper of all. It is a common opinion, since Grotius, that this Simon was known to be an adherent of Christ, and was chosen on that account. This supposition, however, appears to me but little probable, for the reason that, if he were such, he would certainly have been in the city, and present at the examination of Christ ; but since he was coming in from the country, it seems to me the more probable opinion that he had not known Christ previously. Perhaps, however, this service which Simon rendered to the Redeemer may have been the means of leading him to God, so that

* Those who love myths should seek the Christian myths in the Christian poets, where they are found clothed with all the charms of fancy, not in the historical contemporaries of Christ. Dante and Calderon stand prominent among these. In his beautiful drama, "The Prophetess of Morning," the Spanish poet has invented a marvellously beautiful myth concerning the wood of the cross. He makes it to have sprung from a shoot of the tree of life, which withered after Adam's fall in Paradise. Had the history of Jesus been an embellished legend only, there would have been no want of all kinds of fabulous poetic descriptions, concerning the potency of his blood, his garments, and such like, since even in ordinary martyrdoms, superstition has employed itself in misapplying to various purposes the blood and raiment of those who have suffered.

his bodily toil was recompensed with a heavenly reward. At all events, that both Simon and his family afterwards attached themselves to Christ, we infer from Mark's statement (ver. 21) that he was the father of Alexander and Rufus, persons who must undoubtedly have been known to the first readers of the Gospel. (Upon ἀγγαρεύειν, compare the Commentary on Matth. v. 41.) In Christ's progress to the place of execution, he was accompanied by many, especially by persons of the female sex, who uttered their tender sympathy with wailings and tears (Luke xxiii. 27-34). But the words which the Lord spoke to those sympathizing hearts cannot but surprise us. They bear no consolatory, beneficent character, but are rather of terrific import. We cannot, however, suppose that those believing women who, according to Luke xxiii. 48, et seq., beheld the death of the Lord from a distance, were amongst this company of females. To the former, these words would not, in fact, have been appropriate, because they certainly had no reason to be alarmed at the heavy retribution of which Jesus spoke as approaching, since, according to the promise of the Lord, they were, like Noah and Lot, to be preserved from it. (Compare Matth. xxiv. 37, et seq.) And then the sympathy of these women must be regarded less as a true expression of their full consciousness concerning the event that was then occurring, than as that mere natural feeling of pity which we find so frequently expressed by the excitable female sex. Nevertheless, it certainly made a grateful impression on the Saviour, to perceive this warm sympathy and compassion after the rude violence he had suffered. But his lofty spirit, even in the prospect of a bitter death, thought not upon his own personal gratification, which would have been promoted had he tendered these women his cordial thanks, and thus caused the gentle stream of their tears to flow afresh, and secured to himself their praise. Rather did he desire to secure to their well-meaning hearts a permanent blessing. But this could result only from their being brought in sincere repentance to a full conviction of the magnitude of the event, and its necessary consequences. Therefore the Saviour exhorted them to turn their attention from him to themselves, not to weep for him but for themselves. They, as members of the populace, partook of the guilt of the people (compare at Acts ii. 23), and the punishment of the people must therefore fall upon them also. The magnitude of this retribution is described by the Saviour in Old Testament language (Isaiah ii. 10-19; Hosea x. 8; and Rev. vi. 16). With a proverbial form of expression, in which the righteous are compared to green trees, and the godless to dry, he concludes his address to them, whose purport tended to awaken in them a consciousness of their alienation from God, and to occasion them to seek with earnestness the way of salvation. (Upon βουνός compare Luke iii. 5.) Now there were also led forth with Christ two malefactors (Luke xxiii. 32), who were crucified with him on Golgotha, one on his right hand, and the other on his left (Matth. xxvii. 38 ; Mark xv. 27, 28 ; John xix. 18). The word of prophecy (Isaiah liii. 12), μετὰ ἀνόμων ἐλογίσθη, *he was reckoned among transgressors*, was therefore literally fulfilled in Christ, in a manner which could not have been expected (Mark xv. 28). The quotation in the text of Mark is wanting, however, in several codices, especially A.B.C.D. ; it appears therefore here not to be authentic, but to have been derived from Luke xxii. 37, as its having been thus supplied is easily explained, whilst its omission would be difficult to account for.

As regards the crucifixion itself, it was accomplished at the common place of execution, called the *κρανίου τόπος*, or according to Luke xxiii. 33, the *κρανίον*, (the latter is a literal translation of the Hebrew גֻּלְגֹּלֶת, Chaldee גֻּלְגַּלְתָּא—skull,) the place of a skull, from the accumulated skulls of the wretched persons who had there lost their lives.* Respecting the *manner* of the crucifixion, only one point further needs to be investigated, viz., whether it was also customary to nail the feet of the crucified, or only to bind them.

The whole church, both ancient and modern, understand this in accordance with the prophecy of Psalm xxii. 17, in connexion with Luke xxiv. 39, in which latter passage the risen Redeemer even shews his pierced feet. The first person in modern times who has asserted the contrary is Dr. Paulus, and he is followed by Rosenmüller, Kuinoel, and Fritzsche. The only positive fact which they have adduced in support of their view, is that the feet were bound. But this was done also with the arms, whilst it is acknowledged that the hands were pierced through. Hence the binding does not exclude, but rather implies the nailing. Again : there are several distinct authorities for the nailing of the feet, particularly Plautus Mostellaria, Act. ii. sc. 1. v. 13 : Tertullian adv. Marc. iii. 19. The principal work is that of Justus Lipsius de cruce, Antwerp, 1595. Amongst modern works, Hengstenberg's Christology, Bd. i. s. 183, ff. should be compared, and the very circumstantial and erudite treatise of Bähr, preacher in Baden, in Heidenreich's and Hüffel's Zeitschr. f. Prediger-Wissenschaften, Bd. ii. h. 2 and 3. The two latter oppose Dr. Paulus. This scholar, in his rejoinder, appeals to Socrat. H.E.I., i. 17, according to which, Helena, the mother of Constantine, found only two nails near the cross. But to this legend we can attach no historical importance, for it is not founded upon any proved fact. The Zeitschrift fur die Giestlichkeit des Erzbisthums Frei-

* According to the Christian myth, Golgotha was the place where Adam was buried. Out of the grave of the *Old* Adam sprung forth the *second* Adam, who, like ripe fruit, hung on the tree of life. With this myth should be compared the Manichæan view of the Ἰησοῦς παθητός, who is regarded as being diffused throughout all nature

burg (Jahrg. 1830, heft 5, s. 1, ff.), also contains very instructive statements on this subject.

Just before crucifixion, the Romans were accustomed to present to the wretched culprits a stupefying drink—wine mingled with myrrh—in order to deaden their sensibility to the awful agonies of this dreadful punishment. Mark xv. 23, contains the usual expression *οἶνος ἐσμυρνισμένος* (from *σμύρνα*, = מֹר, Matth. ii. 11); Matthew, on the contrary, has the expression, *ὄξος μετὰ χολῆς μεμιγμένον*. This expression, indeed, and that of Mark, may be reconciled as to signification. For *ὄξος* was nothing else than the common sour wine, and *χολή*, like רֹאשׁ (for which word it is employed by the LXX. in Psalm lxix. 22), was used for bitters of every kind. Compare, however, Luke xxiii. 36, where it is expressly included under the acts of mockery practised by the soldiers, that they gave *ὄξος* to the Saviour. And in Psalm lxix. 21, it is reckoned amongst the sufferings of Messiah that he should receive *ὄξος* and *χολή*. Thus there is certainly no doubt that the Evangelist understood this very event to be an aggravation of his sufferings. That such cruelty was not the original intention in giving the drink by no means contradicts this conclusion. For, although apparently an act of charity, still it was the expression of a most unholy charity. To the Saviour it assumed the appearance of a fresh mockery; therefore as soon as he had tasted the drink, he rejected it, for he did not desire to meet death otherwise than in the full possession of his consciousness. Probably it was whilst being nailed to the cross that the Lord uttered the affecting prayer: *πάτερ ἄφες αὐτοῖς· οὐ γὰρ οἴδασι τί ποιοῦσι, Father, forgive them*, etc. The address "Father" directly expresses the fact that even at this moment, when he was fixed upon the cross, he was vividly conscious of his sonship to God. In his prayer, he included not only the soldiers who were carrying the crucifixion into effect—these were mere irresponsible instruments, and even guiltless in what they were doing, that guilt excepted which they themselves incurred by unnecessary violence. The Saviour's prayer, in its widest comprehension, embraced all those who were in any way inculpated in his death. It had reference, therefore, also to the high priests, and to Pilate. But if *ignorance* of the true character of the deed they perpetrated seems to be rendered prominent as a ground for their forgiveness, it is still true, as we remarked at Matth. xxvii. 1, that as their very ignorance of the fact that they were murdering the holy one of God was itself their guilt, the high-priestly intercession of the Lord was necessary in order to their forgiveness. Compare, further, the observations upon Acts iii. 17, and 1 Cor. ii. 8.

The Synoptical Evangelists notice but briefly the parting of the raiment of Jesus, and the superscription upon the cross. But these events are very circumstantially narrated by John xix. 19–24. It was customary among the Romans, as it is still, in the Turkish empire, in all executions of persons, to suspend a tablet which expressed the cause of their punishment. In the official language of the Romans, this was called Titulus. (Suetonius. Caligula, cap. 32, and Domitian, cap. 10.) At the beginning, Pilate may have ordered the superscription to be made out without special regard to its import; but when he noticed that the form in which it was composed was unacceptable to the priests, whom he detested, he adhered firmly to it, and would admit of no alteration. The subtle priests apprehended an evil impression from the circumstance that Jesus was represented as "King of the Jews," without limitation of meaning to the title: this was thought to correspond too closely with those passages of the Old Testament, in which the Jews are described as despisers of their king, and the king himself as deeply humbled, passages which might thus be employed as means of proving that Jesus was the true Messiah; hence in their position their fear was not without reason. After the crucifixion had been completed, the four soldiers who had been appointed to that duty, took their stations round the cross, and divided the garments of Jesus into four parts, but cast lots amongst themselves for his tunic, which was formed of a single web. The Evangelist here makes a reference to Psalm xxii. 18, in which this proceeding is foretold with astonishing precision, furnishing a new proof of the manner in which the Lord, in himself and in his fate, represents the greatest and the least in unparalleled union. (The citation follows the LXX. closely. In the passage, Matth. xxvii. 35, the same quotation occurs, but it is rejected by the best critics. Without doubt it was written on the margin from John, and gradually became incorporated with the text.) The *χιτών*, = כְּתֹנֶת, was the under garment, and was made in one piece. The epithets seem to intimate its costliness, so that thus the Saviour was not clothed remarkably meanly. Even in this respect he observed the middle course. The expressions *ἄρραφος* and *ὑφαντὸς δι' ὅλου*, occur only in this place. They signify the unity of the weft, which was without seam, or the uniting of several pieces.*

Thus hung the Son of God between earth and heaven, sacrificed upon the beam of the cross as upon his altar, like a patient lamb, bearing the sin of the world, and still the measure of his sufferings was not yet filled up. They who passed by blasphemed him, and the priests, with venomous malignity, shouted out in mockery, the words he had spoken (Matth. xxvii. 39, et seq.) According to Luke xxiii. 36, even the soldiers also mocked him. (These partic-

* The ecclesiastical fathers understand this account of the garment of Christ in an allegorical sense, and explain it to signify the one indivisible Church of the Lord upon earth.

ulars were partially prophesied in Psalms xxii. 7, et seq. The wagging of the head is often mentioned in the Old Testament as a gesture of ridicule. Compare Job xvi. 4; Psalm cix. 25; Isaiah xxxvii. 22. Luke xxiii. 35 has the word ἐκμυκτηρίζειν, on which compare our remark at Luke, ch. xvi. 14.—As regards the allusion to the words of Christ concerning the destruction and rebuilding of the Temple, the same holds good which we remarked at Matth. xxvi. 61; the language is perverted, in that to the Saviour is ascribed the destruction (καταλύειν) whilst he vindicates to himself only the building (οἰκοδομεῖν). The abbreviated form κατάβα for κατάβηθι, occurs frequently in the New Testament. In Rev. iv. 1, we find ἀνάβα, and in Acts xii. 7, and Ephes. v. 14, ἀνάστα, but the longer form is the more usual. (Compare Winer's Gramm. p. 72.) In Matthew xxvii. 42, and the parallel passage of Mark xv. 32, the readings vary remarkably in the construction of πιστεύειν, for it is sometimes without an object, and sometimes connected with αὐτῷ or ἐπ' αὐτόν. The Evangelists probably read variously, and indeed the readings ἐπ' αὐτῷ in Matthew, and αὐτῷ in Mark, are respectively correct. In Matth. xxvii. 43, the εἰ θέλει αὐτόν is after the LXX. in the passage, Psalm xxii., where these words stand for כִּי חָפֵץ בּ׳.

Luke xxiii. 39-43.—Whilst now it is stated without any distinction by Matth. xxvii. 44 and Mark xv. 32, that those who were crucified with Jesus ridiculed him also, Luke records more precisely the fact that but one thus inculpated himself. Concerning the other, he remarks, on the contrary, that in the prospect of approaching death, he besought Christ that he might be admitted into his kingdom, and that the Saviour granted him his prayer. Over this little narrative is shed a mysterious charm.

First, so unexpected is the joyful and sublime incident which it recounts in the midst of a multitude of the most mournful events, that it takes us by surprise. Whilst all the disciples disperse themselves, the faithful John alone excepted, who stands at the foot of the cross—whilst Judas betrays his Lord, and Peter denies him—whilst, from both the priests and the people, wild enmity pours forth against the Saviour—and whilst Pilate displays his weakness, living faith appears under the most unfavourable circumstances in a robber and murderer, with most marvellous power. As long as Christ remained unfastened to the cross, many a votary might have cherished the hope that he would even yet free himself by a miracle. But who could have deemed the pierced right hand of Him who was fastened upon the cross sufficiently powerful to sustain and conduct the spirit through the dark valley of death? Who could have esteemed him who was himself dying the death of a criminal, worthy to command the gates of Paradise?

Even granting that this unhappy man still possessed some nobility of character; granting that he might also have previously heard something concerning Christ, and have experienced many powerful emotions, he still remains for ever an actual demonstration of the fact that Jesus Christ came to save *sinners*, and stands whilst time endures, as a hero of the faith, since he believed when faith forsook even the very persons who had previously professed aloud that they acknowledged in Christ the Son of the living God. *Again*, the unprejudiced observer will perceive, in the history of Christ's sufferings, a certain character which our introduction hinted at, and which has been but too frequently misunderstood, that is, its symbolical character.* The suffering Christ, as a symbol of a fulness of truths the most profound, and relations the most significant, speaks a language to the world which his living word could scarcely have uttered.

Conceive now, apart from this or that dogmatic view, the history of the dying Jesus just as it is given by the Evangelists, and we are constrained to acknowledge that even the most boundless imagination could never have produced a romance corresponding to this reality. The imagination usually pictures forth its objects according to analogy, but there is here something altogether transcending analogy; a new product of Divinely creative power. The same being, who was in the beginning with the Father, who could say, "he that seeth me seeth the Father," that "men should honour the Son even as they honour the Father," relinquishes all his glory in order to assume our flesh and blood (John i. 1–14, v. 23, xiv. 9, xvii. 24), and hangs naked upon the tree of the cross. Already sunk deep in poverty, he now abandons *everything*, in order, by his poverty, to make us rich, 2 Cor. viii. 9. Yet do all his own forsake him and throw away their faith. But murderers and heathens, consciously and unconsciously, believe, and bear witness of his Divine sonship, and of his work of redemption. Above his head, which is crowned with thorns, as typical of the suffering which the sin-defiled earth, the mother of thorns, prepared for him, stands his sacred name. The cross, like an unfolded banner, publishes, in the three chief languages of the earth, that it is the king of honours whom humanity has nailed to it. His arms are extended as if they would embrace the world for whose salvation he yet thirsts, though it thrusts him from it (John xix. 28). On his left hangs the infidel malefactor, who with the barbarous mob ridicules the holy one of God. On his right is the sinner brought to repent-

* Compare Calderon's Prophetess of the Morning, as translated by the Lord of Malsburg, vol 4, s. 76, et seq., where the symbolic character of the history of the crucifixion is employed with profound sagacity. To each also of its picturesque descriptions this character lends its due charm and spiritual import. Christianity is thus also a fruitful principle in regard to art, since it presents the most profound ideas in a pictorial form.

ance; so that around the Saviour of the world the various representatives of the human race are assembled—representatives alike of those who are lost and of those who are saved. In his deep humiliation, however, the Saviour now exercises none the less acts of Divine glory. He receives the homage of a believing soul, he opens to him the gates of the kingdom of heaven. The cross of Christ becomes a throne; the place of skulls, the tribunal of universal judgment.* As regards the particulars of this record, there have not been wanting attempts to rob them of their grand character; yet, without exception, these attempts have issued in utter weakness.

The prayer of the thief: *μνήσθητί μου, κύριε, ὅταν ἔλθῃς ἐν τῇ βασιλείᾳ σου, Lord remember me*, etc., some would understand, as requesting a mere friendly reminiscence in the world of the blessed. But it is clear that *ἔρχεσθαι ἐν τῇ βασιλείᾳ σου, come in thy kingdom* (*i. e.*, entering into his kingdom, and then *abiding* there), cannot possibly be said of mere happiness. But if the man thought that in Christ he addressed the Messiah, and had applied to him the representations concerning the suffering Messiah; then the astonishing circumstance would be, that this man could do so whilst the disciples themselves failed to make the application. On this matter, however, there is nothing explained further. But the sublime promise of Christ: *ἀμὴν λέγω σοι, σήμερον μετ' ἐμοῦ ἔσῃ ἐν τῷ παραδείσῳ, verily I say unto thee, to-day*, etc., has been superficialized to such a degree by some, that they render the words thus: "I *to-day*, say unto thee" (*i. e. now*, so that the comma is made to stand after *σήμερον*), "thou yet shalt enter into Paradise. God is love, and he will yet make thee also happy." But, as Kuinoel observes on this passage, the impressive *ἀμὴν λέγω σοι*, does not at all harmonize with such a mere assurance, one which any person could have expressed.

It is manifest that the evangelical history so represents the incident that the two essential elements of salvation, faith and repentance, existed in the mind of the man. That these elements might have had their preparatory causes is very probable. But that does not destroy the astonishing character of the occurrence, that with a faith generating repentance, this man could embrace Christ at a moment in which it could be done by no one else.

As to the term *παράδεισος*, it appears, as we remarked at Luke xvi. 24, et seq., by no means synonymous with *heaven, heavenly world*. This passage leaves, on this point, no doubt whatever. For

* The suffering Christ is also naturally a type of the church's destiny, and of that of many of its individual members. The church also will yet appear as abandoned of God, and forgotten by her children. And murderers and heathen, to whom grace is given, will be the only witnesses in her to bear testimony to her Divine origin.

since σημερον, *to-day*, is annexed, and since it is expressly stated that the soul of Christ, at his death, went into *Hades to the dead* (1 Peter iii. 18), it follows that Christ could say, "Thou shalt be with me" (ἔσῃ μετ' ἐμοῦ), only if the soul of the person crucified with him went also to the general assembling-place of the dead.*

Further, the entire condition of the robber will lead us to this conclusion. For readily as we acknowledge him a truly converted man, yet we cannot in any way speak of him as a regenerated man, one to whom it is allowable to apply the word of promise, "Where I am, there also shall my servant be;" especially since as yet Christ was not exalted to the right hand of God. True, in 2 Cor. xii. 4, the heavenly world (τρίτος οὐρανός), seems to be styled *Paradise:* but as we observed previously, the Jews distinguish the *upper* or heavenly paradise (Παράδεισος τοῦ Θεοῦ, Rev. ii. 7), from the *lower* Paradise. The latter is synonymous with Κόλπος 'Αβραάμ, *bosom of Abraham*, and signifies the place of joy in the kingdom of the dead, as Γέεννα signifies the place of suffering. (The form of the name Παράδεισος = פרדס Hosea iv. 13; Ecclesiastes ii. 5, springs confessedly from the Persian. The word primarily denotes a pleasure garden, a park, and hence is used for any pleasant place of residence.

John xix. 25-27.—To this infinitely sublime scene, where the Saviour acts as Lord of the heavenly world, another event attaches itself which shews how the Lord, in his most violent struggle, along with the sublimest objects of his life, remembered also the little earthly interests, from which he seemed to have been far removed. In the power of perfect love, which is ever regardless of self, and consults the happiness of others, he remembers Mary his mother. Whilst her Divine Son hangs upon the cross, that sword of which Simeon once prophesied to her, pierces through her soul (Luke ii. 35). All that she had experienced in the happiest periods of her life, now becomes darkened to her; doubts agitate her soul. The moment of her own new birth is come: the earthly mother of Christ must now also spiritually bear the new man, the Christ within us! To John, the faithful disciple, it is natural to suppose that no exhortation was necessary to induce him to take to his own home the mo-

* Samuel, whose spirit had been evoked from the dead by the witch of Endor, addressed Saul in the contrary sense where he said, "to-day shalt thou and thy sons be with me (in Sheol)." 1 Samuel xxviii. 19. [To those who reject the above interpretation of 1 Pet. iii. 18, in regard to Christ's descent into the place of departed spirits, this argument of Olshausen's will of course have no weight. To me this interpretation seems indefeasible by any legitimate exegesis. Also the distinction here drawn between conversion and regeneration seems unfounded in the New Testament. And if the dying robber was to be with the Saviour in Paradise, and this conceived by the Jews as the "bosom of Abraham," the abode of the faithful of all previous ages, it is difficult to see what higher blessings the Saviour *could* have promised him, or to recognize any distinction made between *him* and other believers.—[K.

ther of his Lord.* She dwelt indeed in the bosom of love, so that nothing could ever have been wanting to her. But for her sake the Lord spoke from his cross the word of consolation. The feeling of abandonment would have been too powerful to her, therefore Jesus presents to her a second son, instead of the beloved one she deemed herself to have lost.

In reference to the persons who are mentioned as standing near the cross (John xix. 25), it is to be observed, that according to Matth. xxvii. 55, and the parallel passages, the persons named along with others (Luke xxiii. 49, even says πάντες οἱ γνωστοὶ αὐτοῦ, where it is plain the πάντες is not to be pressed), beheld the occurrence from a distance (μακρόθεν). This statement harmonizes very simply with the description of John, if we suppose that afterwards some few of them approached near to the cross. Of the disciples, only the faithful John seems to have thus ventured. Amongst the women yet a third Mary is named, besides Mary the mother of Jesus, Mary Magdalene, and Salome. John (xix. 25), expressly calls her the sister of the mother of Jesus, and the wife of a certain Cleopas. But Matthew and Mark distinguish her as the mother of James (whom Mark xv. 40, names "James the less,") and of Joses. If on this point we compare Matthew xiii. 55, it will appear, that amongst the so-called brethren of the Lord (ἀδελφοῖς τοῦ κυρίου), were the two persons thus named. Hence the supposition is rendered very probable, that those brothers of Christ were sons of his mother's sister, and consequently his cousins. The name "James the less" seems employed to distinguish, as an ordinary disciple, that brother of the Lord thus named, from James the Apostle. According to John vii. 5, and Acts i. 14, it is quite certain that amongst the twelve there was no brother of Jesus.

Matthew xxvii. 45–50.—After these affecting incidents upon Golgotha, the moment at length approached in which "the prince of life" expired (Acts iii. 15). The sublimity of this moment seems to have been symbolically solemnized even by nature herself; whilst the light of the world appeared to be extinguished, darkness, from the sixth until the ninth hour, extended itself over the whole land. (Γῆ is to be understood of the land of Palestine.) Luke remarks further, and very expressly, "the sun was darkened" (ἐσκοτίσθη ὁ ἥλιος). This might be explained by the supposition of a solar eclipse, were it not that, the full moon occurring at the period of Easter, forbids such an hypothesis.

But, on the other hand, nothing hinders the supposition of other general physical causes to account for this darkening, for neither is

* This passage is to me decisive on the question, that Mary had no actual son, else would not the Saviour have entrusted his mother, as a solitary widow, to a stranger. This would have been an open slight to the brother.

it mentioned that anything peculiarly miraculous was involved in it, nor can there be any object subserved in making such an assumption. There is merely suggested the *idea*, that with the Lord of Nature the creation itself suffered: that it spread around the tragedy of Golgotha the curtain of night, to veil the guilt which was now being consummated, and for that object God could control and direct even natural phenomena.* The Scriptural doctrine of Providence, which excludes all chance coincidences, warrants no other view of this event than that which we have given.† As the moment of his death drew near, there returned yet a severer trial for the Saviour. It was the last of his mortal life, replete with trials, but perhaps the severest, since the soul was forcibly divorced from the bonds of the sacred body, which was of necessity the more exquisitely sensible to agony because of its freedom from sin. To this event applies in general what was observed on Matthew xxvi. 36, et seq., in reference to the conflict of Christ in Gethsemane; but what we had to assume, in order to explain the phenomena of that conflict, is here clearly expressed. Here the Saviour, in the words of Psalm xxii. 1, openly complains of his being forsaken of God. Every attempt to superficialize this mysterious exclamation must be rejected at the outset. The Saviour does not give utterance to this sentiment because the 22d Psalm contains it. In accordance with the essential truth and harmony of his whole life, the Saviour spoke no

* Concerning the darkness at the death of Jesus, compare the treatise by Grausbeck, Tübingen, 1835. How deeply it lies in human nature to regard natural events symbolically as manifesting a sympathy between the life of nature and the incidents of humanity, is shewn by parallel passages from the profane writers. Amongst the passages of Virgil, Georgic i. 463, et seq., is particularly worthy of note:

> Sol, tibi signa dabit; solem quis dicere falsum
> Audeat? Ille etiam cæcos instare tumultus
> Sæpe monet, fraudemque et operta tumescere bella.
> Ille etiam exstincto miseratus Cæsare Romam;
> Quam caput obscura nitidum ferrugine (*i. e.* caligine) texit,
> Impiaque æternam timuerunt sæcula noctem.

Such parallels are so little calculated to favour a mythical interpretation of the evangelical history, that they afford decisive evidence of its historical character. In the history of Immanuel, appear realized in their perfect truth the confused and variously darkened presages and presentiments of humanity. The passage quoted from Virgil acquires a peculiar interest, if we compare the description by Dante (Inferno, Canto 34), where the death of Cæsar and that of Christ are brought forward in connexion, in that the poet discovers in the former sufferer, the representative of all earthly power, and in the latter the possessor of all spiritual might. Judas, Brutus, and Cassius appear to the poet as the greatest criminals in the history of the world, and as such are placed in the lowest depth of hell.

† The darkness and the earthquake seem clearly *intended* to be represented by the Evangelists as miraculous. That this miraculous character is not *mentioned* is in accordance with their general mode of describing such events. But how else are we to account for those phenomena; and assuredly if miracles clustered about the commencement of our Lord's earthly life, they are no less fitting attendants on its tragic and awful close.—[K.

word which did not perfectly correspond with the reality. But to refer the abandonment merely to his outward sufferings, is forbidden by every more profound conception of it; for the most extreme physical suffering is no abandonment to him whose internal nature is filled with Divine energy and happiness. But the magnitude of the sufferings of Christ consisted in the fact that his physical torments were united with the divestiture of his soul of all spiritual energy. His bodily nakedness was, as it were, a type of his being inwardly divested of all heavenly adornments. When we reflect that such abandonment was experienced by *him* who had said, "I and my Father are one; he that seeth me seeth the Father also; the Father leaveth me not alone" (John viii. 29), we shall perceive that the object of that abandoment, like that of the death of Christ generally—(which is to be regarded only as the acmé of all sufferings)—must have been unique and infinitely great. (Compare the Comm. on Matth. xxvi. 36, where intimations of the ensuing dis cussion have been given.)

According to Scripture itself, this object was twofold. First, the course of suffering, and the agonizing withdrawal of God from him, were necessary to render perfect the human personality of the Lord himself. In the epistle to the Hebrews we have the clearest and most direct statements to this effect. Sufferings, it is said (Heb. ii. 10), had made the captain of salvation perfect; and, although he was the Son of God, yet, in that which he suffered, did he *learn obedience* (v. 8, 9, vii. 28). In this epistle especially, prominent reference is made to the compassion of Christ. Thus it is said, ii. 17, in all things it behooved him to be made like unto his brethren, that he might be a merciful and faithful high priest in things pertaining to God. (Compare Heb. iv. 15.)

But, secondly, the Saviour in himself, and in his personality, at the same time perfected all those whom he, as the second Adam, bore potentially in himself; as it is mentioned in Heb. x. 14, "by one offering, hath he perfected for ever them that are sanctified." But this "perfecting of all" has both a negative and a positive character, which indeed always stand in close connexion, yet cannot be regarded as interchangeable. The negative character consists in cancelling the guilt of the sinful life, *reconciliation* with God;* the

* Compare on the idea of satisfaction, the profoundly intelligent essay, published, with a particular reference to Göschel, on this question, in Tholuck's "Litter. Anzeiger, Jahrg. 1833, Num. 10, ff.," with which should be compared the particulars in the observations on Rom. iii. 25. When Schleiermacher, in his "Glaubenslehre," interprets reconciliation as merely "reception into the community of the blessedness of Christ," there disappears manifestly the necessary *objective* feature (which with him is always thrown into the background), namely, the harmonizing of justice and grace in the Divine nature itself. Ritzsch Christl. Lehre. s. 186, in the forcible style of a realist, expresses this opinion

forgiveness of sins. As will be explained at Romans iii. 25, and Hebrews ix. 22, this negative efficacy would have been impossible, in consequence of the absolute justice of God, without the shedding of blood; in submitting to which condition the Saviour presented the most exalted manifestation of the voluntary self-devotedness of sacrificial love. In this respect, therefore, the dying Redeemer appears as the "lamb of God, that taketh away the sins of the world." The *positive* character consists in the communication of a higher principle of life; emancipation from the slavery of sin; the creation of the new man, of Christ within us. This *latter* element is indicated by the *resurrection* which is the necessary sequel of Christ's death. The *death* of Jesus indicates the former (or negative character), the ultimate point of his self-sacrificing love (Rom. vi. 1, et seq.) In regard to the idea of his abandonment, it is necessary still to remind the reader that no Gnostic ideas, such as the withdrawal of the celestial Christ, so that only the man Jesus suffered,* are to be accepted.

Passages such as John viii. 29, xvi. 32, shew that the union of the Divine and human natures in Christ was such that they were and are immiscible, and at the same time inseparable. The abandonment therefore took place as a *hiding* only of Divinity, not as a proper removal of it. (As regards the form of the citation, Mark xv. 34 gives the Aramaic text more closely. For the Hebrew Ἠλί, = אֵלִי, he has Ἐλωΐ = אֱלָהִי. For the Hebrew עֲזַבְתָּנִי both have the Aramæan שְׁבַקְתָּנִי. The vocative form Θεέ in Matthew is entirely unusual. Compare Winer's Gramm. p. 62, and upon ἵνα τί in the signification of "Wherefore," p. 145.)

In the following verses (47 et seq.) we are informed that the bystanders misunderstood the exclamation of Christ. They thought

very fitly thus: "Christ, following the impulse of Divine mercy, constituted himself a principle of life and death."

* Sartorius, in the excellent treatise upon the relation of the Divine and human natures in Christ (in den dorpatischen Beiträgen, ersten Heft, im auszuge in der Evang. K. Zeit. Feb. 1833), expresses himself concerning the relation of the Divine nature in Christ to the sufferings of his human nature, in the following manner:—"God limited the fulness of the Divine nature in the human by the veil of the flesh, but without, on that account, altering it. In the same manner as the eye, when it lets down the eyelid, suffers no change or limitation in the nature or possession of its peculiar faculty of operating at an immense distance; but merely experiences a restraint in the exercise of this faculty. Without this enshrouding, no incarnation, in the form of a servant, would have been possible, because the infinite brightness of deity would have repelled altogether the darkness of human suffering. But the shadows of death in this manner surrounded the veiled majesty. Or rather, not merely do its shadows obscure that majesty; but through the unity of the Divine and human consciousness, the veritable *feeling* of sufferings penetrated the very mind of deity. Thus, though the soul, by its very nature, is immortal and lives, whilst the body is dying, and *after* the body is dead, yet by reason of its personal union with the body, it experiences, in the unity of consciousness, all the bodily pains of sickness, and all the horror of death.

he called for Elias, who was expected as the forerunner of the Messiah. Several commentators have been disposed to regard these words as additional mockery, but this is not intimated by a single syllable. We must rather infer, that a secret horror now overspread their minds, a feeling which the most daring are often the first to experience, and that it subsequently affected them powerfully (Matth. xxvii. 54, Luke xxiii. 48). Those rude mockers may have feared that there might be something real in the Messiahship of the crucified Jesus, and have trembled at the thought that Elias might appear in a tempest. Psychologically considered, this conclusion is very probable. For even the rudest nature, when it has wearied itself with mockery and insult against suffering innocence, feels it necessary to pause, and some nobler feeling, if only the terror of a guilty conscience, for a time assumes the mastery. Hence, when the Lord cried out "I thirst" (John xix. 28, 29), a person immediately ran and presented him with a draught. (John calls to mind that even this exclamation fulfilled a prophecy, Psalm lxix. 21. In the ἵνα τελειωθῇ = πληρωθῇ, the ἵνα must not be referred to Jesus as if his only object in uttering the exclamation was the fulfilment of this prophecy; it must be referred to the general purpose of God. The reference of the formula to εἰδώς, which is maintained by Bengel and Tholuck, I regard as entirely untenable; ἵνα in this passage must be taken τελικῶς.—Whilst Matthew and Mark mention that the sponge filled with sour wine (ὄξος), was tied upon a reed, John says more particularly it was tied upon a stalk of hyssop. This plant has indeed but a short stalk, but the cross was very low, and only a short reed was requisite for the object contemplated.) After Jesus had received the drink, he cried yet again, with a loud voice, and expired. According to John xix. 30, the Redeemer uttered the words, "it is finished" (τετέλεσται). That this expression did not refer to what was merely physical, is evident from the preceding sentence, "Jesus knowing that all things were now accomplished" (εἰδὼς ὁ Ἰησοῦς, ὅτι πάντα ἤδη τετέλεσται). But, irrespective of this, reflection upon the personal character of the Lord will lead to a more comprehensive sense of this weighty expression. Ever filled with the remembrance of the sublime objects of his mission, he now regarded them as completely fulfilled and accomplished.* His victory over all the assaults of darkness, was the pledge of his complete triumph, just as by Adam's fall all was lost. (Compare Rom. v. 12, et seq.) According to Luke xxiii. 46, Jesus,

* The Christian poet has expressed himself in accordance with this interpretation:

"That too, which day and night I perfect,
Is by e'en thee, in me perfected."

The perfection of every particular is therefore not needed in the first instance, but will be received in faith from the riches of Christ.

in conformity with Psalm xxxi. 5, added the words, *πάτερ, εἰς χεῖράς σου παραθήσομαι τὸ πνεῦμά μου, Father, into thy hands*, etc. In the address, "Father," he expresses the full consciousness of his sonship, which was undisturbed even by his extreme sufferings. But while the *soul* of Christ went to the dead in Sheol (1 Pet. iii. 18), his *body* rested in the grave, and his *spirit* returned again to the Father. In the resurrection, all three were again conjoined in harmonious unity.

Ver. 51–54.—To this plain description, given without comment or reflection, of the greatest incident in the history of the world, the turning-point of the old and new worlds, the Synoptical writers add an account of certain phenomena which accompanied and followed it, in which the material universe, by physical occurrences, gave witness of that which was accomplished,* as in the visions of angels the sympathy of the spiritual world took utterance at the birth of Jesus.† At the moment when the Prince of Life (Acts iii. 15), expired, the earth quaked, the rocks were burst asunder, and the veil of the Temple was rent. (In Matth. the *καὶ ἰδού* affirms that these were simultaneous occurrences.) Luke has anticipated their date in his account xxiii. 45. The *καταπέτασμα* corresponds to the Hebrew פָּרֹכֶת, which signifies the curtain in front of "the Holy of Holies:" the curtain in front of the holy place was called מָסָךְ, which is rendered by *κάλυμμα* in the LXX. (Compare the words in Gesenius' lexicon.) Here again it is quite indifferent whether we regard the earthquake as a usual one or not. For mere chance, as is self-evident, must be totally excluded; and therefore the event must for ever remain a profoundly significant symbol. With the death of the Saviour, a light penetrated into all that was hidden. The graves were opened. Hades and its dead beheld the celestial radiance. The barred entrance to the heaven of God, which was typified in the earthly temple, was thrown open to man. Now when those who stood around observed those movements of nature, an indistinct apprehension led

* In the Christian Treasury of Song, the ethical importance of these occurrences is strikingly represented in those celebrated lines:

If, when Christ dies, creation heaves around,
Thou too, my soul, shouldst not unmoved be found.
Da selbst die creatur sich regt,
So, sey auch du, mein herz bewegt.

† In the critical periods of man's moral history, the creation always appears in peculiar co-operation with the spirit. Interesting parallels of this kind are furnished by a comparison of the history of the fall with the history of Christ's sufferings. By the *tree* of knowledge, mankind fell: by the *tree* of the cross, he was restored. In the *garden* (Eden), the first Adam ate the fruit and fell; in the *garden* (Gethsemane), the second Adam conquered, and in the *garden* he enjoyed in the grave the Sabbatic rest. In *fruit* (of the tree of knowledge) the first man ate to himself death: in the *fruit* of the vine believers at the Lord's supper enjoy eternal life. Sin caused those *thorns* to grow which were to form the regal coronet of the Son of God.

them to the correct conclusion, that there was a connexion between these appearances and the crucifixion of Christ. The Roman centurion even uttered his conviction, that this person might well have been a Son of God. (According to Luke xxiii. 47, he gave glory to God, [ἐδόξασε τὸν Θεόν]—he was probably a proselyte—and termed Jesus a δίκαιος, *righteous man.*) (Comp. Matth. xxvii. 19.) In Mark xv. 39, the description is inaccurate, in that there appears not the proper reference to the earthquake. Even the rest of the multitude, who came merely to see a sight, were seized with a feeling of horror. They smote upon their breasts and turned away; they knew not that they had just beheld an event which the angels desired to contemplate (1 Peter i. 12). Matthew subjoins, by way of anticipation, a very remarkable statement. He informs us, that at the earthquake not only did the graves (cut in the rocks) open, but that many of the saints arose, and (subsequently) went into the holy city, and appeared there to many. The only interpretation of this statement which, next to the *literally historical* one, can gain currency, is the mythical. For the so-called *natural* one which connects the loss of some dead bodies, which the earthquake had thrown from their graves, with certain casual dreams of some citizens of Jerusalem, is assuredly too meagre.* But the mythical interpretation in so extraordinary an occurrence, certainly *appears* to commend itself; and hence it is no wonder that the numerous opponents of the doctrine of a bodily resurrection all incline towards it.

Here, however, as in all similar cases, the *nearness of the time* would not permit the construction of a myth, since numerous contemporary witnesses of the event would have been able to contradict it. The defenders of the mythical view may, however, in this case, take refuge under that hypothesis respecting this Gospel which assumes it to be not written by the Apostle Matthew himself, in the form in which we possess it. Now, improbable as this conjecture appears to me, yet we may at any moment concede its probability, and still maintain decisive ground against interpreting the passage mythically, namely, that this view is formed wholly in contradiction to analogy, and even to the generally received dogmas of the faith. Christ himself was regarded assuredly as the πρωτότοκος ἐκ τῶν νεκρῶν, *the first-born from the dead* (Coloss. i. 18; Rev. i. 5)—a view with which this statement (of Matthew) appears to be irreconcilable. Hence a myth would undoubtedly have interpolated this statement into the account of the *resurrection* of Christ, not into that of his *death*. But, if the resurrection of the dead in general has been once recognized by Christian consciousness, then this occur-

* Just as little does the notion of Stroth, that the passage is not authentic, need a particular contradiction. (Compare Eichhorn's Bibl. B. ix.) For this latter conjecture, no proofs, external or internal, can be adduced.

rence expresses merely the simple thought (which in another relation was previously mentioned at Luke xiv. 14, respecting the righteous of the New Testament dispensation) that the resurrection took place gradually, and that with the Saviour the saints of the ancient covenant attained to the glorification of the body (Isaiah xxvi. 19). In any case, the hypothesis of the late Steudel ("Glaubenslehre," p. 455), with which Krabbe ("Von der Sünde," p. 297) agrees, is altogether untenable; namely, that there is no mention at all of a bodily resurrection, but only of mere apparitions of the dead, thus furnishing a guarantee of their life. This hypothesis is contradicted in the most decided manner, by the plain meaning of the words "many *bodies* of sleeping saints arose" (πολλὰ σώματα τῶν κεκοιμημένων ἁγίων ἠγέρθη). A bodily resurrection, with which there should be associated a subsequent liability to death, is, of course, inconceivable; hence there remains no other tenable view than that which we have explained, and which corresponds most closely with the entire Scripture doctrine of the resurrection. The difficulty just touched upon respecting the relation of these risen ones to Christ, as the "first-born of the dead" (this discussion cannot be affected by the cases of Enoch and Elijah, because they did not taste death at all) might be removed by supposing that the actual going-forth out of their graves did not occur until after the resurrection of the Lord; so that "after the resurrection" (μετὰ τὴν ἔγερσιν) should be taken in connexion with "coming forth" (ἐξελθόντες). The death of Christ thus appears as a *blow* which vibrated through and shook all things, but his resurrection as the proper act of *quickening* to the sleeping world of the saints. The first advent of the Saviour possesses in this event a peculiar grace, by which it appears all the more recognizable as a type of the future glorious appearing of the Lord. Everything which shall yet occur in its fullest extent in the Parousia,* was thus indicated partially in Christ's first advent.

§ 6. THE BURIAL OF JESUS.

(Matthew xxvii. 57–66; Mark xv. 42–47; Luke xxiii. 50–56; John xix. 31–42.)

After the soul of Jesus had forsaken the pure temple wherein it had dwelt, his sacred body was not left unregarded, as the mere insignificant envelope of a heavenly phenomenon; a wondrous providence of God hovered over it, and averted from it every kind of injury revolting to the feelings. John (xix. 31–37), conscious of

* Compare Rev. xi., where the resurrection of the two witnesses, the earthquake accompanying that event, the opening of the temple of God, which stands parallel with the rending of the veil, and other incidents, are described.

the importance of this circumstance, has given the most careful information concerning its particulars. In this account we possess as decisive a guarantee as was possible, in a physical point of view, of the reality of the death of Jesus; and also a proof of the significance which Christian feeling attaches to our corporeal nature. Christianity is far from conforming to that comfortless view which regards the body as merely the prison of the human spirit; a view which conducts to rigid asceticism only. And just as foreign is it from the hollow notion that sin arises merely from the attractions of sense, and hence that death and sin cease along with our sensuous appetites, a view which favours Epicureanism. Rather does the Gospel regard it as the object of the connexion between body and soul, that the former should be glorified as the temple of the Holy Spirit, so that the language of a profound thinker is thoroughly scriptural, "without body no soul, without corporeity no bliss."

According to the Jewish custom (Deut. xxi. 22, 23), the bodies of persons who had been executed, were required to be removed on the same day on which they died. The Jews besought Pilate, therefore, that they might end the lives of those who were crucified, as it was then the preparation day before the Sabbath.* (*Παρασκευή*, so named also by Mark xv. 42, and by Luke xxiii. 54, who calls the succeeding Sabbath "great" because occurring during the Paschal festival.) It was customary to break the limbs of those who were suffering crucifixion, and who were invariably persons of the meanest condition, in order to hasten their death. This was done

* Compare the observations on Matth. xxvi. 17, and John xix. 14. Locke erroneously supposes, from John xix. 31, that a view of the *παρασκευή* contrary to that conveyed by the above passages may be deduced, since he says, "The annexed expletive would have no object, if the *παρασκευή* was the ordinary Sabbatical one." On the other hand, however, Tholuck has correctly remarked (on John xiii. 1, s. 250) that the addition is sufficiently explained, from the circumstance that the Sabbath, falling during the Paschal festival, although not coinciding with the first holy-day of the Passover, thereby gained a particular dignity. Besides, in the latter case no mention would have been made of a great Sabbath day, by way of distinction, for if the first day of the Passover were to fall upon a Sabbath, so must the last also. As we have already remarked on Matth. xxvi. 17, all the Evangelists are agreed unanimously in respect to the week days of the passion week; it is only concerning the time of the paschal feast that they seem to vary in their accounts. Hitzig's representation of the case ("Easter and Pentecost," p. 38), which concedes the correctness of John in opposition to the Synoptical writers, is untenable, for the following reason, namely, because, between the Sabbath, in which the Lord lay in the grave, and the day of the resurrection, he quite arbitrarily intercalates a *σάββατον δευτερόπρωτον*. But this hypothesis nothing in the evangelical history can justify, except, apparently, the statement (Matth. xii. 40) that the Messiah would rest in the earth three days and three nights. Yet, however we may explain this passage, in no case could the succession of the days of the passion-week be determined from it; and least of all, in its explanation, could so obscure an expression as *σάββατον δευτερόπρωτον*, be here introduced. Compare Luke vi. 1.

hands and feet, yet without destroying or altering his perfect organism.

After this event, the Synoptical Evangelists (see Matth. xxvii. 57–61, and parallels, and compare therewith John xix. 38–42), record the exertions of certain influential friends of Jesus in reference to his body. John (ver. 39) names Nicodemus, and alludes to his former visit to Jesus by night (John iii. 1, et seq.) The principal person, however, was Joseph of Arimathea. (Ἀριμάθαια is either הָרָמָה, *Ramah*, in the tribe of Benjamin, mentioned in Matth. ii. 18, and called in Syriac אָרָמְתָא, or since that town is called Ῥαμᾶ by Matthew, it was probably רָמָתַיִם, a city in the tribe of Ephraim (1 Sam. i. 1), which the LXX. call by the name of Ἀραμαθαίμ.)

This city, it is true, stood originally in the territory of the Samaritans, but it was afterwards annexed to Judea, 1 Maccabees xi. 28–34: and hence Luke xxiii. 51 might with propriety designate it as a city of the Jews.

This worthy man was a disciple of the Lord, but the fear of man had hitherto prevented him from openly professing his attachment to Jesus, John xix. 38. Meanwhile what he could not prevail on himself to do whilst Jesus was living, he had resolution to do now that he was dead. He besought Pilate for the body of Christ. Notwithstanding his infirmity, Joseph certainly belonged to the nobler minded class of the Jewish people, who waited with longing expectation for the fulfilment of all the prophecies. (Compare upon the προσδέχεσθαι τὴν βασιλείαν τοῦ Θεοῦ, the Comm. on Luke ii. 25.) He was a man of a benevolent character (Luke xxiii. 50, ἀγαθὸς καὶ δίκαιος), wealthy (Matth. xxvii. 57), and an influential member of the Sanhedrim (εὐσχήμων βουλευτής, Mark xv. 43).

Many would have him to have been a counsellor of Arimathea; but this supposition is forbidden by Luke xxiii. 51, in which passage it is expressly mentioned that he had refused his concurrence in the sentence against Jesus, or rather that he opposed it. Jesus then may have been sentenced by a *majority* of voices in the Sanhedrim, whilst such men as Gamaliel and others may have voted in opposition to the view of the majority. (Συγκατατίθεσθαι scil. ψῆφον, signifies calculum adjicere—to add one's vote. It occurs here only in the New Testament, yet in Acts i. 26, the synonyme συγκαταψηφίζεσθαι. It is frequent in the Septuagint. Compare Exodus xxiii. 1–32.) After Pilate had learned that Jesus was dead, from the centurion, who had been commanded to hasten the death of those that were crucified, Mark xv. 44, he granted his body to Joseph. (The ἐδωρήσατο, in Mark xv. 45, is to be understood in its proper force; but thoroughly avaricious men, such as Verres (Cicero in Ver. v. 45, 51), required to be paid for delivering up the bodies of condemned persons to be interred by their relatives or friends.) Joseph, when he had received the boon, enfolded the body of Jesus in a roll of linen, with a mixture of sweet spices (John xix. 39), placed it in a new sepulchre in his garden, and rolled a stone to its front. The fact of the sepulchre having been new, and unused, is noticed as a mark of honour. It was probably the vault intended for the interment of his own family, which Joseph devoted to the body of Christ. But the whole proceeding took place hastily, for the Sabbath was already drawing nigh, Luke xxiii. 54. Still some of the devoted women who had faithfully accompanied their beloved Master from Galilee, followed him even to his grave, where they sat down, sunk in dejected sorrow (Matth. xxvii. 61), in order to see precisely how his body was placed.

After their return, they prepared at home an ointment of sweet spices, in order, immediately after the Sabbath, to place the beloved body in a meet condition for its rest. For on the Sabbath-day itself they reposed, according to the ordinance (*ἐντολή*) of the law (*νόμος*) of Moses. (Upon *σινδών*, compare at Mark xiv. 51. John, for the same word, employs, xix. 40, *ὀθόνια* = *κειρίαι*, compare at John xi. 44, by which are meant the swathes in which it was customary to enfold the corpses—'Εντυλίσσω (Mark has *ἐνειλέω*), to wrap up. In Hebrew כָּרַךְ. Compare Buxtorf's Lexicon, p. 1089.)

The burying places of the Jews were frequently hewn out in rocks (*λατομέω* from *λᾶς* and *τέμνω*): a block of stone closed up the door-way, or horizontal entrance. (Comp. at John xi. 38.) Luke has the usual expression *λαξευτός*, xxiii. 53, from *λᾶς* and *ξέω*, to polish, to hew out smoothly.) A difficulty still appears in the narration of John, where he states that Nicodemus provided a mixture of myrrh and aloes of about 100 pounds (*μίγμα σμύρνης καὶ ἀλόης ὡσεὶ λίτρας ἑκατόν.*) (John xix. 39.) If we take the pound here, as with the Romans and Greeks, to have contained twelve ounces, the quantity appears too great. Hence Michaelis would understand under the litra a lesser weight. But that this can signify such a lesser weight, is entirely without proof. We must consider, therefore, that this extraordinary quantity of spices was employed, partly as an expression of profound reverence (like the superfluous quantity of ointment used by Mary, John xii. 1, et seq.), and partly in order to surround with it the whole body of Jesus.

Ver. 62-66.—"The morrow, which is the day after the preparation" (*τῇ δὲ ἐπαύριον, ἥτις ἐστὶ μετὰ τὴν παρασκευήν*), is a remarkable mode of characterizing the Sabbath. Such a designation could not of course be ordinarily applied, since the most important day would not be mentioned after the less important one. Yet here this mode of expression is perfectly in place, because the *preparation*, from the fact that the death of Christ occurred upon it, had acquired a greater importance than belonged to the Sabbath. (Compare the particulars in my programme upon the authenticity of Matthew.)

The struggle and contest being completed, the Sabbath was now the day of rest* for the friends of the Lord. Yet the enemies of Christ rested not. The torture of a guilty conscience drove them again to Pilate. They told him of the prophecy concerning the resurrection, and requested that a watch might be placed over the sepulchre until the third day. At this communication, what a feeling must have agitated Pilate, may be conceived, by reflecting how powerfully he had been affected already, upon learning that Jesus had called himself the Son of God. Perhaps he gave his consent so hastily, in order that he might receive certain information as to what might occur relative to Jesus. True, the least conceivable thing to him, in *theory*, was the return (to life) of a dead person, yet the diviner element often prevails over unbelief, through the medium of *sentiment;* and the most sceptical may still be deeply superstitious, since the uneradicable *feeling* of invisible realities maintains its ground in spite of speculation. (*Κουστωδία* is among the many Latin words, which specially, in reference to military transactions, passed over to the Greeks and other people.) But as to the sepulchre of Christ being surrounded by a Roman guard, modern criticism† has disputed the fact upon very specious grounds. Many objections to it disprove themselves, as, for instance, that it is improbable the Jews would on the Sabbath have requested the guard from Pilate, or that the apostles would subsequently, when arraigned before them, have appealed to this fact. Other arguments however, require investigation.

And first, the silence of the other three Evangelists is remarkable, since this event so strongly confirmed the truth of the resurrection. If, however, we take in connexion the subsequent statement of Matthew xxviii. 11–15, it will be evident that the Evangelists might have had a positive reason for leaving untouched the occurrence regarding the guard. For if once such a report, as that the disciples had stolen away the body of Christ, gained currency, it

* The significance of the great (quiet) Sabbath is not yet rightly understood in the church, as is shewn by the fact that it is not solemnized as it ought to be, and not less by our own want of more suitable hymns for the day, which yet as the day of rest of him who is life itself, as the repose, after his creation of the second Adam, has so lofty a poetic significancy.' But the two chief features of the great Sabbath, in a dogmatical sense, are—that it constitutes a type of the rest of the general church in the kingdom of God—and that the soul of Jesus was meanwhile active in Sheol. But the church has not yet rightly tasted the rest, nor carried out completely in practice the important doctrine of the descent into hell. Hence the neglect of this day.

† Comp. Stroth in Eichhorn's Repertorium, vol. ix., and Dr. Paulus' Comm. "de custodia ad sepulchrum. Jesu disposita, Jenæ, 1795."

is manifest that they could not employ the occurrence (of the watch) against sceptics as a *proof* of the resurrection ; as in fact Matthew does not apply it to that purpose, but merely reports it.

But, secondly, some have adduced an important objection from this very narrative itself (Matth. xxviii. 12), which states that the Sanhedrists held a *formal sitting* (*συμβούλιον λαβόντες*), in consequence of information given by the soldiers, and in this assembly passed a resolution to bribe the soldiers. Such a proceeding appears inconsistent with the decorum of such a college, and also with the later declarations of Gamaliel (Acts v. 34), who desired merely to leave it to time to discover whether or not there was anything Divine in the newly arising church of Christ. It would seem also that such a piece of deception could not have escaped the knowledge of Pilate, who, considering the position he stood in towards the Pharisees, would have been well inclined to expose it. To the fact that the women, whilst going to the sepulchre, had no thought about the watch, I should attach no importance, for the guard had received no orders to prevent the body of Jesus from being properly arranged. Besides, they may not have had any knowledge of the entire occurrence during the Sabbath. Whether these difficulties can be completely obviated or not, I do not know ; but a certain hesitancy still remains in my mind. Pilate indeed might himself also wish that the resurrection of Jesus should prove to be without foundation, oppressed as he was by a feeling of guilt, and hence remain silent about the matter. But I cannot believe that such a cheat would have been sanctioned by the resolution of a college, especially since such men as Gamaliel, Joseph of Arimathea, and Nicodemus, were members of it. Still, equally untenable is the hypothesis that the whole account is but a tradition of a later date. Matthew, who, as an eye-witness of the event, wrote in Jerusalem at a time when many persons must still have been present there who had a contemporaneous knowledge of the fact, could not have adopted an entirely false statement of this kind concerning an event which had become so notorious. Hence, the most prudent course is to accept the statement as essentially correct in its facts, but to concede an inaccuracy in the account of the assembling of the Sanhedrim.* Probably Caiaphas, as officiating high priest, dis-

* This concession to neologizing scepticism on the part of Olshausen, is almost inexplicable. He would seem to have forgotten his own vivid portraiture of the growing and bitter hatred with which the heads of the Jewish Theocracy regarded the Saviour, and to overlook the anxious and breathless interest with which they would await the results of that recent crucifixion which had occurred amidst such solemn phenomena. It was surely natural that they should procure a guard to watch the tomb (with a sort of *latent* hope, not so much of preventing the stealing of the body, as of preventing its miraculous resurrection), and when this guard unanimously assured them of the Lord's wonderful

posed of the case alone, in an underhand way, and in this acceptation the narrative contains nothing at all improbable. Compare Hase's Leben Jesu, p. 194.

disappearance, it is not only probable that the Sanhedrim should assemble, but *incredible that it should not.* The attempt to bribe the soldiery to a falsehood, is the resort of desperation—a natural consummation of their malignant and infatuated opposition to one whose life had been a career of miracles. Nor would Joseph, Nicodemus, and Gamaliel, be more likely to arrest their fury in this crisis of the tragic scene, than in its previous stages.—[K.

SECOND PART.

OF THE RESURRECTION OF JESUS CHRIST.

(Matth. xxviii.; Mark xv.; Luke xxiv.; John xx., xxi.)

THE death of the Lord, and the shedding of his blood (Heb. ix. 22), were essentially involved in the prosecution of the work of redemption. But it was equally necessary that death should be vanquished* by his subsequent *resurrection.*† The very notion of a Saviour from sin and death, involves, as a necessary consequence, the idea of that Saviour being himself *sinless;* and therefore incapable, except by his voluntary self-devotion to that death which was necessary to the redemption of man, of dying, but, on that very account, incapable also of being holden by death. By his death, and by the resurrection essentially connected with it, he stripped of authority him who had the power of death (Heb. ii. 14), in order that men, his *brethren* reconciled to God by his death, might be redeemed and translated into a new life. Hence the death and resurrection of Jesus represent the two parts of his collective ministry; the negative as well as the positive. (Rom. vi. 1, seq.)

From what has just been stated, it appears that the resurrection was an event in the highest degree essential to the completion of the sublime development of the Saviour's life, and it is in this light that the history of the apostolic church represents it. The resurrection was the great fact which the apostles published, properly *that alone.* After the ascension to heaven, and the outpouring of the Holy Ghost, which were the first acts of the glorified Saviour, those disciples who exhibited such weakness but a few days

* Amongst interesting treatises upon the resurrection, the reader should consult Griesbach, "De fontibus unde Evangelistæ suas de resurrectione Domini narrationes hauserint," Jenæ 1793. Niemeyer, "De evangelistarum in narrando Christi in vitam reditu dissensione," Halle, 1824. Further, compare the treatises by Velthusen in "Sylloge Commentt., vol. iv. page 77, et seq.," and by Seiler in the same work, vol. vi. page 503, et seq. (The latter treats rather of the ascension.) And especially as regards the nature of the resurrection, Krabbe on the doctrine of sin and death (Hamburg, 1836), p. 275, et seq.

† In connexion with the following observations upon the resurrection, consult what is stated at Acts i. 11, concerning the ascension into heaven.

before when Jesus was arrested, appeared thoroughly transformed in their moral nature; endowed with invincible boldness, with wisdom, calmness, and clearness of intelligence.

The origin of the Christian church is an incontrovertible matter-of-fact proof, that a great event, a decisive transaction, must have taken place, which was capable of supplying to its founders the persevering energy necessary for such an enterprise.* But this significance of the resurrection appears only as we hold that the Saviour did not rise again with the *mortal* body which he bore before his crucifixion.† Should we think, like many well-meaning persons, that the Saviour, when truly dead, was again quickened by an act of Divine Omnipotence, without any transformation having taken place in his body, we fail to see in what the importance of this fact consists. The raising of Lazarus would in that case have been a precisely similar event, and in no manner could the apostle Paul (1 Cor. xv.), have been able to represent this occurrence as the foundation of the faith, and the consummation of the victory over death and the grave, since the body of Christ would have still continued subject to death. It would in that case be the *ascension* (to which the advocates of this view are accustomed to attribute the glorification of Christ's body), that must be viewed as the victory over death; but this cannot be, since all the apostles regarded the ascension as only a *consequence* of the resurrection, which last event was to them the chief and peculiar fact. Assuredly then this mode of apprehending the resurrection, and of which even Tholuck approves (on John xx. 19, 20) could never have been maintained for a moment, if the statements relating to the appearances of the risen Redeemer did not seem to vouch for its correctness. The Lord, for instance, appeared with a body possessing flesh and bone (Luke xxiv. 39), a body which bore in it the wounds he received (John xx. 27); one that partook of food (Luke xxiv. 42); one, in short, bearing a complete resemblance to an ordinary mortal body: such expressions and statements seem unsuited to the idea of a glorified body. Yet, weighty as these remarks appear at the first view, they will be found, upon more careful investigation, to be altogether untenable.

In the first case, for example, the *spiritual body* (*σῶμα πνευμα-*

* Hase, in his "Leben Jesu," s. 199, says, with entire correctness, "It is not the essence of Christianity that depends on the resurrection, but its *manifestation*. The *church* was founded by means of it." But it is hard to discover how the scholar just named can ascribe this importance to the event of the resurrection, whilst he regards it as merely an awakening from apparent death.

† This has been ably demonstrated by Krabbe (loc. cit. p. 300, et seq.) In the passage, Rom. vi. 9, the apostle asserts the impossibility of a recurrence of death to the risen Saviour. This passage, taken in connexion with Philippians iii. 21, where a *σῶμα τῆς δόξης* is attributed to Christ, warrants the inference, that Paul himself regarded the body of Jesus as glorified in the resurrection, since with the resurrection the glory of Christ commences.

τικόν) must not be confounded with the *spirit* (πνεῦμα), properly so called.* According to the express representation of the Apostle Paul, the animal body (σῶμα ψυχικόν) becomes a spiritual one (πνευματικόν) in the resurrection, but it still remains a true *body*. Further, if we consider that whilst the body of Christ, from his birth upwards, with all its similarity to ours, was yet also very different (since to it appertained a *possibility*, but not the *necessity* of death†), and hence the alteration it underwent during the process of glorification was less striking; we shall understand on the one hand how the disciples could recognize him, and examine the marks of his wounds, and on the other hand, why they discerned in him an alteration so great that frequently they did not know him. This consideration acquires the greater weight if we assume that the process of glorification went on during the forty days (after his resurrection), and was not thoroughly perfected until the period of his ascension to heaven. Lastly, in the history of the resurrection (Luke xxiv. 42), no mention is made of his partaking of food from necessity: its sole object was to convince those who were present of the *reality* of his body. But finally, it is always assumed in Scripture (Rev. xxii. 2), that the bodies of the glorified partake of food, though indeed, any accompanying physical process is expressly excluded (1 Cor. vi. 13). According to Gen. xviii. 8, even the three men who appear to Abraham—(of whom one was the Angel of the Lord, κατ' ἐξοχήν, that is, Jehovah), actually partake of food, though they must be regarded as destitute of corporeity, and merely invested with apparent bodies. The difficulties involved in the hypothesis, of the glorified nature of the Lord's body in the resurrection, may therefore be thus removed; and at any rate they are not of a nature to lead us astray in the essential point of this whole occurrence, namely, that the Redeemer must have so arisen that henceforth it is impossible for him to die again, which could only be the case with a glorified body. The case is entirely different with those who are not merely doubtful as to the *time* of the glorification, but who regard with suspicion the doctrine, although they do not deny the resurrection. Alas, that modern philosophy, in accordance with its predominating idealism, should not yet be able to appreciate the idea of a glorification of the body and of matter generally! (Compare at Romans viii. 19, et seq.) But a few men (especially Schubert and Steffens), distinguished equally as natur-

* Hase ("Leben Jesu," p. 202), is chargeable with this confusion in representing the doctrine of a glorified body as docetic. The entire distinctness of the two doctrines is best shewn by the opposition of the earliest Christian Fathers to doceticism, while yet, without exception, they taught the glorification of the body.

† That this character belonged to the body of Christ is indicated, for instance, by the walking of the Lord upon the sea, his transfiguration, and other events of the evangelical history.

alists and as philosophers, have acknowledged its truth and importance.*

The sacred Scriptures do not recognize that Dualism, which is involved in the doctrine of an absolute separation of matter and spirit. As in man the spirit appears in matter and united with it, so are we taught by Scripture that it exerts an influence on matter, defiles, sanctifies it, and, at last, even transforms it. Instead of making this profound and comprehensive doctrine their own, and gradually testing its philosophical power, some persons at once transfer everything it includes into the region of *mythology*. The mere idea of a return of one who had come from the world of spirits into that world is all that, in their view, is expressed in the resurrection. But the sober narratives of the Evangelists, which have descended from a purely historical period, and were written by actual eye-witnesses of the fact, stand—as we have already observed more than once—in the most glaring contrast with the hypothesis of a *myth*. And, besides, when we resolve the fantastic splendour of the myth, we discover beneath it a reality that annihilates the idea of a Redeemer, and which yet must be received for truth, if we reject the representation of the Evangelists. If, to wit, the bodily frame of the Lord did not in fact arise, and that in a glorified state, then the very victor over the grave must somewhere, and in some way, have become a victim of the grave,† were his spirit to have returned to the realm of spirit.

After these remarks, there still remains to be noticed a view which does not so much conceive the resurrection in a peculiar light, as totally *deny* it. One class of the advocates of this view (Dr. Paulus and Henneberg), maintain the fact itself, but in the

* It is surprising that the Holy Scriptures do not, for the purpose of elucidating the relation between the new body and the old nature from whose elements it evolves itself, make use of so immediate an analogy, as that of the butterfly and the chrysalis, from which it releases itself. Its reason seems to spring from the fact that Holy Scripture leaves animal life generally in the background, and borrows its figures more frequently from vegetable nature. The twilight existence of animals, and their half-developed, psychical, and yet unconscious character, unfits them for the illustrating of the phenomena of that conscious *spirit-life* which struggles forth even from the faint dawn of childhood.

† Thus Hase, in his "Leben Jesu," s. 204, expresses it openly.

‡ The view that Christ's body was raised spiritual and glorified, seems not only confirmed by the general character of the risen Saviour's intercourse with his disciples (which was occasional, rare, and mysterious), but demanded by the relation which his resurrection sustains to that of his people. If they rise from the dead with spiritual bodies, he, who in all things was made like unto his brethren, should, as the "first fruits," rise in like manner. Nor need we suppose a *process* of glorification continued to his ascension, nor, again, appeal to his walking on the sea, as proof of an *original* difference of his body from that of men in general. The walking on the sea was a miracle; and resulted, not from any peculiarities of his physical organism, but, like all his other miracles, from the power of the indwelling Divinity.—[K.

resurrection of Christ allow only an awakening from a swoon. By the holders of the view we first touched upon, who maintain that the Saviour rose again in his mortal body, this opinion of Dr. Paulus and Henneberg cannot be easily confuted from external grounds. For the medical proofs of the reality of Christ's death, from the wound made by the spear-thrust, are at least not irresistible.* But, on the other hand, according to our interpretation, this hypothesis has not the slightest degree of importance. For, assuming that the Redeemer was only apparently dead, yet that circumstance by no means impairs the significance of this event. For this does not consist in the return of Jesus to life (this had also happened in the case of others without possessing any special weight), but in the *impossibility of dying* again, which, with this return, was given in the glorification of his body. This latter view necessarily assumes a peculiar agency of God in the resurrection, and can never be deceived by the flimsy hypothesis of an *apparent* death. But, leaving aside all uncertain physical proofs, we have further, in Christ's prophecies of his death, an immovable foundation whereon to base our conviction of its reality. As in the case of Lazarus, and all other dead persons who were awakened to life, it is only from the word of Christ we can conclude with certainty that they were *dead;* (since he openly declared, in cases where death had not taken place, that the persons only slept†). So the word of Christ—the true witness—is the rock whereon alone rests the certainty that "He was dead, and is again alive" (Rev. i. 18).

Attempts have not been wanting to obviate those clear, direct expressions of Jesus, in reference to his prospective death and resurrection, which we have in Matthew xvi. 21, xvii. 22, xx. 19; in Mark viii. 31, ix. 31, x. 34; and in Luke xviii. 33; besides the less definite passages, Matthew xii. 40, xvi. 4. But so very weak are the grounds upon which it is sought to make it appear probable that these were put into the mouth of Christ, post eventum, by the

* Compare Bretschneider's essay in opposition to Dr. Paulus concerning the apparent death of Jesus, in "Die Studien," 1832, h. 3, p. 625, et seq. He exposes an instance in which Dr. Paulus misunderstands Josephus, vit. c. 75, from which he concluded that men, after having hung three days upon the cross, had been restored to life; but, as Bretschneider shews, the passage contains nothing of the kind.

† Compare my explanation of the awakening of the daughter of Jairus, Comm. Part I. on Matth. If we must invert the signification of the simple, distinct declaration of Christ, "The maiden is not dead, but she sleepeth," into the assertion, "The maiden sleepeth not, but she is dead," I confess that I cannot see how we can speak of any certain results of Exegesis. [But see the notes of Ebrard and the present editor on that passage. There can be, of course, no doubt that the Saviour uttered the truth: the only question is, how he *meant to be understood.* Here the whole discussion of the evidences of the real or apparent death of Jesus is totally irrelevant with one who admits the historical authority of the Evangelists. We have the same reason to believe that he was *dead* as that he was *crucified.*]—[K.

disciples, that only the irresistible consciousness that in this way alone was the great fact itself likely to be rendered suspicious, could have induced the originators of this attempt to lend to these grounds the slightest importance. For in the first place it is said "the risen Redeemer appealed to the prophecies of the Old Testament (Luke xxiv. 46), but not to his own."* But any one may easily see for what reason the Lord made reference to the Old Testament; because, for example, it plainly devolved upon him, under such circumstances, to demonstrate to the disciples the common connexion of the New Testament and the Old Testament economies with his personal fortunes. A reference to his own former words would therefore be of no importance to his object.

Again—some persons refer to the hopelessness of the disciples, which would not have been conceivable, if they had known anything of the resurrection. But if we consider how hard it is to believe in the fact of the resurrection, so hard, indeed, that even after the lapse of 1800 years, many are still unable to believe it, although the church has received the doctrine among its most indispensable articles of belief, we shall be disposed to form a milder judgment of the apostles' inability to believe in the resurrection *before* it had taken place, nor shall we be able to ascribe to that circumstance the slightest force in disproof of the clear prophecies of the Redeemer. Peter did not believe that he could deny Christ, although it was foretold to him, not to mention other circumstances, which shew that the Lord had uttered many sayings which the disciples were not able entirely to comprehend.† There now remains to be noticed by us, only that obsolete opinion, which (like the Wolfenbüttle Fragmentist) employs the seeming discrepancy that exists amongst the four Evangelists, in order to make it probable that there was a deception in the whole occurrence of the resurrection. Now the account would have been far more suspicious, if, in unessential points, it were entirely free from discrepancy. It is now perfectly harmonious in the main facts of the narrative, but moves independently in reference to secondary matters. Assuming, further, that

* Luke xxiv. 6–8. The angel, too, refers to Christ's prophecies concerning the resurrection. This circumstance leads to the conclusion, that the apostles had noticed similar pre-announcements of it in his discourse, which in after times they called to mind. The Lord's appealing to the Old Testament had besides the most important significance in his lips, since he acknowledged it as the eternal word of God, Matthew v. 17.

† A remarkable external evidence of the resurrection of Jesus is contained in the passage, 1 Cor. xv. 6, from which it appears that many of the 500 disciples who beheld the risen Lord in Galilee, were living at the time when the Apostle wrote to the Corinthians. A more striking fact, in contradiction to the hypothesis, that the history of the resurrection is of a mythical character, is scarcely imaginable. The defenders of the myth have not, in the feeling of their weakness, attempted to invalidate such decisive evidences as these—evidences which, in connexion with the admitted authenticity of the Pauline epistles, possess all the more importance.

the discrepancies were utterly inexplicable, yet even this circumstance would not damage the credibility of what is essential in the narrative. But an explanation of particulars will shew that these variations are but free modes of conceiving the same occurrences, such as generally occur where several persons, unconnected one with another, recount the same event. (Upon the literature of this question compare Hase's Leben Jesu, p. 196, § 135, and the subsequent paragraph.)

The history of the resurrection possesses a peculiarity of character from the fact that the Holy Scriptures themselves make use of it, to typify the spiritual and corporeal resurrection, alike of the individual Christian and of the whole church. Particularly Paul (Rom. vi.) treats of baptism, in the twofold reference of that ordinance, to immersion and emersion, as symbolizing the death and resurrection of Christ.

§ 1. History of the Resurrection.

(Matthew xxviii. 1–15; Mark xvi. 1–11; Luke xxiv. 1–12; John xx. 1–18.)

The act of the resurrection itself, like every new process of production, is enveloped in obscurity. The writers of the New Testament make mention only of what they themselves saw when the sepulchre was already empty. The creative energies wrought in silence, and unobservedly, and wove, for the sublime person of the Lord, as it were, a raiment of celestial light, worthy of investing the King of the world of light. Even so, no human eye beheld how, at that moment, when the energies of life flowed into them, the bodies of the saints arose, to typify that the anticipated resurrection at the end of time will also be an unseen act of Divine omnipotence. The great Sabbath on which the Lord rested from his work, was spent by the male and female friends of Jesus, in pious association, still thinking that they had lost him whom their souls loved. But, in their love, this mistake did not lead astray their love, for, carried out to its proper consequences, it would have forced them to conclude definitely that Jesus was not the Messiah. Nay, scarcely had the light of another day begun to dawn, when they hastened to complete the anointing of the Lord's body. Now in the account of this visit of the women to his tomb, very remarkable differences appear amongst the Evangelists. These require to be stated at the outset. In the first place, then, the Synoptical writers are in the main unanimous.

Mary Magdalene, and Mary the wife of Cleopas (and according to Mark, Salome, and to Luke, Johanna, the wife of Chuza, Luke

xxiv. 10, comp. Luke viii. 3), went about day-break (Mark xvi. 2), to the sepulchre with spices. On their way, they were conversing on the difficulty they should find in rolling away the stone from the entrance to the sepulchre (Mark xvi. 3). But as they drew nigh to the tomb, they found that the stone was removed, and near the sepulchre they saw an angel.

Here the first discrepancy occurs; Luke (xxiv. 4) deviates from Matthew and Mark, by mentioning two angels, whilst they make mention of one only. These angels address the women, inform them of the Saviour's resurrection, and direct them to publish the tidings to the disciples. Luke (xxiv. 7, 8), in the address of the angel, contains something indeed which the other two writers have not, but the only formal discrepancy appears at Mark xvi. 8, in which passage it is said: "They said nothing to any one."

At this point Luke breaks off his account, only remarking in a cursory manner at xxiv. 11, 12, that the apostles did not believe the report of the women, but yet that Peter hastened to the sepulchre. The other two append the additional fact, that Christ himself appeared on the occasion. Matthew observes that he met the women when they were returning. Mark speaks merely of his appearance to Mary Magdalene, without particularizing how she had separated herself from the other women (Matth. xxviii. 9, 10, and Mark xvi. 9, 10). Now if we had only the accounts of the Synoptical Evangelists, the narrative might be regarded, to all intents and purposes, as unanimous. For, so far as the number of the angels is concerned, to any one who desires such minute accuracy, it is sufficient to say, that that apparent diversity occurs in the statement, because Matthew and Mark allude only to the angel that spoke to the women, whilst Luke mentions also the less active heavenly messenger. And the words of Mark, *οὐδενὶ οὐδὲν εἶπον, they said nothing to any*, ver. 8, will harmonize easily with the whole account, provided we limit them, by supplying the clause: "in the first moments" of their astonishment. To this we are guided by the following *ἐφοβοῦντο γάρ, for they were afraid.* The deviation of Mark's account appears to be most conspicuous (Mark xvi. 9) where he suddenly names Mary Magdalene alone, and states that Jesus appeared first to her. Still, if we had not the narrative of John, even this diversity would not appear at all essential, for we need only to suppose that a separation took place between Mary and the other women, which has been left unmentioned, in order to regard the two statements as nearly coincident. But the question assumes a totally different aspect, when we compare the synoptical narrative with that of John. According to the latter, Mary Magdalene went alone to the sepulchre, whilst the morning was yet dark; she found the stone rolled away from it, and hastened back immediately to Peter and John, to whom she expressed her apprehensions that the body of the Lord had been taken away by some persons. On hearing this, the two disciples ran to the sepulchre. John arrived at it first, but Peter ventured to enter the sepulchre before him. After they had convinced themselves that the body of the Lord was not there, they returned back. Mary, however, still remained at the sepulchre weeping. Whilst she sat thus, she beheld two angels, and immediately after this vision, she beheld Jesus also, upon which she hastened to the disciples, and mentioned what she had seen. (John xx. 1–18.)

On a first view, there appears no similarity whatever between this account and that of the Synoptical Evangelists. Only in the passing observation of Luke xxiv. 12, that Peter entered into the sepulchre, is there any appearance of an echo to the narrative of John, and so also in Mark xvi. 9, 10, where it is stated that Jesus appeared first to Mary. But upon closer investigation it will be seen that this great discrepancy, by the help of some inconsiderable assumptions, resolves itself into perfect harmony, and that the several accounts blend together exactly as they might be expected when several persons, in narrating the same transaction, state merely those portions of it which they had observed themselves.

Even the accounts of several eye-witnesses concerning events that occur in their very presence, almost always present a diversity of character, since the manner in which these events are conceived of, varies with the point of view from which each has contemplated them. Griesbach and Hess have therefore adopted the following method of harmonizing the several narratives in opposition to the unhistorical objections to the truth of the resurrection, which have been founded upon these discrepancies.

The narratives of the Synoptical writers form two parallel series: John recounts merely what he himself had witnessed, but the others derived the knowledge of what they relate from others, probably from one of the women. Now, by simply assuming that Mary separated herself from the other women, came at first to the sepulchre alone, and then summoned Peter and John thither, the parallelism of the two accounts will become plain and perspicuous. The order of the events will then be as follows: early in the morning, Mary betakes herself to the sepulchre in company with the other women. But, hastening in advance of her female companions, to her astonishment she finds the sepulchre empty. Immediately Mary runs in haste to Peter and John. In the meanwhile, the other women arrive, see the angels, and receive their commands and tidings. After they had gone away, Mary arrives with the two disciples, who, having seen the empty sepulchre, return home. Mary still remains by the tomb, weeping. And now the angels appear to her also, and next the Lord himself. After this appearance of the Lord which was witnessed by Mary alone, the Saviour again revealed himself to the women, who were returning from the sepulchre. With this interpretation all discrepancies vanish.

There is only one circumstance against which any one can object, namely, if the events occurred so near one to another, how could Mark (xvi. 9, 10) have declared so decisively that the Lord appeared first to Mary? The other women certainly saw him about the same time, or at least so soon afterwards that the fact of Mary's having seen him first could not be specially remarked. Now add to this that Mark, in this account, deviates from Matthew, and thus the latter alone relates that Jesus shewed himself to the women on their return, then, in relation to this point, it is perhaps more probable that Matthew somewhat loosely extended to all the women the appearance, which had been witnessed by Mary only. This discrepancy, however, is so unimportant that it serves rather to establish that freedom and independence of the Evangelists, which they exhibit in connexion with the most perfect accuracy in the principal details. After these general remarks, we shall treat the particular events according to the above sketched parallel.

Ver. 1–10, and the parallel passages in the Synoptical authors. As respects, first, the fixing of the dates, the expression *διαγενομένου τοῦ σαββάτου*, in Mark (xvi. 1), serves to explain the *ὀψὲ σαββάτων* in Matthew. For instance, *σάββατον* = שַׁבָּת, also in the plural (*τὰ σάββατα*), was used for the *one* day of Sabbath. (Compare the Septuagint version of Exodus xx. 10, and Leviticus xxiii. 32.) *Ὀψέ* is, however, used in the sense of "after." It occurs, indeed, in the New Testament only here, but it occurs also in this signification in profane writers. (Compare Philostratus, Vit. Apoll. iv. 18, *ὀψὲ μυστηρίων*, "*after* the mysteries." Thucyd. iv. 93, and Ælian, V. H. ii. 23. With *ἐπιφωσκούσῃ* supply *ἡμέρᾳ*, to which *ἀνατείλαντος τοῦ ἡλίου* (Luke xxiv. 1), and *ὄρθρου βαθέος* (Mark xvi. 2), correspond. John (xx. 1) has *σκοτίας ἔτι οὔσης*, which must be understood of the morning twilight, and thus coincides with the statements of the other Evangelists.) Now, the day itself on which the women went forth to the sepulchre is called by all the Evangelists unanimously *μία σαββάτων*, that is, the first day of the week, since *μία* is used = אֶחָד (the same phrase occurs in 1 Cor. xvi. 2), and *σάββατα* also signifies "the week" (Luke xviii. 12).

The following verses (2–4), peculiar to Matthew, describe the occurrence of the resurrection itself, or at least of the incidents immediately accompanying it. We might suppose Matthew intended here no historical account, but merely inferred the facts from the existing phenomena, the *ἰδού*, *lo*, thus merely giving vivacity to his picture. But the slight, definite touches, the *ἀπεκύλισε τὸν* *λίθον, rolled away the stone*, and more particularly the *ἐκάθητο ἐπάνω αὐτοῦ, sat upon it*, do not allow this hypothesis. Hence we must refer the account to witnesses, perhaps to one of the watch. (Ἰδέα = מַרְאֶה. Like every celestial vision, this one also appears amid a halo of light, *ἀστραπή*, Luke xxiv. 4, *ἐν ἐσθήσεσιν ἀστραπτούσαις*. To this the white raiment also points.) On ver. 4, and the passage (xi. 15), which is connected with it, compare the remarks made at Matth. xxvii. 62–66. As the women approached the sepulchre, they beheld the angels.* Luke only (xxiv. 5) describes the profound impression which this vision made upon them. These celestial messengers, as the women drew nigh, made known to them the resurrection of the Lord† (verse 6, *the Lord* [*ὁ κύριος*], in the mouth of the angels, is significant); and reminded them (Luke xxiv. 6–8), of the promise of Jesus relative to this fact.

Here, too, the women were commissioned to make known to the disciples, that he would go before them into Galilee. This we learn from Matthew, and from Mark xvi. 7.‡ The latter, moreover, expressly names Peter. In verse 10, Jesus himself repeats this injunction, and in verse 16, it is stated that the disciples went to Galilee. The object of this arrangement, which Jesus had previously intimated, on the occasion of the supper, Matth. xxvi. 32, was, without doubt, no other than this:—The Lord regarded it as more appropriate for the disciples to receive his last commands amidst the stillness and seclusion of Galilee, than in the tumult of the metropolis.

The first appearances of the Lord in Jerusalem, were only intended to convince the doubting disciples that he was truly risen. In the verses 9, 10, with which Matthew concludes the subject, the *κρατεῖν πόδας, clasping his feet*, is to be understood merely as a gesture of supplication which had been elicited by fear. Compare the closer investigation at John xx. 17. Mark (v. 9–11), makes mention only of the vision seen by Mary Magdalene, with the remark that out of her Jesus had cast seven devils. (Compare at Luke viii. 2, and Matthew xii. 45.) This circumstance renders strikingly prominent the fact that the gracious Saviour revealed himself first to the meanest and most wretched of his followers who stood most in need of his assistance, but who receiving it were also inflamed with the most ardent love towards him. The disciples, meanwhile,

* Like the commencement of the Lord's life upon earth, this beginning of his glorified life was also adorned with kindred angel-visions, visible to many persons. The other visions of angels, of which we meet with occasional mention, as having appeared to Christ, seem to have been internal revelations only.

† In Luke xxiv. 5, the sentence, *τί ζητεῖτε τὸν ζῶντα μετὰ τῶν νεκρῶν*, the word *ζῶντα* must be interpreted emphatically, "him who is the life itself." Compare John i. 4.

‡ On the authenticity of the concluding portion of Mark's Gospel, see our observations on Mark xvi. 15.

in consequence of the death of Christ, were as yet so bewildered in mind, that they yielded no credence to the joyous tidings of their Lord's resurrection, notwithstanding that he himself had previously so often and so positively foretold it to them. (According to Luke xxiv. 14, they declared that the report of the women was mere λῆρος, that is, like the Latin, nugæ, a deceptive, vain word or thing.)

John xx. 1-18.—From this point the narrative of the Synoptical Evangelists has its parallel in that of John. The latter proceeds first to relate of himself and Peter, that they were led to the sepulchre by Mary, who had previously hastened thither. Impelled by love, John was swifter in running than Peter. But he shrank from entering the sanctuary of the resurrection. The daring, resolute Peter, on the contrary, went directly into the sepulchre. Although at this time Peter had not as yet obtained immediately from the Lord the pardon of his grievous sin, yet, so steadfast was his faith in Christ's pardoning love, that not for a moment would he acknowledge himself to be excluded from his Lord. But how deeply the affectionate soul of John was impressed by the scene of that great event is manifest from the simple circumstance that he (ver. 6, 7), minutely describes how the interior of the sepulchre was furnished. The grave clothes = ὀθόνια (Luke xxiv. 12, compare John xi. 44) and the napkin which had enwrapped the head of Jesus, lay there, the latter folded and in a separate place. ('Εντυλίσσω, means "envelope," but means also "to fold." Compare Matth. xxvii. 53.) As the same circumstance is also noticed in Luke xxiv. 12, it must have had some special meaning. Tholuck very properly observes that it determines the *ἐπίστευσεν, he believed*, ver. 9. For instance, at the first, when John was speaking to Mary, he like her, might have believed that the body of Jesus had been *stolen away;* but when in the sepulchre he perceived not the slightest trace of disorder, but found everything *carefully arranged*, there arose in him real faith in the Lord's resurrection. Hence the ᾔδεισαν which follows in ver. 9 is not, as Tholuck would have it, to be taken as pluperfect. We need only translate the passage thus: "they understood not the Scripture in this relation." This application of the words to their faith in the resurrection is at all events more appropriate than to conjecture with Lücke and others that they refer merely to their credence of the report of Mary. (On the Old Testament prophecies of the resurrection, compare the observations made at Luke xxiv. 46, and 1 Cor. xv. 5.) After this occurrence, whilst the disciples betook themselves to their homes, Mary remained behind, weeping alone at the sepulchre. Looking into it she now beheld two angels, who were sitting, the one at the head and the other at the feet, where the body of Jesus had lain. This passage justifies the inference that angels can at pleasure render themselves visible or invisible. For we are without doubt to understand that these were the same angels whom the women had seen previously, and who had remained present, but invisible. Mary Magdalene might not at first have thought they were angels: hence, probably, her quiet, childlike answer to their question. In like manner she did not at first know Jesus when, on turning round, she saw him. As she happened to be in the garden, she supposed that he was the gardener.* (Κηπουρός, from κῆπος and οὖρος, overseer, occurs here only in the New Testament.) But immediately upon hearing his voice she knew the Lord, and exclaimed with exultant transport Ῥαββουνί. (Comp. Mark x. 51.)

Probably Mary, whilst thus speaking, ran to embrace the Lord's feet (according to Matth. xxviii. 9, the other women did likewise). Then the Lord addressed to her the enigmatical words, *μή μου ἅπτου*. Of the many attempts which have been made to explain these words, all those which would alter the text should be rejected at the very outset. Of this kind are the conjectures of Gersdorf and Schulthess, *σύ μου ἅπτου, do thou touch me;* and of Vogel, *μὴ σὺ πτοοῦ*, fear not. The critical authorities perfectly establish the correctness of the usual reading *μή μου ἅπτου*. But of its import various explanations have been suggested, which must also be deemed obsolete, and may, therefore, be dismissed at once. To these belong, first, the interpretation, which makes *ἅπτεσθαι* = דָּבַק, *adhærere*, "to delay;" so that the meaning of the passage would be, "hasten to thy brethren without delay," etc. Another is, that which regards the attempt at touching the Lord on the part of Mary, as designed to assure herself whether the body of Christ was real or not, so that the *μή μου ἅπτου* would be a reproof to her unbelief. But apart from all other grounds, the context by no means harmonizes with either of these interpretations. For, on such an occasion, the momentary homage which Mary offered to her heavenly friend was not at all an action to deserve the repulse that "she should not delay!" And how the subsequent *οὔπω γὰρ ἀναβέβηκα* is at all consistent with the alleged unbelief, we cannot see.

There remain therefore only the following interpretations of the words which merit particular notice. And first, the view promulgated by Augustine, and commended by Beza, which regards *ἅπτεσθαι* as employed figuratively of "a *mental* concerning one's self

* Even Tholuck, referring to this circumstance, offers the suggestion that after his resurrection Jesus might really have worn clothes belonging to the gardener. Questions such as, "Whence did Christ get the necessary raiment?" "How could he walk with his pierced feet?" are suggested only by the belief that he rose again in a mortal body. According to our interpretation, as little do such queries merit any answer as does the analogous one, "From whence did the angels obtain their white raiment?"—[This is treating the matter far too leniently. To concede Christ's *miraculous resurrection*, and then seriously ask questions like the above, is, on any hypothesis, simple stupidity.]—[K.

about a thing;" so that the meaning would be, "Cling not to this my *earthly* appearance, for I shall yet experience a *heavenly* exaltation." This sense is appropriate, and harmonizes with the connexion; but the tropical interpretation of ἅπτεσθαι is so harsh, and the οὔπω would follow it so unfittingly, that we cannot assent to this mode of explanation. Secondly, other interpreters, especially Tholuck, understand ἅπτεσθαι as referring to the attitude of worship (προσκύνησις), and supply ποδῶν or γονάτων, like the embracing of knees which frequently occurs in Homer, and in the Old Testament, 2 Kings iv. 27. The meaning would then be, "Do not worship me, I am not a heavenly being, I must first be glorified." But how could *he* utter that who had said, "all men should honour the Son even as they honour the Father;" "he who seeth me seeth the Father" (John v. 23, and xiv. 9); and who, immediately after, permitted Thomas to exclaim, "My Lord and my God" (ὁ κύριός μου καὶ ὁ θεός μου, John xx. 28)? But granting we concede that the Divine worship of Christ was not to begin until after his ascension to the Father, then the subsequent words of Christ, "to my Father and to your Father, to my God and to your God," would not at all consist with this prohibition of worship. It is manifest that these words of the Saviour express the idea of an *approximation* of the disciples to the person of Christ. So that the meaning of the words is, "The same God is mine, and yours; we are brethren." But if the μή μου ἅπτου referred to the prohibition of worshipping Christ, then the language should have brought out *the infinite difference* between Christ and his disciples, in which case the course of thought would be as follows: "Worship me not, for I am not yet glorified; but when I shall have been glorified, and thereby exalted above you infinitely, then worship me." There remains,* therefore, thirdly, only

* Krabbe, in his work "on Sin," p. 316, et seq., presents another explanation of this difficult passage, somewhat similar to that previously given by Chrysostom and Erasmus. He thinks the meaning of the words to be this—"Do not touch me; that is, think not that the former intimacy can still subsist between us. My relation to you has become different from what it was, and, as such, you must henceforth regard it. Still thou hast not erred by calling me ῥαββουνί, for such I am, thy risen Lord: but I have not yet ascended to my Father." This interpretation commends itself to us, when taken in reference to the account of Mary's anointing of the feet of Jesus. But Krabbe himself has already observed that the οὔπω γὰρ ἀναβέβηκα which follows, does not, according to this view, connect itself naturally with the μή μου ἅπτου. For the supplying of the sentence, "thou hast not erred in calling me ῥαββουνί, for such I am," etc., is manifestly altogether arbitrary. Neither will the difficulty be avoided by taking this latter interpretation of the passage in a somewhat modified manner. If, for instance, we should conclude, according to the view of Augustine, that the meaning of the words is this, "Rest not satisfied with my tangible nature, but become exalted by faith to an apprehension of the spiritual nature of the Son of God. The former will vanish from you. The latter will remain with you, ever present. For I go to my Father, to whom you also shall hereafter approach," then the οὔπω, as we have already observed, entirely militates against this thought. This combination, "touch me not, for I am not yet ascended," etc., leads me

the interpretation proposed by Schleiermacher.* If we conceive the occurrence of the resurrection and of the glorification of Christ, in their essential nature, it becomes a natural thought that all which checks this is to be avoided. In the "ascending to his Father," is thus indicated, as a necessary consequence, the completion of the Saviour's glorification. Thus also the words *ἀναβαίνω πρὸς τὸν πατέρα μου, καὶ πατέρα ὑμῶν*, *I ascend to my Father and your Father*, which follow, completely harmonize with the preceding. For in the *μή μου ἅπτου* there seemed something repulsive; this impression the following thought does away, in that the Lord seems to say to his disciples, "Since I became like you, ye shall become, as I am, by regeneration true children of God, my brethren."

§ 2. FURTHER APPEARANCES OF CHRIST ON THE DAY OF THE RESURRECTION.

(Luke xxiv. 13–43; Mark xvi. 12–14; John xx. 19–29.)

The Lord, according to his promise, would probably have shewed himself to his disciples only in quiet Galilee, if they had been able immediately to attain to a living faith in his resurrection. But the statements of the women who were first privileged to behold the Saviour did not satisfy them. They were unable, on the strength of those statements, to rise to an unwavering faith. John, however (xx. 8), was probably convinced of the truth of Mary's report. After the first day the risen Redeemer does not appear to have again revealed himself to the disciples in Jerusalem. The other acknowledged appearances all took place probably in Galilee. Yet that we may understand precisely the character of Christ's association with his disciples after his resurrection, so far as the documents before us

back from every other exegesis, to the interpretation of Schleiermacher, which is sustained by the context, although I am by no means insensible to the singularity of the thought. The explanation given by De Wette, perhaps allows more of its proper force to the *οὔπω*, where he gives the following as the meaning of the passage: "Mary finds her entire satisfaction in the appearance of Jesus, and with this feeling would embrace him. But Jesus reminds her of the fact that this content of hers was as yet premature." But in this view, we hardly see how the *touching* can be an expression of satisfaction, or how the prohibition, *μή μου ἅπτου*, can be an injunction not to seek such satisfaction.

* Schleiermacher's festival sermons, the fifth collected edition, Berlin, 1826, p. 303, in the incomparably beautiful sermon entitled "The Resurrection of Christ a type of our new life." His words in reference to this passage are as follows: "When the Saviour at first appeared to Mary, he then, as if fearful and susceptible, his glorified life being new to him, said, 'Touch me not; I am not yet ascended to my God and to your God;' but, after a few days, he presented himself to Thomas, and required him heartily to test the reality of his body, to thrust his hand into his side, etc."

allow, we must first investigate minutely several difficulties, which are presented to us in this part of the evangelical history. For, in the first place, the question suggests itself, have the Evangelists recorded all the appearances of the Lord ? or may there not have occurred many others, of which we are not informed ? Upon comparing 1 Corinthians xv. 6, et seq., we find that the Apostle Paul even there makes mention of certain revelations of the Saviour, concerning which the Gospels are silent ; particularly those with which Peter and James were privileged. The omission of these by the Evangelists is explainable, however, from the fact that the Saviour, for special reasons, shewed himself to these two disciples *alone*—to Peter probably the appearance was made on account of his denial of the Lord, but to James (the brother of the Lord) because hitherto he had never been able to believe in Jesus. (John vii. 5, Acts i. 14.) Both these appearances had thus, as their object, individual instruction, and hence presented nothing of general interest.

The Apostle Paul speaks of another appearance still, besides the two noticed. At this over five hundred brethren were present, many of whom were yet living at the time when Paul wrote his epistles to the Corinthians. But this appearance was probably that of which the Synoptical Gospels make mention, as having happened in Galilee (compare at Matth. xxviii. 16, et seq.) Hence it appears to me most probable that *no other appearances took place* than those of which we are informed. Jesus shewed himself, as he had promised, *only* to his disciples, and even to them but in unfrequent visions. On this account his association with his disciples after his resurrection, acquires a certain peculiarity of character. To the *Pharisees*, and to all who had not turned to Christ with a full purpose of heart, his resurrection was a sign, like that of Jonah, invisible, and presented merely to their faith. The Lord could not reveal himself to them in his glory, for had he done so, and they had then resisted him, their culpability would have been greatly aggravated ; and if, on the other hand, they had yielded themselves to him, the presumption would have been, that a change thus wrought through the senses could be no truly spiritual one, but produced by fear only. But if any, by the influence of the risen Redeemer, were brought to render honour to the truth without having seen him, it might be taken for granted that they had yielded their hearts to the light. Had the risen Saviour, therefore, appeared to all or to any of his opponents, nothing but injury could have been the result ; no good would have been effected.

But, as regards the disciples, they had previously enjoyed fully the privilege of the Lord's constant intercourse with them. And now it was only necessary to give them, as it were, their complete perfection, and to consecrate them to their work, that they might become complete instruments for the service of God's kingdom. Hence the Lord, after his resurrection, shewed himself to them only on particular, sacred occasions, and in the most impressive and mysterious manner. We find, also, that the disciples, as often as they beheld the Saviour, were invariably seized with a secret *dread*, which mingled in a peculiar manner with their joy at possessing him who was the beloved of their soul. Still, they knew distinctly that they now possessed him in a manner *different* from what they had formerly; for when, in his ascension into heaven, the Saviour withdrew altogether from them, they were filled with joy, and did not in any way sorrow, as previously, for they knew that Christ would remain present with them in spirit, and be at the same time himself exalted to sit at the right hand of God.

The questions, Where the Lord abode in the time intermediate between his appearances, and how he supported himself, have arisen in modern times, from indistinct views concerning the nature of the risen Redeemer's life. (In Christian antiquity, the fundamentally correct views of the resurrection which prevailed, afforded no ground for such questions.) But if we reflect that, even prior to the resurrection, the Saviour walked upon the waves of the sea, and fed thousands with a few loaves, we may well take it for granted that after the resurrection the glorified Saviour would have been still less restrained by physical laws; and therefore that the necessities incident to human nature could have had no application whatever to him when glorified.

Ver. 13–24.—The first appearance of Jesus on the resurrection day itself (besides those at the sepulchre) was that which Luke details at length (xxiv. 13–24), and which Márk briefly glances at (xvi. 12–14). Two disciples were on their way to Emmaus. Of these one was named Cleopas (Κλεόπας = Κλωπᾶς. He was perhaps the relative of Jesus, John xix. 25). It was then the afternoon, for it was evening when they returned, John xx. 19. (Ἐμμαούς or Ἀμμαούς, was, as is mentioned by Josephus, B. J. vii. 6, 6, a little village distant from Jerusalem a Sabbath day's journey, that is, sixty stadia. This village must not be confounded with the city of the same name, which lay at a distance of twenty miles from Jerusalem, and which in after times received the name of Nicopolis. It was at this latter city that Judas Maccabeus defeated Georgias, the Syrian general. Compare 1 Maccab. iii. 40–57; also Winer's Real-lex. p. 382.) The two disciples were conversing together concerning the great events of the few past days, when, without being recognized, Jesus himself joined company with them. On this Luke (xxiv. 16) remarks that "their eyes were holden" (*οἱ ὀφθαλμοὶ αὐτῶν ἐκρατοῦντο*). But Mark (xvi. 12) gives prominence to the fact that

Christ himself appeared in another form (ἐν ἑτέρᾳ μορφῇ). We may assume both: on the part of the Lord a veiling of his person, and of the disciples that their eyes were holden. But all conceptions of disfigurement by sorrow and the like, should be rejected as utterly unscriptural. We should rather maintain that the strangeness of the Lord's appearance was in part a consequence of his very glorification, and might partly be intended by him. There is a greater difficulty in the question, "What were the Lord's reasons for not revealing himself openly at first, and for withdrawing when he was recognized?" They were drawn probably from the personal character of the two disciples. They appear (ver. 21) to have been entirely in error as to the Messiahship of Jesus, and hence were in need of some powerful support to their faith. This the Saviour vouchsafed, by explaining to them the doctrine of Christ's vicarious death, as taught by the Scriptures. But if Jesus had made himself known to them before he had convinced them by the force of Scriptural proofs, his appearance would have overpowered them so far that they would have been incapable of calm investigation. For this reason, the revelation of his person did not take place till his chief object was effected.

The Saviour opened the conversation by inquiring the cause of their sadness. (Σκυθρωπός, consult Matth. vi. 16.) To this Cleopas made answer, and recalled to him the great and well-known events of the few preceding days. (Παροικεῖν, like יָשַׁב, does not merely signify to tarry as a stranger in a place, but means also generally, "to dwell," "to belong to the place." See Genesis xxiv. 37.) Dr. Paulus thinks that the summary account of the fate of Jesus contained in the 19th and following verses, contains the language of the two disciples, and that one spoke the 19th and 20th, and the other those that follow. To this supposition he has been led by the circumstance that verses 19 and 21 seem to contradict each other: according to the 21st verse they would seem to have given up all hope, whilst, according to verse 19th, Jesus is still called a prophet. If, then, we suppose that the two disciples held different views of Christ, that one, for instance, still preserved more faith than the other, this apparent contrariety would be explained.

But as it is not intimated, by a word, that verse 21 follows as from a different speaker, this supposition can be scarcely maintained. It is more correct to understand the expression "he who was to redeem Israel" (ὁ μέλλων λυτροῦσθαι τὸν Ἰσραήλ), of the Messiah, and to separate it from the idea of the prophet, ver. 19. The disciples might have doubted whether Jesus was the Messiah, and yet have believed him to be a prophet. Many of the prophets had been put to death, therefore the death of Jesus could not have destroyed their belief in his prophetic dignity. But of the Messiah they seemed still to have entertained the indistinct popular notions (which, however, were by no means the general views of the enlightened classes amongst the Jews, compare at John i. 29); hence they were convinced that by the death of Jesus his Messianic work was annihilated. In their view, then, the "redeeming of Israel" had certainly but a very subordinate, perhaps in part a political significance. The words that ensue, in verses 22–24, express finally the reports concerning the resurrection of Christ, to which, however, these disciples could as yet yield no credence. Their words, however, corroborate the twofold appearance of Jesus, that to the women, which the Synoptical writers relate, and that witnessed by Peter and John, which is recorded by the latter; and this testimony is the weightier, that it cannot have been intentionally introduced into the narrative of Luke, as he has not mentioned at all the transaction with these two disciples.

Verses 25–35.—Upon this lament of theirs the Lord addressed to them his discourse of reproof and of consolation. He first reprehended the want of susceptibility manifested by the disciples, as to the predictions so clearly made by the prophets. (Ἀνόητος is by no means synonymous with *βραδὺς τῇ καρδίᾳ*: the former signifies an incapacity of the *νοῦς*, the latter an unsusceptibility of the *καρδία*: so that, taken together, the two expressions describe the want of susceptibility of the whole man, both in head and heart.) Secondly, Christ adduces the individual prophecies of Scripture concerning himself, and expounds them to the two disciples, shewing them that the suffering of the Messiah was necessarily connected with his entire work, and with his glorification. (Comp. on this subject the remarks made on John xiii. 31, and on Matthew xxvii. 46.) It was this divinely decreed necessity which was expressed in the prophecies of the Old Testament. They refer as well to the resurrection of the Lord as to his death. (Comp. Luke xxiv. 46, and 1 Corinth. xv. 3, 4.) Christ now led the disciples into the true spiritual apprehension of those prophecies by going through them singly (Luke xxiv. 44, specifies Moses, the prophets, and the Psalms). This passage affords a proof that our present classification of the Old Testament Scriptures into תּוֹרָה, נְבִאִים, and כְּתוּבִים, prevailed, even at the time of Christ, for the last class is named "the psalms," because the psalms constituted the first book of the division.) This last statement is of the utmost importance to us, inasmuch as it justifies us in regarding the explanations of the Old Testament prophecies which the apostles give us in their writings, as the authentic expositions of the Saviour himself. They thus acquire a degree of security and stability, which, to all unprejudiced judges, must elevate them to the character of demonstrations of the faith which cannot be shaken. The prophecies given by the Spirit of God are also again interpreted by the Lord of all Spirit (2 Peter i. 20), so that a secure ground of faith is afforded to all doubts springing from a genuine feeling of want, and only to wilful scepticism, as is fit, does it remain possible in regard to *every* prophecy to say, "the Lord would certainly not have applied *this* with the others to himself." These passages, together with Matthew v. 17, constitute the most certain demonstration of the Divine inspiration of the Old Testament from the lips of the Lord himself: so that with faith in the Redeemer, we receive not merely prospective faith in the divinity of the New Testament, but also retrospective faith in the divinity of the Old.

After this conversation the Lord desired to withdraw, since his chief object had been attained. But he, unknown though he was, so dear when known, had filled their hearts with the marvellous energy of love. They were not able to bear separation from him. He therefore entered the house with them, and disclosed himself to them, in the act of breaking of bread. But immediately afterwards vanished from before their eyes.

It needs no argument to prove that, alike in the αὐτὸς ἄφαντος ἐγένετο ἀπ' αὐτῶν, *he vanished from their sight*, ver. 31, and in the αὐτῶν διηνοίχθησαν οἱ ὀφθαλμοί, *their eyes were opened*, no mere *ordinary* recognition and quick departure were intended by the Evangelist. Their zeal was so great, that they would certainly have followed him. The only correct interpretation of the passage is that all the incidents of his appearance, his coming, his allowing himself to be recognized, his departure, involve something mysterious. Although his identity remained, yet were his being and nature more exalted, more consecrated than formerly. His appearances, although corporeal, were yet similar to those of celestial beings.

Finally, the ἐγένετο ἀπ' αὐτῶν, in the words quoted, need not be so connected that the γενέσθαι ἀπό τινος should be employed in the sense of, "to withdraw from one." The ἄφαντος is evidently not in harmony with this construction. Rather the ἀπ' αὐτῶν (with which we might supply πορευόμενος) is a subjoined intimation that Jesus not merely became, or remained invisible, but withdrew himself *entirely*. After this occurrence, therefore, the two disciples hastened thence, to the assembling-place of the apostles, where the latter met them, with the tidings that the Lord had appeared to Peter (1 Cor. xv. 5). This intelligence they requited with an account of what they themselves had experienced.

John xx. 19-23.—Scarcely had the two disciples from Emmaus entered the place, when the Lord himself also stood in the midst of them. In their accounts of this new appearance Luke and John mutually supplement each other. The latter describes the scene itself. The former passes over the scene, but labours to give the strongest and most direct assurances of the reality of the Lord's corporeity, a matter of which John makes but cursory mention. As regards, then, the place in which the disciples were assembled, John (ver. 19), mentions that they had shut the doors through fear of the Jews. Even in early times, interpreters discovered something miraculous in Christ's entering, when the doors were closed. Some thought that the doors were opened in a miraculous way. So Jerome, who here employs the words: creatura cedente Creatori. Others would make it appear that the Lord entered through the closed doors, as if the words were *διὰ τῶν θυρῶν κεκλεισμένων*. So thought Theophylact, who also expresses the unscriptural notion, that the Saviour arose without the stone having been removed from the sepulchre. (Comp. Matthew xxviii. 2.) It is plain that the text in no way justifies such hypotheses, and that the passage is falsely applied in support of *any* dogmatical views, as by the Lutheran divines, to prove the doctrine of the ubiquity.

Still, definitely as we reject the view which makes the act a *monstrous* one, we are equally compelled to combat that which designates this appearance of Christ as an *ordinary* coming. This is contradicted, not only by the *ἔστη εἰς τὸ μέσον*,* *he stood in their midst*, which points to something of a sudden character, but also by that important passage, John xx. 30, in which the appearances of the Lord are designated as *signs* (*σημεῖα*): compare the particulars at this passage. In every one of those *σημεῖα*, for instance, according to the correct interpretation of the disciples, there was revealed to them something exalted and celestial; for the Lord himself appeared to them as of a super-terrestrial nature; and this extraordinary characteristic was indicated by his entering suddenly, without any previous intimation.

In this view alone the subsequent pains taken by the Lord to convince them that his was a real body, becomes explicable. Had he entered in the same manner as the others, no such effort would have been required.

It is here, for the first time, mentioned that the Lord said to the assembled disciples: *εἰρήνη ὑμῖν, peace be to you*; which saying he afterwards (verse 21), repeated with emphasis. This was quite a usual form of salutation amongst the Jews (שָׁלוֹם לָכֶם). But in the lips of the glorified Redeemer, it bore not only a higher *significance*—as wishing them temporal and eternal peace, but also an essential *power*. As the Lord entered, they were thrilled with a feeling of sacred peace. They felt that they were in immediate proximity

* The repetition of these words, when taken in connexion with the formula, *τῶν θυρῶν κεκλεισμένων*, verse 26, without in the latter case any mention being made concerning "their fear of the Jews," points to something of profound significance. Moreover, *φανεροῦσθαι* is employed descriptively of the appearances of the risen Saviour, in which is manifestly expressed the fact, that they were the entrances of an exalted being, like the Divine or angelic visions (John xxi. 1).

with the Holy One. Hence then the supposition, that in the form of Jesus a *spirit* had appeared. (Luke xxiv. 37, πνεῦμα is employed similarly to φάντασμα, Matth. xiv. 26.) To the apostles the notion of a spirit may have been just as obscure as is that of a ghost to persons in our day. But in both cases opinions agree, that it consists in a bodiless apparition.

It was for the Lord to disabuse their minds of this docetic illusion. The essential character of the resurrection did not consist in the returning again of the spiritual principle: but in the *renewal of corporeal life*. When, therefore, the Saviour, to prove that his was a real body, shewed them (Luke xxiv. 38–43) his hands and his feet, bearing the marks of his wounds, and even ate in their very presence ; no argument can be raised from this occurrence, as was previously remarked, in disproof of the fact, that the body of Christ was a *glorified* body, for though it was glorified, it was still truly a *body*. Yet we are not warranted to infer, that he ate from any real necessity of food, a thing incompatible with the nature of a glorified body. His eating should be simply regarded as a proof of the *reality* of his body. The reason why many most estimable theologians imagine that such passages as these militate against the opinion that the body of Christ was glorified at the resurrection, is, that they do not in reality believe in the glorification of the body at all, but hold the monophysite view of its complete annihilation by the spirit. The thoroughly idealizing tendencies of our day have conducted to this view, which, is nevertheless, in the most decided terms, repudiated by holy writ. (Comp. 1 Cor. xv., and 2 Timothy ii. 18.) Profoundly characteristic of human nature is the remark (ver. 41), that the disciples were filled with joy, and yet could not bring themselves to believe firmly that it was the true Jesus whom they saw before them ! Man feels a secret horror in the presence of all purely spiritual being divested of the corporeal covering. The appearance of Christ became precious to them, and a source of blissful transport, only when they felt certain as to the reality of his body.

In this circumstance an indirect support is afforded to the conclusion that God is not the author of death (Wisdom of Solomon i. 13) ; that the severance of the connecting bonds between the soul and body is opposed to nature, and that only in this union can the soul find its full satisfaction. (Ὀπτός, from ὀπτάω, broiled or roasted (Luke xxiv. 42). Μελίσσιον κηρίον, the honey of bees, in distinction from that of grapes or of fruits.) John xx. 20 barely hints at this incident, as he wished immediately to recount it still more minutely in connexion with Thomas. He mentions, however, another and very remarkable circumstance. He states that the Lord once more and most impressively uttered the words, "Peace be unto you," then reminded them of their Divine mission, and, breathing upon them, said, "Receive ye the Holy Ghost." These words may be regarded as renewing their installation in the apostolic office, and as confirming their exalted prerogatives. (Upon the forgiving and retaining of sins, compare at Matthew xvi. 19.)

That something of this kind should be performed by the risen Saviour seems in the highest degree appropriate; the disciples must as it were receive from him fresh assurances of that which had been previously promised; but this event seems less suited to the resurrection day itself, since, in addition to other considerations, Thomas was not present, who was not to be excluded from the apostleship. This renewed consecration would seem to have occurred far more appropriately at the *end* of the forty days, for the ratification of the choice of the apostles would have formed a noble conclusion to the earthly ministry of Christ. To this also the accounts given by the Synoptical Evangelists of the last commands of Jesus, by which the apostles were anew authorized as messengers to mankind, would be admirably suited. I feel almost inclined to suppose that John (as shall be presently proved of the Synoptical writers) here narrates compendiously, and therefore assigns to this appearance things which did not transpire until afterwards. The account that follows concerning Thomas is not contradictory of this hypothesis, for it is manifestly only supplementary; its object being to describe the means by which that disciple was brought to believe in the resurrection of Christ.

John concludes his Gospel at the 20th chapter and 31st verse; for the 21st chapter is beyond question a subsequent addition to the completed work. But, besides, I regard the opinion that the *λάβετε πνεῦμα ἅγιον*, *receive the Holy Ghost*, should be understood barely of the anticipated outpouring of the Spirit at the Pentecost, as altogether untenable. The symbolical act of breathing on the disciples becomes an empty ceremony, if it be regarded as unaccompanied by any spiritual *influence*. The communication of the Spirit to the disciples should rather be understood as proceeding by gradual augmentation. Upon their being sent forth the first time (Matth. x.), the disciples received a superior degree of spiritual power; the Lord here augments that gift; and at Pentecost the fulness of the Spirit was poured out upon them. With the possession of the Spirit was connected the power of forgiving sins and that of not forgiving, that is, of retaining them; for, in *his* nature lie the conditions through which alone such power becomes explicable and secured against abuse. (Compare at Matth. xvi. 19.) To draw a distinction between this communication of the Spirit and the pouring forth of the Holy Ghost at the Pentecost, not merely in degree but also in kind, and indeed so as to refer the former to sanctification and to the apostolical office, and the latter (the outpouring at the Pentecost) to miraculous gifts, is inadmissible, for the reason that, according to Matth. x. 1, et seq., the apostles, long previously to Pentecost, had been endowed with miraculous gifts. The symbolical act of breathing does not occur elsewhere in the sacred Scriptures. But, with the meaning of πνεῦμα (from πνέω, to breathe), it is self-explained how in all languages, the expressions that have been framed to convey the signification of spiritual communications have all been borrowed from "*breathing.*" On this statement compare Knapp. Scr. Var. Arg. pp. 29, et seq., in the treatise upon 2 Pet. i. 19–21. Compare also in my Opusc. Acad. the treatise upon Heb. iv. 12, 13, pages 4 and 8.

Ver. 24–29.—At the beginning of this paragraph we remarked that probably none of the later appearances of Christ occurred in Jerusalem. Amongst these I include that which was witnessed by Thomas eight days after the resurrection, verse 26. John relates this appearance less for its own sake than to explain the absence of Thomas on the former occasion. At the same time, however, his precise description of the way in which Thomas was convinced of the reality of Christ's body, might have been especially intended by John for such of his readers as held docetic views, and who likewise found it difficult to believe in the true humanity of the Lord. It has been already observed that Thomas's conduct indicates a predominance of the reflective faculties; so that we may style him the *rationalist** amongst the apostles. To such characters the *essential* reception of the Divine nature is usually very difficult, for in them the active powers of the mind have a controlling influence over the passive, and they deem it possible only to attain *conceptions* of Divinity, never to arrive at its true possession. If, however, the power of Divine truth once assert its supremacy in their moral nature, then the ideal edifice which their reason had framed is razed effectually, and their recognition of the heavenly element expresses itself in bold faith. Thus it was with Thomas. Once convinced, he exclaimed, "My Lord and my God" (ὁ Κύριός μου, καὶ ὁ Θεός μου. The nominative with the article stands, by a Hebrew idiom, for the vocative). Many attempts have been made to represent these words of Thomas as a mere exclamation, not at all indicating belief. But they are all disproved by the grammatical connexion of the words taken in their psychological relation to the character of Thomas. That the evil custom preva-

* On this passage Tholuck strikingly remarks: "We may see that a passion for the marvellous was by no means a fault common to all the Jews. Moreover, it can hardly be a myth that a disciple had doubted thus. His incredulity becomes to us, accordingly, a very convincing proof of the tr.th of the resurrection. 'Dubitatum est ab illo,' says Leo the Great, 'ne dubitetur a nobis.'"

lent among us of using the name of God as a mere exclamation existed also among the Jews, cannot be demonstrated; and is incredible, when we consider the stringent character of their law. Such an exclamation would have been a transgression of the command, "Thou shalt not take the name of the Lord thy God in vain." Besides, the words, "he said to him," demand a personal reference to Christ, and the only conclusion to which we can come is, that Thomas styled Jesus *God*.

Some have asserted that on this occasion Thomas applied to the Redeemer an epithet which expressed more than he would have uttered in moments of self-possession and consciousness. Were this assertion made in reference to the earlier condition of the apostle, I should readily grant it; but to affirm it of his subsequent state of mind, as if in a moment of excitement he had said more than he meant, is altogether unpsychological. Such natures as that of Thomas, when once conquered by heavenly influences, hold their belief the more firmly, that they have been brought to conviction by almighty power itself, which must have been employed to subdue their obstinate resistance. We must hence rather thus conceive this incident, to wit, that this manifestation of Christ was the moment in which Thomas was thoroughly illuminated by Divine light, and renewed in his inner nature, so that now for the first time the Lord was manifested to him, not merely in his outward form, but also to the inner man, in his Divine glory.

But beyond all question, the name "my God" presupposes that, as Thomas knew, Christ had claimed Divine honours for himself, and these previously unintelligible or offensive expressions now dawned upon him in their full import. Thus Christ's revelations of himself were attended by the most exalted effects; in the case of Peter, of James, and of Thomas, especially; completing, as they did, the gradual renewing of their minds, and their regeneration. Upon these disciples the appearances of Christ produced an effect exactly similar to that produced upon the Apostle Paul by the revelation made to him on his journey to Damascus.

The reply of Jesus to the address of Thomas still further confirmed the humbling impression experienced by the apostle from the whole transaction. For Jesus directed his attention to the fact, that his scepticism was the result of sin, especially of the one-sided predominance of one mental power, the understanding, by which susceptibility to Divine influences, and the power of spiritual perception are narrowed and circumscribed. (Upon the relation between faith and sight, compare at 2 Corinthians v. 7.)

§ 3. CONCLUDING VERSES OF THE FOUR EVANGELISTS.

(Matth. xxviii. 16-20; Mark xvi. 15-20; Luke xxiv. 44-53; John xx. 30, 31.)

In comparing the concluding portions of all the four Gospels with one another, we discover that they involve a certain indefiniteness. In Matthew xxviii. 16, it is indeed expressly stated, that the Lord appeared to his disciples in Galilee, as he had promised; and even the locality of the appearance is particularly mentioned. But as he says nothing of the ascension into heaven, we are left in darkness as to the manner in which the discourses delivered at this appearance, and which seem to have been his final farewell discourses, stand related to the great concluding event of the Lord's life upon earth. Mark alludes briefly to the ascension into heaven, but gives, in the verses immediately antecedent, 15-18, the elements of discourses which are closely related to those at the conclusion of Matthew. These, however, unite themselves so loosely by the vague transition, "and he said to them" (ver. 15), with the preceding, that we might easily believe the Redeemer had uttered them at his appearance on the evening of the resurrection-day. In like manner, Luke separates, indeed, his account of the ascension from the rest of the narrative; but the verses 44-49, connect themselves so loosely with the preceding, that it is doubtful whether the discourses they record were uttered during the Saviour's last appearance or not. Finally, John, after his account concerning Thomas, concludes his gospel at xx. 30, 31, with a brief statement of a general character: for chapter xxi. is a supplement afterwards added to the work. Here, therefore, the parting words of the Saviour, as given in the Synoptical Gospels, are entirely wanting, nor do the passages in chapter xxi. which mention the Saviour's appearance in Galilee, contain any account of them; they touch merely on personal matters, chiefly relating to Peter.

This is a very striking fact, and requires explanation. We should have supposed that the Evangelists would have felt bound to relate the history of the resurrection in the most circumstantial manner, since each successive appearance of the risen Lord, with all that happened on each occasion, would have been additional evidence of the truth of the resurrection. But, instead of this, they record them in a general and indefinite manner, without distinguishing accurately the several appearances of the Lord, and leaving it quite uncertain whether the discourses which they adduce were delivered on this or the other occasion. Yet upon a closer examination, we shall find in the very features of their narrative a striking internal truth.

Omitting these purely personal references, which mark, for example, the appearances on behalf of Thomas and Peter, one common character belonged in all probability to all the appearances of the Lord. They were in no way designed to impart any new information, or unfold any fresh aspect of his ministry, but rather to confirm that faith in his person, the foundation of which had been already laid. Hence the appearances were upon the whole few in number, and probably also but brief and transitory. In comprehensive intimations, the Saviour informed the disciples of things pertaining to the kingdom of God, Acts i. 3, of the prophecies of the Old Testament concerning himself, Luke xxiv. 44 ; and of their own destination as labourers in the cause of God. The Evangelists, therefore, on account of the similarity of the truths uttered on these occasions, might easily not only confound the several appearances, but might also with entire appropriateness comprehend under a few leading thoughts the different discourses of the Lord. A more particular investigation is here necessary* of the critical question as to *the authenticity of the conclusion of Mark's Gospel* (xvi. 9–18).

The testimony afforded by codices and other critical aids, is of such a kind as to render the opinion perfectly conceivable that this section is not authentic. J. D. Michaelis declares himself favourable to this view, and is followed by Griesbach, Grats, Bertholdt, Schulthess, Schultz, and Fritzsche. Fully as the last-named scholar thinks the spuriousness of this section proved, that conclusion can be by no means regarded as established, since the celebrated names of Storr, Matthäi, Eichhorn, Kuinoel, Paulus, Schott, and Saunier, among its defenders, shew that much may be adduced in proof of its authenticity. But perhaps the most decisive points in reference to the question have been overlooked even by the defenders themselves. These we shall briefly place before the reader.

If we consider the critical authorities only, they undoubtedly make the section appear suspicious. The passage is wanting in all the existing codices, except in codex B. Some, however, have asterisks, and others scholia,† at this section. Several fathers of the church also mention that Mark xvi. 9–18 is wanting in many codices. This is plainly asserted, not only by Euthymius, and Victor of Antioch, but even by Jerome and Eusebius: ancient and unimpeachable witnesses. The former of these, in one passage (opp. vol. iii. 96), even

* On the critical opinions concerning the conclusion of Mark, compare the Appendix to Rödiger's Synopsis, p. 235, etc.

† In the codex L. there certainly occurs in a marginal note an entirely different recension of the concluding section of Mark. It reads as follows: *φέρεταί που καὶ ταῦτα. πάντα δὲ τὰ παρηγγελμένα τοῖς περὶ τὸν Πέτρον συντόμως ἐξήγγειλαν. Μετὰ δὲ ταῦτα καὶ αὐτὸς ὁ Ἰησοῦς ἀπὸ ἀνατολῆς καὶ ἄχρι δύσεως ἐξαπέστειλε δι' αὐτῶν τὸ ἱερὸν καὶ ἄφθαρτον κήρυγμα τῆς αἰωνίου σωτηρίας.*

mentions that almost all the Greek manuscripts want the section in question: yet in another passage (opp. vol. ii. 193), he himself limits this to *a number*. Probably Eusebius did not meet with the section in his manuscripts, or at least regarded it as unauthentic; for his canons conclude with verse 8. Irenæus, however (iii. 16), early as he wrote, acknowledges the section in question as part of the Gospel of Mark. Now, that these are very remarkable phenomena, cannot be denied; yet they embrace substantially all the arguments against the authenticity of the passage. Some have indeed adduced the fact, that the manuscripts which retain the passage furnish a multitude of various readings, by which, spurious additions to the text usually betray themselves. If, however, we compare this section with the history of the adulteress, John viii. 3–11, we shall be ready to acknowledge that this argument rests upon a very slender foundation. There are many passages of unquestioned authenticity, which exhibit many more discrepancies than the concluding portion of Mark. In like manner there is no weight whatever in the objection, that as Mark had said, xiv. 28, and xvi. 7, that Jesus would reveal himself to the disciples in Galilee, if he had written this concluding section, he would undoubtedly have recorded the appearance of Jesus in Galilee; and as this is not done, the composition must be attributed to some other person. For, a comparison of ver. 15–18 with Matth. xxviii. 16, will manifestly shew that Mark actually describes Christ's appearing in Galilee, and therefore the omission of any express mention of Galilee merely exhibits a want of circumstantial precision in the narrative, such as is frequent even in the best historical writers.

But let us, in deference to those important critical doubts, admit for a moment that the passage is not authentic, in that the addition of it to the defective codices may be explained, but not its omission from those which contained it at first. Will the whole matter, then, be quite plain and easy of comprehension? I very much question it. How then has this appended section originated? Is it perchance from materials furnished by tradition, or from apocryphal gospels? This no one will maintain; for the conclusion of Mark contains no peculiar accounts marked by fulness of detail. Is it then from our received gospels? If so, its composer must have intentionally excluded the Gospel of John from his notice, because he recounts nothing which that Gospel contains! Now, such an exclusion would be altogether inexplicable; for it is certain that, in after times, when the Gospel collection had been formed, no one would have taken his information from Matthew and Luke to the utter neglect of John! And any one who might have desired to conclude the Gospel of Mark by adding a compendious survey of the appearances of Christ, would without doubt have drawn materials from John.

But even making the improbable supposition that, in order to construct a conclusion to the Gospel of Mark, some person availed himself *merely* of Matthew and Luke, does this supposition suffice to explain its character? At a first glance it seems sufficient, inasmuch as Mark gives, in a condensed form, all that the other two Evangelists narrate in detail. Upon inquiring more particularly, however, we must acknowledge that even this hypothesis cannot be maintained. For, if the conclusion of Mark's Gospel were such a mere compilation as we have supposed, we should discover in it a slavish adherence to the sources from whence its information was derived. But, on the contrary, although this section contains no entirely new account (the same indeed is true of the whole Gospel of Mark), yet it exhibits new and peculiar features which accord perfectly with the entire manner and style of this Evangelist, so that it is impossible to suppose it the work of any mere compiler. To these features belong the words in ver. 12: ἐφανερώθη ἐν ἑτέρᾳ μορφῇ, *he appeared in another form*, and that entirely peculiar expression, γλώσσαις καιναῖς λαλεῖν, *to speak with new tongues*, in ver. 17, and similarly, all which is adduced in ver. 18, under the signs to be expected by the apostles in their ministry, such as the touching of serpents, the drinking of deadly substances, and the praying over the sick. Now, since no foreign character betrays itself in the *style*, we must acknowledge that the spuriousness of this concluding section cannot be regarded as completely established; especially since we can assign no imaginable reason why Mark should have left his narrative uncompleted. He certainly never could have meant to conclude with the words ἐφοβοῦντο γάρ, at ver. 8. The hypothesis put forth by Michaelis to explain this circumstance betrays, by its weakness, how little that is satisfactory can be said on this point. He is of opinion that Mark derived his information from Peter; that Peter, when he was thrown into prison, was unable to make further communications to the Evangelist, and consequently that Mark was obliged to break off his narrative abruptly. But surely we must not imagine that the Evangelist so carefully restricted himself to the narrations of Peter. Even assuming that such had been the case, still Mark could have found the means of composing a brief conclusion to his Gospel; to say nothing of the fact that other persons, besides Peter, had knowledge of the appearances of Christ, from whom he could derive the necessary information. What a plain aspect does the case assume when, on the other hand, we proceed upon the supposition that this concluding section is authentic! The concluding portion was severed from the manuscript. It might have been written upon a separate parchment from that which contained the rest of the Gospel. This principal parchment concluded with the words ἐφοβοῦντο γάρ. The transcriber, who followed this codex, left out of his copy the concluding verses; and persons who noticed this want attempted of themselves (as is proved by codex L.) briefly to finish the Gospel. In the greatest number of manuscripts, meanwhile, the authentic conclusion was preserved, and by these means the two recensions of Mark, the complete and the incomplete one, have come down to us.

Matth. xxviii. 16–20.—As regards particular incidents, the narrative of Matthew alone requires any special investigation, with which that of Mark blends into a continuous account. The statements of Luke were in part (xxiv. 44–46) explained at Luke xxiv. 26 (partly on account especially of the κηρυχθῆναι μετάνοιαν), what follows is to be compared (see remarks at Acts v. 31). Finally, the last two verses (48, 49) contain only the promise of the outpouring of the Holy Ghost, and the command to tarry in Jerusalem till it should be accomplished. Upon ἐξ ὕψους, compare at Luke i. 78. Ἐνδύσασθαι = לָבַשׁ, like the parallel expression Χριστὸν ἐνδύσασθαι, *putting on Christ*, must be understood of a process that thoroughly penetrates and takes possession of the soul. Upon the brief narratives of Mark and Luke relating to the ascension, as well as upon all which comes under discussion in connexion with it, and especially on the omission of this narrative by Matthew and John, compare particulars at Acts i. 9, et seq.

The concluding words of Matth. xxviii. 16–20, are strikingly significant. First, this Evangelist remarks that the ensuing discourses of the Lord were delivered by him upon his having appeared as he had promised, Matth. xxviii. 7, in Galilee; he even mentions that the Lord, whilst uttering them, stood upon a mountain. Tradition itself does not specify the locality more particularly. This appearance of Jesus, however, is perhaps identical with that alluded to in 1 Corinth. xv. 6, at which five hundred of the brethren were present. True, the words of Christ, as given in the narrative, appear to have been addressed to the twelve merely, or at most to them in common with the seventy. We can only suppose, however, that the Lord, on this occasion, as on several others of a similar kind, directed some parts of his discourse to those who were standing nearest to him. There is then nothing to militate against the opinion that these appearances were identical. For on the whole, the solemnity of the discourse appears well suited to an elevated scene which the vast numbers assembled together on the occasion also indicate, consisting probably of all the persons who, up to that time, had become believers in the Lord. This helps also to explain how it was possible (as stated in verse 17) that many could still doubt. Such incredulity, on the part of the apostles themselves, at that time, is certainly hardly conceivable; but to many of the disciples in Galilee, who then saw the Lord for the first time, it might have been, as it was with the apostles in the beginning. Beza conjectures *οὐδέ* for *οἱ δὲ ἐδίσταραν*; but no manuscript supports that reading. Now, during this appearance in Galilee, at the termination of which it is probable the Lord took a solemn leave of his disciples, he represented himself to them as the Lord of both heaven and earth. Compare Matth. xi. 27, John xiii. 3, and xvii. 2. From the context it might seem that the expression merely referred to Christ's moral dominion, since, in immediate connexion with it, there follows the command to teach the nations. But the *ἐν οὐρανῷ*, *in heaven*, is so very express, that it must necessarily refer to more than moral dominion; but even apart from this, the teaching of all nations, as commanded by Christ, presupposes on his part more than mere earthly power. For under it a mere *διδάσκειν* (communication of opinions) cannot be intended, which, in fact, at the conclusion of the verse, is expressly distinguished from it. Their mission was to win over the whole man to the Gospel, to accomplish which no power would be sufficient except that which they were to receive from a higher, a Divine spirit. From this point of view, the connexion of ideas between verses 18 and 20 becomes perfectly clear. For the bold mandate to go forth and make disciples of all nations, which, in the feeling of their impotence, may have humbled the apostles, appeared practicable through the might of him who was sending them.

In the 19th verse there follows the important *institution of the sacrament of baptism.** The words which directly refer to this institution, standing in the midst of the sentence, constitute, as it were, the very kernel of the command. This kernel, however, is enveloped, as it were, in the thoughts, both immediately preceding and following. We shall first consider these latter.

Some have manifestly altogether misunderstood this passage (as we have already intimated) in interpreting the *μαθητεύσατε* as something which should precede baptism, as if the meaning of the words had been, "*first* instruct, *then* baptize them." But the grammatical construction does not warrant such a mode of interpretation, for the two participles *βαπτίζοντες* and *διδάσκοντες* are precisely what

* There is something remarkable in the fact that baptism was instituted after the Lord's Supper. It seems to be implied in the relation of the two sacraments, that baptism should occur antecedently to the supper. For only the baptized, who has been born again, may partake of the heavenly food. However, as the disciples, according to John iv. 2, baptized at a still earlier period, we are compelled to regard the transaction in the following light: Baptism was not now instituted for the first time, but was appointed by Christ for every one who should afterwards enter the Church, and at the same time filled with power from on high. Doubtless the disciples at first baptized Israelites only, and their earlier baptism was not essentially different from the baptism of John.

constitute the *μαθητεύειν*. And again, that view is contradicted by the apostolic practice, in which instruction never preceded baptism. On the contrary, baptism followed upon the mere confession that Jesus was the Christ. But when, through baptism, the believer had become a member of the community of the saints, then, as such, he participated in the progressive courses of instruction which prevailed in the church. To this the *διδάσκοντες αὐτοὺς τηρεῖν πάντα, ὅσα ἐνετειλάμην ὑμῖν*, *teaching them to observe all things*, etc., which follows the command concerning baptism, immediately refers (comp. at Acts ii. 38).* But as the object of this ministration, appear "all the nations" (*πάντα τὰ ἔθνη*). In this passage, therefore, we behold Christ occupying the position of comprehensive universality, in accordance with which the whole human race is the object of his reconciling efficacy. (On the more restricted view of his ministry, comp. at Matthew x. 5, 6.) Under his sacred influence, sent to them from above, and which shall never cease, the Lord desired that all the nations of the earth should attain to spiritual life, and development. Yet his church was not assuredly to remain as a *merely spiritual* community in love and faith. It was also to exhibit itself visibly in external manifestation. To this leads the institution of an external rite, by which all his disciples were to be consecrated. But that at the beginning even the apostles did not catch this comprehensive meaning of the words, is shewn in the history of Peter (Acts x. 9, et seq.)—to whom it was gradually unfolded by the Spirit. The recension of Mark xvi. 15, who connects the *πορευθέντες εἰς τὸν κόσμον ἅπαντα* with the *κηρύσσειν τό εὐαγγέλιον πάσῃ τῇ κτίσει*, is somewhat peculiar. Now, a glance shews that the latter expression, the *κτίσις*, is here equivalent to the foregoing *κόσμος*. When Lightfoot, therefore, on this passage, appeals to that Rabbinical use of language which makes בְּרִיּוֹת, that is, creatures, created beings, to be used of the *heathen*, he unwarrantably restricts the meaning of the expression; for the gospel was surely still to be preached to the Jews also. Hence, chiefly with reference to Colossians i. 15 and 23, and Hebrews iv. 13, this phrase is usually interpreted as of like significance with *πάντες ἄνθρωποι*. These latter passages, however, should be differently rendered. In Col. i. 15, the *κτίσις* is put for creation universally. In Col. i. 23, it should be rendered as referring to the whole earth, all that is under heaven. In Heb. iv. 13, *κτίσις*, without the article, stands for an individual created thing. Still, without the article, *κτίσις* may doubtless signify humanity; yet *πᾶσα κτίσις* certainly cannot. The latter formula, from the nature of the case, must always denote the universe.

* The connexion of the *μαθητεύσατε* with the *βαπτίζοντες* and *διδάσκοντες*, however, undeniably intimates, that in uttering these words the Saviour had no immediate thought of infant baptism. Compare on this subject the observations at Acts xvi. 14, 15.

Hence the passage under discussion must not be taken as indicating mankind in positive separation from the world of created things generally, as it is understood by most. This view tends to efface a profound idea which pervades the whole New Testament, viz., that with the gospel is united the glorification of *all* created things, by a process which commences, it is true, with the human race, but gradually penetrates all things. (Compare the particulars at Rom. viii. 19, seq.) The κτίσις is therefore put for humanity, but only in so far as humanity is the flower of the whole creation.*

The *baptismal formula* itself, is all that now remains to be explained. It is plain from the outset, that the Lord intended to institute a *perpetual* rite which should be binding upon the church in all ages, and in which alike baptism and teaching refer to *all nations*. From this it follows, therefore, that the baptism ordained by Christ differed essentially from the baptism of John, which possessed but a temporary significance. (Compare at Matth. iii. 13.) The Christian sacrament of baptism was not to be merely a baptism of repentance (βάπτισμα τῆς μετανοίας), but rather a symbol of the second birth, coincident with the external ordinance. (Comp. at John iii. 5.) Hence, as at John iii. 3, salvation is made dependent on regeneration, so in the parallel (Mark xvi. 16) could it be made dependent on *baptism* and the *faith* which it necessarily presupposes. The second half of the verse, however, which merely opposes to "believeth" "believeth not" (without adding "and is not baptized") serves to indicate that the internal process of regeneration is essentially necessary to salvation; but that in certain cases the external ordinance of baptism, which, according to the original institution, coincides with it, may be dispensed with.† By the introducing of pædo-baptism,‡ the position which this ordinance occupied

* The expression of the pious Hildegard is full of spirit: "When God created the world, he impressed on man the stamp of the whole creation, as we inscribe on a small bit of parchment the events and dates of a whole year. For this reason, in the language of God, man is designated 'every creature.'" Compare Sailer's Letters from all Centuries, vol. iv. p. 14.

† The ancient church was therefore perfectly correct in acknowledging even unbaptized persons, who, during the persecutions had confessed Christ, and been put to death in consequence, to be true believers. But had these confessors remained alive, obedience to the command of the Lord would have impelled them to seek baptism.

‡ Under the correct impression, that infant baptism cannot itself be regeneration, our church has ordained that baptized children cannot partake of the Lord's supper before confirmation, which otherwise, as regenerate persons, could not be refused to them. But yet infant baptism is not without effect. The Holy Ghost can, even in the mother's womb, operate upon the babe. Luke i. 41. The operation of the Holy Ghost in infant baptism, cannot, however, be regarded as overthrowing the dominion of hereditary sinfulness. This has never been asserted in the Lutheran doctrines. (Comp. the observations on Acts xvi. 14, 15.) Taken in this sense, namely, as destroying the dominion of hereditary sin, regeneration, without consciousness, and without a personal appropriation of grace, is perfectly inconceivable. Upon the application of Christian baptism to those

is changed. Pædo-baptism is certainly not apostolic. But it became necessary in the church, when once the supernatural communication of the powers of the Holy Spirit had ceased. The external rite then retrograded to the position occupied by the baptism of John, and receives its necessary completion only through confirmation.*

The meaning of the words : *βαπτίζειν εἰς τὸ ὄνομα τοῦ πατρὸς, καὶ τοῦ υἱοῦ, καὶ τοῦ ἁγίου πνεύματος, to baptize into the name*, etc., is best learned from such passages as 1 Cor. i. 13, x. 2, in which baptism, *εἰς τὸ ὄνομα* Παύλου and *εἰς τὸν Μωσῆν*, is spoken of. The *βαπτίζειν εἰς τινα, baptizing into any one*, signifies baptism as involving a binding obligation ; a rite, whereby one is pledged ; and the sublime object to which baptism binds, consists of Father, Son, and Holy Ghost. (*Ὄνομα* = שֵׁם, signifies here again the very essence of God himself.)

The unbaptized are therefore regarded as not possessing essential connexion with God ; as separate from God. This sinful alienation, which is, at the same time, the source of all human misery, both external and internal, is removed by baptism and regeneration. The Divine power is wedded to the human soul, which thus becomes itself the parent of a higher heavenly consciousness.† But it is worthy of notice that the Saviour does not here give the name of God directly, but the names of the Father, Son, and Holy Ghost, as the exalted object to which the votary of baptism becomes pledged. This is the only passage in the Gospels in which the Lord himself names the three Divine persons together. In many passages the Saviour, it is true, describes both the Son and the Holy Ghost individually as Divine personalities. Here, however, they appear together, and are styled in common the object to which believers bind themselves by baptism. The elements of the doctrine of the Trinity are thus given in Christ's identical words. But the dogma is presented in an entirely undeveloped form, and the unfolding of the mystery is committed to the scientific activity of the church. The established doctrine of the church on this subject is

who had received the baptism of John previously, comp. the observations at Acts xix. 1, et seq.

* According to this, it cannot be asserted that infant baptism is necessary to salvation, for the inward act of regeneration, which is possible only with consciousness, cannot be supposed in connexion with it. The confusion of the baptism of John (and of pædo-baptism, which stands parallel to it), with the baptism which is specifically Christian, was first made prevalent in the church by *Augustine*, and has since prevailed in it.

† In Ullman's Studien, 1832, H. 2, s. 410, et seq., Dr. Bindseil of Halle explains the words *βαπτίζειν εἰς ὄνομα τοῦ πατρός, κ. τ. λ.*, "first, as an expression of subjection (better, of obligation) to Father, Son, and Holy Ghost; and secondly, as also necessarily intimating an elevation of the recipient to superior dignity." But the formula, in itself, does not at all signify the latter thought, although it is implied doubtless in the relation of the ordinance.

essentially that of the Bible also, but the symbolically derived term *Person* involves a degree of inconvenience, and may easily lead to error. Human language, however, furnishes no expression by which the connexion between a unity of essence with an independence of consciousness, in Father, Son, and Spirit can be more appropriately indicated. We cannot therefore charge the teachers of the church with error because they have made choice of this expression. We can only lament the imperfection of human language, which renders it inadequate to designate the most exalted and absolute relations which are clearly comprehensible to the purified reason only, by precise ideas, and words corresponding with them in clearness.

The chief error to which the word "Person" leads, and which has constantly been opposed by all the more profound teachers of the church, and especially by Augustine, in his acute and profound work on the subject of the Trinity, is this. We are led by it to conceive of Father, Son, and Spirit as locally or mechanically *distinct* from one another, whilst we should view them as livingly interpenetrating one another. To this view we may advantageously oppose whatever there is of truth in Sabellianism (which rightly recognizes this unity in the existence of the Deity), yet without adopting at the same time its erroneous denial of the individual independency of consciousness in Father, Son, and Spirit. In the commentary on Matthew xii. 32, and John i. 1, I have intimated my views of the Trinity. But to facilitate our survey, I shall here state them again in a condensed form. The only means we possess for illustrating the unity of the essence, and the severalty of consciousness in the Godhead, consists in the corresponding analogy which we find in the spiritual nature of man, the image of God. As in man there is not only spiritual being, but also the knowledge of that being, so also in the Divine nature, if we apprehend it as a living God, not as a dead notion, we must suppose both being and the knowledge of its peculiar being. This knowledge which God possesses of himself is designated as the Son: in him dwells the Father himself, and through him effects everything that he does effect. But, as all the powers of the Father concentrate themselves, as it were, in his self-consciousness, so do they also continually revert from the Son to their primary source, the Father, and this return is designated as the Holy Ghost. This view explains the phraseology of Scripture, where it is said that "the Father draws to the Son," but, "the Son leads, in the Holy Ghost, back again to the Father." The manifestation of the *influence* of Father, Son, and Holy Ghost, thus presents a climax. All knowledge of God proceeds *from* the Father, as *absolute power, through* the Son, as *perfect love, to* the Holy Ghost, as *complete holiness*. But regarded conversely, the Holy Ghost leads back directly to the

Father, so that the end again issues in the beginning. And thus, in Father, Son, and Holy Ghost is represented the eternal being of God in its essential internal movement and interaction. If according to this explanation it may appear difficult to understand how inward *actions* of the Divine Being can appear as an individual consciousness, it is explained by the consideration that the activities of the *absolute* Spirit are, in accordance with its nature, pure life, being, and consciousness. To apprehend, however, the idea of the *individual* as something limited and bounded within itself, and totally separated from all other spiritual life, would be the very error which has been already pointed out; and the Scriptures, in their entire mode of expression, shew that *in this sense* it apprehends neither the Son nor the Holy Ghost as a person. The Son, indeed, appears individualized in the person of Jesus, but he labours by regeneration to transform all humanity into his own nature, on which account the whole church is simply called Christ (1 Cor. xii. 12); and the Holy Ghost also appears shed abroad in the hearts of all believers, like the Father, who is omnipresent throughout the whole universe. As, therefore, the consciousness of God in itself can be conceived of only as all-comprehending, so also must the notion of *Person* under the true idea of the doctrine of the Trinity, be understood in an all-comprehensive sense. By this means a great deal of the difficulty which, from the earliest times, has surrounded the doctrine of the Trinity, will be obviated.

Apart from this, the important passage before us presents yet another question for discussion, namely, "*Whether, in the institutory words quoted, the Lord did or did not intend to establish a fixed formula of baptism?*" This question would not have been suggested at all, had the other portions of the New Testament Scriptures shewn that the disciples, in administering baptism, employed these words. But, instead of this, we find that, even in the history of the Acts of the Apostles, as often as baptism is mentioned it is performed only *εἰς*, or *ἐπὶ τὸ ὄνομα*, *ἐν τῷ ὀνόματι Ἰησοῦ*, or *Χριστοῦ*.* In the first place, however, the *act* of baptism itself is in no passage thus *described*, but the fact of baptism merely *indicated*. We cannot, therefore, infer from the use of these phrases that the complete formula given by the Saviour was not employed. These phrases might have been intended merely to distinguish baptism as a *Christian* ordinance, from that of John. Add to this that there are several passages (Acts xix. 2, comp. with ver.

* From this circumstance, and because the formula of baptism is not mentioned in Mark, Teller would deduce the conclusion that the passage in Matthew is not authentic! —a hypothesis which has no foundation whatever, and arose merely from hostility to the doctrine of the Trinity.

5, Tit. iii. 4, ff.), in which the Son and the Holy Ghost are named in such a connexion with baptism as to render it highly probable that the names form part of the formula used in that ordinance, whilst at the same time the most ancient Christian writers (Justin Martyr, for instance), quote the words of the passage before us as the baptismal formula. (Compare Just. Mar. Apol., 1, p. 93, in my "Monum. Hist. Eccl." vol. ii. p. 167.) As in the institution of the holy supper, so also in the institution of baptism, the Saviour would without doubt have employed the most suitable words to signify the spiritual character of the ceremony. And from this, therefore, arises the church's obligation to retain the practice of using these words as the formula for the administration of this sacrament. The ancient church, however, exercised considerable freedom in everything that regarded the mere externals of the ordinance; and therefore it may well have happened, that in single instances they baptized in the name of Jesus only. That this was the fact appears from the later controversies maintained by Cyprian on the baptism of heretics. (Compare Cypriani epist. 73, in my "Monum. Hist. Eccl." vol. ii. p. 118, note.) Such a baptism, performed solely in the name of Jesus, was however not less valid than if accompanied by the complete formula. For Christ implies alike the Father, and the Holy Ghost; but the converse will not hold, that the Father implies the Son. Such modern phrases, therefore, as "to baptize into the eternal love," are to be rejected as unchristian. They would be more accordant with the Old Testament dispensation.

The Saviour now in conclusion sustains his command to the little band of his disciples, to impart new life to the whole world, by the promise of his own almighty assistance, which should never fail them. (The *συντέλεια τοῦ αἰῶνος*, must here again be understood as referring to the period of growth and development assigned to the *βασιλεία τοῦ Θεοῦ*, for only during this period lasts the struggle which renders the help of Christ necessary. In the kingdom of God, the Lord Jesus is also present, it is true, but there his presence is to be regarded as the fountain of blessedness, not as a protection amidst dangers. On this subject, compare at Matth. xxiv. 3.) The passage in Mark xvi. 17, 18, describes particularly the abundant assistance which the church is to receive from the presence of Christ, during the continuance of her struggles, and especially mentions the tokens (*σημεῖα*) of his power which the disciples should experience.* Sufficient examples occur in the Acts of the casting out of

* Some would hold this passage also as unauthentic. But the critical authorities, and even its own contents, clearly testify to its authenticity. For, surely the mention of the drinking of deadly substances would not have been introduced if the passage had been interpolated, because no accredited example of that sign can be adduced.

demons, and of the healing of sick persons, and even of the touching of serpents there occurs one well known account (Acts xxviii. 3). On the other hand, there is no instance whatever of the drinking of deadly poisons (θανάσιμον scil. φάρμακον), and, as we noticed previously, this very fact affords evidence of the genuineness of this passage in Mark.* (Upon the γλώσσαις λαλεῖν, compare particulars at Acts ii. 4.) The expletive clause καιναῖς γλώσσαις λαλήσουσι occurs here only. Every hypothesis concerning it encounters some difficulty, since neither the languages nor the tongues were in the proper sense of the word *new;* and it is certainly harsh to understand *new* (καιναῖς) as completely synonymous with *other* (ἑτέραις, Acts ii. 4). The simplest course perhaps is to suppose, in accordance with 1 Cor. xiii. 1, that the speech of him who spake with tongues (γλώσσῃ λαλῶν) was sometimes regarded as an angelic language, and hence designated as a new language.† The plural form may be explained from the fact that (as is shewn by 1 Cor. xiv.) the speaking with tongues manifested itself in several distinct forms, especially in praying and singing in the spirit.

John xx. 30, 31.—If we compare the conclusion of the fourth gospel, that of John, with the beginning of the same work, we discover an admirable closing up. John concludes the history of Thomas with the words: "blessed are they who have not seen and yet have believed" (μακάριοι οἱ μὴ ἰδόντες, καὶ πιστεύσαντες). In this is contained, though indirectly, the most powerful admonition to the reader, namely, that although we have not beheld the Lord with the bodily eye, we should believe in the announcement of him who dwelt amongst men full of grace and truth. And to awaken this faith, to convince his readers of the fact, that Christ the Messiah was the true Son of God, was the great object of John's Gospel. For as the logos, who is the life (John i. 4), imparted this life to John, through faith, so the disciple of love would render this blessed life accessible to his readers. In order, meanwhile, to leave to his readers an open eye for further surveys of the infinitely copious life of Christ, John intimates that he had not related everything, but only many things, so that much still remained for that spirit of inquiry which his own work should have awakened in them. As Lücke and Kuinoel correctly interpret it, the "signs" (σημεῖα), in the present connexion, can refer only to the appearances of the risen Redeemer. Tholuck, on account of the concluding verse (ver. 31), would refer the expression to all the miracles previously mentioned. But we

* It is mentioned, in an apocryphal writing, that John drank poison without sustaining any injury, Fabricii codex, apocr. vol. ii. p. 575, et seq., but the legend was perhaps suggested by this passage in Mark.

† Rather explain *new* as "new *to them,*" such as the apostles were before unacquainted with; new not absolutely, but relatively.—[K.

shall be more correct in supposing that ver. 30 stands in immediate connexion with that which directly precedes it, and then follows the conclusion. This therefore will be the connexion: "Much still remains to be narrated concerning the appearance of the Lord, but what has been here stated, as well as what was stated formerly, furnishes a sufficient basis of faith in the Redeemer." But again, the appearances of Christ are themselves called *σημεῖα*, *signs*, just as *φανεροῦσθαι*, *manifested himself*, is used elsewhere in reference to them, a circumstance which must be regarded as favouring the hypothesis, that in the opinion of the Evangelists, the Saviour arose from the grave with a glorified body.* Finally, verse 31 expresses directly the main object of the gospel, as we observed in our introduction to the Gospel of John. John's representation, however, of Jesus as the true Christ and the Son of God, was immediately designed for a special class of opinions in the ancient church, though without losing sight of more general objects. Finally, "Son of God" (*υἱὸς τοῦ θεοῦ*), in this passage, is evidently to be regarded from the Christian point of view, as explanatory of the Χριστός; so that from this it cannot be inferred that *υἱὸς τοῦ θεοῦ* was a well-known and usual name for the Messiah amongst the Jews of that age. Compare on this point the remarks made at Luke i. 35.

With this statement of his object, John appropriately concludes his work in a manner calculated to excite in his readers a consciousness of the obligation laid upon them by the announcement that the promised Saviour had appeared.

§ 4. APPENDIX OF JOHN'S GOSPEL.

(John xxi. 1–25.)

The fact that the last chapter of John's gospel forms a supplement to the entire work is so plain, and now so generally acknowledged, that it needs no further proof. But on the question, "Who should be regarded as the composer of this appendix?" commentators have not, as yet, been able unanimously to agree. The only result of all the investigations of this subject which commends itself as tenable, is that which regards the last two verses only as not written by John, while the whole remaining portion of the chapter was added to the complete Gospel by the Evangelist himself.†

* Doubtful. His appearances would be *signs* (*σημεῖα*) simply as proving his *resurrection*, and the term *φανεροῦσθαι* (*shewed himself*), might apply simply to the *rareness* of these appearances. The risen Lord did not, as before, *associate* with his disciples, but only occasionally *appeared* to them. Still the *fact* of his glorified body seems indubitable.—[K.

† Compare, on the authenticity of the concluding chapter of John, Guerike's Beiträge, vol. i., s. 67, et seq.

To this effect, Tholuck, in particular, expresses himself. Those scholars who deny the authenticity of the whole chapter (at the head of whom stand Schott and Lücke), whether they assume as its author some definite person (*e. g.*, the presbyter John), or even some one unknown, or with Grotius attribute its composition to the Ephesian church, borrow their weightiest reasons for this view merely from the last verse. The natural hyperbole of ver. 25 certainly does not accord with the spirit of John, which dictated the most beautiful moderation of expression. Just as little does the use of the plural *οἴδαμεν* in verse 24 correspond with the beginning of the statement, *οὗτός ἐστιν ὁ μαθητὴς ὁ μαρτυρῶν περὶ τούτων καὶ γράψας ταῦτα*. Kuinoel and Weber have proved most satisfactorily that no sufficient reason can be adduced for rejecting the larger part of the chapter, since all the manuscripts contain it; the ideas are characteristic of John; and even in style it presents no distinguishable differences.

The only objections, therefore, against the authenticity of the chapter must arise from its *contents*. These contents unquestionably present much that is surprising, and in any case, therefore, the question is forced upon us, "What could have influenced John to append such statements to his gospel, after he had already brought it to a conclusion?" To reason from the contents of a passage to its genuineness is always a questionable course, even though it contain matter deviating widely from the spirit and modes of thought of the alleged author. No such deviation can here be pointed out, though the contents of the chapter, when compared with the earlier portions of this Evangelist's gospel, appear poor and without significance. This will hold good of the first half at least of the chapter so long as it is interpreted literally, since a successful draught of fishes is the only incident it recounts. But in the second half, on the other hand, an event is recorded, which might certainly have occasioned the Evangelist to touch upon it in a special supplementary note, namely, a report that he should remain living until the future advent of the Lord. But if this had been the sole motive of John for composing this appendix, what purpose could be subserved by such a lengthened, unmeaning preface concerning the occurrence upon the lake of Gennesareth? To this question, no completely satisfactory reply can be afforded by those who defend the authenticity of the chapter, so long as they controvert the *symbolical** mode of interpreting it, which formerly obtained currency amongst the most spiritual and intellectual fathers of the church,† and

* Upon the symbolical acts of Christ generally, compare in the Commentary, Part I., at Matthew xxi. 19.

† I shall here quote the words of Augustine, who in essentials correctly explains the passage, although perhaps he goes too far in discovering the significance of minutiæ. He

which in this section of the evangelical history receives the most undeniable supports from the narrative itself.

Through the entire second half of the chapter, the symbolic character manifestly prevails. The "girding," the "stretching forth of the hands," the "following," the "tarrying," cannot in any case be understood in a merely literal sense. The same symbolical character may therefore be very simply extended to the first half also, to which the application of such a character is the more justifiable and appropriate, that the very words of Christ in reference to a perfectly similar incident recorded elsewhere (Luke v. 4) entirely authorize the symbolical interpretation. (On this point compare the full investigation in the Comm. Part I.) The fact that throughout the entire chapter, not John, but Peter, plays the principal part, testifies manifestly and emphatically in favour of its authenticity, and against the assumption that it was composed at a later period by any other historian. Had it been subjoined by some teacher in the church, who was a disciple of John, he would, without a doubt, have drawn his picture more to give prominence to John. But here we have an entirely candid history, written sine ira et studio.

John xxi. 1-6. The two concluding verses of the Gospel, (xx. 30, 31) are ignored, and the subsequent narrative attached directly to the last appearance of Christ, by the μετὰ ταῦτα, *after this.* (Compare chap. xxi. 14.) The fact, that according to the narrative in the twenty-first chapter, the disciples prosecute their worldly vocation, loses its surprising character when we reflect that even Paul, during the course of his apostolic labours, constantly practised

refers the draught of fishes to the anticipated spiritual agency of Peter. But he places the draught of fishes in parallelism with the analogous account of Luke v., and declares himself on the subject in the following manner:—Hoc loco qualiter in seculi fine futura sit ecclesia dominus significat, alia piscatione significavit qualiter nunc sit. Quod autem illud fecit in initio prædicationis suæ hoc, vero post resurrectionem suam, hinc ostendit illam capturam piscium, bonos et malos significare, quos nunc habet ecclesia; istam vero tantummodo bonos, quos habebit in æternum, completa in fine hujus seculi resurrectione mortuarum. Denique ibi Jesus non sicut hic in littore stabat, quando jussit pisces capi: sed ascendens in unam navim, quæ erat Simonis, rogavit eum, ut a terra reduceret pusillum et in ea sedens docebat turbas, ut cessavit autem loqui, dixit ad Simonem: "duc in altum et laxate retia vestra in capturam." Et illic quod captum est piscium in naviculis fuit, non sicut hic rete extraxerunt in terram. His signis et si qua alia potuerint reperiri, ibi ecclesia in hoc seculo, hic vero in fine seculi figurata est; ideo illud ante, hoc autem post resurrectionem domini factum est, quia ibi nos Christus significavit vocatos, hic resuscitatos. Ibi retia non mittuntur in dexteram, ne solos significent bonos, nec in sinistram, ne solos malos, sed indifferenter: "laxate," inquit, "retia vestra in capturam," ut permixtos intelligamus bonos et malos. Hic autem inquit: "Mittite in dexteram navigii rete ut significaret eos, qui stabant ad dexteram, solos bonos." Ibi rete propter significanda schismata rumpebatur, hic vero quoniam tunc jam in illa summa pace sanctorum nulla erant schismata, pertinuit ad evangelistam dicere: "et cum tanti essent, non est scissum rete. Tanquam illud respiceret ubi scissum est et in illius mali comparatione commendaret hoc bonum." Cf. Opera Augustini edit. Benedict. vol. iii. p. 591, et seq.

his handicraft also. On this occasion, the appearing of Jesus was again sudden: without the disciples having observed his approach, he was standing before them.

(In verse 4, εἰς is not = ἐν: rather connect with the ἔστη the previous movement. Προσφάγιον = ὄψον, a relish, that which is eaten with bread.)

Ver. 7–14.—By the miraculous draught of fishes, the beloved disciple discovered the gracious presence of the Lord, and the excitable Peter at once hastens to him by swimming. (Γυμνός expresses here one merely clad with his under garment. He therefore wrapped an over-garment around himself, in order probably to appear fully clothed on the shore. Some have falsely interpreted the ἐπενδύτης of the under garment, but that is called ὑποδύτης, as indicated also by its etymology.) In the sequel of this account, verse 9, it is surprising, that when the disciples were come with the ship to the shore, they found a fire of coals, food (ὀψάριον, here fish roasted on the coals), and bread. Some writers have abandoned themselves to very wild notions in the explanation of this circumstance (as, e. g., that all this was produced out of nothing!) which need no particular disproof. Still, in whatever manner we regard the statement, the fact is very remarkable, even if we adopt the simplest supposition, viz., that the Lord had caused these preparations to be made upon the shore. It may be asked for instance, for what purpose all this? Such refreshment was alike unnecessary for the risen Redeemer and for the disciples, who had their dwellings in the neighbourhood; and, would not these external preparations hinder that powerful influence upon their inner nature, which Jesus assuredly contemplated in appearing to them? These questions are answered only by the supposition that the whole account is symbolical. To the inhabitants of western countries, this style of conveying instruction may appear somewhat strange; in the East, however, it is the usual method, and upon all less developed capacities of conception, is calculated to produce a deep impression.

How powerfully, for example, would the draught of fishes remind the disciples, and especially Peter, of their first vocation by the Saviour, and the blessed results promised to their ministry! In like manner the food provided for them here by the Saviour after their completed toil, would intimate that blissful feast which he prepares for his people with Abraham, Isaac and Jacob, in the kingdom of God.* Viewed in this light, the whole transaction attains

* Augustine (loc. cit. a. 594) in his interpretation of the passage, considers that it contains an allusion to the Lord's Supper, for he says; "Piscis assus, Christus est passus; ipse est panis, qui de cœlo descendit; huic incorporatur ecclesia, ad participandum, beatitudinem sempiternam."

meaning and significance, and the connexion of what follows with it becomes obvious. (The remark that this was the third appearance of Jesus is correct, if it be limited to those appearances which were witnessed by several disciples at the same time.)

Ver. 15-17.—According to the interpretation just given, the second half of the chapter follows the first naturally and easily, and the two form a complete whole.

After the prophetic glance, vouchsafed to the apostle, at the greatness of his future ministry, the Lord directs his attention to the *conditions* on which it should depend. Love to Christ, and voluntary self-devotion, are its indispensable requirements. That the threefold question of the Lord had a reference to the threefold denial of Peter, is too obvious to be overlooked. But Tholuck's conjecture that the Lord, after some intermediate speech with the other disciples, which is omitted in the narrative, turned, first with the second question, and next with the third, to Peter, to me appears anything but probable. For the immediate reiteration of the question directly and consecutively, would powerfully contribute to the impression, which the Lord intended to produce. At the first, Peter remains perfectly tranquil, and appeals to the knowledge of the Lord himself; but at the last question he is sensible that the object of Jesus is to produce within him a salutary feeling of humiliation, and he becomes troubled. Yet he could with heartfelt truth appeal to his love of the Saviour, and because that was the case, the Lord therefore now affixed the seal to his blessed commission, in the *βόσκε τὰ πρόβατά μου, feed my sheep.* There is still, however, another circumstance, which Tholuck, in his exposition of this passage seems to me to have mistaken. For example, he would have the question "lovest thou me more than these?" (*ἀγαπᾷς με πλεῖον τούτων*;) in ver. 15, to refer retrospectively to Matth. xxvi. 33, where Peter is stated to have said, "though all should be offended for thy sake, yet will not I be offended;" as if Christ had desired to awaken in Peter the conviction that he had erred respecting his own character. But, as we remarked in our comment upon Matth. xvi. 19, Peter did in fact possess a certain spiritual eminence above the other disciples, in the power of effective, external action.

It might therefore be said of him with perfect truth, that he loved the Lord with more energy than did any of the others. And that the Saviour would not deny this, is manifest from the fact that, without Peter's having made any such apology as, "I love thee far less than do the others, since I could deny thee," he yet appointed him the shepherd of his flock. The object of Jesus was, therefore, not to prove to Peter that he felt no love to him, for Peter really did possess it, nay, he possessed it even when he denied him, or he would never have been able to rise again so speedily to the enjoyment of faith, after the waves of darkness had rolled over his head. The object of the questions was therefore this alone: to lead the apostle to perfect poverty of spirit, and to emancipation from the thraldom of self. But this consists not in affirming that we have no love, when we really possess it; such a profession would indicate an ignorance of ourselves or a false humility. It rather so reveals itself as to lead man not to ascribe all that he discovers within himself of the operations of grace to himself, as a secure unalienable possession; but to regard them as presents of no absolutely enduring character, but which the Lord, who bestowed them, can again, whenever he pleases, withdraw. Thus the *soul* remains humble, feeling its own littleness even amid all the adornments of Divine grace, which it never claims as its absolute possession. But that was what Peter had done! The ardour of love which, in the fulness of the spirit, inflamed his soul, took entire possession of him; he felt himself strong as a hero; but when this fulness of power forsook him, he denied his Lord, in the prospect of imagined dangers.

Finally, as to the Catholic church referring this passage to the primacy of the Pope, the remarks hold which were made at Matth. xvi. 19. What is here said to Peter, as the representative of the apostles, refers equally to them all. But that Peter must certainly be regarded as their representative, cannot be denied.* The assertion that this representative character involved a superior plenipotentiary power, or a succession, is, however, just as incapable of proof, and as unlikely as that in general the collective body of the twelve was perpetuated after their death.

Ver. 18, 19.—Upon the promise by which the Saviour confided to Peter the office of pastor over believers, there follows immediately a solemn admonition concerning the end of his earthly pilgrimage. Although he was to be great in the kingdom of God, still the issue of his career was to be painful and abhorrent to the natural human will. The figurative words in which this admonition was couched, would have been surrendered still more than they have been to the caprice of interpreters, had not the Evangelist himself subjoined their explanation. According to tradition, Peter died upon the cross, Eusebius' Hist. Eccles. ii. 35. And the most ancient teachers in the church understood the words as referring to his† crucifixion.

* Chrysostom, who knew nothing of any primacy, expresses himself to the same effect on this passage: ὁ Πέτρος τὴν προστασίαν ἐνεπιστεύθη τῶν ἀδελφῶν. Cyprian also acknowledges Peter as the representative of the apostles, but even at that period transferred this character to the Bishop of Rome. Compare Cypriani Ep. 55, in my Monum. Hist. Eccles. ii. p. 50.

† Tertulliani Scorpiace, cap. 15, tunc Petrus ab altero vincitur, cum cruci adstringitur.

It is only in modern times that it has been thought the words might be understood merely of his arrest, since, if they were referred to the crucifixion, the girding must have taken place previous to the stretching out of the hands. A fitting parallel with this is furnished in Acts xxi. 11, where the prophet Agabus binds his hands and feet with Paul's girdle, as a sign of his imprisonment. Yet it has been justly stated that, like all prophetic intimations, the passage is both brief and obscure. Hence it remains indefinite whether the girding (ζωννύειν) should be referred to the binding of his hands on his being arrested, or to his being bound to the cross. It is sufficient meanwhile that the expressions selected *might* refer to his crucifixion, and it may well have happened that this more definite meaning of the words first dawned upon John when he heard of the martyrdom of Peter. But the passage refers not merely to the stretching forth of hands, and to being bound, but also to the contrasted conditions in youth and in old age. The mention of Peter's youthful condition is commonly wholly overlooked; it is regarded as void of significancy in itself, and as merely placed in antithesis to death in old age. It is plain, however, that we should not understand the one half only as typical, and the other half as literal; both must be taken figuratively, and both literally.

Primarily, therefore, the passage asserts simply, that, in youth, man exults in the full freedom of his powers, but in old age, feels himself bound in many ways by his infirmities, and requires the help of others. *Both* these divisions then are *significant*. They refer to youth and age in the spiritual life (1 John ii. 13, 14). In the fulness of spiritual power, Peter acted boldly and vigorously, in the manner which seemed best to himself. But, in his age, he was to be restrained in many ways; fiercely persecuted, and necessitated against his own will to be an active agent in various circumstances. These dealings had a *disciplinary* object: they were to cause the disciple to forego his own will, and to divest him of all selfishness. The climax of the discipline was the death by crucifixion of Peter himself, in which was literally fulfilled that which in its more general sense, he had long previously experienced to be true. The interpretation proposed by Fikenscher—"with increasing age, thou shalt become more and more the servant of another (namely, of God)—who will gird thee and employ thee as he may please,"—is in itself, no doubt, very appropriate, but does not harmonize with the connexion.

Verses 20–23.—Upon this particular discourse of the Lord to Peter, there follows another, which, in connexion with the accompanying declarations of the Evangelist, presents a very enigmatical character. The Redeemer says to Peter, Follow me. That the words were accompanied by an *action*, seems plainly intimated by what follows. The "follow me" (ἀκολούθει μοι) cannot possibly be understood as a mere trope, for the scene is circumstantially described. Christ went some distance away, Peter followed him —but, on the way, Peter looked around and perceived that John also was coming after them. This occasioned him to ask the question, "Lord, and what of this man?" (κύριε, οὗτος δὲ τί;) The reason of the Evangelist for writing so expressly concerning himself on this occasion, suggests itself immediately. This order in which they followed, reminded him of the last paschal-feast of Christ (xiii. 25), when John occupied a nearer place to the Lord than Peter. On that occasion Peter did not venture to put a question directly to the Redeemer, but conveyed it to him through John. Now their relations to Christ seemed inverted; Peter appears to be the nearer, and to have, as it were, supplanted John. This addition was therefore very important, in order to make manifest the relations of Peter and John respectively to Christ. To the apparently jealous, or at least anxious-sounding question of Peter, Jesus now replied: *ἐὰν αὐτὸν θέλω μένειν, ἕως ἔρχομαι, τί πρός σε; σὺ ἀκολούθει μοι, if I will*, etc.

Many of John's contemporaries understood the tarrying of the continuance of his earthly life. This explanation is rejected by the Evangelist, who then merely repeats the words of Christ just cited, but without assigning their meaning. Let us now inquire how this passage may be understood. First, let us take the words in a merely external sense, and try how their meaning may be apprehended. We suppose that Jesus desired to make some private communication to Peter, and on that account commanded Peter to follow him. John, who may not have known this, follows Peter, and the latter therefore calls out to Christ: "Lord, what shall this man do?" But in this case, the reply of Christ, "If I will," etc., is wholly inappropriate. For there are but two cases conceivable: *either* it seemed right to Christ that John should accompany them, and he intended a reproof to Peter, in which case his language should have been, "let him come with us quietly," or, "he may hear what we say," or something similar, *or*, he meant to reprove John's ill-timed attendance upon them; the words would then have been, "do not follow us, remain where you are." It is impossible to discover how Christ could then employ the *μένειν, tarry*, for the disciple did not remain, but went with them. Besides, in this interpretation of the passage, the *ἕως ἔρχομαι, till I come*, is altogether unintelligible. For if we take it in the simplest sense, "until I return," viz., from his walking aside with Peter, the reply would not be *against*, but *favourable* to Peter. For while it was his wish that John should not come after them, yet the reply appears plainly to convey a reproof to Peter. Besides, apart from the difficulty of understanding the words in themselves, it would be inexplicable how the report concerning John could have arisen from an occurrence so purely commonplace; for that report, although false, unquestionably originated from some cause. We are therefore compelled to admit that the interpretation of the occurrence, as a merely external event, is untenable, and that all who have sought to establish it, have dealt in arbitrary conjecture. They take, for example, the *μένειν*, *tarry*, either as "be with me," or, "remain with me," and then the *ἕως ἔρχομαι*, *until I come*, has no meaning; for we speak of returning only to one in whose presence we are not; but, in this case, according to the hypothesis, both Peter and John remained present with the Lord. For what purpose, then, this added clause? Or, again, they supply with the *μένειν* the word *ὧδε*, "If I will that John remain *here*;" but it was precisely Peter's wish that John should not go with them; thus the language would have been in accordance with the desire of Peter, which does not correspond with the fact.

Finally, if we decide that the emphasis should be laid upon the *θέλω*, *I will*, "I can command him either to remain or to come with us, thou hast nothing to say in the matter," then, as we have not *ἐγὼ θέλω*, this mode of completing the thought is too harsh to allow our supposing that John required it of his readers; especially since it must have been his chief object here to make himself clearly understood, as he had to controvert a false interpretation of the words.

But the whole passage, dark as it appears, becomes plain and luminous, if, as we have already proposed, the whole be understood as a symbolical transaction, to which we are further guided by the girding in verse 18. The Lord desired to point out still more precisely to Peter the way which *he* should walk on earth. It was the way of following Christ, and bearing the cross in a severe conflict with the world. By certain steps which he took, Jesus symbolically represented this; which steps occasioned Peter again to draw nearer to the Lord. Whatever may appear surprising in the representation will be removed, if we imagine ourselves spectators of the living scene. That which now lies before us cold and dry, in lifeless letters and words, was, in the actual scene, enlivened by the Saviour's significant and spiritual expression. Whilst he communicated to the disciple the final disclosures regarding his destiny, his look, his bearing, formed a living commentary upon the external act which he performed. We must therefore suppose that the disciple perfectly understood all that was thus signified. Without this, the whole proceeding would have been absolutely devoid of meaning. This assumed, all that follows has a significancy in perfect accordance with our explanation. Peter, somewhat depressed by the prospect of the difficult way which he was to travel, asks, when he sees John following them, "Lord, how then will it fare with this man?" As this question, however, did not proceed from a perfectly pure state of mind, but from a somewhat envious glance at the more tranquil destiny of John, the discourse of Christ assumes a certain tone of reproof. Jesus explains to him "that his, Peter's, part was to follow the Lord; that he was not to look to the course of another," and that "John should remain until he would come." Now it is plain that "tarry" (μένειν) is the converse of "follow" (ἀκολουθεῖν), namely, a peaceful, quiet, waiting for the coming of Lord. But some referred this coming to the second advent, and concluded that John should live to behold it (2 Cor. v. 4).* The Evangelist denies this interpretation, and in an impressive manner repeats the words of Jesus, leaving the discovery of their import to the acuteness of the reader himself. The Lord's coming manifestly referred only to the death of the disciple.† Hence the meaning is, "John shall tarry, living in quiet and peace, until the moment when the Lord shall come to call him hence. Peter, in the midst of trials and contests, shall follow his Lord even to the cross." But here the reflection will occur to many, that to follow the Lord in this sense could not have been enjoined as the peculiar duty of Peter, since the same obligation devolves equally upon all Christians, whence it cannot be admitted that John was to be exempted from it. This remark is perfectly true in some respects, and certainly no person can be entirely exempted from the duty of thus following the Lord. But with equal certainty experience testifies that the spiritual development of believers assumes very distinct aspects. In one it is a continuous, heavy, and bitter series of sufferings; his whole life is a constant bearing of the cross. With many, life glides smoothly onwards, unchequered by any grievous disasters, and gently also do they pass into their eternal home. Such differences, it is obvious, do not occur by chance, but according to the providence of the Lord; since all destinies, which are wisely ordered in congruity with the characters of men, must subserve the object of perfecting the moral life. Now in Peter and John (compare the introduction to John) we perceive, as it were, the representatives of two entirely different courses of life; of that which is powerfully

* When, regardless of this passage, many persons, both in ancient and modern times, would attribute to John a longevity extending to Christ's second advent, it is certainly a strange misinterpretation of his most public declaration. Augustine mentions the report, that although John was buried, he still breathed in the grave, so that the earth which covered him moved.

† The selection of the expression ἕως ἔρχομαι can be explained only from the view entertained by the first Christians, that the second coming of Christ was near at hand. (Compare at Matth. xxiv. 1.) But in this passage the meaning of the expression is modified by its connexion.

agitated, and of that which attains its development in tranquillity and peace. The prophecy of the Lord directly points to this fact, and that without at all limiting the general truth, that to every man "strait is the gate, and narrow the way which leadeth unto life."

Ver. 24, 25.—It has been already observed in the critical introduction to this chapter, that its concluding words never proceeded from John the Evangelist, but were probably appended to it by some person unknown. When penning the first words, he may probably have had in view the parallel passage in John xix. 35 (compare also 3 John v. 12); and in what follows them, may have had regard to John xx. 30. But he pursues the two parallels with so little skill that he immediately betrays himself to be an imitator. The concluding hyperbole, particularly, is altogether foreign to the spirit of John. It must have been very early interpolated, however, for it is found in all the manuscripts.

Here we close our observations upón the history of the Lord's sublime life—a life which, issuing from the depths of Divinity, and planting itself in the depths of humanity, reveals even in its humiliation,* an incomparable, all-transcending lustre, glory, and beauty. The glorified Saviour, as the perfected fruit of this life's development, returns to the bosom of the Father, from which the impulse of love had sent forth the eternal Word. But Christ left behind him in the world the impress of his own character, and also a little circle of friends, in whose hearts his spirit had found an abode. This little company was the germ of a new world—the embryo of an unimagined future. A single millenium had not elapsed before this newly created world began to assert the sovereignty of Christianity over the earth. "The life, nature, and essence of Christ had become a legacy to the world. One century struggled for his sepulchre; a second contended concerning his flesh and blood; and a third made his revealed will the subject of their disputations." Yet however painful it was, and still is, to see sin thus frequently striving, there is an abundant source of consolation in the reflection, that the object of such strife is he who came to make an end of all animosity, the Prince of Peace. He will also finally tranquillize the strife about himself.

* An appropriate conclusion to this account is furnished by that noble passage in the "Dämmerungen Für Deutschland" of Jean Paul:—"There once trod our earth a single being, who, by his sole moral omnipotence, controlled other ages, and founded an immortality peculiarly his own. He, gently blooming, and tractable to influences from on high, like the sunflower, but in his ardour and power of attracting, a sun, he, still with mildness of aspect, drew alike himself, nations and ages to the universal and original sun. It is the meek Spirit whom we name 'Jesus Christ.' If he was, then there is a Providence—or rather he was it."

THE

ACTS OF THE APOSTLES

Poena linguarum dispersit homines, donum;
linguarum dispersos in unum populum collegit.

GROTIUS.

INTRODUCTION.

It has been our practice hitherto to treat but briefly the introductions to the several books, inasmuch as we must refer for special investigations to discussions embraced in the science of Introduction. In the case of the Acts of the Apostles, there is need of still fewer introductory remarks, because, in the first place, with respect to most of the questions which are handled in introductions, there is little to be said in reference to this treatise: their importance is smaller here than in the other books of the New Testament; the genuineness of the work, to give but one example, having scarcely ever been doubted. In the second place, the necessary biographical notices, especially respecting Paul, will naturally present themselves both in the exposition of the book of Acts itself, and also more fully still in the exposition of the Pauline epistles and in the general introduction to them, on which account, to save repetitions, they are here entirely omitted. And finally, with respect to chronology, although it is certainly a very important subject and plainly belongs to an introduction to the Acts, yet its peculiar nature is such that, on account of its mathematical and astronomical aspects, a fundamental and independent investigation of it is practicable only to a few, and yet without this investigation, detailed communications on the subject are of little value. I have therefore satisfied myself with giving in the exposition short notices, according to the best authorities, as hints to those readers who wish to see their own way in this intricate region: for deeper researches application must be made to the chronological works themselves.

It has already been remarked in the introduetion of the Gospel of Luke (see Comm. Part I., sect. 6), that the Acts of the Apostles forms only the second part of the historical work which that Evangelist prepared for Theophilus (Luke i. 1; Acts i. 1).* This con-

* In the Gospel all references to the Acts are wanting; the question therefore suggests itself, whether Luke, while composing the one designed to add the other. Perhaps the plan of the Acts was first formed after the completion of the Gospel; yet it is highly probable that there was no great interval of time between the composition of the two.—The opinion of Mayerhoff, which he has expressed in his introduction to the writings of Peter, that it was not Luke, but Timothy, who wrote both the Acts of the Apostles and the Gospel that bears Luke's name, has already been sufficiently refuted.

nexion with the Gospel furnishes a powerful argument in defence of the genuineness of the book of Acts. Everything in fact which serves for a proof of the genuineness of the Gospel, proves the same thing in reference to the Acts, in consequence of their unity as a literary production. And as withal there is nothing in the book itself tending to awaken suspicion, no one has affirmed its spuriousness in the proper sense of the term; the most that has been attempted has been to bring into doubt the credibility of some of the sources which Luke has employed. In this way, for example, are we to understand the doubts which De Wette (Introd. to the New Test. p. 203) has expressed against the book of Acts. And the history of the book in the most ancient times accords entirely with what we have stated. The Acts of the Apostles was never assailed in the church catholic; and therefore it was ranked among the homologoumena. (Compare Euseb. H. E. III. 25.) Individual sects indeed of later origin, as the Severians (Euseb. H. E. IV. 29), the Marcionites (Tertul. cont. Marc. V. 2), the Manichæans (August. Epist. 237) rejected the Acts, but only on dogmatical grounds, and without holding the work to be fictitious. It is quite recently that Baur (Tübing. Zeitscrift, 1836, H. 3) has attempted for the first time to transfer to the Acts of the Apostles the mythical character which Strauss has ascribed to the Gospels. He sets it down altogether as a historical romance, and regards the whole work as an apologetic fiction in defence of the Apostle Paul against the assaults of the followers of Peter; and this he holds to be proved by the circumstance that the author always gives designed prominence to the fact, that Paul preached first to the Jews, and then went to the Gentiles when the Jews rejected him. But the utter emptiness of this hypothesis has been already exposed by Kling. (Studien, 1837, Part 2.)

Yet, although the Acts of the Apostles was always acknowledged by the great body of the primitive church, it was not one of those books of the New Testament that were widely circulated and much read. The Gospel of Luke, it is probable, excited more general interest, particularly as the history of Paul and Peter, wherever these apostles had been heard themselves, would be orally communicated; and therefore the former half of Luke's work was more frequently transcribed, and was placed at an ealier period in the Gospel collection. With most correct appreciation, however, the church admitted the Acts of the Apostles also into the Canon of the New Testament; here it forms a more essential link in the chain: it is as it were, the stem, shooting up immediately from the root of the Gospels, and bearing the rich crown of the epistles as its blossoms.

(Compare on this point Tholuck's Credibilty, p. 136, and Bleek's Review in the Studien, 1836, No. 4.)

The separation, however, of the book of Acts from the Gospel has had the effect, first, of causing a separate title to be affixed to it, and secondly, of exposing its text to greater corruption than that of the Gospel. The corruptions of the text appear particularly in the codices D. and E., which exhibit very marked interpolations in the Acts of the Apostles. They are not, however, to be regarded as constituting a separate recension of the book; the interpolations bear evident traces of having sprung incidentally from the difficulties of the narrative, or of being short notices that have been appended. Their great prevalence in the Acts could spring only from the fact that for a long period this book was but little read in the church,* and thus the opportunity was wanting of immediately removing spurious additions, by the comparison of different copies. The more widely, it is plain, that any composition is circulated, and the more numerous the copies which are taken from it, the more difficult must it be for spurious additions to spread themselves through the whole mass of manuscripts in circulation. The title of the book *πράξεις τῶν ἀποστόλων* was certainly not prefixed to the Acts by Luke: for the manuscripts differ very much with respect to it; he would himself probably have named it *λόγος δεύτερος*. But still the name would very readily suggest itself, after the separation of the book from the Gospel, since even in profane authors *πράξεις* occurs in the signification of "*res gestæ*," proceedings. (Comp. Xenoph. Cyrop. I. 3, 1.) It is certain, however, that the name of the canonical book was not derived from the apocryphal *πράξεις*, but the reverse; the canonical is the older work, and furnished the occasion for the forgery of the other.

As to the *time* and *place* of the composition of the book of Acts, the necessary statements have already been made in the remarks upon the Gospel of Luke. I have only here to add, that De Wette is certainly wrong when he concludes from Luke xxi. that the Gospel as well as the Acts of the Apostles must have been written after the destruction of Jerusalem. The exact references of that chapter to this great event, can furnish no ground at all for supposing the predictions which it contains to have been written after the event; because even in the Old Testament there are found entirely similar predictions. (Comp. the Commentary on Matth. xxiv.)

Again, the *design* and *language* of the Acts of the Apostles are determined by the fact that the book is addressed to Theophilus.

* Even at the close of the fourth century, Chrysostom, at the commencement of his exposition of the Acts, writes: *πολλοῖς τοῦτο τὸ βιβλίον οὐδ' ὅτι ἐστὶ γνώριμόν ἐστιν*. In this, however, there is probably something of rhetorical exaggeration. We know that the book of Acts was regularly read in the Greek Church between Easter and Pentecost, and according to Augustine, the same custom prevailed in Africa too. This book of Scripture therefore could not possibly be so utterly unknown to Christians. (Comp. Bingham orig. vol. vi. 63, etc.)

As to its design, the circumstance in question clearly shews that it was primarily of a private nature: it was intended to give Theophilus, who, as was remarked at Luke i. 3, was probably a distinguished Roman, and had been converted to the gospel, information both respecting the character of Christ and the first formation of the church. Theophilus accordingly stands before us as the representative of enquiring heathens in general; and the Acts of the Apostles is a book most thoroughly adapted to the wants of such. It makes its readers accurately acquainted only with the individuals who had laboured among the Gentiles, especially in Rome itself, viz., Peter and Paul; and yet it treats only of their labours *beyond the limits* of Rome and Italy, for what happened there is presupposed by Luke to be known. In like manner we find the way in which the gospel passed from the Jews to the Gentiles described with peculiar minuteness, as in the history of Cornelius, and how the relation between the Jewish and the Gentile Christians was settled; yet so that we are not entitled to regard it as the main design of the author, to exhibit the transference of Christianity from the Jews to the Gentiles. The marked prominence which is given to points relating to this matter, is rather an incidental result of the very ample account we have of Paul, by whose ministry this transfer was effected. Any aim of a different kind, such as perhaps a history of all the apostles, or a general history of missions, or of the Christian church, is not to be ascribed to the author, because there is none to which the contents of the book properly adjust themselves. Now, these circumstances plainly lead to the conclusion that the Acts of the Apostles could not have been written in any other than the Greek tongue: and the same remark has already been made as to the first part of the work, viz., Luke's Gospel. The Hellenic tongue, in fact, was the general medium of literary communication at the time; and as Luke himself was of Greek origin, nothing was more natural than that he should use this language. The decided Hebraisms of the work have been supposed to furnish an argument, rendering it probable that Luke wrote the Acts in Hebrew, or rather in Aramaic; but it has been forgotten that the author's own style must be carefully distinguished from the language of the original documents which he employed. (Comp. Comm. on Luke i. 1–4.) For as we have seen that Luke employed documents in preparing his Gospel, we must suppose the same thing with respect to the Acts of the Apostles. Unfortunately we have never yet received from the celebrated critic, to whom we are indebted for so accurate an investigation of Luke, the promised treatise on the Acts; but, at all events, the leading idea stands secure, that in the case of the Acts too, Luke elaborated his work from documentary sources. Whether Schleiermacher entertained the same view of the Acts of the Apostles, which he has defended in reference to the Gospel, viz., that the author inserted his documents without change, I know not; but at all events I cannot acquiesce in this idea. As in the Gospel, so I find in the Acts too, upon the whole, with the exception of a few passages (see, for example, what is stated at chap. xiii. 1), a free treatment of the documents employed, which for the most part, betray themselves to us only by the style, deviating perceptibly from that of Luke himself. To specify, therefore, with precision, where one document ends and another begins, I hold to be a very questionable proceeding.

In like manner, it is impossible to state with certainty any particulars respecting the origin of the documents; but we may reject without scruple, all conjectures as to the use of the apocryphal πράξεις by Luke. For these apocryphal Acts came into existence, as was formerly remarked, at a much later period; and, besides, the historical documents of the Acts of the Apostles have not a syllable in them that savours of the apocryphal character. Far more probable is it that Luke, in reference to events which he had not observed as an eye-witness, consulted, for information on single incidents, journals or memoirs whose credibility he had sufficiently ascertained (Luke i. 4). It has, indeed, been doubted in recent times, whether Luke ever relates anything as an eye-witness. Schleiermacher even alleged that the passage in which the narrative proceeds in the plural, furnish no certain proof that Luke journeyed along with Paul, for the plural might proceed from the author of the travels consulted by Luke, who appears to have been Timothy. Mayerhoff followed out this supposition so far, as to declare that Timothy was the author of the whole book of the Acts, as has already been mentioned. Bleek, in the review of Mayerhoff's work, referred to above (p. 159), while he is opposed to the idea that Timothy was the author of the Acts, yet thinks that there is certainly some truth in the supposition, that Luke is not to be viewed as included under the plural form. The same view has also been maintained by Ulrich in the Sudien. for 1837, Part 2. Now, although there is certainly much that appears to favour this new observation, yet I have not been able to convince myself of its soundness, and I shall adduce the grounds which have determined my judgment at Acts xvi. 12. Here I only remark that, if the view were established, it could have no influence upon the credibility of the Acts; for this rests not upon the circumstance of Luke's being an eye-witness, which in any case applies only to the smallest and least important part of the work, but upon the apostolic authority of Paul, and upon the testimony of the ancient church, which had the gift of trying not only the genuine and the spurious, but also the Divine and the human.

And what holds good of the historical parts of the Acts of the Apostles, that for the most part at least they were compiled from written documents, must also be supposed in reference to the speeches, which, doubtless, in general formed integral portions of the documents which Luke employed. Only, of course, it cannot be supposed, that these speeches were written down on the spot as they were delivered. We have only to imagine to ourselves affecting situations, the parting, for example, of Paul from the Ephesian elders at Miletus, Acts xx. 17, etc., to feel the incongruity of this supposition. The speech of Paul on the occasion referred to, so greatly moved the minds of all who were present, that they burst into tears. Who, in such circumstances, thinks of mechanically writing down the spoken living words? It may be apprehended, indeed, that, if no writing took place at the moment, all security for the credibility of the speeches is gone. But this fear, as has already been remarked in the introduction to the Gospels, plainly proceeds from a want of faith in the power of the Spirit of truth. If we do not suppose this Spirit to have been at work in the mind of the writer of the Acts, and of the apostles under whose eye he wrote, then we have no guarantee at all for the contents; but, if such an influence of the Spirit be acknowledged, then no harm can result from the freer view of the speeches indicated above. This, however, does not oblige us to deny that notations might be made of many impressive speeches, a few hours or days after they were delivered. Rather is it in the highest degree probable that this was the case from the nature of many discourses, as, for example, the speech of Stephen; for the contents of this speech are so peculiar, that we can scarcely conceive it to have been constructed without any notations.* We must not, however, insist upon a *literal* reproduction of what was spoken, but rather be satisfied with holding that the essential matter of the most abbreviated discourses, and, above all, the spirit which breathed in them, is communicated to us. And thus these discourses perfectly fulfil the important service which, as also the whole book of

* This is rather strongly expressed. Still, it is true that the inspiration possessed by the sacred penmen does not require us to suppose that they employed none of the ordinary methods of preserving the memory of important events and declarations. Doubtless they made notations of such things as they wished to remember, and doubtless they investigated with care whatever they were about to record. Luke plainly mentions that he had perfect understanding of all things from the very first, or, as the words rather mean, that he had carefully examined or traced out, παρηκολουθηκοτι, all things from the very first, before proceeding to write to Theophilus. The inspiration of the Holy Ghost did not suspend the faculties of the apostles: their powers of memory and judgment and imagination were all in vigorous exercise when they wrote and spoke, and hence the individual peculiarities that characterize their writings. But their unequalled distinction was this, that they were infallibly guarded from error, and guided to truth. The Spirit of the Most High gave them understanding. They spake as they were moved by the Holy Ghost.—Tr.

the Acts in its historical portions, they were designed to perform for the later ages of the church. They afford us a perfectly just view of the labours of the apostles in teaching, and of the collective inner life of the earliest churches. In this respect the Acts of the Apostles is a work whose value to the church is quite inestimable; and, if by any mischance she had been robbed of it, there would have been a gap in her history which nothing could supply. Even although the lost writings of Papias and Hegesippus were still at our command, the want of the book of Acts would be most sensibly felt, because it communicates to us nothing but genuine information, whereas in those works truth appeared largely mingled with error, and we should have been unable in all cases to separate the one from the other with certainty.

With respect to *treatises* upon the Acts of the Apostles, the expositions of Clemens Alexandrinus (in the ὑποτυπώσεις), of Origen, of Diodorus of Tarsus, of Theodorus of Mopsuestia, have perished. Of Chrysostom only there are preserved to us fifty-five homilies on this book. But they are not to be ranked amongst the best productions of this great preacher, so that some have been disposed even to doubt their genuineness. Their inferiority, however, is accounted for by the consideration that he must plainly have composed this commentary amid manifold interruptions, and therefore must have bestowed less pains upon it than upon his other expository works. From a later period, we have the commentaries of Œcumenius and Theophylact. In more recent times, with the exception of expositions of the Acts contained in the general works of Grotius, Wolf, and others, we have very few special commentaries upon the book. Besides Limborch's great work (Rotterdam 1711), we must particularly notice the Dissertationes in Acta Apostolorum of J. E. Chr. Walch (Jena, 1756–1761, 3 vols.); the exposition of Morus, edited by Dindorf (Leipsic, 1794, 2 vols.); a translation of the Acts, with Annotations, by Thiess (Leipsic, 1800). In Koppe's New Test., vol. iii., there is an exposition of the Acts by Heinrichs (Göttingen, 1809). The most recent exposition is that of Kuinoel (Leipsic, 1818). Stier has written upon the speeches in the Acts (2 parts, Leipsic, 1829, 1830).* Menken's work, styled "Blicke in das leben des Apostels Paulus" (Bremen, 1828), embraces an exposition of chapters xv.—xx. of the Acts. Among recent commentators upon the whole New Testament, Meyer as yet is the first who has handled

* Stier attempts to point out most precise arrangements in the speeches of the Acts; but in my judgment this method of treating the book, which had already prevailed in the school of Baumgarten, is not serviceable to the exegesis of it. In another quarter too, I refer to Seyler (in Ullman's Studien, 1832, part i., page 44, etc.), a similar treatment of the text of the New Testament is recommended. But the thoughts in the New Test. and in the Holy Scriptures generally, appear to be not so much arranged after a logical method, as united by a higher unity of spirit.

the Acts. [De Wette's Kurze Erklärung der Apostol. Geschichte, Leipsic, 1848. Commentary on the Original Text of the Acts of the Apostles by H. B. Hackett. Boston, 1852.]—[K.

Finally, as respects *chronology*,* it is only here and there that Luke specifies the interval of time between the occurrences which he narrates, and even then only in general periods of two or three years. (Compare Acts xx. 31, xxiv. 27, xxviii. 30.) He usually confines himself to indefinite expressions "in those days," "at that time" (*ἐν ταύταις ἡμέραις, κατ' ἐκεῖνον τὸν καιρόν*), from which chronology can derive but little assistance. However, he mentions some occurrences which are recorded in profane history, and whose date therefore can be in some measure ascertained. From these points chronologists have endeavoured with remarkable sagacity to form an arrangment of the leading events in the Acts of the Apostles. Among such points may be mentioned particularly, (1) the famine under Claudius Cæsar, which the prophet Agabus predicted (xi. 28); (2) the expulsion of the Jews from Rome by the same Emperor (xviii. 2); (3) the entrance upon office of the procurator Porcius Festus (xxiv. 27). By means of these ascertainable points we may with some probability arrange in chronological order the leading events of the Acts; though how far our arrangement falls short of *historical certainty*, is apparent from the great multitude of different computations which have been derived from them. The uncertainty, besides, of the year of Christ's birth and death increases the chronological difficulties. I confine myself to the task of laying before my readers two chronological tables. The one presents a view of political circumstances in connexion with the parallel events of the Acts, according to my own opinion of the chronology, in which, upon the whole, I have followed Hug; the other presents a comparative view of the different computations that have been made respecting the leading events of the Acts. For the latter the learned world is indebted to Dr. Gröschen (see Ullmann's Studien, year 1831, H. 7), who has most kindly permitted me to insert it in my exposition of the Acts. For the relationships which subsisted between the different branches of the Herodian family, I refer to the genealogical tree, which Karl von Raumer has admitted into his geography of Palestine. (2d Edit., p. 373.)

* Compare the chronological work: Rud. Anger de temporum in Actis Apostolorum ratione. Lipsiæ, 1833.

FIRST CHRONOLOGICAL TABLE.

Æra of Dionysius.	*Emperors.*	*Rulers of Palestine.*			*Rulers of Neighbouring States.*		*Events in the Book of Acts.*
		JUDEA.	GALILEE.	GAULONITIS	ABILENE.	CHALCIS.	
14	Tiberius.	Roman procurators govern the country.	Herod Antipas.	Philip.			
33				Philip†.			33. Ascension of Christ.
35							35. Conversion of Paul.
36		Pilate displaced.					
37	Caligula.		Antipas displaced.				
38							38. Paul's first journey to Jerusalem, Acts ix. 26, compared with Gal. i. 18.
40		Herod Agrippa governs the whole of Palestine.					
41	Claudius.				Lysanias.	Herod, brother of Agrippa.	41. Paul goes with Barnabas to Antioch, Acts xi. 25.
44		Famine in Palestine. Agrippa†. Acts xii. 20, etc. Roman procurators govern the land.					44. Paul's second journey to Jerusalem. First missionary journey of Paul, Acts xiii. 1, xiv. 28.
49						Herod† Agrippa min. follows.	49. Paul's return to Antioch, Acts xiv. 28.
52		Expulsion of the Jews from Rome, Acts xviii. 2.			Lysanias†.		52. Paul's third journey to Jerusalem, Acts xv.; Gal. ii. 1. Towards end of the year second missionary journey.
53				Agrippa minor receives Gaulonitis and Abilene.		Chalcis is assigned to Syria.	53. Paul in Corinth.
54	Nero.						
55							55. Pentecost. Paul's fourth journey to Jerusalem. Third missionary journey.
56, 57							56, 57. Stay in Ephesus.
60							60. Paul's fifth journey to Jerusalem. Imprisonment.
62		Porcius Festus is procurator.					62. Paul's trial before Porcius Festus.
63							63. Paul's arrival in Rome.
65							65. Completion of Book of Acts. Second imprisonment.
66		Gessius Florus, procurator.					
67							67. Death of the Apostle. Jewish war.
68	Nero†.						

SECOND CHRONOLOGICAL TABLE.

EVENTS.	1 *Eusebius.*	2 *Hieronymus.*	3 *Baronius.*	4 *Usher*	5 *Calvisius.*
Birth of Christ.	2 or 1 before Chr. æra, 6 Jan.	2 or 1 before Chr. æra, 25 Dec.	3 before Chr. æra, 25 Dec.	5 before Chr. æra, 25 Dec.	3 before Chr. æra, in October.
Baptism.	29	29	29 6 Jan.	30	29
Death.	33	32	32 March.	33 3 April.	33 3 April.
Stoning of Stephen.	33		32 26 Dec.	34	33
Conversion of Paul.	33		34	36	34
Paul's first journey to Jerusalem, Acts ix.; Gal. i. 18.			37	38	37
The second, Acts xi. 12.			42	44	38
The third, Acts xv.; Gal. ii. 1.			49 14 years after conversion.	52 14 years after first journey.	48 14 years after conversion.
The fourth, Acts xviii. 22.				56	52
A problematical journey to Jerusalem, Gal. ii. 1.					
The fifth journey and imprisonment.			56	60	56, about Pentecost.
Paul's journey to Rome.	55	57	56, Nov. the 2 years refer to Felix.*	62	58
Paul's arrival in Rome.			57, May	63	59 in Spring.
Deliverance from imprisonment.	After 2 years	After 2 years	59	65	61
Return to Rome.	67 ?			66	
Death.	68	69	67 29 June.	67 29 June.	64

* See note page 172.

EVENTS.	6 *Bengel.*	7 *Vogel.*	8 *Süsskind.*	9 *Eichhorn.*	10 *Schmidt.*
Birth of Christ.	4 before Chr. 25 Dec.	3 before Chr. æra.	3 before Chr. begin. of Mar.	4 before Chr. æra?	
Baptism.	27 8 Nov.	28	29 begin. March.	30?	
Death.	30 6 April.	31	32	32	
Stoning of Stephen.	30		32	37	
Conversion of Paul.	31	33	32	37 or 38	41
Paul's first journey to Jerusalem, Acts ix.; Gal. i. 18.	33	36	35	40 or 41	Never made.
The second, Acts xi. 12.	41–44	44	Gal. ii. 1, 46, 14 yrs. af. conversion.	44	44 Gal. i. 18.
The third, Acts xv.; Gal. ii. 1.	47, 14 years after the first journey.	47 14 years after conversion.	47?	52	55
The fourth, Acts xviii. 22.	49	54	50	56	
A problematical journey to Jerusalem, Gal. ii. 1.					
The fifth journey and imprisonment.	53, about Pentecost.	57	53, about Pentecost.	60 in Summer.	59
Paul's journey to Rome.	55	59	55	62	61
Paul's arrival in Rome.	56 in Spring	59 or 60		63 in Spring.	62 in Spring.
Deliverance from imprisonment.	58	62		Did not take place.	Did not take place.
Return to Rome.	?	?		Did not take place.	Did not take place.
Death.	67 29 June.	65		65–68	64

EVENTS.	11 *Hemlien.*	12 *Bertholdt.*	13 *Heinrichs.*	14 *Kuinoel.*	15 *Hug.*
Birth of Christ.				?	1 before Chr. æra in Feb.
Baptism.				?	29, in Feb.
Death.	33		33	33	29
Stoning of Stephen.	36		36	37 or 38	
Conversion of Paul.	36–38	40	37	40	35
Paul's first journey to Jerusalem, Acts ix.; Gal. i. 18.	39–41	43	40	43	38
The second, Acts xi. 12.	14 years after conversion Gal. ii. 1.	44, 4 years after conversion.	44, 4 years after first journey.	44, 4 years after conversion.	44
The third, Acts xv.; Gal. ii. 1.	49?	52	?	52	52, 14 years after first journey.
The fourth, Acts xviii. 22.	54 Easter.	55	52	Not made.	55, about Pentecost.
A problematical journey to Jerusalem, Gal. iii. 2.					
The fifth journey and imprisonment.	59 or 60	58, after Pentecost.	60	57	59 Pentecost.
Paul's journey to Rome.	61 or 62	60	62	59	61
Paul's arrival in Rome.	62 or 63 Spring.	61 Spring.	63 Spring.	60 Spring.	62 Spring.
Deliverance from imprisonment.	64 or 65	63	65	62	64
Return to Rome.	66 or 67	?		?	66
Death.	68	67		67	67

EVENTS.	16 a. *Sanclemente and Ideler.*	17 *Schrader.*	18 *Hemsen.*	19 *Schott.*	20 *Feilmoser.*
Birth of Christ.	1 before Chr. æra, in 25 Dec.				?
Baptism.	25 end, or 26 beginning.				29
Death.	29, 15 April, acc. to Ideler.	35			33
Stoning of Stephen.	16 b. De Wette.	35	•		
Conversion of Paul.	35–38	39	35	40 or 41	35
Paul's first journey to Jerusalem, Acts ix.; Gal. i. 18.	38–41	42	38	42 or 43	38
The second, Acts xi. 12.	44	44	44	44 end, or 45 beginning.	44
The third, Acts xv.; Gal. ii. 1.	52	47	52, 14 years after first journey.	47 or 48, 4 years after first journey.	52 14 years after first journey.
The fourth, Acts xviii. 22.	56 16 b. De Wette.	51, about Pentecost.	55, about Pentecost.		55
I problematical journey to Jerusalem Gal. iii. 2.		56, 14 years after the first journey.			
The fifth journey and imprisonment.	60	59 Pentecost.	59	57	58 Pentecost.
Paul's journey to Rome.	62	61	61	59	60
Paul's arrival in Rome.	63 Spring.	62 Spring.	62 Spring.	60 Spring.	61 Spring.
Deliverance from imprisonment.		Did not take place.	Did not take place.		63
Return to Rome.		Did not take place.	Did not take place.		?
Death.		64	64	64 or 65	?

NOTATIONS FOR THE SECOND CHRONOLOGICAL TABLE.

1. Eusebii Chronicon. Hist. Eccl. i. 5, ii. 1, 22, 26, iii. 1, vii. 32, vii. 1.

2. Hieronymi Chronicon. Ed. Vallarsii, T. viii. Catal. Viror. illust. c. 5. Comment. in Jes. c. 2.

3. Baronii Annales, vol. I.

4. Usserii Annales. Genevæ, 1722, p. 568.

5. Calvisii opus Chronologicum. Francof, 1620, p. 424.

6. Bengelii ordo temporum. Stuttg. 1741, p. 218.

7. Vogel, Versuch über Chronologische Standpunkte der Lebensgeschichte Pauli. In Gabler's Journal für auserlesene theologische Literatur, Bd. 1, st. 2.

8. Süskind, neuer Versuch uber chronolog. Standpunkte in Bengel's Archiv. Bd. 1, st. 1.

9. Eichhorn's Einl. ins N. T., B. i. s. 440; Bd. ii. s. 48; Bd. iii. s. 32, ff., 364, ff.

10. Schmidt (J. E. Chr.) Chronologie der Apostelgeschichte, in Keil's und Tzschirner's Analecten, Bd. iii. st. 1, s. 128, ff. Einl. in N. T. Giessen, 1804, s. 184, ff.

11. Hänlein Einl. ins N. T. 2te Aufl. Erlangen, 1809, Bd. iii. s. 158, s. 298, ff.

12. Bertholdt, Einl. Bd. v. 2te hälfte s. 2693, ff.

13. Heinrichs Acta Apostolorum, Gott. 1809.

14. Kuinoel Comment. in Acta Apostolorum, Lips. 1818.

15. Hug's Einl., 3te Aufl. Bd. ii., s 307 ff.

16. [a]Sanclementii de vulgaris æræ emendatione Rom. 1793. Ideler's Handb. d. Chronologie Th. ii. s. 366, ff.

16. [b]De Wette's Einl. ins N. T. s. 212.

17. Schrader's Apostel Paulus.

18. Hemsen, der Apostel Paulus.

19. Schotti Isagoge in N. T. P. 189, sqq.

20. Feilmoser's Einl. ins N. T. 2 te. Aufl. Tübingen 1830. S. 306, ff.; 318, ff.

In the second chronological table, see page 168, where Paul's journey to Rome, as fixed by Baronius, is stated, the words are added, "the two years refer to Felix." The two years meant are those mentioned in Acts xxiv. 27, which all chronologists, with the exception of Baronius, have understood to refer to Paul's captivity; but Baronius understands them to refer to Felix, and therefore he places the apostle's arrival in Rome in the same year as his fifth journey to Jerusalem. In this he is undoubtedly wrong, for the administration of Felix had lasted a number of years, as is plain from Acts xxiv. 10; and there being no special event in his life mentioned to which the two years can apply, we are shut up to the conclusion that they refer to the imprisonment of Paul in Cæsarea.—Tr.

EXPOSITION

OF THE

ACTS OF THE APOSTLES.

I.

PART FIRST.

FROM THE ASCENSION OF CHRIST TILL THE CONVERSION OF PAUL.

(Acts i. 1—viii. 40.)

§ 1. Christ's Ascension. Choice of an Apostle.

(Acts i. 1–26.)

The first part of the Acts of the Apostles contains a short general survey of the earliest occurrences in the church. With the ascension, which was already noticed at the close of the Gospel, Luke here sets out, that he may first describe in connexion with it the outpouring of the Holy Ghost, and then recount the first results of the preaching of the Gospel. Respecting the source of the information which is here communicated to us, unfortunately we are not now able to state any particulars. The hypothesis has indeed been advanced, that Luke, in this first part of the Acts of the Apostles, may have used documents belonging to the school of Peter, because notices of Peter predominate in it. But this is the case only in appearance, and consequently the hypothesis is deprived of all foundation. It is true, indeed, that after Pentecost Peter stands forth almost as the only speaker; but this happens, not because we have Petrine documents, but because, in fact, Peter was the leading speaker of the young community. From whatever quarter therefore the accounts might come, provided only they were true, Peter must occupy the most prominent position. As early, however, as the v. and viii. chapters, this apostle begins to appear incidentally, and in the vi. and vii. his name does not occur, a circumstance by no means favourable to the hypothesis in question. We think it best, therefore, to leave undetermined what is unknown, and to content ourselves with a careful examination of the precious fragments themselves, respecting the apostolic church, which the narrative of Luke presents to us.

Vers. 1, 2.—The Evangelists commence their narratives with the *coming* of the Redeemer from the world of holiness and bliss into this world of sin and sorrow; Luke, on the other hand, in this second part of his work, commences with the *return* of the Lord into the bosom of the Father. This return itself, however, is also in another point of view, a *coming* of Christ (see Comm. on John xiv. 3), because his departure was the condition on which was suspended the communication of the fulness of the Spirit (John xvi. 7), through whom the Lord now lived among his disciples, not in a mere bodily and outward manner, but dwelling in them constituted the principle of their life. Hence the grand history of what Jesus did and taught (Acts i. 1) does not conclude with his departure to the Father; but Luke now first begins it in a higher strain; for all the subsequent labours of the apostles are but an exhibition of the ministry of the glorified Redeemer himself, who was the principle that operated in them all.

Before our author particularly describes the sublime scene of Christ's departure (already indicated in Luke xxiv. 50–53), he expressly connects his second book with the first, viz., his Gospel. (Λόγος is to be taken in the signification of book, treatise, = סֵפֶר, comp. 1 Chron. xxix. 29, in the Septuagint.) In the clause, ὧν ἤρξατο ὁ Ἰησοῦς κ. τ. λ., interpreters commonly take ἤρξατο as pleonastic; but it is better to retain the proper meaning of this word, and to make the implied contrast lie between the ministry of our Lord upon earth, and his subsequent invisible ministry. (Compare Winer's Gram. p. 539, etc.) As forming the conclusion of Christ's work upon earth, the ἀνάληψις is named (compare at ἀνελήφθη the parallel ἀνεφέρετο in Luke xxiv. 51), which took place after all his commands and charges to the apostles were completed. (Compare John xiv. 15, xv. 12–17.) In the construction there is an uncertainty about the connexion of διὰ πνεύματος ἁγίου; and there is difficulty alike whether we connect it with ἐντειλάμενος or with ἀνελήφθη; hence, the general opinion has been in favour of joining it with οὓς ἐξελέξατο. Finally, the entire period is somewhat incomplete, the μέν having no δέ to follow it. The author would have added: "from this point I now continue my narrative in a second treatise," but was drawn aside from his proposed construction by the mention of the apostles.' (Comp. Winer's Gram., p. 500.)

Vers. 3–5.—The first sentence (ver. 1, 2) is plainly shewn, by its connexion with the following one, to want its conclusion: the τὸν μὲν πρῶτον should naturally have had a ὁ δὲ δεύτερος following it. But from the word ἀνελήφθη Luke immediately takes occasion to proceed to the fact of the ascension, after briefly touching upon the interval between the passion and the final departure of Christ. The presence of the Saviour, for forty days, he mentions first of all, as a perfectly authenticated fact,* and then he brings into view what was the great subject of our Lord's conversations with his disciples, viz., the whole compass of the interests of the kingdom of God. For we must distinguish between λέγων περὶ τῆς βασιλείας and λέγων τὰ περὶ τῆς βασιλείας, the latter of which phrases expresses the thought just indicated. The circumstances also lead to the conclusion that Christ would confide to his disciples, during these last moments of his personal presence, all that he had yet to say respecting the kingdom. (It is plain, finally, from verse 6, that the word βασιλεία cannot here denote the Christian religion, as Kuinoel supposes. On the idea of the βασιλεία consult the Comm., Part I., upon Matth. iii. 2.)

The only particular command of Christ to his disciples, given during this period of forty days, which Luke mentions, is the one to wait patiently for the promise of the Spirit's baptism: with this baptism the public ministry of the apostles was to take its rise. (On this subject compare Luke xxiv. 49, and Matth. iii. 11.) The style changes suddenly from the indirect form to the direct, as is frequently the case with Luke (*e. g.*, Acts xvii. 3, xxii. 24, xxiii. 22). There is a grammatical difficulty in this passage connected with the word συναλιζόμενος in ver. 4. First of all, as respects the reading, many codices have συναυλιζόμενος, which means "dwelling together, living together." The codex D. reads συναλισκόμενος μετ' αὐτῶν, meaning, according to the signification of the verb, "to make expenses together," "to be at joint expenses," "to live together." But both readings are unanimously rejected by critics, and the conjecture of Hemsterhusius (who would read συναλιζομένοις) as little deserves to be approved or admitted into the text, though this reading certainly would make the construction much more simple. But as to the reading which must stand as the right one, the question presents itself how the participle συναλιζόμενος ought to be understood. It may be connected with αὐτοῖς as passive, or be taken as a middle with αὐτούς supplied. The latter view has been preferred by Heinrichs and Kuinoel, on the ground that παρήγγειλεν requires αὐτοῖς to be connected with it: yet there is no certain example to be found of the use of the word in the middle voice. The verb συναλίζω finally = συναθροίζω, to assemble, convene: it comes from the Ionic ἀλής, = the Attic ἀθρόος, "confertus": from which is derived the adverb ἅλις, meaning "in crowds," also equivalent to ἅλις, "enough, sufficient." It is the Latin "salis," from which "satis" was formed.

Vers. 6–8.—From Luke xxiv. 49, 50, it may be plainly perceived

* The word τεκμήριον, which occurs in no other part of the New Testament, embodies the idea of settled, fixed, accredited. See Wisdom of Solomon, v. 11, xix. 13.

that the meeting mentioned in verse 4, and the one in verse 6, are not the same. The promise of the baptism of the Spirit, and the command to tarry for it at Jerusalem, were given by the Lord before his last meeting with the disciples upon the Mount of Olives, where the words that follow were spoken. (Compare verses 9 and 12.) The connexion accordingly is this: "After Jesus had collected his disciples, he commanded them not to leave Jerusalem. When they were afterwards assembled together anew, and that for the last time, they inquired of the Lord whether he would now establish the kingdom to Israel (and whether they perchance should have to continue waiting in Jerusalem for the inauguration of it"). Meyer supposes that it is not the earlier appearance of Christ in Jerusalem which is incidentally mentioned by Luke in the 4th verse; but that the 4th and 6th verses relate to the very same meeting, at which Jesus only enforces anew the direction previously given. But the supposition is inadmissible, because the last appearance in verse 6 is introduced as quite a new topic by *οἱ μὲν οὖν*, whereas verse 4 follows only as a brief reference to *ὀπτανόμενος* and *λέγων* in verse 3: verse 4 contains as yet no independent narrative, but merely forms the connexion with the close of the gospel, and the introduction to what follows in the declaration of the continued presence of the apostles in Jerusalem. The meaning of the question respecting the nearness of the kingdom of God cannot appear in any respect doubtful. The disciples expected, in accordance with their earthly views of the Messiah, a splendid visible introduction of the kingdom of God, accompanied perhaps with a political movement against the Romans, and with respect to this event they inquire whether it should take place just now. Ideas, therefore, like those of Lightfoot—"thou wilt assuredly not now set up thy kingdom for the wicked Jews, who killed thee upon the cross?" or "wilt thou indeed now, when the hatred of the rulers is so strong, and our power so small, wilt thou erect the banner of thy kingdom?"—need no serious refutation.* But, at the same time, there is no tolerable pretext for conceiving the answer of Christ to be of such a nature as would take away all prospect of a future manifestation of his kingdom as a dominion. It is obvious rather, as has been already remarked (Matth. iii. 2, xix. 28), that the very idea of the "kingdom" implies that it shall one day burst out from its secret character, and display itself in a visible and external shape. Although, therefore, there were still obscurities in the views of the disciples respecting the kingdom, yet the Re-

* This latter view was not that of Lightfoot, but of Barkeyus, advanced in the Biblioth. Hagana, T. i. p. 603. He supposed that the words of the disciples expressed astonishment and admiration that, in the circumstances of the case, with so little apparent probability of success, their Master should propose to restore the kingdom to Israel.

deemer did not judge it necessary to sift them, because they could not fail to attain the more spiritual idea by the power of the Spirit whom they were to receive. He expresses himself only in reference to the *time*, but in such a manner as neither to fix anything respecting it, nor yet to deny, which would have been a negative fixing. (See on this subject at Matth. xxiv. 1.) The time of the manifestation of God's kingdom, he declares, it is not given to the disciples, nor to any of mankind at all to know, but it is a thing reserved for the omniscience of the Father. And the circumstance that *father* stands here in the text, and not *God*, renders the passage similar to the words of Mark xiii. 32 (consult the Comm. Part I. p. 902), where the knowledge of this period is denied even to the Son. However, the two passages are by no means to be identified: the passage in Mark xiii. 32 might indeed be explained from the limitation (*κένωσις*) of the Son of God, but here such an explanation is negatived by the connexion, for the words were spoken by the *glorified* Redeemer, in whom humiliation (*κένωσις*) can have no more place. Here, therefore, we must suppose our Lord only teaches his disciples that such knowledge reaches beyond the position of man as such, for whom it would not be advantageous: of his own relation to the Father he says nothing at all here; but as the invisible Father dwelt in him, and was glorified in him (John xiii. 31), so could his knowledge in no respect be different from the knowledge of the Father himself.

(Respecting *ἀποκαθιστάνειν*, see Comm. on Matth. xvii. 11. Here the idea "of bringing again into the ancient condition" looks back to the splendour of the kingdom of David, which the Jews expected the Messiah to restore. The excellent among them, however, conceived this glory to rest upon true godliness and devotion, which they expected the Messiah to instil into his people. The expression *χρόνοι καὶ καιροί* probably follows that of Daniel ii. 21, עִדָּנַיָּא וְזִמְנַיָּא, for which the Seventy employ the same two words. In *χρόνος* it is rather simple time that is expressed, "tempus," in *καιρός* the relations and circumstances of time, "opportunitas.")

As if to compensate for the knowledge which he thus denied to his disciples regarding the times, the Redeemer promises them the power of the Holy Ghost (Luke xxiv. 49) by which they were to be constituted, not so much prophets of the future,* as witnesses of the past. It is the mighty works of God in and upon Christ, for the salvation of the world, especially his resurrection from the dead, which the apostles were to proclaim to the world. From Zion the light goes forth (Isaiah ii. 2), and spreading in ever-widening circles, it fills the globe. We are not required by the phrase *ἕως ἐσχάτου*

* The gift of prophecy is not, of course, here denied to the apostles: it is only represented as not lying at the very foundation of their office. The unveiling of the future appears in a decided manner only in some of them, as, for example, the Evangelist John.

τῆς γῆς, *to the extremities of the earth,* to defend the untenable position that the apostles themselves went into all lands: these words of Christ rather apply through the apostles to all future generations of teachers, and find in them their fulfilment. (See Comm. on Matth. x., where Christ's instruction of the apostles embraces, at the same time, the elements of all the instruction needed by teachers.) To refer the words to Palestine is wholly unsuitable, for the parts of Palestine have been already mentioned: ἔσχατον τῆς γῆς corresponds to the Hebrew קְצֵה הָאָרֶץ. Ps. xix. 5.

Ver. 9–11.—In these verses the act of the ascension itself is described.* With respect first of all to the scene, it is portrayed so simply that we cannot possibly misunderstand it, but by some over-refinement. The Redeemer was raised on high before the eyes of his disciples, and then received by a cloud, most probably a cloud of light, which removed him from their view. (Instead of ἐπήρθη here Luke has, xxiv. 51, διέστη ἀπ' αὐτῶν καὶ ἀνεφέρετο εἰς τὸν οὐρανόν, and Mark, xvi. 19, ἀνελήφθη εἰς τὸν οὐρανόν, as in Acts i. 2.) Luke names (xxiv. 50) as the place where the ascension took place, the neighbourhood of Bethany (ἐξήγαγε αὐτοὺς ἔξω ἕως εἰς Βηθανίαν), with which agrees the statement in verse 12, that the disciples returned from the Mount of Olives, at the foot of which Bethany lay. The same place, therefore, where the deepest humiliation of our Lord occurred, viz., in the conflict of Gethsemane, witnessed also his sublimest elevation. (Compare Zech. xiv. 4, Ezek. xi. 23.) Blessing his disciples, and setting them apart as the champions of truth and righteousness, the Saviour left the scene of his tears and prayers. (Compare Luke xxiv. 50, 51, καὶ ἐπάρας τὰς χεῖρας αὐτοῦ εὐλόγησεν αὐτούς, καὶ ἐγένετο ἐν τῷ εὐλογεῖν αὐτὸν αὐτοὺς διέστη ἀπ' αὐτῶν.) And while the disciples were gazing intently after him, suddenly there stood by their side (without their having noticed whence they came), two men in white raiment, that is, in heavenly robes of light, who suggested to them the fruitlessness of thus looking with the bodily eye after Christ, and rather directed their thoughts to his future return, when they should behold him coming as they had now seen him depart. That this view of the scene is the only one which corresponds to the mind of the narrator, should be acknowledged even by those who deny the reality of the fact: if we compare particularly Mark xvi. 5, Luke xxiv. 4, with Matth. xxviii. 2, John xx. 12, it is manifest that the latter passages represent as angels the men in white robes named in the former; and therefore it admits of no doubt at all, that here too we must understand angels to be meant by the sacred historian. In like manner the phrase οὕτως ἐλεύσεται, ὃν τρόπον ἐθεάσασθε κ. τ. λ., refers, beyond all question, to the visible

* Compare the discussion of Seiler in Velthusen Sylloge Commentt. vol. vi. p. 503, seq.

return of our Lord in his glorified humanity, which is taught by all the New Testament writers (comp. Comm. on Matth. xxv. 31, xxiv. 1), and, with this at the same time his previous departure is also described as a going to the Father, a sitting down at the right hand of God. (Mark xvi. 19.)

All attempts, therefore, to explain the facts of the case on *natural* principles, by referring them to a withdrawment of Christ amid thunder and lightning and thick clouds, are liable to the objection of thrusting into the text what is not there. And again to take this view of the matter, that the narrators supposed indeed their Master to be exalted to heaven, but this merely from a misunderstanding of some such occurrence as is indicated above, is a view alien to the moral character of Christ, who never could lend himself to the device of using accidental external circumstances to deceive his disciples, that they might be led to suppose him elevated to heaven, while he continued to live concealed in some unknown region.*

There is far more plausibility in the *mythical* view of the occurrence before us, which makes a reference to analogous cases in history, such as those of Hercules, Romulus, and others.† The fundamental fact is, on this principle, altogether set aside: we only retain the idea that he who comes from God must again return to God; this idea is legibly stamped upon the account even as it is given to us by Luke. Yet in truth this view is only in appearance more moderate and historical than the former. To leave the fact uncertain, embraces the very same error, from which the explanations on natural principles take their rise. For every one must immediately say to himself, since Christ was a historical personage, he must have left the earth upon which he lived in a definite manner. Now, if his departure did not take place in the way recorded, which some will have to be mythical, then there remains no other than the common exit; and thus we see ourselves conducted to conclusions which impair the character of Christ, equally with those to which the former view led us.‡ Add to this what was

* The utmost extreme of this view was presented in the hypothesis of Brennecke (Lüneburg, 1819), who supposed that Christ continued to labour for twenty-seven years after his crucifixion, in concealment; for he considers the appearance of Jesus to Paul as proof of his continued presence upon the earth. The absurdity of this view is its own refutation.

† With respect to these analogies, let it not be overlooked that they are in no way correspondent: of a glorification of the σῶμα, no mythology knows anything: the heathen apotheoses are only deifications of the ψυχή.

‡ The beautiful conclusion of the life of Jesus by Hase (p. 204), "His departure was not the sad parting of a mortal, but the blessing of a glorified being, who promised yet by his love with the deity to love on immortal among his disciples; and he does remain with us," sinks down, therefore, to mere words; because shortly before, Christ's grave was presupposed, and with it the sad parting of a mortal

formerly remarked in reference to the mythical view of the history of the Saviour's childhood, that the composition of the Acts of the Apostles lies too near the historical occurrences, to allow time for a circle of mythical legends to have formed themselves around the person of Jesus. However, the advocates of this view make their appeal here to a circumstance which at first sight must appear surprising. They remind us that the ascension, if it really occurred, is so important an incident in the history of Christ, that in none of the gospels could it be overlooked; it is the keystone of the whole, without which the building cannot be completed. Nevertheless, this keystone is wanting in the Gospel of Matthew, who yet was an eye-witness; nay, it is even wanting in John, for whose delineation of Christ it would have been doubly important; setting out, as he does, from the original state of the Logos with the Father, thither also there would have been an evident propriety in following him back. Besides, it is remarked that no other apostle speaks of the occurrence, neither Peter, nor Paul, nor James: it is only the two penmen of the New Testament who were not eye-witnesses, Mark and Luke, who narrate the ascension, whence it would seem not improbable that they drew their narrative from impure sources. This observation is by no means without weight, and I confess that for a long time I was disquieted by it, because I could nowhere find a satisfactory explanation of the fact. What at last presented itself to me as an explanation, after carefully considering the circumstances of the case, I will now attempt shortly to unfold.*

First of all, it has already been often justly remarked, that references to the ascension are not so entirely wanting as has been supposed. In the Old Testament, it is true, passages, such as Ps. cx. 1, contain but mere hints, which can be directly applied to the ascension only on the authority of the New Testament; but yet, in 2 Kings ii. 11, we are presented with an obvious prefiguration of it in the history of Elijah.† It would therefore, very readily suggest itself to the Rabbins, who transferred everything glorious and beautiful in the Old Testament to the Messiah, to suppose also that he should ascend to heaven. (Compare Schoettgen, Jesus der wahre Messias, Leipsic, 1748, p. 844, etc.) And, what is of more weight, Jesus himself refers to it, not only in the expression, so often repeated in the last chapters of John, "I go to the Father" (ὑπάγω πρὸς τὸν πατέρα), but also more definitely in the passage John vi.

* Hase, in his life of Jesus, who decides in favour of the mythical view of the resurrection, declares the silence of the eye-witnesses to be altogether inexplicable. And to what point he was led by this mythical view appears from the words, "as the grave of Moses, so also his was not seen." Had he then a grave, he who swallowed up death for ever?! (Hase, as cited above, page 204.)

† I designedly mention only Elias, because the departure of Enoch and Moses is not represented expressly as a bodily glorification.

62, "if then ye see the Son of Man ascending where he was before" (*ἐὰν οὖν θεωρῆτε τὸν υἱὸν τοῦ ἀνθρώπου ἀναβαίνοντα ὅπου ἦν τὸ πρότερον*), where the connexion, as well as the words "Son of Man" plainly point to an exaltation of his *human* nature. In the apostolic epistles, in fine, there are passages, such as 1 Tim. iii. 16 (*ἀνελήφθη ἐν δόξῃ*), which contain manifest allusions to the fact in question; and even other passages, such as Ephes. ii. 6, iv. 8, and 1 Pet. iii. 22 (*πορευθεὶς εἰς τὸν οὐρανόν*, where, besides, the mention of the *ἀνάστασις* immediately precedes), are not to be overlooked, nor yet any of those declarations which represent Christ as sitting continually at the right hand of God, particularly Matth. xxvi. 64. However, it must be acknowledged that in most of these passages the specific circumstance distinctive of Christ's ascension, viz., his *bodily* elevation, is not expressly brought forward, and, therefore, many of them might be applied to persons who have blissfully fallen asleep, *e. g.* the words "he has gone to heaven."*

But, again, suppose that the declarations of Mark and Luke regarding the ascension were wanting likewise, and that we were quite at liberty to imagine to ourselves the end of Christ's earthly life; should we then be able to conceive any other departure of the Lord, that would recommend itself to the consciousness of Christians? Since allowing that the Saviour was not a mere phantom, as supposed by the Docetæ, but lived in a real human body upon the earth, we are necessarily driven to suppose, if the glorification of his body be not admitted, that a *separation* of his soul from his body again took place. But this separation must be death, and therefore we must say that in some way Christ died again, and that his soul returned to his Father. But where, then, is the victory of Christ over death? What becomes of the significancy of the resurrection, which all the apostles have celebrated as the great work of God, and as the foundation of faith? (Comp. Comm. on 1 Cor. xv.) It has already been remarked, in the history of the resurrection, that the raising of Christ is significant only as being the climax of *ζωή*, *life*, in that Christ conquered death in his humanity, and rose with a glorified immortal body. But what boots a resurrection, that is followed by a new death? If the Redeemer, therefore, is at all to be and to continue what he is to the church, the conqueror of sin and death, his departure from this world *cannot* be conceived to have been different from what the Evangelists declare. Now let this be granted, and the question will present itself in quite a different shape. The *fact* of the ascension is certain, on internal grounds, and the only question that now remains is, why this con-

* Ephes. ii. 6 is a passage particularly worthy of notice, because Paul there views the resurrection and ascension of Christ as an image of the resurrection and exaltation of believers.

cluding scene receives so little prominence in the apostolic writings? To this question we find a sufficient answer in the relation, which the resurrection and the ascension necessarily bear to one another. The ascension, as the concluding act of our Lord's career upon the earth, did not by any means appear to the apostles so significant as it does to us: in their view it was only a *consequence* of the resurrection. They had already become accustomed, after their master's death, to regard him as absent and gone; they had no continuous enjoyment of his presence after he rose from the dead: there was always something sudden and unexpected in his individual appearances, and each might be the last. And though, indeed, the ascension was an express leave-taking and a solemn departure, yet even after it, Jesus appeared again, for example, to Paul.* The ascension itself, therefore, was really not an act of special significance; the moment of our Lord's departure appeared like a fleeting instant, and therefore there was no feast of the ascension known to the ancient church.† Everything of importance, in a doctrinal point of view, was concentrated in the resurrection; with it closed the earthly career of Christ: the ascension, and also the outpouring of the Spirit, which was connected with the ascension and dependent upon it, are only results of the resurrection, viewed as the glorification of the body, and consequences of the victory over death. Whilst in the incarnation divinity was born into flesh, the resurrection is, as it were, a birth of the flesh into spirit; and the ascension is the return of the glorified body into the eternal world of spirit, with which the sitting of the glorified Redeemer at the right hand of God, and his participation in the Divine government of the world, must necessarily be viewed as connected. As therefore the earthly sinks by the essential tendency of its nature down to the earth, so likewise does an inward impulse guide the heavenly back to its source. The Redeemer, therefore, glorified in a body, *could* not leave his spiritual body upon the earth, but he took it with him into

* Hence, too, the apostle Paul (1 Cor. xv. 8) enumerates, along with the other appearances of Christ, the appearance of him with which he himself was favoured, although it did not take place till after the ascension, and he speaks of the resurrection without making any mention of the ascension at all.

† In the days of Augustine and Chrysostom, the ascension was indeed celebrated in the church, and because they did not know the origin of the feast that commemorated it (adscensio, ἀνάληψις), they traced it back to the apostles; but in the writings of the fathers of the first three centuries, there is no trace of it to be found. (Comp. Binghami origg. eccl. vol. ix. p. 126, seq.) How much, too, the importance of the feast of ascension has fallen below that of the feast of Easter, in the estimation of Christians, is plain from our collections of sacred psalmody. The abundance of admirable hymns for Easter stands in glaring contrast with the few and rather unimportant songs which refer to the ascension. The cause of this fact undoubtedly is nothing but this, that the imagination of poets has not found in the event any peculiar idea, but a mere consequence of the resurrection.

the world of spirit. And in accordance with the representative character which Christ bears in relation to mankind, the whole race was elevated in him, and he now draws up to his own elevation his faithful people, and grants to them to sit upon his throne, as God has granted to him to sit upon his throne. (Rev. iii. 21.) If but one Evangelist, therefore, had neglected to mention the resurrection of Christ, the omission would have been inexplicable, but the omission of the ascension in the Gospels of Matthew and John is merely to be regarded as a record of one fewer of the appearances of Christ. That the risen Redeemer has ascended to heaven with his glorified body, and sits on the right hand of God, lies at the foundation of the whole apostolic view of his ministry; and without this idea neither the significant rite of the supper, nor yet the doctrine of the resurrection of the body, can be retained at all with consistency. And, therefore, in fact, the New Theology has not hitherto been able properly to incorporate with itself either the one or the other, because, on account of its prevailing ideal tendency, it has misunderstood the import of the ascension.

Vers. 12–14.—Luke next gives an account of the return of the disciples to Jerusalem from the Mount of Olives. (The usual name of this mountain [see Comm. on Matth. xxi. 1] is ὄρος τῶν ἐλαιῶν. The name here employed, ὄρος τοῦ ἐλαιῶνος, is found in this passage only of the New Testament, but it also occurs in Josephus, Ant. vii. 9, 2. It comes from the ἐλαίων, olivetum, a place planted with olive trees. The LXX. use it for זַיִת. Exod. xxiii. 11.) This mountain lay, it is well known, near to the city, at the distance of a Sabbath day's journey. (The Jews might walk on the Sabbath two thousand yards, or seven and a half stadia or furlongs. Josephus states the distance of the Mount of Olives sometimes at six furlongs [Ant. xx. 8, 6], and sometimes at five [Bell. Jud. i. 5, 2], according as he reckoned from the top of the mountain or the foot. Here we have only an indefinite statement.) When Luke intimates in verse 13 that the apostles assembled in a private house (ὑπερῷον = עֲלִיָּה an upper chamber,* which was usually constructed in the form of a hall, and therefore commonly served for meetings, Acts ix. 37, xx. 8); it is but an apparent contradiction to the statement in Luke (xxiv. 53), that they were in the temple. For the added διαπαντός, *continually*, shews that it is not there meant to be affirmed that they went directly from the Mount of Olives to the temple, but rather that, as pious, God-fearing men, they were frequently to be found in the common sanctuary of the nation. But in the passage before us the discourse relates to an immediate meeting, after the return from the Mount of Olives. (Respecting the list of the apostles, see the

* Undoubtedly it was in the house of a family friendly to them, perhaps in the same where the last supper was observed.

Comm. on Matth. x. 2. Mary, the mother of Jesus, is mentioned by name, as a mark of respect, and indeed for the last time. It is not to be overlooked that the brothers of Christ are distinguished from the eleven apostles, for this circumstance clearly shews that none of them can have belonged to that body. It is not to be doubted, however, that they were now attached to the Gospel, and perhaps had been so from the time of Christ's appearance to James, 1 Cor. xv. 7. Comp. the Comm. on John vii. 5, and Matth. xiii. 55.) Although the Lord had now left the disciples, and they stood alone like sheep among wolves, yet they were filled with a blessed joy. (Luke xxiv. 52.) They had learned that by means of the resurrection of Christ, the foundations of the kingdom of God were immoveably laid, and that all their hopes should be realized. Therefore they joined together in heartfelt prayer, that the purposes of God towards mankind might be carried into effect through them. From the definite statement of the individual fact (*ὅτε εἰσῆλθον, ἀνέβησαν*), the words *οὗ ἦσαν καταμένοντες* and *ἦσαν προσκαρτεροῦντες*, form a transition to a more general statement. Here in the place indicated they were *wont* to assemble for prayer. (Comp. verse 15.) The word *ὁμοθυμαδόν*, *unanimously*, in verse 14, also in chap. ii. 1, 46, is significant: it occurs elsewhere in the New Testament only in Rom. xv. 6. It denotes that oneness of life in the disciples which was displayed in a living community of feeling and consciousness.

Ver. 15–17.—During the days that intervened between the ascension and the day of Pentecost (ii. 1) the apostles proceeded to the election of a new member of the apostolic college in the room of Judas. First of all, in reference to this transaction, it seems strange, that when the Redeemer himself had not supplied the vacancy during the forty days that followed his resurrection, the apostles did not wait till they received the Holy Ghost. In that case they might have been able to dispense with the use of the lot, which necessarily betrays a deficiency of the gift of discerning spirits: if Peter, for instance, had had this gift of the Holy Ghost, then he could at once, by heavenly guidance, have selected a new apostle. But this would have been a proceeding obviously opposed to all propriety, for one apostle could not nominate another: all of them required to be appointed by the same Lord.* Their use of the lot therefore only gave expression to the idea, that they wished to

* In this circumstance probably we can find the reason why in the ancient church the teachers of religion were not also appointed by lot. The apostles were named immediately by the Lord, and therefore the filling of the vacancy which had occurred was also left to him. But the overseers and teachers of the individual churches were always named by the apostle who planted them, and the church kept up the number by election. It is only at a late period that traces of election by lot are to be found in Spain (see Binghami orig. eccl. vol. ii. 80), but it was probably the very passage before us which led to the adoption of the practice when it did arise.

decline the decision themselves, and put it wholly into the hands of the Saviour. But, at all events, this occurrence will always remain a remarkable proof of the lawfulness of the lot, in those cases where a decision needs to be given, in which it transcends the ability of man to discover what is right. It is well known that in such cases the church of the United Brethren use the lot; and, according to the latest accounts regarding the practice, they use it with such prudence that scarcely any well grounded objection can be made to it.

But further, in the speech of Peter there is exhibited a manifest consciousness of the importance of the office which was conferred upon him and all the apostles, and of the completeness of the body which the twelve were designed to form. And just because they were to stand purely as the representatives of Israel (comp. Comm. at Matth. x. 1), even Paul himself afterwards could not be ranked in the apostolic circle, for as the apostle of the Gentiles, he did not belong to the number of the twelve.

And finally, our admiration is excited by the calmness and the clear conscience with which Peter speaks of Judas in this first speech which he delivers. Though he had himself so deeply fallen, he could, after receiving pardon as a penitent, take that lead among the disciples to which the Lord had called him, without being held back by a false humility, and proceed to supply the place of Judas who had destroyed himself in despairing remorse. So greatly do sins differ from one another in their consequences, according to the state of mind from which they proceed! Only let the heart be at bottom sincere and true to God, and the soul may soon rise again from a very deep fall.

The whole body of the little church at Jerusalem amounted at that time only to one hundred and twenty souls. (Ὄνομα, *name*, is here employed to denote the person himself. The word is used in the same manner in Rev. iii. 4, where it stands plainly for "men" (ἄνθρωποι). Among profane authors this usage is only to be found in poetical diction. For *ἐπὶ τὸ αὐτό*, = יַחְדָּו, we find only once *κατὰ τὸ αὐτό*, viz., in Acts xiv. 1. This phrase, *ἐπὶ τὸ αὐτό*, occurs chiefly in the writings of Luke and Paul, though also in Matth. xxii. 34. In signification it refers usually to place [sc. *χωρίον*], yet sometimes also, as in Acts iii. 1, to time, in the sense of "at the same time, together." It unites therefore in itself, like יַחְדָּו, different references.) The passages to which Peter refers in this speech, as relating to Judas, are cited in verse 20. In accordance with the universal doctrine of Scripture, the word of prophecy is here considered as *necessarily* reaching its fulfilment. That this objective necessity does not interfere with the subjective free determinations of the mind, but that God recognizes free actions as such, has already been repeatedly noticed. (It is probably in such passages as verse 17, *κλῆρος τῆς διακονίας*, comp. verse 25, that we are to seek the origin of the word clerus, as applied to the spiritual functionaries of the church. At the very beginning of the church, it was supposed, we must find the commencement also of the spiritual office; and this name very naturally presented itself in the case of the apostles as the representatives of that office. Κλῆρος denotes the lot, then, whatever is distributed by lot, as נַחֲלָה, and then generally that which is distributed; here it means a thing conferred by God, which of course implied that the individual who had received the special blessing was laid under special obligations to God in return.* *Κλῆρος διακονίας* must therefore be translated, "munus ministerii," but the expressions are by no means synonymous, as Heinrichs and Kuinoel assert.)

Vers. 18, 19.—These two verses appear not to belong to the original speech of Peter. As the miserable end of Judas was universally known in Jerusalem (ver. 19), it is improbable that Peter should have here detailed it so minutely.† The verses, therefore, are most properly to be regarded as a historical supplement of Luke, who in his Gospel had mentioned no particulars respecting the fate of Judas. This supposition will appear the more plain and natural, when it is considered that this view must at any rate be taken of verse 19, because we must suppose that Peter spoke in Hebrew, and therefore we cannot imagine that a translation of the word *Ἀκελδαμά* would occur in his speech. Meyer, however, is right in saying that, *in form*, these verses are to be considered as belonging to the apostle's speech. Regarding the particular circumstances mentioned in them, as well as the fate of Judas generally, and the purchase of the piece of ground made by the priests, see the details in the Commentary at Matthew xxvii. 5.

Ver. 20.—According to this view, then, the citations from the Old Testament connect themselves immediately with the 16th verse where mention of them is made. The first passage is taken from Ps. lxix. 25.‡ In the LXX. it stands thus: *γενηθήτω ἡ ἔπαυλις αὐτῶν ἠρημωμένη καὶ ἐν τοῖς σκηνώμασιν αὐτῶν μὴ ἔστω ὁ κατοικῶν.* Probably the passage is quoted only from memory, for the variations from the LXX. are not material. The employment of the singular number, however, is plainly intentional, to mark the better

* Thus speaks Jerome, Epist. ii. ad Nepot., ministri Dei propterea vocantur clerici, vel quia de sorte sunt Domini, vel quia ispo Dominus *sors* id est pars clericorum est. See Binghami orig. eccl. vol. i. 50.

† So most interpreters, perhaps correctly. The English translator regards the verses, however, as necessary to the speech of Peter, as preparatory to the citation from the Psalms, ver. 20. Yet this certainly required no such minute account as is here given.—[K.

‡ In the Hebrew it is the 26th verse, which runs thus: תְּהִי־טִירָתָם נְשַׁמָּה בְּאָהֳלֵיהֶם אַל־יְהִי יֹשֵׁב.

the reference of the passage to Judas. But in this there is by no means any disfigurement or essential alteration of the sense. Judas is rather viewed as representing the ungodly in general, and the sentiment which is applicable to them all, holds good of him pre-eminently. On this principle it is to be explained how the passage admits of being applied to Judas, and the word ἔπαυλις (= οἰκία, and occurring only here in the New Testament), to his apostolic office.* We need not at all suppose that David, in the strict and proper sense, had a view of Judas and his office clearly before his mind; but he scanned deeply the fundamental relations between good and evil, as developed in the history of the world. For it is God's plan to permit evil indeed to bear sway for a time over the good, but he at length sends forth judgment, and drives evil from its possession. Then the place of evil is supplied by a good which repairs its disasters. This deep thought was exhibited typically in the life of David, and it was realized in a great historical event in the case of Judas, but it shall one day be fully vindicated in the complete triumph of the good. The second passage is quoted from Ps. cix. 8, and corresponds word for word with the LXX. To this Psalm the same remarks are entirely applicable, as have been made regarding Ps. lxix. There too, David, the representative in his day of all godly living, is described as being in his persecutions a type of the Messiah. (Ἐπισκοπή corresponds to the Hebrew פְּקֻדָּה, office.)

Vers. 21, 22.—It is not inward qualifications which Peter here brings forward as requisite to an apostle, but something altogether external, viz., constant intercourse with Christ and his circle of followers. This might in fact appear a mistaken view when we consider that Paul, who enjoyed no such intercourse, yet laboured far more than Matthias, who was chosen. But it must not be overlooked that three years' intercourse with Christ was the farthest possible from a thing purely external, and that it must influence most decidedly the character of the individual: either he would enter upon a really pious life, or he would sink as deep into sin as Judas. The heavenly light which proceeded from Christ left no room for indecision. The idea of Peter, accordingly, must be conceived in this manner, "we can choose none, but one who has already approved himself." We do not find any respect at all paid to richness of natural endowments in the choice of the apostles. The majority of those who were chosen by Christ himself appear to have been in no way preeminently distinguished by talents. Integrity, truth, and experience were the only qualities that were looked to, and these qualities are still of most importance in the church of Christ. Again, it is the resurrection only (ἀνάστασις), which Peter prominently exhibits, although he also mentions the ascension. It was not witnesses of

* On the 69th Psalm in general, see the Comm. on John ii. 17.

the ascension the church needed, but of the resurrection, for the former was a necessary consequence of the latter. (The phrase *εἰσέρχεσθαι* and *ἐξέρχεσθαι* is formed upon the model of the Hebrew בּוֹא וְצֵאת, and denotes the close and intimate intercourse of life.)

Ver. 23.—Two persons, who possessed the qualifications required, were now appointed as candidates, viz., Barsabas and Matthias. The former had three names, like Thaddeus among the apostles. (Comp. Comm. on Matth. x. 3.) For Ἰωσήφ, however, some codices read Ἰωσῆς, and for Βαρσαβᾶν, codex D., in particular, has Βαρνάβαν. Both names appear to have been frequently interchanged with the kindred forms. This Joseph Barsabas has been confounded by transcribers with the well known Joses Barnabas mentioned in chap. iv. 36,* and there, too, indeed, some codices read Βαρσαββᾶς. (The etymology of Βαρσαβᾶς is unknown. Grotius explains it to mean son of an oath, from בַּר and שֶׁבַע. The name Justus was borrowed by the Jews from the Latin tongue, and assumed the form of יוּסְטִי.)

Vers. 24-26.—The question presents itself, to whom is this prayer addressed? The word *κύριε*, *lord*, placed absolutely, denotes in the New Testament almost universally the Son;† and, besides, the words *ἀνάδειξον ὃν ἐξελέξω*, *show whom thou hast chosen*, are decisive. The apostles are messengers of Christ; it is he who selects them, and of him they are to bear witness. Here, therefore, we have the first example of a prayer offered to the exalted Redeemer, which furnishes indirectly the strongest proof of his divinity. (*Καρδιογνώστης* is equivalent to חֹקֵר לֵב, Jerem. xvii. 10; comp. John ii. 25.) Of Matthias, who was chosen, history gives no particular information. (*Διδόναι κλήρους* = נָתַן גּוֹרָל, Lev. xvi. 8. *Συγκαταψηφίζεσθαι*, "to be chosen with general consent," occurs nowhere else in the New Testament.

There has been found some difficulty in the statement these verses make concerning Judas, that he went into his own place (*εἰς τὸν τόπον τὸν ἴδιον*). False principles of moderation have created a wish to shun the obvious sense of the words, and therefore *πορευθῆναι*, *go*, has been made to refer back to *λαβεῖν*, *take*, and *τόπος*, *place*, has been understood to mean office; so that the sense of the whole has been made this: shew, Lord, whom thou hast chosen to receive the office, and to enter into the situation thus devolving upon him. But this exposition is so ungrammatical and violent, that it cannot maintain its ground for a moment; for as the words *ἐξ ἧς παρέβη Ἰούδας* stand between *λαβεῖν* and *πορευθῆναι*, it is perfectly clear,

* Against the identity of the two men you have decisive evidence in the chapter mentioned above, iv. 36; where, certainly, if Barnabas had been the same with Barsabas, some reference to this fact was to be expected. What Ullman (Studien 1828, ii., page 377, ff.) has adduced in favour of their identity, has not convinced me of it.

† Consult Winer's treatise, de sensu vocum, *κύριος* et *ὁ κύριος*, in actt. epist. apost. Erlangæ, 1828.

that without *καί* these two infinitives cannot be connected. The explanations too, which, referring the clause to Judas, understand the word *place* of the grave, or of his habitation, and make the meaning to be that he withdrew himself entirely from the company of believers, deserve just as little attention. Nothing is left, therefore, but to regard "his own place" (*τόπος ἴδιος*) as a euphemistical designation of the place of punishment, to which it was befitting that Judas should be consigned on account of his sins. (One codex has *δίκαιος τόπος*, meaning, according to the fundamental signification of this word: "What is due to any one, what righteously belongs to him.") Although this undoubtedly is the meaning of the words, yet interpreters have not brought into clear relief the contrast formed by *τόπος ἴδιος* with *ἔπαυλις* and *ἐπισκοπή* in ver. 20. The heavenly position in the kingdom of light and truth to which Judas was called, but which he lost by his unfaithfulness, has standing opposed to it the kingdom of darkness, whose powers drew him down to themselves. As the iron between two magnets, so stands the soul between the powers of light and of darkness; and the principle to which it yields the supremacy, draws it upwards or downwards to itself.

§ 2. CELEBRATION OF THE FIRST PENTECOST.*

(Acts ii. 1–47.)

Ver. 1.—And now the sacred number of the twelve was again restored to its completeness, and the closed circle of the disciples were waiting in prayer for the promise of the Father (i. 4). Nor did the Redeemer, exalted to heaven to the right hand of power, leave them long alone (John xiv. 18); he opened the streams of the celestial world, and in the language of Isaiah xlv. 8, made the heavens drop from above, and the clouds pour down righteousness. The fulness of the Spirit from above, which had vanished with the sin of mankind, returned once more; and by means of that fulness there was laid in the church of Christ the foundation of the kingdom of God upon earth. Broken into fragments by sin, mankind were melted together anew into a holy unity; and to seal this restored unity, the diversity of languages, which was the consequence of the breach made by sin, was neutralized. The effect, it is true, lasted only for a brief period, but still it served as a real pledge of the permanent condition one day to be expected. This great fact,

* See the discussion by Hase in Winer's Zeitscrift f. wissench. Theol. part ii. page 264. ff. Likewise Schneckenburger über die Pfingstbegebenheit in den Beiträgen. p. 76, etc.

however, the birthday of the young church, the new birth of Israel according to the Spirit, is preserved to us only in the one short narrative of Luke; and therefore it is not easy to form to one's self a clear conception of the event, the more especially as there are difficult collateral points connected with the main question. We begin our statement with an explanation of the text, that we may first investigate carefully what the author *designed* to communicate; we shall then subjoin a vindication to the consciousness of Christians of what he declares, as also remarks upon other views that have been taken of the event.

And first, with regard to the *time* of the occurrence, there is a difficulty in the words, *ἐν τῷ συμπληροῦσθαι τὴν ἡμέραν τῆς πεντακοστῆς, when the day of Pentecost*, etc. The word *συμπληροῦσθαι* or *πληροῦσθαι*, applied to points of time, denotes invariably, in the New Testament, the reaching of a limit which refers back to an earlier period. Here the view is directed back to the feast of the Passover, and on the arrival of Pentecost, the interval between the two feasts was, as it were, filled up. The words before us therefore cannot be translated, "when the day of Pentecost approached," but "when it was reached." (*Συμπληροῦσθαι* occurs elsewhere in this sense only at Luke ix. 51; but *πληροῦσθαι*, like מָלֵא in the Old Testament, occurs with singular frequency, especially in Luke. Also in Mark i. 15, John vii. 8.) Further, the phrase *ἡμέρα τῆς πεντηκοστῆς*, must not be translated "the fiftieth day;" the Greek for that would be *ἡμέρα πεντηκοστή*; but "the day of Pentecost," *πεντηκοστή* having acquired quite the force of a substantive. The supplying of *ἑορτή* is altogether unnecessary, but it is not absurd, as Meyer maintains, any more than our phrase "feast of Pentecost" (Pfingstfest). He erroneously supposes that *πεντηκοστὴ ἑορτή* would mean the fiftieth feast; but that this is not the case, is clear from a passage in Tobias ii. 1, *ἐν τῇ πεντηκοστῇ ἑορτῇ, ἥ ἐστιν ἁγία ἑπτὰ ἑβδομάδων*. 2 Macc. xii. 32. Among the Jews Pentecost was called חַג הַשָּׁבֻעוֹת, the feast of (the seven) weeks, that is, of seven weeks (Deut. xvi. 9, Tobias ii. 1). It was celebrated as a memorial of the giving of the law of Moses on Mount Sinai, and also as a harvest festival.* It corresponded therefore entirely to the Christian Pentecost, inasmuch as it celebrated the establishment of the Old Testament covenant, when God wrote his law outwardly upon tables of stone, while now he wrote it with the finger of the Spirit upon the living tables of the heart. The reference also to the harvest had its spiritual significance, because at the Christian Pentecost the complete harvest, as it were, of the Jewish people, those, to wit, who had been brought to the fruit of true repentance and renewal of heart, were gathered in and con-

* In the former respect it is called שִׂמְחַת הַתּוֹרָה, the festival of the law. In reference to the first fruits it is called by Philo *ἑορτὴ πρωτογεννημάτων*, equivalent to יוֹם הַבִּכּוּרִים. See Numb. xxviii. 26.

secrated to God. The name *πεντηκοστή*, *pentecost*, takes its rise from the relation of this feast to the Passover; for it was to be celebrated on the day following the completion of seven weeks or forty-nine days, and consequently fell upon the fiftieth day. Still, there is a question respecting the point from which the fifty days were counted. According to the appointment of Moses (Lev. xxiii. 15), the fifty days were reckoned from the day after the first day of the Passover, or from the sixteenth day of Nisan; for it is said in the passage referred to מִמָּחֳרַת הַשַּׁבָּת, where שַׁבָּת denotes the first day of the Passover, which was observed as a Sabbath. Now since, according to the accounts given regarding the time of the feast, the Passover, in the year of our Lord's death fell so, that the first day of the feast lasted from Thursday evening at six o'clock till Friday evening at the same hour, it follows of course that it was from Friday evening at six o'clock that the fifty days began to be counted. The fiftieth day fell, therefore, it appears, upon Saturday, while the whole church, so far as we can trace the history of Pentecost, have celebrated the feast on Sunday. For a solution of this difficulty, an appeal is made to a different exposition of Lev. xxiii. 15. While the Jews, trained in the schools of the Rabbins and Pharisees, explain שַׁבָּת of the first day of the Passover, the Karaites understand it of the real Sabbath, that occurred during the paschal feast, which it is known lasted eight days. But it is at once an objection to this view, that we cannot well transfer the custom of the Karaites back to the time of Christ; at least we have no evidence at all to warrant us to do so. The practice of the church, however, when more narrowly considered, is not at all inconsistent with the reckoning stated above, and, therefore, we may entirely discard that uncertain hypothesis. We must merely avoid being misled by the different commencement of a Jewish day. Undoubtedly the Jewish Pentecost in the year of our Lord's death fell upon Saturday, but it began at six o'clock in the evening, when the Sabbath was at a close, and it lasted till six o'clock on Sunday evening. As the church, therefore, has quite rightly fixed the day of the Redeemer's death upon Friday, although the Passover began on Thursday evening at six o'clock, so also has it with equal propriety fixed the first Pentecost upon the day which occurred exactly seven weeks after the resurrection. In those congregations of the primitive church, which, at first, according to Jewish custom, observed Easter on the day of the week on which it fell by the reckoning, they would also, without doubt, assign Pentecost to the day of the week which came round at the expiration of seven weeks after Easter, but, when the custom became general of statedly observing Easter upon Sunday, the whole church likewise celebrated Pentecost on the seventh Sunday after Easter.*

* The state of the case would, indeed, be quite different, if Hitzig's view were right,

There is another considerable difficulty, with respect to the *place* where the event recorded occurred. As we know (ii. 15) the hour of the day exactly, viz., nine o'clock in the morning, which was one of the solemn hours of prayer among the Jews, we cannot suppose that in the morning of the first Pentecost, the apostles would not be assembled in the temple for prayer. The great multitude of men, too, of so many different nations that streamed in upon them, appears to point to the temple, the central point to which all eagerly flocked. Yet, on the other hand, the expression ὅλος οἶκος in verse 2, seems to indicate a private house, in which case the scene would be entirely altered; and particularly it would be inexplicable, how so many persons, and of so various classes, could assemble round the apostles. But the accounts given by Josephus respecting the construction of the temple, guide us here to the right conclusion. According to his description, the main building was surrounded by thirty rooms, which he names οἴκους (Joseph. Antiq. viii. 3, 2), and it is probable the apostles, along with their little company, assembled in one of these spacious apartments. And thus the solemn inauguration of the church of Christ presents itself as an imposing spectacle in the *sanctuary of the old covenant*. The weightiest objection which can be brought against these views, arises from the idea that the Pharisees would hardly have permitted the apostles to assemble in the temple. But let it be considered that hitherto the apostles had been treated as quite harmless people, and that probably there was no need of any special permission for such a meeting, because these halls, being employed for various purposes, stood to some extent open, and were accessible to every person, and the objection loses all its force. Without this supposition, the whole occurrence must appear of a far less significant character. As the crowning inauguration of Christ took place in the temple (John xii. 28), so behoved it also to be the case with the founding of the church. Here the hundred and twenty assembled (i. 15) (that is ten times twelve), and by their preaching and help at baptizing (ii. 41) the number immediately grew to three thousand (that is twenty-five times one hundred and twenty). Without doubt, therefore, we must suppose that not the twelve only, but the whole hundred and twenty received the Holy Ghost, for this gift was to be common and accessible to every believer. It was therefore bestowed upon the first little company of decided believers for further diffusion among all who should become connected with them. Certainly,

which is developed in the circular letter to Ideler, entitled "Ostern und Pfingsten zur Zeitbestimmung im Alten und Neuen Testament," Heidelberg, 1837, page 7, etc. According to the view there given, the Passover and Pentecost were not moveable feasts at all. But the correctness of this view appears to me a matter of doubt. However, I venture no judgment on this difficult question. I have rather desired that it might please the venerable man to whom the letter is addressed, to express his opinion of Hitzig's views.

however, the twelve possessed the Holy Ghost in a different way from the other believers, as is indicated particularly by the circumstance that they only at first appear to have been gifted with the power of *communicating* the Spirit. (See Commentary on Acts viii. 15.)

Vers. 2, 3.—If we examine the text, then, quite without prejudice, it will be seen that the historian presents the astonishing occurrence in this light. While the disciples were sitting in the apartment, there suddenly arose a rushing noise (ἦχος means any sound, but especially a rushing or whistling sound), which appeared to come downwards from heaven: it might be compared to the rushing of a mighty wind that sweeps along, and it filled the spacious hall gradually, although moving quickly onwards. The whole description is so picturesque and striking, that it could only come from an eye-witness. After these sounds, there are described the sights that accompanied them. The disciples saw (ὤφθησαν αὐτοῖς can only be understood thus: "there appeared to them," that is, they saw, not "there were seen upon them," "visæ sunt super illos") fiery flames, which seemed to proceed from a common centre, but disparted and divided themselves: these flames touched each of the company, and rested upon them, and they now all felt themselves to be filled with a high and holy principle of life, and they began to speak with tongues, as the Spirit gave them utterance.

(In the phrase γλῶσσαι ὡσεὶ πυρός, *tongues as of fire*, the word γλῶσσα, *tongue*, like לְשׁוֹן in Isaiah v. 24, must be understood in the sense of flame.* And ὡσεί, *as if*, is inserted, because, although the appearance was indeed one of fire, yet its effects shewed it to be different from an actual earthly flame. The word διαμεριζόμενος refers to an original unity, which resolved itself into parts. The author manifestly intends that we should form to ourselves the idea of a fiery stream, which divided itself, and whose radiations spread over all and rested upon them. The μένειν of John corresponds entirely to καθίζειν.)

As respects the explanation of this occurrence, it may be alleged, *in the first place*, that the disciples saw and heard everything in a state of ecstacy or trance, and that accordingly the gathering crowds (verse 6) heard not the rushing noise, but were attracted to the place by the sound of the disciples' voices. But a trance happening at the same time to many persons, let it even be but to twelve, is a thing utterly unheard of. We must therefore suppose assuredly something external which produced this common ecstacy, the more especially as it was attended with real consequences, since the apostles after this occurrence suddenly stand forth and teach as

* Better perhaps to regard the flame as tongue-shaped (and hence symbolical) which disparted so that a like flame sat on each.—[K.

inspired witnesses of Christ, and preach the Gospel. *Others*, therefore, are inclined to suppose there was some physical phenomenon in the air, a thunder-storm or electric meteors, which as declarations of God from heaven in favour of the apostles, were *interpreted* as the fulfilment of the promise of the Father. But neither can this supposition prove satisfactory; for, in the first place, other men, too, must have seen these atmospheric phenomena, and could not therefore have had occasion to wonder at the event; and, secondly, an interpretation put by the apostles upon a thunder-storm, could never have secured that lasting power which accrued to them from the scene, and least of all could it have given rise to such peculiar exhibitions as the γλώσσαις λαλεῖν, "speaking with tongues," which lasted for many years in the church. Nor again is the *mythical* view of the occurrence, which is grounded upon the idea prevalent among Jews as well as Gentiles (see Schoettgen on this passage, Liv. i. 39, Virg. Æn. ii. 680, seq.), that in peculiar circumstances rays of light have played around distinguished persons, here at all admissible. For, not to advert to the circumstance that we cannot allow the possibility of myths arising in the time of the eye-witnesses, and passing over the consideration that this myth would be formed contrary to all analogy, the gift of tongues being a thing wholly unprecedented; this view would lead to the conclusion that the power which subsequently displayed itself in the ministry of the apostles was a mere heightened action of their own life, a conclusion that would entirely set aside the peculiar work of the Holy Ghost. Those who cannot reconcile themselves, therefore, to the occurrence, must still confess, that it is the author's design to declare that a higher and a heavenly power came upon the apostles, amid audible and visible manifestations; and the very existence of the church obliges them in any case to suppose that there must have been something to produce so mighty a change in the timid disciples. Many have found this in the resurrection of Christ (Hase's Life of Jesus, page 196); but not one of the disciples taught publicly *before* Pentecost: it was on the day and in the hour of the outpouring of the Spirit, that the church was first permanently established, and thereafter it grew from day to day and from century to century.

Now, let us only disengage ourselves from the prevailing ideas respecting the relation between spirit and matter (of which we have already said something in the history of the resurrection), and much of the difficulty which these ideas have been the means of spreading over the history of Pentecost will disappear. An absolute separation of the spiritual world from the material is altogether incapable of proof, and is in the highest degree improbable, because the very constitution of man himself furnishes us with an example of spirit acting in matter. The essence of the Absolute Spirit, which is love, implies moreover the power of imparting himself, and the supposition that spirit can receive spirit, that two such homogeneous natures may be united, involves nothing which should restrain us from adopting it: nay, the consciousness of spiritual poverty, along with the greatness of man's conscious destination, necessarily gives indication that a higher fulness shall one day supply the want that is felt. Hence, too, throughout the whole of the Old Testament, the longing desire and promise of a spiritual fulness to be poured down upon mankind. The only thing in the narrative before us, according to the view we have given, which might still occasion doubt, even to the man who readily admits the idea of spiritual communication, is the fact that here the spiritual power displays itself in *physical* effects, which it is feared may tend to materialism. But this, too, on closer consideration, is very easily explained. It is not said that the spiritual is itself material, which certainly would be inconceivable, but only that the spiritual, in its manifestation, was accompanied with physical effects. And to assume even this to be contradictory, is to regard every outward manifestation of the inward spiritual life in man, nay his very existence, which exhibits spirit in a material covering, as also a contradiction, which will be maintained by none.

Vers. 4–11.—The entire following description of the occurrence, serves for the illustration of the mysterious gift of tongues, which was now manifested in accordance with the promise given in Mark xvi. 17. The feast had brought Jews from all parts of the world to Jerusalem, who were assembled in the Temple at the hour of prayer; and pressing forward where the sound proceeded from the chamber of meeting, they were astonished to hear the company speaking in their several dialects. We are at once led to ascribe to the historian the idea, that an effect was here wrought exactly the reverse of the separation that once took place among the nations by the confusion of tongues (Gen. xi. 7). The outpouring of the Spirit of God, through the instrumentality of the gift of tongues, melted together again the broken fragments into a new unity. Hence the minute catalogue of nations, which are enumerated according to their order of position, from east to west, from north to south, in order to indicate the whole world: every one hears his own speech, and feels that the wall of separation which divided him from his brethren is taken away. The *γλώσσαις λαλεῖν*, *speaking with tongues*, appears therefore plainly to mean speaking in various dialects, so that all who were present understood what was advanced. There is some inexactness certainly in the words: *εἷς ἕκαστος ἤκουον τῇ ἰδίᾳ διαλέκτῳ λαλούντων αὐτῶν* in verse 6; for every one of the multitude could not hear every disciple speaking in his own language: manifestly, however, it is merely an indefiniteness of expression: the meaning must be, that every one of the collected throng heard his own language from *some one* of the disciples. This is clear from the speech which Luke, in the 7th and following verses, puts into the mouth of the multitude, for of course these words could not be spoken in such a shape: what individuals may have actually said or thought of individual speakers, is exhibited by Luke in the form of their collective judgment respecting the whole.

(Respecting *εὐλαβής* in verse 5, see the Comm. on Luke ii. 25.—Κατοικεῖν = ἐπιδημεῖν, denotes a short stay or sojourn in a place, like the Hebrew יָשַׁב, in Gen. xxvii. 44. *Τῶν ὑπὸ τὸν οὐρανόν* scil. *ὄντων*, "that are under heaven," is a picturesque form of expression to denote extension on every side.—Ver. 6, *συγχύνομαι*, in the sense of being amazed, perplexed, "confundi," occurs in the New Testament only in the Acts [ix. 22, xix. 32, xxi. 31.]—Verse 7. The question, "Are not these Galileans?" [*οὐχ οὗτοι Γαλιλαῖοι*;], is to be explained on the ground of the well-known deficiency of education which prevailed in Galilee, and which left no room for expecting strange and distant languages among them.—Vers. 9-11. The catalogue of the nations of the Græco-Roman world is plainly constructed according to a rule. Those in the east are first mentioned, then those in the north, next those in the south, and finally those in the west. The western nations are thrown together under the title of Ῥωμαῖοι;* and in conclusion, it is remarked of all the nations mentioned, that both Jews and Proselytes (for the passage does not refer at all to Gentiles, who had no occasion to come to the feast) were present from amongst them. And by way of supplement, Cretes and Arabians are mentioned, somewhat unconnectedly with the rest. The only strange thing in the list of countries is that Judea, *Ἰουδαία*, verse 9, is likewise mentioned; as it is foreign nations that are to be enumerated, and the discourse relates to an event that happened in Jerusalem, the mention of Judea obviously does not seem appropriate. But when it is considered that Luke wrote in Rome, one easily sees why in his enumeration, commencing with the distant east, he should also name Judea; respect is had to the position of his Roman readers. Theophylact, however, has omitted the word: Tertullian and Augustine read Armenia; others have conjectured India, Bithynia, or the like. India is inappropriate, for being the most easterly country, it should have stood first, but Bithynia fits admirably. The very difficulty, however, of the reading *Ἰουδαία*, must prevent conjecture from prevailing against

* The addition of *ἐπιδημοῦντες* shews that they were not merely Roman citizens dwelling elsewhere, but that they resided in Rome itself, and were therefore properly Romans—"Strangers of Rome."

the manuscripts.—Verse 11, *μεγαλεῖα* scil. *ἔργα*, equivalent to גדלות Ps. lxxi. 19.*)

But to consider more closely the gift of speaking with tongues (*γλώσσαις λαλεῖν*) first exhibited at Pentecost, it certainly is a most remarkable phenomenon. Whilst of almost all the great features in the gospel history, there are not only intimations in the Old Testament, but also anticipations among the Rabbins and analogies among other nations, this phenomenon has absolutely nothing akin to it, a circumstance of itself sufficient to divest the mythical explanation of every shadow of probability. And yet it is this very wonder of speaking with tongues which occurs with such frequency in the church, for in the apostolic times, and in the times too of primitive Christianity, it very copiously accompanied the communication of the Holy Ghost. Without the detailed information, however, which the apostle Paul gives us in 1 Cor. xiv. respecting this gift and its relation to "prophecy" (*προφητεία*) and to the "interpretation of tongues" (*ἑρμηνεία γλωσσῶν*), it would be quite impossible for us to acquire clear views on the subject. And for that reason the particular consideration of it must be delayed till we reach the passage referred to. At present I shall only give a preliminary abstract of my view, and also a survey of the principal opinions respecting this mysterious gift.

First, with respect to the names which this gift (1 Cor. xii. 4–11) bears in the New Testament, we find, besides the phrase *ἑτέραις γλώσσαις λαλεῖν* also *καιναῖς γλώσσαις λαλεῖν* in Mark xvi. 17, and further simply, *γλώσσαις* and *γλώσσῃ λαλεῖν*, also *γλώσσῃ προσεύχεσθαι*, *ψάλλειν* or *ψαλμὸν ἔχειν*, *γένη γλωσσῶν* (xii. 28); also simply, *γλῶσσαι* (xiii. 8), or *γλῶσσα* (xiv. 26). In Irenæus (v. 26) the phrase *παντοδαπαῖς γλώσσαις λαλεῖν* occurs. (Comp. the leading passages in 1 Cor. xii. and xiv.) It is probable that the words *λαλεῖν*, *προσεύχεσθαι*, and *ψάλλειν* denoted the different forms in which the gift appeared, the last word, for example, denoting the poetical and musical form of it. (See the Comm. on 1 Cor. xiv. 15.) As to the point whether the name *γένη γλωσσῶν* also denotes a peculiar form of the gift, consult the Commentary on 1 Cor. xiv. 10.

Again, with respect to the views which have been entertained of the gift of tongues, we may consider some of them as abandoned. To this class belongs the old orthodox opinion, that the gift of speaking all the languages of the world was bestowed once for all

* The passage adduced by the Apostle Paul, in 1 Cor. xiv. 21, from the Old Testament, is of such a kind, that apart from his citation of it, it would never have been regarded as referring to the *γλώσσαις λαλεῖν*. See the exposition of this passage, 1 Cor. xiv. 21. Ps. lxxxvii. 6, is a passage of the Old Testament particularly deserving of attention, because undoubtedly we may recognize in it an intimation of the gift of tongues.

upon the apostles, as a permanent endowment to fit them for their apostolic office. This idea is repugnant to history, because, not only had the apostles their interpreters, but many persons also received the gift of tongues whose office it by no means was to preach the gospel to all nations. (Compare Acts x. 46 regarding Cornelius.) In like manner we may regard as set aside the view which Cyprian, Gregory of Nazianzen, and at a later period, Erasmus and Schneckenburger have defended, that the miracle lay not in the speakers but in the hearers, the apostles speaking in their usual manner, and the hearers supposing each that he heard his own language. If this hypothesis, which rests particularly upon the form of expression used in verse 6, were tenable, then we must at the same time suppose that the *primitive tongue* was again made known by the Spirit to the apostles, and that each of the hearers thought he found his own dialect in it. This is the view of the gift which Billroth (on 1 Cor. xiv.) has attempted to uphold, and I confess that his argument, taken in connexion with this statement of Baur, has made me waver in my opinion. This explanation is attended with the special advantage of bringing out quite clearly the contrast between Pentecost, as the period of a restored unity of speech, and the confusion of tongues at the building of Babel. But I feel myself too much hampered by the text, both here and in 1 Cor. xiv., to be able to adopt this opinion as my own. Especially does the expression *γένη γλωσσῶν* (1 Cor. xii. 28), appear to me incompatible with this hypothesis.*

And if these explanations are untenable, equally must we dismiss the so-called *natural* explanation of the event, which makes the whole fact, so full of significance, degenerate into a mistake. We are required to suppose that the Christians who spoke were Persian and other Jews, and that they prayed in their own language, and when a great storm brought many others to the place, who took the Christians for men of Galilee, they were filled with astonishment, and fancied it was speaking with strange tongues which they heard. In this manner even Meyer understands the gift of tongues, but at the same time he supposes that Luke has disfigured the historical fact, and imagined there really was a miraculous speaking in strange languages. Most extraordinarily, he supposes that he has found a support for this superficial view in verse 15, because he imagines that if all present, even the apostles, who were Galileans by birth, had spoken in strange languages, then Peter would not

* Yet with Neander (Apost. Zeitalt. B. I. p. 172, note 1) we might explain this expression of the different forms in which the gift of tongues presented itself as *προσεύχεσθαι, ψάλλειν*, and the like. (Comp. 1 Cor. xiv. 15.) But if we observe the manner in which, with reference to the name *γένη γλωσσῶν*, the words *γένη φωνῶν* are employed in xiv. 10, we find ourselves obliged to renounce this expedient.

have said "these are not drunken" (*οὐ γὰρ οὗτοι μεθύουσιν*), but "*we* are not drunken" (*οὐ γὰρ ἡμεῖς μεθύομεν*). But on the principle of this conclusion the apostles would be the only persons who did not speak with tongues, while yet Paul declares, in 1 Cor. xiv. 18, that he spoke with tongues more than all of them. That this explanation suits none of the later passages, in which mention is made of the communication of the Spirit, is so clear that there is no need of any remarks upon the subject.

Between the extremes which have been mentioned, there lie intermediate views, which may be the subject of controversy. This much we may regard as generally acknowledged at the present day, that an elevated tone of mind, and one bordering upon ecstacy, was an essential element implied in speaking with tongues. A more vivid conception than the older theologians had reached, of the way and manner in which the Spirit works upon the mind, has gradually brought about this acknowledgment. (Compare the remarks on the *ἔκστασις* at Acts x. 9.) The description given by Paul leads also necessarily to the same conclusion, as the particular exposition of 1 Cor. xiv. will further shew. The power of the higher Spirit seized the soul of the inspired person so strongly, that his own consciousness (*νοῦς*) was depressed, and he declared things that lay quite beyond his own individual point of view. The state of tranquil clearness under the full influence of the Spirit, and of perfect consciousness, constitutes the *προφητεία*, *prophecy*, which stands higher than the gift of tongues. That on the occasion of Pentecost the whole company were under a powerful excitement, is plain from the expressions (verses 12, 13) that were uttered by the gathering crowds. But here the question presents itself, how this exalted spiritual condition was manifested, and why it received the name it bears, for every state of ecstacy (*ἔκστασις*) was not speaking with tongues. The answer of this question brings out views which differ widely from one another. At this point, however, the philological investigation of the word *γλῶσσα* becomes indispensable. *Γλῶσσα* has three significations: 1, tongue; 2, language; 3, an antiquated poetical or provincial word.

The first signification Bardili and Eichhorn have attempted to establish here, supposing that when the disciples spoke in the state of ecstacy, they did not utter distinctly articulate sounds, but only a kind of stammer. They appeal in defence of this view particularly to 1 Cor. xiv. 7–9, where speaking with tongues is compared with indistinct tones from an instrument. But this comparison does not refer to the single sounds of an instrument, but to the whole melody produced upon it; and therefore it can only be the obscurity usually prevailing in the speeches *taken as a whole* of the person who spoke with tongues (*γλώσσαις λαλῶν*) that is indicated, and not the inarticulateness of single words, which would have made the discourse unintelligible even to the interpreter. Besides, there is the philological argument against this supposition, that it would always require the phrase γλώσσῃ λαλεῖν to be used, while yet we have the plural γλώσσαις applied even to an individual speaker (1 Cor. xiv. 6). This first signification of the word must therefore, at all events, be abandoned. All the greater vigour, however, has been displayed of late in defending the third of the significations specified above. Bleek* has shewn, by ample details, what indeed was not doubted, that γλῶσσα may mean "an old provincial expression." [Besides other passages, he appeals in particular to the words γλῶσσαι κατὰ πόλεις occurring in the "Anecdotis Græcis" of Becker, by which are meant the provincialisms of particular Greek cities. Γλώσσημα is used quite synonymously with γλῶσσα, and is by no means the explanation of a provincialism or rare poetical expression, as is usually supposed. Dionysius of Halicarnassus (de verb. or composi. c. 25) calls poetical expressions γλωσσηματικαὶ λέξεις. Now, following this signification of γλῶσσα, Bleek supposes that the γλώσσαις λαλεῖν, meant an inspired address uttered in the common language, but intermixed with unusual poetical expressions. But he himself confesses, that although all other passages of the New Testament in which this gift is mentioned might appear favourable to his hypothesis, yet the history of Pentecost is not so; for the first and abiding impression made by Luke's statement is, that the gathering strangers heard the disciples speak not in poetical and uncommon diction, exhibiting here and there an Arabic and Egyptian phrase, but in their own language, and accordingly γλῶσσα and διάλεκτος are interchanged with one another in verses 6, 8, 11. Bleek, therefore, can only construct a negative argument here, in that he attempts to shew that the idea of the use of foreign tongues involves an inconsistency, and ought therefore, notwithstanding what the text seems to affirm, to be rejected.† But the correctness of this assertion may

* In Ullmann's Studien, 1829, part i., page 33, etc.

† A *miracle* always involves "an inconsistency" with the ordinary laws of nature. To explain it by these laws is to destroy it. The only required warrant for admitting it is the clear declaration of the word of God, and this most assuredly, when we can see a high moral purpose to be subserved by it. Both conditions are here fulfilled. The sacred writer obviously *intends* to describe a miracle; and the *occasion*, viz., that on which the glorified Redeemer signalizes his return to his Father by sending forth the Spirit, and formally inaugurating the spiritual dispensation, as manifestly justifies it, as did the introduction of the old dispensation, or the birth of Christ. And as the miracle is timely, so in character it is strikingly appropriate. The old economy was ushered in amidst storm and earthquake; the birth of Christ by a vision of angels to the Jews and of a star to the Gentiles, intimating that the light of the world was born: and so the special epoch of the Spirit is inaugurated by a miraculous gift of tongues, intimating that all nations are to share in its blessings. No miracle could be more striking as a *sign* to the assembled strangers, or as a *symbol* of the character of the apostolic ministry. The subsequent appeal

be easily controverted, and this leads us to the consideration of the second meaning of γλῶσσα, viz., language.

Of the appropriateness of this signification in the passage before us there can be no question, for, in Acts ii. 6, 8, 11, as has already been remarked, the words γλῶσσα and διάλεκτος are manifestly interchanged, of which the latter can never stand for poetical expressions: besides the whole description accords with the supposition, that the apostles spoke in foreign languages. But it appears surprising that in no other part of the New Testament is there anything expressly said of speaking in foreign languages: on the contrary, it is only the sublime and the obscure which are exhibited in the speeches of those who speak with tongues (γλώσσαις). For this reason I dissent from the old and certainly untenable supposition, already opposed in these pages, that the gift of tongues was the *permanent* power of speaking foreign languages. To me it appears that the gift of speaking with tongues was frequently manifested, simply in the way Bleek describes, as a kind of elevated speaking in which single uncommon words might be introduced; but *first*, it was not always so; and *secondly*, I am persuaded that the name was not borrowed from the unusual expressions. We must rather maintain, in accordance with the account of Pentecost given by Luke, that on that occasion the gift undeniably displayed itself in the employment of foreign languages. But the power of using them was not a permanent endowment, but only an ability communicated for the time, and was displayed as part of the gift, only when the gift was exhibited in its highest form. The miraculous features of the gift must of course be acknowledged as such, although there are analogies which enable us to soften down its startling aspect.* The foreign tongues in which

to magnetism is every way gratuitous. If it *had* force, we ought to see the powerful impulses of Christian love operating similarly now. But, although its ardour *stimulates* the mental powers, and accelerates the processes of study, it exhibits not the slightest tendency to *supersede* them.—[K.

* Neander, in his excellent and exceedingly instructive work on the times of the apostles (part i. p. 17), affirms that different foreign languages cannot here be spoken of, because in all the regions that are named, the Greek tongue was at that time the prevailing one. But this view, I think, is only the consequence of the general notion which this learned man entertains of the nature of the gift of tongues. Neander considers this gift only as the original index of the great change which Christianity accomplishes in the hearts of men, and he appeals for proof to such passages as Luke xxi. 15. (Apost. Zeit. p. 19.) He supposes, however, that afterwards the expression, "speaking with tongues," was fixed particularly to denote that inspired speaking, in which the consciousness of the speaker himself disappeared. But, in reference to the passage before us, this view appears to have little to recommend it: for Luke's intention in giving the catalogue of nations could be nothing else, than to indicate that all the languages of the world were understood. Neander supposes he is able to justify his view by passages from the Fathers, but the places he quotes are of such a kind as are quite compatible with other views of the gift of tongues. The passage from Irenæus, v. 26, in particular, presenting the expression παντοδαπαῖς γλώσσαις λαλεῖν, which does not at all occur in the New Testa-

these persons spoke, were only such as were used by strangers actually present: no apostle spoke Chinese, because no individual from China was there. If we think of the imparted Spirit as the principle of love and true communion (κοινωνία), then we may imagine how his communications rendered a meeting of hearts possible, and in this way led to a transference of one into another. When the fire which filled the apostles, passed from them into the hearts of the strangers, so as to make them also believe, then too the language of the strangers went over from them to the apostles. There is presented, in the very different sphere of animal magnetism, a phenomenon which affords an illustration of this transference. We find that somnambulists speak languages, of which at other times they are ignorant, when they are brought into connexion with those who know them. This in like manner is a fact which can only be explained by supposing the inward life of different individuals to be communicated to one another. At Pentecost the gift of tongues appeared in its full power, and displayed itself in the speaking of foreign languages. From this first exhibition of it it took its name, which in the full form ran thus; "to speak with other or new tongues" (ἑτέραις or καιναῖς γλώσσαις λαλεῖν), or more shortly, "to speak with tongues or a tongue" (γλώσσαις, or γλώσσῃ λαλεῖν), also "kinds of tongues" (γένη γλωσσῶν), see 1 Cor. xii. 28, and Comm. on 1 Cor. xiv. 10, and the same name continued to be employed afterwards, even when the gift was not so fully manifested. In the phrase γλώσσαις λαλεῖν, then, the signification of *language* is the only one that is applicable to γλῶσσα, and this signification too brings out plainly the meaning of γλώσσῃ λαλεῖν, for this form arose from the fact that sometimes there was only speaking in one foreign language. But, with Bleek's view of γλῶσσα, this phraseology is always improper, because no person could display the gift of tongues in a speech by the employment of a single provincialism or antique word.

(Regarding the details, see Comm. on 1 Cor. xiv. Of works on the subject before us, a full enumeration is given by Kuinoel at the passage, and by Bleek in the work mentioned above. The most important are: J. A. Ernesti opusc. theol. pag. 455–477. Bardili significatus primitivus vocis προφήτης. Gotting. 1786. Eichhorn, allgem. Bibl. der biblischen Literatur Bd. I. iii. Herder, von der Gabe der Sprachen, Riga, 1794. Storr, notitiæ hist. in epist. Pauli ad Corinthios, Tubingæ, 1788. Melville observationes de dono linguarum, Basil, 1816. Again Bleek's excellent treatise in the Stu-

ment, points evidently to an actual speaking in different languages. But the declarations of the Fathers, proceeding as they did upon the principle that the gift was known from observation, are of too general a kind [illegible] be inferred from them respecting its nature.

dien of Ullman und Umbreit as cited above, together with the supplement to it, 1830, part i. page 45, etc. The latter has reference to my remarks, which are to be found in the same journal, 1829, Part III. p. 538, etc.; 1830, P. I. p. 65, etc.; 1831, Part III. p. 566, etc. The papers of Baur and Steudel in der tübinger Zeitscrift für Theologie, are unusually instructive, 1830 and 1831. Consult also the article of Scholl in Klaiber's Studien, Bd. iii. p. i., 1831, p. 168, ff., and that of Baümlein in the same work, Bd. vi. p. 2, 1834, p. 40, ff. On the Catholic side Weihart has expressed himself on the subject in the Jahrb. für Theol. und Christl. Phil., Bd. v. p. 2, p. 288, ff. Frankf. A. M. 1835. Again, the gift of tongues is handled by Flatt, in a special appendix to the first epistle to the Corinthians, p. 414–448, and by Billroth at the 14th chap. of the first epistle to the Corinthians, and finally by Jäger, in his exposition of the epistles to the Corinthians, Tübingen, 1838, appendix, p. 186, etc.)

Verses 12–16.—In few words, Luke further describes the uncertainty of the strangers who had come together: the more timid natures among them apprehended some danger from this violent excitement, the more bold mocked at it. Yet plainly this mockery is not to be regarded as bitter and malignant mockery, but as good-humoured jesting. Their observation of the scene was in fact accurate, for the outward appearance did resemble drunkenness (Ps. xxxvi. 9); and therefore Peter, in the speech that follows, censures their allegation but mildly.

Here Luke communicates to us the first preaching of the Gospel by the apostles, and thus the institution of the preacher's office appears connected with the very founding of the church. All the peculiarities of the apostolic preaching (κήρυγμα) we discover in this first discourse. It embraces no reflections or reasonings upon the doctrine of Christ, no enunciation of new and unknown dogmas, but simply and alone the *proclamation of historical facts.* The apostles appear here quite in their proper character as witnesses of what they had experienced; the resurrection of Jesus forms the central point of their testimony. In the later development of the church, it is true, preaching could not be limited to this bare proclamation: it was gradually directed to the additional object of guiding believers onward in knowledge. Yet never in preaching ought the simple declaration of the mighty works of God, such as is here made by Peter, to be wanting for those whose hearts have not yet been penetrated by the word. This disciple is here again presented to us, notwithstanding his denial of Christ, as the organ of the apostolic company: he is, as it were, the mouth by which they make themselves understood—their speaker. (Διαχλευάζω = the more common χλευάζω, corresponds entirely to ἐμπαίζειν.—Γλεῦκος =

יַיִן, Job xxxii, 19, LXX.—Ἐνωτίζεσθαι = הַאֲזִין appears to belong to the Alexandrian dialect.

Ver. 17–21.—For the purpose of leading the assembled Jews to the meaning of the spectacle before them, Peter quotes in detail a remarkable prediction from the Old Testament (Joel iii. 1–5), in which the outpouring of the Spirit was promised. The idea of spiritual communication was quite familiar to the prophets of the Old Testament, as has already been remarked; they had themselves experienced, in a lively manner, the breathing of the Spirit, and yet still there remained to them the feeling of a void and of longing desire: hence they were able to conclude, from the analogy of development, which displays itself in ever-enlarging results, that one day an infinitely richer fulness of the Spirit would be poured out, not upon a few merely, but upon all flesh, upon the entire community of those who were concerned for salvation. And to this conclusion the Spirit of prophecy affixed in their minds the seal of perfect certainty. Hence, besides Joel, several other prophets speak of the effusion of the Spirit to be expected. (Comp. Numb. xi. 29; Isaiah xxxii. 15, xliv. 3; Ezek. xxxvi. 25, xxxix. 29); but Peter quotes the passage before us, because it describes not only the outpouring of the Spirit, but also its *effects*, and that too in such a manner as to furnish an explanation of the inspired state in which the assembled believers were seen to be. The speaking with tongues, together with the whole excitement, which displayed itself not only in the men but also in the women (i. 14), Peter comprehended under the *προφητεύειν, prophesying*, which Joel promises. He says, therefore, as it were, "behold, we *all* prophesy! instead of the few single prophets of the Old Testament, the whole people are now filled with the prophetic spirit." The words quoted agree essentially with the original text and the Septuagint, but as they are quoted from memory, it is not surprising that there are transpositions and unimportant additions. One deviation, however, from the Hebrew and the Septuagint, must not be overlooked. Just at the beginning, Luke (verse 17) writes *ἔσται ἐν ταῖς ἐσχάταις ἡμέραις, it shall be in the last days.* This expression is surprising, because it was not yet the last time when the Spirit fell upon the apostles. Besides, the Septuagint has only *ἔσται μετὰ ταῦτα*, and the Hebrew הָיָה אַחֲרֵי כֵן, which expression appears far more suitable to Peter's purpose. But this passage is to be explained from the idea of the apostles, which pervades the whole of the New Testament, that with the advent of Christ in the flesh the end of things was really at hand. Therefore the apostle quotes also the verse in which mention is made of the terrible signs connected with the future: this description is designed to excite to repentance by means of fear, while verse 21* allures to it by the exhibition of mercy. (See the particulars in the Comm. on Matth. xxiv. 1. Respecting the promised wonders, too, compare the prophetical passages of the New Testament, Matth. xxiv. 2 ; 2 Pet. ii. 8 ; Rev. viii.) Besides this deviation, there is also in the Hebrew text of Joel, a remarkable difference from the Septuagint, with which latter the passage as given by Luke entirely agrees. While in the Hebrew it is said, with comprehensive generality, אֶשְׁפּוֹךְ אֶת־רוּחִי, Luke and the Septuagint have *ἐκχεῶ ἀπὸ τοῦ πνεύματός μου*. By this latter mode of expression, the outpouring of the Holy Ghost, powerful and mighty as it was, is yet characterized as a *partial* effusion ; so that the prediction of Joel in its original form still remains for the future, when the complete fulness of the Divine Spirit is to be conferred upon the church, which shall then have received into her bosom the countless races of mankind. (Comp. Comm. Part I., at Luke iv. 18, 19.)

Vers. 22–24.—The predictions of the Old Testament referred to by Peter afforded a proof that the new economy, now brought under the notice of the gathering multitude, was the fulfilment of prophecy, the flower, as it were, of the ancient stem. The apostle, therefore, now appeals to his hearers with the view of awakening their hearts to repentance, and thus preparing them to receive the rich grace of the Gospel. He reminds them of their wickedness in putting Jesus to death. But it would seem that Peter was accusing the innocent, for it is inconceivable that the strangers from afar, who had come to Zion only under the impulse of longing desire, and in obedience to the law, should have taken part in the murder of the Holy One ; and even supposing there were some of the multitude who had joined in the cry, "crucify him, crucify him," why does Peter accuse them all, without distinction, of so heinous a crime, when assuredly they were not all in the same condemnation ?† Now, strange as such language sounds to man in his natural isolation, in which he fancies himself separate from all his brethren, and bearing alone his own guilt and merit, it yet appears a simple truth to him who feels himself connected by the social principle with the great whole of humanity. What any one member of the community

* Regarding verse 21, see Comm. on Rom. x. 13.

† Meyer makes the apostle's charge rest simply upon the fact, that Jesus was put to death by the Sanhedrim, the highest court of justice among the Jews, and that therefore his death was a judicial murder, perpetrated in the name of the whole nation. But in that case Peter should have said the very thing which Meyer improperly starts as an objection to my view, "*We* have killed him," for Peter and the other apostles belonged to the Israelitish nation too. What Peter here says to the Jews, may be said at all times and among all nations. It was the sin of mankind that brought Jesus to the cross. And he only is free from this sin who has confessed it with penitence and faith, and received pardon. Now as this was the case with the apostles, Peter could not speak in the first person.

performs, he recognizes as the deed of the community; what any one man performs, he recognizes as the deed of the race. Everything good, therefore, awakens in him sympathetic joy; everything evil, pity; for he shares in them both. Of all evil, in particular, he discovers the root in his own heart, which, in unfavourable circumstances might have borne all the bitter fruits which it anywhere tends to produce. But the murder of the Holy One of God is the very highest point of development which sin could reach; and always and everywhere it is the nature of sin to hate him (and hatred is murder itself, 1 John iii. 15) who has come to exterminate it. Just as far, therefore, as sin prevails in man, does hatred against the Lord possess him; for Christ and sin are always opposed to one another, they seek each other's destruction; first of all, sin kills the Prince of Life, but, when his life is reproduced by its own power, it finally destroys sin. This profound connexion of the individual with the whole race, the hearers of Peter apprehended, although properly as matter of *feeling* only, with entire correctness. Not one of them declares he is innocent of the death of the Lord, but on the contrary the word of the Spirit, like a sword, pierced them through the heart (verse 37), and they recognized in the death of Christ a common act of the human race, which contracted a common guilt. For a fuller consideration of this subject, see Comm. on the leading passage respecting it, Rom. v. 12, etc.

(On the ideas expressed by δύναμις, τέρας, σημεῖον, see at Matth. viii. 1. The word ἀποδείκνυμι here indicates the authentication which the miracles referred to were intended to give to the Divine mission of Christ. Ἀπό is not = ὑπό, as Kuinoel supposes, but indicates that the miraculous power proceeds from God.—Ἔκδοτον with λαμβάνειν, as with δοῦναι, occurs frequently, especially in Josephus, in the sense of "delivering into the power of any one, or receiving." With προσπήξαντες supply σταυρῷ.—The higher necessity that existed for the death of Christ has already been treated in detail in the history of the passion at Luke xxii. 22. Βουλή and πρόγνωσις denote will and knowledge, which in God must necessarily be viewed as one. Ὡρισμένος expresses the fixedness and absoluteness of the Divine will. See particulars at Rom. viii. 29.)

The sin of man, however, was retrieved by God's mercy, which called back the crucified Redeemer into life. In the simple thought of ver. 24 there is only one thing doubtful, how we are to understand the words οὐκ ἦν δυνατὸν κρατεῖσθαι αὐτόν, *it was not possible that he should be holden;* whether it was impossible that the bonds of death should hold him, because he was himself the life, and consequently also the resurrection, or because God designed to raise him. But both reasons coalesce, when we keep in view, that it was even the will of the Father, that the Son should have in himself the fountain of life (John v. 26); whence also it is sometimes said the Father raises the Son, and sometimes the Son himself resumes life (John x. 18). (The expression ὠδῖνες θανάτου corresponds entirely to the Hebrew חֶבְלֵי מָוֶת. The Septuagint sometimes renders the phrase by σχοινία [Ps. cxix. 61], and sometimes by ὠδῖνες [Ps. xviii. 5], because the Hebrew word unites the two significations of "cord" and "birth-pains." In the pure Greek tongue, ὠδῖνες has only the latter signification, but in the Hellenistic it acquired the other, too, as they are conjoined in the Hebrew word. In the passage before us, λύειν and κρατεῖν plainly point to the signification of "band or cord" as the proper one.*—The reading ᾅδου instead of θανάτου, is supported by such weighty authorities, that it stands at least upon a level with it; in the sense there is no difference, for Hades is to be conceived only as the place of the dead, and thus identical with θάνατος.

Vers. 25–31.—To exhibit the correspondence between the fact of the resurrection and the predictions of the Old Testament, Peter quotes a passage (following the Septuagint exactly) from Ps. xvi. 8–11, and subjoins an exposition of these verses (29–31). In this exposition he shews that the words of the psalm were not applicable to David, because he was dead and buried. His explicit declaration makes a typical view of the words quite inadmissible; for in no sense has the prediction been fulfilled in David, that he should not see corruption. We must here accordingly, as in Psalm cx., acknowledge a real direct prophecy. Yet we are not to view it as having no subjective connexion with David: even in direct predictions some such connexion must always be supposed as the groundwork. In the case before us, it may be thus conceived, that in David the dread of corruption and of the dark valley of death awakened the longing desire of victory over it; and this the prophetic Spirit led him to see realized in the person of the Messiah. Now in Psalm xvi. death is contemplated in its twofold operation, first, in relation to the body, and secondly, to the soul. The body is represented as guarded against the last effect of death, viz., corruption (διαφθορά), and the soul is described as beholding indeed the dark place of shades, but as speedily delivered from it, and restored to the kingdom of light. The exactness with which these points were realized in the development of Christ's life, makes the prediction one of the most remarkable in Holy Writ. While his sacred body was untouched by corruption, and rose from the grave, his soul went to the dead (1 Pet. iii. 18),† but speedily returned again, and

* Meyer, on this passage, doubts whether, in the Hellenistic dialect ὠδίν was used in the signification of "band, fetter." The passages quoted by Schleusner in his Lexicon on the Septuag., tom. v. p. 571, sqq. might teach him better.

† The passage, properly interpreted, furnishes no support to this opinion. "My soul," — נַפְשִׁי, is a well-known emphatic Hebraism for "me." Hades, the abode of the dead· then, by metonymy, for death. Thus the two clauses are in strict parallelism, the

ascended with his glorified body to the eternal mansions of light. '

(Προωρώμην, in verse 25, expresses the idea of contemplating an object, "having it before the eyes." The expression *ἐκ δεξιῶν* = מִימִינִי, involves here the idea of help, support. For *ἡ γλῶσσά μου* the Hebrew text has כְבוֹדִי, = *ἡ δόξα μου*. Probably the Seventy, who, like Luke, have *γλῶσσα*, already read the original differently: perhaps their Hebrew MSS. had לְשׁוֹנִי. Κατασκηνοῦν = שָׁכַן, denotes rest in the grave. On the subject of Hades, comp. Comm. on Luke xvi. 23. With *εἰς ᾅδου* we must obviously supply *οἶκον*.—Ver. 27. As to the reading חֲסִידֶיךָ, in Ps. xvi. 10, see De Wette's Commentary on the passage before us. In the expression *ὁδὸς ζωῆς*, in verse 28, the material and the spiritual are intimately combined. The train of thought would refer *ζωή* primarily to the outward life; but the highest manifestation of the life that overcomes death is never to be conceived apart from the inward life which is bestowed by the *Spirit* [*πνεῦμα*]. In verse 29 David is called the patriarch, which the Seventy, in 1 Chron. xxiv. 31, put for רָאשֵׁי הָאָבוֹת. Comp. Acts vii. 8, 9; Heb. vii. 4. The supposed tomb of David was pillaged by Joannes Hyrcanus and Herod. Comp. Joseph. Arch. vii. 15, 3, xiii. 8, 4.—In verse 30, Peter refers to Ps. lxxxix. 4, 5, and cxxxii. 11, which represent David in his peculiar relation to the Messiah, not simply as one of his ancestors, but also as the prefiguration of the theocratical kingdom. This position pre-eminently fitted him for receiving those prophetic views into the future, which the apostle had just explained to his hearers. The reference, however, to these passages is only of a general kind; and therefore *καρπὸς τῆς ὀσφύος* is put for פְּרִי בֶטֶן, while more strictly *κοιλίας* would have been employed. With *ἐκ καρποῦ* supply *τινά*.)

Vers. 32–36.—Along with the resurrection of our Lord, Peter also mentions his ascension, with which the outpouring of the Holy Ghost was most closely connected. In this respect, too, Peter again compares David with Christ, and shews that he himself styled the Messiah his Lord, and foretold his sitting at the right hand of God. And thereupon the apostle demands of the house of Israel that they acknowledge him who a few weeks before was crucified as their Lord and Messiah: *And they believe!* A stronger proof cannot well be imagined than this, that it was the power of the Holy Ghost which made the words of the preacher move the hearts of the hearers! To all Jews the cross of Christ was a stumbling-block, and yet they recognize, on the word of a private individual, the crucified and deeply abased Jesus as their Saviour.

(In verse 32 *οὗ* is not to be understood as neuter. The apostles

latter interpreting the former:—"Thou wilt not leave me in the power of death, nor suffer thy Holy One to see corruption."—[K.

are the witnesses of Christ, and not merely of his resurrection. This is clear from the parallel passage in chap. v. 31, where it is said *ἡμεῖς ἐσμεν αὐτοῦ μάρτυρες τῶν ῥημάτων τούτων*. In ver. 33, *τῇ δεξιᾷ ὑψωθείς* is not to be understood as meaning "exalted by the right hand of God," but "exalted to the right hand of God," as is shewn by ver. 34 and the parallel passage in chap. v. 31. The connexion, it is true, of the dative with verbs of motion is rare, and occurs almost solely in poetical diction. But the representation here given partakes somewhat of a poetical strain. For particulars on the point consult Winer's Gramm. p. 191, seq.—Ver. 33, respecting *ἐπαγγελίαν λαβὼν παρὰ τοῦ πατρός* see Comm. on John xiv. 16.—Ver. 34. The quotation is taken from Ps. cx. 1. Comp. on the Psalm remarks at Matth. xxii. 44.)

Vers. 37–41.—To the question of the hearers, "What shall we do?" the apostle replies by admonishing them to repentance and faith, both of which are presupposed in baptism. It is not to works of one kind or another he points, but to an inward change of heart. *Μετανοήσατε* in ver. 38 defines more narrowly the import of *κατανύττεσθαι τῇ καρδίᾳ*. This expression, as here employed, denotes not predominantly the idea of pain, as is usually alleged, but indicates in general the idea of being struck or arrested. The discourse of Peter touched them to the inmost soul, and excited feelings of every kind, sad as well as joyful, for the apostle had let them see, that the promises of the prophets were now fulfilled. (The proper signification of *κατανύττω* is "to pierce," "compungere," hence "to excite," "to awaken.") In *μετάνοια*, *repentance*, on the other hand, the idea of pain predominates. The admonition of Peter is accordingly to be conceived thus: "First of all, enter profoundly into your sin, that you may feel the full sorrow it should inspire, and long for a thorough conversion." With this repentance baptism is then connected, which necessarily presupposes faith, because it requires an acknowledgment of Christ as the Messiah. And baptism is accompanied with the remission of sins (*ἄφεσις ἁμαρτιῶν*), as a result. This is the negative side of the blessing, the removal of the *old man*, which is a necessary preparation for the positive side, the communication of the Spirit, with which the establishment of the *new man* takes place. Quite correctly, therefore, does Luther say, that "where there is the forgiveness of sins, there is life and blessedness;" for a reconciled heart, as such, possesses the gift of the Holy Ghost, although not in the form in which it was displayed in the apostolic church. (Compare Acts viii. 15.) If now we compare the description given in Matth. iii. 11 of the baptism of John, its relation to the baptism of Christ will appear quite obvious. The former aims at the awakening of repentance (*εἰς μετάνοιαν*), the latter begins where the former ends: it presupposes repentance (μετάνοια) together with faith, which it confirms and seals, and it communicates a real heavenly power. There is a difficulty still in ver. 39, where Peter represents those likewise who are far away (οἱ εἰς μακράν), as called to receive the Holy Ghost. The question presents itself, whether Peter here referred to the Gentile world. It has been supposed that what is mentioned in the tenth chapter obliges us to doubt this, and to refer the expression either to the Jews scattered through the Gentile world, or taking the idea of time, as Beza does, to the remotest posterity. Let it be considered, however, that Peter, according to chap. x., did not doubt the calling of the Gentiles, but only whether they were to be called without passing through Judaism, and it will be evident that all reason disappears for excluding from the language of the apostle a reference to the Gentiles. Rather the words, "Whomsoever the Lord our God shall call" (ὅσους ἂν προσκαλέσηται κύριος ὁ Θεὸς ἡμῶν) necessarily point to the Gentiles, for the Israelites could not then be called for the first time, as they were already in possession of God's gracious covenant. (Respecting baptism in the name of Jesus, see Comm. on Matth. xxviii. 19.) The words of Peter which are recorded, are only a brief specimen of his more detailed admonitions, from which the author adduces yet one other exhortation: "save yourselves from this perverse generation" (σώθητε ἀπὸ τῆς γενεᾶς τῆς σκολιᾶς ταύτης.) Σώζεσθαι, *saved*, is here to be understood as referring to the judgments, described above in verses 19 and 20 as near: so that there is plainly suggested a comparison with the flood or the destruction of Sodom. "Save yourselves like Noah or Lot, getting out from amongst this untoward generation, that is doomed to destruction." Γενεὰ σκολιά agrees with Deut. xxxii. 5; comp. Phil. ii. 15. Σκολιός denotes primarily "crooked" (Luke iii. 5), then, as applied to moral subjects, "impure, sinful."

As the hearers received with joy (ἀσμένως) the intelligence of salvation presented by Peter, baptism was immediately administered to three thousand persons. Thus, along with the preaching of the word, the sacrament of baptism was at once dispensed on the day of Pentecost, and that too no longer, like the apostolic baptism which preceded the outpouring of the Spirit, as a mere baptism of repentance, but as the *baptism of regeneration.*[*] This baptism,

* Respecting the question, whether those who had been baptized by John the Baptist were again baptized by the apostles, see the remarks on chap. xix. 5. It is difficult, however, to answer the question how the baptism of three thousand persons could be performed in one day, according to the old practice of a complete submersion, the more especially as in Jerusalem there was no water at hand with the exception of Kidron and a few pools. But to have baptized so many persons in these would necessarily have excited in the highest degree the attention of the authorities. The difficulty can only be removed by supposing that they already employed mere sprinkling, or that they baptised

however, took place without any preparatory instruction. It was after baptism that the teaching (διδαχή), mentioned in verse 42, was first given, which was probably, however, confined to the proof of the Messiahship of Christ from the Old Testament ; and hence we may see that it was not dogmas upon which the apostles laid stress, but the disposition and bent of the mind.* The man who received the proclamation of the Gospel with susceptible mind, who professed faith in Christ, who was penetrated with the new principle of the higher life brought by the Saviour to mankind, was for that reason baptized, and by this means his faith was confirmed and sealed, the powers of the Spirit were imparted to him, and he was thus separated from the world, and became a saint, ἅγιος, ἡγιασμένος. But in proportion as the original power and fulness of the Spirit disappeared in the church, the necessity would become the more urgent for making instruction precede baptism, because the communication of clearer views respecting the specific nature of Christianity, was the only means, in the more lifeless period of the church, of giving to the weaker influences of the Spirit, as they came upon the mind, that right direction which he himself at an earlier period had instinctively, as it were, imparted to sincere minds, by his more powerful working. The church, therefore, in its gradual development, followed exactly the course of development in the individual. As in the child simplicity of mind prevails, and though life certainly is present, there is not the clear consciousness of the properties of life, so was it in the young church : it is in youth that the intellectual faculties begin to assert their pre-eminence, and so also in the church the need of Christian knowledge gradually made itself apparent, a need which, in the great mass, presents itself as the requirement of instruction before baptism. The perfection of the church will be the return of the original *immediateness* of life, connected with perfect clearness of knowledge.

Vers. 42–47.—With the special account of the first Christian discourse of Peter and its effects, there is connected in the following verses a general view of the life of the church in Jerusalem. Passages thus bearing a general character are intermixed in the

in houses in tubs ; formal submersion in rivers or larger quantities of water probably took place only where the locality conveniently allowed it.

* Neander, in the work cited above, page 28, observes correctly, that we must not regard the three thousand who were converted in one day as all at once transformed into thorough Christians : without doubt the very suddenness of the change that took place in their condition would leave much of a heterogeneous character connected with them. But, on the other hand, again, it must not be overlooked, that this sudden conversion undoubtedly produced in the thousands mentioned a specific change. As a tree always continues an improved one, although below the precious graft water shoots continue to grow ; so also were those minds, which had been put by the leaven of the Gospel into spiritual fermentation, really born again, although in them the old man was not yet annihilated.

Acts of the Apostles with special accounts of particular occurrences; at first the general statements are longer (iv. 32-35, v. 12-16), then they become shorter (v. 42, vi. 7, viii. 25, xii. 24, 25), and at last they cease altogether after xiii. 1, and the narrative becomes a connected particular account. Now, as this coincides exactly with the point where the particular accounts of the apostle Paul and his journeys commence (xiii. 1), it is certainly more than probable that this interchange of special accounts with general views, in the first half of the Acts of the Apostles, is to be traced to the manner in which the book was formed. The general observations have *either* proceeded from Luke himself, and been inserted between the special accounts drawn from documents of particular occurrences, or they are the concluding statements of those documents themselves. I would declare myself for the former view, if in the general observations there appeared any perceptible difference of style; but so little is that the case, that in them, just as in the special accounts, the Hebrew colouring of the language can be very plainly recognized. The language from the beginning of the xiii. chapter has a far less heterogeneous stamp; and therefore it is in the highest degree probable, that in the second half of the work, Luke wrote less from documents lying before him, than from his own knowledge.

Further, the general view itself, which is presented to us in this passage, is by no means without interest, because with a few touches it describes the mode of life in the most ancient Christian church, and exhibits the *earliest elements of worship.** The peculiar spirit of the gospel is exhibited by this description quite clearly before our eyes. Those men who had poured in from curiosity to see what

* Although the gospel teaches that God is to be worshipped in spirit, it yet requires an outward form of worship. The Redeemer designed to found a visible church, which necessarily presupposes an external service of God (cultus). Worship accordingly exists in the Christian church not merely for the sake of the weak, but also for the most advanced, in whom the old natural man that needs an outward form still lives; worship too is instituted, not merely for the proclamation of the Gospel to unbelievers, but it also embraces an element of pure adoration for the faithful. The worship of the church is designed for a perpetual thank-offering of believers, which is presented to the Lord for his propitiatory sacrifice of ever-during validity (1 Pet. ii. 5; Heb. xiii. 15). This element of adoration, with spurious objectiveness, has acquired in the Catholic church an undue predominance, while in the Reformed church, with spurious subjectiveness, the preacher and his discourse have too much supplanted the element of adoration. The middle course is the right one, and it requires the two to be so distributed that the minister may stand forth, not only in his subjectiveness as a teacher, but also as a true "liturgus," that is, as the organ through which the adoration of the church receives expression. According to this view Divine service has two essentially different halves; *first*, the preaching of the gospel, which is designed partly to convert unbelievers, and partly to advance believers in knowledge; *secondly*, adoration, which has its central point in the eucharist, the great thank-offering of the church, and a symbolical representation at the same time of the sacrifice of Christ. For these ideas I am indebted to the spirited preface of the Romish hymn book, in which (page lxxxvi. etc.) they are developed in an uncommonly attractive and convincing manner.

was going on, we find here knit together by the uniting spirit of Christ into a living brotherhood. The young church of Christ had but few peculiarities in its outward form, or even in its doctrine: the single discriminating principle of its few members was, that they all recognized the crucified Jesus of Nazareth as the Messiah. This confession would have been a thing of no importance, if it had only presented itself as a naked declaration, and would never in such a case have been able to form a community, that would spread itself in a few years over the whole Roman empire; this confession of Jesus as the Messiah acquired its value, only through the power of the Holy Ghost passing from the apostles as they preached to the hearers, for he brought the confession from the very hearts of men (1 Cor. xii. 3), and like a burning flame made their souls glow with love. By the power of this spirit, therefore, we not only behold the first Christians in a state of active outward fellowship, but we find them also internally changed: the narrow views of the natural man are broken through, they have their possessions in common, and they regard themselves as one family.

The first thing which is named as an element of Christian worship, is the διδαχὴ τῶν ἀποστόλων, *teaching of the apostles.* As the original form of church order was borrowed from the Jewish Synagogue, we may conclude that the apostolic teaching would have writings of the Old Testament for its basis. Its specific Christian character was derived from the circumstance, that predictions of the Old Testament were exhibited in their fulfilment in the person of Jesus of Nazareth. As, however, no instruction preceded baptism, the teachers of the church, in their lessons from the Old Testament, must have provided, according to circumstances, for the advancement of believers in all parts of knowledge, which, particularly among the Gentile churches, must have been imperatively necessary.

The second point, viz., the κοινωνία, *fellowship,* is attended with more difficulty. The word cannot possibly be understood of the general fellowship of the Spirit, for this could not have been represented as a separate particular, being in fact the general principle from which everything else proceeded. And to connect the word with κλάσις ἄρτου, *breaking of bread,* so that κοινωνία and κλάσις may be viewed as a hendiadys, is plainly precluded by the repetition of καί, which places κοινωνία upon a level with the other three particulars. It only remains therefore that we understand κοινωνία, as not only Mosheim (de rebus Christianis ante Const. p. 113, seq.), but also the most recent interpreters of the Acts of the Apostles do, to signify the bestowment of outward means of support, whether in money or goods.* To express this idea, the Apostle Paul uses the

* Neander supposes that κοινωνία can only mean the whole of the common intercourse

word frequently (Rom. xv. 26; 2 Cor. viii. 4, ix. 13), and in so far as such a physical *κοινωνία*, if I may use this expression, was collected and remitted to strangers, it was called also *διακονία*, *ministry*. (Acts xi. 29, compared with 2 Cor. viii. 4, ix. 13.) As the passage before us, however, speaks of the meetings of believers for the worship of God, this circumstance gives to *κοινωνία* a modified signification. It must denote such gifts as were presented in the *public assemblies*. But these are precisely what were named at a later period *oblations*, in which therefore we must recognize a primitive Christian institution. Mosheim rightly observes that the offering of Ananias, mentioned in chapter v., must have been such an oblation.

There are fewer difficulties connected with the third point, viz., the *κλάσις τοῦ ἄρτου*, *breaking of bread*.* The whole question, whether common or sacred repasts should be understood by the expression, loses its importance, when it is considered that the ancient Christians were in the habit of eating together daily, or holding the love-feast, and never took the common meal without observing the Lord's Supper. In the apostolic church at Jerusalem there appears to have obtained, as is plain from the very idea of a community of goods, a family union of all believers in the strictest and most proper sense. Accordingly, they took food together daily (verse 46), that is, they celebrated the "agapæ," and to the common meal the Lord's Supper likewise was daily appended. In the African church, where the ancient Christian institutions maintained their ground, in other respects, for the longest period, we yet find even in the days of Tertullian the supper separated from the "agapæ." (See Neander's Tertullian, p. 153, etc.) In the first century it was probably everywhere celebrated, conformably to the last meal of Christ, in connexion with a common meal.

In the last place, prayers are mentioned, which are connected especially with the celebration of the Lord's Supper. There is no mention made of singing, but it is certain that at a very early period† it was an element of Divine service. (Plin. Epist. x. 97, in Olshaus. Histor. Eccles. veteris Monum., vol. i. p. 24. Affirma-

of Christians, of which two parts, viz., the fellowship of meals and that of prayer, are particularly brought into view. But this supposition, as it seems to me, is untenable, because everything in the enumeration refers to the worship of God, as the first named word διδαχή plainly shews: if Neander's view were the right one, then κοινωνία would necessarily have been mentioned first. See Neander's Geschichte der Pflanzung und Leitung, etc., page 30, note.

* The Catholic church employ this expression for the purpose of proving from Scripture the administration of the Lord's Supper "sub una specie" in the days of the apostles. (Compare the confut. conf. Aug. in Meyer's Ausg. der symbol. Bücher, p. 543.) Of course, however, this name has been given to the whole act only a potiori.

† According to Acts xvi. 25, Paul and Silas sang in prison, but this perhaps should only be understood of the rythmical utterance of a psalm in prayer.

bant Christiani quod essent soliti stato die* ante lucem convenire, carmenque Christo quasi Deo dicere secum invicem.) Perhaps we may suppose that the prayers were spoken, not merely by one in the name of all, but by all in common; and if we suppose, at the same time, that perhaps psalms were read as prayers, then we might find something of the nature of song in the rhythmical utterance which the Jews were accustomed to employ in the reading of Scripture. Yet it is more probable that church singing first arose along with Christian poetry, which did not appear before the beginning of the second century.

To render the blessed joy of the little company of believers the more conspicuous by contrast, the fear (φόβος) of those who did not believe is brought into view. All who were of susceptible minds traced the mighty power of the Spirit, and this could not but first of all excite fear. Yet from these did the church recruit her ranks (ver. 47). In contrast with the fear of the unbelievers, the active unity of the Christians is pourtrayed. As to the meaning, first of all, of the phrase *εἶναι ἐπὶ τὸ αὐτό*, the number of the converts (ver. 41) forbids us to refer it to one place of meeting; and, indeed, the words *κατ' οἶκον* in verse 46 lead to the conclusion that there were houses in several parts of the city where they met. The collective body of the faithful had therefore been obliged to divide themselves into smaller societies, and thus was the establishment of various churches, and the appointment of church office-bearers brought about, as we find was the case at an early period in the larger cities. The more particular consideration of the community of goods, intimated in verses 44, 45, we defer till we come to the exposition of chap. iv. 32, etc., a passage that is more decisive on the subject. From the passage before us, taken by itself, nothing further can be gathered than that a highly excited spirit of beneficence led the followers of Christ to regard their property and goods as common, and to support the poorer brethren. But from chap. iv. 32, etc., it has been supposed that a common chest was formed of the proceeds of all goods that were sold, a view which will be afterwards more narrowly considered. (*Κτήματα* denotes here "houses, lands, real property;" *ὑπάρξεις*, on the other hand, means "moveable possessions.") Verse 46 may appear a repetition of verse 42, but in this verse the stress is to be laid upon the opposition between *ἐν τῷ ἱερῷ* and *κατ' οἶκον*. The latter expression cannot be understood to mean, as

* According to this question, it appears that by the time of Pliny the daily meeting had been given up; and, according to the nature of things, it could only continue so long as the number of believers was small. In the lesser churches, however, they might meet daily till a later period. The observance, too, of love feasts, became difficult as the churches became larger. The church of the United Brethren, it is well-known, have introduced them again. See respecting their rise, Spangenberg in his life of Zinzendorf vol. iii., page 446, etc.

Erasmus and Kuinoel suppose, from "house to house." Doubtless there must have been, on account of the large number of believers, several places of meeting, and they may have changed from one to another; but this is not expressed in the words before us. It is rather the private that is placed in opposition to the public. The earliest Christians of the church at Jerusalem had not ceased to associate with the Jews in the services of the Temple, they only held their Christian institutions in connexion with the ordinances of the Old Testament, and, so little did this appear to the people an incompatible thing, that they wished well to the Christians. But so soon as the fickle multitude perceived, in addition to the loving spirit of the brotherhood of believers, the moral earnestness which reigned among them, they changed their views, and began to persecute the Christians. (See chap. xii. 1, etc.) The Christian church in Jerusalem in its outward appearance may have had at first much resemblance to the societies of the Essenes, because like them it presented the spectacle of an intimate union of hearts. But in its inward character the church stood immeasurably higher, because in it the union of souls was a reality, established by a uniting heavenly power, while among the Essenes, it was something wrought by themselves, and therefore, as in all associations of a sectarian kind, unreal, and mingled with much impurity.*

(*Προσκαρτερεῖν* is commonly construed with the dative, when we are speaking of *things* to which the continuance relates; but in Rom. xiii. 6, it is connected with *εἰς*. Applied to *place* it is followed by *ἐν*, as in the apocryphal book of the history of Susanna, verse 7.—The word *ἀφελότης* occurs no where else in the New Testament. It is similar to *ἀφέλεια*, which Josephus (Arch. iii. 12, 2) uses for *ὁλοκληρία*, "integritas," in a physical sense. Transferred to spiritual things it denotes, like *ἁπλότης*, simplicity or singleness of heart. The adjective *ἀφελής* is derived from *φελλός*, *φελός*, *φέλα*, in the Macedonian dialect, which denotes a stone, and therefore the words *πεδία ἀφελῆ* mean level fields, without rocky inequalities.)

§ 3. Cure of a Lame Man.

(Acts. iii. 1–26.)

Vers. 1–10.—After the general description which has now been presented to us, there again follows a detailed particular statement respecting the cure of a lame man, with which a discourse of Peter is connected. Luke had already, in chap. ii. 43, made mention in general terms of the miracles of the apostles; but now for the first

* In particular, a spiritual conceit was spread among the Essenes, which went so far that the members of the higher classes regarded themselves as polluted by simple contact with the humbler brethren.

time there is an occurrence of the kind described in detail. The narrative itself, however, embraces nothing peculiar (see the remarks on miraculous cures in general, in the Commentary on Matth. viii. 1), only it must not be overlooked that Peter (ver. 6) performs the cure not in his own name, nor in the name of God, but in the name of Jesus. By no means therefore did he consider himself as possessing independently the power of healing, but simply as the instrument of Christ: he was conscious to himself that it was the power of the Lord which wrought by him. There is here presented indirectly a striking proof of the higher nature of Christ. The view of Thiess, that the man only pretended to be lame, is a lame view, and needs no serious refutation. As to the particulars of the narrative, we are informed that Peter and John went to the Temple at one of the usual hours of prayer, and found a lame man at one of the gates.

(It has already been mentioned in reference to *ἐπὶ τὸ αὐτό* at chap. i. 15, that it must be understood here not of place, but rather of time, and be taken in the signification of "together," "at the same time." This idea was lost sight of by a number of transcribers; and therefore they annexed *ἐπὶ τὸ αὐτό* to the close of the second chapter, while they left out *τῇ ἐκκλησίᾳ*. The new chapter they then began with *Πέτρος δὲ κ. τ. λ.*, or with *ἐν ταῖς ἡμέραις ἐκείναις*. The critical authorities, however, sufficiently establish the common text.)

The gate beside which the lame man sat, is named *ἡ ὡραία, the beautiful*. The name probably took its rise from the magnificence of the gate, and it is likely that the same gate is here meant to which Josephus (Bell. Jud. v. 5, 3) gives this name, and which is styled by the Rabbins שושן, probably from the bas-relief lily work in Corinthian brass (see 1 Kings vii. 19), with which, according to the account of Josephus, the door was covered. In reply to the entreaty of the infirm man, Peter declares that he has no earthly help to give, but he has something greater to bestow; and at his touch the lame man rises and is able to walk. (Verse 3. *Λαβεῖν*, by a well-known Greek idiom, with words of giving, is redundant.—At verse 5 supply *νοῦν* to *ἔπειχε*; the outward look is necessarily implied along with the attention of the mind.—Ver. 7. *Ἐστερεώθησαν* indicates that the man's lameness had its origin in debility. *Βάσις* denotes commonly the step, but here in connexion with *σφυρά*, the ankles, it denotes the sole of the foot, together with its muscles and ligaments.)

Vers. 11–13.—The man who was healed immediately attached himself to his benefactors, and followed them with a great multitude of people to the porch of Solomon. (With respect to this porch, see Comm. on John x. 23.—*Κρατεῖν*, *to hold*, is here employed like דָּבַק, to denote an inward attachment, a cleaving of the mind to another.* The LXX., in 2 Sam. iii. 6, have translated חָזַק in a similar connexion by *κρατεῖν*.) And here Peter began (see on *ἀποκρίνεσθαι* the Comm. at Luke i. 60), and spoke to the people. The address of the apostle which follows has very much resemblance to the first one: the very same ideas in substance are expressed; the Messiahship of Jesus is proved from the Old Testament, and the people are summoned to repent and believe on him. Only in verses 20 and 21 there is introduced a peculiar thought, in the promise of times of revival. In the first place, the apostle puts away from himself all the honour of the cure, and ascribes it to the Lord, whom God had glorified. (In verse 12, some transcribers have taken offence at the connexion of *δύναμις* and *εὐσέβεια*; and have therefore, instead of the latter word, written *ἐξουσία*. But there is no ground at all for this change. Piety is viewed, on account of the connexion of the pious individual with God, as imparting a real power.) In verse 13 there is the peculiarity of the name *παῖς Θεοῦ* being applied to Christ, and it is repeated in chap. iii. 26, iv. 27–30. After the observations of Nitzsch (in Ullmann's Studien, 1828, Part II. page 331, etc.), no one probably will ever again be disposed to maintain that the expression is identical with *υἱὸς τοῦ Θεοῦ*. It has already been remarked, in the Commentary on Luke i. 35, that *παῖς* corresponds to the Hebrew word עֶבֶד, which is so frequently applied to the Messiah, particularly in the second part of Isaiah. The LXX. translate it by *παῖς*, which word occurs also in Matth. xii. 18 in a citation from the Old Testament. According to the same usage, David also is called *παῖς* in Acts iv. 25, and the people of Israel in Luke i. 54–69. This name accordingly stands less related to the *person* of our Lord than to his office; and, considering the frequent use of עֶבֶד in the Old Testament, we may with more propriety wonder that in the New Testament *παῖς* is so seldom applied to Christ, than that it is so used at all. In verse 13, *κατὰ πρόσωπον* is to be explained with Meyer: ye denied him in the presence of Pilate.

Vers. 14–16.—For the purpose of placing their sin in all its hideousness before the minds of the people, Peter contrasts their conduct towards the Redeemer with their conduct towards Barabbas. The name, *ἀρχηγὸς τῆς ζωῆς*, *prince of life*, is in this passage peculiarly applied to the person of our Lord. In Acts v. 31, we find

* Meyer, on this passage, insists that the physical signification of holding fast ought to be here retained. His translation is: "but when he held Peter and John fast, that is, seized them and held by them." But in this case undoubtedly *χερσὶ* would have been added. The signification of *κρατεῖν* is not altered by my view of the passage; the word is only explained as referring not to a physical seizing and holding, but to a spiritual.

ἀρχηγὸς καὶ σωτήρ, and in Heb. ii. 10 ἀρχηγὸς τῆς σωτηρίας. Critics in general attempt to shew that the proper signification of ἀρχηγός is "author." Much light is thrown upon the meaning of the word by the passage in Heb. xii. 2, where ἀρχηγός and τελειωτὴς τῆς πίστεως stand together. According to this connexion the signification of "beginning, conducting to something," suits the word; although indeed this by no means stands in contradiction to the sense of "producing." The word life must here (comp. John i. 4) be taken in the absolute sense, and in the most comprehensive application. It embraces not only the higher spiritual life, which Christ has introduced into the world, and to which he guides his followers; but also the conquest of physical death by the resurrection. And now in verse 16 to this Jesus whom they had despised, the miracle is ascribed, which was filling the multitude with astonishment. The construction of the sentence, however, is not quite plain. If with Kuinoel we translate ἐπὶ τῇ πίστει τοῦ ὀνόματος αὐτοῦ: "propter fiduciam in Christi auxilio repositam;" then the second half of the verse exhibits a complete tautology, which is not removed even by putting a point after ἐστερέωσε, and attaching τὸ ὄνομα αὐτοῦ to what follows. The passage becomes intelligible only by translating ἐπὶ τῇ πίστει, "for faith," or "to faith;" that is, healed the infirm man for the purpose of leading him, as well as others, to faith in his name. So Heinrichs rightly. With respect again to the expression ἡ πίστις ἡ δι' αὐτοῦ, *the faith which is through him*, in the second half of the sentence, Kuinoel likewise errs in regarding it as quite synonymous with the forms πίστις εἰς αὐτόν or πίστις αὐτοῦ. This mode of expression is plainly designed to represent the πίστις as something called into existence by grace, in opposition to a self-originated and therefore inefficient opinion. Ὁλοκληρία is here to be understood only of physical "integritas:" the substantive (see James i. 4) occurs no where else in the New Testament.

Vers. 17–19.—After addressing them with severity, the apostle turns round again, and brings into view the higher necessity which the prophecies have declared to be connected with the death of Christ,* and thus mitigates their guilt. It has already been remarked at Luke xxiii. 34, that their ignorance (ἄγνοια) by no means entirely removes their guilt, since it was itself deserving of blame; but certainly it has a mitigating effect (1 Cor. ii. 8); and we cannot well say, in accordance with these passages, that the chief priests and members of the Sanhedrim who put Christ to death, committed the sin against the Holy Ghost. (See Comm. Matth. xii. 32.)

By the extenuation thus made, the way is now paved for a sum-

* There is mention here expressly made of *all* the prophets, which many regard as a hyperbolical expression, and therefore modify it to mean *some*. But, according to the typical view of sacred history, it is perfectly true that they *all* prophesy of Christ.

mons to repentance and conversion. Conversion (ἐπιστρέφειν) implies also the faith, of which mention has already been made in the 16th verse. As the first consequence of penitence and conversion, appears the forgiveness of sins, which again must be considered as involving life and blessedness. To denote this remission (ἄφεσις τῶν ἁμαρτιῶν) ἐξαλείφω, *blot out*, is here employed, which occurs in a figurative acceptation only in this passage. At the bottom of this figurative usage lies the idea of a bond (Col. ii. 14) which is cancelled. The same image is found in the Old Testament, for example in Isaiah xliii. 25, אָנֹכִי מֹחֶה פְשָׁעֶיךָ, where the Seventy also use ἐξαλείφω.

Vers. 20, 21.—A peculiarity, as has already been observed, of this discourse of the apostle, is its mention of times of refreshing. The very different explanations which have been given of this passage, are to be judged of altogether in accordance with the observations which I have prefixed to the leading passage respecting the last things, viz., Matth. xxiv. 1. The alleged fact that the apostle conceives the times of refreshing (καιροὶ ἀναψύξεως) to be quite close at hand, has led some interpreters to regard the time of death as what is meant, others the abrogation of the Jewish ceremonial law, or perhaps a delay of the judgments impending over the Jews, or the warding off of persecutions. These different conjectures, however, need no serious refutation. They may be looked upon as antiquated, as the only tenable reference of the words is to the times of the Messiah. Still, it is a question whether the times of restitution (χρόνοι ἀποκαταστάσεως) in verse 21, and the times of refreshing in verse 20, be identical, or whether the former expression refers to the future, and the latter to the present. According to the fundamental ideas of the New Testament, both views, considered in themselves, might be entertained, for we notice a double form of representation in the doctrine of the "kingdom of God," of which the seasons of refreshing are the realization ; *first*, one which represents the kingdom of God as already present ; *secondly*, another, as still future. (See Comm. Part i. at Matth. iii. 2.) But the grammatical connexion admits only the first view, which regards the two expressions as identical, and as not referring to the present time. Without doubt the apostle Peter, as well as all the disciples, and the whole apostolic church, regarded the coming of Christ as near at hand, but still always as future. If the reference of verse 20 to the present be maintained, then the words ὅπως ἂν ἔλθωσι—καὶ ἀποστείλῃ must be translated "cum venerint, et Deus miserit," as Kuinoel supposes. But this translation is inconsistent, not only with the particle ἄν, which is not connected with the conjunction ὅπως, except when the end is conceived as attainable only in the future, but also with the employment of ὅπως with the subjunctive, for it can mean "when, as" only with the indicative. (Comp. Passow's Lex. under this word, and Winer's Grammar, p. 285.) The coming of Christ (*i. e.*, his parousia) is therefore to be conceived as coincident with the times of refreshing, and his sojourn in the heavenly world closes with his return to the earth for the completion of his work. The conversion of men, therefore, and the diffusion of faith in Christ, are the *condition* of the speedy approach of that blessed time, a thought which occurs again in 2 Pet. iii. 9. The expression occurring here, *καιροὶ ἀναψύξεως, times of refreshing*, is easily explained. Life in this sinful world is conceived as a time of conflict and distress, and it is followed by rest in the kingdom of the Messiah. The phrase is only to be found in this passage of the New Testament, and has but feeble parallels in the Old Testament, as for example, 2 Sam. xxiii. 7. Probably it takes its origin from a comparison of the Messianic era with a Sabbath day in the higher sense, which, it is known, was very current among the Jews.

(The *ἀπὸ προσώπου* = מִפְּנֵי, which is by no means quite synonymous with *πρὸ προσώπου* = לִפְנֵי, embodies the idea that the refreshing *proceeds* from the Lord, that he himself produces it. Instead of the common reading, *προκεκηρυγμένον*, many and important manuscripts [A, B, C, D, E, and fifty-three others], besides several versions, read *προκεχειρισμένον*, which, as the more unusual reading, certainly deserves the preference. *Προχειρίζεσθαι* occurs only in the Acts of the Apostles [xxii. 14, xxvi. 16], in the sense of "appointing," "electing to something." Properly it means "to take in hand, to purpose, to determine." It is found in the best profane writers, and the Seventy also use it frequently, as in Joshua iii. 12, for לָקַח.) The 21st verse contrasts with the coming of Christ to this world, his heavenly condition, described in the words *δέχεσθαι οὐρανόν*, which is not to be referred so much to the act of reception as to the state of possession and authority. For the view of the words which takes *οὐρανόν* as the subject in this sense, "the heaven must receive him," which, after Beza's example, Ernesti, Kuinoel, and Schott have defended, although it is certainly not inadmissible on grammatical grounds, yet must give place to the other, because it is an unscriptural view to conceive heaven like an independent agent, receiving Christ into itself, while it is he, as Lord and King, who takes it and holds it in possession. With as little propriety can we take the former of these statements, as we can say the throne receives the king upon it. Beza, without doubt, has been led to this idea by his views as connected with the reformed Church.*

* This passage has always been differently interpreted by the Lutheran and the Reformed churches; and if Beza might be unduly biassed to the one side, Olshausen himself might lean in a similar manner to the other. The Lutheran Church has viewed ὃν as the subject, and understood the meaning of the clause to be that Christ took

The form of concord expressly rejects this interpretation (sol. declar. art. vii. towards the end).*

As the period of the Redeemer's return, the Messianic era is again mentioned, which is here styled the "time of the restitution of all things" (χρόνος ἀποκαταστάσεως πάντων). This connexion of ideas occurs only here, though in Hebrews ix. 10, there is to be found the very similar expression καιρὸς διορθώσεως. On the import of the limitation, however, no doubt can arise, if we keep in view the relation of the Redeemer to this sinful world: Christ is the *restorer* of the fallen creation, and therefore the word ἀποκατάστασις derives from his redeeming power its peculiar meaning, viz., that of bringing back to its originally pure condition. It would seem, indeed, from the connexion of the passage, that πάντων, *of all things*, had reference only to what the prophets have spoken, but not to the universe of things or relations. But the prophets have really spoken of all things, and therefore the expression ἀποκατάστασις πάντων denotes the restitution of everything. That πάντων is not to be understood as masculine, is self-evident.

(The substantive ἀποκατάστασις does not occur elsewhere in the New Testament, but the verb does, being applied to physical restoration, as in Matth. xii. 13; Mark viii. 25; Luke vi. 10, and also

possession of the heavens: their feeling has been that the omnipresence of Christ would be compromised by saying that the heavens receive or contain him. The Reformed Church, again, make οὐρανόν the subject, and translate, as in our version, whom the heavens must receive: their idea has been that the simple object of the clause is to describe Christ as dwelling now not on earth, but in heaven. The words, doubtless, are ambiguous in construction, and admit of either rendering, for the verb δέχεσθαι is to be found in both shades of meaning. The cases, however, are more numerous where it is applied to a place receiving or containing a person, than to a person taking possession of a place. Indeed, only one passage has been produced from Euripides, Alc. 817, in support of the latter meaning,* and the bearing of it has been disputed, so that on mere philological grounds the interpretation of the Reformed Church deserves the preference. Nor is there much force in our author's argument that it is unscriptural to conceive of the heavens as receiving Christ, receiving him as a place does the person who enters it. Was he not, without prejudice to his omnipresence and Divine authority, in this world for a term of years; and why might he not, with as little prejudice to these attributes, be described as received into heaven when he left this world, to remain there till the period specified in the text? Calvin expresses himself with more moderation than those who followed him in the Reformed Church. Ceterum loquutio est ambigua: quia tam intelligere possumus Christum cœlo capi vel contineri quam cœlum capere. Ne ergo verbum dubiæ significationis urgeamus: sed eo contente simus quod certum est, Christum, interea dum speratur ultima rerum omnium instauratio non alibi quam in cœlo quæremdum esse. Calv. in loc.—[TR.   * It has here no such meaning.—[K.

* The Form of Concord (Concordienformel) here mentioned is one of the symbolical books of the Lutheran Church, though not so important a one, nor so universally acknowledged as the Confession of Augsburg. It was called the book of Torgaw, from the place where it was composed in the sixteenth century, and the book of Concord, from the purpose it was designed to serve. It became the source, however, of many disputes, and was violently opposed, not only by the Reformed Church, but by some also of the most distinguished Lutheran churches and divines.—[TR.

to spiritual, as in Matth. xvii. 11 ; Acts i. 6.—At the close of verse 21 there are some various readings. The text. rec. has inserted πάντων before ἁγίων προφητῶν, but it should be erased, as doubtless an interpolation from the 18th verse. But ἀπ' αἰῶνος, is improperly omitted in some manuscripts ; it is not so definite a period as is immediately specified in what follows, and may hence be referred to the whole series of God's promises with respect to the restoration of men, in that there are also prophets mentioned in the New Testament who were prior to the deluge. See Jude ver. 14.)

Vers. 22-26.—Looking back to the admonition to repentance (ver. 19), the apostle adduces some passages from the Old Testament,* in which the necessity of recognizing the great Messianic prophet is exhibited with peculiar force. First of all, the well-known passage in Deut. xviii. 15, 18, 19, is cited. The language of the Septuagint is followed in the main ; but the words of the 15th and 18th verses are united, and in the 19th, instead of ἐκδικήσω ἐξ αὐτοῦ, we have ἐξολοθρευθήσεται ἐκ τοῦ λαοῦ (Heb. אֶדְרֹשׁ מֵעִמּוֹ). From the connexion, certainly, the passage seems to refer primarily to the order of prophets in general, but as the prophetical character is exhibited in the Messiah in the highest, nay, in absolute perfection, the passage applies to him too in the very highest sense. In this view the words ὡς ἐμέ (כָּמֹנִי) must have a decided reference to the legislative character, which was exhibited in Moses, and afterwards appeared only in Christ. In its relation to the Old Testament, the threatening of the 23d verse refers to external, in its relation to the New, to spiritual punishment, and in this respect corresponds entirely to the words of our Lord, "he that believeth not is condemned already" (ὁ μὴ πιστεύων ἤδη κέκριται, John iii. 18). All promises belong primarily to the seed of Abraham, according to the Divine appointment, and upon that consideration Peter grounds the invitation to his hearers, to appropriate to themselves the blessing that is in Christ. The quotation in verse 25 is taken from Gen. xii. 3, or xviii. 18, xxii. 18. It is almost exactly in the words of the Septuagint, which, instead of πατριαί reads ἔθνη or φυλαί. The words ὑμῖν πρῶτον ὁ Θεὸς—ἀπέστειλεν αὐτόν, in verse 26, contain an intimation of the *universality* of the grace that is in Christ, that is, of the introduction of the Gentiles into the Christian church, which the prophets had so frequently foretold ; for it was not against this introduction, considered in itself, that Peter at a later period (chap. x.) entertained scruples, but only in so far as it was to take place directly, without the reception of the law on the part of the Gentile converts.

* Respecting the want of precision in the words: πάντες οἱ προφῆται ἀπὸ Σαμουὴλ καὶ τῶν καθεξῆς ὅσοι ἐλάλησαν, consult Winer's Grammar, p. 464.

§ 4. FIRST IMPRISONMENT OF PETER.

(Acts iv. 1-31.)

The auspicious opening bloom of the young church of Christ could not fail speedily to attract the attention of those who occupied the seat of Moses. But as they were themselves the murderers of the Son of God, and would not humble themselves before him to receive themselves also the pardon of their sins, which was offered to them by the apostles preaching in their presence, they fell of consequence into the new sin of seeking to quench the Spirit. Yet their first undecided procedure against those who announced the resurrection of the crucified Jesus, plainly evinces that a smitten conscience bore witness to them, of their alienation from God and their struggle against the defenders of true piety. But soon we behold them grow more daring, and by gradually working upon the mass of the people, they excite the fickle multitude against the Christians, as despisers of the national sanctuaries.

Vers. 1-7.—In the power of the Spirit the apostles continued to preach, and their word wrought so powerfully, that already about five thousand men believed. (In verse 4, compared with chap. v 14, it seems that men only are named exclusive of women. It might, therefore, be supposed that the number of the Christian community was much greater. But at first perhaps it might be only men that were added to the church. In all likelihood this occurrence must be placed only a few days after Pentecost, for it is hardly to be supposed that the priests would not interfere at once, for the purpose of extinguishing the flame as speedily as possible.) The conversion of so many was the source of vexation to the whole party of priests, but above all to the Sadducees; whose views were directly impugned by the preaching of the resurrection. (Compare the Commentary on Matth. iii. 7, and xxii. 23.) The person who took the active part in the arrest of Peter (for John appears in all these transactions only as the companion of Peter, without any independent agency),* is described as the στρατηγὸς τοῦ ἱεροῦ, *captain of the temple.* It has been erroneously supposed that the expression denotes a Roman officer; but it should rather be understood as meaning the captain of the Levitical guard of the Temple who was on duty. This guard had the charge of preserving tranquillity in the

* This may be explained partly from the circumstance, that these sections of the Acts of the Apostles were taken from some writing or from several short memoirs, which originated with the school of Peter; but the character of John, too, on the other hand, renders it probable that he did not at the first display very great energy. (Compare the Commentary on John, page 4.)

neighbourhood of the Temple; and the pretence, that the apostles were disturbing the peace, was made to furnish an occasion for their arrest. Comp. Josephus, Arch. xx. 6, 2. B. J. ii. 12. 6; in 2 Maccab. 4, where προστάτης τοῦ ἱεροῦ is the title used. As it was already late (verse 3), the examination was delayed till the following day, when the Sanhedrim assembled.

(The form ἐγενήθη, in verse 4, does not occur in the Attic writers, though frequently found in the κοινὴ διάλεκτος. Compare Lobeck ad Phryn. page 108. Respecting ἄρχοντες πρεσβύτεροι and γραμματεῖς, as also respecting Caiaphas and Annas, see particulars at Matth. xxvi. 57. At the same place too see regarding γένος ἀρχιερατικόν. Nothing is known of the two other persons whose names are mentioned. Lightfoot on this passage supposes that John corresponds to an individual, of whom intelligence is preserved in the Talmud. He is called Rabban Jochanan ben Zaccai, and is described as a priest of distinction. Far more improbably has it been conjectured, that Alexander may be the brother of Philo; for he was Alabarches of Alexandria, and could not therefore be a member of the Sanhedrim in Jerusalem. (Compare Eusebius Hist. Ecc. ii. 5, and the note of Valesius on the passage. Alabarches meant the highest magistrate of the Jews in Alexandria and all Egypt.)

Vers. 8–12.—The Sanhedrim had interrogated the apostles respecting their authority to teach publicly, a question which undoubtedly was competent to them. (Consult the Comm. on Matth. xxi. 23.) Peter now replies to their question, by appealing to a decided miracle, the healing of the lame man, as his authority; and he ascribes this miracle to the power of Jesus of Nazareth.* The adducing of the miracle was entirely natural, for miracles were to be the means of establishing the authority of a prophet (compare the passage quoted, viz., Ps. cxviii. 22), but the second point is remarkable. According to Jewish principles, the prophet was required to perform his miracles in the name of Jehovah the true God; but the apostles wrought theirs in the name of Jesus. In this way, therefore, they indirectly declared him to be their Lord and God: they announced that in him God dwells and is manifested; and the members of the Sanhedrim would undoubtedly understand their words to mean, that they proclaimed themselves to be messengers

* In verse 8 it is expressly mentioned, that Peter spoke these words πλησθεὶς πνεύματος ἁγίου. The same thing is said in iv. 31, xiii. 9, and very frequently of Paul. In this we are not simply to recognize the general idea, that the apostles spoke at the suggestion of the Holy Ghost, and not by their own ability; but we are rather to see an evident proof, that the Holy Ghost, who was always really working in them, was at these moments producing effects that were peculiarly palpable. In the inward spiritual life of the apostles, therefore, we must distinguish between periods of high excitement and periods of less elevation (see Comm. on 2 Cor. xii.); and the expression before us denotes the former.

of Jesus, and recognized in him a Divine majesty. With undaunted boldness Peter now reproaches them with having rejected this corner stone of the spiritual temple, while yet it was Christ only in whom there was salvation for them. He therefore, the impeached humble citizen, preaches the way of salvation to the godless ministers of the sanctuary! (Respecting the quotation from Ps. cxviii. 22, consult Comm. at Matth. xxi. 42.)

The 12th verse is attended with peculiar doctrinal difficulties: it confines the "salvation" so strictly to Christ, that the question may present itself, How then can those who have never heard of him, be or become σωζόμενοι, *saved?* Quite inadmissible is the expedient to which some have had recourse, of making the σωτηρία relate only to what is physical, because the subject previously under consideration has been the healing of the lame man. It is plain from the preceding citation in the 11th verse, that σωτηρία can only mean the Messianic salvation, which Christ bestows. Nevertheless it was a total misunderstanding of this passage, from which however the primitive church stood clear, to explain it so as to exclude unbaptized children and Gentiles from the salvation. The ancient fathers rightly conceived every exhibition of superior excellence, even in the heathen world, to be the effect of the λόγος σπερματικός (so expressly says Justin Martyr, page 51 c.), and for all, to whom no ray of Divine light had penetrated, they opened up in the "descensus Christi ad inferos" the possibility of obtaining salvation. But as the circle can only have one centre, so also the Divine being alone can be the Saviour, and this is the deep thought of the apostle's language. Not without reason, therefore, is the general expression οὐκ ἔστιν more narrowly defined in the second clause by the words ἐν ᾧ δεῖ σωθῆναι, by which the possibility of any other way of salvation is most decidedly excluded. But the one Logos (λόγος), has very various forms of manifestation; in consequence of which there arises an *apparent variety* of ways of access to God. (On the expression δεδομένον ἐν ἀνθρώποις, consult Winer's Grammar, page 177.) In respect to the *sense*, it may be said that ἐν stands for the dative; but grammatically it is more correct to give it the signification of "among," making the thought this: "there is no other name given," that is, "exhibited" *among* men, and at the same time, *for* men.

Ver. 13-18.—The Sanhedrim were unable, partly because they were restrained by the power of the Spirit of truth speaking in the apostles, and partly because they feared the people (verse 18), to adopt any severe measures against the preachers of the resurrection of the crucified Jesus. They dismissed the apostles with an unmeaning admonition. (The two expressions ἀγράμματοι and ἰδιῶται appear to be synonymous, for the latter as well as the former frequently denotes the unlearned as opposed to the learned. Suidas explains it by ἀγράμματος, ἀμαθής. But the word is also applied to the *lowly* as distinguished from the great and the wealthy, and therefore it is best to give it this sense for the purpose of making a distinction between it and ἀγράμματος. This latter word, finally, implies nothing more than the want of formal Rabbinical training; for, where this was wanting, the Pharisees, whose minds were quite ossified, were unable to recognize any higher knowledge as existing. Διανέμω, "to divide, to disperse," and thence "to propagate," occurs in no other part of the New Testament.)

Vers. 19-22.—Although the apostles openly declare that they cannot comply with the admonition given to them, yet the chief priests dismiss them without punishment, merely adding a threat Perhaps it was their hope that by mildness they might most efficiently suppress the growing sect, which appeared to them so dangerous. But the apostles at once gave utterance to the great principle, which is repeated by them (chap. v. 29) at their second imprisonment, that we must obey God rather than man. The relation of this principle to the general command, to obey "the government" as the minister of God (Rom. xiii. 1), is attended with some difficulty, especially when, as in the case before us, that power enjoins no positive sin, but only negatively forbids something. Many enthusiasts and rebels have misapplied this principle to the defence of their insane or mischievous undertakings. Now, such an abuse cannot be prevented by restrictions and regulations, because this principle, like every other, is regulated in practice by the character of those who apply it, whose depravity may pervert what is most excellent. But, in its purely objective character, the highest freedom of the believer maintains no conflict at all with his unqualified obedience to the government, even though it be an unrighteous one. He moves, in fact, with his old and new man, as it were, in a twofold world. In the one character he is placed in subjection to earthly relations, and therefore willingly gives to Cæsar what is Cæsar's; but in the other he is a member of the spiritual world, and therefore gives to God what is God's. And because he thus leaves to the earthly power whatever belongs to it, he secures to himself perfect liberty of deciding in accordance with a higher will, in whatever does not belong to it. But every misapplication of the principle has really the earthly element in view, to obtain which, the heavenly is only used as a means. Where such obliquity does not disturb the inward vision, the proper relations of the two commands will be easily perceived. Peter appeals, therefore, with respect to the truth of the principle that God's command rises above that of man, to the moral feeling of the Sanhedrim themselves, and they were unable to resist it. (In verse 20 we must with Lachmann prefer *εἴδαμεν* as the more unusual Alexandrian form, which is also found sometimes in the LXX. See 1 Sam. x. 14; 2 Sam. x. 14. In verse 21 *μηδέν* must be taken as an absolute accusative; it stands for *μηδαμᾶ* or *μηδαμῶς*.)

Vers. 23–31.—After their release the apostles repaired to their friends, who broke out into a prayer of thanksgiving to God. (Ἴδιοι cannot mean all Christians, for all could not assemble in one place, but only the household church of the apostles, those with whom they were accustomed to unite in social prayer, compare xii. 12; it cannot mean, as Meyer supposes, the other apostles.) It is self-evident, that this prayer of thanksgiving was either uttered by one in the name of the rest, or that the common feeling of all is exhibited in these words. The latter idea is favoured by the expression; "they with one accord raised their voices to God" (*ὁμοθυμαδὸν ἦραν φωνὴν πρὸς τὸν θεόν*). And in this case the form of the thoughts belongs either to Luke, or perhaps rather to the author of the memoirs which he employed in constructing his narrative. Meyer's supposition is quite inadmissible, that the prayer which follows may have been a form that was in use in the church of Jerusalem; we thus improperly transfer to the primitive church the usages of a later time. In the prayer, the concluding verses only (29, 30) touch upon the fact to which the whole scene refers; and they do so only cursorily, in the entreaty that the threatenings may be averted. The first verses are entirely occupied with the fruitless persecutions of the Redeemer, a thing which appears unseasonable. But on closer consideration this is seen to express a very deep feeling, which affords a strong warrant for the correctness of the narrative. The apostles were so thoroughly engrossed with the person of Christ and his affairs, their own individual concerns were thrown so much into the background, and it was so exclusively Christ's cause which appeared to them intrinsically important, that they saw even in their own sufferings nothing but persecutions directed against Christ. Their prayer therefore concerned itself only about *him*; and their desire looked exclusively to this, that they might be enabled to glorify him. Of the omnipotence of God, mention is made, to bring into view the fact, that he is able everywhere to give help. (On *δεσπότης*, comp. Comm. on Luke ii. 29.) This power of the Almighty, which protects against all the rage of men in rebellion against heaven, is strikingly portrayed in Psalm ii. 1, 2, which passage is quoted exactly according to the LXX., and explained as referring to Christ. (Vers. 27, 28.) The second Psalm is very frequently applied to Christ in the New Testament.* (Acts xiii. 33; Heb. i.

* Peter ascribes it to David, although both the Hebrew text and the LXX. have no inscription. In this he follows the general opinion of the Jews, which ascribes to David

5, v. 5; Rev. ii. 26, 27, xii. 5, xix. 15.) Granting even that the Psalm may have a historical basis, and may relate to the installation of a king in Israel, yet the peculiar reference of it to the Messiah, the universal king, cannot be mistaken. (Comp. Hengstenberg's Christology, vol. i. page 95, etc.) The hostility of the world is so little able to overthrow God's plan, that it is compelled to become the means of accomplishing it. (Ver. 29.) This idea of a Divine necessity in the free actions of men has already been considered at Matth. xxvi. 24.

(Respecting *ἱνατί*, see at Matth. xxvii. 46.—*Φρυάττω* = צָהַל, is applied primarily to neighing horses, then it denotes, "to storm," "to rage."—In verse 27, *ἐπ' ἀληθείας* is used, as in Luke iv. 25, xxii. 59, by way of asseveration. According to the common text it connects itself immediately with *ἐπὶ τὸν ἅγιον παῖδά σου*; while Griesbach, following codices A. D. E. and others, has inserted *ἐν τῇ πόλει ταύτῃ*. If we compare such passages as Matth. xxiii. 37, Luke xiii. 33, this addition acquires very great force. The *holy* city, Luke means to say, they have made the seat of infamous treachery.—*Ταννῦν* occurs again in Acts xvii. 30, xx. 32, xxvii. 22. It is used also by profane writers as synonymous with *νῦν*. Compare Herod. vii. 104.) After the prayer was concluded, the place where the disciples were assembled was shaken, and they were all filled with the Holy Ghost. It has already been remarked at chap. iv. 8, that the being filled with the Holy Ghost, must be regarded as denoting a state of unusually high spiritual excitement; for at Pentecost the apostles had received the Holy Ghost once for all. The common excitement which here found place in all who were assembled was, like the outpouring of the Spirit described in chap. ii. 2, accompanied with an external manifestation, viz., the shaking of the place. Now, a common earthquake is as little to be supposed in this place, as a common storm at chap. ii. 2; for both of these must have struck the city, and not merely the place of meeting. But certainly there is something parallel to this occurrence in the view of the ancients, for they regarded earthquakes as a sign from the gods. (Virg. Æn. iii. 89.) The earthquake was to them as a gigantic exhibition of the power of the gods, a token of their presence, and thus of their favour.

§ 5. The Community of Goods.

(Acts iv. 32—v. 11.)

After the special narrative thus given, there follows again a general view of the state of the church in Jerusalem. (Compare at ii.

all Psalms whose authors are not definitely marked. With respect to the second Psalm, the correctness of this view is not to be doubted.

42–47.) This passage only brings more prominently into view a particular usage, viz., the community of goods, of which mention has already been cursorily made in the passage just referred to.* And in connexion with the general statement respecting the community of goods, two particular narratives are presented, in which the use and the abuse of the practice are described. With respect to this ancient Christian institute, we may now, after Mosheim's enquiry ("de vera natura communionis bonorum in ecclesia Hierosolymitana" contained in "diss. ad hist. eccl. pertin. vol. i. diss. i."), regard the old view as exploded, which supposed that all property had ceased among Christians. They must in this case have lived upon a common fund, which would have speedily wasted away; and, instead of the dwellings which were sold, others must have been hired anew. The passages ii. 45, iv. 35, appear at first sight to favour this view, because it is there said, "they sold their possessions and goods" (τὰ κτήματα καὶ τὰς ὑπάρξεις ἐπίπρασκον), language which seems to include all possessions, whether moveable or real, and because in the latter passage, iv. 35, the distribution is represented as so general, that one is tempted to think of a common fund out of which *every one* received what he needed. But when we investigate the circumstances more narrowly, we come upon invincible difficulties, and find ourselves compelled to admit only an active liberality, which led the more wealthy to sell much for the support of their poorer brethren; and so disposed every one that he managed his own private property as the common property of all. There is only one circumstance which seems to lead to the conclusion, that in the earliest time there did in fact prevail in Jerusalem a proper community of goods. We find the church there remarkably poor, so that Paul, in particular, is continually occupied with collections for the mother church. The fact might be explained in this manner: in the first glow of love, the believers in Jerusalem really went too far; they sold all their possessions, they lived upon the common fund, and hoped the Lord would soon return to conduct them into his kingdom. But, when the advent was delayed, they fell into temporal destitution, and needed support. From this circumstance too it might be explained why there is not even a trace of this institute to be found in any other church. It may be said that the apostles, taught experience by this trial, ceased

* That in the progress of mankind there is a tendency to the abolition of private property, is illustrated by the sect of the Simonians in France, whose case is worthy of attention in a history of the church. But this party ridiculously pervert a right feeling, because they strive to establish by external regulations, what can only be effected by the power of love operating from within. No power or plan can supply the place of the omnipotence of love. The gospel establishes in a truly spiritual manner a community of goods, because, without any external revolutions, it awakens the pure love, which teaches us to regard and treat the need of a brother as our own.

to form after the manner of the Essenes, such a common stock, and nowhere else established it. In opposition to this view, it would be no proper argument to say, that the apostles must in this case have either made or allowed an unsuitable regulation; for the apostles do not by any means appear infallible, excepting where a matter of faith is concerned: in a regulation for the church, therefore, they might perhaps have conceived wrongly for a moment, and especially *thus* as they would have erred in this case: their whole error would have consisted in applying too pure and heavenly a standard to the circumstances of an earthly church.*

But other considerations forbid me to regard the foregoing argumentation as proving that a complete community of goods prevailed among the primitive Christians. First of all, Peter expressly declares to Ananias (chap. v. 4), that it was in his own power either to sell the field or to retain it: it is inconceivable, therefore, that it could be a law in the church, as it was among the Essenes, that every one *must* sell all his goods. Again, we find in chap. xii. 12, an example of the private possession of a house. The poverty therefore of the Christians in Jerusalem, which is certainly a very remarkable phenomenon, must be accounted for in some other way. Either the church was formed from amongst the poorest inhabitants of the city, or many, without the restraint of any law, went so far under the influence of spontaneous affection in selling their possessions, as to impoverish themselves too much, or finally both causes may have operated together, which is perhaps the most probable opinion. And the way in which the apostles might be led to the idea of a community of goods, is very easily conceived, when we consider that separate possession is nothing but a consequence of sin. (Comp. Comm. on Luke xvi. 1, etc.) The ideal perfection of man's condition is just that, in which neither poor nor rich are to be found, but every individual has his wants supplied. Intimations that such a condition must one day be realized, are to be found, not only in the reckless cry after freedom and equality, but also in the most exalted of our race. Pythagoras and Plato were captivated with this idea: the Essenes† and other small sectarian bodies attempted to

* The statement here made regarding the apostles is pushed too far, nor is there any ground for it in the practice under notice, for this practice resulted out of the spontaneous love of believers, and was not wrong. The apostles were appointed by Christ not only to proclaim the truth, but also to plant and regulate churches, and they received the promise of the Holy Ghost to fit them for these duties. Their infallibility therefore went beyond mere matters of faith, and extended also to the ordinances and institutions which they established for the churches. Apostolic practice, clearly made out, is a good rule to us.—[TR.

† The Essenes really and truly had no private property; all that they earned went into a common fund, out of which all were supported. (Comp. Joseph. Bell Jud. ii. 12.)

realize it. But the outward realization of it requires certain internal conditions; and just because these were wanting, the attempts referred to could not but fail. These conditions, however, were secured by the Redeemer, who poured pure brotherly love into the hearts of believers; but as the church herself still appears in this world externally veiled, so the true community of goods cannot be outwardly practised: this will only take place when the kingdom of God is openly manifested as the victorious and ruling power at the advent of the Lord.

There are but few individual points to be noticed in these words. In the first place, it is not without reason that in verse 32 the expression is employed: "The heart and the soul was one" (ἦν ἡ καρδία καὶ ἡ ψυχὴ μία). It could not have been said, "the *spirit* was one" (τὸ πνεῦμα ἓν ἦν), at least this would have conveyed quite a different meaning; it would have referred rather to knowledge than to feeling. But here the idea to be expressed is, that the church was feelingly sensible of its community of life; hence the soul (ψυχή) and its central point the heart (καρδία), as the seat of feeling, are rendered prominent. Again, at first sight, verse 33 appears to interrupt the connexion, because verse 34 treats anew of the community of goods. But closer observation makes it plain that verse 34 does not look back to verse 32, but refers immediately to verse 33. It was the brotherly love, which displayed itself among the Christians, that won for them in so high a degree the favour of the people. In verse 35 τιθέναι παρὰ τοὺς πόδας τῶν ἀποστόλων, *place at the feet*, etc., is a symbolical expression, meaning, to place under their control.

Vers. 36, 37.—Regarding the well-known Joses, surnamed Barnabas, of whom mention is so frequently made in the sequel, the information is here communicated, that, with an upright purpose, he sold a field, and handed over to the apostles the money realized by the sale. The alleged identity of Barnabas with Barsabas, and the different reading of the names, have been already sufficiently considered at chap. i. 23. In this passage the tribe to which Barnabas belonged and the land of his birth are mentioned. (For the purpose of exhibiting the import of the name Barnabas, Luke gives a Greek translation of it, υἱὸς παρακλήσεως, *son of consolation*. It is uncertain, however, what etymology he had before his eyes: one is most readily led to think of נָבָא, but this word denotes "to foretell, to prophesy." Admonition, however, and consolation, are

The question, whether the Essenes had any influence upon the Christian institute of a community of goods, I would thus answer: "Not upon the institute as such, which originated solely in Christian love; but their regulations may perhaps have exercised an influence upon individual Christians who knew them, and may have recommended the institute to them, and led them to prize it."

certainly a part of the functions of a prophet; and therefore Luke might put *παράκλησις* for *προφητεία*. At least this idea is certainly not so harsh as the supposition of Grotius, that *παράκλησις* stands strictly for "prophecying," which cannot at all be made good.)

Chap. v., vers. 1–6.—The event which follows embodies a case of a totally different kind, viz., an example of the abuse which sordid individuals were tempted to make of the institute of a community of goods. This is the first trace of a shade, which falls upon the pure bright form of the young church. A member of the Christian body misguidedly attempts, along with his wife, to deceive the apostles and the whole church, by bringing forward a smaller price than he had received for a piece of ground which he had sold. Hypocrisy was therefore the proper sin of Ananias and Sapphira. It is probable that among the new Christians a kind of holy rivalry had sprung up: every one was eager to place his superfluous means at the disposal of the church: now this zeal swept along many a one, who was not in heart properly freed from attachment to earthly possessions; and thus it happened that Ananias too sold some property, but afterwards secretly kept back part of the price. *Vanity* was the motive of the sale, *hypocrisy* the ground of the concealment: he wished to appear as disinterested as others, and yet he could not let go his hold of mammon. But still the punishment with which he was visited appears very severe, especially when compared with the treatment given to far more dangerous persons, Simon Magus (chap. viii.) and Elymas (chap xiii.) Appeal indeed is made to the fact that the hypocrisy of Ananias and his wife was uncommonly daring, and must have undermined, if it had succeeded, the consideration of the apostles; and certainly this remark is not without force. But the proper solution can only be found in this, that these persons had experienced the power of the Holy Ghost, and yet could abandon themselves to so gross a sin. It is not the deed therefore itself alone, but also the condition of him who perpetrates it, which determines the measure of the guilt. Simon and Elymas were free from the great responsibility which lay upon Ananias, because they had not the experience of the power of the Spirit, which we must ascribe to him. Where this experience existed, even an apparently smaller sin required a severer punishment.

Ananias (חֲנַנְיָה) and Sapphira (from שַׁפִּיר) his wife sold a piece of land, for the purpose of putting the proceeds into the chest of the church, but they secretly kept back a part of the price. (*Κτῆμα* might mean a moveable possession, but verse 3 shews that it here denotes *χωρίον*, a field.—*Νοσφίζεσθαι* from *νόσφι*, "remote, apart." In Homer *νοσφίζεσθαι* occurs both in the sense, both of physical and moral withdrawment, that is turning away from one out of hatred. Later writers use it also as active, in the signification of "removing, *i. e.*, robbing, stealing." And still more frequently is the middle voice to be found in this sense in Xenophon, Polybius, and others. In the New Testament we find it again in Titus ii. 10, and in the LXX. it occurs in Joshua vii. 1.)

In his address, Peter first exhibits the greatness of the guilt of Ananias, ascribing the idea of the deception to diabolical influence, and representing it as directed against the Holy Ghost. The unholy accordingly appears here in conflict with the Holiest; as the representatives of whom, the apostles are to be regarded (comp. Acts xv. 28) as filled with the Holy Ghost. It would almost seem as if the act of Ananias were represented as a sin against the Holy Ghost, which would explain the fact, that all admonition to repentance is wanting, and all mention of pardon; the apostles in this case only exercise their prerogative of retaining sin. (Comp. Comm. on Matth. xvi. 19.) And from this it follows that the peculiar procedure of Peter in this affair is inexplicable, if we suppose that he learned by information from others that Ananias committed this fraud: an external communication respecting the fact could not place the apostle in a position to determine the degree of the man's inward guilt. Yet such a determination was necessary to him, if he would not do injustice to Ananias, and for this therefore nothing but the power of the Spirit could qualify him. It has already been remarked on verse 4, that the words of Peter clearly shew, there was no obligation resting upon Ananias to sell the ground; yet that he might not be outstripped by others, he parted with it, but hypocritically kept back a part of the price. Further, the fact that verse 4 ascribes to Ananias himself, what verse 3 imputes to Satan, involves no contradiction at all; nor is it right to say that the ascription of the evil thought to Satan is only a popular expression for the simpler idea, that the thought came from the heart of Ananias himself. The twofold form of expression in these verses, is one quite suitable to the nature of the circumstances, because the influence of the devil is not compulsory; and accordingly the reception into the heart of an evil thought suggested by him requires the consent of the will. In like manner, the expression in verse 4, "thou hast not lied unto men, but to God" (*οὐκ ἐψεύσω ἀνθρώποις, ἀλλὰ τῷ Θεῷ*), does not deny that Ananias had lied also to men; but as this aspect of his misdeed came not at all into consideration, in comparison with the deceiving of God, the apostle in energetic speech denies it. Explanations therefore such as these, "not only to men, or not so much to men as to God," are to be rejected as enfeebling the thought. With regard, finally, to the sudden death of Ananias, mentioned in verse 5, many interpreters, on the one hand, explain it as an apoplectic fit brought on by terror;

and many, on the other, as a purely supernatural occurrence. This total separation between the natural and the supernatural is another mistake; there is nothing to prevent us from supposing that the death of Ananias might be quite a natural event; but this supposition does not destroy its marvellous character. What is natural in itself may become miraculous by connexion with circumstances and adjuncts; and so also here the death of Ananias as connected with the penal sentence of the apostle, which was spoken in the power of the Spirit, and like a sword pierced him, while alarmed on account of his sin, is the miraculous result of a higher and supernatural adjustment.

The sudden death of Ananias naturally excited a solemn awe in the minds of all who were present. The servants of the church buried the lifeless body. Certainly Mosheim is right (comm. de rebus Christ. ante Const. p. 114), and he is followed by Kuinoel (Heinrichs leaves the question undecided), in supposing that νεωτέρους (= νεανίσκοις in verse 10) denotes not merely some young men, but the regular servants of the church, who were also in Hebrew styled נְעָרִים. The article plainly leads to the conclusion, that it was not any young people who pleased that took charge of the interment, but certain definite persons, and as, moreover, they performed this duty unsummoned, we are led to suppose that they regarded it as belonging to their office. These young men (νεώτεροι) are best conceived as occupying a position similar to that of the acoluthi or acolytes at a later period.* The agapæ or love-feasts, and the numerous meetings held, must in fact have made the need of servants be felt, as early as that of rulers. (Συστέλλω or περιστέλλω is, like συγκομίζω in Acts viii. 2, applied to the burial of the dead, and the whole preparatory steps, like the Latin "pollingere." In the New Testament it is found only here; but it occurs also in the Septuagint, Ezek. xxix. 5, and in profane authors, *e. g.*, Herod. ii. 90. It denotes, primarily, the dressing of the dead body with a shroud, from στέλλω, "to place, to set in order, to prepare, to dress," whence στολή. In like manner, ἐκφέρειν = efferre, is a common expression for performing the interment of the dead.)

Vers. 7-11.—After the lapse of a few hours, the wife of Ananias

* Neander (Apost. Zeitalt. p. 39) advances the opinion that the νεώτεροι here mentioned might be no regular church officers, but only younger members of the church who undertook the interment. But in this case, doubtless, another expression would have been chosen instead of νεώτεροι, and at all events τινὲς would have been added: the article points to known individuals. It might rather be supposed that the expression denotes the deacons, if the existence among deacons of such men as Stephen and Philip did not render it improbable that employments of this outward kind would be imposed upon them. Certainly there were in the church at a very early period persons who were entrusted with the care of mere external matters, such as the cleaning of the places of meeting and the like: these might also take charge of the interment of the dead.

likewise appeared—and, as she boldly persisted in the concerted fraud, the same fate befel her. The precision of the narrative discovers itself in the careful fixing of the time (verse 7). The only peculiarity of these verses is the idea of "tempting the Spirit of the Lord" (πειράσαι τὸ πνεῦμα κυρίου). Though the expression "to tempt God," נִסָּה אֶת־הָאֱלֹהִים, occurs frequently, especially in the Old Testament, yet the phrase "to tempt the Spirit" is found only in this passage. There is expressed in it the idea that Ananias and Sapphira not only in general tempted God, as he is made known in the remoter manifestations of his character, but even supposed that they were able to conceal their sins from the Holy Ghost, the highest exhibition of the Divine agency (ψεύσασθαι τὸ πνεῦμα ἅγιον, ver. 3), although he searches not only the depths of the hearts, but even the deep things of God. (1 Cor. ii. 10.) The view of Pott and Kuinoel is quite wrong, that to tempt God is exactly the same thing as sinning in general. It is rather a species of sin, viz., that sin which displays itself audaciously and presumptuously. Man frequently puts God's love, and mercy, and omniscience, as it were, to the proof, by his sins; and this boldness of the creature against the Creator is called "tempting God." That in this case covetousness was also at work, by no means excludes the idea indicated; for a mere common covetousness would have either wholly restrained Ananias from joining himself to the church, or at least would have been a motive to forbid the sale of his property. In ver. 9 the phrase τί (ἐστι) ὅτι συνεφωνήθη ὑμῖν, "wherefore have ye agreed or concerted together," must be explained on the principle of the well-known construction of the passive with a dative. Compare Winer's Gram. page 196. In the words ἰδοὺ οἱ πόδες κ. τ. λ., we recognize the expression of immediate knowledge:. "behold, we hear the tread of the young men returning.")

§ 6. SECOND TRIAL OF THE APOSTLES.

(Acts v. 12–42.)

This narrative of matters in the bosom of the church is followed by a scene of a more public kind, an account of a new imprisonment of the apostles. It is introduced by a general description of the healing powers of the apostles (verses 12–16), especially of Peter. This excited attention in so high a degree, that even from the neighbouring cities sick people were brought to Jerusalem; which indicates that probably in these cities, too, small bodies of believers would be formed, because, according to God's appointment, outward circumstances were always designed to be a means of drawing attention to the inward spiritual truths which the apostles proclaimed.

(Respecting the porch of Solomon, comp. Comm. on Acts iii. 11. It appears to have been the usual place where the apostles met. In verse 13 the expression "but of the rest" [τῶν δὲ λοιπῶν] is undoubtedly to be understood of the multitude of those who were not yet converted, but whose attention, at the same time, was arrested by the spiritual power of Christianity.—Κολλᾶσθαι, equivalent to דָּבַק, is frequently applied to scholars and their attachment to teachers. The believers remained together, and a certain awe restrained the multitude from mingling themselves with them According to verse 14, there were many women also who believed: their baptism rendered the appointment of deaconesses necessary, who, it is probable, existed from a very early period in the church at Jerusalem, although they are not expressly named. The devout women among the followers of the Lord himself were probably not baptized, any more than the disciples, who had only received the baptism of John. The baptism of the Spirit compensated, in their case, for the outward baptism.—Verse 15. What is mentioned of the shadow of Peter is to be regarded primarily as a view of the people, but this does not imply that the view was a mere notion: we must rather suppose that where pure and childlike faith existed, it was not put to shame. Certainly, however, it was not the shadow that could heal, but only the wondrous influence which streamed from the apostle in conformity with his will. The passage is analogous to what is said of the touching of the hem of Christ's garment.* Comp. Comm. on Matth. ix. 20.—Verse 16. Πέριξ, in the signification of "round about" occurs nowhere else in the New Testament. On the position of the adverb with respect to the substantive, compare Bernhardy's Syntax, page 323.)

Vers. 17–23.—The statement that follows, of a new imprisonment of Peter and several other apostles (verse 29) agrees in substance with the account of the first imprisonment (iv. 1–22). The only things peculiar to this narrative, are the mention of their deliverance by an angel (verses 19, 20), and the information respecting the proceedings in the Sanhedrim itself (verses 33–42). The first circumstance, however, we pass over here, because it will receive a minute consideration at the passage in xii. 7, etc., connected with xvi. 26, etc., where deliverances quite similar are narrated far more in detail.

(Ver. 17.—The expression ἡ οὖσα αἵρεσις τῶν Σαδδουκαίων, *which was the sect of the Sadducees*, which stands related to the preceding words, ἀρχιερεὺς καὶ πάντες οἱ σὺν αὐτῷ, *the chief priest and all who were with him*, denotes that the high priest and even his family were attached to this sect, and in a manner represented it.—Verse 20. The phrase ῥήματα τῆς ζωῆς ταύτης is a singular one, because

* Something similar is related of Paul in Acts xix. 12.

the expression ζωὴ αὕτη, agreeably to the analogy of αἰων οὗτος, might appear to be employed in opposition to ζωὴ μέλλουσα or αἰώνιος; but, in the first place, such a mode of speaking does not occur in the language of Scripture, although it is quite common in German and English, and, in the second place it does not suit the connexion, which would rather have required ζωὴ αἰώνιος. The forced conjecture has been made that for ζωῆς we should substitute ὁδοῦ; which indeed removes the difficulties, but for want of critical authorities it cannot be admitted. It is common to regard the expression as a hypallage for ῥήματα ταῦτα τῆς ζωῆς, *these words of life*, but Winer [Grammar, p. 519] supposes that the phrase might be better understood thus: "words of the salvation, in proclaiming which the apostles were just engaged." But this idea is harsh here, because there has been no mention at all previously made of the proclamation of the gospel. Meyer prefers to understand it thus: "the words of this life, that is, of the life present to your thoughts and to your interest," but neither is this simple or plain. Perhaps it is best, as the hypallage of the pronoun is doubtful, to explain the words on the principle that reference is made to the fact that it is the angel, a being from heaven, who is speaking. In this view the sense will be: "the words of this heavenly life, of which I speak to you."—Ver. 21, Γερουσία means "council, assembly of the elders:" it is not found elsewhere in the New Testament. This council of elders is here distinguished from the Sanhedrim; it must denote experienced men, who in particular cases were associated with that body in their deliberations. In the Apocrypha the word denotes the Sanhedrim itself. Compare 2 Macc. i. 10, iv. 44.)

Ver. 24–28.—Freed from imprisonment, the apostles immediately resumed preaching in the temple, which they only left when brought away by the astonished officers to be placed before the court. (The word ἱερεύς, in ver. 24, is remarkable on account of ἀρχιερεῖς which follows; and hence may be explained the omission of it in A.B.D. and other authorities. Without doubt, however, it is genuine, because it is inexplicable how it could be inserted. Ἱερεύς is here used absolutely for the high priest, while ἀρχιερεῖς denotes the members of the Sanhedrim.—Ver. 28 παραγγελία occurs again in Acts xvi. 24; 1 Thess. iv. 2; 1 Tim. i. 5. In connexion with παραγγέλλειν, however, it is only to be found here, and this addition as usual gives force to the thought. The chiding words of the Sanhedrim, contain the peculiar expression: βούλεσθε ἐπαγαγεῖν ἐφ' ἡμᾶς τὸ αἷμα. These words doubtless express, not only the apprehension that the people may hold them guilty of the death of a righteous man, but also the consciousness of guilt itself.)

Vers. 29–32.—Peter first of all reminded them of his former public declaration (iv. 19), that we must obey God rather than men;

and then he again proclaims to them that Jesus, who had been put to death by the Sanhedrim, was raised from the dead, and exalted to the right hand of God. At the same time, however, he shews that there was pardon even for their sins in the Saviour.

(*Διαχειρίζεσθαι*, "to kill, murder," occurs again in chap. xxvi. 27. *Κρεμάσθαι ἐπὶ ξύλου* = תָּלָה עַל הָעֵץ, the usual expression in Hebrew for crucifixion. *Ἀρχηγὸς τῆς ζωῆς* occurred in chap. iii. 15: we need not here, with Kuinoel, suppose the signification to be different, because *ἀρχηγός* stands alone. The leading idea implied in it is, that the Redeemer goes before men, and prepares the way for them. In the first passage the *ζωή* is only stated definitely as the object, which here is not named. The most important idea in these verses is that embodied in *δοῦναι μετάνοιαν*, *give repentance*, in verse 31. We have already, in Luke xxiv. 47, found repentance in conjunction with remission, appearing as the object of the preaching of the Gospel. Here, however, there is a more precise intimation given in the word "give" [*δοῦναι*] that repentance [*μετάνοια*] is not a thing which can be produced by the will of man, but must be effected by grace. To all Pelagian modes of conception therefore, this passage stands in most decided opposition. Ver. 32.—Their testimony to the events described, the apostles conceive as borne and supported by the Holy Ghost, whose influences they at the same time presuppose in the hearts of their hearers.)

Vers. 33-35.—The wild hatred of the rest, which this discourse of Peter had excited, was opposed by the wise Gamaliel alone, and he guided them back to reason.* (*Διαπρίω* occurs again in chap. vii. 54: it denotes properly "to saw through or in pieces," then "to gnash with the teeth, to grow furious." *Γαμαλιήλ* גַּמְלִיאֵל [Numb. i. 10; ii. 20] was the instructor of the Apostle Paul. [Acts xxii. 3.] According to the Talmud, he was the son of one Rabbi Simeon, and grandson to the celebrated Rabbi Hillel; and on account of his piety and rabbinical learning, he had acquired much fame, and at the time of Christ was president of the Sanhedrim. [Comp. Lightfoot on this passage, and Comm. on Matth. xxvi. 3.] The expression *ἔξω ποιεῖν*, which occurs nowhere else in the New Testament, bears in verse 34 the signification "to put forth, remove." It is found also in the best profane authors, *e. g.*, in Xenoph. Cyrop. iv. 1, 3.)

Vers. 36, 37.—Gamaliel strikes into a historical path, for the purpose of leading the Sanhedrim to a temperate view of the new

* Respecting Gamaliel and the character of Jewish learning, compare the discussion of Tholuck in the Studien. 1835, Part ii., on the life and character of the Apostle Paul, page 367, etc. According to the tradition of the church (Recognit. Clem. i. 65. Phot. bibl. cod. 171), he was a Christian secretly.

phenomenon, which was presenting itself to their eyes. He reminds them of Theudas and Judas Galilæus,* who both represented themselves as the Messiah, but were soon unmasked as deceivers, and he predicts a similar speedy destruction to Christianity also, if no higher power were at work in it. First, as to Theudas, Josephus informs us (Ant. xx. 5, 1) of a rebel of this name, who appeared under the Proconsul Cuspius Fadus, declared himself to be a prophet, and promised to the multitude whom he had collected together, that he would divide the Jordan before them, and lead them through it. But Roman troopers scattered the multitude, and killed Theudas. We naturally at first think of this man; but he lived under Claudius Cæsar, and therefore much later than the time when Gamaliel uttered this speech. Many interpreters have supposed, that Luke here gives the speech of Gamaliel freely, and that he falls into an anachronism, by making him mention a man who appeared at a much later period. If we consider that Luke could hardly possess such accurate information of the proceedings within the Sanhedrim, as to be able to give word for word the speech of Gamaliel as it was spoken, we might feel disposed to conclude that there was such an oversight committed here. The character of Holy Scripture would in no respect suffer by this supposition; but only the literal theory of inspiration, which must be given up at any rate as opposed to truth, and as presenting a weak side to the assaults of adversaries. Infallibility belongs to the Scriptures only in matters of a religious and moral kind; in circumstances purely external, it has the full "fides humana," as much as any other work can deserve it; but it is no rule on such points, and therefore not infallible. But there is one consideration which prevents me from adopting this opinion as my own; in verse 37, Judas is expressly placed after Theudas (*μετὰ τοῦτον ἀνέστη Ἰούδας*), and according to the above supposition, Luke must have committed a double oversight: in the first place, he has let Gamaliel name a man who lived after him: and in the second place, he has put Judas, who appeared under Augustus, after Theudas who lived under Claudius. That Luke should have committed the latter mistake, is in fact altogether improbable, because such false prophets and false Christs must have strongly attracted the notice of all believers who lived along with them; and the time therefore of their appearance we must regard as universally known among their contemporaries. I decide therefore in favour of the other view, which supposes an earlier Theudas under Augustus, of whom Josephus has made no men-

* Comp. on chap. v. 36, 37, the ample discussion of Dr. Kuhn, in the kath. Zeitschrift. Jahrb. für Theol. und Christl. Philos. Von Kuhn, Staudenmaier and others. Frankf. a. M. 1834. Vol. i. Part i. Also Tholuck über die Glaubwürdigkeit der evang. Gesch. p. 388, etc.

tion.* And this is quite consistent with the circumstance, that according to the statement of Luke, the whole number of his followers was so insignificant that it only amounted to four hundred.

(Respecting the phrase, *λέγων εἶναί τινα ἑαυτόν*, in verse 36, compare the parallel passage in chap. viii. 9, where the same is used in full of Simon Magus, with the addition of *μέγαν* to *ἑαυτὸν λέγων*. Some codices have added *μέγαν* here too, but critical authorities are wanting to prove its genuineness, and it is not even necessary as a supplement.—The phrase *εἶναί τινα* forms a contrast with the phrase that follows, *γίνεσθαι εἰς οὐδέν*.—Instead of *προσεκολλήθη*, there are found in manuscripts the readings *προσεκλίθη*, *προσεκλήθη*, *προσετέθη*. The first of these three, the reading *προσεκλίθη*, has the most critical authorities in its favour, and perhaps, as being the more unusual expression, it is to be preferred to the common reading.—*Διαλύω*, "to unloose," here applied to the band of rebels, "to scatter," = *διασκορπίζω* in ver. 37.)

The second false prophet was Judas Galilæus, who, as has already been mentioned, appeared in the days of Cæsar Augustus. On the occasion of the census under the Proconsul Quirinus (comp. Comm. on Luke ii. 1), this Judas (Josephus Ant. xviii. i. 1) raised a disturbance, and declared that it was not at all allowable to the Jews, as the people of God, to pay taxes to the heathen Romans. Josephus, though not with entire propriety, considers the followers of this man, whom we must regard as political fanatics, as the fourth Jewish sect. The followers of Judas actually maintained their position till the great Jewish war under Titus.

Vers. 38, 39.—By referring to these rebels, Gamaliel made way for the declaration, that God's power displays itself in shaping historical events, and that without his will nothing can acquire enduring stability. Now, with respect to the idea embodied in this celebrated judgment of Gamaliel, we should of course greatly err, if we conceived it to mean that man should allow everything to proceed in its own way, on the ground that that only can secure success which is accompanied with the blessing of God; for, according to this view, it would be necessary to leave untouched every

* Olshausen seems here very needlessly to go out of his way, to make the statement that Luke might fall into a mistake, while after all it appears he is convinced there was no mistake. It is a very large promise which Christ gives to his disciples that he would send the Spirit, who should bring all things to their remembrance, and guide them into all truth. Certainly these words of our Lord do not suggest the idea, that it was in some respects only they were to be infallibly guided, while in others they were to be left to the risk of mistake. But how, we are asked, was Luke to know what Gamaliel said in the Sanhedrim? Doubtless, he gathered it from some sure source, for he tells us that he investigated every point with accuracy and care (ἀκριβῶς). But in whatever way he might learn this and a hundred other things he describes, our security rests not upon his diligence, but upon the fact that he enjoyed the direction of the Holy Ghost. Like the holy men of an earlier age, he spake as he was moved by the Holy Ghost.—Tr.

germinating form of evil. The words of Gamaliel can only claim to be reckoned wise, if we suppose that he regarded Christianity neither as a thing manifestly to be rejected, nor yet to be entirely approved: he knew not what to think of this new phenomenon; and therefore he left the explanation of it to time, which could not fail to develope fully its true character. Had he recognized it as decidedly to be reprobated, he would have felt constrained to crush it; had he recognized it as decidedly good, he would have been obliged to acknowledge it openly as such. It might be said indeed, that Gamaliel ought rather to have investigated what the nature of Christianity was, than to wait for the development of it; but undoubtedly he had instituted researches,* though without being able to come to a decision. Yet this must not be made a ground of reproach against him, for the old man probably was no longer sufficiently plastic to be transplanted into the new element of the gospel life, and perhaps it was rather his destination, like the Baptist, to be perfected in the Old Testament life. (θεομάχος occurs in no other part of the New Testament.)

Vers. 40-42.—In consequence of Gamaliel's advice, the Sanhedrim dismissed the apostles again; and they continued with joy to preach the gospel. (Ver. 40.—On the beating of the apostles comp. Luke xxiii. 16. Ver. 41.—With respect to the joy that was felt under the suffering of persecutions, comp. the remarks on Matth. v. 10. Ver. 42.—The expression κατ' οἶκον stands opposed to ἐν τῷ ἱερῷ, and denotes the private meetings which the apostles held in various parts of the city. Comp. chap. ii. 46.)

§ 7. HISTORY OF STEPHEN.

(Acts vi. 1—viii. 1.)

Vers. 1-7.—With respect to the first division of this paragraph (vi. 1-7), it might be supposed that the evangelist's design in it was to communicate information regarding the public regulations of the church at Jerusalem. But a closer consideration of the connexion of the passage with what follows renders this supposition quite improbable. If this were the author's design, we should

* I entirely agree with Neander (Apost. Zeitalter Th. i. s. 56, etc.) in my view of the state of Gamaliel's mind. It is not to be supposed that this Jewish scholar was secretly attached to the gospel: on the contrary he was honoured to the end of his life as a model of Pharisaic piety. But as a Pharisee, he was moderate and well-intentioned; and he may therefore, upon the whole, have received an impression of the character of the apostles, which gave him the conviction that these men aimed at nothing decidedly objectionable. He prevented, therefore, violent means of suppression, and rather left to the cause its free course, supposing it would probably soon come to nothing of its own accord.

undoubtedly be informed, not only respecting the deacons, but also respecting the presbyters and their election: nay in this case the narrative even of the choice of the deacons must have proceeded quite differently from what it has done; because the seven that are mentioned, as will be more clearly shewn immediately, could not be the only deacons of the church at Jerusalem. The whole complexion of this narrative makes it nearly certain, that it could only be designed for an introduction to the history of Stephen: Luke wished to inform his readers briefly of the occasion on which this celebrated martyr received an office in the church, and thus to introduce him as a distinguished member of the body.

With respect to the position of the seven individuals who were chosen, there can be no doubt that they are to be regarded as deacons.* We are led to this conclusion not only by the expressions *διακονία καθημερινή* in ver. 1, and *διακονεῖν τραπέζαις* in ver. 2, but also particularly by primitive exegetical tradition. The ancient church did not venture, in consequence of the number here specified, to go beyond seven deacons in any church. In the third century there were in Rome, along with forty presbyters, not more than seven deacons. (Compare Euseb. H. E. vi. 43.) Certain however though it be that those newly-chosen individuals are to be regarded as deacons, it is equally certain that they could not be the first nor the only deacons. For the service of the church, even at an earlier period, must have required persons to manage the funds, to take charge of the sick, and to attend at the love-feasts. At the first these were chosen from amongst the Jews of Palestine; but when the Greek Jews complained of the neglect of their poor, it is probable that the church proceeded to the election of these seven men from amongst the Hellenists, for they all bear Greek names. Now if the poor of the Jews of Palestine had been committed to the care of these men, the same complaint might readily have been repeated on the other side. Undoubtedly, therefore, there were more than these seven deacons instated in office in the ancient church of Jerusalem. (Compare Moshemii Comm. p. 118, etc.) That there were also presbyters appointed from the earliest date in the church of Jerusalem, is rendered probable by the very mention of the *νεώτεροι* in chap. v. 6; and besides, they are expressly named in the passages xi. 30, xv. 2.† The ecclesiastical duties to be performed, especially

* Some learned men have been disposed to regard as presbyters the individuals whose election is described in this passage: so the celebrated Canonist J. H. Bohmer (in his diss. Jur. eccl. ant. diss. vii. p. 373, etc.) But this view does not at all admit of being properly established, and ought decidedly to be rejected.

† Neander (Apost. Zeitalt. page 40, etc.) supposes that the deacons were first appointed, and that until their election all the members of the church at Jerusalem stood upon a level, so that the apostles themselves were the only rulers and guides. During the first weeks or months this may have been the state of matters. But if we consider how rapidly

baptizing and the internal government of the church, rendered the speedy appointment of presbyters absolutely necessary. The proper work of teaching (διακονία τοῦ λόγου) the apostles appear at first to have reserved entirely to themselves. (Compare ver. 4.) It is certain, however, that from amongst the number of the presbyters, no bishop had as yet assumed the rule, because the college of apostles retained the prime direction of affairs. It was when the apostles left Jerusalem that the need was first felt of unity; and from that time James, the brother of the Lord, governed the church as bishop. (Euseb. H. E. II., 23.)

With respect to the particulars of this section, the indefinite expression "in those days" (ἐν ταῖς ἡμέραις ταύταις), does not permit us to fix precisely the chronology of the event. Still, however, it must be placed in the earliest times of the church, and accordingly the fact is undeniable, that at a very early period differences displayed themselves in the Christian community. The pure ideal conception of the apostolic church cannot stand before these and similar facts, which we shall have to consider in the sequel; but they prove by no means prejudicial to a temperate estimate of the life displayed in it. Never can the earthly fellowship of believers be without blemishes, partly because it always comprehends individual unworthy members, partly because even in the best the sinful principle is not yet entirely extinguished; but never was the life of faith more purely and powerfully exhibited than in the apostolic age. And particularly as to the contest before us, it was really but an emulation of love: each party would have their own poor taken care of in the best possible manner: we are not to suppose there was any deceitful overreaching of either party by the other.

The two contending parties, mentioned in this passage, are the Hebrews ('Εβραῖοι) and the Hellenists ('Ελληνισταί). By the former expression we are undoubtedly to understand the Jews of Palestine who spoke Hebrew, and by the latter the Jews who spoke Greek, and who had come to Jerusalem from abroad.* The only point

the church increased, how much the time of the apostles was occupied by transactions with magistrates, by imprisonment, and the like, it will appear, I think, more probable that very soon men with the gifts of teaching were appointed by them as presbyters, and persons with powers of management chosen for deacons. (Compare at Rom. xii. 4.) If we only give up the idea, that Luke designs here to inform us expressly of the election of the deacons, and if we suppose instead that the whole narrative is just intended as an introduction to the history of Stephen, then there is nothing which can be advanced against this supposition. Now, that it is not Luke's primary object here to make formal communications respecting the nature of ecclesiastical offices, plainly appears, in the first place, from the conciseness of the whole account, and in the second place, particularly from the circumstance that he says not a word of the presbyters, although they come before us in chap. xi. 30, and xv. 2, as office-bearers already appointed in the church.

* The word 'Ελληνισταί never has the same signification in the New Testament as

about which there can be any uncertainty, is whether the Ἑλληνισταί include proselytes or not. But since (verse 5) there is one proselyte to be found among the seven deacons who were chosen, there is no doubt that this class is included; and indeed it is difficult to imagine that the proselytes who went over to Christianity should be kept back in any way, or separated from the rest. It was language only which established a distinction between the Hebrews and the Hellenists; and all proselytes on the very ground of their language belonged to the latter class.

Again, as to the *subject* of the contest, the Hellenists affirm that their widows were neglected in the daily ministration. This passage confirms the view we have already expressed at chap. iv. 32, that it was only the poor and the destitute who could be supported out of the common fund: the widows are here put by synecdoche for all poor and needy persons. And the expression "daily ministration" (*διακονία καθημερινή*) leads to the conclusion, that the assistance was not given in money, but in food, which is also confirmed by the phrase "serving tables" (*διακονεῖν τραπέζαις*) in verse 2. It is probable that in various parts of the city, in the places of meeting belonging to the church, there were apartments for eating prepared, in which the poor were fed free of expense. And thus we see appearing at the very origin of the church, the charitable feeling, which is so peculiar to the gospel, and which has produced so many institutions in the church. (The adjective *καθημερινός*, formed from *καθ' ἡμέραν*, is found in the New Testament only here.)

The matter in question was laid by the apostles before the whole body. Here accordingly we find the democratical element prevailing in the church; but it gradually passed through the aristocratical into the monarchical.* This transition was by no means merely a result of priestly ambition (though certainly at a later period that passion was often enough displayed in the church) but a necessary consequence of the course of events in the church as a whole. So long, for example, as the Christian spirit continued to display itself vigorously in the church, the public voice might well be consulted; but when this spirit afterwards disappeared, it would have been ruinous to the church if the plurality of voices had been allowed to decide. A glance at the rudeness of the masses in the middle ages may convince us of the necessity of their being guided by those

Ἕλληνες, Greeks, who were not proselytes. In chap. xi. 20, Ἕλληνες is the right reading.

* It must not be overlooked that the multitude here certainly exercise the right of election, and yet the apostles retain the right of ratifying the choice (*οὓς καταστήσομεν*, verse 3). But, according to the pastoral epistles, the bishops appear to have possessed the appointment of office-bearers: there is no trace in them of an election by the church. Among the Gentile churches, which were often but little confirmed in the faith, it might be early found by the apostles that a general election was impracticable.

above them. Even in the latter part of the apostolic age, as is plain from the pastoral epistles, the democratic element appears to have lost ground in the church, and the predominating influence in the management of affairs proceeds from the body of the teachers. Finally, the great number of believers, without doubt, made several places of meeting necessary for them, in which the assemblies might be conducted by individual apostles.

In ver. 3, *σοφία*, *wisdom*, is taken in the more restricted sense, as prudence in outward affairs: it is not to be conceived, however, as a natural talent, but as a gift of the Spirit, for Paul enumerates the *διακονίαι* among the Charismata, 1 Cor. xii. 5. The word *χρεία*, "want, need," is also used synonymously with *λειτουργία*, "office, employment;" on the principle that every employment presupposes some need. So also in profane authors, *e. g.*, Polyb. vi. 12, viii. 22.

Ver. 5.—Of the seven deacons that were chosen, Stephen and Philip (chap. viii.) only are known. Nicolaus has been falsely supposed to be the founder of the sect of the Nicolaitanes: on this subject see more at Rev. ii. 6.—Ver. 6. Although it was the church that made the choice, yet the apostles had the right of confirmation and consecration, as being endowed with the gifts of the Holy Ghost. The form of consecration was the imposition of hands with prayer. The *χειροθεσία*, סְמִיכַת יָדַיִם, is a usage found even in the Old Testament in Gen. xlviii. 14, Numb. xxvii. 18, and which also occurs in the New, as in Matth. xix. 13, Mark vi. 5. It was a standing ordinance in the church for the communication of the Holy Ghost (Acts viii. 17), and for the consecration of office-bearers (1 Tim. iv. 14; 2 Tim. i. 6). The idea embraced in the laying on of hands was doubtless no other than this, that by means of it there was effected a communication of the Spirit from the individual consecrating to the one ordained. It is further expressly stated in verse 7, that among the increasing number of believers there were many priests even to be found. They belonged probably to the sect of the Pharisees, who were far more likely to be subdued by the power of the truth than the sensual Sadducees. The Essenes had no priests.

Vers. 8–10.—After the account of the election of Stephen along with the six other deacons, the narrative proceeds immediately to a more particular statement respecting him. First of all, it is mentioned of him that he wrought miracles. In him accordingly we see this gift already removed one step further from its source, for Christ bestowed it upon the apostles, and they upon Stephen. Later traces of the gift of healing are to be found even in the second and third century of the church (compare Justin Martyr, apol. i. p. 45; Iren. adv. hær. ii. 56; Orig. cont. Cels. vii. p. 334); but the further we recede from the apostolic age, the more do these very striking exhibitions of the power of the Spirit become lost to our view. (Regarding the particular Charismata, see details at 1 Cor. xii.) Of the Jews, who were connected with the foreign synagogues existing in Jerusalem (compare Comm. on Matth. iv. 23), several now fell into disputation with the zealous Stephen; but he overpowered them all.

It is remarkable that the Libertini are mentioned along with the names of nations, and that they had a separate synagogue. Perhaps freedmen (and beyond all doubt, as the name indicates, Roman freedmen, not Palestinian, as Lightfoot supposed, for the institute of freedmen was entirely of a Roman character) built the synagogue, and from this circumstance it derived its name; yet we need not suppose that freedmen only were connected with it, any more than that the other synagogues numbered among their members only men of Alexandria or Cyrene. They had their names either from their founders, or from the preponderating class of people who were connected with them. Valckenaer's conjecture of Λιβυστίνων is very attractive, but wants all critical authority. The supposition of a city named Libertum is not sufficiently confirmed to permit us to think of Jews from it. Sickler, in his Ancient Geography, recognizes no city of this name.

Vers. 11–15.—The success of Stephen's ministry raised up a keen opposition to him. His enemies accused him before the Sanhedrim as a blasphemer of God and of the law. And just as in the case of the accusation brought against the Lord himself (comp. Comm. on Matth. xxvi. 60, etc.), so here likewise it is said, that false witnesses appeared against him. These give testimony that Stephen said, Jesus would destroy the Temple, and change the Jewish manners and customs. In this the Jews, according to their ideas, might find a blasphemy against the Temple and against Moses, who had founded and regulated its services, but not any blasphemy against God.* It may be said that indirectly there is blasphemy against God, inasmuch as Moses arranged his religious institutions by a Divine command; but that is not sufficient, for it is only on account of this circumstance that a word against Moses could be regarded as blasphemy at all: if he were not viewed as a messenger sent from God, then no reproachful word uttered against him would be different from the reproaches thrown upon any other man. The blasphemies against God (ῥήματα βλάσφημα εἰς Θεόν) must therefore still have some special reference; and that without doubt is no other than that which was formed in his assertion of the Divine dignity of Christ. (Comp. Comm. on Matth. xxvi. 65.) But

* In the Talmudic tract styled Sanhedrim (chap. vii. 4) it is said: Lapidator profanator Sabbathi, magus et qui ad apostasiam impellit.

here again the question presents itself, as at Matth. xxvi. 60, how these witnesses can be named false (μάρτυρες ψευδεῖς), when in fact Stephen did teach Christ's Divine dignity, and declared that God dwells not in temples made with hands (chap. vii. 48), which contains an indirect intimation that the Temple at Jerusalem might be dispensed with? One would expect, not that the witnesses should be accused of falsehood, but rather the Sanhedrim of a deficiency in discernment, which prevented them from perceiving that the ideas promulgated by Stephen did not at all contradict the true sense of the Old Testament, and consequently the Divine will. This difficulty, however, will be solved, if here again we suppose that the Jews, with a disposition of mind that regarded things merely in their outward and *material* aspects, did not rightly comprehend the thoughts of Stephen, but took a distorted view of them. What he had represented as a *consequence* of the operation of the Spirit of Christ, whose design it was to consecrate the world as a great temple of God, and to guide religion from externals to the heart: *that* the Jews conceived as a *purpose* to be accomplished by violence; and thus they ascribe to him the destruction of the Temple, and the abolition of Jewish usages, things which he had never attempted. Stephen, in fact, blames the Jews that they had not kept the law of Moses (vii. 53), while, if he had been aiming at the positive abolition of it, they would have been acting exactly according to his wish. The New Testament, therefore, does not abolish the Old in a violent manner, but only in the way of organic development, that is, in such a manner, that the eternal and permanent substance of the Old Testament is preserved, and passes over into the New Testament life itself. The Holy Scriptures testify against all revolution, whether in political or ecclesiastical affairs; they, on the contrary, recommend the gradual remodelling of what is old, in accordance with the necessities of the times. The fact, however, that this relation of the gospel to the external aspect of the Old Covenant, which was thus placed as a hedge between Gentiles and Jews, came into question in connexion with the person of Stephen, and not in connexion with one of the twelve apostles, undoubtedly had its ground, as Baur (in a holiday programme of the University of Tübingen, of the year 1829), and Neander (Apos. Zeitalt., page 60, etc.), rightly remark, in the course of culture through which Stephen had passed. As a Hellenist, he had undoubtedly from the very first entertained freer notions of the Old Testament, than was possible for a Jew of Palestine; and therefore the Spirit might more readily bring into his view that aspect of Christianity, by which it was to draw the whole heathen world within the circle of the higher life, an object that necessarily presupposes the dissolution of that bond and centre of opinion formed by the Temple at Jerusalem. Rightly, therefore, may Stephen be styled the forerunner of Paul, the apostle of the Gentiles. Out of *his* blood grew this powerful preacher of the heathen world, and the echo of the words heard from Stephen may have been to Paul, after his conversion, a leading means of drawing out his ministry in the direction of the heathen world.

(Ver. 11.—Ὑποβάλλω occurs nowhere else in the New Testament: it means primarily "to lay under, to push under," then like the Latin subornare, "to contrive, instigate, abet," and therefore *ὑπόβλητος* is a secret accuser. Josep. Arch. vii. 8, 4. Ver. 13. Βλάσφημα is undoubtedly spurious: it is merely an interpolation from verse 11. Ver. 15. The words *ὡσεὶ πρόσωπον ἀγγέλου* describe the glory that brightened the features of Stephen, supported as he was by the consciousness of the Divine favour. Similar is the expression in 2 Sam. xiv. 17, כְּמַלְאַךְ הָאֱלֹהִים, כֵּן תְּפִלָּה.)

Chap. vii. 1–3.—The speech of Stephen which follows, exhibits both in its general structure and in its particular parts, much that is striking and difficult.* *First of all*, the address does not seem strictly appropriate in its general relation to the position of Stephen. It makes only an incidental reference to the charges that were brought against him (verses 48, 49), and the rest of the discourse embraces nothing but a review of the history of the Jewish nation till the time of Solomon. But this peculiar character unquestionably imprints upon it the seal of genuineness, for no one certainly would have thought of framing a discourse of this kind for the circumstances in which Stephen was placed. Moreover, as there were many priests, according to chap. vi. 7, connected with the church, the question can occasion no difficulty, how the speech delivered before the Sanhedrim could become known. In order to explain the peculiar character of this discourse, many interpreters have supposed, that the narrative it gives of the fortunes of the Jewish people embraces a concealed parrying of all the charges which had been brought against Stephen. But this view leads to forced interpretations, as for example, that the history of Abraham was intended to intimate that there were pious men even before the building of the Temple, and that accordingly it cannot be service in the visible temple which alone is acceptable to God. So Grotius. The simplest view is, that Stephen's reason for narrating the history of the Old Testament so much in detail, is just to shew the Jews that he believes it, and thus to induce them, through love of their national history, to listen with calm attention. For, although the

* Comp. in Heinrichs' Commentary, the sixth and seventh excursus, which refer to this speech of Stephen. Further, the treatise of Luger (Lübeck 1838) respecting this discourse, and the remarks of Lange in the Studien 1836, Part iii. page 725, etc. Above all, Baur's programme de orationis a Stephano habitæ consilio. Tubing. 1829.

nature of the history itself was fitted to make it a mirror to the hearers, and particularly to bring before their minds the circumstance, that the Jewish people in all stages of their progress, and of Divine revelation, had resisted the Spirit of God, and that consequently it was not astonishing they should now again shew themselves disobedient;* yet it does not appear to me that this object was definitely kept in view in the discourse, and that for the following reasons: First, because in this case the mode of exhibiting the history of the people of Israel would have been different. Stephen would have brought out the contrast far more decidedly, and would have paid less attention to secondary points than he has done. And further, the Jews would not have listened so quietly, if they had noticed any trace of such a design. We should therefore be obliged to suppose that the speech of Stephen had failed of its object, inasmuch as the Jews did not at all perceive that it inflicted any censure upon them.

Again, it is a characteristic of this address, that it contains so many references to the Rabbinical tradition, of which traces are also exhibited in the translation of the LXX., which is frequently followed by Stephen.† Reference has already been made in an earlier part of the Commentary (at Luke iv. 18) to those deviations of the LXX. which are received by the New Testament writers; and I have remarked that they are by no means at once to be rejected.

* Even Baur, in the treatise already quoted, regards this as the main thought of the discourse: Quo ampliora fuerint Dei beneficia, eo alieniorem a Deo se gessisse populum. But if this really stood before the mind of Stephen as a definite purpose, while he was speaking, then it will be difficult to give any reason for the fulness with which accessory points are handled, which admit of no reference to this main thought. We shall be obliged therefore to suppose, at the least, that there are other objects besides this, as for example, to shew that he is well acquainted with sacred history, that he believes it, and that he holds it in high honour. Such detailed references to the points of charge against Stephen, as Meyer and Luger suppose to be in this speech, I cannot find in it, and I regard the effort to make them apparent as quite calculated to mislead. Luger supposes that, according to my representation, the design of Stephen's discourse was not answered, inasmuch as the Jews after all did not listen to him when he came to the main point. In so far as the Jews interrupted him, the failure certainly is a fact; but on every other explanation, the martyr's speech appears equally in this sense to have miscarried, and in particular according to the view brought forward by Luger, that his object is to parry the individual charges, it certainly failed, for the Jews after all killed him. It did not fail, however, in so far as Stephen obtained ample opportunity of declaring his faith in the word of God and making it plain to every lover of truth that he was innocent.

† This reference to traditional elements in the discourse of Stephen is particularly striking in this respect, that his whole tendency of mind, more free as being a Hellenist, does not lead us to expect the like. This circumstance has never, amid the numerous investigations to which the remarkable speech of Stephen has been subjected, been sufficiently considered, nor anywhere satisfactorily explained. In any case it obliges us to suppose that Stephen, though a Hellenist, had yet received a thorough rabbinical education, without, however, having allowed himself to become a prey to the narrow-hearted spirit of Pharisaism.

And with respect to these references to tradition, they render it in fact very probable, that ancient genuine elements were preserved traditionally among the Jews, which received their higher confirmation by admission into the New Testament. If we consider the general prevalence of oral tradition among all ancient nations, and particularly the stationary posture of things which was common among the Jews, such a descent of genuine traditionary elements through a succession of centuries will lose the astonishing character which it seems to have.

The speech commences with Abraham, the ancestor of the Jewish nation, and the first appearance of God with which he was favoured. In the very first verses, however, the historical statement does not appear to be purely connected with the original sources, for there is no mention made in Genesis of any appearance of God before the departure from Ur. The words which are here (ver. 3) quoted as spoken *before* the residence in Haran, were spoken, according to Gen. xii. 1, during the appearance with which Abraham was favoured *in* Haran. It has been attempted to remove the force of this circumstance by the remark that, according to tradition, the departure from Ur likewise took place at the command of God. (It is probable that this opinion was formed in consequence of the passages in Gen. xv. 7 ; Neh. ix. 7. Compare Philo de Abrah. p. 11, 12. Vol. ii. edit. Mangey. Joseph. Arch. i. 7, 1.) However, the words of the quotation always appear to stand in the way of this view; they are to be found literally, according to the LXX., in the passage Gen. xii. 1. (But the LXX. has, in accordance with the Hebrew, the additional words, καὶ ἐκ τοῦ οἴκου τοῦ πατρός σου. The words καὶ δεῦρο are wanting in the Cod. Alex.) Even if therefore, we chose to refer to that tradition, still we must confess that the words contained in ver. 3 appear to be transferred from a later appearance of God to an earlier one. For the supposition of Luger, that, according to the narrative of Genesis, the theophany recorded in Gen. xii. 1, did not take place in Haran at all, but in Ur, the accounts in the eleventh chapter being anticipated simply for the purpose of completing the external history of Abraham, before the author begins to communicate the spiritual (as if the external history of Abraham did not continue to be recorded even after the 12th chapter), is, on account of the connexion between xi. 31 and xii. 4, quite untenable. It is only the notice of Terah's death that is anticipated (xi. 32); in other points the narrative advances regularly forward.

Another difficulty, that Haran (חָרָן, Χαῤῥάν Κάῤῥαι, Carræ) is really situated in Mesopotamia itself, while Abraham here seems to have departed out of Mesopotamia to go to Haran, is more easily disposed of. Ur, which Genesis transfers to Chaldea (xi. 31), is itself, in a somewhat wider sense, a city of Mesopotamia, because the Chaldeans inhabited the north of Mesopotamia. (Compare Winer's Reallex. page 258, etc.) There might, therefore, even before the arrival of Abraham in Haran, be mention made of his residence in Mesopotamia.

Vers. 4, 5.—In the account of Abraham's migration from Haran to Canaan, there likewise appears an inconsistency with the narrative in Genesis. It is alleged here that the migration followed after the death of Terah, the father of Abraham; but according to Genesis xi. 32, Terah reached the age of 205 years, and therefore he lived for sixty years after the period in question, for he was 70 years old when he begat* Abraham, and Abraham was 75 when he removed to Canaan. By altering the number 205 into 145, the inconsistency would indeed be removed, but that is plainly too violent a measure; the only method which is here of any avail, and which is therefore followed by Michaelis and Kuinoel, is to summon tradition to our aid. And in fact, among the traditions of the Jews, the opinion has arisen, that Abraham (because the opposite appeared like a violation of the fourth (fifth) commandment) first left Haran after the death of his father. But as the book of Genesis expressly places the *literal* death of Terah later, they understood the former death *spiritually* of his apostacy to idolatry, which obliged Abraham to leave him.† This view appears to have been followed here by Stephen, and such indications of his Rabbinical learning may have been peculiarly attractive to his hearers.‡ (Compare Philo de migrat. Abrah, p. 463, and Lightfoot on this passage.) In verse 5 the faith of Abraham is commended, who, although no part of Canaan was yet actually in his possession, and although he had no children, believed that the land was bestowed upon him and his posterity. (In *οὐκ ἔδωκε οὐκ* = *οὔπω* [compare John vii. 8]; on his first arrival, God in fact had not given him anything which he could call his own in the land. *Βῆμα ποδός* = מִדְרַךְ־רָגֶל in Deut. ii. 5. *Κατάσχεσις* occurs again in verse 45 as the rendering of the Hebrew נַחֲלָה, אֲחֻזָּה. Compare Gen. xvii. 8, Numb, xxxii. 5, in the LXX. version.)

* We may indeed understand Gen. xi. 26 to mean that Terah was seventy years old when he began to have children, and we may suppose that Abraham was not the oldest of his family: but this will not suffice to fill up sixty years.

† That Terah was odious among the Rabbins as an idolater (Jos. xxiv. 2) is shewn too by other traditions. Thus it is related that Abraham had broken down the idols of his father, and was therefore delivered by him to Nimrod. And Nimrod threw Abraham into a fiery furnace, from which however he escaped without injury. Compare Lightfoot on this passage.

‡ Other explanations, like that of Bengel in the Gnomon: "Abram, dum Thara vixit in Haran, domum quodammodo paternam habuit in Haran, in terra Canaan duntaxat peregrinum agens; mortuo autem patre, plane in terra Canaan domum unice habere cœpit," must be rejected as forced.

Vers. 6, 7.—The words of the promise itself are now quoted agreeably to the passage in Gen. xv. 13; but Stephen, or rather the translator of the speech, which undoubtedly was delivered in Hebrew, does not follow the LXX. closely. The deviations, however, have no effect upon the thoughts, excepting that the last words of verse 7, *καὶ λατρεύσουσί μοι ἐν τῷ τόπῳ τούτῳ*, are entirely wanting in the passage in Genesis; they have probably been taken from Exod. iii. 12, and blended with the former passage into one whole. According to Exod. xii. 40, the bondage really lasted 430, but here the round number merely is given as in Gen. xv. 13. Respecting the difficulty that springs from the statement in Gal. iii. 17, compare the remarks on that passage. *Κακόω* occurs likewise in chapters xii. 1, xviii. 10, and in 1 Pet. iii. 13, in the signification of "persecuting, maltreating."

Vers. 8–12.—In what follows, the history is pursued further; and particularly Joseph's fortunes are treated in detail. It is very probable that in this detail there floated before the mind of Stephen a typical relation of the history of Joseph to the Redeemer. (In the phrase *καὶ ἔδωκεν αὐτῷ διαθήκην περιτομῆς*, there is to be seen a blending of two thoughts: fully expressed, the clause must run: *ἔδωκεν αὐτῷ περιτομὴν, τῆς διαθήκης σημεῖον.* It is not admissible to understand *διαθήκη* directly in the signification of "command, ordinance." For *οὕτως* some codices have the easier reading *οὗτος*, but this has certainly resulted from a correction of the unusual use of *οὕτως*. We are not to suppose an interchange of *οὕτως* and *οὗτος* [compare Winer's Grammar, page 434], and therefore it only remains that we understand *οὕτως* here as a particle of transition in the sense of our words "then, so," as it occurred in common language. Compare Passow's Lexicon under this word. In the New Testament, it is similarly used in Acts xvii. 33, xxviii. 14.—The twelve sons of Jacob are styled *πατριάρχαι*, as the heads of the twelve tribes or *πατριαί*. Compare ii. 29.—*Χορτάσματα* denotes properly the fodder of cattle; but it is here used generally in the wider sense of "means of subsistence.")

Vers. 13–16.—In the statement of the number of Jacob's family that went down to Egypt, another difference presents itself, for only seventy persons are mentioned in Gen. xlvi. 27; Exod. i. 5; Deut. x. 22; but here seventy-five. As the Septuagint likewise mentions seventy-five souls in the passages referred to, we cannot well say that Stephen only meant to state a round number, but rather that he must have followed this version; and probably the Seventy, or the tradition which is preserved in their version, included the children of Ephraim and Manasseh, and so made up the number, which in this case, of course, does not so much specify the number of those that went down, as the number of all the posterity of Jacob.

Other difficulties are presented in verse 16, according to which all the patriarchs were buried in Sychem, which Abraham bought from the sons of Emmor. But, according to Gen. xxxiii. 19, Jacob bought this field (it was the cave of Machpelah in Hebron that Abraham bought), and Jacob, moreover, according to Gen. l. 13, was buried in Abraham's sepulchre in Hebron: of the other patriarchs there is nothing mentioned in Genesis, with respect to the place of their interment. Joseph, however, was buried, according to Gen. l. 25, in Sychem, and the other sons of Jacob likewise, according to tradition. Yet there is another tradition, which says they were buried with Abraham in Hebron (Joseph. Arch. ii. 8, 2), and such a twofold account might readily arise, as Genesis presented nothing decisive either in favour of the one or the other. In the passage before us, therefore, *οἱ πατέρες ἡμῶν* may be regarded as supplying the subject to *μετετέθησαν*, and thus the one difficulty is solved. For the removal of the other it has been conjectured that instead of Ἀβραάμ we should read Ἰακώβ, or that Abraham's name should be thrown out, and *ὠνήσατο* taken impersonally; but the manuscripts do not support these conjectures; and nothing therefore remains, unless we are disposed to use violent measures, but to confess that here Abraham has been put for Jacob by the speaker or by the narrator, a confession which, according to my view of the relation of the spirit to the letter, is not in the smallest degree dangerous.*

Vers. 17–19.—In these verses the speech passes on to the history of Moses, which is treated very fully in what follows. The quotation in verse 18 is taken from Exod. i. 8. The expression "knew not" (*οὐκ ᾔδει*) is not to be understood of ignorance properly speaking, but rather of a want of regard for the merits of Joseph. *Κατασοφίζεσθαι* is found nowhere else in the New Testament. It is borrowed from Exod. i. 10; and conformably to the Hebrew [illegible]: it denotes "to circumvent or mislead in a crafty manner," "dolose agere." *Ζωογονεῖσθαι* means primarily to be born alive, and then to be preserved in life. (Comp. Comm. on Luke xvii. 33.)

Vers. 20–22.—Down to verse 44, the history of Moses is now related very fully. In these first verses, the remark (ver. 22) that Moses was instructed in the wisdom of the Egyptians, contains another reference to Jewish tradition, for Genesis mentions nothing of the kind. As Moses was brought up in the palace of Pharaoh, it was very natural to suppose that he was instructed in the sciences and arts of Egypt. But certainly, in making this supposition, the ancients were far from the notion of modern infidelity, that it was the training he received in Egypt which put him in the condition of

* The same thing is said by Calvin also on this passage: in nomine Abrahæ erratum esse palam est, quare hic locus corrigendus est.

becoming the founder of the political and religious life of the Israelites. All the education of the Egyptians was in the hands of the priests; and if their influence therefore had determined the inward life of Moses, he would necessarily have spread their idolatry among the Jews, and yet he abolished at once all the traces of it that had crept in among them. Just as little, therefore as Paul became an apostle, in consequence of his Grecian education in Tarsus, did Moses become the great founder of religion, in consequence of the wisdom he had learned in Egypt. And yet God might employ the outward education which Moses had received in Egypt, so as to make him impart it, under the hallowing influence of the Divine Spirit that filled him, in an improved shape to the Jews.

(The conjecture that in verse 20, the reading should be *ἀστεῖος τῇ θεῷ* instead of *ἀστεῖος τῷ Θεῷ* is quite unnecessary; for *τῷ Θεῷ* is to be understood like לִפְנֵי יְהוָה in Gen. x. 9. In verse 22, the expression, *δυνατὸς ἐν λόγοις* is remarkable, for Moses we know had no gift of eloquence. Nor can the expression be applied to the eloquence of Moses in writing; but it admits very well of being applied to the spiritual power, which fitted him for filling men's minds with enthusiasm in favour of his convictions. All true eloquence, in fact, rests pre-eminently upon the power of the soul to win the hearts of men.)

Vers. 23–29.—Respecting the age of Moses, when he went among his people, there is nothing determined in the Holy Scriptures: here too Stephen follows tradition,* which however was not uniform, for there are other passages which represent him as having been twenty years old at the time. The slaughter of the Egyptian, Stephen appears (verse 25) to understand generally as a type of the office of Moses to protect and to help, for he declares that Moses hoped his brethren would discover his true character from this action. Of this there is nothing contained in the statements of the Pentateuch; the thought appears to be a reflection of Stephen's upon the circumstances of Moses; for there are no traditional elements that bear upon this passage, at least there is nothing upon the point in our remains of Rabbinical literature. (The expression, *ἀνέβη ἐπὶ καρδίαν* is formed upon the model of the Hebrew, עָלָה עַל לֵב. Respecting it comp. 1 Cor. ii. 9.—In verse 26, the Septuagint has *ἡμέρᾳ δευτέρᾳ* instead of *ἐπιούσῃ*.—*Συνελαύνειν* is used in the signification of "admonishing urgently," "compellere."—Verse 29. *Μαδιάμ* = מִדְיָן.)

Ver. 30–32.—Of the important occurrence that follows the exposition belongs to the interpretation of the Pentateuch; but

* In Bereshith Rabba, fol. 115, it is said: Moses in palatio Pharaonis, 40 annos degit, in Midiane 40 annos, et 40 annos Israeli ministravit. (See Lightfoot on this passage.)

on the subject of the interchange of *ἄγγελος κυρίου* and *κύριος*, we may refer the reader to Steinwender's treatise: Christus Deus in Vet. Test. Regiom. 1829, p. 6, seq. The words of God are not accurately repeated: verse 33 should have stood, according to Exod. iii. 5, 6, before verse 32. (Instead of *πατέρων σου*, in verse 32, the Septuagint has *πατρός σου*, after the Hebrew.)

Vers. 33–36.—In connexion with the words of God, by which he sends Moses as a messenger to his people, appears (verses 35, 36) the first definite allusion to the person of Jesus, on whose account Stephen stood accused before the Sanhedrim's tribunal. As the Jews formerly rejected Moses, so now do they reject Jesus; and yet God has appointed the one as he did the other to bring them help. As Moses literally conducted the people out of Egypt through the Red Sea into the land of promise, so does Christ spiritually guide through conflict and struggle into the eternal home of heaven.

It is a peculiarity of this passage that in verse 35 Moses bears the name of *λυτρωτής*, Redeemer. In the Old Testament this word is used by the Seventy to represent גֹּאֵל, but it is only applied to God (Psalm xviii. 17, lxxvii. 15); in the New Testament it does not occur elsewhere, the term usually employed to express the idea being *σωτήρ*. This, however, is to be regarded as merely accidental, because all the other words that are formed from *λύτρον* are in other passages applied to Christ. In the case of Moses the epithet *λυτρωτής* to course bears only an external reference to the deliverance from Egyptian bondage; but this is to be conceived as a prefiguration of the redemption from sin, which was accomplished by the Messiah. (Ἐν *χειρί* corresponds obviously to the Hebrew בְּיַד, and denotes simply interposition, medium = *διά*.)

Vers. 37–40.—Further, we have in regard to Moses his prediction respecting the Messiah, and his intercourse with God, exhibited to view; and, in connexion with these points, the unfaithfulness of the people, and their apostacy from God. (Respecting the quotation from Deut. xviii. 18, contained in verse 37, comp. Comm. on Acts iii. 22. In verse 38 *γίνεσθαι*, followed by *μετά*, corresponds to the Hebrew הָיָה עִם.—The *ἐκκλησία* is the collective body of the Jews who were in the wilderness, between whom and God, Moses acted as mediator.—On *λόγια ζῶντα* consult Comm. on John vi. 63; 1 Pet. i. 23, And if here the *ζωή*, *life*, is ascribed to the Mosaic law, this holds of its essential character, which is good and holy [Rom. vii. 12]; but in the preceptive form, in which it appears among men, it has no power to *communicate* the life.—The quotation in verse 40 is from Exod. xxxii. 1.)

Vers. 41–43.—The following verses give more precise information respecting the idolatry of the Israelites in the wilderness. It was undoubtedly the Egyptian worship of Apis which led to the formation of the golden calf, under which they adored the creative principle in nature. (The word *μοσχοποιεῖν* was probably first formed either by Stephen, or if he spoke before the Sanhedrim in Hebrew, by the narrator of his speech. It is found nowhere else.) In this apostacy of the Jews, Stephen rightly discovers a judgment of God, who punishes sin by sin. Compare Rom. i. 24, etc. But besides the golden calf the Israelites also practised in the wilderness the worship of the stars, in reference to which Stephen appeals to a passage in Amos v. 25, 26, which he quotes exactly according to the Septuagint, with the exception that in the conclusion Βαβυλῶνος stands instead of Δαμασκοῦ: which variation without doubt results simply from the fact, that the captivity was better known under the name of the Babylonish.

(*Στρατιὰ τοῦ οὐρανοῦ*, = צְבָא הַשָּׁמַיִם, *host of heaven*, denotes the sun, the moon, and the stars; inasmuch as these bodies were contemplated under the idea of heavenly beings. The adoration of the stars (Sabeanism) formed an integral part of all the ancient systems of natural religion, because the splendour and magnificence of the starry sky attracted even the rudest minds, and excited to the worship of a superior power.—*Βίβλος τῶν προφητῶν* denotes the collection of the twelve prophets, which it is known were regarded as one whole.)

The quotation from Amos, however, is not unattended with difficulty. First of all, the question put with *μή*, requires undoubtedly a negative answer, so that the meaning is "Ye have offered unto me no sacrifices in the wilderness." But the children of Israel did offer sacrifices repeatedly to Jehovah the true God in the wilderness; and therefore the accusation appears unfounded. This difficulty, however, is very easily dispelled by the remark, that we have here an absolute expression for what is true only relatively, and the sense accordingly is this, "Ye have served me not alone, not always." It is an ingenious proposal of Fritzsche (Comm. on Mark, page 65) to put the mark of interrogation first after the words *προσκυνεῖν αὐτοῖς* in verse 43; for then we escape the whole difficulty, because Stephen, according to this arrangement, certainly acknowledges the worship that was paid to Jehovah, but finds fault that it was connected with the worship of idols.

Again, we have here an example to shew that the prophets themselves recognized ancient traditions. The books of the Pentateuch certainly make no mention either of the worship of Moloch, or of the worship of the stars by the Israelites in the wilderness; and Amos, therefore, without doubt, followed in his statements very ancient traditions. Nothing can be more preposterous than Vatke's procedure in his biblical theology of the Old Testament, when he chooses the passage of Amos for a basis upon which to build a new history of religion, and denies completely the antiquity of the worship of Jehovah, thus rejecting, on account of this single notice, the connected accounts of the Pentateuch. With respect to the first point mentioned, the worship of Moloch, the name (מֹלֶךְ, מֶלֶךְ, מַלְכָּם) denotes nothing else than "king, lord," it corresponds therefore to the name Bel or Baal, which the Canaanitish nations gave to their idols. Under this name they adored the sun, as the generating principle; while the moon, under the title of the queen of heaven (Jerem. vii. 18, xliv. 25), was viewed as the female or conceiving principle. (Compare Winer's Reallex under this word.) The *σκηνὴ τοῦ Μολόχ* is to be regarded as a little portable temple, in which the image of the idol deity (*τύπος = εἴδωλον*) was set up, and which could be carried about in travelling. The Kalmucks and other nomadic tribes have to this day such portable sanctuaries. As to the second deity that is mentioned, the unknown name Ῥεμφάν is very differently written in the manuscripts: we find Ῥεφάν, Ῥεφφᾶ, Ῥομφᾶ. According to the Coptic, however, the name Remphan, is the right reading, and it denotes the planet Saturn.* The Seventy have taken this name from the Egyptian dialect, which was familiar to them, and employed it for the Hebrew כִּיּוּן, which stands in the passage of Amos. In the Arabic the same consonants, only with different vowels כֵּיוָן, likewise denote Saturn, with which too the statement of Stephen that Remphan is a star (*ἄστρον*) exactly agrees; and thus all indications concur in leading to this point.

Vers. 44–47.—In the progress of Stephen's speech, there is contrasted with the worship which the Israelites, when led away by temptation, paid to the tabernacle of Moloch, the worship in the tabernacle of testimony, instituted by God himself under whose protection and defence they had been able to take possession of the holy land of promise. It is obvious that this juxtaposition renders only the more conspicuous the guilt of that idolatry, from which the peculiar guidance vouchsafed by God's grace should have guarded the Jews. (The *σκηνὴ τοῦ μαρτυρίου* = אֹהֶל מוֹעֵד, denotes, it is obvious, the moveable sanctuary which the Israelites used till the time of Solomon. The Seventy derived מוֹעֵד from עוּד, and therefore translate it as = עֵדוּת. The usual derivation of the word is from יָעַד, "to assemble," and thus the phrase signifies the tabernacle of meeting.) In verse 46, etc., finally, there is a transition to the charge brought forward at chap. vi. 13, that Stephen had spoken against the Temple, which receives in what follows a pretty direct refutation.

* Compare a singular treatise by Jablonski, the great Coptic scholar, upon this name (Lips. 1731), and in his Pantheon Ægypt prol. p. L. Jablonski, however, certainly errs in regarding Moloch and Saturn as identical; the former was rather the creative principle in nature, and the latter the conservative. The passage before us too, by the juxtaposition of the two idols, indicates their difference.

Vers. 48–50.—Without disparaging the sanctity of the Temple, as an image of the heavenly dwelling-place of God, Stephen yet shews that, according to the words of the prophet himself, no external dwelling-place can contain the eternal ruler of heaven and earth. By this reference to the prophetic word, he hallows in the very eyes of his accusers the view of the temple which he had expressed, and confutes their audacious charge against himself. (On the idea expressed by the words, ὁ ὕψιστος κ. τ. λ., comp. the parallel passage in xvii. 24. The quotation is taken from Isa. lxvi. 1, 2, somewhat freely indeed, yet without essential variations.—The expression ναὸν χειροποίητον contrasts directly with ἀχειροποίητον, to which the passage in Acts xvii. 24 points. To the temple of stone reared by men stands opposed the universe, as the glorious temple of the Lord, fashioned by the fingers of Deity; the former is only a figure of the latter, and has therefore only a conditional value.)

Vers. 51–53.—There is plainly here an interruption of Stephen in his speech, as indeed the better editions indicate. The profounder spirit of prophecy had struck root so little into the people, that the mention of prophetic declarations respecting the temple was actually regarded as a violation of the reverence due to it. On beholding the obduracy of his hearers, therefore, Stephen altered the tone of his discourse: and instead of the gentle manner in which he had hitherto spoken, he preached now in the fiery language of rebuke. He declared to his hearers that the same spirit of disobedience and unfaithfulness, which, according to the testimony of sacred history, had been displayed by their fathers, bore sway also in them, and had made them the murderers of the righteous one.

(Σκληροτράχηλος is found nowhere else in the New Testament; in the translation of the Old Testament it occurs pretty frequently for the Hebrew קְשֵׁה־עֹרֶף. Compare Exod. xxxiii. 3, 5. It expresses the stubbornness and obstinancy which stand out so prominently to view in the national character of the Israelites.—The word ἀπερίτμητος = עָרֵל, points to the signification of "unholy, impure," and the same expression is also in the Old Testament applied to the heart and the ear, as the internal and external organs of spiritual susceptibility. Compare Jerem. vi. 10; Ezek. xliv. 9. In verse 52, Jesus is again styled, as in chap. iii. 14, ὁ δίκαιος, the absolutely righteous, the perfect one.) Special consideration is due to the concluding clause of the speech in ver. 53, which declares that the Jews, though they relied upon the law, and though it had been given to them with such splendour, yet had not kept it. Without doubt, Stephen, if he had not been interrupted, would have gone on to shew, that, with such unfaithfulness, their resistance of the Holy Ghost who spoke through the apostles was not to be wondered at. There is something remarkable in the clause here added, εἰς διαταγὰς ἀγγέλων, for the Holy Scriptures make no mention of angels at the giving of the law upon Mount Sinai. Undoubtedly, therefore, this circumstance must also be traced back to tradition. Traces of it are to be found even in the Septuagint, which, at the passage in Deut. xxxiii. 2, adds the words: *ἐκ δεξιῶν αὐτοῦ ἄγγελοι μετ' αὐτοῦ*, while the Hebrew text runs thus: מִימִינוֹ אֵשׁ דָּת לָמוֹ, that is, on his right hand there is the fire of the law for them (or, as in the English version, from his right hand went a fiery law for them), which probably denotes the Shechinah, the pillar of cloud and the pillar of fire. Perhaps, however, the Seventy had a different reading before them, and besides they might very naturally be led to their translation by the Hebrew words which go before, viz., מֵרִבְבֹת קֹדֶשׁ, which denote the angelic hosts. The same idea that the giving of the law took place through angels, is to be found likewise in Psalm lxviii. 17, and in Josephus Arch. xv. 5, 3, who, in his recital of the history of the Israelites, has adopted many traditional elements. The question, however, still remains, how the words *εἰς διαταγάς* ought to be understood. It has been proposed to understand *διαταγαί* of the hosts, the ranks of angels; in which case the sense would be: "ye have received the law in the presence of angels." But the substantive does not occur in this signification, and besides, the preposition *εἰς* is not suited to it. If we compare the parallel passages in Gal. iii. 19, and Heb. ii. 2, in which the same idea is to be found, then we cannot doubt that *διαταγή* ought here to be taken in the signification of "appointment, ordination," in which case *εἰς* takes the signification, here quite appropriate, "in consequence of, according to, by." The angels appear therefore here as the powers mediating between God and man.

Vers. 54–56.—This keen reproof of Stephen, however, did not bring the hearers to repentance, but only excited their fury to the highest pitch. With this raging madness contrasts strikingly the calm serenity of the martyr, absorbed in contemplation of the Lord. (On *διαπρίω* comp. Comm. on chap. v. 33.) With respect to the vision of Stephen, we are not to think of any external spectacle, but of an internal vision in the state of ecstacy. Meyer's remark, "that Stephen may have been able to see heaven through the windows of the chamber of session," is therefore, to speak mildly, entirely gratuitous. His countenance beamed with a heavenly glory, but what he beheld, those who were around him learned only from his words.

(*Δόξα Θεοῦ* is to be understood like the Hebrew כְּבוֹד יְהוָה, and to be explained of the heavenly splendour which surrounds every Divine appearance.—Respecting the opening of the heavens, see the Comm. on Matth. iii. 17.—The special object, however, of his glorious vision was the person of the Lord; elsewhere Christ alone applies to himself the name Son of Man (υἱὸς τοῦ ἀνθρώπου); but Stephen here gives it to Jesus for the purpose of making it plain that he sees him in his human form, in the well-known beloved form in which he walked upon the earth. There is a peculiarity in the expression here twice repeated, "*standing* on the right hand of God" ἑστῶτα ἐκ δεξιῶν τοῦ Θεοῦ [comp. Comm. on Matth. xxvi. 62–64], for it is usually *sitting* at the right hand of God that is spoken of. But long since Gregory the Great undoubtedly gave the right explanation of the phrase, in a passage adduced here by Kuinoel. He says: "sedere judicantis et imperantis est, stare vero pugnantis vel adjuvantis. Stephanus stantem videt, quem adjutorem habuit."* Hom. xix. in festum adscensionis. Compare Knapp. scr. arg. p. 47, Note.)

VERS. 57–60.—In these words of the martyr the Jews saw another act of blasphemy, and therefore they only hastened his death. As the Romans had taken away from the Jews the power of life and death (compare at John xviii. 31), the execution of Stephen must be regarded as a tumultuous act; at the same time this supposition is not without difficulty, because the whole occurrence, according to vi. 12, took place before the Sanhedrim. Perhaps the Sanhedrim, for the purpose of avoiding any collision with the Roman authorities, pronounced no formal judgment, but connived at the execution, which was perpetrated by some fanatics. The witnesses (vi. 13) were required, according to the Jewish custom, to throw the first stones at the condemned individual, as if to shew their conviction of his guilt. (The first ἐλιθοβόλουν, ver. 58, is to be regarded as anticipating the subsequent more minute narration of the event.) In the passage before us the circumstance too is worthy of notice, that we find *a prayer expressly addressed to Jesus.* What the Redeemer said to his heavenly Father: "into thy hands I commend my spirit," the same thing does Stephen say to Christ, "receive my spirit" (δέξαι τὸ πνεῦμά μου). There lies in this a stronger argument for the doctrine of the Divine dignity of Christ, than in many other passages which are usually adduced as proof-passages in favour of it, when it is considered with what severity the Old Testament denounces every ascription of Divine prerogatives to any being who is not God. The opposers of the divinity of Christ must therefore, in consistency, pronounce every prayer to the Lord Jesus to be idolatry. But Stephen, on the contrary, proceeds quite in accordance with the command contained in John v. 23; and the same view of it has been taken by the church in all ages. In order, therefore, to set aside this troublesome passage, it has been proposed to understand the words κύριε Ἰησοῦ thus, "God, who art the Father

* That is "*sitting* marks the judge, and the ruler; *standing*, the combatant and auxiliary. Stephen saw him standing in his character of defender."—[K.

and Lord of Jesus!" an explanation which is sufficiently characteristic, and deserves to be known.

Here Paul comes before us for the first time as a furious persecutor of the church of God: the murder of Stephen he regards as a deed pleasing to God. The word *νεανίας*, *young man*, affords only an approximate determination of his age, because it is applied to persons between the ages of twenty-four and forty. (In the prayer of Stephen that his enemies might be forgiven, in ver. 60, the phrase *μὴ στήσῃς* deserves to be noticed. It is used in the sense of "retribuere," as in Matth. xxvi. 15, agreeably to the Hebrew usage of שָׁקַל, to weigh, to weigh for one. In its complete shape the expression stands thus, *ἱστάναι ἐν ζυγῷ*, to place upon the balance. Compare Schleusner's Lexicon on the LXX., under the word *ἵστημι*. Herodotus ii. 65 uses *ἱστάναι σταθμῷ* in the same manner.

§ 8. Spread of the Gospel Beyond Jerusalem.

(Acts viii. 1–40.)

Vers. 1–4.—Thus now the blood of the first martyr of the church was shed; but even here there was exhibited a proof of the truth of Tertullian's declaration: "sanguis martyrum semen Christianorum." The dispersion of the Christians from Jerusalem had the effect of spreading the Gospel through the neighbouring regions. Only Judea and Samaria are immediately named, because it is probable that Galilee had churches from the beginning, for many friends of Christ lived there (compare ix. 31); but there can be no doubt that Christianity spread itself at this period through Phœnicia also and Cyprus and Antioch. See chap. xi. 19, 20. The apostles (viii. 1), however, considered it their duty for some time at first to abide in the central point of the church.

With respect to the arrangement of the first verses of this chapter, the 2d and the 3d ought properly to stand at the beginning, because they are immediately connected with the death of Stephen. The concluding words too of the foregoing paragraph: *Σαῦλος δὲ ἦν συνευδοκῶν τῇ ἀναιρέσει αὐτοῦ*, with which the sentence *ἐγένετο δὲ κ. τ. λ.* stands connected, do not appear to fit well their place in the arrangement. The supposition of a process of abridgment, applied to the sources of information lying before the author, furnishes the best explanation of the present state of the text.—(On *συγκομίζειν*, in verse 2, compare the parallel passages in v. 6, 9, 10.—Κοπετός, from *κόπτεσθαι*, "to smite oneself in token of sorrow," denotes lamentation for the dead, compare Gen. l. 10.—The *ἄνδρες εὐλαβεῖς*, *devout men*, who buried the corpse of the martyr, are not to be viewed as believers, but as pious Jews who regarded Stephen as innocent: believers would have been styled brethren.—*Λυμαίνομαι* is only found here in the New Testament; it is = *πορθέω*, which Paul himself, in Gal. i. 13, applies to his persecutions of the church.)

Vers. 5–8. –Luke does not proceed to give us comprehensive accounts of the missionary labours of the Christians who had fled from Jerusalem: he only communicates some particulars respecting the ministry of another of the seven deacons, viz., Philip: he gives an account first of his preaching in Samaria, and next of the conversion of the chamberlain of Queen Candace. As to the question who this Philip was, it would seem that he was not the apostle of this name, for the apostles had not yet left Jerusalem, and besides, in viii. 14, he is expressly distinguished from them. Probably he was Philip the deacon, vi. 5, who also appears in chap. xxi. 8 as "the Evangelist, being one of the seven" (*εὐαγγελιστῆς, ὢν ἐκ τῶν ἑπτά*). The city of Samaria, in which Philip first preached the gospel, is not named: perhaps it was Sychem, where, according to John iv., Christ had already found so much acceptance.* In general, Samaria with its inhabitants appears to have been very much disposed to receive Divine things; but, at the same time also, very accessible to the misleading influence of false teachers. The remoteness of the district may have guarded the inhabitants from that corruption into which the inhabitants of Judea had to a great extent fallen; and thus there might be preserved actively among them the simple faith in a restorer of all things, viz., the Messiah, whom they styled תָּאֵב or תָּהֵב. Compare Gesenius progr. de theol. Samarit. a. 1822. Philip too paved for himself an entrance into their minds, by deeds of striking external aspect, which both turned the eyes of men upon him, and proved him to be the messenger of God to their souls.

Vers. 9–11.—In Samaria Philip now came in contact with a man named Simon, who belonged to that numerous class of religious deceivers (*γοηταί*), by whom the various countries were overrun in the days of the apostles. This Simon is no other than the one who is distinguished in church history by the surname of Magus. According to the account of Justin Martyr, he was a native of Gitton in Samaria (Just apol. p. 69, ed Sylb.), which agrees well with the circumstance, that here he is represented as pursuing his practices

* Kuinoel understands the words *εἰς πόλιν τῆς Σαμαρείας*, in ver. 5, to refer to the capital city itself, which bore the same name as the country; but in this case the article should have been prefixed to *πόλιν*. The 14th ver. on which the critic in question relies, because he supposes the whole land had not yet received the gospel, is only to be understood of a very wide diffusion of the truth. That Samaria means here the land and not the city, is clearly shewn by the 9th verse, where, if the opposite were the case, *αὐτῆς* would be the reading, as *πόλις* has preceded.

among the Samaritans. The accounts given by Josephus (Arch. xx. 7, 2) of a similar individual of the same name, who at the instigation of Felix (xxiv. 24) lent himself to the seduction of Drusilla from her husband, are not applicable to Simon Magus.* For the former, as Josephus relates, was a Cyprian by birth, the latter, according to Justin, was a Samaritan; but it seems altogether unreasonable to doubt the correctness of Justin's narrative, as he had every opportunity of knowing the native country of Simon, being himself a Samaritan of Sychem, and he could have no possible interest in misrepresenting the truth. Besides, Felix lived too late to allow us to suppose that Simon Magus could still be actively engaged in those regions where he was Procurator; for Simon appears to have early left the East, and to have betaken himself to Rome, the rendezvous of all deceivers of this kind.

The ancient Fathers of the church consider Simon Magus as the Father of the Gnostics, nay, of all heretics. This view is certainly wrong, inasmuch as we cannot trace the doctrines of the later false teachers directly from Simon; but there is this amount of truth in the idea, that in Simon we first behold the heretical element penetrate into the church, and it is this that constitutes the peculiar interest of the occurrence that follows. The essence of heresy, according to the proper Christian sense of the word, as it is defined in the pastoral letters and catholic epistles, is not merely error in matters of faith, which might find place in many an upright believing mind in the earliest times of the Christian church simply from a want of thorough mental training, but the intermixture of Christian ideas and doctrines with a totally foreign element. This intermixture we first find in Simon Magus: he was indeed overcome by the power of the Christian principle, but he did not enter with sincerity into it. His conduct externally was not so gross as that of Ananias; the ideas of the Gospel moved him mightily, and the powers which it displayed threw him into astonishment; but as Ananias could not let go his gold, so Simon could not prevail upon himself to give up his spiritual possession, viz., his dominion over the souls of men: but he mingled with his circle of notions the Christian ideas, and, as it were, drew down the Christian element into that sphere of life, in which he himself continued. This mode of procedure could not but neutralize the whole purpose of Christianity, whose power was designed to establish a new principle of association among men, and to draw all to it; measures were therefore

* Yet Neander declares himself inclined to the supposition of the identity of the two. (Compare Zeitalt. part i. page 80.) Let it be considered, however, how many such sorcerers there were at that time in all the provinces of the Roman empire, and how common the name of Simon was among the Jews; and we must admit, without hesitation, that the two men were different, particularly as the minuter circumstances, which are communicated by equally unsuspected witnesses, vary so much from one another.

necessary against such heretical systems, severe in proportion to the ruinous character of the deceptive appearance, which they acquired from the Christian ideas admitted into them. At first it is probable Simon Magus had no formal system: he was merely one of that numerous class of men, who, under the equivalent names of Chaldæi, mathematici, *γοηταί*, *μάγοι*, ensnared the minds of men with delusive practices, and might also state some particular philosophical speculations respecting angels and the world of spirits, or at the least, pretended an acquaintance with them. It was Christianity, with its fulness of ideas, which first gave an impulse to systematic development. Whether Simon Magus, with the help of infernal powers, may have performed real wonders, or only imposed upon men, is a question which cannot be definitely settled, since the text of the narrative before us gives no decision upon the point. At all events he had sufficient audacity to represent himself as a superior and heavenly being. The conflict which arose between this man and the Gospel, gives an uncommonly vivid picture of the proceedings of that age of excitement, which witnessed the promulgation of Christianity. The longing everywhere awakened after something higher, led them to attach themselves to all who affirmed that they had been favoured with glimpses of the spiritual world: every one of these persons pretended to have the power of working signs and wonders; and thus they beguiled the minds of men still more. Through this mass of superstition, through the labyrinth of this wild endeavour, Christianity could penetrate only by means of a fullness of spiritual power which might destroy all those phantoms and illusive systems that were endeavouring to copy it. The miracles performed by the messengers of God, and the power of the Gospel to transform the heart and mind, excited not only the astonishment of the multitude, but also of the sorcerers themselves, who perceived here the genuine power of God, to which they only pretended. An example of this we behold in Simon: he bowed before the power of the cross, and was baptized; but his corruption was a barrier to his reception of the Holy Ghost, and therefore he blended with his own unsanctified feelings the heavenly ideas which he had learned, and became a more dangerous adversary of the church, than either Jews or Gentiles were or could be.

As from *μάγος* (on this word see at Matth. ii. 1) *μαγεύω* and *μαγεία* were formed, so from *γοής* came the forms *γοητεύω* and *γοητεία*. Both words are found in the New Testament only here. As Simon's own declaration respecting himself, we find first adduced merely the words "saying that he was some great one" (*λέγων εἶναι ἑαυτὸν μέγαν*); but this expression is more narrowly defined by the words employed to describe the opinion of the people respecting him, "saying this is the Great power of God" (λέγοντες οὗτός ἐστιν ἡ δύναμις τοῦ Θεοῦ ἡ καλουμένη μεγάλη), which can only be regarded as the echo of what the sorcerer had boastfully given out respecting himself. Now, in the first place, this vain ostentation forms a glaring contrast with the humility of the apostles, who, although really filled with the powers of the heavenly world, yet most sharply reprehended all undue estimation of their own persons; they desired to be regarded as nothing but weak instruments, and their illustrious works were designed to glorify not themselves, but only the eternal God and his Son Jesus Christ. Again we find in the expression "the great power of God" (δύναμις τοῦ Θεοῦ ἡ μεγάλη), precisely the mode of speaking which was adopted afterwards by the Gnostics. Heinrichs supposes that the Samaritans had only by some misunderstanding applied this name to Simon, that he may only in reality have said "God's great power works this and that by me," and that they have imagined he meant to give himself this name. But this is by no means in accordance with the spirit of those sorcerers. They supposed, like the Gnostics, a multitude of Divine δυνάμεις who had emanated from the eternal first principle of light, and that one of these elevated beings styled Æons, now appeared among men in the person of Simon. Jerome mentions (Comm. on Matth. ch. xxiv.) that Simon said of himself: ego sum sermo Dei, ego sum speciosus, ego paracletus, ego omnipotens, ego omnia Dei. Now, although this declaration refers doubtless to the views of Simon after he was acquainted with Christianity, yet it points out of what the man was capable; and if he ventured, at a later period, to arrogate to himself all the prerogatives of Christ, in acknowledgment of whom he had submitted to baptism, it is surely not at all improbable that before this he had persuaded himself that he had brought down the powers of the angelic world to the earth. And the magnitude of his pretensions, as often happens, imposed upon men to such a degree that they resigned themselves entirely to his influence, from which nothing but the higher power of the gospel, vanquishing all the wiles of the sorcerer, could extricate them.

Vers. 12, 13.—Without external miraculous signs, it would have been altogether impossible for the heralds of the gospel to gain the attention of men engrossed with what struck the senses, to their doctrine of the crucified Son of God, and their preaching of repentance and faith; but the mighty works which they performed, brought to them all susceptible hearts, and proved the exciting means of faith. Even Simon was astonished when he saw the miracles of Philip, which had nothing of the deceitful appearance of his tricks, but, on the contrary, bore the impress of real miracles of God, and he had himself baptized. Some may be disposed to regard this as an act of deceit on the part of the sorcerer, and they may think Philip should rather not have baptized him, in order not to aggravate his guilt. But it is far more probable that the request for baptism really indicated a temporary improvement in the life of Simon: he was overcome at the moment by the heavenly power of the truth, and he surrendered himself to it for a time, and to a certain degree. Yet it was only to a certain degree! He allowed not the light to penetrate into the concealed depths of his heart; there was no thorough humiliation of the man. And therefore it naturally happened that he soon attempted to apply Christianity itself, as a more efficacious instrument, to the same purposes for which he had hitherto emyloyed his arts of sorcery.

Vers. 14-17.—The occasion for this attempt was furnished to Simon by the journey of some of the apostles to Samaria. This journey took its rise in the circumstance, that the Samaritans who believed, although they were baptized by Philip, yet had not received the Holy Ghost through him: to impart the Spirit, the apostles now hastened to the new churches. This information contains something very remarkable, for one naturally inquires, why did not Philip himself communicate the Holy Ghost, of which he was assuredly a partaker? That he had the Holy Ghost is shewn, partly by the miracles which he performed in the power of the Spirit, and partly by such passages as chap. viii. 29, 39. Kuinoel attempts to set aside all that seems surprising in this, by the observation that the apostles really had in view the further instruction of those who were baptized on the simple confession of Jesus as the Messiah, and that then along with this instruction the communication of the Holy Ghost was first to take place. He appeals on this point to Hebrews vi. 2, in which passage baptism appears to be followed by instruction, and then by the laying on of hands. But this learned man has himself, in his exposition of the epistle to the Hebrews, which has just appeared, rectified this mistake. In the passage referred to, vi. 2, the phrase, βαπτισμῶν διδαχῆς is not to be separated in translating, as if mention were first made of baptism and then of instruction; but the two words are to be taken together, and βαπτισμῶν regarded as the genitive of the object. We must therefore go back to what has been already remarked at John iv. 2. As the Redeemer did not himself baptize, but only caused it to be done by his disciples, so also the apostles, after the outpouring of the Holy Ghost, did not themselves baptize, but left the rite to be performed by their associates.* (Compare Comm. on Acts x. 48, and 1 Cor. i. 14, etc.)

* The manner in which this practice was transmitted to the church in after times, may be seen in Binghami origg. vol. i. page 319, iii. 548. The custom which still prevails in the Catholic church, of confining confirmation, as a symbol of the communication of the Spirit, to the episcopal office, is to be traced up to the fact before us.

The ground of this arrangement was probably, first, that in the earliest times of the church, when thousands connected themselves with it at the same time, the act of baptizing so many would have encroached too much upon the time of the apostles; and again, the Holy Ghost wrought, as it were, with more concentrated power in the Twelve than in other believers, and therefore the laying on of hands, as the means of imparting the Spirit, was confined to them alone. When the act of baptism thus appeared dissociated from the communication of the Spirit, it then acquired a position similar to what infant baptism obtained at a later period, from which it may be concluded that in the latter there can be nothing opposed to the spirit of Christianity. Finally, how variously baptism stood related to the communication of the Spirit in the apostolic age, may be seen from chap. x. 44, etc., where we find that the Holy Ghost was imparted to Cornelius and his household even before they were baptized. It cannot, therefore, be said that the restriction of the power of imparting the Holy Ghost to the apostles was founded upon any intrinsic necessity: it was rather a practice peculiar to that time. After their death, when, it is true, the intensity of the Spirit's operations had already greatly diminished, others communicated the gift of the Spirit by the laying on of hands; and even at a later period, when the extraordinary phenomenon which at first accompanied the communication of the Spirit had entirely disappeared, the laying on of hands was efficacious in imparting powers of the Spirit that wrought inwardly. (Verse 16. On the expression Βαπτίζειν εἰς ὄνομα Ἰησοῦ, compare the remarks at Matth. xxviii. 19.)

Verse 18–23.—When Simon perceived the extraordinary effects of the laying on of the apostles' hands, in the gifts which were exhibited, particularly the speaking with tongues, he attempted to procure for himself with money the power of communicating the Spirit, an attempt upon which the brand of infamy, as is known to all, was afterwards fixed in the church, when the name of *simony* was given to every purchase of spiritual dignities. It is a characteristic feature of Simon that he not only wished to obtain the Spirit himself, but also to purchase the power of communicating the gift to others. Hence we plainly perceive that spiritual ambition, the *secret source of the efforts of all founders of sects*, animated him; the power which he desired, he believed would furnish him with the means of still further imposing upon men.* Yet, although Peter

* Striving after the noblest gifts, after the Spirit himself, after virtue and perfection, is pleasing to the Lord only when it proceeds from an humble heart, which does not wish to make a show with his gifts, and to rule, but to serve. Nay, a self-willed striving after powers from on high, with a sordid purpose in view, is an abomination to the Lord, and, as the history of all enthusiasts shews, it brings the greater ruin upon themselves and the church.

rebukes him with the utmost severity on account of this proposal, he does not by any means cast him off entirely, but rather calls upon him to repent, and to pray for the forgiveness of his sins. Now, here the *mildness* of the apostle apppears as surprising as the *severity* shewn in the case of Ananias. We have already noticed the fact at chap. v. 1, that Simon had not yet experienced in himself the power of the Holy Ghost; and sordid therefore as he was, it might still be said of him that he knew not what he was doing. The circumstance that he had made a trade of religion, was the cause why he had never received it in its heart-changing power, but only prized it according to the amount of show which it was capable of making. Peter might appear to him a greater conjuror than he supposed himself to be, and it was his hope that he might procure from him, for a good recompense, the art of acquiring control over the powerful principles which govern the universe. His susceptibility, however, of spiritual impressions, similar to what we find in the Old Testament in the case of Balaam, the father of all false prophets, still left room for hoping that the truth would gain the victory in his heart, and therefore Peter preaches repentance to him. Ananias, on the other hand, was possessed of a thoroughly sordid disposition, and this prevented even the attempt being made to exert any further beneficial influence upon him.

(In ver. 20 the words *εἶναι εἰς ἀπώλειαν* are to be understood neither of ecclesiastical excommunication, to which the expression is never applied, nor yet of eternal perdition, because this idea would be inconsistent with the admonition to repentance which follows. The expression is rather to be understood only relatively, as pointing to the result of the course which Simon was pursuing, if no change should take place.—In ver. 21, *κλῆρος* is used agreeably to the analogy of the Hebrew word נַחֲלָה. Compare Col. i. 12.—Λόγος is not to be taken here like דָּבָר in the signification of "thing," "matter," as if denoting the Holy Ghost, the promised gift of God: but it means the gospel generally, in whose blessings it is here denied that Simon has any share.—The phrase *καρδία εὐθεῖα*, = לֵב יָשָׁר, denotes internal purity of heart. The gospel sets no value upon the opulence of talents with which a man may have been endowed, but only upon the disposition of the mind in reference to the will of God; it is the upright only to whom God shews favour.—In verse 22, *ἐπίνοια* = *διανόημα, διαλογισμός*. On the connexion of the word with *καρδία*, see the Comm. on Luke i. 51. The idea of an *evil* thought is not necessarily embraced in the meaning of *ἐπίνοια*; it is only by the connexion that this idea is here associated with the word. In verse 23, *εἰς* does not stand for *ἐν*; but the previous idea of motion is rather to be supplied: "I see that thou hast fallen into sin, and art now in it."—*Χολὴ πικρίας*, equivalent to *χολὴ πικρά*, denotes, according to Hebrew usage, what brings mischief and ruin, because the ideas of bitterness and poison run together. Compare Gesenius' Lexicon, under the word מְרֹרָה. The word *σύνδεσμος*, "bond, fetter," occurs in Ephes. iv. 3; Col. ii. 19, iii. 14, in a good sense, being applied to love and peace. Sin is here conceived as a chain, from whose power man needs to be released. The first half of the verse, *ὄντα εἰς χολήν*, might be thus understood: "thou hast become bitterness itself," *εἰς* being taken agreeably to the analogy of the Hebrew לְ; but the second half requires the meaning of *εἰς* indicated above, because it is an incongruous image to regard the sinner himself as *σύνδεσμος*, a bond.)

Vers. 24, 25.—The rebuke was not without effect. Simon besought the apostles for their prayers, because he felt that his conduct could not be pleasing to God. But true humility does not appear to have called forth this appeal, for the subsequent course of his life shews that he continued in his evil ways. (The government of *εὐαγγελίζεσθαι* varies between the dative and the accusative.)

Vers. 26–28.—With this narrative of the progress of the gospel among the Samaritans, there is connected another, which points to the diffusion of the doctrine of the cross among the remotest nations. Withal, too, the simplicity of the chamberlain of Meroe forms a remarkable contrast with the craft of the magician who has just been described. The same Philip received an intimation to betake himself to the road leading to Gaza. (*Γάζα*, a very ancient city, is mentioned even in Gen. x. 19, and is called in Hebrew עַזָּה. It was one of the five principal cities of the Philistines. Alexander the Great destroyed it, but it was rebuilt by Herod the Great. The additional clause [*αὕτη ἐστὶν ἔρημος*] might indeed be referred not to the city, but only to the way leading to it; but Josephus [Bell. Jud. ii. 33] mentions that a band of insurgents destroyed among other places Gaza also. The word *ἔρημος* may therefore be properly referred to Gaza itself. See Tholuck on the credibility of the Gospel History, p. 381.)

An officer of Queen Candace, who probably had journeyed to Jerusalem to a festival, was pursuing this road to Gaza, and he was reading in his chariot the prophet Isaiah. This latter circumstance points to the Jewish origin of the man, for proselytes were seldom acquainted with the Hebrew tongue;* he is called *Αἰθίοψ*, only from the place of his residence. (Eunuchs proper could not enter into

* The reading of Isaiah is not, indeed, a decisive proof of his Jewish descent, for he might be reading the Septuagint. But the word *περιοχή* refers probably to the division into Haphtaroth, which we cannot suppose existing in the Septuagint. Besides, there were many Jews living in Arabia and Meroe, so that the supposition of his Jewish descent cannot appear improbable.

the congregation of the Lord, Deut. xxiii. 1, and therefore probably this Ethiopian was only a distinguished officer of his princess, viz., her treasurer. The word *εὐνοῦχος*, like סָרִיס, is used to denote in general a high officer of state, a signification which even *δυνάστης* has here, though it commonly denotes an independent ruler. The name Ethiopia was employed by the ancients to denote indefinitely the lands of South Africa, as India was applied to the south of Asia. But here it is the kingdom of Meroe in Upper Egypt that is meant, as we learn from the accounts of Pliny,* who mentions that it was governed by queens, who bore the name of Candace as a title of office.)

It is worthy of notice here that in ver. 26 we find *ἄγγελος κυρίου*, *angel of the Lord*, but in ver. 29, *πνεῦμα*, *spirit*. This confirms the view we have expressed at John i. 52, that by angels we are by no means always to understand beings appearing as individuals, but often spiritual powers. Hence also in ver. 26, we are not to suppose the actual appearance of an angel, but an inward spiritual communication which was made to Philip. Now here we behold this disciple surrendering himself with child-like faith to the guidance accorded from above: he goes not his own way, but the impulses of the Spirit guide all his steps. Without cavilling he lets himself be taken by the Spirit to a desert road: and lo! even there he finds an opportunity of preaching the word.

Vers. 29–33.—Philip heard the Ethiopian reading (either he read himself aloud, or listened to one that read to him), and began conversation with him by asking whether he understood what he read. With touching simplicity the eunuch acknowledges that the sense eluded him, and he receives Philip as a messenger sent from God into his chariot, who straightway saw, that it was the celebrated passage in Is. liii. which he had been reading.

(*Κολλᾶσθαι* in ver. 29, corresponds exactly to the Hebrew דָּבַק.—In ver. 31 *ἀρά γε* is interrogative, and differs from *ἄραγε*, which indicates a conclusion. See at xi. 18.—Ver. 32. *περιοχή* occurs only here in the New Testament; it denotes, as *τμῆμα*, and *χωρίον*, a section in a book.) The verses of Is. liii. 7, 8, are quoted exactly according to the Septuagint, even to unimportant deviations; but the Hebrew text differs from the translation of the Seventy, in verse 8 very considerably. Gesenius renders the original text exactly thus: "From calamity and judgment he was taken away, and who of his contemporaries regarded it that he was taken from the land of the living." Instead of מִמִּשְׁפָּט the Seventy appear to have read בְּמִשְׁפָּט, and דורו

* Plin. Hist. Nat. vi. 35. He makes mention of Meroe, an island in the Nile, where the chief city lay, and then continues: "ædificia oppidi pauca, regnare feminam Candacem, quod nomen multis jam annis ad reginas transiit; delubrum Hammonis, et ibi religiosum et toto tractu sacella.

they have understood as referring to the life of the party himself that is spoken of, and not to his contemporaries. However, this variation does not at all affect the connexion in which the words are here presented; it is a more important question whether Philip rightly explains the passage, in referring it to the Messiah. For the solution of this question, it is necessary to view the fifty-third chapter in connexion with what goes before from the fortieth chapter onwards, as well as with what comes after. The same servant of the Lord (עֶבֶד יְהוָֹה) who is here presented as suffering, is described both before and afterwards, partly in similar, and partly in different situations. If we survey therefore the whole scope of the discourse, we shall understand why doubts should be entertained about referring the passage to the Messiah, because the servant is often directly called Israel or Jacob, and is described in the plural, for which reason either the people of Israel, or distinguished personages among them, or the whole order of prophets, have been supposed to be meant. Other views, such as those which regard the prophet Isaiah himself, or king Hezekiah, as the subject of the passage, are to be altogether dismissed; but the views first mentioned do not at all stand in direct contradiction to the Messianic: on the contrary, the Messiah is the representative of the people, and especially of the better and enlightened part of them, and the people again are a type of the Messiah. To him, therefore, in the last resort, and with the highest emphasis, the whole refers, without excluding however subordinate references. From this point of view the whole majestic picture of the second half of Isaiah is sketched; and therefore the comprehensive exposition of it must have a respect to all these different points. (See Umbreit's Abhandl. über den Knecht Gottes. In the Studien, 1828, p. 2, page 295, etc.)

Vers. 34–38.—Nothing hinders us from supposing in this case, that Philip entered into more detailed explanations than was possible in preaching to great multitudes, whose wants were very various, and answered questions proposed by the stranger. The passages of Scripture only formed a ground-work for his instructions. (Γραφή, denoting single passages of Scripture, is of frequent occurrence: see Mark xv. 28.) And in this way are we to account for the desire of the chamberlain to be baptized, because Philip, without doubt, had made mention of the institution of baptism by the Lord. At a later period, however, offence was taken at the precipitation with which the baptism appeared to have been administered, and therefore an ample clause was added, embracing a kind of confession of faith of the treasurer. But the different shapes in which this clause appears are of themselves sufficient to raise doubts of its genuineness, which are carried to certainty by the agreement of the best codices A.C.G. and others, in omitting it.* It has already been remarked that baptism ensued upon a single confession of the Messiahship of Jesus, of which the treasurer, whose heart had obviously been prepared by grace, might readily be convinced.

Vers. 39, 40.—After the discharge of this duty Philip returned, and came by way of Ashdod to Cæsarea, where (Acts xxi. 8) he dwelt. (The phrase πνεῦμα κυρίου ἥρπασε, *the Spirit of the Lord snatched*, does not authorize the supposition of a supernatural removal: ἁρπάζειν only expresses the idea of speed, and πνεῦμα that of suggestion from above.—Ἄζωτος, Hebrew אַשְׁדּוֹד, *Ashdod*, like Gaza, was one of the five cities of the Philistines, and lay north of this city.—Καισάρεια, *Cæsarea*, is here the well known city lying upon the Mediterranean Sea, which was the seat of the Jewish procurators. It was built by Herod the Great, and named in honour of Augustus. At an earlier period there stood upon the site of it a tower, which bore the name of Straton [Joseph., Arch. xiv. 8–11], and therefore the city was often called Cæsarea Stratonis, in distinction from Cæsarea Philippi, Matth. xvi. 13; Mark viii. 27.)

The Abyssinians, it is known, trace up their conversion, though erroneously, to the influence of this treasurer, whom tradition names Indich; their conversion was first effected in the fourth century by Frumentius and Ædesius. The conversion of the treasurer appears to have produced no effects upon the country from which he came, but to have been limited to his own personal benefit.

* The clause here referred to is the whole of the 37th verse.—Tr.

II.

PART SECOND.

FROM PAUL'S CONVERSION TILL HIS SECOND MISSIONARY JOURNEY.

(Acts ix. 1—xviii. 22.)

---

§ 1. History of the Conversion of Paul.

(Acts ix. 1–30.)

The second part of the Acts of the Apostles loses to a great extent the *general* character which was apparent in the first part: the work indeed becomes almost entirely an account of the life of Paul. Peter, it is true, does not altogether disappear from the narrative, but the principal communications which are made respecting him, have reference to the great controversy of apostolic times about the calling of the Gentiles, which must have been peculiarly interesting to Luke in respect to his general aim, and the specific purpose of his work. We cannot therefore regard the paragraphs, from chap. x. 1, to xi. 18, and in chap. xv. 6, etc., as introduced for the sake of Peter, but rather to justify the conduct of Paul by the authority of another apostle. Yet there are some other sections, such as chap. ix. 31–43, and xii. 1, etc., which have reference simply to the Apostle Peter, and discover therefore still a tendency to contemplate other apostles besides Paul, and a gradual transition of the work into a form completely special. General observations respecting the condition of the whole church, such as those we found in the first part, are now altogether wanting. On the other hand, the powerful character of the Apostle Paul, whose entrance into the church imparted, as it were, a new activity to the Christian life, stands forth so prominently in this second part, that it engrosses all attention to itself.* The ground of this fact, that Paul occupies so conspicuous a place in the apostolic church, is to be sought not alone in the greatness of his intellect, and in his zeal and faithfulness, but mainly in the circumstance that the Twelve were primarily destined for the people of Israel, and only turned

* A connected view of the life of Paul is prefixed to the Commentary on the epistles of Paul.

in part to the Gentiles when the Jews, with obstinate unbelief, rejected the word of reconciliation. Paul's proper destination, on the other hand, was to be a messenger to the Gentile world. Although, therefore, the Twelve were not wanting to the work set before them, yet their power did not reach so full a development, as we perceive in the case of Paul.

But it was in a very wonderful manner that the grace of the Lord made Paul so important an instrument in the church; for without any traceable process of transition it converted him at once from being a persecutor into a most devoted advocate. And thus Paul, quite irrespectively of the force of his eloquence, proclaimed at once, by the simple fact of his conversion, the power of Christ, which could not be said equally of those who had followed the Lord from the beginning. Of the remarkable occurrence itself we possess, not counting the numerous passing references to it in the letters of Paul, three detailed accounts; first the one here given by Luke, and then two others by Paul himself. (Acts xxii. 1–16, xxvi. 9–18.) In the former of these two passages, Paul explains, in a public speech at Jerusalem, the grounds which had led him to become a believer in Christ. He mentions his birth in Tarsus of Cilicia, his being reared in Jerusalem, and instructed in the law by Gamaliel; and he appeals, in reference to his zeal for the Mosaic institutions and against the Christians, to the testimony of the high priest and the whole Sanhedrim. And then follows a detailed account of the appearance of the Lord. In the other passage, Paul speaks before King Agrippa and Festus, and describes the occurrence to them with the same minuteness. The credibility of these accounts is not a little heightened by the circumstance that they do *not literally* agree, but treat the subject with freedom of narration. Along with exact agreement in essentials, we find therefore unimportant variations, by which doubts of the credibility of the accounts, involving the fictitious character of both speeches of Paul, are rendered exceedingly difficult. Besides, if we consider that his change of views brought no honour to the Apostle Paul but disgrace, procured for him no earthly happiness but only sufferings, then every attempt to exhibit the occurrence as a fraud or a delusion must fall to the ground. Further, we cannot suppose a trance in which everything appeared to the apostle internally,* because the occurrence was witnessed by his attendants; and therefore there are only two views of the event left which can possibly be defended: either we are to

* The passage in 2 Cor. xii. 1, etc., in which Paul describes a trance that happened to him must not at all be taken into account here, as Neander (Apost. Zeitalter, Th. 1, s. 110, note) has already excellently remarked. For that trance constitutes an *exalted moment* in the renovated life of Paul; but the appearance at Damascus coincides with the commencement of his new life.

suppose a real appearance of the glorified Redeemer, or we must explain the change in the apostle on psychological grounds, which coincided accidentally with a natural phenomenon in which Paul supposed he saw an appearance of Christ.

The latter view is defended by the most recent theologians, Heinrichs, Rosenmüller, Kuinoel, Eichhorn (Allgem. Bibl. der bibl. lit. Bd. 6), Böhme (Henke's Museum, vol. 3), and others. The older theologians defend the former view; and the work of an Englishman named Littleton (translated by Hahn, Hanover, 1751), who was himself converted by the history of Paul's conversion, is particularly worthy of notice. The older theologians however erred in this, that they frequently overlooked the importance of those psychological processes in the mind of Paul, to which later theologians have drawn attention. It is not to be denied that the mind of a Paul, who persecuted the Christians with an honest purpose, but ignorantly, must have been deeply impressed with the joyful faith of a Stephen. His knowledge of the Scriptures, too, could not fail to suggest to him passages which appeared to confirm the Messiahship of Jesus. In his heart, therefore, there might be a violent struggle, and he might have to fight against the truth forcing itself upon his mind, a state which, although not outwardly apparent, yet internally would prepare the way for the designs of God in reference to him. We may therefore quite properly connect the supposition of internal preparations in the apostle, with the miraculous appearance which Christ made to him.

But on the other hand, modern theologians of any impartiality must confess, that they do violence to the text when they assert that these psychological processes, assisted merely by some natural phenomenon, effected the conversion of Paul. Were they to say it can be conceived *possible*, that Paul might have been converted by means of a flash of lightning darting down before him, much doubtless might be said in favour of this idea: the holy Norbert, it is well-known, was converted by such an occurrence: but here we have to do, not with possibilities, but with facts respecting which we have most precise accounts. The defenders therefore of the natural view of the occurrence in question, must say that Paul persuaded himself he saw the Lord in the flash of lightning, and that this view of the natural phenomenon was communicated by him to Luke and to the whole Christian church. In that case the three accounts that are given could at least be explained without any subtle refinement. However, no proof is needed to shew how much this supposition is opposed to sound psychological views. The Apostle Paul certainly exhibits in his whole conduct, if ever any person did, the utmost distance from all fanaticism: in the visionary, feeling and fancy have the unqualified mastery, but this is so little the case with Paul, that in him the dialectic element preponderates, which implies a predominance of the intellect. And would a man so constituted have been able to imagine that he held a long conversation with some person, while a flash of lightning darted near him to the ground; and that not merely at the first moment of the occurrence, but many years afterwards? The thing is not merely improbable, but altogether unnatural. To this, it must be added, that if we should suppose Paul deceived himself once as to his having seen the Lord, then we must suppose this to have occurred repeatedly with him; for we find that he declares himself that he had seen Jesus several times (comp. Acts xviii. 9; xxiii. 11; 2 Cor. xii. 9), which manifestly renders the whole hypothesis more contradictory still to the character of Paul. We may therefore say, without being unjust, that it is nothing but dogmatic views which have recommended to so many recent theologians the explanation on natural principles: if they had been able to adopt the biblical doctrine of the glorification of the Lord's body, they would not have regarded an appearance of the glorified Redeemer as a thing so inconceivable. But where it is supposed that, though a spiritual immortality must be conceded to Christ, yet he laid down his body again, there certainly a personal appearance of the Lord, such as is here related, must occasion great difficulties.

Vers. 1, 2.—The commencement of the account of Paul's conversion plainly looks back to chap. viii. 1-3. Saul was so furious against the Christians, that he was not satisfied with persecuting in Jerusalem, but also endeavoured to destroy believers at a distance. Why he went particularly to Damascus, which lay north from Jerusalem beyond the boundaries of Palestine, it is difficult to determine:* perhaps numbers of the Christians, who fled after the martyrdom of Stephen, had gone to that quarter, where perhaps there may have been formed immediately after Pentecost a small Christian society. (The word ἐμπνέων is taken from the image of a wild raging beast; it is usually construed with the accusative, though sometimes also with the genitive. In chap. xxvi. 11, we find instead of it, ἐμμαινόμενος.) The passage in xxvi. 10, 11, brings into view some additional notices respecting the persecutions which Saul stirred up; in particular, he mentions there that he had given consent to the death of numbers of Christians, as well as to the murder of Stephen; that is, by his authority as the commissioned agent of the Sanhedrim, with whose president, the high priest, Paul stood in direct communication, he had sanctioned these deeds. (The phrase, καταφέρειν ψῆφον, is applied to judicial suffrage: it retains almost exactly this proper signification, when we view Paul, in

* According to chap. xxvi. 12, however, Paul before his journey to Damascus, had already persecuted the Christians in other cities.

these persecutions, as representing in a certain measure the authorities.) Without any reason, this plain declaration of Paul has been doubted, because no other who died in the persecution is named but Stephen; and it has been supposed, that using the plural, he only employed an enallage numeri. But the powerful impression which the persecution made upon the Christians in Jerusalem, leads directly to the supposition that Stephen was not the only sufferer in it; he only was mentioned, simply because he was the most distinguished among those who died. Further, in chap. xxvi. 11, it is adduced as a peculiar mark of the hatred which burned in the bosom of Paul against the Christians, that he sought to compel them to utter blasphemies (βλασφημεῖν). It is not indeed expressly said whom they were to blaspheme, but it is self-evident, that Christ is the being meant. And this incident certainly presupposes a fearful height of rage in the heart of Paul; and the conviction afterwards reached of its great wickedness, explains the deeply humble feeling which he expresses, whenever after his conversion he makes mention of his earlier state, and compares it with the compassionate grace which the Lord had nevertheless poured out upon him. Finally it is plain from chap. ix. 14, xxii. 5, xxvi. 12, that Paul acted in these persecutions as the official agent of the authorities. But the Sanhedrim considered all Jews in all lands as under their jurisdiction, and as Damascus at that time (see Comm. 2 Cor. xi. 32) was under the government of a prince very favourably disposed to the Jews, viz., Aretas, they could easily effect the removal of Christians from this city to Jerusalem. The Jews, moreover, were so numerous in Damascus, that according to Josephus (Bell. Jud. i. ii. 25), ten thousand of them perished there in the reign of Nero.

Vers. 3, 4.—In the neighbourhood of Damascus, and according to tradition, upon a bridge near the city, a brilliant light shone around the apostle, and he heard himself called by his name. The account of Luke here, as respects both the facts and the speeches, is shorter than either of the accounts given by Paul himself. But it admits of no doubt that in both respects the latter, as full accounts, are to be preferred. Luke might readily present the narrative in an abbreviated form, as not feeling so lively an interest in the particulars; but Paul himself would naturally be disposed to describe the occurrence in all its details. It is a remark quite in harmony with the constitution of the mind, that in the case of events which exert a deep influence upon the life, even apparently trifling circumstances are deeply imprinted upon the memory; and it excites an agreeable feeling, when recalling the fact, to make mention also of these minute points, because the mind is assured as it were by them of the reality of the occurrence, and of the accuracy of the recollection of it. Thus Paul, besides mentioning the sudden light and the voice, brings into view also these circumstances, that it was about mid-day (xxii. 6, xxvi. 13), that the light surpassed the brightness of the sun (xxvi. 13), that the voice spoke in the Hebrew tongue (xxvi. 14), and that all his attendants fell along with him to the ground (same passage). Now, although it must be allowed that φῶς, *light*, and φωνή, *voice*, might signify lightning and thunder, yet the additional circumstance of the voice speaking in Hebrew, totally overturns the possibility of thus explaining the words; not to mention that in chapter ix. 17, 27, Ananias and Barnabas declare in plain terms, that Paul saw Jesus, a fact upon which moreover Paul, in his whole apostolic ministry, grounds the peculiar position which he took in relation to the other apostles who had lived with the Lord. In the parallel passage, xxvi. 14, there is added to the words of Jesus, "Saul, Saul, why persecutest thou me?" (Σαοὺλ, Σαοὺλ, τί με διώκεις;) the peculiar expression, "it is hard for thee to kick against the pricks" (σκληρόν σοι πρὸς κέντρα λακτίζειν). As to the words, κέντρον denotes, as also βούκεντρον, a scourge furnished with sharp points (from κεντέω), employed for driving horses and oxen. Λακτίζειν denotes to strike with the foot (from λάξ), to strike out behind like a horse. To kick against the pricks therefore means to increase one's pain by resistance, a proverbial mode of expression which often occurs in Latin and Greek authors. (See Terent. Phorm. i. 2, 27, adversus stimulum calcare. Pindar. Pyth. ii. 174. Æschyli Agamemn. v. 1633. Euripidis Bacch. v. 791.)

Further, this passage is one of the most striking of those in which grace is apparently represented as irresistible. The meaning of the words is really nothing else than this: "thy resistance to the urging power of grace helps thee not: thou must surrender thyself to it." It might indeed be alleged that it is not said ἀδύνατόν σοι, but only σκληρόν σοι; and that therefore a degree of resistance might be imagined in Paul, which grace might not have overcome. But according to my conviction, this explanation has more verbal subtilty than truth; according to the sense and connexion of the passage, σκληρόν σοι must mean here much the same as ἀδύνατον, so that what is meant is that Paul really could not at that time resist the constraining power of grace. But although we readily acknowledge this sense in the passage before us, we do not therefore approve of Augustine's doctrine of gratia irresistibilis. This doctrine is that the gratia in the elect overcomes resistance not only at particular times, but throughout the whole of life, so that the loss of grace by unfaithfulness is impossible. Although we assert that the appearance of the Lord to Paul at this time carried along with it an overcoming power of grace, yet we do not deny that later in the life of this apostle there were moments when by unfaithfulness he might have forfeited the grace given to him.* Yet that grace at particular junctures may display itself thus irresistibly in the heart, is sufficiently confirmed by the experience of countless numbers. And it is not difficult to see, in the case of the apostle Paul, how this experience must not only have operated with decisive influence upon the development of his future life, but also have been a leading principle in the formation of his doctrinal system. He, so proud of his legal piety, saw himself, by his very zeal for the law, which he imagined well-pleasing to God, converted into a murderer of the saints of God and an opposer of the Messiah, the prince; and yet the Lord did not cast him out of his sight, but even chose him for a witness of his power over the souls of men, for a herald of the gospel to the heathen world. In this contrast there must have been something so overpowering, that even the strong soul of a Paul broke under it; and this very rupture and fall of what was old, was at the same time the commencement of a new condition in the world of the apostle's mind. The outward appearance of the Redeemer therefore, and the outward light which dazzled his bodily eye, were but the outward aspect of the whole occurrence; its true inward meaning is to be found in the entrance of the light of a higher world into the depths of the apostle's mind, where, hovering over the waters of his soul humbled and purified in repentance, that light called forth from the water and the spirit, a new, a higher, a heavenly consciousness, the new creature in Christ Jesus. After such an experience it naturally became the business of Paul's life to preach the power of grace, and to shew by his own example, how possible it was for the Lord of glory, to make even his bitterest enemies a stool for his feet, that is, to transform them into the most enthusiastic friends.†

Vers. 5-7.—In the verses which follow, it is necessary first to

* That the most exemplary Christians do frequently in fact resist both their own convictions and the motions of the Spirit within them cannot be denied; but whether any one who has been truly regenerated ever so resists the Spirit as to forfeit grace altogether, and to become a child of the devil again, is a very different question. Admonitions to perseverance, warnings against resisting the Spirit, do not prove that such forfeiture ever takes place; for the progress of believers is secured not by physical force, but by influences operating upon them as rational and immortal beings. There are passages of Scripture which seem to place it beyond all doubt that where regeneration has really taken place, the new spiritual life, whatever fluctuations it may undergo, is never extinguished. John manifestly proceeds upon this principle when he concludes from the apostacy of certain individuals that they had never really been Christians: "They went out from us, but they were not of us; for if they had been of us they would no doubt have continued with us: but they went out that they might be made manifest that they were not all of us." 1 John ii. 19.—[Tr.

† All powerful preachers of grace, especially Luther and Augustine, have in a similar manner, by the power of inward experience, reached their conviction of it, and by means of the powerful utterance of that conviction they have been able to win whole centuries to the same belief.

settle the text. As the three narratives do not agree in all points, transcribers endeavoured to smooth down the differences. In particular, they supplemented the shorter statement of Luke, from the two longer ones in Paul's discourses. From chap. xxii. 8 they have added to Ἰησοῦς in chap. ix. 6 the word ὁ Ναζωραῖος; and after διώκεις there occurs a very long addition in the textus receptus, in which particularly the phrase σκληρόν σοι πρὸς κέντρα λακτίζειν is borrowed from chap. xxvi. 14. According to the testimony of Codices, however, these words are inserted here from the speech of Paul in chap. xxvi. 14, and therefore they are omitted by the best critics. Besides, we find real variations in the narratives. According to chap. ix. 7, all the attendants of Paul stood, according to chap. xxvi. 14, they fell to the ground: according to chap. ix. 7, they heard indeed the voice but saw no person, according to chap. xxii. 9, they heard nothing, but they saw the light. How this difference is to be explained, in accordance with the principle that literal agreement must exist between the different narratives of Holy Writ, I do not see. To say that some of the attendants remained standing, while others fell, and that some of them saw the light and others heard the voice, is inadmissible here, because it is expressly said in chap. xxvi. 14 that they all fell down. And to suppose two occurrences of the kind, and distribute the varying accounts between them, would produce still greater confusion, for how can it be made probable that the Lord would appear twice to Paul on the way to Damascus? We must therefore take the Scripture account simply as it presents itself to us. There are plainly here variations in the narratives, exactly like those we often find in the Gospels, but they refer to unessential incidents, and are so far therefore from affecting the credibility of the event as a whole, that they rather confirm it. Certainly, however, Paul's own statements deserve the preference above those of Luke, whose accounts, moreover, are represented in a very abbreviated form, and who might readily transpose some of the circumstances, as he was not an eye-witness.*

* Olshausen recognizes the inspiration of the Holy Scriptures, but some of the statements made above seem rather to trench upon that fundamental principle. Plenary inspiration undoubtedly implies that, whatever apparent discrepancies may be found between different portions of the Word of God, there can be no real disagreement. Now, surely the discrepancies commented upon by the author are merely apparent, and too much has been made of them. The two statements, "they heard the voice, but saw no man," and "they heard nothing, but saw the light," are by no means opposed to one another; for surely they might see the light and yet see no person, and they might hear the voice so far as the sound of it was concerned, and yet not hear the words that were addressed to Paul. The two statements combined intimate that they saw the light, but saw not the person of Jesus, that they heard the sound of his voice, but did not catch his words. And, as to the other alleged disagreement between the statements, that they fell to the ground and stood speechless, they may be reconciled on the principle that they refer to different instants of time. They might stand speechless for a little, and then fall during the pro-

And finally, the speeches too in these verses differ from one another. The passage xxii. 10 agrees indeed in substance completely with ix. 6, but it differs so much the more from xxvi. 16–18. Instead of the short direction contained in the first two narratives, to go to Damascus and there learn everything, chap. xxvi. 16–18 presents a detailed speech of Christ to Paul. Of Ananias and his speeches there is no mention made at all in chap. xxvi., while, on the other hand, in chap. ix. 15, 16, and xxii. 14, the very same points occur in the speech of Ananias which are to be found in chap. xxvi. 16, etc., in the speech of Jesus. The idea, therefore, very naturally suggests itself, that in chap. xxvi. Paul has transferred what Ananias said to Christ himself, on the principle: quod quis per alium facit, id ipse fecisse putatur. It may be objected, indeed, to this idea, that Paul expressly appeals to the fact of the Lord's having appeared to him, and instructed him (comp. Galat. i. 12), and therefore it may be alleged that the words in question must be ascribed to Christ himself. But on closer consideration new difficulties rise up against this view, which oblige us to go back to the former one. In the first place, the declaration in the Epistle to the Galatians refers to the doctrine of Christ, which Paul professes to have received from no apostle, but immediately from the Lord by inward revelation; but here in chap. xxvi. there is no mention made of doctrine at all in the speech of Christ. And again it appears that we cannot well suppose Jesus to have uttered a long speech, because it is expressly remarked that Paul would receive the necessary communications in Damascus. The appearance of Christ, therefore, was to operate more by power of impression, and calm instruction was afterwards to be given by Ananias. This arrangement, at the same time, was wisely adapted to the character of Paul. To him, as a proud Pharisee, well versed in law, it might be a wholesome humiliation to receive from a man of little education, as Ananias probably was, instruction respecting the way of eternal life. The only way, therefore, in which we can hold the speech of chap. xxvi. to be real words of Christ, is to suppose that Paul has transferred words of the Lord that were spoken on the occasion of a later appearance (compare xxii. 18–21) to the earlier one, and blended them with it. Which of these views may be preferred is to me indifferent.* (In chap. ix.

gress of the scene, overcome by their augmenting alarm, or they might fall at first, struck down by the suddenness of the occurrence, and afterwards rise, but only to stand in speechless terror. Or perhaps εἱστήκεισαν in Luke may not refer to the standing posture as distinguished from prostration, but simply to the fact of their being rivetted to the spot as distinguished from advancing on their journey. Even in the case of an uninspired author, a charge of contradiction is not advanced if any plausible method of reconciling two statements can be pointed out; and surely the sacred penmen are entitled, at the very least, to the benefit of the same rule of judgment.—[Tr.

* There appears to be no good ground for the conclusion to which Olshausen here

7, the rare word *ἐννεος* deserves notice, instead of which we find in chap. xxii. 9, *ἔμφοβος*. The better mode of writing it is *ἐνεος*, and the word denotes properly "dumb," then also, "speechless through terror." It occurs nowhere else in the New Testament.)

Vers 8–16.—Blinded by the splendour of the appearance, which was designed for him alone (a flash of lightning must have equally blinded his attendants), Paul was led by the hand to Damascus (xxii. 11). The whole of the scene which follows is peculiar to the narrative before us. Luke describes minutely what happened to Ananias, and that too with a local knowledge of the city (verse 11 specifies the street and residence of Paul), which presupposes a very sure source of information. A remarkable thing in this account is that mutual adaptation of the operations of Divine grace, which is so manifestly displayed. The same God who hears prayers prompts them also, and works again in another heart to bring about their fulfilment. So here the Lord shews to Ananias Paul in prayer, and to Paul again Ananias approaching with the needful aid. Whether we suppose Ananias and Paul to have been previously acquainted with one anothet or not, does not at all materially influence the state of the fact. The objections of Ananias, and the removal of them by the Lord, display, in a very touching manner, the childlike relation of the believing soul to its Redeemer: Ananias speaks with him as a man does with his friend.

(The word *ἅγιοι* in verse 13, corresponding to the Hebrew קְדֹשִׁים, denotes in the New Testament, as applied to Christians, not the highest degree of moral excellence, but only the fact of being distinguished from the great mass of Jews and Gentiles, and living in the fellowship of the Spirit of Christ. [See particularly at Rom. i. 7.] Respecting *σκεῦος ἐκλογῆς*, ver. 15, comp. Comm. at Rom. ix. 21, etc. The expression here is plainly opposed, not to the reprobate, but only to those who have a less extensive sphere of influence. In verse 16 the apparent threatening, *ὑποδείξω αὐτῷ ὅσα δεῖ . . . παθεῖν*, embraces really a promise of grace, and thus forms a striking thought; for to suffer for the Lord is the highest grace of which the believer can be accounted worthy. Matth. v. 10, etc.)

Vers. 17–19.—Of the relations of the passage in chap. xxvi. 16–18 to the speech of Ananias, we have already spoken at vers. 5–7:

comes. It rests simply upon the fact that Paul is directed to go to Damascus for the information he needs, whence it is concluded to be improbable that Christ would say so much to him personally. But there is no inconsistency in supposing that Christ might say to him all that is mentioned in the three verses 16–18, of chap. xxvi., and that yet he might be instructed at much greater length by Ananias. We are not to suppose that Ananias said nothing to Paul but what is stated in the 17th verse of this 9th chapter He probably conversed with him much during his sojourn in Damascus, so that the address of Christ might just suffice for an introduction to the fuller communications to be received in Damascus, and a means of authenticating them to Paul.—[Tr.

the narrative before us gives the words of Ananias, but very briefly, and at xxii. 12, etc., they are found a little more full. On the other hand, chap. ix. 17–19 describes most minutely the healing of Paul: it is represented as effected very suddenly, and through the laying on of the hands of Ananias. We are not to suppose from the words ver. 18, *ἀπέπεσον ἀπὸ τῶν ὀφθαλμῶν αὐτοῦ ὡσεὶ λεπίδες*, that there was an actual falling off of anything; the word *ὡσεί* sufficiently shews that there was only a feeling in the eyes, when they received the power of light again, similar to what usually accompanies the falling off of scales—*Λεπίς* denotes properly a scale or scurf: it is applied to diseases of the eye in Tobit ii. 9, vi. 10.*

In the passage xxii. 14, etc., the speech of Ananias confines itself to the general calling of Paul to the apostolic office for all men, which indeed indicates his destination to the Gentiles, though it does not clearly express it, like xxvi. 16. We need only remark that chap. xxii. ver. 16 (*ἀπόλουσαι τὰς ἁμαρτίας σου*) plainly represents baptism as an act of cleansing from sin (the *ἄφεσις τῶν ἁμαρτιῶν*). Comp. at Titus iii. 5.† In chap. xxvi. 16, etc., however, Paul is expressly appointed as the witness of Christ among the Gentiles, and by this appointment he receives the peculiar position in reference to the Twelve, which we find him through his whole life maintaining. At the same time it is intimated that he, as the representative of the world of light, is called to the exalted duty of delivering men from the power of darkness and its prince. (In ver. 17, *ἐξαιρούμενος* is to be referred to deliverance from dangers: the phrase *ἐκ τῶν ἐθνῶν* forbids our regarding it as synonymous with *ἐκλεκτός*. On the expression *κλῆρος ἐν τοῖς ἡγιασμένοις* in ver. 18, see at Colos. i. 12.)

And here now it is a highly important circumstance, that the Apostle Paul by no means becomes, simply by this wonderful calling, received from the Lord himself, a member of the church, but he must also receive baptism. In this the objective character of the sacraments appears beyond all mistake: they cannot be set aside on account of the immediate operations of the Spirit, but require to be administered, if it be at all possible; for exceptions must be admitted, as when martyrdom for the faith supplies the want of

* Olshausen seems here to have fallen into a mistake. The word that is used in Tobit in both the passages referred to is *λευκῶμα*. In another passage, however, of the same book, xi. 13, the verb *λεπίζω* is employed to denote the falling off of the *λευκώματα*. *Καὶ ἐλεπίσθη ἀπὸ τῶν κάνθων τῶν ὀφθαλμῶν αὐτοῦ τὰ λευκώματα.*—[Tr.

† It should, however, be added, that the expression is not to be *literally* interpreted. The rite of baptism standing in close connexion with the forgiveness of sins, following upon and symbolizing it, comes very naturally in emphatic, figurative phraseology to be put for it. "Wash away thy sins" in baptism, is thus an elliptical and forcible expression, equivalent to "submit to that baptism which attends upon and indicates the remission of sin." Baptism without faith could certainly not bring salvation, and faith under circumstances where baptism is impossible, will be accepted of God.—[K.

baptism. We must not, however, suppose that Paul in his baptism received the Holy Ghost by the laying on of the hands of an apostle in the usual manner. In that case he would have been placed in a position of dependence with reference to the Twelve, which he himself most keenly repudiates. (Galat. i. 12.) Probably the true state of the case was this, that Paul, like Cornelius, chap. x. 45, etc., received the Holy Ghost directly, and that before baptism. Baptism of itself placed him in no position of dependence, any more than the baptism of Christ made him dependent upon John the Baptist: but probably the communication of the Spirit would have had this effect, if it had taken place through the instrumentality of an apostle.

Vers. 20–25.—According to Acts Paul went immediately (εὐθέως) after his conversion into the synagogues of Damascus, and preached Christ: according to Galat. i. 17, he withdrew soon after it to Arabia. How long he remained there is not mentioned in Galatians. We may unite the two accounts by supposing that Paul at first made the attempt to teach immediately, but then felt that he required a period of quietness to collect himself and to commune with his own mind, and therefore went for some time to Arabia.* Such an interval of repose must indeed have been essentially necessary to the apostle, because the revolution of his ideas was too violent, not to require an arranging of them, and a settling of them by the Old Testament. The point to which all the effort of the apostle

* This view, which is also supported by Schrader, of the object of Paul's residence in Arabia, has recently found an opponent in Neander (Apost. Zeitalt. Th. i. S. 115, Note). The grounds, however, upon which this learned man attempts to make it appear that the apostle went to Arabia only for the purpose of preaching, have not appeared to me satisfactory. In the first place Neander is of opinion that Paul, if he had retired for the purpose of collecting himself, would have written "into the desert of Arabia" (εἰς ἔρημον Ἀραβίας), or simply "into the desert" (εἰς ἔρημον). But one does not see the necessity why this form of expression should have been chosen to express that idea; Paul did not need to go to a desert to collect his thoughts, and to arrange his new ideas, he might reside for a time in any city in Arabia. Besides, it does not appear to Neander probable, psychologically considered, that Paul, after Ananias had comforted him in solitude, should again have gone into solitude; he would rather have sought society. But intercourse with believers, and preaching of the gospel as an apostle, are surely to be distinguished from one another. As Paul himself, in his pastoral letters (see 1 Tim. iii. 6), gives the injunction that novices are not to teach, it appears to me very unlikely that he should himself have immediately entered upon his apostolic office. His first preaching in Damascus is probably to be regarded only as a testimony borne to what God had done in him: such testimony was necessary, because otherwise his conversion would have assumed the appearance of something clandestine. But after this testimony was publicly given, the apostle could not but feel the necessity of having his thoughts absorbed with the new world which had unfolded itself to him, which was hardly possible during his apostolic journeys. As three years, therefore, had been spent by the disciples in immediate intercourse with the Lord, so the same period was enjoyed also by Paul as a time of training. During this time the glorified Redeemer, unseen, but inwardly near to the apostle, formed him into the powerful instrument, which he was afterwards honoured by the Church as being. For further particulars consult the exposition of Galat. i. 17.

was first directed was naturally the Messiahship of Jesus* and that in the higher view in which Christianity exhibits the Messiah, namely, as the Son of God. (Συγχύνω denotes here "to confound, to bring into perplexity." See Acts ii. 6. Συμβιβάζω properly means "to join to one another," in which sense it occurs, *e. g.*, in Ephes. iv. 16. Here it denotes "to prove, to confirm, to join, as it were, reasons firmly to one another." It refers doubtless to Rabbinical arguments, such as Paul had been conversant with in the schools of the Pharisees.)

Luke mentions but briefly (Acts ix. 23–25) the persecutions which the Jews at Damascus raised against Paul, whom they regarded as an apostate. From 2 Cor. xi. 32, where Paul himself makes mention of these occurrences, we learn that the governor of king Aretas of Arabia (ἐθνάρχης Ἀρέτα τοῦ βασιλέως), supported the hostile Jews in their designs against the apostle. Aretas, in his conflicts with Herod Antipas, had made himself master of a part of Syria. (Joseph. Arch. xviii. 5, 1.) Paul escaped from Damascus, only because the Christians let him down in a basket through an opening in the city wall. (Comp. Comm. on 2 Cor. xi. 32.)

Vers. 26–30.—The account of Paul's return to Jerusalem, which Luke here gives, may lead to the supposition, that after a short time he went back thither: but the passage in Gal. i. 17, 18, shews that, after fleeing from Damascus, he withdrew to Arabia, then came back to Damascus,† and first revisited Jerusalem after three years. Probably this time, respecting the employment of which no express information is given to us, was spent by the apostle in making a thorough revision of his ideas. The internal change in Paul was exceedingly violent; he needed repose, that he might free himself entirely from his old principles, and become thoroughly grounded in the new to which he had been drawn. And this long absence perhaps explains, why the believers in Jerusalem were still afraid of Paul. Certainly they had heard of his conversion, but as nothing had been known of him for three years, they might fear that he had fallen away again. But Barnabas brought him to the apostles, and bore witness to the reality of his conversion. Yet it is surprising that Barnabas needed first to describe to the apostles how he had been converted. But as three years had elapsed, during which time they had heard nothing of him, the true state of matters might have escaped their memory: at first they might not consider the

* In verse 20, instead of the common reading Χριστόν, Ἰησοῦν should stand.

† The incident of being let down through an opening in the wall appears to have occurred on the occasion of Paul's second visit to Damascus, which Luke does not distinguish from the first, because he entirely omits the journey to Arabia; for farther particulars, see Comm. on Gal. i. 16, etc.

event of his conversion to be so important, as his commanding personal qualities afterwards shewed it to be. Further, according to Gal. i. 18, 19, Paul met only Peter and James in Jerusalem. And of course the more definite words of the apostle there exhibited, must be allowed to modify the more general statement of Luke. The evangelist had not been personally acquainted with the early occurrences in the life of the apostle; and therefore this account of them could not be expected to be so precise.

In Jerusalem too Paul made the attempt to preach the Gospel (verse 28), but it was to be anticipated, that here his labours would be few. The Christians recognized him as the old enemy of their church, and might not be able to admit him so soon to their full confidence. The Jews viewed him as an apostate, and therefore shunned him. Besides, according to Acts xxii. 17, etc., the apostle was favoured with a vision of Christ in the Temple, although it was one purely spiritual (ἐν ἐκστάσει), by which he was directed to the Gentile world as the scene of his apostolic ministry. As soon, therefore, as some opposition to Paul appeared in Jerusalem on the part of the Hellenists,* the brethren there sent him away, after a stay of fourteen days (Gal. i. 18), by way of Cæsarea, to his native city Tarsus, the metropolis of Cilicia. It appears from Acts xv. 23–41 that churches existed in Cilicia, and there can be no doubt, therefore, that Paul employed his time in Tarsus in preaching the Gospel to his countrymen, for during his first missionary excursion he did not touch upon Cilicia at all.

(According to Gal. i. 21, Paul's journey to Tarsus lay through Syria, and therefore Cæsarea must not be understood as the well-known city upon the Mediterranean sea, but Cæsarea Philippi, on the borders of Syria. Proceeding by land from Jerusalem to Tarsus, Paul would not have chosen the longer way by Cæsarea Stratonis. The phrase κατήγαγον εἰς must mean merely "to bring on the way to Cæsarea," because that place is too far removed from Jerusalem to render it probable that an escort would go all the way.)

§ 2. FIRST PREACHING TO THE GENTILES.

(Acts ix. 31—x. 48.)

It has already been observed at the commencement of the second part of Acts, that the accounts which it embraces respecting Peter, were not communicated so much to set before us the minis-

* There is no inconsistency between this and the statement of Acts xxii. 17, 18, that the vision of Christ caused him to depart, because they would not receive his testimony.

try of Peter, as to shew in what manner the Gospel was first carried to the Gentiles. As Luke wrote mainly for Gentile readers, he would naturally feel very solicitious to make it plain to them, that this important event was brought about quite in accordance with God's purpose. It is true the accounts respecting Æneas and Tabitha have no necessary connexion with this object: they might have been omitted without causing any essential deficiency. But the reason, probably, why Luke inserted them in his work was, that he found them in his Petrine documents connected with the history of Cornelius which follows, and considered that, as striking proofs of the power of that Spirit who wrought in believers, he ought not to withhold them from his readers. To this add that these events exerted the most direct influence upon the spread of the Gospel in Palestine (ix. 35–42), and for that very reason could not but appear important to Luke. With respect to the *time* of these occurrences we find only quite general intimations in what follows, as in ix. 43, x. 48, and in xi. 2, according to the fuller reading. Without doubt, however, the statement of Paul's return to Jerusalem (ix. 26, etc.) is anticipated, and therefore these accounts of Peter are to be referred to the time of Paul's sojourn in Arabia. Were we, with Meyer, to refer them to the time of Paul's abode in Cilicia, then we should have too great an interval, respecting which no account was given. In chap. xi. 19, Luke glances back to the consequences of the sufferings inflicted upon Christians in the time of Stephen, but only as to something already past. (See the particulars at that passage.)

Vers. 31–35.—The first verse embraces only a general description of the peaceful condition of the apostolic church in Canaan. (Respecting *οἰκοδομεῖν* see Comm. on 1 Cor. iii. 10, etc.—On *φόβος τοῦ κυρίου*, see at Luke i. 12.—*Παράκλησις* is considered at John xiv. 16.) The Apostle Peter appears, from verse 32, to have made a journey of visitation among the existing churches, and during this journey the cure of Æneas took place. (Lydda was a country town near to Joppa (verse 38), which Josephus also mentions, Arch. xx. 6, 2.—*Σάρων* is a well-known fruitful region in the neighbourhood of these places. Consult Gesenius on שָׁרוֹן).

Vers. 36–43.—The account of the above cure is followed by a narrative of the raising of a certain woman, Tabitha, from the dead in Joppa, to which Peter was called from Lydda. There is nothing however peculiar in the occurrence, and therefore I simply refer the reader to the observations made at John xi. 1, respecting the general subject of raising from the dead. (The name *Ταβιθά*, which is found only here, is explained by Luke himself by the Greek word *δορκάς*, a gazelle, which, on account of the loveliness of the creature, was frequently employed as a proper name for women. The Hebrew name comes from צְבָה, or צְבִיָּה, a roe, a gazelle, of which the Syriac form is טְבִיתָא. See Buxtorf. Lex. Talm. p. 848.—Ver. 36, πλήρης ἀγαθῶν ἔργων. In a similar manner, James iii. 17 uses μεστός. It is a Hebraism, the adjective מְלֵא being thus applied to invisible possessions. Further, verse 39 shews in what the good works of Tabitha consisted.—(On the import of ἔργα, see at Rom. iii. 21.—In verse 36, μαθήτρια is a peculiar form, found in the New Testament only here. Elsewhere it occurs in Diog. Laërt. iv. 2. The more common form is μαθητρίς. Consult Lobeck ad Phryn. p. 256.)

Chap. x. 1.—With these occurrences is connected the important narrative of the conversion of Cornelius, the first-fruits of the whole Gentile world to the church of Christ. It appears surprising that the Apostle Peter, who laboured in the power of the Holy Ghost, and to whom the prophecies of the Old Testament respecting the calling of the Gentiles (see Comm. on Matth. viii. 10) could not be unknown, needed a special lesson on the point that the Gentiles were to be admitted into the church. But here it must not be overlooked that Peter was by no means uncertain about the entrance of the Gentiles into the church considered in itself, but only about the point whether they could be admitted without being circumcised, and taking upon themselves the obligation of the law.* The Divine authority of the Old Testament being presupposed, it was by no means so easy to regard this as possible, and agreeable to the will of God. In the law of Moses, circumcision was instituted for all times, with the threatening that the uncircumcised should be cut off from the people of God (Gen. xvii. 10, 14) ; no prophet had expressly predicted that circumcision was ever to cease : the supposition therefore that would most readily suggest itself was, that the Gentiles must first go through the intermediate stage of Judaism, in order to reach the church of Christ. The proper idea of the position of the Gentiles in reference to the church was first given by the typical view of circumcision, which indeed is expressed with sufficient clearness in the Old Testament (Deut. x. 16, xxx. 6 ; Jerem. iv. 4) ; but without an explicit exhibition of the relation between the circumcision of the Spirit, and that of the flesh. One might indeed suppose that the Spirit who guides into all truth (John xvi. 13), would have immediately disclosed to the apostle this relation ; and that he would have needed therefore no further instruction on the point. But let us only conceive the Spirit, not as a power suddenly overwhelming the mind with truths of every

* This solves the doubts which De Wette expresses on Matth. xxviii. 19, how the apostles could have any scruple to baptize Gentiles, when the Lord had expressly commanded that all nations should be baptized. Peter had no scruple at all with respect to this point, but only how far he could baptize Gentiles, without at the same time binding them to the observance of the whole Old Testament law, and therefore also of circumcision.

kind, but as a higher principle which, penetrating the soul, leads it on *gradually* from step to step into the depths of Divine knowledge; and then the event, which is here related to us respecting Peter, will stand in no way opposed to the statement, that he was filled with the Holy Ghost. Yet the reason why a peculiar arrangement of God took place, for the purpose of instructing Peter respecting this question, and through him guiding to certainty all who were in doubt, is to be found in the importance of the question. The reception of the Gentiles into the church, without laying upon them the obligation of circumcision and the law, was, on the one hand, the public declaration of the universal character of the Gospel, the removal of the hedge which separated Jews and Gentiles (Ephes. ii. 14); but, on the other hand, this very reception was also the signal for an internal division of the church into Jewish and Gentile Christians. The Jews of the Pharisaic sect who had entered into the church, could not raise themselves to the purely spiritual and typical view of circumcision; they held firmly by the necessity of entering through the old covenant in its outward form into the new, and according to the literal view of the Old Testament, as well as the words of Jesus in Matth. v. 17, they had so much in their favour, that it was difficult to refute them: They were able therefore, even at a later period, to make a strong impression upon Peter (Gal. ii.), and for this very reason this apostle needed that powerful support to his conviction, which the occurrences here narrated must have furnished him. The need of being confirmed in so extraordinary a manner, in the principle of the freedom of the Gentiles from the law, does not stand in any contradiction to the character of Peter, in which firmness and depth were conspicuous, but arises necessarily out of it. His very depth was the reason why he found the question exceedingly difficult to answer; his earnest faith in the word of God in the Old Testament, his reverence for every syllable of it, made him feel keenly the difficulties which the objections of the strict Jewish Christians started; and in order that here, in a business of decisive moment, he might not be without certain warrant, nor follow any merely subjective opinion of his own, but act according to the will of God, he received this extraordinary assistance through a symbolical vision.

Vers. 1–8.—First of all, Luke gives a description of the character and circumstances of Cornelius, and of the vision which was imparted to him. He dwelt in Cæsarea, the political capital of the country, and the seat of the highest Roman authorities; he was a centurion in the Italian band or cohort, and without doubt therefore a Roman by birth, or at least from Italy. (The legions that were stationed in the eastern provinces consisted for the most part of native soldiers. Particular cohorts, however, were formed of Italians, and these were called Italian cohorts.) And here it is surprising that Cornelius is described exactly as a proselyte, "pious and fearing God" (εὐσεβὴς καὶ φοβούμενος τὸν Θεόν), with which character the representation of ver. 22 particularly harmonizes, "and attested by all the nation of the Jews" (μαρτυρούμενός τε ὑπὸ ὅλου τοῦ ἔθνους, τῶν Ἰουδαίων). This circumstance appears in fact to destroy the importance of the whole narrative, for if Cornelius was already a Jewish proselyte, his conversion cannot be regarded as the commencement of the entrance of Gentiles into the church; yet it is surely represented as such in what follows (x. 45, xi. 1), and Peter too names Cornelius (x. 28) ἀλλόφυλος (= נָכְרִי Isaiah xi. 6), while he adds that it was not permitted to him as a Jew to hold intercourse with him. On account of this difficulty it has been proposed to take the expression φοβούμενος τὸν Θεόν in a more general signification, without reference to the condition of a proselyte: but first this phrase, like σεβόμενος τὸν Θεόν and προσήλυτος, is the usual description of Gentiles favourable to Judaism, and again the singular with the article τὸν Θεόν does not permit that it be regarded as a description of heathen devoutness. The difficulty under consideration is best explained by considering minutely the condition of proselytes among the Jews. There were, it is known, two classes of proselytes, those of the gate (גֵּרֵי הַשַּׁעַר), and those of righteousness (גֵּרֵי הַצֶּדֶק). The latter received circumcision, and formally passed over into the Jewish church; the former, on the other hand, bound themselves only to the observance of the so-called precepts of Noah (see Comm. on Acts xv. 20); these proselytes of the gate, therefore, as being uncircumcised, were always regarded as unclean, and at the best were viewed as a kind of middle class between Jews and Gentiles. It was probably supposed that all proselytes of the gate would gradually allow themselves to be circumcised; and this intermediate stage was perhaps only appointed, not to frighten away by too rigid requirements at first those Gentiles who displayed a leaning to Judaism. If then we suppose that Cornelius was a proselyte of the gate, and consequently uncircumcised, which accords with the words in chap. xi. 1–3, in which Cornelius and his friends are styled uncircumcised (ἀκροβυστίαν ἔχοντες), then all the descriptions which occur in what follows are quite appropriate; and the new feature of the case was this, that Cornelius, without becoming a proselyte of righteousness, was immediately baptized in the name of Jesus. Meyer's objection to this view, that it is improbable there were no proselytes before this who had entered the church, and that therefore, according to our supposition, the history of Cornelius would present nothing at all peculiar, is easily obviated by the supposition, which has a solid ground in the circumstances of the case, that proselytes of righteousness, who were of course circumcised, had already been admitted into the Christian community, but no proselytes of the gate, that is, none who were uncircumcised: this first took place in the case of Cornelius, and herein lies the great importance of his admission. For on account of the high value which the Jews attached to circumcision, the grand question was, whether persons could become Christians without circumcision.

With respect to the vision of the angel next mentioned, with which Cornelius was favoured, nothing leads to the conclusion that it occurred otherwise than as a purely internal phenomenon (*ἐν ἐκστάσει*), as in the 10th verse.* As it was late in the day, viz., three hours after noon, it is altogether probable that the fasting of Cornelius had augmented his susceptibility of spiritual impressions (for in fact we do not find that any one has had such appearances immediately after a full meal), but it does not follow from this, that the whole occurrence was the mere product of an excited imagination; at least that is certainly not the meaning of the narrator, which we must first of all ascertain by exegetical means. It is not improbable (see at chap. x. 37) that Cornelius had already heard of Christianity, and that the object of his prayers was to obtain light from above respecting this new religion.

(In verse 4 the words *ἀνέβησαν αἱ προσευχαί σου εἰς μνημόσυνον*, *thy prayers have come up for a memorial*, are a well-known form of expression adapted to human views and feelings. See Exod. ii. 23. Probably it takes its origin from a comparison of prayers with sacrifices, as the smoke rising up to heaven was viewed as an index of the acceptance of the sacrifice. In the 5th and 6th verses there is no particular stress to be laid upon the circumstance that the trade of a tanner, on account of his being occupied with the skins of slain beasts, was held in contempt among the Jews: were anything of the kind designed, a clearer indication of it would have been given.)

Vers. 9–16.—In conjunction with the vision of Cornelius there occurred by God's direction another, which was imparted to Peter about the same time. Of this vision it is expressly said in verse 10: *ἐπέπεσεν ἐπ' αὐτὸν ἔκστασις*.† The word *ἔκστασις* denotes prima-

* The word *φανερῶς* seems inconsistent with the view advocated by Olshausen, and rather favours the idea that an angel actually appeared to Cornelius in his waking moments. The statements made too regarding the entrance and departure of the angel in verses 3–7, as well as the hour of the day when the occurrence took place, lead to the same conclusion. Olshausen appeals to the 10th verse, but it tells against himself, for it is there plainly said that an *ἔκστασις* fell upon Peter, while nothing of the kind is said regarding the angelic vision of Cornelius.—[TR.

† The word *ἔκστασις* is used by Philo (quis rer. div. hær. edit. Pfeiffer. vol. iv. p. 111, seq.) in a fourfold sense. In the highest form it denotes the *ἔνθεος κατοχωτική τε μανία ᾗ τὸ προφητικὸν γένος χρῆται*. An example of this sort he finds (p. 114), in the history of Abraham, in Gen. xliii. 10, where it is said: *περὶ δὲ ἡλίου δυσμὰς ἔκστασις ἐπέπεσεν ἐπὶ τὸν Ἀβραάμ*. And this form of the *ἔκστασις* can only be imparted to the wise man, for

rly the condition of being put out of one's self; and is therefore frequently applied to terror and astonishment, as in Mark v. 42; Luke v. 26; Acts iii. 10. By way of eminence, however, it is applied to a state of spiritual excitement, which is also indicated by the expressions *εἶναι* or *γίνεσθαι ἐν πνεύματι*, *being, or becoming in the Spirit*, as in Rev. i. 10;* and *φέρεσθαι ὑπὸ τοῦ πνεύματος*, *being moved by the Spirit*, in 2 Peter i. 21, denotes something similar. It is a remarkable description of the *ἔκστασις*, which Paul gives in 2 Cor. xii. 2, 3, when he declares that he knew not whether that which occurred to him occurred in the body or out of the body. And hence it plainly follows, that the depression or removal of the human consciousness, which, however, must be conceived as connected with an exaltation of the heavenly consciousness, constitutes the specific character of the *ἔκστασις* (which has its analogies in somnambulism), during which, too, the Spirit exerts a mighty influence upon the soul. States which at least came very near to *ἔκστασις*, appear also to have prevailed among the prophets of the Old Testament. Sudden seizure by the power of the Spirit (expressed here by the *ἐπέπεσεν ἐπ' αὐτόν*, *fell upon him*), is indicated by the well-known phrases, רוּחַ יְהוָה עָלַי, *the Spirit of Jehovah was upon me*, and יַד יְהוָה עָלַי, *the hand of Jehovah was upon me;* and Ezekiel, in particular, shews how states of ecstacy were connected with this seizure. Now, although such occurrences are represented as operations of grace, yet Paul, who describes them most carefully in his Epistles to the Corinthians, intimates, that they by no means form the highest stage of development in the spiritual life; it is better under the full influence of the Spirit, to be able to maintain† a

to him alone does God draw near, that he may inspire him as his instrument and permeate his soul: *μόνῳ δὲ σοφῷ ταῦτ' ἐφαρμόττει, ἐπεὶ καὶ μόνος ὄργανον Θεοῦ ἐστιν ἠχοῦν, κρουόμενον, καὶ πληττόμενον ἀοράτως ὑπ' αὐτοῦ.* In the sequel of his representation (p. 119), Philo then describes more minutely the nature of such a genuine prophetic ecstacy, and gives an allegorical exposition of the passage respecting Abraham. As the day lasts so long as the sun shines, so the earthly lower consciousness endures while the understanding continues active. But when a higher Divine power drives back the lower human power, then the earthly consciousness fades, but a higher and more comprehensive consciousness dawns upon the man. The mortal, says Philo, cannot dwell along with the immortal, and therefore must the earthly light evanish at the entrance of the Divine light, and it is only when the latter is withdrawn that the former reappears. This description is so lively and picturesque, that undoubtedly we must suppose Philo had not only observed such ecstacies in others, but had also been partaker of them himself.

* It is by no means meant, that wherever the words *ἐν πνεύματι* occur, a state of ecstacy is to be understood: on the contrary, it is only the two forms of expression specified that are so used. The Holy Ghost frequently, nay commonly, appears to operate in the state of consciousness, without producing a remarkable exaltation of the spiritual life.

† A mistake on this point was the peculiar error in the doctrine of the Montanists respecting the state of ecstacy; they erroneously regarded this lower form of the revelation of the Spirit as the highest, and thus hindered the advancement of the church to a higher life.

state of clear consciousness, (For further particulars, see at 1 Cor. xiv. 32.) Accordingly we do not find that the Redeemer himself ever appeared in states that even bordered upon the ἔκστασις: in him the highest influence of the Spirit was always connected with the clearest consciousness.

(The sixth hour was one of the usual hours of prayer; and the Jews frequently went to pray upon the flat roof (ἐπὶ τὸ δῶμα), where they were alone under the open sky.—Πρόσπεινος occurs nowhere else in the New Testament; it signifies very hungry, for πρός frequently heightens the signification.—In verse 11, the words σκεῦός τι ὡς ὀθόνην, denote something indefinite and general that belonged to the vision; the appearance perhaps might be compared to a great sheet fastened to the corners of the sky.—Ἀρχή stands here as in xi. 5, in the signification of "end, extremity," in which sense it is also found among profane writers. The repetition mentioned in verse 16, denotes the certainty and reliableness of the instruction imparted by the vision.)

And here the question presents itself, in what relation the arrangements of this vision stood to the laws of food in the Old Testament. (Lev. x. 11.) Assuming, indeed, that those laws of Moses were not at all designed to suggest higher instruction, and that the vision here described was a mere imagination of Peter, then there is no difficulty in allowing one fancy to be abrogated by means of another.[*] But the dignity of the word of God cannot consist with such suppositions. According to Matth. v. 17, nothing entitles us to choose out portions from the Old Testament, that may deprive them of their Divine character; and as little does the New Testament permit the supposition, that events so important as the con-

[*] With much ingenuity Neander (Apost. Zeitalt. p. s. 92, etc.) handles this occurrence. He says: "There came together two tendencies of his nature, the higher want of his Spirit, the power of the Divine, which overcame his Spirit, and the power of the animal want over his lower nature. In this way it happened that the Divine and the natural were mingled together, not so, that the Divine was obscured by the mixture, but so, that the Divine employed the reflection of the natural as an image or vehicle for the truth to be revealed. The Divine light, which, breaking through the atmosphere of traditional notions, was about to rise in his soul, displayed itself in the mirror of sensuous images that proceeded from the present want of his animal nature." This representation, however, might be readily misunderstood. In the first place, it might be imagined that Peter's view of the difference between clean and unclean beasts, as well as of the separation between Jews and Gentiles, was absolutely false, as belonging to the circle of traditional notions. But this, on the supposition of the Divine authority of all the Old Testament institutions, cannot be allowed; on the contrary, the ordinances respecting unclean beasts, and the separation of the Jews from the Gentiles, though only temporary appointments, were yet really valid until the coming of the Messiah, and therefore their abolition for the Messianic times required to be then expressly declared. Again, Neander's representation might be misunderstood, as if it intimated that the feeling of hunger was the real cause of the whole occurrence; while according to his view it was only the subjective handle which Divine grace laid hold of, for the purpose of making the apostle acquainted with a point which was peculiarly difficult to him.

version of the Gentiles were brought about by the dreaming of an apostle. But according to this stricter view, the New Testament appears in this case to abrogate the Old, which assuredly stands opposed to the express declaration of Christ in Matth. v. 17. Now here we might just say, that in Christ all the types of the Old Testament attained their end, that the laws of food were part of these types, and that accordingly in their outward form they have ceased, after they have been spiritually fulfilled. But it is very difficult to make out a real typical character for the laws of food: for although here unclean beasts plainly denote the Gentiles (verse 28), yet they have this reference only because the Gentiles, on account of their eating unclean beasts, were themselves esteemed unclean. The conjecture therefore forces itself upon us, that in the distinction between clean and unclean beasts, some other circumstances were looked to. It is difficult indeed in regard to all to make this good, but the eating of serpents and other reptiles was probably forbidden on no other ground than this, that in fact in such disgusting beasts they saw something impure.* A clear intimation in favour of this idea is furnished in ver. 15, where it is said: *ἃ ὁ Θεὸς ἐκαθάρισε, σὺ μὴ κοίνου, what God hath cleansed*, etc. Here the idea of the impurity of certain beasts is recognized, because "cleansing" (*καθαρίζειν*) can only be applied to that which is unclean. And it makes no difference whether we take the word in the sense of "making clean," or "declaring clean," for the latter necessarily presupposes the former. (Consult Comm. on Matth. viii. 3.) According to the connexion indeed the aorist has reference to the vision, and the first announcement made in it, *θῦσον καὶ φάγε, slay and eat* (verse 13); but the reason why at this time, and under these circumstances, the declaration ensued, is to be sought in more general grounds, viz., in the completed redemption, which is regarded as a restitution of the whole creation. The laws of food accordingly, from their nature, retained their importance only until, by the redemption of Christ, that which occasioned them was overcome. We cannot therefore say that they are here *abolished* as something opposed to Christianity, but they only appear like all else, *fulfilled* by the work of redemption.

Vers. 17–22.—Peter, still uncertain about the purpose of this vision, received upon the spot an inward notice from the Spirit (*εἶπεν αὐτῷ τὸ πνεῦμα*, see chap. viii. 29), that some strangers were waiting for him. (Verse 19. The common reading *ἐνθυμουμένου* has been rightly regarded by Griesbach as inferior to the other reading *διενθυμουμένου*: this compound is found in the New Testament only here, and, as the more unusual form, deserves the preference.—

* Respecting the degradation of the unconscious creature, see the remarks made at Romans viii. 18, etc.

Verse 20. Respecting *διακρίνεσθαι* compare Matth. xxi. 21; Mark xi. 23.—Verse 22. Respecting *χρηματίζειν*, see Comm. on Matth. ii. 12.)

Vers. 23–29.—The behaviour of Cornelius on the arrival of Peter at his house (verse 25) shews plainly how undeveloped his religious views still were. To judge by the apostle's words, his adoration was no mere form of courtesy, but he regarded Peter as a being endowed with supernatural powers. Probably therefore he had not been able altogether to disengage himself from heathen ideas, and he might suppose Peter to be the son of some god or a hero. Now, as Cornelius, notwithstanding this, received the Holy Ghost, and that too before baptism (verse 44), we see here again how incomparably more important in the religious life are the desire and inward longing of the heart, than correctness of ideas; it was such feelings alone which made the Roman captain so acceptable to God.*

(In verse 25, the codices A.B.D.E. insert *τοῦ* before *εἰσελθεῖν*, which, as the more difficult reading, ought to receive the preference. Yet this connexion of the genitive of the infinitive with *ἐγένετο*, is to be viewed as an extreme use of this construction with the infinitive, of which there is elsewhere no example. [See Meyer on this passage.]—Verse 29, *ἀναντιῤῥήτως* occurs nowhere else in the New Testament. Hesychius explains it by *ἀναμφιβόλως*. The phrase, *τίνι λόγῳ*, occurs again in 1 Cor. xv. 2. It may be explained by *ἐπί* supplied; *λόγος*, like דָּבָר, is used in the sense of *χρῆμα* or *πρᾶγμα*.)

Vers. 30–33.—The minuteness with which Cornelius describes his vision, gives to the narrative an air of simplicity, which renders it probable, that the account as communicated to us by Luke, has been drawn from a very excellent source, to be sought for perhaps among the friends of Cornelius himself.† (Verse 30.) Heinrichs,

* The supposition that the prostration of Cornelius was intended as an act of worship, seems quite inconsistent with the character of Cornelius as one who feared God (τὸν Θεόν), the Jehovah of the Hebrews. The act itself does not necessarily imply such worship, nor is this proved with any certainty from the address of Peter, "Arise, for I also am a man." This language may spring from a misapprehension of Cornelius' purpose, or (which seems to me more probable), may be simply an emphatic mode of deprecating such excessive honour:—"Arise, I am no Divine being that I should receive such marks of reverence."—[K.

† This remark of Olshausen seems to lead to the conclusion that he considered some portions of Scripture as more entitled to credit than others, on account of the sources from which they have been drawn. Such a notion is utterly inconsistent with sound views of inspiration, and would render valueless the whole word of God, for who is to decide what portions came from the best sources? Paul gives us the right view, when he says "that all Scripture is given by inspiration of God, and is profitable for doctrine, for reproof, for correction, for instruction in righteousness." Yet the remark of Olshausen embodies a certain amount of truth. The several portions of Scripture, though all equally inspired, yet differ from one another, and all exhibit the impress of the mental peculiarities of their respective penmen, who must have written therefore not as mere machines,

who is followed too by Meyer, errs in understanding the words, *ἀπὸ τετάρτης ἡμέρας—ἤμην νηστεύων*, to mean that Cornelius had been fasting four complete days, down to the time when Peter arrived, for in that case the present tense must have been used; the meaning rather is: "I was fasting at the time I received the vision, viz., four days ago, down to the same hour of the day at which we are now speaking." Meyer, however, differs from Heinrichs in this, that the latter places the vision upon the fourth day of the fast, the former upon the first. Meyer's view is plainly quite untenable, for the idea of the writer is that God, in consequence of the disposition first manifested by Cornelius, favoured him with the vision; but this disposition shewed itself by means of the long fasting, and consequently the vision must have taken place at the end of it.*

Vers. 34-36.—This statement of Cornelius awakened the astonishment of Peter at the proceedings of God's grace. (Respecting *προσωπολήπτης*, consult Comm. on Matth. xxii. 16.) He saw that the Gospel in its comprehensive agency was appointed to draw to itself all those who, whatever nation they might belong to, bore within themselves a holy longing and upward striving after God.† This passage is one of those which, through a complete mistake of the depth of the Gospel principles, are misapplied to the purpose of proving from the Holy Scriptures themselves, the pretended superfluousness of Christianity, and the sufficiency of virtue. It has been supposed to prove that the apostles themselves taught, that the fear of God and virtuous conduct (*ἐργάζεσθαι τὴν δικαιοσύνην*) are perfectly sufficient to guide to blessedness, and that for gaining this end there is no need of faith in the specific doctrines of Christianity. But the shallowness of the religious indifference displayed in these

but as intelligent beings exercising their different powers of mind. The peculiar air of simplicity therefore, which pervades this passage, may have originated in the circumstance that Luke, who was very diligent in the investigation of facts, had some document before him, which had been written upon the spot, and which therefore preserved the minutest details. But this could be no reason for our receiving the narrative with peculiar favour. The claim of the narrative to our implicit belief, rests altogether upon the fact, that Luke wrote by inspiration, though the peculiar hue it wears may have originated in the manner supposed by Olshausen.—[TR.

* Meyer's view seems improbable, both on account of the verb "I was" (*ἤμην*), and because it seems aside from Cornelius' purpose to speak of his continued fasting *after* he saw the vision: Heinrich's still more, as it allows no time for the sending for and coming of Peter. If the fasting continued four days, it must, I think, have been a period terminating with the angelic appearance. I think, however, Olshausen right, and the *ἀπὸ τετάρτης ἡμέρας*, I regard as a loose construction meaning, "four days ago from the commencement of the day up to this hour," etc.—[K.

† The holy longing and striving after God here spoken of, cannot be supposed to be the native growth of man's own corrupt heart. Doubtless the Spirit of God was at work in the breast of Cornelius, while he fasted and prayed, previously to the visit of Peter; and the desires excited within him were gratified by the good providence of that God who turns not away from those who seek him. The appetite, as well as the food, in spiritual matters, comes from God.—[TR.

statements, appears plainly from the circumstance, that they ascribe to man, without any help beyond himself, the ability to fear God truly, and to practise righteousness in the full sense of the term. And again the connexion of the whole narrative clearly shews that the position hitherto occupied by Cornelius did not suffice for him, because he now received baptism; not to mention that the right view of verse 36 requires that the words *δεκτὸς αὐτῷ ἐστι τὸν λόγον* be connected together. There is indeed a great difference between those Gentiles who labour according to their knowledge, to keep the law, and those who make no such effort (Rom. ii. 13, 14); but the operation of this difference is, that those who do by nature the works of the law, are in the way of being more easily led to the higher stage of spiritual life which the Gospel discloses. The general principle therefore, that out of Christ there is no salvation, is only confirmed by this passage, which makes the blessing of an earnest faithfulness to the law consist in its leading to Christ. Hence the expressions *φοβεῖσθαι τὸν Θεόν* and *ἐργάζεσθαι δικαιοσύνην* denote, according to the connexion, devoutness of a legal kind, the *δικαιοσύνη κατὰ νόμον*. (On this point see the remarks at Luke i. 6, and Rom. iii. 21.)

In the grammatical connexion of verses 35–37, unnecessary difficulty has been found. As *ὃν* in verse 36 is wanting in some codices, *τὸν λόγον* has been understood by some in the sense of "*this* doctrine," and the passage has been translated "this doctrine," viz., that God accepts also pious Gentiles, God has sent or imparted to the Israelites. But first the omission of *ὃν* is not the reading critically established, and again the idea does not suit the connexion, for the calling of the Gentiles into the church of Christ had not hitherto been seen to be founded in the principles of the Gospel. Nor can the conjectural reading of *ὡς* for *ὃν* at all make good its claim, as it is wholly destitute of critical authority. It would be better to decide in favour of the connexion of *ὃν λόγον* with *ὑμεῖς οἴδατε* in the 37th verse, which has been defended, not only by Heumann and Bolten, but also by Heinrichs and Kuinoel.* With this view, however, there are two important difficulties connected,

* Meyer too has decided in favour of this view: he so understands the passage as to make three accusatives dependent upon *οἴδατε* in verse 37, viz., *τὸν λόγον* in ver. 36, *ῥῆμα* in ver. 37, and *Ἰησοῦν* in ver. 38; but the highly forced character of this connexion, appears in the translation which he appends, not to mention that, according to this view, the clause *οὗτός ἐστι πάντων κύριος* must be taken as a parenthesis, although the connexion requires the main emphasis to fall upon it. It is upon the principle that Christ is Lord of all, that the warrants rests for the calling of all. My view of the passage has been completely misunderstood by Meyer. It does not govern the accusative τὸν λόγον by *καταλαμβάνομαι*, in verse 44, but connects it with *δεκτὸς αὐτῷ ἐστι*, in this sense: "he is acceptable to him in reference to the word which God sent to the Israelites, that is, so as to have part in this word."

viz., first the parenthesis *οὗτός ἐστι πάντων κύριος*, and secondly, the clause that follows, *τὸ γενόμενον ῥῆμα*, which must be taken as in apposition with *λόγος*, so far removed from it. On the other hand, everything is plain, when we understand *ὃν λόγον* as the accusative absolute, and connect it with *δεκτὸς αὐτῷ ἐστι*. The expression, *ὃν ἀπέστειλε τοῖς υἱοῖς Ἰσραήλ*, must then be understood in this manner: which word he sent *first* to the children of Israel, but as Christ is Lord of *all* (*πάντων* being masculine, and not neuter for the universe*), it appertains also to all men.

Vers. 37-43.—Peter next brings forward an account of the leading occurrences in the life of Christ, and in conclusion presents him to the view of his heathen hearers, as the judge and Saviour even of the Gentile world. It is worthy of notice that Peter here, in the words "ye know," presupposes the history of Christ to be already known to Cornelius and his friends: *ὑμεῖς* refers to the *πάντες ἡμεῖς* of verse 33. It is not improbable, therefore, as we have already intimated at verse 1, that Cornelius was in a state of inward conflict, uncertain whether he should regard Christianity as of Divine origin or not. And from this uncertainty might proceed his earnest prayer, which God, on account of his sincerity regarded, and in an extraordinary manner gave him full assurance respecting the way in which he should go.

(The phrase *καταδυναστευόμενοι ὑπὸ τοῦ διαβόλου* in verse 38 occurs only here, as being a designation of demoniacs. The verb occurs also in James ii. 6. It may be remarked that Peter, without any special occasion, touches here upon the doctrine of the Devil, even before Gentiles who did not know it, which is not favourable to the theory of accommodation.—Ver. 41. *Προχειροτονέω* is found nowhere else in the New Testament. On *συμφαγεῖν* and *συμπιεῖν*, see Luke xiii. 26. It is a most important idea in these verses, that Christ is appointed *κριτὴς ζώντων καὶ νεκρῶν*, *a judge of living and dead.* Of the *thought* itself mention has already been made at Matth. xxv. 32; John v. 27; see also 2 Cor. v. 10; 2 Thess. i. 5, etc. And the *expression* here chosen occurs again in 2 Tim. iv. 1, and 1 Pet. iv. 5,† in which latter epistle the language manifestly is quite similar to that of Paul. The only question that still presents itself is this, what is the distinction drawn between the living and the dead? Does it mean this: "Christ judges not only those who shall still be

* Winer in his Gramm. p. 499, decides in favour of the supposition that the construction is left incomplete (anacoluthon), and remarks in opposition to my explanation, that it would deprive the words which follow of all proper grammatical connexion. I cannot see wherein he can fail to trace the connexion in what follows: if we understand the words *οὗτός ἐστι πάντων κύριος*, as forming an independent sentence in the sense, "he is Lord of all, and therefore also your Lord," the discourse moves on in the very best connexion.

† In the passage in 1 Pet. iv. 5, the connexion points primarily to those who are *literally* dead, but to such as are at the same time *spiritually* dead.

alive at his return, but also those already dead?" This certainly appears very improbable, when it is considered that in this view all the pious of preceding times would be styled *dead*, while yet the Redeemer expressly says of them: "God is not the God of the dead, but of the living; they all live to him." Luke xx. 38. Comp. Comm. on Matth. xxii. 32. And besides, the division of mankind would thus be very unequal, because the number of those who have died in the course of thousands of years, can by no means come into comparison with those who shall be alive at the end of the world.* Certainly, therefore, it is more correct to understand the *living* of those who enjoy spiritual life, and the *dead* of those who remain spiritually dead; which makes the distinction a more important one, and renders the phrase parallel to all those passages which treat of the judgment of the good and the bad.)

Vers. 44–48.—It is quite a peculiarity in connexion with the account of the conversion of Cornelius, that the Holy Ghost, who manifested himself here also by the gift of tongues (γλώσσαις λαλεῖν). was imparted *before* baptism. A consideration of the import of baptism, and its relation to the gift of the Spirit, makes this appear a remarkable occurrence; for it is first in baptism, and in regeneration which coincides with it, that the new man in whom the Holy Ghost dwells is fully born. We must suppose, in the case of Cornelius, that regeneration took place before baptism; as indeed the baptism of adults always presupposes faith, and therefore also the commencement of regeneration. The outward act of baptism, therefore, is not to be regarded as absolutely indispensable; and accordingly the church has always considered unbaptized persons, who suffered martyrdom for the faith, as having in the baptism of blood received at the same time the baptism of water and of the Spirit. Still, however, there is something singular in the case before us: there is nothing similar to it to be found: and probably, therefore, the correct view of the subject is, that this unusual proceeding took place *for the sake of Peter*. It appears from his subsequent conduct that the immediate reception of the Gentiles into the church of Christ had always appeared to him a matter of difficulty; and therefore in this first decisive case the Divine compassion came to his

* Yet we cannot for a moment suppose that the Redeemer means to deny the *literal* death of those whom he declares to live to God. On the contrary he is *speaking* expressly of the dead. Nor is there weight in Olshausen's second argument founded on the unequal distribution which is *thus* made of the races; for this is a matter of no importance whatever to the statement, whose purpose was simply to represent Christ as the judge of *all*. And as, at the Saviour's second coming, there were to be two widely-distinguished classes, those who slept in their graves, and those who had never tasted death, it was appropriate, in describing his judicial functions, to represent them as extending over *both*; and this the more, as it was uncertain to which class the persons addressed might belong.—[K.

help, and revealed to him in an undoubted manner that the Gentiles were not to be excluded from the noblest privilege of believers, the gift of the Holy Ghost. The importance of this circumstance Peter himself afterwards (chap. xi. 15) expressly sets forth. The view of Meyer, that the communication of the Holy Ghost before baptism, has its ground "only in the elevation of the mind to the proper pitch for receiving the gift," is untenable; because this might be the case with many, to whom nevertheless the Spirit was not imparted before baptism. This takes place not at all by any internal necessity, but in consequence of a free action of God.*

§ 3. FIRST PROCEEDINGS ON ACCOUNT OF THE GENTILE CHRISTIANS. PAUL'S STAY IN ANTIOCH AND JOURNEY TO JERUSALEM.

(Acts xi. 1–30.)

Vers. 1–18.—In what a momentous aspect this event of the entrance of the Gentiles into the church of God was viewed, plainly appears from the account that follows. Not only all believers in Jerusalem, but even the apostles themselves, were unable rightly to explain the conduct of Peter, and therefore they called him to account. It is plain therefore that they occupied essentially the same position, and it would probably have been difficult for Peter to justify himself fully before them, if he had not been able to appeal to such extraordinary occurrences. The simple statement of them, however (xi. 4–17), sufficed to convince the whole body of believers, that it was the will of God that Gentiles should be received into the

* Some further remarks will be made on the author's views of baptism and regeneration at chap. xvi. 15, where he more fully expresses them. He seems in general to regard regeneration as the consequence of baptism, and yet in this paragraph he allows that the inward change of regeneration should at least be begun before the outward rite of baptism takes place. It is plain too from his remarks on Lydia, xvi. 15, that he considers the very first inclination of the mind to God as the result of a Divine influence. Faith and a change of heart, then, ought to go before baptism. They are the proper preparation for it; and if they are wanting, baptism will be found altogether unable to produce them. Baptism will never of itself regenerate a soul. The author seems to overlook the distinction between the ordinary and extraordinary influence of the Spirit. There were ordinary influences, such as Lydia experienced, which were absolutely necessary to the very first right feeling, and which of course must precede the faith and baptism of adults, not follow them. But there was also in primitive times an extraordinary influence of the Spirit, which displayed itself in a palpable manner, and which was often exhibited after baptism. This extraordinary influence, though following baptism, was not connected with it, our author allows, by any internal necessity, but depended altogether upon the will of God. And much less could the ordinary influence that produced faith, and that of course preceded baptism, be itself in any sense a consequence of baptism. The regeneration of faith should always go before baptism, and it is vain to look to baptism for it.—[TR.

church without being placed under the Mosaic law. Yet it appears, from the course of the proceedings respecting the Gentile Christians, that the doubts of the stricter Jewish party were not absolutely set at rest by Peter's statement. (See Comm. on chap. xv.) As the narrative of Peter agrees entirely with the account already given, it needs no special explanation.

(In verse 3, διακρίνεσθαι denotes not simply "to be uncertain," as in verse 12, but also "to dispute." It is so used in the Septuagint in Ezek. xx. 35.—In verse 15 it is not necessary, because Peter had already spoken a long time, to understand ἄρξασθαι as a pleonasm, for the word only presupposes the intention of proceeding yet much further.—In ver. 16 there is a reference to chap. i. 5.—Verse 18. On ἄραγε, see Matth. vii. 20, xvii. 26. It must doubtless be distinguished from the interrogative ἀρά γε in Acts viii. 30.—On δοῦναι μετάνοιαν, see Acts v. 31.)

Vers. 19–24.—This first attempt to preach the Gospel to Gentiles was speedily followed by others; and it was in Antioch first, beyond the limits of Palestine, that Greeks were admitted into the church. Kuinoel supposes that this happened in consequence of the intelligence of the conversion of Cornelius, but there is not a word to indicate this. On the contrary, the mission of Barnabas to Antioch makes it more probable, that they had ventured there on their own responsibility to baptize Gentiles. To prevent however the abuses which might possibly in this way creep in, the mother church sent down Barnabas on a visitation. This notice is very important, because it discloses the apostolic conception of the church. The apostles did not allow churches to spring up here and there in a state of isolation, but they connected them all with themselves, and with the living organization which they represented. The church as an organic whole, as the body of the Lord, needs a controlling power, an ecclesiastical government. With respect to the mention made of those who were scattered abroad by the persecution *after* the death of Stephen,* it is not Luke's object here to narrate this circumstance as for the first time; he simply looks back to it, as something that is past (see Comm. on Acts ix. 30), in order to shew that even in Antioch the Gospel was at first preached only to Jews; it was not till the arrival of some men of Cyprus and Cyrene that an alteration took place. Who these men were is not known; perhaps they might be the individuals named in chap. xiii.

* Winer, in his Grammar, p. 374, hesitates whether ἐπί with the dative Στεφάνῳ, in verse 19, should not rather be understood in the sense of *against*. It seems preferable, however, to give it the meaning of *after*. The reading Στεφάνου is a subsequent correction. ['Επί with dative properly "on condition of, on occasion of, regarding." So probably here, "on occasion of Stephen." To render it "*after* Stephen," is harsh. Besides, as the English translator justly observes, the persecution, though it continued after Stephen, commenced before his death.]—[K.

1; at all events they were Jews or proselytes, but in their native country, holding intercourse with honourable Gentiles who had adopted milder views of their position in reference to the Divine economy of grace.

(In verse 19, the phrase *διασπαρέντες ἀπὸ θλίψεως* is best understood with Winer [Gram. p. 356] to mean, "on the occasion of the persecution."—Verse 20. The question here presents itself, whether the reading of the textus receptus Ἑλληνιστάς, or the reading Ἕλληνας, deserves the preference. The greater number of manuscripts certainly support the former reading, but A.D., and several versions and fathers, present Ἕλληνας. Besides, the connexion absolutely requires this reading. The preaching of the Gospel to Hellenists, that is, to Jews who spoke Greek, or to proselytes of the gate, could not at all be brought forward as a new thing, for it had already taken place at the first Pentecost. But Ἑλληνιστής can by no means be employed to denote Gentile or heathen Greeks.—Verse 21. *Χεὶρ κυρίου* corresponds to יַד יְהוָה. See Gesenius under the word יָד.—Verse 22. On *εἰς* or *πρὸς τὸ οὖς ἀκούειν*, see Comm. on Luke i. 44, xii. 3; Matth. x. 27. The words *διελθεῖν ἕως* intimate that Barnabas, even on the way to Antioch, had churches to visit. Verse 23. Πρόθεσις must be understood of "a firm purpose, a resolution of the will," as in 2 Tim. iii. 10.)

Vers. 25, 26.—Barnabas, who appears to have been the first to recognize the importance of Paul to the Christian cause, did not immediately return to Jerusalem, but probably sent a written statement in reference to the commission with which he had been entrusted. He rather set out for Tarsus, brought Paul thence, and remained with him a whole year in Antioch. Through their influence Christianity spread extraordinarily, and it was here first that the name of "Christians," which afterwards became the predominant one, originated. This name proceeded from the Gentiles, and, as the form of it shews, from Romans, to whom the acknowledgment of Christ appeared to be the distinguishing feature of the new sect; they were called Ναζωραῖοι by the Jews, to indicate their despicable origin. (Acts xxiv. 5.) The name certainly did not take its rise among the Christians themselves, because it is not used in the New Testament in a good sense.* (See Acts xxvi. 28; 1 Pet. iv. 14.) In reference to *χρηματίζειν* consult the Comm. at Matth. ii. 12. The meaning of the word here "to give a name," which is very common among profane writers after Polybius and Diodorus, occurs else-

* See Tacitus, Ann. xv. 44, auctor nominis ejus Christus Tiberio imperitante per procuratorem Pontium Pilatum supplicio affectus erat. But at a later period the Christians took the name to themselves, and frequently, as is plain from the Fathers, made use of a play upon the word *χρηστοί*, which, pronounced according to the Itacism, sounds like *χριστιανοί*, to shew that even their name declared they were good people.

where in the New Testament only at Rom. vii. 3. It is used especially where mention is made of giving names or titles of office, according to the radical meaning of the word, "to manage affairs of state."

VER. 27–30.—There is only one circumstance connected with the time of Paul's sojourn in Antioch mentioned by Luke, viz., the arrival of a prophet named Agabus (according to Grotius from עָגַב to love), who foretold that a famine was at hand in Palestine. (See a particular consideration of the nature of the New Testament prophets in Comm. at 1 Cor. xiv.) Since we know that in the fourth year of Claudius Cæsar a famine did prevail in Palestine (three other such calamities befel Greece and Italy under the government of the same Cæsar), we thus obtain, as has already been remarked in the introduction to the Acts of the Apostles, an important chronological datum. According to the reckoning of Hug, which in the main we follow, the fourth year of Claudius coincides with the forty-fifth year after the birth of Christ.* The delegates from Antioch might perhaps reach Jerusalem about the time of Easter, to deliver their gifts of love. (Compare Hemsen's Apostle Paul, p. 50. Note, according to Acts xii. 4 and 23.) From the fact that they delivered these to the presbyters, and not to the apostles, it cannot be concluded that the latter had left the city: the account that follows rather contradicts this conclusion. But we perceive from this circumstance, that the apostles had already completely relinquished the government of the church, and committed it to the hands of the elders. So soon as the apostles began to labour out of the city, although they returned to it again as their head-quarters, it became indispensable to establish a regular government for the church. Yet that the apostles always retained the supreme direction of the whole, is manifestly apparent from Acts xv. 2.

§ 4. PETER'S IMPRISONMENT AND DELIVERANCE. HEROD'S DEATH.

(Acts xii. 1–25.)

During the continuance of Paul and Barnabas in Jerusalem, respecting the length of which† nothing is stated (see chap. xii. 25),

* According to the account of Josephus (Arch. xx. 2, 6, and 5, 2), Queen Helena of Adiabene had corn brought from Eygpt and distributed among the poor, in this famine.

† Bengel (ordo temporum, p. 274) fixed it without any ground, at three years, because he had dated the conversion of Paul so very early. If the interval had been so long, we should certainly have had more accounts of it. (Compare Hemsen's Apostle Paul, p. 51.) Besides, if we suppose, as we must, that the journey of Paul to Jerusalem mentioned in Galat. ii. 1, is not the one here recorded, then it becomes the more probable that the stay on this occasion was only short and unimportant, and therefore was not

there occurred a new persecution of the Christians, in which one of the apostles themselves suffered martyrdom. This is the last narrative in Acts which has reference to Peter, and perhaps Luke recorded it only because Paul was present at the time, and might often therefore have made mention of it. Besides, the contrast between the deliverance of Peter and the terrible death of the persecutor of believers, contained something so striking, that for that reason Luke might suppose he ought not to withhold this occurrence from his readers. Meyer's idea that the things mentioned respecting Peter in what follows, took place during Paul's journey to Jerusalem, and not while he was there, is improbable, because the distance to Antioch was not so considerable. The supposition that Paul may have first visited the other churches of Palestine, and therefore have been very late in reaching Jerusalem, is not favoured by what is said in chap. xi. 30, xii. 1-25.

Vers. 1, 2.—The new persecutions against the Christians proceeded from King Herod Agrippa. After Caligula's death he received from Claudius, who favoured him greatly, the sovereignty over Judea and Samaria (Joseph. Arch. xix. 4). This circumstance enabled him to persecute the Christians in Jerusalem itself, and James the elder, the son of Zebedee, was put to death there. Of the ministry and fortunes of this man nothing further is known; only Clement of Alexandria (in a fragment of his Ὑποτυπώσεις preserved in Eusebius, Hist. Eccl. ii. 9), states that the accuser of James, when he was led to death, agonized by the gnawings of conscience, professed faith himself in the crucified Redeemer, besought the forgiveness of James, received it, and then suffered martyrdom along with him.

Vers. 3-5.—To gratify the people, whose first good will towards the Christians (Acts ii. 47) had speedily changed into hatred, Herod went further, and about the time of the Paschal feast, threw Peter also into prison, probably with the view of exhibiting in his execution a very startling example to the numerous visitors at the feast. Peter was guarded according to the custom of the Romans: four times four soldiers had the charge of him, changing according to the night-watches. Two of these, according to verse 6, kept watch in the prison itself, and two before the door of it. Meanwhile the church prayed fervently to God for the imprisoned apostle. Ἐκτενής is often applied to prayer, as in Luke xxii. 44; Acts xxvi. 7. It expresses the spiritual effort put forth in earnest prayer.

Vers. 6-11.—The account which follows of the deliverance of Peter from imprisonment, illustrates the shorter account of a similar occurrence which is communicated in chap. v. 17, etc.; and it

counted by the apostle in the enumeration of his journeys to Jerusalem. (See a more particular consideration of this point at Gal. ii. 1.)

also readily admits of being compared with the wonderful deliverance of Paul and Silas from imprisonment at Philippi, recorded in chap. xvi. 26, etc. An impartial comparison of these narratives may perhaps leave it uncertain for a moment, whether real visible appearances of angels are meant in them; and this again accounts for the fact, that we find the more recent interpreters adopting very different views of these occurrences. According to Hazel, it was a thunder-storm combined with an earthquake which delivered Peter, and this natural phenomenon was described by him after the Jewish mode of speaking as an angel. According to Eichhorn,* who is followed by Heinrichs, Peter was delivered by Christian friends, or by the keeper of the prison himself, but he did not well know himself to whom he owed his deliverance, and therefore supposed he must ascribe it to a Divine messenger. Kuinoel expresses himself undecidedly; while all the old interpreters understood the angelic appearance in the literal sense. Now with respect to the first view, it is undeniable that natural phenomena of a certain kind are styled angels (comp. Comm. on John v. 4); and there can be no doubt that in chap. xvi. 26, etc., it is an earthquake only that must be thought of, for even the text refers to nothing else; but the representation made in the passage before us does not permit this supposition, because the 7th and 8th verses describe the angel as acting wholly like a person: the like description is never found where natural powers are styled angels. Far more plausible is the other view, which supposes Peter himself not to have known how his deliverance was effected. This idea appears to be favoured by the words in verse 9, οὐκ ᾔδει, ὅτι ἀληθές ἐστι τὸ γινόμενον διὰ τοῦ ἀγγέλου, "*he knew not that it was true*," etc., taken in connexion with verse 11, according to which latter passage Peter first comes to himself in the street, and appears now to conclude that an angel must have delivered him. But these words cannot establish that view, because in the *first* place, it was contrary to the principles of the Christians to deliver either themselves or others from such dangers by fraudulent artifices. But certainly on this view it must be supposed that either the jailor or the soldiers were *bribed* by Peter's deliverer; and should it be said that the jailor himself might be favourably disposed to the apostles, yet not the less would he have violated his duty, if he had let the prisoners escape. *Again*, this view gives no explanation of the unconscious condition of Peter: amid so many occurrences and incidents, he could not fail to overcome the oppression of sleep, and to recognize the friend that was helping him. *Finally*, the fact that the soldiers did not awake, as is plain from verse 18, till the morning, but little accords with this view. They must therefore have been thrown into so profound a slumber by a

* Compare Eichhorn in the "Allgm. Biblioth. der bibl. Literatur. Bd. iii. p. 361," etc.

sleeping-draught, which would make the hypothesis rather complicated; for we are debarred from supposing that they were privy to the transaction by the 19th verse, which informs us that the king caused them to be punished. The only matter therefore which can properly be made a question here, is whether we are to suppose a real angelic appearance or only a vision. Now certainly the occurrence did bear some resemblance to an ecstatic vision, for Peter himself took this view of it for a time (verse 9): but the *reality of the effects* which were connected with it (which in reality is denoted by the expression *ἀληθὲς εἶναι* in vers. 9 and 11) does not permit the supposition of a mere vision (*ὅραμα*), and it was on this very ground that Peter himself came to the conclusion that he had been favoured with an actual visit from an angel. A mere mental vision is never accompanied with physical effects. That he might be uncertain, however, for a moment, whether it was a vision he saw or a real angelic appearance, is to be explained from the fact, that every manifestation from the higher order of existences is attended with a powerful excitement of soul, which produces a state of mind akin to ecstacy. And this may easily render it uncertain whether the whole be something purely internal, or whether there be also something outward: the grand criterion in favour of the latter is the appearance of real visible results.

(Ver. 7.—Some codices, instead of the stronger word *πατάξας*, have the milder *νύξας*. The stronger word, it is probable, appeared to many transcribers not quite suitable to an angel.—Ver. 11. *Προσδοκία* stands for the thing expected, namely, the act of punishment.)

Vers. 12–19.—Peter repaired, after he had assured himself as to the neighbourhood where he was, to the residence of a certain woman Mary, where he knew that the disciples were in the habit of meeting. According to the concurrent view of all interpreters, this Mary was the mother of the Evangelist Mark, who is mentioned here by his full name John Mark. The great precision of the account given of the arrival of Peter furnishes a proof of its coming from original sources; perhaps it was obtained from Mark himself. Finally, there is presented to us here at this early period, an example of assemblies of Christians held during the night: these were probably introduced at first only for the purpose of eluding observation when they met and separated, but afterwards in a securer state they were retained for a length of time, on account of the greater solemnity of nocturnal meetings. Yet it was these meetings which not only gave occasion to the heathen to fabricate many malicious reports, but also in all probability made it easy for the immoral Gnostic parties to practise their excesses. The church therefore acted wisely in forbidding, at a later period, all assemblies during the night.*

* Compare Bingham origg. vol. v. p. 329, seq.

A difficulty is presented in verse 15, in which it is stated that the disciples who were assembled, on being assured by the maid Rhoda that Peter was at the door, exclaim: "It is his angel" (ὁ ἄγγελος αὐτοῦ ἐστιν). We have already, at Matth. xviii. 10, referred to this passage, and intimated that it expresses the idea of guardian angels, who are assigned to each individual person. Some indeed have tried to take the word ἄγγελος here in the sense of messenger, but it is obvious that the connexion is altogether opposed to this idea, because it could not be conceived that Peter should have sent a messenger out of the prison during the night. It might be imagined however that ἄγγελος here, like πνεῦμα in Luke xxiv. 39, bears the signification of "apparition, phantom;" and in this case the disciples might have supposed that the spirit of Peter appeared to them before his approaching death, as if bidding them farewell, or giving them a sure premonition of his decease. But, in the first place, there is no indication in the Bible that such appearances of the soul during the life-time of a man were considered possible; and again, it not only cannot be proved, but it is intrinsically improbable, that ἄγγελος should be used to express this idea. The phrase ἄγγελος αὐτοῦ therefore cannot well be understood otherwise than as meaning "his guardian angel," so that here again we find the idea indicated in Matth. xviii. 10. In the exposition of our Lord's words occurring in that passage, we left it undetermined, whether these guardian angels were to be considered as assigned to each individual person, or as the representatives of certain larger bodies, whole nations for example, or classes. The passage before us plainly favours the former idea, because the Apostle Peter has an angel attributed to himself alone. In this shape the idea was taken up by the church in the first century (compare the treatise of Schmidt referred to at Matth. xviii. 10),* for they assigned to every man not only a good, but also an evil angel. But how far these ideas can be reckoned as belonging to the specific circle of Christian doctrine, is certainly a matter of question, because the exclamation in the text proceeds from persons who cannot be regarded as authorities by us. They were indeed believers, and were under the influence of the Holy Ghost, but it is only to the apostles that we are warranted to ascribe such an influence of the Spirit as excluded all admixture of uncertain and one-sided popular notions. Certainly the popular view of guardian angels here expressed is grounded upon a saying of Christ; but this, as we have seen, is presented in too general a shape for firm doctrinal principle to be derived from it. I feel therefore most inclined, according to the intimation already made in the Comm. at Matth. xviii. 10, to

* Schmidtii historia dogmatis de angelis tutelaribus, in Illgen's Denkschrift. Leips. 1817.

suppose that there is here expressed the thought that there lives in the world of spirit a pre-existing ideal of every individual, to be realized in the course of his development, and that the higher consciousness, which dwells in man here below, stands in vital connexion with kindred phenomena in the spiritual world. In the case where a human conscience resigns itself to the influence of evil, its development in evil will likewise be completed in the kindred existences that correspond to it in the world of evil.*

(Ver. 12.—The word συνιδών is not to be referred to the reviving consciousness of Peter, but to the consideration of what was around him, agreeably to the sense it bears in chap. xiv. 6. Otherwise there would be a manifest tautology between this and ver. 11, where mention has already been made of the return of perfect consciousness.)

In this passage James, the brother of the Lord, is first presented as an important personage in the church at Jerusalem.† He is expressly distinguished in verse 17 from all the other brethren, and to him first information of the occurrence which had taken place is sent. Undoubtedly therefore he already stood forth distinguished as a bishop among the presbyters, as leader of the whole body. The name Episcopus (ἐπίσκοπος) indeed as indicative of the first among the presbyters, may have come into use at a subsequent period, but certainly in all churches of any considerable magnitude the office very early existed, for their affairs must by all means have required a guiding head.‡ (In ver. 19 ἀπαχθῆναι must be understood, like the

* This is a very strange idea. The author does not attempt to furnish any argument in its support, nor is it easy to see where such argument could be found. At the passage in Matthew to which reference is made, he throws out the same idea, though with more hesitation, and describes the angels mentioned as corresponding to Zoroaster's Fervers. These imaginary existences of the Median Reformer were the original archetypes of all rational beings, and particularly of men. They existed before men, but with a view to their existence, and every man has one of them mystically united to himself, his original spiritual double self. Among the Parsees every man sincerely adores his Ferver. The whole is a mere fancy, and Olshausen's idea is no better. It is a needless and groundless mystification. There may not, as he argues, be ground in the words of our Lord, Matth. xviii. 10, for the inference that each individual has a guardian angel; and if, for the reason stated by our author, we are not warranted to regard the words of those who were assembled in the house of Mary as more definitely settling the question, surely the natural inference is that, without assigning individual angels to individual men, we should rest satisfied with the general principle that the angels do take an interest in the affairs of this world? Because the Scriptures only teach the general doctrine of the guardianship of angels, and do not assign particular angels to particular men, are we therefore warranted to jump to the conclusion that every man has an "alter ego," another self, in the world of spirits, growing with his growth, and forming the same habits? The words of our Lord seem to refer to the same truth as the apostle does in Heb. i. 14, Are they not all ministering spirits sent forth to minister to them? etc.—[Tr.

† That no other James than the brother of the Lord is here referred to, is undoubted, because the elder James, the brother of John, was already killed (xii. 2); and the other apostle of this name, the son of Alpheus, receives no further notice in history.

‡ Olshausen here allows that at first bishops and presbyters were the same. And in

Latin "ducere," of being "led away to punishment." By itself it might mean simply being led away to prison; but the preceding *ἀνακρίνας* manifestly shews that Herod had condemned the soldiers upon the spot.)

Vers. 20-25.—In contrast with the miraculous deliverance of Peter, the evangelist now exhibits the appalling fate of the persecutor of the children of God, for he proceeds at once briefly to narrate the circumstances in which the punishment of the Almighty overtook him, and then this account is concluded by a short general statement.*—Luke first mentions (verse 20) a difference that took place between Herod and the inhabitants of Tyre and Sidon; it was this probably, together with the festivities, which brought the king to Cæsarea (Stratonis). The presence of Herod at Cæsarea, for the purpose of attending the sports there, is mentioned also by Josephus (Arch. xix. 7, 2), although he says nothing of any quarrel with the Tyrians and Sidonians. It is probable matters had not proceeded to any open rupture between the parties, but had only gone the length of exasperation on the part of the king. The Romans would certainly not have permitted a war in the immediate neighbourhood of their territories. But even the displeasure of the king was regarded by the inhabitants of the sea-port towns, as so little in accordance with their interest, that they sued for peace by

fact it admits of no doubt, that in the New Testament the two words are applied to the same individuals. See Acts xx. 17 and 28; 1 Tim. iii. 1; Phil. i. 1; Titus i. 5-7. The use of *ἐπίσκοπος* in the singular, to denote the first among the presbyters, arose after the days of the apostles; there is not an instance of it to be found in any apostolic writing. That the office of a bishop, as defined by our author, existed in the primitive church, cannot be proved; and certainly the argument suggested by him that it was indispensable, is devoid of all weight. The name *πρεσβύτεροι* was borrowed from the offices of the Jewish synagogue, and the name *ἐπίσκοποι* was taken from the common stock of the Greek language, in which it denoted individuals entrusted with the management of any business; and the difference between the two names did not lie in their being applied to different office-bearers, but in the fact that the former expressed the dignity of the office, and the latter the nature of its duties. The history of these two words furnishes a striking instance of the capricious changes which language often undergoes: for the word *πρεσβύτεροι*, the more dignified expression, analogous to senators and descriptive of the reverence due to the men, was degraded to denote the lower order of office-bearers, while the word *ἐπίσκοποι*, descriptive of the charge with which the presbyters were entrusted, was elevated to denote an order of men who had charge of the presbyters themselves. From denoting the oversight which the presbyters took of the church, the only idea suggested in the Scriptures, it was perverted to denote the oversight which a class unknown to the Scriptures took of the presbyters. The reference to James in the chapter before us, furnishes no ground for the conclusion Olshausen has drawn; for whatever may be the position which he occupied in the church at Jerusalem, it is to be remembered that he was an apostle, and the question of the authority vested in the apostles is a totally different one from the relations subsisting among the ordinary office-bearers of the church.—[TR.

* Regarding the historical incidents here referred to, consult the excellent remarks of Tholuck in his Glaubw. der evang. Gesch. p. 165, etc.

sending deputies, who secured the good grace of Blastus the king's favourite.

(In ver. 20, θυμομαχεῖν does not denote, as elsewhere, "to fight, to wage war with fury," but "to be exasperated in mind." The word has this sense in Polybius and Plutarch.—'Ο ἐπὶ τοῦ κοιτῶνος = cubicularius, comp. viii. 27.—The words διὰ τὸ τρέφεσθαι κ. τ. λ., point out the ground on which the inhabitants of the maritime and trading towns dreaded the hostility of Herod; they were afraid that he might injure them in their commercial interests.) With respect to the account which follows in verses 21-23, Josephus, in the passage above referred to, describes the occurrence in substantially the same manner. Upon the second day of the public games, the king appeared in splendid attire, and sat down upon his throne (βῆμα). The acclamations which saluted him on the occasion were probably raised by the deputies of the Tyrians and Sidonians, together with their retinue; for the Jews abhorred such proceedings as idolatry. And while the king was witnessing the games, Josephus mentions further, that an owl perched itself over his head upon a rope, which was stretched for the purpose of drawing a screen over the stage as a protection from the sun; the king regarded it as an evil omen, fell sick, and died after five days of a disease of the bowels. The statement of Luke (σκωληκόβρωτος γενόμενος) may be regarded as describing more minutely what is mentioned by Josephus; but that no visible appearance of an angel is indicated by the words, "an angel of the Lord smote him" (ἐπάταξεν αὐτὸν ἄγγελος κυρίου), nor sudden death thus produced, is sufficiently obvious from the connexion of these words with the other phrase, "being eaten by worms" (γενόμενος σκωληκόβρωτος). The angel denotes here merely the invisible Divine influence, which punished the pride of the king, who received with satisfaction the idolatrous reverence, and gave him over to those sufferings which fell upon him. In Acts xiii. 11, the same idea is expressed by the phrase χεὶρ κυρίου, *hand of the Lord*, comp. Comm. on John i. 52, v. 4.—According to verses 24, 25, John Mark joined himself to the deputies of the church of Antioch, who were returning thither from Jerusalem, viz., Barnabas and Saul, and came with them.

§ 5. PAUL'S FIRST MISSIONARY JOURNEY.

(Acts xiii. 1—xiv. 28.)

Although Christianity had already spread from Jerusalem through Palestine, and beyond the limits of Palestine, still the church continued a stranger to formal missionary effort. Casual occurrences had hitherto brought about the diffusion of the Gospel, particularly the persecutions of the faithful in Jerusalem. (Acts viii. 1.) It was from Antioch that teachers were first sent forth, with the definite purpose of spreading Christianity, and organizing churches with regular institutions. (Acts xiv. 23.) These commissioned instructors too maintained a connexion with the church from which they had been deputed; they sent accounts to them of their success; they returned to them after the completion of their journey, and they also doubtless received from them assistance of different kinds.* As Jerusalem had been the central point of missionary effort to the Jewish Christians, so Antioch after this period assumed the like position in reference to the Gentile Christians; the two cities formed the main poles of life in the primitive apostolic church.†

The first missionary journey of Paul extended by way of Cyprus only to some of the south-eastern districts of Asia Minor. It was, as it were, the first timid trial that was hazarded, to carry the Gospel to a distance beyond the limits of the Holy Land. And we can easily imagine that some uncertainty was at first felt as to the success of such journeys. When we consider that a few unlearned and unknown individuals went forth into the wide, heathen world, without any outward help or support, preaching a crucified Son of God, to the Jews a stumbling-block, and to the Greeks foolishness; then indeed nothing appears more natural, than that their labour should remain utterly fruitless, and nothing more wonderful and incredible than that it should produce an effect lasting through centuries. But although such thoughts might intimidate for a moment the Christians of Antioch, yet they soon felt assured that they were only the suggestions of the old man: in the Holy Ghost who filled their hearts, they recognized without doubt a power that could con-

* This circumstance is in the highest degree important; it lets us see that the apostles proceeded upon the principle laid down in Rom. x. 15: "how shall they preach except they be sent." The fact of being thus sent is not to be sought, merely in a subjective inclination, which is ascribed to a supposed movement of the Spirit, but in a regular commission received from the church. Here the church in Antioch sent forth the messengers in an orderly manner; and thus these messengers themselves acquired an objective support, and the new churches became connected with the church universal. Even Paul, although called immediately by the Lord, yet waited for an impulse or invitation from without, that he might enter upon his proper ministry among the Gentiles. From this procedure, important hints may be deduced with respect to missionary undertakings in the present day.

† The Gospel not only in primitive times, but also in the subsequent extension of the church, always fixed itself first in the great cities, and then spread gradually over the country. The greater variety of wants, and the high intellectual activity prevailing among the inhabitants of cities, occasioned Christianity to take root sooner in them. And then in the neighbourhood of great cities there were soon formed, by the influence proceeding from them, churches in the country, and in the smaller cities, which is shewn to have happened in the case of Rome, for example, by Acts xxviii. 13, etc.

quer the world, and, moved by that power, they also accomplished the work.

The form which this narrative wears, renders it highly probable, that it is an extract from a larger account, which was sent perhaps directly to the mother church by the travelling preachers, and which Luke adopted into his narrative just as he had received it. This latter circumstance receives much countenance from the very commencement of the account; for, after the journey of Barnabas and Paul to Antioch has been described, they are mentioned among the other teachers of the church there, as if no one knew of their presence. But the epitomized form of the narrative displays itself in the dissimilarity, which prevails in the statements given of the abode of Paul in different cities: where the original complete accounts furnished nothing interesting, they were either entirely omitted, or abbreviated as much as possible. It needs not to be remarked what authority this supposition imparts even to the *missionary speeches* in the account before us: it is very possible that we have in them the very notations of Paul himself.

Ver. 1.—In the enumeration of distinguished persons collected together at Antioch, the first place is assigned to Barnabas, who enjoyed very great consideration in the old apostolic church, and indeed in the earliest times is always named before Paul: it is only at a later period that he is overshadowed by the great apostle of the Gentiles, and then he disappears from the history. Of the second person, Simeon Niger, nothing more is known: Lucius of Cyrene, on the other hand, is mentioned again in Rom. xvi. 21. The supposition that he is the same person as Luke the Evangelist, has nothing whatever to support it. It is improbable that Luke should have mentioned himself amongst the most distinguished teachers of the church, and besides the name Lucas does not come from Lucius, but from Lucanus. (Comp. Comm. Introd. Sect. vi. Part i. page 147.) The fourth individual, Manaen, is another of whom nothing further is known: his name comes from מְנַחֵם = παράκλητος, for which, in 2 Kings xv. 14, the LXX. have Μαναήμ, but in the verse before us the liquid letters are interchanged so as to make Μαναήν. To mark him out more particularly, it is further stated that he was the foster-brother of Herod the Tetrarch. Σύντροφος = ὁμογάλακτος, denotes one who receives along with another the milk of a mother or nurse, hence naturally, brought up and trained together. The Herod here mentioned, it is obvious from the chronological relations, is Herod Antipas. The last place is assigned to Saul, whose influence had not as yet spread itself very widely.

(The word τινές is wanting in some codices. It was supposed unsuitable to the well-known individuals Barnabas and Paul, who are named along with the others. But for this very reason, the reading must certainly be held as genuine. Our hypothesis, that this narrative is an extract from the original account of the mission, does not appear at first sight to be favoured by the word τινές; for a friend writing to persons who are aware of the circumstances, will not begin thus: ἦσαν δέ τινες κ. τ. λ. But it is self-evident that verses 1–3 are to be viewed as introductory statements, prefixed to the abbreviated account, and they are probably the words of Luke himself: it is in verse 4 that the account itself is first presented to us. On the difference between προφῆται and διδάσκαλοι, consult Comm. on 1 Cor. xii. 28.)

Vers. 2, 3.—While these men were assembled together for prayer, and perhaps for particular conference regarding the work of God entrusted to them, they were guided by the suggestion of the Holy Ghost to the idea of sending forth itinerating preachers (εὐαγγελισταί, Ephes. iv. 11). They prepared themselves for this important work by prayer and fasting, and sent away the missionaries with a formal ordination. Kuinoel here erroneously takes λειτουργεῖν = κηρύττειν, of the public preaching of the Gospel: the fact that such an impulse of the Spirit came upon them, does not comport with this idea. This suggestion rather befits a quiet small circle, where the new and grand idea might be duly weighed. Λειτουργεῖν (see Comm. on Luke i. 23) denotes therefore here, like προσκυνεῖν, absorption in the devout worship of God. In ver. 2, προσκέκλημαι bears a middle signification, as also in chap. xvi. 10, xxv. 12. (See Winer's Gram. p. 239) Here, too, as in the whole ancient church,* we find fasting retained as a good practice: it was a help for gathering in the mind and drawing it away from earthly things. What was false in it, as was shown even in the views of the Montanists, was produced only by the gradual and stealthy introduction of a legal spirit, which converted it into an opus operatum.

Vers. 4–12.—Barnabas and Paul, the chosen messengers of the church, took along with them John Mark,† as a help to them in their apostolic labours. In ver. 5, ὑπηρέτης denotes a less distinguished teacher, who stood to Paul and Barnabas in a relation of dependence, as is shewn too by the gloss ὑπηρετοῦντα αὐτοῖς. (See Comm. on Luke i. 2.) Such ὑπηρέται administered the baptisms (1 Cor. i. 14) and attended to outward concerns, so that the apostles and evangelists (Ephes. iv. 11) might be able to devote themselves en-

* Perhaps even at this period fasting was practised chiefly on Friday, the feria sexta, a custom which was very ancient.

† The words εἶχον δὲ καὶ Ἰωάννην ὑπηρέτην, stand so strangely inserted between what goes before and what follows, that they manifestly appear to be a supplementary remark. Luke probably introduced them into the account that lay before him, because what follows in the fifteenth and succeeding verses rendered it necessary that previous mention should be made of Mark.

tirely to teaching. From this it is plain that a gradation among the teachers of the church is not opposed to the spirit of the Gospel: every organized body, that seeks to develope itself in the visible order of things, must present itself with parts of regular connexion and subordination. And no evil could ever proceed from this arrangement, provided only, as was the case in the apostolic church, that in the higher orders the greater fulness of the Holy Ghost always prevailed.

Barnabas, a Cyprian by birth (chap. iv. 37), was probably the occasion of their going first by Seleucia* to Salamis, which lies on the east side of the island, and thence across the island to Paphos, which lies on the west side of it, where it is known the worship of Venus had a great central establishment. Proceeding upon the principle that the Gospel was designed first of all for the Jews, they always preached first in the synagogues, and only turned to the Gentiles when they found themselves rejected by the Jews. (Comp. ver. 46.) In the chief city, Paphos, the Roman proconsul, Sergius Paulus had his seat, a judicious man (ver. 7), free from Roman superstition, but who had fallen into the toils of a Jewish conjuror, named Barjesus. (In some manuscripts this sorcerer γόης is called also Βαριησουάν or Βαρσοῦμα; perhaps because many transcribers were unwilling to recognize the holy name of Jesus as given to this false prophet. Either this man was a Jew from Arabia, or he had picked up some crumbs of Oriental philosophy: this may be concluded from the circumstance, that he had taken the name of Ἐλύμας, which corresponds to the Arabic עַלִּים, that is, wise man.) The same remarks which were made regarding Simon Magus, at chap. viii. 9, hold good with reference to the spiritual condition of this man. He used his arts for selfish ends, and sought, therefore, to obstruct the work of the Spirit in the soul of the proconsul, that he might hold him fast in his snares, The address of Paul to him is keen, but still the words ἄχρι καιροῦ in verse 11, plainly discover the design of bringing him to the consciousness of his guilt and to true repentance. Such sorcerers were commonly clever notorious men, but the slaves of their own notions, and often guided in their undertakings by sordid desires: Paul therefore endeavours, by stern rebuke, to rescue the good germ that might be in his heart.

(Ver. 10.—Ῥᾳδιουργία occurs nowhere else in the New Testament: it denotes properly "dexterity, quickness in action," then particularly, in a bad sense "daring cleverness in sin." Ver. 11. Ἀχλύς denotes primarily darkness, then a peculiar disease of the eyes. Here the connexion with σκότος shews that the latter signification is to be adopted, the obscuration of sight (σκότος) resulting from an

* Which also bears the name Pieria, and situated at the mouth of the Orontes, is the harbour of Antioch, that lies much further up the river.

affection of the eyes (ἀχλύς). It is worthy of notice that Paul succeeded in gaining over so distinguished an individual as the proconsul: it is not indeed said that Sergius formally attached himself to the church by baptism, but the word ἐπίστευσε points at least to an acknowledgment of Jesus as the Messiah. Now as Saul from this time (ver. 9) is always called Paul, the ancient supposition* that he received this name from his protector, is probable in a high degree. If the apostle had borne two names from the first, and if it were only intimated here, as Heinrichs supposes, that he had one name in common with the proconsul, it would remain unexplained why, in the Acts of the Apostles, and in the Epistles, the name Saul from this time so completely disappears.

Vers. 13–15.—From Cyprus they proceeded to Perga in Pamphylia. Here John Mark left the company, for reasons which cannot have been good, as subsequent events (see at xv. 37, etc.) shew. From Perga, the metropolis of Pamphylia, they went far into the interior to Antioch in Pisidia, upon the borders of Phrygia. Here Paul and Barnabas on the Sabbath-day entered into the synagogue and sat down, and were invited, as was customary (see Comm. on Luke iv. 16), to deliver an address.

Vers. 16–22.—The beginning of the discourse, which Paul, in consequence of this invitation delivered, and in which he expressly (ver. 17) distinguishes between Israelites and proselytes, bears a resemblance to that of Stephen, which is contained in chap. vii.: it embraces a brief review of the history of the people, and of God's gracious dealings with them. The Jew listens (then as now) to nothing more readily than to the narrative of Jehovah's dealings with his people; such a historical recapitulation therefore formed a natural captatio benevolentiæ.†

(Ver. 17.—The connexion of ὕψουν with the παροικία in Egypt [see chap. vii. 6] sets aside the idea of exaltation and elevation, for the people were oppressed; rather the signification to be adopted here is "increase of numbers," which embraces indirectly the idea of elevation. This is decisively favoured by Sirach xliv. 21, where ἀνυψῶσαι is used as parallel with πληθῦναι: less appropriate is the

* See Jerome de viris illus. sub voce Paulus. The father says: apostolus a primo ecclesiæ spolio Proconsule Sergio Paulo Victoriæ suæ trophæa retulit, erexitque vexillum, ut Paulus ex Saulo vocaretur. Augustine gives a singular view of the apostle's design in choosing the name Paul in the passage: de spir. et litt. c. 7. Paulus apostolus, cum Saulus prius vocaretur, non ob aliud, quantum mihi videtur, hoc nomen elegit, nisi ut se ostenderet parvum, tanquam minimum apostolorum. (1 Cor. xv. 9.)

† From the resemblance of this first speech of Paul to that of Stephen, one might perhaps conclude that there was an effect produced by Stephen upon the character of the apostle. According to chap. vi. 13, 14, we already see in Stephen a very expanded view of the Gospel and of the effects which it would produce, and it is in the highest degree probable that, much as Paul might at first struggle against his view, it yet afterwards exerted a very important influence upon him.

reference to Sirach l. 22, where *ὑψοῦν ἡμέρας* does not mean "to increase the number of days," but to "make respectable and important in life." The expression *μετὰ βραχίονος ὑψηλοῦ* corresponds to the Hebrew בִּזְרוֹעַ נְטוּיָה in Exod. vi. 6, that is with an arm raised up high and ready to help.—In verse 18 the reading *ἐτροφοφόρησεν* is to be preferred to the usual reading *ἐτροποφόρησεν*. This latter, indeed, gives also a sense not unsuitable, *τροποφορεῖν*, denoting "to bear with the manners and ways of any one" (Cic. ad Attic. xiii. 29); but as Paul designs here to exhibit the gracious aspect of God's dealings, this idea does not strictly harmonize with the connexion. Again, too, *τροφοφορεῖν* is the rarer word, and transcribers might readily substitute for it one better known. It denotes "to carry in the arms like a nurse" (*τρόφος*), hence "to cherish, to take care of." Thus the word is used in 2 Maccab. vii. 27, of a mother who is speaking to her son. In a wider sense, too, it is applied to men, as in the Septuagint, Deut. i. 31.—Ver. 19. Regarding the seven nations, see Deut. vii. 1.—Instead of *κατεκληροδότησεν* contained in the textus receptus, and not found elsewhere in the New Testament, Griesbach has rightly preferred the reading *κατεκληρονόμησεν*. The use of this word with a Hiphil signification, "to cause to possess, to give into one's possession," as in Judges xi. 24, might have escaped many transcribers, and they might therefore suppose themselves obliged to prefer that other form.—Ver. 20. The number of 450 years down to Samuel appears to stand in contradiction to 1 Kings, vi. 1, where 480 years are counted to the building of the Temple. Interpreters have employed the most violent measures to remove the contradiction, either declaring the passage before us or the one in the Old Testament to be interpolated, or altering the number, or supposing that the time is not counted when the Israelites were subject to foreign nations, in the days of the Judges. Others again have supposed that Paul follows a traditional chronology, which they suppose also to be found in Josephus [Arch. viii. 3, 1, Bell. Jud. iv. 9, 7]. But this writer is not consistent with himself, and gives in other passages [Arch. xx. 10, cont. Apion. ii. 2] quite different chronologica. The difficulty cannot indeed be completely solved, and therefore the supposition, that either here or in 1 Kings vi. 1, there may be something wrong in the numbers, is not altogether without plausibility:* still this is a violent remedy. The following may contribute towards a solution. It is not Paul's design here to make exact chronological statements, he gives them only by the way. They are therefore wanting in reference to the period from Abraham till the departure out of Egypt, of the leadership of Joshua, and again of the reign of David. Besides, the *ὡς* indicates that 450 is a round number. To this add, that while the accusative

* See Winer's Lex. under the word Zahlen.

is employed in stating the other numbers mentioned in the passage, the dative is used for the number 450. Now, according to more exact Greek usage [see Bernardy's Syntax, p. 116, Kühner's Gr. B. ii. p. 218, etc.], the dative denotes not the duration of time, but the time in which something has resulted or ensued; the words might therefore mean: after that, God, in the space of 450 years, gave Judges till Samuel, and then (from Samuel, viz.) Saul during forty years, and so on; so that these forty years, and what follows till the building of the Temple, were included in the 450 years. This latter view has been communicated to me by my worthy friend, Dr. Hofmann, assistant teacher. It by no means altogether satisfies me, because the expressions, μετὰ ταῦτα and κακεῖθεν, appear to fix the limit of the 450 years, a quo and ad quem; and it is a question whether the usage of the dative, in reference to the fixing of dates, be so constantly observed in the New Testament [comp. Winer's Gram. p. 194]. The view, however, is worthy of consideration. [Consult the article, Köster on the chronology of the Old Testament, in the first part of Pelt's Theol. Mitarbeiten.]—Ver. 21. Regarding the duration of Saul's reign, the Old Testament is silent; but Josephus sets it down also at forty years. [Arch. vi. 14, 9.]—Verse 22. The phrase, μεταστήσας αὐτόν, *removing him*, refers to Saul's death, but at the same time it indicates the fact, that his death was the consequence and expression of God's rejection of him. The quotation is taken partly from Ps. lxxxix. 20, and partly from 1 Sam. xiii. 14, and is given freely from memory.)

Vers. 23–31.—The speech of Paul mentions the fulfilment of prophecies, in the sending of Christ and his forerunner John the Baptist. To Jews and proselytes (verse 26) Jesus is proclaimed as the promised Messiah.—(In verse 23, the reading σωτηρίαν is indeed the more difficult, but Kuinoel is wrong in allowing himself to be led by this consideration to prefer it, for then the name is entirely wanting of him, who in the sequel is always treated as the Messiah, an omission which the context does not at all warrant. Mill's supposition, that the abbreviated mode of writing ΣΡΑΙΝ, for σωτῆρα Ἰησοῦν, gave origin to the reading σωτηρίαν, is more than probable.—Verse 24. The words πρὸ προσώπου do not, according to ordinary usage, refer to the person, but to a fact, viz., the εἴσοδος of Christ; the original idea consequently expressed in the phrase has quite disappeared. Further, the mention of the Baptist's preaching leaves no doubt as to the fact, that εἴσοδος does not refer to the birth of the Redeemer, but to the commencement of his public ministry.—Verse 25. Kuinoel is right in stating that the words, ὡς ἐπλήρου τὸν δρόμον, do not refer to the completion or ending of John's ministry, but to its *continuance;* otherwise, the aorist must have been employed. Regarding the words of the Baptist, see Comm.

on Matth. iii. 11.—Verse 27. On τοῦτον ἀγνοήσαντες, see at Acts iii. 17. We need not, with Kuinoel and Heinrichs, supply αὐτόν to κρίναντες ἐπλήρωσαν; the participle rather stands for ἐν τῇ κρίσει, "in their decision they fulfilled, without knowing it, the Scriptures." Ver. 31. On ἐπί with the accusative in statements of time, see Winer's Grammar, p. 385.)

Vers. 32, 33.—The exhibition of Jesus of Nazareth as the Messiah, is now with the utmost propriety followed by proof adduced from passages of the Old Testament.—(Ver. 33. Ἐκπληρόω is found only here, but the substantive ἐκπλήρωσις occurs in Acts xxi. 26. The preposition augments the force of the simple word. The participle ἀναστήσας is not to be referred to the resurrection of our Lord, as ἐκ νεκρῶν is wanting (compare verse 34), and the proof passage for the resurrection is first brought forward in verse 34; but according to the analogy of the Hebrew הֵקִים or הוֹצִיא, it must be understood in general of the sending of Jesus. The quotation is manifestly from Psalm ii. 7. It is remarkable, therefore, that the reading, which critical grounds require to be preferred, is ἐν τῷ πρώτῳ ψαλμῷ. This is to be accounted for on the principle, that the first Psalm forms merely a general introduction to the whole collection, and that our second Psalm is properly the first in order. Even in Hebrew codices we find our second Psalm marked as the first. [See Rosenmülleri scholia in Psalm. edit. sec. Vol. i., p. 31, 32.] With reference to the Psalm itself, see the particulars at Acts iv. 25, 26; and with reference to the doctrinal import of the words here adduced from it, see Comm. on Acts ii. 29.)

Ver. 34–36.—That something new is now brought forward, and that therefore verses 32, 33 cannot have referred to the resurrection of Jesus, is plain from the words ὅτι δὲ—οὕτως εἴρηκε. The point of advancement cannot be sought in the words μηκέτι μέλλοντα κ. τ. λ., for they only describe a subordinate thought, illustrative of the leading idea of the resurrection. In confirmation of the resurrection of Jesus, as a fact predicted by the prophets, the apostle refers first to the passage in Isaiah lv. 3, of which the leading words τὰ ὅσια Δαβὶδ τὰ πιστά are taken from the Septuagint; the words ὅτι δώσω ὑμῖν are only added by Paul to bring the passage into connexion, because the words of the Septuagint διαθήσομαι ὑμῖν διαθήκην αἰώνιον represent the appearance of the Messiah as something future. The Messianic reference of the passage cited admits of no doubt, because the words חַסְדֵי דָוִד can only denote the promises of the Messiah given to David, whose certain fulfilment is declared. But the question presents itself, how could Paul employ these words to prove the resurrection? Undoubtedly the words have no direct reference to this fact, but indirectly they presuppose it, for since an eternal kingdom was promised to David, the ruler of this kingdom could not remain under the power of death. To strengthen, however, the indefinite prediction by means of a more definite one, the apostle adduces another passage, Ps. xvi. 10, which has already been considered at chap. ii. 27, where Peter gives the very same explanation of it as Paul does here, for they both deny the possibility of its proper reference to David.

(In ver. 34, there are verbal allusions to the second quotation in ver. 35, for *ὑποστρέφειν εἰς διαφθοράν* corresponds to *ἰδεῖν διαφθοράν*, and *δώσω ὅσια* to *οὐ δώσεις ὅσιον*.—Μηκέτι by no means requires to be taken for *μή*: I understand the passage with Winer, Gram., p. 498, thus: "he will no more be laid in the grave, and in this way be given over to corruption." The particle refers only to that portion of the meaning of the verb which had already actually been realized, viz., the being laid in the grave.* The one phrase therefore, *ὑποστρέφειν εἰς διαφθοράν*, distinguishes itself from the other *ἰδεῖν διαφθοράν* in this manner, that the latter denotes corruption and the actual experience of it, the former the fact of being exposed to it. The one of these really happened to the Redeemer, the other not.—Ver. 36. *Γενεά* is equivalent to דּוֹר "lifetime," and the whole phrase *ὑπηρετεῖν τῇ βουλῇ τοῦ Θεοῦ* represents David in his higher position as an instrument of Divine grace for founding the kingdom of God. The words *προσετέθη πρὸς τοὺς πατέρας αὐτοῦ* correspond to the well-known formula נֶאֱסַף אֶל אֲבוֹתָיו, and denote his reception into the happy portion of Hades.)

Vers. 37-41.—It appears remarkable to the Christian consciousness of the church in latter times, that here the Apostle Paul, as Peter too had done in the speeches of the first half of Acts, lays stress upon the resurrection only, and not upon the death of our Lord. Nay, here as it seems, Paul connects the remission of sins immediately with the resurrection, while yet in his letters he represents the death of Christ as the source of the forgiveness of sins. But the mode of instruction pursued by the apostles in this respect will be fully accounted for, when it is considered that in the missionary discourses by which men were first to be convinced of the Messiahship of Christ, they could not aim at a minute development of the principles of the Gospel: it was of more importance first to establish the conviction that Jesus was the Messiah. But the death of Christ was a point that gave offence, and required to be thrown into the background; while, on the other hand, the resurrection

* I think it however still better (in accordance with a common use of *μηκέτι* and *οὐκέτι* both in the classics and in the New Testament), to take the clause with *μηκέτι* in the following way, "he raised him up from the dead, being no longer about to see corruption," *as he would have done had he not been thus raised.* The *μηκέτι* thus marks not that which has occurred and will occur no more, but that which *would have occurred*, but which, under the circumstances described, is no more to be apprehended. Hence its logical use. See Rom. vii. 17.—[K.

contained the proper power of proof, and to it therefore reference was mainly made. But Paul did not write his Epistles to unbelievers, for the purpose of guiding them to the truth, but to believers for the purpose of confirming them in the faith; and in them therefore the proper relation of the death of Christ to God's plan of salvation required to be definitely exhibited. The same object of confirming in the faith, Paul had in view also in the discourse which he addressed to the Ephesian elders, who of course were already believers, and we notice accordingly that in it too (see chap. xx. 28) the significance of the death of Christ is clearly displayed. Further, in verses 38 and 39 the grand idea characteristic of Paul, regarding the unfitness of the law to guide to true righteousness (*δικαιοσύνη*), is set forth in such a manner, as to confirm most powerfully the genuineness of the speech.

And now the joyous proclamation of grace is followed in the end of the discourse with an earnest warning, not to disregard through unbelief the invitation of God. The apostle utters this warning, in words which are cited by memory from Habak. i. 5.—In ver. 39 the connexion of *δικαιωθῆναι* with *ἀπὸ πάντων* sc. *ἁμαρτημάτων*, denotes the union of the negative and positive aspects in the work of redemption,* because not merely is the old removed, but something new is also created in the mind. (Comp. Rom. vi. 7.)—In ver. 40, the plural *ἐν τοῖς προφήταις* indicates, as in Matth. ii. 23, that Paul did not so much design to quote a particular passage, as to express in words of the Old Testament a thought of frequent recurrence in the prophets.—*Ἀφανίζεσθαι* combines, like שָׁמֵם, the two significations of "destruction or removal out of the way," and the "being thrown into astonishment or terror," and the bond of union between the two significations is to be found in the physical effect of terror, by which the consciousness of the individual is for the moment as it were taken away.

Vers. 42-44.—And now the power of the Spirit, who spoke through Paul, first laid hold of the minds of the hearers: and they besought him to speak again in the synagogue. (In ver. 42 the codices vary so much in their readings, that we see how Kuinoel was led to regard the whole verse as a gloss. This supposition, however, cannot well be maintained, because the request to speak

* Neander (ap. Zeitalt. s. 136, Note) is right in observing that the expression *δικαιωθῆναι ἀπὸ πάντων* is not to be understood as if Paul supposed two justifications, an imperfect one under the Old Dispensation, and a perfect one under the New. The expression is rather to be regarded simply as an explanation of the *ἄφεσις ἁμαρτιῶν*. As under the Old Testament no true forgiveness had place, but only the hope of forgiveness was awakened by the hope of a coming Saviour; so the law too could produce no true righteousness. But the real blessing was bestowed by the Gospel, and therefore men received in it everything, which the Old Testament could only offer prefiguratively (Heb. ix. 1, etc.)

on the next Sabbath stands in connexion with verse 44. I prefer therefore, with Griesbach, the shortest reading, which supplies "Jews" as the subjective or nominative to παρεκαλουν. They first became hostile, it is plain from the 45th verse, when they saw the throng of Gentiles. The circumstance that Paul and Barnabas appear to have departed before the meeting was ended, is easily explained by the consideration, that the ἐξιόντων αὐτῶν is not placed historically before the phrase λυθείσης δὲ τῆς συναγωγῆς, but is only anticipated as being the occasion of the leading circumstance in the narrative, viz., the request that they would appear again.—Μεταξύ occurs here, as elsewhere too in the later Greek [see Passow in Lex.], in the sense of μετέπειτα. [Comp. Plut. inst. lac. c. 42. Joseph. Bell. Jud. v. 4. 2.] Here the word is sufficiently explained by the parallel ἐχόμενος in verse 44. See on this word Comm. at Mark i. 38; Luke xiii. 33.)

Vers. 45–49.—The perception of the heart-felt interest taken by the Gentiles in the Gospel of Christ awakens the envy of the Jews, who in their narrowness wished to restrict to themselves the blessings of the Messiah. They begin therefore openly to contradict and revile Paul, which obliges him to withdraw himself entirely from them.—(Ver. 45. In the best codices, particularly A.B.F., the participle ἀντιλέγοντες is omitted on account of the foregoing ἀντέλεγον. But unless we suppose this word to have originally belonged to the text, it is inexplicable how it should have been added: it is better therefore to view the phrase ἀντιλέγοντες ἀντέλεγον as emphatic: "they contradicted vehemently," as in 1 Sam. vi. 12.—Ver. 47. Paul shews, from Isaiah xlix. 6, that there was nothing arbitrary in the calling of the Gentiles, or at all opposed to the plans of God, but that it was an event already predicted by the prophets. The words are addressed to the "servant of God," the personage with whom the predictions of the second part of Isaiah are connected: on the reference of this designation to the Messiah, we have already spoken at chap. iii. 13. The citation finally is given in the words of the Septuagint, yet with an omission and slight change, for in the Septuagint the first words run thus: ἰδοὺ, δέδωκά σε εἰς διαθήκην γένους, εἰς φῶς ἐθνῶν.—Ver. 48. In the words ὅσοι ἦσαν τεταγμένοι εἰς ζωὴν αἰώνιον, we must recognize the idea which pervades the whole Scriptures, of a prædestinatio sanctorum. The attempts which have been made to evade this idea are in the highest degree forced, for example the connecting of ἐπίστευσαν with εἰς ζωὴν αἰώνιον. Regarding the relation of the prædestinatio sanctorum to the gratia irresistibilis, and to the reprobatio impiorum, compare Comm. at Rom. ix.—In ver. 49, the words δι' ὅλης τῆς χώρας probably indicate the diffusion of the Gospel in the villages and over the country, of which few traces are found elsewhere in the New Testament.)

Vers. 50–52.—The envious Jews meanwhile rested not until, by their influence, they had driven away the heralds of peace. Their influence exerted itself particularly upon honourable women, who were attached to Judaism. We find that in the apostolic age the female sex were peculiarly disposed to receive the better elements of the Jewish system, partly without doubt on account of their more susceptible nature, and partly also because they could attach themselves entirely to the economy of the Old Testament without the troublesome rite of circumcision.

(Vers. 51.—On the symbolic act of shaking off the dust, see at Matth. x. 14.—Iconium lay on the borders of Lycaonia, Phrygia, and Pisidia, and therefore it might be sometimes assigned to the one province and sometimes to the other, the more especially as the boundaries of particular districts in Asia Minor were very variable.—Vers. 52. On the joy of the disciples, that is, of the new converts, notwithstanding the removal of their faithful teachers, which would in the first instance tend to excite their sorrow, see v. 41.)

Chap. xiv. 1–7.—After this detailed account of the labours of Paul at Antioch in Pisidia, Luke subjoins only brief notices of his further labours, partly because, from the nature of the case, his discourses must have embraced nearly the same topics, and partly because the consequences that resulted assumed quite a similar shape. In Iconium also the influence of the doctrine of the cross displayed itself as a powerful leaven; but here too the envious feeling of the Jews took offence at the calling of the Gentiles, and drove the apostles onwards to Lystra and Derbe. (Ver. 1, the phrase *κατὰ τὸ αὐτό* can be taken in no other than the usual meaning of "at the same time," "together."—Ver. 2. On *κακόω*, see at chap. vii. 6. Here it is used in the sense of exacerbare, "to excite, to inflame." It frequently bears the same signification in Josephus. [See Arch. xvi. 1, 2.]—In ver. 3, the signs and wonders are represented as quite independent of the power of him, through whose instrumentality they are wrought: the glorified Redeemer is called their author.—Ver. 6. The name Lystra is employed sometimes as a feminine noun, and sometimes as a neuter plural, as in verse 8.)

Vers. 8–12.—In Lystra (on the borders of Lycaonia and Isauria), the cure of a lame man performed by Paul excited great attention, and gave rise to a singular scene which Luke minutely describes. The Gentiles recognized the presence of supernatural powers in the work of the strangers, who had come to their city; but swayed by their mythological notions, they regarded Paul and Barnabas as Mercury and Jupiter, come down again to visit men, as once they had visited Philemon and Baucis, who had lived in those very regions, and they wished to offer sacrifice to them. This occurrence is interesting, particularly because it shews, that faith in the old doctrine of the gods was still more deeply rooted in the popular mind, than one would have been disposed to imagine. At the same time, it must not be overlooked that this occurrence took place in a remote town, to which the philosophical illumination of the age of Augustus had not yet penetrated. And here the question presents itself, whether the unsophisticated simple faith reposed by the inhabitants of Lystra in the old divinities, made them more disposed to receive the Gospel, than if they had broken loose from ancient notions? When this latter state was connected with an earnest longing after the true knowledge of God, then certainly it was more favourable to the reception of the Gospel, but it was generally accompanied with a complete despair of all truth; and compared with this unhappy position, the state of the people of Lystra undoubtedly deserves the preference. The idea of the influence of a higher world of spirit upon this lower world, was still current among them; and from this they might the more easily be guided to the one true God, the beams of whose glory they reverenced in their numerous divinities.

(In ver. 11, mention is made of the speech of Lycaonia. Jablonski, in a treatise contained in the collection of his dissertations by te Water, has rendered it probable that this was only a corrupted Greek dialect.—Ver. 12 shews plainly that Paul possessed the gift of oral address in a high degree: he always took the lead in speaking on missionary journeys. In ver. 13, the words, Ζεὺς ὁ πρὸ τῆς πόλεως ὤν, *Jupiter, who was* BEFORE *the city*, lead to the conclusion that there was a temple of Jupiter also in the city. The peculiar form of expression here exhibited, is to be explained on the principle, that according to the rude popular notion, the image was really taken for the God; a supplying of ἱερόν or ναός is quite inadmissible, as it would require the repetition of the article. Among the ancients, the πρόπυλος, or God dwelling in the suburbs, is often distinguished from the πολιοῦχος, or God protecting the city itself. The covering of the gates with garlands has respect to the residence of the two apostles.)

Vers. 13-20.—Paul and Barnabas were naturally confounded at these tokens of reverence, and attempted to raise the heathens from the natural powers which they worshipped in their divinities, to the one Creator of nature and of all its powers. They succeeded in restraining the men from their purpose, but the malignant Jews of Antioch and Iconium wrought against the apostles, and contrived speedily to estrange from them the fickle multitude.—(In ver. 14, the textus receptus reads εἰσεπήδησαν, but Griesbach has adopted the more difficult and rare reading, ἐξεπήδησαν: the view to be formed of the scene is this, that the multitude surround the dwelling of the apostles, and the apostles rush forth from it into the midst of them. In ver. 15, Paul places the living God Θεὸς ζῶν = אֵל חַי, as the wonder-working Creator, in contrast with the impotent [ματαίοις] idols, and himself upon a level with all other men. Ὁμοιοπαθής occurs also in James v. 17, in the same signification, "subject to like sufferings, to like infirmity."

Vers. 16 and 17, embrace thoughts of great dogmatic importance, which however are to receive further consideration in Acts xvii. 27, 28, and especially in Rom. i. 19, 20, ii. 14, iii. 25. In the first place, Paul contrasts the present time, as the time of the Messiah, with former times, in which the heathen world, with no such light as the Jewish nation possessed, lived on in their own ways. In this thought is to be found the apology for the design of the people of Lystra, so blasphemous considered in itself. But again this situation of the Gentile world was not sufficient to free them altogether from guilt; for nature herself, with all the wonderful arrangements which she exhibits, furnished the means of rising to the idea of the true God, who summoned the whole fabric into being. This declaration of the 17th verse is worthy of notice, not only because it embraces the elements of the argument upon which Natural Theology rests, but also particularly, because it suggests the idea, so important with reference to the biblical view of man, that fallen human nature is not absolutely dead to every higher feeling, a thought which stands in close connexion with the whole circle of Paul's ideas. It need scarcely however be mentioned, that those persons err egregiously, who employ this and the parallel passages cited above, for the purpose of proving the sufficiency of man's own powers. Here too truth lies in the middle. Finally, the words ἀμάρτυρος and καρποφόρος are not found elsewhere in the New Testament.)

Vers. 21–28.—Without communicating any particulars regarding the stay of Paul in Derbe, Luke only informs us of the journey back, which lay through the same places that the apostles had formerly visited. His second appearance among the churches was employed in confirming the disciples in the faith, and he also ordained elders over them, and settled, as such ordination implied, their ecclesiastical arrangements. The expresssion in verse 23 is a peculiar one, χειροτονήσαντες αὐτοῖς πρεσβυτέρους, *electing for them elders*. It does not permit us to suppose there was a free choice on the part of the church, but intimates that the apostles themselves sought out the parties qualified for office. The general mind might not yet be so much developed, that the business of choosing could be committed to the young churches themselves. Often too the number of those from amongst whom a choice could be made, might be so small, that the persons were apparent at a glance, to whom alone offices in the church could be entrusted.

At last the travelling messengers of Christ returned by Attalea in Pamphylia to the mother church at Antioch, and presented a report of their proceedings. They regarded themselves therefore as dependent upon the church in Antioch, an important intimation, from which it may be concluded, that a loose and isolated itinerancy of detached individuals for the preaching of the Gospel is not proper. The individual messenger, extraordinary cases excepted, must always retain his connexion with the church universal, and therefore must belong to some particular Christian community. The time the apostles remained in Antioch, is only described in very general terms as not short, *οὐκ ὀλίγον*, ver. 28. It is common to regard the afflictions (*θλίψεις*, ver. 22), for which Paul prepares the brethren, as referring only to the persecutions with which the primitive church had to contend. But the words of the apostle hold good in reference to Christians of all times. (See Matth. v. 11.) For in the Gospel itself, and in the spirit which it inspires, there is an element opposed to the world, and tending to excite its opposition. The world feels that in this power lies its death, and therefore it makes resistance against it, and seeks to kill the life. It is only the forms of afflictions therefore that change; they themselves touch every believer more or less, but in the hand of God they form a process of training for eternal life. 2 Tim. iii. 12.—Ver. 27. Regarding *θύρα τῆς πίστεως*, see 1 Cor. xvi. 9; Colos. iv. 3.

§ 6. The Apostolic Council.

(Acts xv. 1–35.)

The transaction which follows is one of the most remarkable communications to be found in the Acts of the Apostles, although Luke by no means mentions everything of importance that occurred during this visit of Paul to Jerusalem: his account must be supplemented from what is stated in Gal. ii. 1-10. (See at that passage.)

And in the first place, as respects the outward *form* of the transaction, this section exhibits the first example of a regular and public consultation regarding a subject that affected the whole church.* As the result too of the deliberations was communicated in a letter to all individual churches, the application to this assembly of the name of the *first council* is really not unsuitable. The practice of dealing

* The transactions which are mentioned in chap. xi. 1, etc., have more the form of a private conference, than of an official public consultation.

with controverted subjects by means of synods, is deeply grounded in the nature of Christianity: there is displayed in it that spirit of fellowship (κοινωνία), which regards everything single and individual as belonging to the whole body. This first council, however, does not appear to have been composed of deputies from all particular churches, but the mother church of Jerusalem still stands forth as predominant. Yet it is not by any means to be regarded as an assembly of one church, but the presbyters of this church rather bear in the apostolic college, to which they are subordinate, a relation to the whole church. (Chap. xv. 2, 4, 6, 22.) Whether all the apostles who were yet alive, or only some of them, were collected together on this occasion, is not expressly mentioned; but it is the more probable view, that they were all present.* For, as the messengers who were sent from the church at Antioch, returned from time to time to that church, so it is probable that the apostles, journeying from place to place, would occasionally visit the mother church at Jerusalem, partly to give an account of the success of their labours, and partly to receive spiritual refreshment from renewed intercourse with the brethren. If we take this view of the circumstance, then it becomes apparent that Jerusalem would be the heart, as it were, of the body of the church, from which all life streamed out, and to which it again flowed back. *James*, therefore, the bishop of Jerusalem, must necessarily have been of great importance in the church, because, altogether irrespectively of his spiritual worth, his position made him as it were the fixed central point of the church.

And as the form of the transactions here described is highly important, so also is their *substance*. They have respect to the point, which had already at an earlier period come under consideration, of the conditions under which the Gentiles should be received into the church. (See chap. x. xi. 1–18.) At that time all had been convinced of the propriety of Peter's conduct (chap. xi. 18); with many however there must have been doubts remaining, which gradually forced themselves again into notice, and even assumed the form of a fixed conviction of the opposite. We find this different view represented by certain presbyters of Jerusalem (chap. xv. 4, 5, 7), who had formerly belonged to the sect of the Pharisees. These men, on account of the importance which they attached to the legal forms, must have been very suspicious of a principle, whose prevalence, it might be foreseen, would one day bring the law into utter disuse; they held themselves therefore obliged, only to permit such

* From the circumstance that of the apostles only John and Peter are named in Gal. ii. 9, it cannot be concluded that Paul met only these two in Jerusalem: it is not his purpose in this passage to mention all who were present, but only the leading men in the apostolic college.

a reception of the Gentiles into the church, as was consistent with maintaining the divinity and perpetual obligation of the Mosaic law even in its outward forms. It has already been remarked, that this opinion of the strict Jewish Christians is more plausible than in our times we are disposed to imagine, a circumstance which accounts for the numerous and obstinately conducted controversies that existed in the primitive church regarding this point. When the divinity of the Old Testament is more or less doubted, as it so commonly is in our day, so that even many believing men entertain very subordinate views of this portion of God's word, it is very easy to dispose of the question regarding the relation of the Gentiles to the law; but when we proceed upon the Divine original of the Old Testament, and consider the strong declarations which it makes regarding the perpetual obligation of its ordinances, and the curses which it pronounces upon those who disregard them, and when we take into consideration the declarations of Christ himself, for example, in Matthew v. 11, apparently to the very same effect; we then can readily comprehend, how persons of a somewhat anxious and timid disposition might not be able to soar up to the free spiritual view of the law, which Paul, with all the might of the Spirit vindicated, and which assigns perpetuity not to the outward form of the ordinances of the law, but only to the ideas wrapt up in these coverings, which receive their absolute fulfilment in the Gospel, and are therefore not lost although the external forms perish.

This position of circumstances we see that the apostles with great wisdom consider. They are very far from dismissing, as obstinate opposers of the truth, the rigid Jewish Christians with their scruples; they rather recognize these scruples up to a certain point; but still they cannot deviate from the practice already introduced, of admitting the Gentiles into the church without circumcision, and the burden of the law; they therefore strike upon the middle way of satisfying the one party by some concessions, while yet they do not discourage the Gentiles by too burdensome requirements. But although up to this period the rigid Jewish Christians must appear to us less worthy of blame, yet their position became essentially changed *after* the decrees adopted by the apostles. Those who even after this still maintained, in opposition to the mind of the apostles and elders, their former view of the necessity of the Gentiles observing the whole law, betrayed a wilfulness and regard for their own opinion, which were manifestly sinful, and which became more and more censurable the longer they were clung to.

It was from this party, who occasioned so many conflicts to the Apostle Paul, that the sect of the Ebionites took its rise. The one error, by which they were separated from the living body of the church, speedily gave rise to another, viz., the vulgar Jewish view of the Messiah as merely a distinguished man, by the maintenance of which they removed themselves entirely from really Christian ground. Fortunately however during the lifetime of the apostles, this party had no defenders of any note. James, indeed, the brother of the Lord, and bishop of Jerusalem, together with the greater part of the apostles who remained in Palestine, observed for themselves, like the Nazarenes of a later period, the law according to the manner of their fathers, but without wishing to impose it upon the Gentiles. It has been falsely inferred from Gal. ii. 12, that James himself might be the head of this party of rigid Jewish Christians. The parties there mentioned, τινὲς ἀπὸ Ἰακώβου, *certain ones from James*, are not to be regarded as messengers and legates deputed by the bishop, but only as members of his church, who without and against his will had stirred up disturbance in Antioch; and accordingly the expression corresponds entirely to the words in the apostolic epistle (chap. xv. 24) τινὲς ἐξ ἡμῶν, *certain ones from us*, who assuredly could have no commission, since the apostles altogether disavow them. Still, however, it remains a remarkable fact, that these wrong-headed Jewish Christians were able to exercise such an influence over Peter and Barnabas, as Paul mentions in Gal. ii. 11, etc., after the question had been so decidedly settled in their experience. It has been imagined that this strange circumstance might be explained, by supposing the Epistle to the Galatians to have been written before the Apostolic Council; but, in the first place, chronology is too decidedly opposed to this supposition, for Paul, at the time of his first journey, had not yet visited Galatia, and again, even if it could be made probable that the Epistle to the Galatians was written so early, it would be of no avail to the main point under consideration. For surely in the case of Peter, what occurred with Cornelius, recorded in the tenth chapter, and undoubtedly prior to Paul's writing to the Galatians, was decisive; and the question accordingly presents itself, how it is conceivable that Peter, after such communications from on high, could again waver? In the first place, it must here be remarked, that all parties in the church have always taught in accordance with the Scripture itself (see Acts xiv. 15), that the apostles did not cease, even after they received the Holy Ghost, to be sinful men: along with the new man, the old man too still lived in them: sinful men, therefore, they remained subject to the possibility of error.* But, in the second place, should

* Excellently does Steudel show (in his discussion on Inspiration in der Tubinger theol. Zeitschrift Jahrg. 1832, h. 3), that the truth of the doctrines preached by the apostles is quite independent of the degree of their personal holiness and advancement, and rather rests upon purely objective communication of the truth to them from on high. The same holds good of the Old Testament prophets, some of whom, as the history of Jonas shows, were very deficient; and the principle too applies to the servants of the church in our own and in all times. The Christian minister does not fashion the truth,

it be said, "certainly the apostles were liable to error, but not in matters of faith, and the question here relates to a religious point;" then let it be considered that, even in the apostles, we must suppose moments when the power of the Spirit that wrought in them retired, and their own subjectivity prevailed. Now if we suppose that in Peter his own natural biases were for a moment in the ascendant, when the Jewish Christians came from Jerusalem, and that they probably assailed him on his weak side, and called him apostate, the whole occurrence receives a satisfactory explanation. And the authority of Peter* could have been injured only by his obstinately persisting in his error; but, as he humbly acknowledged his mistake to Paul, his stumbling only became a triumph to the cause of the truth. The apostles, like all other believers, were distinguished from the world, not by never going wrong, but by the fact that, when they did go wrong, they were sufficiently humble to acknowledge their mistake, and immediately to correct it. Nor is the authority of Scripture in any degree affected by the facts before us: this would only be the case if the error of Peter were inserted as a truth: then indeed the Scriptures could not have been composed by the sacred penmen under the full influence of spiritual illumination, and could consequently furnish no rule of faith for all succeeding times. But since they represent the error of Peter as one removed and overcome by the power of the Spirit, they are on this very account shewn to be altogether pure and genuine, because they openly acknowledge what is apparently prejudicial to their authority. But finally, it is decisive of the whole question, that we cannot, on close consideration, say that the error of Peter and of the strict Jewish Christians was one properly *doctrinal;* the blessings of the Gospel are certainly not neutralized by the observance of the law. Suppose therefore the ancient church had stood to the principle, that every Gentile who wished to join the church must keep the law; then indeed the speedy diffusion of Christianity

nor yet the Divine effect springing from it, by his own personal qualities, but that effect rests upon the inward power residing in the Divine word and in the preaching of Christ. Yet we mean not to deny, what is evident of itself, that a pastor of eminence and experience is able to labour more comprehensively and judiciously than one who is deficient in these qualities; it is only meant to oppose what has become prevalent in our times and in the evangelical church, an undue estimate of the subjective element, and to vindicate the objective character of the Christian scheme of salvation.

* With regard to this subject the circumstance must not be overlooked, that Peter was particularly called, as also the rest of the Twelve, to labour among the Jews, while the Gentile world was expressly assigned to Paul. This was not an arbitrary arrangement, but was made with a due respect to their entire constitution and habits. Peter was really more at home in the Jewish element, and for that reason was the less able to sympathize with the wants of the Gentile Christians. (On this point see Comm. on Gal. ii. 7, 9, where the formal distribution of the labours of the apostles among the Jews and Gentiles is considered.)

would have been greatly hindered, but its essential character would not have been destroyed. That observance of the law, of which Paul speaks in the Epistle to the Galatians (v. 4), "Christ is become of none effect unto you, whosoever of you are justified by the law ; ye are fallen from grace," is plainly not to be confounded with the observance here supposed. Paul is opposing the idea, that it is the observance of the law which makes men righteous before God, an idea which obviously destroys the essence of the Gospel ; but Peter might suppose that the reception of the law was a suitable method of introducing Gentiles into the church, without at all placing justification in anything else than faith in Christ. It was this only that the strict Jewish Christians wished at first, otherwise the apostles would have sternly rebuked them, and made no approaches to them at all : it was afterwards, when polemical ardour sharpened the points of opposition, that the Judaizing party, out of a false zeal for the Old Testament and its forms, gradually went to the extent of impairing entirely the essential character of the New Testament.

And if the proceeding of Peter is excusable on the grounds stated, it may also be readily understood and explained how it occurred, if we consider that the question regarding the relation of the Gentiles to the law by no means exhausts the whole subject. Paul laboured, although not positively, yet negatively, to free even the native Jews on their entrance into the church from the observance of the law. Now, that was a step further, and it might be exceedingly difficult to make the lawfulness of it plain to one like Peter, who probably held that the native Israelites were bound perpetually to observe the law, and in this way his doubts would be revived in reference even to the relation of the Gentiles to the law.* This whole ques-

* To guard as much as possible the difficult question of the apostle's liability to error from all misunderstanding, I submit the following additional remarks. As the prophets of the Old Testament, according to the remark already made, were not perfect men, so also the apostles carried their heavenly treasure of the new birth and of the Holy Ghost in earthen vessels. They are not witnesses of the truth on account of their own subjective perfection, but only because God chose them according to his free grace to be instruments of his revelation. In accordance with this destination, indications of their liability to error could only appear in those moments, when they spoke in the mere exercise of their own powers. (Comp. 2 Sam. vii. 3, 4.) But so soon again as they spoke with Divine authority in the power of the Spirit, as heralds of the truth intrusted to them, they were infallibly directed by the Spirit who guides into all truth. In earthly matters, therefore, so far as these were not connected with the faith, or they had received no particular instruction regarding them, the apostles might err. But with respect to their work as writers of the Scriptures, no fault or error can be supposed in the religious and moral ideas, because the work was performed in the most elevated moments of the inward life of faith, and when their personal character was in the background. When therefore Scripture makes mention of the error of an apostle, the truth of the account lies in this, that it represents the error as an error. In this way we may recognize the Scripture, as we must do, to be an infallible witness of the truth in religious and moral ideas, and a clear light shining upon

tion, however, regarding the relinquishment of the law in the case of Jewish Christians, will receive a further consideration at chap. xxi. 17, etc.

Vers. 1-5.—The whole question regarding the relation of the Gentiles to the law was brought under discussion by certain emissaries from Jerusalem. (*Τινὲς ἀπὸ τῆς Ἰουδαίας* is most closely defined by *τινὲς ἐξ ἡμῶν* in ver. 24.) These men demanded that the Gentiles should receive circumcision, which, as the more important and burdensome part stands for the observance of the law in general. (Comp. ver. 5.) By the expression however, *οὐ δύνασθε σωθῆναι*, according to the remarks already made, we are not to understand that the Jewish party, instead of connecting salvation (*σωτηρία*) with Christ and his redemption, connected it with circumcision—in that case Paul and the whole church must have altogether denied their claim to be Christians (see Comm. on Gal. v. 4)—but it must be understood only as intimating, that the Gentile could not come in the regular way to the salvation that is in Christ, excepting through circumcision and the observance of the law. To this the apostles might suppose it necessary to yield, conceding somewhat to the weakness of the advocates of this view.

(Vers. 1.—The additional clause, *τῶν πεπιστευκότων ἀπὸ τῆς αἱρέσεως τῶν Φαρισαίων*, although correct as to the substance of the statement, as is plain from ver. 5, is yet not a genuine reading here, but has been interpolated from the verse in question.—Ver. 2. The "certain others" are not more particularly defined, but from Gal. ii. 1, where the same journey of Paul to Jerusalem that is here mentioned is spoken of, it may be concluded that Titus accompanied the apostle.* This attendant Paul refused, notwithstanding the demands of the opposite party, to circumcise, that he might shew practically the decided character of his principles: it is known that he acted otherwise in the case of Timothy [chap. xvi. 3].† In the connexion between verses 4 and 5 a difficulty has been supposed to

the dark pathway of life; and yet we need not mistake the subjective imperfection of the apostles (as well as of the mere outward form of Scripture).

* See the particulars regarding the journey, both in the general introduction to the Epistles of Paul, and at the passage itself in Gal. ii. 1. Probably it took place in the year 52, after the birth of Christ (compare the second chronological table), although accounts fluctuate between the year 47 and 52 after Christ.

† Paul acted differently in the case of Timothy, but still in both cases he acted consistently with his principles. He refused to circumcise Titus, because those who asked him to do so attached undue importance to circumcision, and made it essential to salvation. They had fallen from grace, Gal. v. 4, and he could not countenance them. Besides Titus was a Greek, Gal. ii. 3. But Timothy was a Jew, by the mother's side, Acts xvi. 1. And Paul circumcised him that he might shew he did not maintain the unlawfulness of circumcision in the case of the Jews, provided only they did not substitute it in the room of the redemption of Christ. As a Jewish custom it was not wrong; but made indispensable to salvation under the Gospel, it was derogatory to the Saviour.—[Tr.

exist: Paul and Barnabas were dispatched for the express purpose of procuring for the Gentiles exemption from the observance of the law, and hence it has appeared remarkable that they say nothing of the occasion of their journey. It has therefore been proposed to supply *λέγοντες* before *ἐξανέστησαν δέ τινες*, so that the 5th verse might contain an account of the arrival of the persons mentioned in ver. 1, with whom the controversy had arisen. But this transition from the indirect form of speech to the direct, is manifestly full of harshness, not to mention that the word *λέγοντες* occurs once more in the same verse. It is far more simple to say, that Luke presupposes the occasion of the address delivered by the deputies to have been already mentioned, and introduces them as giving an account of their labours with the view of refuting their opponents. But in Jerusalem too, the strict Jewish Christians rose up immediately against them, and demanded that the Gentiles should observe the law.)

Vers. 6–12.—For the settlement of this difficult question a formal assembly of the apostles and elders was appointed at Jerusalem.* In this meeting opinions were at first divided. It may therefore be concluded with certainty, that some even of the presbyters belonged to the strict Jewish Christians. So far as verse 5 is concerned, it might still remain uncertain, whether the elders formerly mentioned were not simply believers (ver. 4), invested with no ecclesiastical office, but here in the assembly there were only ministers of the church, and yet there arose a warm dispute (*συζήτησις*) about the question. First of all, Peter arose and detailed his own experience, which he had already, at an earlier period, laid before the church (chap. xi. 1, etc.), and by which at that time he had convinced them of the propriety of his conduct. It does not appear clear how Peter can call the attempt to impose upon the Gentiles the yoke of the law, a tempting of God (*πειράζειν τὸν Θεόν*). But the choice of this expression probably takes its rise from ver. 8, where Peter mentions the giving of the Holy Ghost to Cornelius and his friends. This gift furnished an exhibition that could not at all be mistaken of the Divine will: every deviation from it therefore was a wilful tempting of God, because he could not possibly give more convincing proofs of his will.

(Ver. 7.—The phrase *ἀφ' ἡμερῶν ἀρχαίων* is formed after the Hebrew יְמֵי קֶדֶם, Ps. xliv. 2. It points to a considerable time, which must have elapsed since the conversion of Cornelius. It is fitted to make the impression that the question, as to its essential features, has been settled long ago. The *ἐν ἡμῖν* must by no means be regarded as equivalent to *ἡμᾶς*: that idea is negatived by the

* Regarding the section that follows, see Stier in den Reden der Apostel, Bd. ii. s. 28, etc., and Menkens Blicke in das Leben des Apostels Paulus, p. 14, etc.

μου which follows: rather must ἐμέ be supplied, and the passage rendered thus: "God made choice *among us* of me, to preach first to the Gentiles."—Ver. 9. The expression τῇ πίστει καθαρίσας τὰς καρδίας, *cleansing their hearts by faith*, is a peculiar one. The purifying, sanctifying principle is properly the Spirit, but this is received in connexion with faith, and therefore the same effect may be ascribed to the one, which belongs to the other.—Ver. 10. It is a remarkable acknowledgment of Peter, that neither they nor their fathers had been able to bear the law. That the apostle could make this declaration before the venerable assembly without being contradicted, shews that all were penetrated with the truth of the statement. The sentiment illustrates the important passages of Paul's writings contained in Rom. iii. 20 and Gal. iii. 10.—Ver. 11. With the law [νόμος] is contrasted, entirely according to the usage alike of Paul and of John, the grace which has been revealed in Christ [χάρις: see Comm. at John i. 17; Rom. iii. 21.] Finally we must not refer the words καθ' ὃν τρόπον κἀκεῖνοι to the patriarchs, with the older interpreters, but to the Gentiles, as Kuinoel has already rightly remarked.)

Ver. 13-18.—After the deputies of Antioch had availed themselves of the impression made by the speech of Peter, to get their own similar experience made known, James at length arose, and by means of a healing measure endeavoured to soothe the opposite party, and to bring about an unanimous decision of the assembly. First of all the bishop mentions the predictions of the Old Testament regarding the calling of the Gentiles, citing Amos ix. 11, 12. But here we see not, how the quotation bears upon the point under review: the opposite party did not object to the *reception* of the Gentiles considered in itself: the only question raised was about the *conditions* of the reception, but the passage says not in express terms, that the Gentiles were to be received without the observance of the law and circumcision. Probably however James drew his conclusion from the silence of the passage quoted, which does not at all declare that the Gentiles were first to become Jews in order to gain admission into the kingdom of the Messiah, but rather describes them as seeking the Lord in the character of Gentiles.*

(Regarding ἐπισκέπτεσθαι, see Comm. on Luke i. 68. The words ἐπὶ τῷ ὀνόματι αὐτοῦ, are after the Hebrew fashion loosely appended, corresponding to שְׁמִי עַל. They are to be viewed as in apposition with λαός, and denote the near relation of the people of Israel, that is, the true spiritual Israel, to God, Rom. ii. 28, 29.—In the

* On this point, see Hengstenberg's remarks (Christology. B. iii. p. 233, etc.), according to which the quotation acquires significancy only when connected with the declaration of God, made not verbally but virtually in the communication of the Holy Ghost to the Gentiles.

quotation, vers. 16–18, the first verse, upon which less stress is laid, deviates very far from the LXX., but the last two agree almost exactly. In most manuscripts of the LXX., the words *τὸν κύριον* are wanting, but the Alexandrian codex has them. In the concluding words, further, the phrase *γνωσταὶ ἀπ' αἰῶνος* is wanting. But the last verses deviate entirely from the Hebrew, which runs thus: לְמַעַן יִירְשׁוּ אֶת־שְׁאֵרִית אֱדוֹם, that is, "to the end that they may possess the remnant of Edom." In this form the passage could not at all appear suitable to the purpose of James; and therefore, if we can suppose, as is extremely probable, that we possess an exact account of these important transactions, then it may be concluded, that in the bosom of the Assembly at this time Greek must have been spoken, because the passage adduced can only have been cited from the LXX.*

The expression, *σκηνὴ Δαβίδ*, סֻכַּת דָּוִיד, is a figurative name for his house and family, but David's family stands for the entire nation, of which it forms the central point.—Ver. 17. *ἐφ' οὓς*, with the following *ἐπ' αὐτούς*, corresponds to the Hebrew אֲשֶׁר—עֲלֵיהֶם. Moreover the phrase, *ἐφ' οὓς ἐπικέκληται τὸ ὄνομά μου*, divides the Gentile world into two parts, viz., those upon whom the name of the Lord is named, and others upon whom it is not named. The former mean those ordained to eternal life.)

Vers. 19–21.—Instead of laying upon the Gentiles the burden of the whole law, and consequently of circumcision, James recommends to enforce upon them only the reception of certain individual precepts of easy observance. The object of this enforcement was plainly nothing but this, to meet in some measure the difficulties of the Jewish Christians, and to lead the Gentile Christians to shun whatever might prove offensive to their Jewish brethren. In all this, then, it was clearly indicated that the prohibitions had no absolute value; once let the Jewish Christians be more thoroughly freed from Old Testament forms, and the end for which those ordinances were made would no longer exist. Now the ground on which these particular points were brought into view, is explained by the circumstance, that they were wont to be laid upon the proselytes of the gate in the so-called seven precepts of Noah. (Compare Buxtorf. lex. rabb. sub voce גֵּר, pag. 407, seq., and Winer's bibl. Reallex. under the word proselytes.) This, therefore, is the import of the arrangement, that the Gentile Christians should not be obliged to become proselytes of righteousness by circumcision,

* See the note on this subject in the Comm., Part i., at Luke iv. 18, 19. Hengstenberg in the work above referred to, page 235, etc., will not allow there is any difference. Yet he himself confesses, that the Alexandrian translators have substituted a general idea in the room of the particular, which is marked out by Amos as part of the general. Now my words mean nothing more than this: I readily acknowledge that the particular, viz., Edom, is quite suitably extended to the general, viz., the Gentiles (*ἔθνη*).

but only to live as proselytes of the gate. Those of the seven precepts of Noah, which are here omitted, viz., the ones regarding blasphemy, murder, robbery, sedition, were of such a kind that it was self-evident to Christians that the like should have no place among them: in the present instance it was not so much precepts of a purely moral character, which required to be brought forward, as precepts which referred merely to the outward life. That the ἀλισγήματα τῶν εἰδώλων are to be understood of an outward act, viz., the eating of the flesh of sacrifices, is quite clear from the analogous expression εἰδωλόθυτα which occurs in the 29th verse. The more particular distinction made by Paul in 1 Cor. x., between such flesh of sacrifices as was bought like any other in the shambles, and such as was eaten in the temple at an idol-festival, is not entered upon by the assembly: they forbid in the widest sense all eating of sacrifices, because the Jews took offence at it. The same holds good of the eating of blood, and, which is the same thing, of that which was strangled, in which the blood remained congealed.* The Jews had the utmost abhorrence of the eating of blood, which was grounded particularly upon the strong declarations of the Old Testament contained in Lev. xvii. 10, 11. In this passage it is not merely said that Jehovah would set his face against him who eats blood, but the blood is also represented as the support of the soul, that is, of the psychical life, and it is placed in connexion with the propitiation, which can only be made by the shedding of blood. (Heb. ix. 22.) This law appears to have been strictly observed by the primitive church (see Euseb. H. E. v. 1), and even in the middle ages the injunction was frequently given by the spiritual authorities to avoid the eating of blood.†

The mention of fornication (πορνεία) appears to be quite foreign to the nature of the other injunctions, and opposed to our view of the object of these apostolic ordinances. It blends a purely moral precept with ordinances that refer only to matters of outward observance. As the Codices present no various readings, conjecture has been called in to give her assistance, and, instead of πορνείας, it has been proposed to read πορκείας or χοιρείας. The sense thus brought out would indeed be very appropriate, but besides the total

* The omission of the words καὶ τοῦ πνικτοῦ in several critical authorities probably arose from this, that the two injunctions to abstain from blood and from things strangled were regarded as identical. The prohibition of blood, and which is the same thing, of strangled animals, had finally also an internal ground, like all laws regarding food, for physical and psychical elements that cause derangement ought to be shunned. When the mighty power of the Gospel was introduced, most of these might have been abrogated, but it was still found necessary to forbid the eating of blood, until the power of the new Spirit should have entirely developed itself.

† Yet this applies particularly to the Greek church: see the Acts of the second Trullanic Council of the year 692 in Canon 67. In the Latin church Augustine (cont. Faustum xxxii. 13) already took the right view

want of critical authorities to support it, this reading is decidedly opposed by the circumstance, that among the precepts of Noah there is no mention made of abstinence from swine's flesh, while fornication is expressly introduced among them. If the reading then be retained, which is supported too by the parallel in xxi. 25, the difficulty can only be removed by some mode of explanation. Most of the explanations, however, which have been proposed, are little worthy of being received. It has been proposed to understand the word figuratively of idolatry, but it is not possible that among Christians gross idolatry could require to be thus spoken of; and if we refer the word to participation in sacrificial feasts and the eating of sacrifices, then it coincides with the first injunction. Quite a failure must the experiment made by Heinsius be pronounced, of taking πορνεία for θυσία πορνική, by which phrase we must understand a sacrifice purchased with the hire of a harlot. To overlook every other objection, this view refers to a state of matters so grossly sinful as could not be thought of among Christians. Undoubtedly the only proper course is to bring into view the greater freedom of intercourse between the sexes, which prevailed among the Greeks and Romans, which was an abomination to the more serious Jews, and appeared to them in fact a refined species of whoredom. By the word in question, therefore, which comprehends not only gross violations of the seventh commandment, but also more polished sins of this kind, the assembled brethren enjoin upon the heathen Christians greater care and circumspection in their intercourse with the female sex, that they might give no offence to the Jewish Christians.

The 21st verse plainly assigns, though very shortly, the ground for the injunctions laid down. The connexion of thought is made somewhat obscure by the brevity. Some have therefore been led to inappropriate explanations of it. Some interpreters, as for example Grotius, have thought of the reading of the Old Testament in Christian assemblies, and have therefore fancied the idea which connects the 21st verse with the foregoing, to be this, that the complaint of the Jewish Christians regarding the Gentile Christians was unreasonable, since they too read the Holy Scriptures in their meetings. And even Bengel's view is to be rejected, which makes the 21st verse give a reason why James does not adduce, besides the passage from the prophets, one too from the writings of Moses, viz., because they were sufficiently known. This view is plainly quite untenable, because the 21st verse is not connected with the quotation, for the 19th and 20th verses lie between them. The γάρ only permits the concluding verse to be connected with ἀπέχεσθαι, so that the following sense comes out: it is proper to enjoin upon the Gentile Christians the observance of the ordinances in question, because, wherever the Jews reside the law of Moses is read, and thus those ordinances are so deeply impressed upon the people's mind, that they cannot tolerate the neglect of them by the Gentile Christians.

(Ver. 19.—Παρενοχλεῖν is found only in this passage of the New Testament.—Ver. 20. As to ἐπιστέλλειν, the meaning of "enjoin by letter" must be retained, for there were no Gentile Christians in Jerusalem. This is plain also from Acts xxi. 25.—The word ἀλισγήματα from ἀλισγέω, which Hesychius explains by μολύνω, is found only in the Hellenistic dialect. The LXX. use the verb for the Hebrew גאל, see Mal. i. 7. The substantive ἀλίσγημα is not to be found at all in the Greek translations of the Old Testament.)

Vers. 22-29.—After the adoption of the proposals of James, two deputies were sent back to the churches, where the matter had first been brought into controversy. Along with the decrees they took an official letter to the council, which has been preserved to us in the original by the care of Luke. The brevity indeed and artlessness of the letter might make us doubt for a moment whether it be the original of the synod's letter which we have, but a closer consideration renders this in the highest degree probable. If the letter had been copied, it would have been carried out with formal exactness, with an account of the occasion of the controversy and information regarding the proceedings; but in fact this very brevity adapts it to the precise circumstances for which it was intended. It could be supplemented and explained by the oral accounts of the deputies, and everywhere delivered in the churches of the Gentiles as a public letter: for such an object the form adopted was the only one suitable.

(In ver. 22 there is a difficulty connected with the construction of ἐκλεξαμένους. The passive use of the middle form is unusual [see Winer's Gr. p. 233]; and if we refer it actively to the apostles, the accusative seems surprising, as does also the nominative γράψαντες in the 23d verse. The position of ἐκλεξαμένους, however, makes its connexion with τοῖς ἀποστόλοις decidedly more probable, and then the accusative with πέμψαι must be regarded as the accusative before the infinitive. And the following γράψαντες, must be viewed as an instance of incomplete construction.—Of Judas Barsabas, who must not be confounded with Joseph Barsabas mentioned in chap. i. 23, no further mention is made in history. Silas, or in the longer form, Silvanus, is the well-known travelling companion of Paul. The shorter form of the name is peculiar to the Acts of the Apostles, the longer is to be found in the letters of Paul.—Ver. 23. At first the letter appears to have been directed only to the inhabitants of certain provinces, who were particularly interested in the controversy; but that it was designed for general use is plain from chap. xxi. 25, where we learn that Paul delivered the decrees wherever the course of his journeys brought him.—Ver. 24. 'Ανασσκυάζω, means primarily vasa colligere, "to gather articles together on the occasion of departing," and hence to "journey:" next "to destroy, to entangle, to perplex." So in Thucyd. iv. 116. It occurs no more in the New Testament.—Ver. 25. The apostles expressly commend Paul, in order to declare openly that they do not concur with the charges of the Jewish Christians against him. Τιθέναι ψυχήν equivalent to נֶפֶשׁ שִׂים.—Ver. 28. Here we find the formula which has become so famous, in consequence of the general use of it afterwards by councils: ἔδοξε τῷ ἁγίῳ πνεύματι καὶ ἡμῖν, *it has seemed good to the Holy Ghost and to us.** Unfortunately, it cannot be denied that this expression has often been employed, in cases where the Holy Ghost only appeared and acted in specie boni: but such abuse cannot at all prejudice the proper use of the formula, and if its propriety be allowed anywhere, here undoubtedly it must be supposed. In the primitive church, the operation of the Holy Ghost in the apostles was so decidedly recognized, that their decrees [δόγματα], as such, had binding power. [See chap. xvi. 4.] Those therefore who opposed the decrees of the apostles, separated themselves by that very act from the communion of the church; and their parties assumed a sectarian form, which led to gradual decay and final ruin. Connexion with the apostles could alone maintain connexion with the fountain of life, which in the Spirit of God was bestowed upon the church.)

Vers. 30–35.—After the fulfilment of their commission, the deputies of the church at Jerusalem devoted themselves to the preaching of the Gospel, and Joseph Barsabas returned, after the lapse of some time; but Silas remained in Antioch, and attached himself wholly to the Apostle Paul.—(Ver. 32. The clause καὶ αὐτοὶ προφῆται ὄντες, *being themselves also prophets*, is not to be understood primarily, as in chap. xi. 27, of the gift of predicting future events, which is not here under consideration. The connexion of these words with the work of teaching leads to the conclusion, that the gift of prophecy (προφητεία), must be here understood, agreeably to the description of it given by Paul in 1 Cor. xiv., where see the subject more particularly considered. But, of course, the foresight of future events is not in this way excluded: it is only meant that this is not the necessary form in which prophecy displays itself. —Ver. 34 is remarkable on account of the plural ἀπελύθησαν which precedes it: the verse is wanting therefore in several manuscripts. and others add the clause: μόνος δὲ Ἰούδας ἐπορεύθη. Light, however, is thrown upon the arrangement of the clause, when it is sup-

* It is self-evident, however, that the words καὶ ἡμῖν do not represent the apostles as considered separately from the Holy Ghost: they are rather to be understood as if it were written πνεύματι ἐν ἡμῖν. See the discussion by Nitzsch regarding Acts xv. 29, in Velthusen syll. vol. vi. page 385, seq.

posed that Silas wished at first to go back with Judas, but afterwards bethought himself and remained.—The word αὐτοῦ in verse 34 is the abbreviated form for ἐπ' αὐτοῦ τοῦ τόπου.)

§ 7. Second Missionary Journey of Paul.

(Acts xv. 36—xviii. 22.)

The account of the second missionary journey of Paul is connected, quite indefinitely as to time, with the preceding section. Luke neither states how long Barnabas had been in Antioch before his return to Jerusalem, nor how long Paul remained after his departure. It remains therefore quite uncertain, to what the words μετά τινας ἡμέρας, *after some days*, in ver. 36, are properly to be referred. They might be supposed to look back to the return of Paul from Jerusalem, but this does not accord with the words ποιήσαντες χρόνον in ver. 33, on which account it is best to regard the departure of Judas Barsabas, by which the decision of Silas to remain was fixed, as the period to which the formula refers. Accordingly, we can only determine the time of this journey from its connexion with the earlier and later points of Paul's life: the most probable supposition is, that the commencement of it falls in the year 53 This second missionary tour appears to have proceeded at first, solely from the desire of visiting the churches already planted. In the end, however, it took a much wider sweep, for it brought the apostle to Europe. On this account it had quite a peculiar interest for Luke; for it must have been of consequence to him, considering the character of his first readers, to exhibit the introduction of the Gospel into Europe. Besides, it was shortly before the departure of Paul from Troas that Luke himself first joined his company, chap. xvi. 10. He hurries therefore rapidly over the events in Asia, and dwells with peculiar interest on Philippi, the first place in Europe where Paul succeeded in forming a church. Afterwards too Luke gives particular information regarding the stay of Paul in Corinth and Athens.

Vers. 36-39.—But before the time of departure arrived, a contest arose between Barnabas and Paul, who were purposing to visit together the churches which they had planted in common, regarding John Mark, who, as we find from chap. xiii. 13, had left them on the first journey. The manner in which Paul mentions this desertion plainly shews that he blamed it and ascribed it to impure motives on the part of Mark. It is altogether most probable that the hardships and dangers of the journey had alarmed the inexperienced youth. Now the conduct of Paul and Barnabas in reference to this event is striking in more than one respect. Not to mention the sharp contention* which arose between them,† Paul appears, although indeed this cannot be imagined, to have permanently violated the principle of love, for on account of a single fault he entirely threw off Mark; and of Barnabas it might be feared that love for his relative (for according to Col. iv. 10, Mark was related to Barnabas), more than a conviction of his fitness, was the motive for taking him as a companion on his missionary journey. But on closer consideration these surmises are seen to be perfectly groundless. Mark appears in fact to have deserved a severe castigation, and therefore Paul felt constrained to administer it, although with no view of casting him off entirely; and perhaps the severity of Paul's rebuke might be the means, in the hands of God, of moulding him to be a proper instrument for the kingdom of Christ; but if Barnabas had opposed him in the same manner, all hope might have been at once torn from him, of doing anything for the church. The mildness of Barnabas towards Mark, we may therefore ascribe to the conviction that, notwithstanding the momentary transgression of his relative, there were noble traits in him, which ought not to be neglected. The concurrence therefore of two such different influences, in the treatment of his case, may have been just the fitting means for training him aright; and there may be no reproach due to Barnabas or Paul on account of their conduct; both erred only through the heat of self-will, from which the contention arose.

Vers. 40, 41.—After this Paul chose Silas for his companion, and went on this occasion by land, through Syria and Cilicia, into the interior of Asia Minor, to the churches at Derbe and Lystra. Barnabas, on the other hand, sailed first back to Cyprus, but there are no accounts of the further course of his journey. The one stream of missionary labour thus became divided into two parts, and the more regions were in consequence supplied with the water of life.—(Ver. 40. The phrase παραδοθεὶς τῇ χάριτι τοῦ θεοῦ ὑπὸ τῶν ἀδελφῶν, refers to the official sending forth of the messengers of Christ by the church.)

* The attempt of many to justify both completely, or at least Paul, I cannot approve. If both had been perfect men, no contention would have arisen, no exasperation of mind; for there must always be two to a quarrel. Nay, there would have been no contention, if even only one of them had been perfect. Our Lord could never have quarrelled with any individual! In the case before us, both were indeed right, but they defended their views in a one-sided manner, and with the heat of self-will.

† Agreeably to the remarks made at chap. xv. 1, a contention might arise even between apostolic men, just as between regenerate men in general, but only for a short time and doubtless the two apostles soon bethought themselves, and even rebuked their own hearts. The word παροξυσμός denotes any violent excitement of mind. It is to be found in a good sense in Heb. x. 24.

Chap. xvi. 1-5.*—Of the apostolic labours of Paul, Luke only mentions in general, that he delivered (ver. 4) the apostolic decrees (chap. xv. 29) everywhere, and confirmed the churches in the faith. He makes mention of only one particular occurrence, viz., the calling of Timothy, because this man plays so important a part in the subsequent history of Paul. According to the account of Luke, it is doubtful where Timothy really came from. Ἐκεῖ, *there*, in ver. 1 appears to refer mainly to Lystra, which is named again in ver. 2. If the passage in Acts xx. 4, means that Timothy was from Derbe, then the mention of Lystra and Iconium in ver. 2 must be explained on this principle, that Paul adduces in behalf of Timothy not only the favourable testimony, as we must suppose, of his native city, but also that of neighbouring cities. (See the exposition of chap. xx. 4.) The notice in verse 3 is a most important one, that Paul for the sake of the Jews circumcised Timothy, whose father was a Greek: the father, it appears, if he was not already dead, had not joined himself to the church; for it is only the Jewish mother of Timothy who is called a believer. In this the apostle appears to have been untrue to his principles, not only in the general, but also as exhibited in the special fact that he refused to let Titus be circumcised.—Gal. ii. 3. But the narrative about Titus refers to *compulsory* circumcision which Paul could not submit to without coming into direct collision with his principles (*οὐδὲ Τίτος ἠναγκάσθη περιτμηθῆναι*), while Timothy willingly submitted to the rite. Where this voluntary reception of the ceremony took place, nothing could hinder him from permitting it; nay, his great principle of becoming a Jew to the Jews (1 Cor. ix. 20) would rather lead him to desire, that the heralds of the Gospel should be circumcised, in order that they might give no offence to the weak Jews. The procedure of Paul shews accordingly his entire freedom from self-willed dogmatism, and his disinterested devotedness to the work of extending the kingdom of God. There can be no doubt that Paul immediately took Timothy along with him. That this adhesion to Paul is first mentioned in chap. xvii. 15, may be easily explained from the consideration, that Timothy would require to be first initiated in the work, and therefore in the beginning could do but little. Yet it is plain from 1 Thess. iii. 1, that Paul, when he was in Thessalonica, had already employed Timothy on missions.

Vers. 6.-10.—It is remarkable that Luke mentions so briefly the journey of Paul through Galatia and Phrygia: he is impatient, as we have already remarked, to see the apostle arrive in Europe. From this brevity the disadvantage has arisen to us, that the formation of the important churches of Galatia, as well as the places

* On chaps. xvi.—xviii., see the excellent remarks of Tholuck in his Credibility, p. 381, etc.

where they stood, have remained quite unknown to us. (See further particulars in the introduction to the Epistle to the Galatians.) It is a remarkable statement too which Luke here makes, that the messengers of Christ could not preach in Asia (meaning Asia proconsularis with its metropolis Ephesus, corresponding to the ancient Ionia), and Mysia and Bithynia, because the Holy Ghost hindered them. The manner in which Luke describes this hindrance, is well adapted to exhibit the operation of the higher spirit (πνεῦμα) in the souls of the apostles. The soul (ψυχή) of the individual who had received the Holy Ghost, was by no means so identified with the Spirit, that he was not conscious of the difference; but he could distinguish the movements of his soul very plainly from the operations of the Spirit. His own impulses led often, if not to what was sinful (although even this cannot be altogether excluded) yet certainly to what was false, and what was unsuitable to the circumstances. The operations of the Holy Ghost in such a case restrained the soul in its activity, and guided it aright. The influence of the Spirit, however, did not work as a power that violently compelled, but only as one that gently guided the will: a sinful opposition to the impulses of the Spirt always remained, objectively considered, a possible thing, although of course in the apostles as regenerate men the will was *inclined* to follow every intimation of the Spirit. In the passage before us, therefore, ἐπείραζον, *endeavoured*, denotes the natural movement of the *soul*, which regards every place and every time as equally suitable for preaching: the "not permitting" (οὐκ εἴασεν αὐτούς) on the other hand, denotes the restraining influence of the Spirit, who took a wider view, and considered the minds of men in those lands as not yet sufficiently prepared for receiving the Gospel. It is not improbable too that outward circumstances were adverse to their ministry in the provinces mentioned; but Luke cannot refer primarily to these, for then he would have said ὁ Θεὸς, or at least ὁ κύριος οὐκ εἴασεν αὐτούς. The word πνεῦμα always refers mainly to the inward influence which the apostles experienced in their hearts.

Ver. 7.—Πνεῦμα Ἰησοῦ, *spirit of Jesus*, is a peculiar form of expression, found no where else in the New Testament. It is wanting therefore in several Codices, and even in the Textus Receptus. The best critics however have adopted it, on account of the difficulty of the reading, following the authority of the manuscripts A.C.D.F., and several others. The difficulty of the expression πνεῦμα Ἰησοῦ lies in this, that it seems to give countenance to the idea of the Monophysites, of a mixture of the natures of Christ. The Holy Ghost, of whom the Lord says in John xvi. 15, "he will take of mine," may well indeed be styled πνεῦμα Χριστοῦ, and often is so styled; but not, as it seems, πνεῦμα Ἰησοῦ, because the latter word refers only to the human nature, while the former describes the Divine nature of the Son. The employment however of such forms is very instructive, inasmuch as it shews that the apostles, although they avoid grossly Monophysite intermixtures of the qualities of the two natures, are yet far removed from the Nestorian disjunction of them. The Redeemer is always with them the one glorious Divine-human person, in whom neither the Divine annihilates or absorbs the human, nor the human the Divine. And the church would have done well, if with respect to the important doctrine of the person of Christ, it had not gone beyond the forms of expression sanctioned in the Holy Scriptures ; all the sacred penmen discover in the choice of their dogmatic formulæ a moderation, which keeps them far from every false extreme.

A vision by night now summoned Paul to Macedonia, and immediately he hastened away. This vision is commonly supposed to have been a dream, but the text does not necessarily lead to this conclusion, for *διὰ νυκτός*, *by night*, does not exclude the idea of being awake. Paul may have seen the vision while praying by night, as it appears from Acts xvi. 25, he was wont to do. Besides, my fundamental principle as to the gradation of the modes of Divine revelation prevents me from admitting the idea of a dream here. (See Comm. on Matth. i. 18.) Communication by dreams is the lowest form of revelation, and we do not meet with it elsewhere in the case of the apostles, who were endowed with the Holy Ghost. Their visions of ecstacy they always received in a waking condition. (See Acts x.)

In ver. 10, Luke begins his narrative in the first person, whence it is plain that he must now have joined the apostle's company. His modesty, however, does not permit him to enter further on his own personal circumstances. (Regarding *συμβιβάζω*, compare chap. ix. 22.)

Vers. 11-18.—Here the narrative at once assumes a different character, the information imparted by Luke becoming quite minute. The most direct course was taken by the island of Samothrace, from which they came on the following day to the harbour of Neapolis, in the neighbourhood of which lay Philippi. This city, rendered so famous by the battle fought near it, in which the freedom of Rome perished, was originally called Κρηνίδες, but it was enlarged and fortified by Philip of Macedonia, and named after him. Under the dominion of the Romans Augustus formed a colony in it, in consequence of which it received the jus Italicum. It is not clear why Luke calls it *πόλις τῆς μερίδος τῆς Μακεδονίας πρώτη*. Macedonia was divided by Æmilius Paulus into four parts (Liv. xlv. 29), and each of these had a *πρώτη πόλις* ; but the chief city of the part where Philippi lay was Amphipolis. Meyer supposes he removes the difficulty by connecting the words πρώτη πόλις κολωνία, "it was the first Roman colonial city established in Macedonia," but πόλις and κολωνία are never combined so as to express one idea. As the article is wanting before πρώτη, we might understand the passage, as Kuinoel does, thus, "one of the first or principal cities of this part of Macedonia," τῆς being viewed as equivalent to ταύτης. However, Bengel's view, in which Heinrichs also concurs, ought to be preferred, according to which πρώτη is understood, not of the importance of the city, but of its situation. Philippi was the first city of this part of Macedonia, which Paul reached by the course he was pursuing, for Neapolis was only the port of Philippi.

On the very first Sabbath they visited the assembly of the Jews in Philippi, and entered into discourse with the female proselytes whom they found collected there. The Jews commonly had their places of meeting beside rivers, because they found them requisite for their washings. The circumstance that they were often without the city, might be occasioned, as much by the hostility of the Gentiles, as by the desire of the Jews that their usages should attract the less notice.

(The original signification of the word ἐνομίζετο, from νόμος, "to prevail as a custom, statute, regulation," must be retained, and thus we admit here no pleonasm. Regarding προσευχή, see Comm. on Matth. iv. 23. It is the abbreviated expression for בֵּית הַתְּפִלָּה, οἶκος προσευχῆς, Matth. xxi. 13.)

It is here we first find the narrative conducted in the first person, and this leads us to consider more narrowly the view already touched upon in the introduction, and defended particularly by Bleek and Ulrich, that this form does not spring from the fact of Luke's having been an eye-witness, but is to be traced up to the author of the documents which Luke employed, whom the learned men in question suppose to have been Timothy. But the reasons given do not appear to me sufficient to establish this assertion. In the first place an appeal is made to the fact, that Luke does not appear, at least at that time, to have been so intimately connected with Paul as this inclusive form of narrative would indicate: it is in his latest letters that Paul first names Luke, as in Col. iv. 14; Philem. ver. 24; 2 Tim. iv. 11. But the form of the narrative in question proceeds from Luke, not from Paul: in the mouth of the latter it would be an expression of great familiarity, but even the servant may describe the journey of his master in the first person: how much more then the assistant of an apostle, although occupying a subordinate position? Again, it is asserted that the cessation of the inclusive form of narrative, as well as the recurrence of it, coincides with occasions, as to which we know from other sources that Timothy had either left the apostle, or had returned to him. That certainly would be a consideration of no small importance. No doubt Luke *might* have been absent at the same time with Timothy, or have returned along with him; but still undeniably such a fact would support the hypothesis, that Timothy was the author of the inclusive form of narrative. But the supposition does not appear to me sufficiently established. In the very passage before us, the narrative proceeds as far as chap. xvi. 17 in the first person with "we" (ἡμεῖς); and, from the 19th verse onwards, there is mention made only of Paul and Silas as imprisoned. But this does not prove that Timothy had gone to a distance: he was only not present at the moment of the arrest, and the same may be supposed with regard to Luke. These and others might be included among the brethren mentioned in ver. 40, to whom the released prisoners returned. It is true, indeed, at chap. xvii. 1, the inclusive mode of narration ceases; but it cannot be proved that Timothy alone was left behind just at this point. The supposition that Luke, if the first person was designed to include himself in the narrative, would have stated when and why he was anywhere left behind, is plainly of a very precarious nature. On the other hand chap. xix. 22, speaks decidedly against the supposition that "we" in the narrative proceeds from Timothy; for there we find him sent by the apostle with Erastus to Macedonia. Timothy had therefore been with Paul, and yet the preceding narrative is not conducted in the first person, as must have been the case on the supposition we are combatting. But chap. xx. 4 is peculiarly decisive, for there it is said that Timotheus, along with others, went before the apostle to Troas, and then ver. 5 proceeds thus: οὗτοι προελθόντες ἔμενον ἡμᾶς ἐν Τρωάδι, *these going before waited for us in Troas.* The word "us" could not be written by Timothy, for he was among those who waited for Paul: it still remains, therefore, the most natural supposition that the form of the narrative in the first person proceeded from the penman of the Acts himself.

Vers. 14, 15.—Among the women mentioned was Lydia, a native of Thyatira, a seller of purple, who first believed, and immediately received baptism.* It is a significant expression that is here used regarding her, "whose heart the Lord opened" (ἧς ὁ κύριος διήνοιξε τὴν καρδίαν), and shews that the inclination of the heart towards the truth originates not in the will of man. The first disposition to turn to the Gospel is a work of grace. Yet this does not imply that grace is compulsory, for it remained possible that either the fear of men or their favour might have impelled Lydia to quench the workings of it in her heart. There is no trace to be found here of instruction before baptism: without doubt the rite took place merely on a profession of faith in Jesus as the Messiah. But for that very reason it is highly improbable that the phrase οἶκος αὐτῆς,

* On the following sections see Menken's Life of Paul, p. 133, etc.

her household, should be understood as including infant children: relatives, servants, grown children might be baptized along with her, for they would be at once carried away by the youthful power of her new life of faith. There is altogether wanting any conclusive proof-passage for the baptism of children in the age of the apostles,* nor can the necessity of it be deduced from the nature of baptism. To allege that the influences of the Spirit might be at work in the unconscious child in the very womb is not sufficient, for regeneration, of which baptism, in its proper and perfect character, stands forth as the medium, is more than a mere reception of higher powers:† it is a reception of them into the deepest foundations of the life, and consequently implies a change of the whole course of life, which cannot be conceived to exist without consciousness, and a profession of surrender to the holy and exalted possessor of these powers. Still, however, the propriety of infant baptism is undoubted, and the condition of the church after the close of the third century imperatively required its introduction. But in this way Christian baptism sank down to the position, as it were, of John's baptism, and it acquired its full significance only when it was connected with confirmation. And as baptism, so also the whole church, had fallen back to a position of legality, of which the clear consciousness first appeared at the Reformation, and then also the effort was made to return to the primitive Christian model. (See the Comm. at Matth. iii. 1, and John iv. 1.) The commencement of the separation between baptism and regeneration by the gift of the Holy Ghost, we discover so early as the instructive narrative of the conversion of the Samaritans. It was a long time after the administration of baptism by Philip, that the apostle Peter communicated the Holy Ghost to the baptized. The practice, too, of baptism by the disciples of Jesus, before the institution of the sacrament and the outpouring of the Spirit, presupposes that these points might exist separately. It is

* In the words describing the institution of baptism, in Matth. xxviii. 19, the connexion of μαθητεύειν, *discipleing*, with βαπτίζειν, *baptizing*, and διδάσκειν, *teaching*, appears quite positively to oppose the idea, that the baptism of children entered at first into the view of Christ. In the Western church the feeling that infant baptism was not itself the baptism of regeneration, appeared plainly in the fact that from the earliest times baptized children were first admitted to the sacrament of the Supper after their χρίσμα. If the child had really been born again in baptism, then the participation in the sacrament of the Supper ought to have been immediately allowed. According to the Lutheran views of doctrine, moreover, baptism removes merely the *guilt* of original sin, but not its *dominion*, which is first overthrown in regeneration. (See Hutter, rediv. p. 206, not. 10, edit. tert.) Accordingly, the whole question, whether infant baptism be regeneration itself, appears to depend upon our definition of regeneration. We view it as the communication of the higher life of Christ, and consequently as involving the abolition of the dominion of original sin. See the remarks on Rom. vii. 24.

† There is a similar distinction in the life of the apostles, between having the Spirit breathed upon them (John xx. 22), and receiving him when he was poured out on the day of Pentecost.

best, therefore, to express one's self thus, that the elements of repentance and regeneration, united in the sacrament of baptism, and prefigured by immersion and emersion (see Comm. at Rom. vi. 3, etc.), were separated from one another in the later practice of the church, when infant baptism came into use. Only the one half is to be seen in infant baptism itself, the other half appears in confirmation. See also Comm. on Acts viii. 16–24, etc., and John iv. 2.*

Vers. 16–24.—An event worthy of particular notice, which occurred during the stay of Paul at Philippi, is related by Luke, viz., the incident of the soothsaying female slave, who lost her power in consequence of the apostle's threatening expostulation. Her owners, who had employed her as means of gain, brought about on this account the apprehension of Paul. After all that has been said at Matth. viii. 28 regarding demoniacs, the occurrence before us can be attended with no particular difficulty. Paul treats the slave altogether as one possessed, and commands the evil spirit to come out of her. That this woman recognized the spiritual qualities of the apostles, is to be regarded as another instance of a kind of clair-

* The statements here made regarding baptism seem very unsatisfactory. If baptism and regeneration were originally joined together by Christ in the manner supposed by Olshausen, then it could not be right in the church afterwards to separate them. But the concession made by the author, that the commencement of the separation between them appears even in the Scriptures in the case of the Samaritans, might well have suggested the doubt whether he had not misunderstood the original connexion between them. The case of the Samaritans occurring so early, should in all fairness be regarded, not as a deviation from the law of Christ, but as a practical illustration of it. The view here given of baptism, that it is the means or instrument of effecting regeneration, is very open to objection. There is no warrant from Scripture for supposing that the mere ordinance of baptism ever produced, or was intended to produce, such effects. It is not the efficient cause of an inward change, but simply the outward sign: and in the case of adults, the inward change ought to have taken place before the outward sign is used. This is plain from the fact, that adults, before being baptized, were required to make a profession of faith, and on the ground of this profession, supposed to be true and faithful, the ordinance was administered. Genuine faith, therefore, which even our author allows at chap. x. 44, could not exist apart from regeneration, was viewed as necessary to the baptism of adults. The inward change was required to precede the outward sign, and was that indeed which alone made it proper to adhibit the outward sign. Would no blessing, then, it may be asked, follow the use of the sign? Would the baptism be a mere fruitless ceremony? Far otherwise. It would be attended with very important consequences. But these consequences would ensue as the effect of a moral and spiritual influence. It would not be the outward rite that would produce them, by some mysterious power operating like a charm. The very act of making a profession of faith, supposing it to be genuine, and the public relinquishment of the world for God, would be attended with such exercises of mind, and such prayer to God for his help, as would, with the blessing of heaven, give a new impulse to the life of faith in the soul. But suppose no inward change to have taken place —suppose the profession of faith to be hollow and heartless, and the mere administration of baptism, though performed by the hands of the holiest and most legitimately ordained bishop that ever lived, would have no other than a hardening influence upon the soul. Alas for the man who, still unregenerate, trusts to the opus operatum of baptism for an inward change of heart. He is seeking for grapes upon thorns, and for figs upon thistles.—[Tr.

voyance, of which numerous examples are to be found in the Gospel narratives of the cure of demoniacs. (See on this subject the Comm on the passages referred to.) The expression *πνεῦμα πύθωνος*, however, or as A.C.D. read *πύθωνα*, is peculiar to the passage before us. In later times the word *πύθων* was employed to denote a ventriloquist (*ἐγγαστρίμυθοι*, *ἐγγαστριμάντεις*, *ἐντερομάντεις*, in Hebrew אֹבֹת). in which signification Plutarch in particular uses the word. It has therefore been proposed to apply to this occurrence the so-called natural explanation, viz., that the slave possessed the gift of ventrilouqism, but lost it through alarm at the sudden address of Paul. But, in the first place, even the choice of the word *πύθων* shews that the ancients regarded the gift of the ventriloquist, not as something acquired by exercise, but bestowed by Apollo, the possessor and distributor of all soothsaying power. The *πύθων* was always a *μάντις*, too, or *πυθόληπτος*, that is, one filled and inspired by Pythian Apollo. That Luke, as the narrator of the occurrence, had this view of the matter, is plain from the expression *πνεῦμα πύθωνος*; and the address of Paul, too, *παραγγέλλω σοι ἐξελθεῖν* in verse 18, can be explained only on this supposition. On this view, then, the question arises here, whether Paul really believed that the spirit of Apollo was in the slave, and was driven out by him. In answering this question, such passages as 1 Cor. viii. 4, 5, x. 20, present themselves for consideration. In the first, Paul denies that the heathen gods were anything; yet in the second he affirms that one might, by sharing the offerings of idols, place himself in fellowship with demons. Did Paul then imagine that the Greek divinities were demons, as Justin Martyr, for example, did (Apol. i. c. 8, 9)? But on this supposition, 1 Cor. viii. 4 would be inexplicable. The following view explains the difficulty in a simple manner. The individualized divinities, Jupiter, Apollo, Venus, Paul regarded as mere phantoms of the imagination, and therefore he might say with propriety, they are nothing. But that stage of development, at which the Greek poets had delineated those imaginary beings, was the stage of mere natural life, in which man found himself entirely exposed to demoniacal influences. Paul, therefore, again was quite right in representing a descent to this stage of life, as a placing of one's self in fellowship with demons. It is true, he did not believe, regarding this slave, that Apollo's spirit wrought in her, for he did not recognize the existence of any Apollo; but he had the well-grounded conviction, that her soul was accessible to demoniacal powers, who abused their hold of her. Like the Redeemer, therefore, Paul would not be praised by demons, and therefore he drove them out by his threatening word.

(Ver. 16.—*Ἐργασία*, "gain, profit." See Acts xix. 24, 25. The verb is found in the same sense in John vi. 27.—Ver. 17. The ing ὑμῖν, of the textus receptus, is probably only the fault of a transcriber, the second person by no means harmonizes with the connexion.—Ver. 19. The ἄρχοντες, who are called στρατηγοί in verse 20, are the so-called decuriones, who held the office of magistrates in the colonies.—Ver. 21 refers to the Roman law, which forbade the introduction of religiones peregrinæ, and from which all persecutions of the Christians were derived in a legal manner. [See on this point Neander's Ch. Hist. vol. 1. p. 122, etc.]—Ver. 24. Ξύλον, nervus, was an instrument not simply of detention, but also of punishment; a wooden block furnished with holes, into which the feet were put, and according to the severity of the torture, stretched far from one another. Origen, in his extreme old age, was obliged to bear this torture; and for several days to lie in such an instrument, with limbs far spread out from one another.)

Ver. 25–34.—Although removed by their imprisonment from the great scene of labour, the messengers of Christ found even in the prison a field for their preaching, more confined indeed, but not less fruitful; for not only were the prisoners attentive to them, but the keeper of the prison himself with his house believed in consequence of what he saw, and through him the abode of crime was changed for many into a temple of grace. (On the singing of the apostles by night, see Comm. at chap. ii. 42. It must be understood of the musical utterance of a psalm in prayer.) With regard to the deliverance of Paul and the other prisoners, it has already been remarked at chap. xii. 8, that it is quite obviously an earthquake which is here spoken of. But if we compare chap. iv. 31, it will not be doubtful that the earthquake occurring at this precise moment, stood connected in the narrator's view with the prayer of the apostles. It was something like the seal of God for them, and for all who were present.

In the conduct of the keeper of the prison, the unbelieving despair that well nigh led to suicide, forms a mighty contrast with the faith that was rapidly developed in him. Jesus, whose history in its great leading features was stated by the apostle, is the object of his faith: Paul requires no works along with this faith, and mentions *aside* from it no conditions of salvation: in it everything else lies enclosed; good works are its necessary fruits. If we contemplate this statement of Paul to the jailor of Philippi, regarding Jesus who was crucified twenty years before in Jerusalem, merely in its historical aspects, we can see no reason why it should have exerted such an influence upon the man; for in this view there is nothing but gratitude to Paul to form the bridge by which the jailor may enter into his ideas, and in that case the apostle might as well have told some legend, which would have produced for the moment apparently the same effect.

But if we view the preaching of the exalted and glorified Redeemer, in connexion with the living power of the Spirit which proceeded from him, then we may conceive its influence upon the hearts of men. The remark in ver. 32, that Paul preached not only to the jailor, but also to all in his house (ἐν τῇ οἰκίᾳ αὐτοῦ) is plainly not favourable to the view, that infant children are included under this expression, for Paul could deliver no discourse to them.—(Ver. 33. Ἔλουσεν ἀπὸ κ. τ. λ. is a Tmesis for ἀπέλουσε.—Ver. 34. Πανοικί = πανοικεί, that is, σὺν ὅλῳ τῷ οἴκῳ, occurs nowhere else in the New Testament.)

Vers. 35–40.—In the morning the magistrates sent messengers with the command to dismiss Paul from prison. Perhaps the earthquake had terrified them, or, as is more probable, they had become convinced of Paul's innocence. Here too we find that Paul does not understand the command of the Lord in Matth. v. 39, as requiring that a Christian should let the wicked do to him whatever they think proper, but, on the contrary, he defends himself most courageously, and demands, on account of his Roman citizenship, satisfaction for the outrage done to him. He deals with those that are without, quite according to the jus talionis, whose force only they are in a condition to estimate. By the lex Porcia moreover it was decreed, that corporal punishment could not be inflicted upon Roman citizens;* and therefore the right of citizenship was an important means of defence to the apostle against the daring assaults of the opposers of his work. How Paul acquired this right is unknown. His native city Tarsus did not possess it; it was an urbs libera, that is, it had obtained from Cæsar Augustus the liberty of governing itself entirely according to its own laws. Now as Paul, according to chap, xxii. 28, was born a Roman citizen nothing remains but to suppose, that his father or one of his ancestors had acquired the right. It is plain from Josephus, B. J. ii. 14, that even Jews frequently purchased it. (Ver. 35. The ῥαβδοῦχοι were the lictors of magistrates in the colonies.—Ver. 40. Εἰς τὴν Λυδίαν, for which Griesbach has adopted the better supported πρός, stands for εἰς τὴν Λυδίας οἶκον. See Winer's Gram. p. 338.)

Chap. xvii. 1–4.—From Philippi Paul went went by Amphipolis and Apollonia (called also Ἀπολλωνία Μυγδονίας to distinguish it from several cities of the same name), to Thessalonica, the chief city of the second part of Macedonia. Although Paul only taught three Sabbaths in this city, yet he succeeded in planting a flourishing church in it; a circumstance which shews more than

* See Cicero pro Rabirio c. 4, Porcia lex virgas ab omnium civium Romanorom corpore amovit. How frequently use was made of this privilege, is plain from Cic. in Verr. v. c. 57, illa vox et imploratio: civis Romanus sum! sæpe multis in ultimis terris opem inter barbaros et salutem tulit.

any thing else, what an amount of spiritual power must have proceeded from the apostle.

(Ver. 1.—The article ἡ συναγωγή probably refers to the relation in which the synagogue of Thessalonica stood to the other synagogues of that region; they were all probably dependent upon it, so that in Thessalonica there was something like a chief Rabbinate.—In ver. 3, there is a sudden transition from the indirect to the direct style, similar to what occurs in chap. i. 4.—Ver. 4. Προσκληρόω = דָּבַק, which only occurs in this passage of the New Testament, is not at all uncommon in the language of Philo. See Loesneri observ. Philon. p. 209, seq.)

Vers. 5–9.—But in Thessalonica too hostility against the Gospel was speedily manifested, and Jason, in whose house Paul resided, was dragged before the authorities. Here the Christians were accused of political offences (verse 7): for it was affirmed that they regarded Jesus as the true king. This accusation gives us a glimpse of the Chiliastic tendency of the Christians at Thessalonica, of which, according to Paul's letters to them, there was a one-sided development in their views. Why this tendency was displayed particularly in Thessalonica, we are unfortunately unable to shew from want of precise information regarding the state of matters there.

(Ver. 5.—The word ἀγοραῖοι denotes men moving about idly in the market-place.—Ver. 6. Πολιτάρχης = στρατηγός in chap. xvi. 20. The word is found nowhere else in the New Testament.—Ver. 7. Ἀναστατόω is found also in Acts xxi. 38, and Galat. v. 12. It belongs to the later Greek, and is formed from the adjective ἀνάστατος, from ἀνίστημι. It denotes primarily "to stir up from one's seat," then generally, "to excite tumult, disturbance."—Ver. 9. Ἱκανὸν λαμβάνειν and also ἱκανὸν ποιεῖν, are juridical expressions for receiving and giving bail. See Passow's Lex. under this word.)

Vers. 10–15.—Meanwhile, to secure the apostle by all means from further persecutions, the disciples conducted him to Beroea, which lay due west from Thessalonica, where Paul found among the Jews and proselytes a peculiar readiness to attach themselves to the Gospel. But the enemies of the truth in Thessalonica excited the multitude in Beroea likewise against him.—(Ver. 11. The word εὐγενέστεροι does not refer to noble descent, but to the disposition of the inhabitants of Beroea, which is particularly described in the following words of the verse, their very zealous study of the Scriptures being praised, for they searched out the oracles of the prophets that were appealed to by the apostle, and fulfilled in the life of Jesus.—Ver. 14. There is nothing in ὡς ἐπί requiring to be changed, but it is not to be translated as Kuinoel supposes usque ad: on the contrary ὡς with a preposition of motion denotes, either the definite purpose, or the pretext of designing to pursue a certain course. Here undoubtedly the latter is the meaning. See Winer's Gram. p. 559. These words therefore do not indicate, as Hemsen (p. 137) supposes, that Paul proceeded to Athens by sea. The fact that nothing is mentioned of the intervening places, does not at all argue in favour of this supposition; for how often are whole regions left unnoticed, through which Paul passed, and where certainly he laboured, as for example Galatia? And the phrase *ἤγαγον αὐτόν* in ver. 15, which indicates an escort going forward, rather favours a journey by land.—Ver. 15. *Καθιστάναι*, meaning "to accompany, to convoy," is found so used in the New Testament only here. This application springs from the signification "to transport something to a place, to deliver." See Passow's Lex. under the word.) In consequence of the disturbance thus raised Paul went to Athens; but left Silas and Timotheus behind him in Macedonia, without doubt to confirm the young churches there planted in the faith. (See 1 Tim. iii. 1.)

Vers. 16–21.—In Athens Paul now trod the leading seat of Grecian science and art. Neither he himself, nor the philosophers who thronged upon him here, anticipated at the time that from the new doctrine which he brought, a new science and art far transcending antiquity would be developed. But if the great apostle of the Gentiles might not clearly apprehend with what power and freshness the Gospel would operate even in the direction of science; yet he carried within him the lively consciousness, that he brought to the central point of Grecian society, an element of life which as infinitely transcended its highest imaginations, as the eternal went beyond the loveliest scenes of a perishable world, and in this consciousness he moved as a spiritual potentate, as a mature man among a crowd of children, to whom he undertook to explain their presentiments and to express them in words. The numerous temples and altars which Paul found in Athens, led him to perceive clearly the spiritual wants of the inhabitants; and contrary to his usual custom therefore, he spoke here in public places to those whom he met (ver. 17), while elsewhere he was wont to teach only in synagogues and private houses. Moreover that they might acquire a connected view of his doctrine, they invited him to speak upon the hill of Mars; for the well-known fickle curiosity of the Athenians was eager to learn what new thing he was proposing.*

(Ver. 16.—The phrase *παρωξύνετο τὸ πνεῦμα αὐτοῦ* does not so much express the wrath or bitterness, as the vehement emotion of sorrow which Paul experienced, when he found the Athenians so far

* Regarding this loquacious curiosity of the Athenians, Seneca says very well: Alexander, qui quod cuique optimum est, eripuit, Lacedæmona *servire* jubet, Athenas *tacere* (Epist. 94).

led astray in what belonged to religion. *Κατείδωλος* occurs no where else in the New Testament. It denotes, agreeably to the frequent signification of *κατά* in composition, "containing an abundance of idol images," "full of idols." Compare in ver. 22 the word *δεισιδαιμονέστεροι*.—Ver. 18. Of the philosophers only the Epicureans and Stoics are mentioned, probably because the adherents of these schools mingled most in public life, and went abroad into the great world. The word *σπερμολόγος* is found nowhere else in the New Testament.* It denotes primarily, a little bird that picks up seeds, then also a poor man, who gathers up grains of corn for his support. Figuratively it is applied to an ignorant babbler, who attempts to make use of scraps of knowledge picked up here and there, which he does not sufficiently understand. Hesych. explains *σπερμολόγος* by *φλύαρος*. Philostratus [vit. Apoll. v. 20] uses also the verb *σπερμολογεῖν*.—*Δαιμόνιον* is used in ver. 18 in a good sense, as frequently in classic Greek.—Ver. 19. *Ἄρειος πάγος*, Campus Martius, is the well-known name of a hill in the city of Athens, with an open space, where the celebrated tribunal of the Areopagus had its place of meeting.—Ver. 21. *Εὐκαιρέω* corresponds entirely to the Latin vacare, "to be at leisure," with the accessory idea of devoting this leisure to some particular object.)

Vers. 22-25.—Standing in the midst of Mars hill, Paul now addressed the Athenians, and with great wisdom he laid hold of a fact, which had struck him in the city, that he might conduct his hearers to a deeper knowledge of God, and thus convince them of their need of redemption.† He availed himself of the inscription upon an altar, *ἀγνώστῳ θεῷ, to an unknown God*, to preach to them the one true God, and altogether departing from the strain of his discourse in the synagogues, he imparted to them formal instructions regarding the unity and spirituality of God. Now, with regard to the circumstance that Paul applied to his purpose the altar with the inscription mentioned, there are several difficult questions which require to be considered.

In the first place, it might be apprehended that the apostle was here guilty of a kind of pious fraud (pia fraus). For according to Polytheistic principles the inscription, *θεῷ ἀγνώστῳ*, cannot be otherwise understood, than as meaning "to an unknown God," for the article is wanting, and in the room of this one among many gods, Paul seems to have substituted the one and only God. This sus-

* Appropriately does Köster (in Pelt's theol. Mitarb. II. 2, p 133) draw attention to the fact, that in the very place in Athens where Paul spoke, Demosthenes too called his opponent Æschines a *σπερμολόγος*. (Pro corona. p. 269, edit. Reiske.) And the very same accusation, of introducing strange gods (Xenoph. apol. Socr. § 10), was brought against Socrates, which is here brought against Paul.

† See Stier's excellent exposition of this speech in his work in den Reden der Apostel, part ii. p. 121, etc., and Menken's "Leben Pauli," p. 240, etc.

picion is still further heightened by the circumstance, that we have absolutely no information regarding any altar in Athens with such an inscription. In Lucian's dialogue of Philopater, which however is not genuine, there is indeed mention made of this altar, but only in mockery of Paul's speech. On the contrary, Jerome (on Titus i. 12) distinctly affirms, that Paul substituted the singular in the room of the plural: that the inscription ran thus, Diis Asiæ et Europæ et Africæ, Diis ignotis et peregrinis; but as in this form the apostle could not have used it, in his speech he put the singular for the plural. In fact, too, Pausanias (descrip. Græc. i. 1) states that in Athens there were altars of unknown gods to be found, and this we can readily imagine from the principles of Polytheism, which would not be unfriendly to the gods of any people, and therefore it included them all under the comprehensive name of "unknown gods." In this case, however, Paul appears to be guilty of a second error, in having given to the inscription an application, which was altogether foreign to the meaning of its authors. Eichhorn has indeed made the supposition (Allg. Bibl. der bibl. Lit. Bd. iii.), that there might be single altars with the inscription ἀγνώστῳ θεῷ, for altars might continue standing from remote ages without any inscription; and as pious feeling would prevent their removal, it would be supposed necessary to furnish them with such an inscription, because it was not known to what god they had originally been dedicated. But impartiality obliges us to confess that this is a mere supposition, which cannot be confirmed by any positive proof; and therefore it should not at all be taken into account in the discussion.

Apart then entirely from this, I still believe that the conduct of the Apostle Paul is entirely unimpeachable, and that without committing any pious fraud he might act as he did. First of all, whether it was really the plural that stood inscribed upon the altar or not, is a matter of perfect indifference; for let it be considered that, if *many* unknown gods were mentioned, then it is self-evident that *one* might be spoken of. The force of the argument would not have been in the slightest degree altered although Paul had said, that he wished to make known to them *one of the many unknown gods.* The only circumstance then that is really strange is this, that Paul attaches to an expression which could only denote one of the many gods of Polytheism, the idea of the *one true God;* and affirms that they already worshipped, without being aware of it, the God whom he was preaching; an affirmation which would seem to be manifestly wrong, and to contradict other passages, in which it is said that the Gentiles are without God. With reference to this point however it must not be overlooked, that the apostle by no means excludes the heathen world from all knowledge of God (Rom. i. 20); errors of the head regarding the nature of God might very well be coupled in a Gentile with an inward longing of the heart after the Divine Being. Now of this longing, as the proper fountain of religious life, Paul in his wisdom lays hold; and seeks to guide it, by the weak threads which connect it with the higher world, to a profounder knowledge. With perfect truth therefore he might say, that they, in the inward yearning of their soul, worshipping this one unknown God as all others, had always really meant the true living God, although their understanding had remained far from him.*

(Ver. 22.—*Δεισιδαίμων* occurs nowhere else in the New Testament: but the substantive is found in Acts xxv. 19. The word is used by the best Greek authors in a good sense also, as synonymous with *εὐσεβής*. The comparative, which Paul here employs, mingles, in a manner very suitable to the circumstances, praise with delicate censure.†—Ver. 23. *Σεβάσματα* denotes sacred objects in the widest sense of the word; proper temples, and also single altars, or sacred enclosed places. The 24th and 25th verses set out with the most general manifestations of the Divine being, his creative power and all-sufficiency. In the close of the verse many more recent Codices read *κατὰ πάντα* for *καὶ τὰ πάντα*. This reading with the meaning "ubique" undoubtedly gives a suitable sense, but still the critical authorities oblige us to decide in favour of the common reading. And in this case the article before *πάντα* must be referred to all that is necessary to creatures.)

Vers. 26, 27.—From the doctrine regarding God as the almighty and self-sufficient Being, the discourse of the apostle makes a transition to the most important member of the creation, viz., man. First of all, the apostle confirms the doctrine of the Old Testament,

* The longing after God which is here attributed by the author to the Gentiles, must not be confounded with that longing after God, which dwells in the bosom of a Christian, and which David so affectingly describes in Ps. xlii. It is a totally different feeling. It is simply that feature of man's constitution by which he is fitted for becoming a religious being, and by which he is distinguished from the beasts of the field, which are wholly unsusceptible of religious emotions. By his very constitution, man feels that he must look up to some higher being: he is a worshipping creature: and it is in consequence of this that all tribes and kindreds have set up for themselves gods of some kind or other. And these gods are not supposed to be false gods: it is a true God that man desires; but though he feels his need of a higher power to direct him, still his mind, darkened by reason of sin, remains an utter stranger to the character of the God who made heaven and earth. He remains far from God. Still, as our author remarks, the apostle recognizes the groping of the Gentiles in the dark after something to lay hold of, as a search directed towards the great God who made heaven and earth. *Whom* therefore ye ignorantly worship, *him* declare I unto you.—[TR.

† Regarding the multitude of sacred objects in Athens, Pausanias among others says in Attic. c. 24: *Ἀθηναίοις περισσότερόν τι ἢ τοῖς ἄλλοις ἐς τὰ θεῖά ἐστι σπουδῆς*, *the Athenians are beyond others devoted to religion.* (Paul's expression is, "ye are as it were rather too religious" — religious and even somewhat in excess.—[K.)

which, even according to the most recent physiological and geological researches, still presents itself as the most probable, that all men have sprung from one pair. (Αἷμα = σπέρμα, see at John i. 13.) Only one question here presents itself, for what reason does Paul bring this point into view? Some say for the purpose of combatting the error of the Athenians, that they were sprung from the soil (autochthones). But the question still presents itself, on what ground could it appear important to the apostle, to draw the attention of the assembly to that point? Paul undoubtedly designed in this way to represent the contempt in which the Jews were held among the Greeks as absurd, and to humble their conceit of their own superior culture, in room of which the Jews had a far deeper moral and religious tendency. For this reason, he made it appear that all tribes were brethren, and that a higher destiny assigned to the nations their dwelling-places and epoch of development. By this last thought, the apostle indicates that the fortunes of nations exhibit no lawless fluctuation, but a course determined by laws from above.

(Ver. 26.—Πρόσωπον τῆς γῆς = פְּנֵי הָאָרֶץ.—Ὁροθεσία occurs nowhere else in the New Testament. Of habitation there is mention here made, because geographical circumstances and diversities of climate exert a most important influence upon the formation of national character.)

It is then represented as the moral duty of man *to seek* after God. This ζητεῖν indicates of itself a previous apostacy of man from God, for before that apostacy he lived in immediate communion of soul with the source of his being, and of course needed not to seek after him whom he already possessed. And the seeking (ζητεῖν) is very significantly resolved into the two points of feeling after (ψηλαφᾶν) and finding (εὑρίσκειν). The former expresses the immediateness of the emotion in which the eternal truth is first made known, and the latter the higher stage of consciousness in which man plainly recognizes the peculiarity of that emotion. And the *possibility* of finding God, even when man is far from him, lies in this, that God remains perpetually near to man. (See at chap. xiv. 16, 17.)

Vers. 28, 29.—This nearness of God, even to the creature that is estranged from him, the apostle describes in a very expressive manner. The Divine Being is plainly with him the immanent ground of all creatures, in some measure the sea of life, in which they all move. Fear of a pantheistic view of the world has led men, without reason, to refine upon the expression, *ἐν αὐτῷ, in him*, and to understand it in the sense of "by him." The whole sacred Scripture exhibits, as Paul does here, one God who is inwardly near to man; nay, whose eternal word speaks in the depth of his heart. (Rom. x. 8.) The teaching of Scripture sufficiently guards against the abyss of Pantheism,* first, by its doctrine of the reality of evil, which no Pantheistic system can acknowledge; and, secondly, by the doctrine of the glorification of the body and of matter in general. Where these two bulwarks are held fast, we may quietly commit ourselves to God, in whom we live, and who is in us, without falling a prey to the all-devouring, all-producing monster of Pantheism.

The question, however, still presents itself, how the three points of living (*ζῆν*), moving (*κινεῖσθαι*), and being (*εἶναι*), are related to one another. Storr would regard them as forming an anticlimax, understanding *ζῆν* in the pregnant sense of blessed life, and *εἶναι* of mere physical existence. It is better however, with Kuinoel, to view *εἶναι*, as the highest point, understanding by it real existence, the life of the soul; *ζῆν* denotes the physical existence of the body; while *κινεῖσθαι* refers to the free activity of the soul. Such a lively view of God was entertained even by individuals among the heathen writers, and Paul adduces a passage in which it is expressed. It is found in Aratus (Phænom. v. 5), and also in Cleanthes (Hymn. in Jov. v. 5), although in the latter writer the words run somewhat differently, viz., thus: *ἐκ σοῦ γὰρ γένος ἐσμέν.* The probability is, that Paul was thinking of the former writer, who was his countryman: at all events Aratus was a native of Cilicia, although not perhaps of Tarsus itself. There is evidence of Grecian culture in this and other quotations of the Greek poets (see 1. Cor. xv. 33; Tit. i. 12); but that Paul, as has been supposed, attended in his native city, which was famed for schools of rhetoric, a formal course of education in the various branches of knowledge, cannot be inferred from these quotations. As he was destined for Rabbinical culture, it seems more probable to me, that it was rather by private reading and by intercourse with Greeks, that the apostle acquired his knowledge of the Greek

* It were to be desired, that instead of the word Pantheism, so liable to be misunderstood, and so often wrongly understood, another word were chosen to describe the error which has usually been denoted by this name. The Bible itself sanctions the expression, "God is all in all," which lies at the foundation of the word Pantheism. The only question is, how this expression is to be understood. In the East, and also in the Pantheism of Spinosa, the unity of God and of the universe is so grossly conceived, that all individuals are regarded as only passing modifications of the one original substance. (See the passages cited at John x. 14, page 493.) Although the Scriptures also say, *πάντα ἐκ τοῦ Θεοῦ, ἐν τῷ Θεῷ* and *εἰς τὸν Θεόν, all things are of God, and in God, and to God*, yet they take their stand upon a rigorous distinction between the eternal and the created, and the distinctive properties of the created are the possibility of evil and matter. The possibility of evil has reference to this earthly life alone, but materiality forms even for saints after the resurrection the boundary of individuality. Without a glorified body, the assurance of individual existence after death would be nothing but an empty assurance.

classics. Further, from the passage quoted, nothing precise can be deduced in reference to the doctrine of the Divine form, because we cannot ascertain how Paul understood the phrase *θεῖον γένος*. He uses it only for the purpose of shewing from the mind of man who springs from God, that the Godhead ought not to be brought down to a level with objects of sense.

(Ver. 29.—*Χάραγμα* from *χαράσσω*, "to engrave, to cut out," stands very frequently in the Apocalypse for "image, representation," Rev. xiv. 9, 11, xv. 12, xvi. 2, etc.)

Vers. 30–34.—After this introduction, the apostle proceeds in his discourse to invite his hearers to repentance (*μετάνοια*), which he enforces first by the patience of God, who had graciously overlooked the earlier times of their heathen ignorance, and would not reject them, and secondly by a reference to the future judgment, which is to come upon the whole world, at the appearance of him who rose from the dead. (Regarding *ὑπεριδεῖν*, see at Rom. iii. 35, which, though not verbally, is yet really parallel.) But the mention of a resurrection from the dead prevented the unbelieving Athenians from lending ear any further to the witness of the truth: but a few, who were ordained to eternal life, attached themselves to Paul. Among these are mentioned a woman named Damaris, and Dionysius, a member of the Areopagus,* which latter individual acquired great importance during the centuries when mystical writings forged under his name were regarded as genuine.

Chap. xviii. 1–3.—From Athens Paul betook himself to Corinth, where he made the acquaintance of a Jew, settled in Rome, but born in Pontus, named Aquila, who with his wife Priscilla, had recently come from Italy. (*Πρόσφατος* signifies primarily "recently killed or slain," from *πρό* and *σφάζω*, then in general "recent." See Lobeck ad Phrynich. p. 374.) Luke remarks, also, that the occasion of their journey had been the command of Claudius Cæsar, that all Jews should depart from Rome. Now as nothing is stated regarding the conversion of this family by Paul, and as they appear very active in favour of Christianity, the probability is that they had brought their knowledge of the Gospel from Rome. But the first little church there might be annihilated by this command of Claudius, and the Jews, from whom the Christians were not distinguished, might only gather again in Rome very gradually: and this supposition throws light upon some points, which would otherwise appear very dark. (See Comm. on Acts xxviii. 21.) With respect to the ex-

* According to the Constit. Apost. vii. 46, Dionysius was appointed by Paul superintendent of the young church in Athens, an assertion which is only indeed a conjecture, but still not an improbable one. Certainly the number of converts in Athens, and of men fit for office in the church, was r[illegible] there could be much room for selection.

pulsion of the Jews by Claudius, it is of importance in this respect, that it furnishes, as was remarked in the introduction, a point of contact with profane history, which is of use in settling the chronology. Suetonius (Claud. c. xxv.), and Dio Cassius, (lx. 6) mention the occurrence. According to the most probable supposition it falls in the year 54 after the birth of Christ, or in the thirteenth year of the reign of Claudius.

The intimate connexion between the apostle and Aquila was brought about, not simply by the union of their hearts in the faith, but also by the outward circumstance that they practised the same handicraft. According to the Jewish custom, which required even the Rabbins to learn a trade, Paul followed the occupation of a *σκηνοποιός*. The Fathers, as for example, Chrysostom, understood this word to mean a worker in leather, *σκυτοτόμος*, because tents were often made of skins; but it is more suitable to understand it of the trade of a tentmaker, which was very much practised in Cilicia. The hair of a species of very shaggy goat was there wrought into a thick stuff like felt, which was very much employed in covering tents. (See Plin. hist. nat. vi. 28., Veget. de re milit. iv. 8.) The principal reason why the apostle always practised his trade during his apostolic ministry was this, that, on account of the numerous opponents who were watching all his movements, he believed it necessary (xx. 33) to shun every appearance of outward advantage, which he might derive from his office. The passage, however, in 1 Cor. ix. 14, shews that Paul was not unaware of the duty of those who received heavenly blessings in the preaching of the Gospel, to bestow upon the messengers who brought them, a portion of their earthly treasures. Paul was therefore far removed from the pride which is ashamed to take: in suitable circumstances he willingly received gifts of love, as we find from Phil. iv. 14, etc.

It is wrong, certainly, to regard the Jewish custom of learning a trade, in conjunction with the study of the law, simply as a means of securing worldly advancement: the true reason of this practice rather was, that by bodily exercise they might guard against the temptations to which idleness might lead. Monks and mystics have often felt the want of such a defence.*

Vers. 4–11.—In Corinth Paul now began to preach among the Jews and proselytes, and he taught with great zeal, particularly after the arrival of his assistants whom he had left behind in Macedonia. But the stubbornness of the Jews obliged him once more to renounce their society, and to turn to the Gentiles.† (There is a difficulty

* Regarding the procedure of the apostle, in supporting himself entirely by the labour of his own hands, see also the remarks at 1 Cor. ix. 7.

† Baur, in his effort to combat the historical character of the Acts of the Apostles, goes so far as to affirm, that Paul himself may have so far excited the opposition of the

in the expression συνέχεσθαι λόγῳ in ver. 5. The common text reads τῷ πνεύματι. This reading probably arose from the most familiar signification of συνέχεσθαι, which would be supposed the one here employed. It denotes in the first place "to be held together, to be pressed," and then "to be distressed, to be filled with anxiety." [See Luke viii. 41, ix. 43; Matth. iv. 24; Luke xii. 50.] This signification accords best with τῷ πνεύματι; and therefore λόγῳ, which was certainly the original reading, was banished from the text. But the same fundamental meaning of the word, "to be pressed together," leads quite naturally to another use of it, viz., incitari, "to be stirred up," for pressure, as in the bending of a bow, produces an augmentation of power. In this sense Paul plainly uses the word in 2 Cor. v. 14, ἡ ἀγάπη τοῦ Χριστοῦ συνέχει ἡμᾶς, "the love of Christ constrains, impels us." This is the signification which we must employ in the passage before us, and the words accordingly must be translated: "Paul laboured most zealously in preaching."—Ver. 6. On the expression αἷμα ἐπὶ τὴν κεφαλὴν ὑμῶν, see at Matth. xxvii. 25.)

Paul laboured for a year and a half in Corinth (ver. 11), and in this very city, the most luxurious and degraded of Greece, the Gospel celebrated her noblest triumphs; as if for the purpose of presenting us with a vivid proof of the great apostle's fundamental principle, that, where sin abounds, grace abounds much more. In the house of a certain man, Justus, beside the synagogue, Paul held his meetings; and Crispus, the superintendent of the Jews, became himself a believer, together with many Corinthians. In his room, it is probable, Sosthenes, who is mentioned in ver. 17, was chosen; but he appears also, according to 1 Cor. i. 1, to have joined himself to the church of God. It was probably the accession of so distinguished a man as Crispus to the church of Christ, that induced the apostle to depart from his usual custom of leaving his assistants to baptize, and to perform the rite himself. (1 Cor. i. 14.) The resolution of the apostle, to exercise his ministry for so long a time in the one city of Corinth, was confirmed, according to vers. 9, 10, by the peculiar circumstance that he had there a vision of Christ by night, who revealed to him that many chosen persons lived in Corinth. In 2 Cor. xii. 1, etc., Paul gives a detailed description of an ecstatic vision of this kind. (Ver. 7. Συνομορέω occurs nowhere else in the New Testament; it comes from ὅμορος, which appears to be compounded of ὁμοῦ and ὅρος.—Ver. 10. Ἐπιτιθέναι τινί denotes primarily "to lay something upon one:" in the middle it is used

Jews to the Gospel, in order to obtain a good apology for labouring among the Gentiles. It is a proper remark which Kling (Studien 1837, H. 2, s. 307) makes on this notion: "one must be astonished at the critical acumen, which could seduce one into an idea so destitute of all propriety."

for seizing, assaulting, as it were, "to throw one's self upon a person, to fall upon him.")

Vers. 12-17.—The extraordinary success attending the preaching of Paul, might excite the hatred of the Jews particularly against him. With their new president at their head (ver. 17), they accused him before the proconsul Gallio,* and dragged him even before his tribunal. This excellent man was a brother of the philosopher Lucius Annæus Seneca;† he was called originally Novatus, but assumed the other name from one Junius Gallio. (See Grotius on this passage. Tacitus Ann. vi. 3, xv. 73, makes mention of him.) This relationship of Gallio was probably what occasioned the fabrication of the apocryphal correspondence between Paul and Seneca. (See J. A. Fabricii. cod. apocr. N. T., vol. i.) It has been supposed that Gallio was converted by Paul,‡ and that he then brought about an acquaintance between Paul and his brother, who also was won over to the Gospel. (Gallio entirely declined to enter upon the consideration of controverted points in the Jewish law, and required that the Jews should accuse Paul of some moral offence, which, however, they could not do, and this was a testimony in favour of the apostle. Ver. 12. Achaia denotes not simply the district of this name in the

* Regarding Gallio consult the excellent notices of Tholuck (Glaubw. s. 173), which bring into view how minutely Luke shows himself to have been acquainted with all circumstances. Luke styles Gallio proconsul: now these officers were only in the provinciis senatoriis; but Achaia was changed by Tiberius into a provincia imperatoria, and provinces of this kind were only governed by procurators. (Tacit. Annal. i. 76.) But Claudius had given back Achaia to the Senate. (Suet. Claud. c. 25.) Luke's narrative is therefore quite accurate. With propriety does Tholuck draw attention to the circumstance, that it might have been supposed Luke had here committed a mistake, if this one passage of Suetonius had been wanting. How much, therefore, that is apparently wrong, would appear quite right, if all sources lay completely before us.

† Gallio is here spoken of very favourably. And certainly there is but small ground furnished in the text for that obloquy which has been thrown upon this Roman governor. He acted rightly when he refused to be a judge in the case of a religious dispute between the Jews and one of their countrymen. He was ready to listen to any accusation that might refer to criminal conduct, and to sift the evidence that might be adduced; but he would not constitute himself a judge of Jewish controversy. In this certainly he acted a wise and noble part; and it was his conduct that secured for Paul a peaceful opportunity of prosecuting his ministry at Corinth. Why, then, has Gallio been so unsparingly condemned? The reason lies in a misapprehension of one clause in the 17th verse, where it is said Gallio cared for none of these things, which has been understood to mean, that he was wholly indifferent to religious matters, and was an infidel. But this is not the sense of the words. They mean that he would not interfere at all in the way of constituting himself a judge of the disputed points, that he even allowed the parties to come to blows without interposing his authority. Now, Gallio was perfectly right in wholly refraining from giving a judgment on the disputed points; but he was wrong in not employing his authority to prevent all violence. He should have kept the peace between the contending parties.—[Tr.

‡ This, according to Eusebius (Chron. a. 66), is improbable, as Gallio put a period to his own existence.

Peloponnesus, but it was also employed by the Romans to designate the whole of Greece, and the Peloponnesus, which formed one province.—Ver. 14. Ῥᾳδιούργημα = ῥᾳδιουργία in xiii. 10. The first of these words, however, like ἁμάρτημα, as compared with ἁμαρτία, only denotes the single act, or wickedness viewed as an isolated deed.—Κατὰ λόγον, "rightly, conformably to reason."—Ver. 15. The word ὄνομα refers to the name Messiah, which the Jews affirmed should not be given to Jesus.)

Vers. 18–22.—This conduct of the proconsul made it practicable for Paul to remain a long time in Corinth* (see verse 11), and at last he left the city of his own accord, without being further molested by his adversaries. The friendly family of Aquila accompanied him to Ephesus, where they remained behind (ver. 26). Paul took shipping in Cenchrea, the harbour of Corinth, situated on the Asiatic side, seventy stadia from the city; the other harbour, that looked in the direction of Italy, being called Lechæus. In Cenchrea, Paul had his hair shorn in fulfilment of a vow. It has been supposed by many, that the words κειράμενος τὴν κεφαλήν refer to Aquila; but the connexion is decidedly opposed to this idea. It is only quite incidentally that mention is made of Aquila and Priscilla; Paul is the subject of the whole sentence, and also of the one that follows. No reason can be perceived, why so unimportant a circumstance should have been stated regarding Aquila. It is true those learned men who deny the reference of the words to Paul, suppose that the statement cannot be applied to him, because it would have been inconsistent with his principles regarding the abrogation of the ceremonial law of Moses to have taken upon him a vow. But that supposition is grounded upon a total misconception of Paul's view of the law. Strenuously as the apostle contended that the native Gentiles, to whom the law was a foreign institution, should not be compelled to observe it, yet he was very far from forbidding the native Jews to keep it, or from disregarding it altogether himself. It is quite probable that Paul, when he was living among Gentiles, conducted himself very freely with reference to the legal observances of Moses, which was the ground of the charge he was afterwards called upon by the apostles in Jerusalem to confute practically;† but that he should have altogether abandoned, while residing in heathen lands, the observance of the law in reference to his own person, is in the highest degree improbable, because he would thus

* The stay of the apostle Paul in Corinth is worthy of attention on this ground, that it was during it he began his labours in writing. The Epistles to the Thessalonians, the oldest among those preserved to us, Paul wrote from Corinth. The particulars regarding the time and the occasion of composing these, and all the other letters of Paul, will be given in the introductions to them.

† See Acts xxi. 17, etc., and the Commentary on this passage regarding the freedom of the Jewish Christians from the law.

have violated his own principle of respecting the scruples of weak brethren; for there were Jews everywhere, to whom his conduct must have given offence. This passage, therefore, is important, because it shews, and perhaps for this very reason it was introduced by Luke, that Paul had not altogether given up the personal observance of the law, but retained it as a religious usage. With respect to the subsequent accusation, therefore, mentioned in chap. xxi. 17, etc., he is with the readers of the Acts of the Apostles justified in advance. The entire loosening of the whole church, and even of Jewish Christians, from the outward forms of the Old Testament, Paul would not on any account bring about with revolutionary precipitation; but he left it to be effected gradually by the evolution of events; and it was at last accomplished in this way for the mother church of the Jewish Christians, by the destruction of Jerusalem by Hadrian, and by the fact that the Jews were forbidden to dwell in Ælia Capitolina, the city which was built in its room.

The occasion of the vow itself (εὐχή) which Paul had made, is not known to us. Many have imagined that it was the Nazarite vow which he had taken on him, but this certainly is not to be thought of. The probability is, that, according to the custom of the Jews, it was in some danger or difficulty he had made the vow in question; and now therefore, in prosecution of this vow, he cuts his hair, and hastens to Jerusalem that he may there offer the requisite sacrifice within the prescribed term* of thirty days. In this manner we find an explanation of the haste with which he leaves Ephesus (ver. 21), and at the same time of the subsequent repetition of a similar vow, chap. xxi. 17, etc., which best enabled him to confute all accusations of the Jews, just as he confuted them at this time.

In Ephesus, Paul, according to his custom, appeared again in the synagogue. The Jews were quite friendly, particularly as they found him occupied with the performance of a vow, and they requested him to remain. But as he needed to present the offering in Jerusalem itself, he hastened speedily away, promising however to come back. He went by Cæsarea to Jerusalem; but of his stay there Luke mentions no particulars; only the participle ἀναβὰς in verse 22 points to it, for ἀναβαίνειν = עָלָה, is specially applied to the journey to Jerusalem. From Jerusalem he went down to Antioch, for he always regarded the church there as the one which had sent him forth to the heathen.

* See on this point, J sephus (B. J. ii. 15, 1), who makes mention of a vow of Berenice, and then adds: τοὺς γὰρ ἢ νόσῳ καταπονουμένους, ἤ τισιν ἄλλαις ἀνάγκαις, ἔθος εὔχεσθαι πρὸ τριάκοντα ἡμερῶν, ἧς ἀποδώσειν μέλλοιεν θυσίας, οἴνου τε ἀφέξεσθαι καὶ ξυρήσασθαι τὰς κόμας.

A chronological question which presents itself here regarding not only the year, but also the season of the year; for Paul names a feast (ver. 21) which he purposed to observe in Jerusalem, as it coincided with the time when his offering was to be presented, and he would probably at the same time obey the Mosaic injunction, which required that the great festivals should be attended by all the male members of the Israelitish nation. Now most chronologers (see the second chronological table) regard Pentecost as the feast referred to by Paul, and probably Pentecost of the year 55 after the birth of Christ; but still this is only a supposition, for there are no decisive arguments to prove it, and the date of the other events in the life of Paul is not so accurately fixed, that from the earlier or the later we can reckon back to this feast, and determine which of the great festivals Paul here means.

(In the Codices A. E. 13, 14, 15, 36, and others, this clause of ver. 21 is wanting: *δεῖ με πάντως τὴν ἑορτὴν τὴν ἐρχομένην ποιῆσαι εἰς Ἱεροσόλυμα πάλιν.* On the authority of these manuscripts many distinguished critics regard the words in question as a gloss, and even Heinrichs and Kuinoel follow them. They proceed on this principle that the omission of them would be inexplicable, but the insertion of them easily accounted for, transcribers supposing that the fulfilment of the vow required the journey to Jerusalem. But the omission may be very easily explained from a confounding of the similar words *δεῖ* and *δέ* at the beginning and end of the clause; and the statement itself is of a kind which could not well be made by a transcriber desirous of inserting a mere notice: in no case certainly would a transcriber have made mention of a feast, to which there was nothing in the connexion to lead. Any person, designing to supplement the verse merely from the connexion, would have stated something regarding the offering. But if the words be genuine, they determine more particularly the reference of *ἀναβάς* in verse 22, which many interpreters do not regard as pointing to Jerusalem, but to Cæsarea. But as *κατελθὼν εἰς Καισάρειαν* occurs before, and *κατέβη εἰς Ἀντιόχειαν* follows, it is plain that *ἀναβαίνειν* cannot be used with respect to Paul's entrance into Cæsarea, supposing even that it lay upon a high shore. It still remains therefore the most probable supposition, that Paul journeyed to Antioch by way of Jerusalem, where he saluted the mother church and the apostles.)

III.

PART THIRD.

FROM PAUL'S THIRD MISSIONARY JOURNEY TILL THE FIRST CAPTIVITY AT ROME.

(Acts xviii. 23—xxviii. 31.)

---

§ 1. Paul's Third Missionary Excursion. Abode in Ephesus.

(Acts xviii. 23—xix. 41.)

Ver. 23.—Luke gives us but very general information regarding Paul's journey through Asia Minor during which he visited individually the churches of Galatia, and also regarding the time of his stay in Antioch. It is probable that the ardent apostle broke away very speedily again from Antioch, that he might confirm his numerous churches in Asia. This might appear to him the more necessary, if, as is probable, the differences with Peter, of which we have already spoken at chap. xv. 1, arose during his present visit to the mother church of the Gentiles. Perhaps in Antioch Paul found himself, along with a number of preachers of the Gospel, engaged in something like a general consultation regarding the principles of their apostolic ministry; and as on this occasion what was new in the Gospel presented itself most strongly in conflict with the whole ancient forms of religious life, Peter might be led to waver for a moment, particularly as some of the strict Jewish Christians pressed hard upon him. (See further particulars in the exposition of the Epistle to the Galatians, which was written shortly after this journey.)

Vers. 24-28.—Before Luke however describes the labours of Paul in Ephesus, he mentions the accession to the church of Christ of a man of great influence, viz., Apollos of Alexandria, who was at that time sojourning in Ephesus. The statements made regarding this learned and distinguished man, taken in connexion with the notices that immediately follow in chap. xix. 1-7, are among the most interesting parts of the Acts of the Apostles. They give us an insight into the excited state of religious life at that time, such as few other sections of this book afford. True, this passage has its own peculiar difficulties. Apollos himself, like those twelve men mentioned in chap. xix. 7, whom one at first is tempted to distinguish from him, was a disciple of John the Baptist : he had been directed by this faithful witness of the truth to Jesus as the true and long expected Messiah, or, if he had not known John himself, he had been guided by disciples of his school to the Saviour. He himself, however, or his instructors among the disciples of John, had learned nothing regarding the glorification and exaltation of Christ in his resurrection and ascension, nor regarding the gift of the Holy Ghost as the consequence of his elevation. That Apollos taught not only regarding John the Baptist, but also regarding Jesus, is plain not only from ver. 25, where the expressions *κατηχημένος τὴν ὁδὸν τοῦ κυρίου* and *διδάσκειν ἀκριβῶς τὰ περὶ τοῦ κυρίου*, but also particularly from chap. xix 2, where the name *μαθηταί* is applied to disciples of John, who occupied a quite similar position to Apollos. Here then we find Christians who lived, as it were, *beside* the great spiritual fellowship of the Gospel, like an offshoot from the tree of the kingdom of God, without knowing anything of the church.*

Two considerations are pressed upon our notice by this fact. On *the one hand*, we perceive from it with what power the appearance of Christ in the world wrought at that time : even in remote districts he was acknowledged, and the fact of his advent (vers. 25, 26), was spread abroad with zeal and courage, while as yet the full splendour of his light was not beheld. From the school of John there proceeded not merely men like the apostles, who attached themselves wholly to the church, nor merely men who openly opposed Christianity, and, like the later Zabeans, made the Baptist, contrary to his own will and public declarations, their Messiah ; but also an intermediate party, who had been directed by the Baptist to Jesus as the Messiah, and been illuminated with some beams of his light, but had acquired no further knowledge of him, probably because their connexion with Palestine was early broken off, perhaps by journeys which they made into the heathen world before the outpouring of the Holy Ghost. *And, on the other hand*, the fact before us shews how expansive was the brotherly love that was cherished by the apostolic church. Notwithstanding the very weak apprehension which these disciples of John certainly had of the new dispensation of Divine mercy, the apostles recognized them as *disciples*, on the principle that no one can call Jesus Lord but by the operation, known or unknown, of the Spirit, and only endeavoured to advance their knowledge of Divine things. It is true, if the disciples of John had withstood the offered means of advancement, they would have exposed themselves to censure, and would have gone over into heresy, like the Zabeans ; but so long as they were merely ignorant of the

* See Neander's Church History, part ii. p. 646, etc., also Gesenius im Probeheft der Encyclop. von Gruber und Ersch Art. Zabier.

principle of life procured by Christ, the apostles treated them only as immature disciples, who were in a state of transition from the Old Covenant to the New, acquainted indeed with the high priest of the latter by name, but without having felt the power of the blood of sprinkling.

Now if Apollos, according to the view we have given, occupied precisely the same position in respect of religion with the disciples of John subsequently mentioned there arises a difficulty in the account before us, in the apparently different treatment of Apollos and of the twelve disciples of John. They are baptized (chap. xix. 5), but he only receives more minute instruction regarding the Gospel (chap. xviii. 26). We cannot believe that it was the greater learning of Apollos and his talents which occasioned this difference of treatment, because it is self-evident, that such endowments belonging to the natural man could never render the higher principle of the Holy Ghost unnecessary. And just as little is it probable that the apostles would pursue a vacillating course in their treatment of the disciples of John: we must rather suppose that they were guided as to this point by some fixed principle. Now as Apollos received his first clear views of the nature of the Gospel only from Aquila, who, as not being an apostle, could not impart to him the Holy Ghost, the most suitable supposition we can make is, that Apollos was really baptized in the name of Christ in Ephesus by Aquila, but first received the Holy Ghost through Paul in Corinth. In this view the occurrence forms no contradiction at all with chap. viii.: there the apostles do not repeat the act of baptism, because Philip had administered Christian baptism in the name of the Father, of the Son, and of the Holy Ghost: but here the baptism of the Spirit is connected with Christian water baptism, because the disciples had only received John's baptism of repentance.*

(Ver. 24.—The form of the name Apollos, Ἀπολλώς, is abbreviated from Ἀπολλώνιος.—The description *ἀνὴρ λόγιος* may refer either

* If the general practice in the apostolic church was that the apostles alone imparted the gift of the Holy Ghost, the question may be asked, what was the case after their death? The imposition of hands continued, it is known, in the church, and every bishop or presbyter communicated the gift of the Spirit according to the measure in which he had received him; but no one possessed the Spirit in the same rich manner and with such original power as the apostles; and therefore if *χαρίσματα* (gifts) were to be found here and there after the apostles' death, the probability is that their manifestations were far weaker than in the time of the apostles. Paul only had not received the Holy Ghost by the imposition of the hands of another apostle (Gal. i. 12), but immediately from the Lord. When and how this communication of the Spirit was made to the Apostle Paul, we know not: as was remarked at the passage in Acts ix. 17, it almost appears that the Holy Ghost was communicated to him, as to Cornelius, before baptism. At all events, however, the Spirit came to him, without the intervention of an apostle, as is clearly apparent from Galat. i. 12.

to eloquence or to learning; but as the Jewish form of learning is plainly described in the words δυνατὸς ἐν ταῖς γραφαῖς, the idea of eloquence is rather to be preferred in this case. Apollos then possessed a distinguished gift of speaking, and was at the same time very accurately acquainted with the Scriptures, without doubt according to the mode of interpretation prevalent among the Gnostics of Alexandria. If Apollos, as has been supposed, or at least some man very similarly trained, was the author of the Epistle to the Hebrews, then we see in this remarkable composition, how the Spirit of Christ consecrated that form of culture, and purified it from false intermixtures.—Ver. 25. The phrase ζέειν πνεύματι is found also in Rom. xii. 11. Apollos, and probably many other elevated men of that stamp, were already animated to enthusiasm by the idea, that the ancient promise of the Messiah had received its fulfilment in the advent of Christ, and yet they knew not the plenitude of spiritual gifts, which were bestowed through him upon the human race.—Ver. 27. Συμβάλλεσθαι is to be understood in the signification of "conferre," "to be profitable," "to give support and help." And χάρις = χάρισμα, is to be understood of the peculiar gift of teaching and preaching, which Apollos possessed.—Ver. 28. Εὐτόνως has already occurred in Luke xxiii. 10.—The form διακατελέγχεσθαι, which strengthens the signification of the simple verb, is found in no other part of the New Testament.)

Chap. xix. 1-7.—The commencement of this chapter looks back, it is obvious, to the account of Paul's journey interrupted at chap. xviii. 23, and mentions his arrival in Ephesus. (The μέρη ['Ασίας] ἀνωτερικά, *upper parts of Asia*, denote the provinces that lay more in the interior of Asia Minor, as opposed to Ephesus, which lay upon the sea-shore.) Here the apostle found twelve disciples of John (ver. 7), who, like Apollos, were only acquainted with John's baptism of repentance (ver. 3); they had been directed by the Baptist to look to Jesus as the Messiah (ver. 2), but they knew nothing of the Holy Ghost, the higher principle of heavenly life procured by Christ for his disciples (John vii. 39). The only difficulty connected with this account springs from the remark in ver. 2: ἀλλ' οὐδὲ εἰ πνεῦμα ἅγιόν ἐστιν ἠκούσαμεν, *we have not even heard if there is a Holy Ghost*. It certainly appears astonishing that these men should know nothing of the Holy Ghost; while yet the Old Testament frequently speaks of an outpouring of the Spirit. The participle δοθέν has therefore been supplied to ἔστιν, and some Codices too instead of ἔστιν read λαμβάνουσί τινες. In this view the disciples of John, when they used these words, only declared that they had not heard that any outpouring of the Spirit had actually taken place. But if we compare the passage in John vii. 39 (see the remarks there offered), it will appear that this view merely throws back the difficulty, but does not solve it. The meaning of the words undoubtedly is, that those men knew nothing even of the existence of the Holy Ghost. It is true the doctrine was clearly unfolded in the Old Testament that God is a *Spirit*, and that he is *holy;* but that in the Divine Being there exists that peculiar power which the church names the third person in the Godhead, they did not know; and they could not discover it in the Old Testament, because it is only the clearness of the New Testament which enables one looking backward to find it in the Old. It is probable even that they did not regard the Messiah as the only begotten Son of God, but merely as an extraordinary man (*ἄνθρωπος κατ' ἐκλογήν*). The meaning of their words therefore is, that God still appeared to them as a simple, self-contained, indivisible unity, and that they knew nothing of those distinctions of Father, Son, and Holy Ghost, necessarily grounded in the nature of God's spiritual essence, without which we cannot conceive God communicating and revealing himself as the Living one. Now, on account of this imperfect knowledge of God, they needed still to be baptized in the name of the Father, the Son, and the Holy Ghost. What we have supposed therefore in the case of Apollos, is here plainly declared, viz., that those who had received the baptism of John were baptized the second time.

It was a very obvious course for all the advocates of rebaptizing from Cyprian down to the Anabaptists and Mennonites, to adduce this passage in their defence; and the views of it which were adopted by the orthodox, in order to deprive them of the argument based upon it, were certainly more forced than even their interpretation of it in favour of their darling idea. It was said, for example, that ver. 5 still refers to the baptism of John, and is so connected with the words of Paul in ver. 4, that the meaning is, "when they heard him, viz., the Baptist, they were baptized by him in the name of the Lord Jesus." But it is manifest that the baptism of John could not possibly be styled baptism in the name of Jesus: the Baptist only directed those already baptized to Jesus, after he was convinced of his Messiahship by the descent of the Spirit upon him. Yet men like Beza, Calixtus, Buddeus, could allow themselves to be so misled as to adopt this untenable supposition, that they might wrench from the Anabaptists their proof-passage. The best expedient was the one devised by Ziegler. (Theol. Abh. Th. ii.) He supposed that these disciples of John had been infected with the error of those who declared the Baptist himself to be the Messiah, and who were also baptized in the name of the Baptist. They had not, therefore, received the right Johannic baptism, and of course they needed to be baptized again, which would not have been the case, had they been properly baptized by John in the name of the approaching Messiah. Under this view, certainly, we can carry through the principle that the disciples of John were not baptized, as there are no certain traces of it elsewhere to be found. But even this explanation is untenable, being fully refuted by the single consideration that in that case the disciples of John would certainly not have been styled μαθηταί, as they are in chap. xix. 1.

But even taking the words in their obvious sense it does not thence follow that the Anabaptists are right, in adducing this passage in their defence. They only assert, in *the first place*, that no child should be baptized, because in their view the inward baptism, which presupposes consciousness, should always coincide with the outward; and, in *the second place*, that those who have been baptized simply as unconscious children, and thus have not received the true baptism at all, ought to be baptized when they come to maturity. An actual repetition of baptism, therefore, is not taught by the Anabaptists: they merely assail the propriety of infant baptism, of which there is nothing said in the passage before us, which therefore it is clear, on a closer view of the point of debate, ought never to have been applied to the question at all.

If then the apostles baptized anew, on their entrance into the Christian church, those who had been baptized by John the Baptist or by his adherents, the question arises, whether those who were baptized by the disciples of Jesus before the institution of the sacrament of baptism (see John iii. 26, iv. 2) would also require to submit to baptism again? There is nothing certainly in the nature of this baptism, to shew that this might not be the case, for as the power of the Holy Ghost was not yet imparted, it could not be the laver of regeneration; moreover, it is probable that the disciples had baptized but a few, and that only immediately after they were disengaged from the Baptist and connected with Jesus, and while they were still under the influence of the ideas of John. And this explains why it is only at this early period in the passages cited above, that we find any notice of the subject, and nowhere observe any further traces of it. But these few individuals may have attached themselves quite closely to the company of Christ, and thus along with the apostles, who were not afterwards baptized by the Lord, they may have immediately received on the day of Pentecost the Holy Ghost, whose communication would render quite unnecessary the administration of the outward ordinance.

Vers. 8–12.—The following verses give a short account of the ministry of Paul in Ephesus. For three months he preached to the Jews: afterwards he turned to the Gentiles, and laboured for two years among them, teaching in the school-room of one Tyrannus.*

* It was during the period of this residence of Paul in Ephesus that the Epistle to the Galatians, and the two to the Corinthians, were composed. The second of the

Many cures too were performed by Paul in this place. (On σκληρύνεσθαι in vers. 9, see at Rom. ix. 18. Here the hardening is ascribed to the unfaithfulness of the Jews themselves, but there it is attributed to God. The milder form of expression which is here chosen, "the hardening of one's self," is the more usual one in Scripture.—Ver. 9. Ἀφώρισε refers merely to the separation of their places of meeting. Σχολή means a school or lecture room; it is probable that Tyrannus kept a school of rhetoric.—Ver. 12. On σουδάριον comp. at John xi. 44. Σιμικίνθιον, from "semi" and "cingere," denotes an apron, and occurs not again in the New Testament. It is such articles of dress plainly, as could be easily laid aside and used elsewhere, that are named. Regarding cures effected by such objects, see remarks on Acts v. 15. Here, however, the conduct of the multitude exhibits more decided marks of superstition than the case mentioned in chap. v. 15. The person of Peter was always present along with his shadow, but here articles of clothing only make their appearance, and they are regarded as impregnated with the apostle's power. When these have a healing efficacy ascribed to them, which is traced back to God, this can only be regarded as a condescension of the Divine mercy to individuals who, though erring, are yet well-intentioned. The apostles themselves certainly have not given countenance to such ideas, for there is no trace of them anywhere to be found.*)

Vers. 13–17.—With this account of the miracles performed by Paul, Luke connects the description of an occurrence altogether singular. Jewish exorcists who witnessed the mighty works of the apostle, supposed that his power lay in the use of the name Jesus; and therefore they expected that the mere employment of it would enable them to exhibit similar results. (See the remarks at Matth. xviii. 5 on a like occurrence.) However strange this notion may appear to us, still it is in entire accordance with the ideas of antiquity, and particularly those of wonder-workers among the Jews, who imagined that the utterance of certain words or formulæ had a mighty power connected with it. And therefore the Rabbins afterwards explained the miracles of Jesus himself by the supposition that he was acquainted with the holy name of Jehovah. ([illegible].) (See Eisenmenger's entdeck. Judenth. Part I. p. 154.) The employment of the name of Jesus by the exorcists had no effect upon the demoniacs, nay, they even manifested hostility to them; a hos-

latter however was probably written after the apostle was driven away by the proceedings of Demetrius the goldsmith, and most likely in Macedonia. (Acts xx. 1, 2.)

* There is no necessary limit to God's mode of miraculous working. We might connect it alike with the touching of the Saviour's garment, with the shadow of Peter, and with the napkin borne from Paul. So long as there was the actual exercise of miraculous power, and it was ascribed to its right source, there seems no ground for the imputation of superstition.—[K.

tility easily explained from that heightened power of perception developed among such unfortunates, by which they at once recognized the inefficacy of the words uttered. (That the Jews too attempted to exorcise evil spirits,* and that often with success, has already appeared from Matth. xii. 27.—In ver. 13, the words ὁρκίζω ὑμᾶς τὸν Ἰησοῦν are followed by ὃν ὁ Παῦλος κηρύσσει; for the reason, doubtless, that the name of Jesus was so common, that there was need of a more particular description to point out the person indicated. Now as these Jews could not of course recognize Jesus as the Messiah, no other method was left but to mark him out by the person who was preaching him with such zeal in Ephesus. On the construction of ὁρκίζω with the accusative, with which supply διά, see Mark v. 7, and 1 Thess. v. 27.—The persons who made this attempt in Ephesus were seven sons of Sceva, a priest of distinction [ἀρχιερέως], who probably was at the head of the Ephesian Jews.—On the use of τὶς in connexion with numbers, see Winer's Gram. p. 158. It is found again in Acts xxiii. 23. However, it might be better to suppose that τὶς does not here refer to the number, but that Luke states the number by way of addition.—Ver. 15. The phrase πνεῦμα πονηρόν is used by Luke with peculiar frequency: instead of it the other two synoptical Evangelists commonly employ πνεῦμα ἀκάθαρτον.—In ver. 16, the reading ἀμφοτέρων has probably arisen from this, that it was regarded as impossible that one should be able to contend against seven. In demoniacs, however, as in the insane, the power of the muscles is often found augmented to an incredible extent. See at Matth. viii. 28.)

Vers. 18-20.—What occurred with the sons of Sceva only augmented, as was to be expected, the consequence of Paul. Almost the entire mass of the people began to repent, and many, beholding the real wonders of the living God, destroyed the idolatrous charms by which the priests attempted to counterfeit miracles. (In ver. 18, ἐξομολογεῖσθαι and ἀναγγέλλειν τὰς πράξεις cannot, as Kuinoel supposes, apply to the general confession of their sins: in this view it would be impossible to keep the two sufficiently distinct from one another in sense. The πράξεις rather denote, as is plain from the connexion, magical arts, and ἐξομολογεῖσθαι means to make confession of these before the apostle or individual believers; ἀναγγέλλειν, on the other hand, refers to the public acknowledgment of them before all, for the purpose of warning against such delusions.—Ver. 19. Περίεργος, like curiosus, is applied particularly to those curious and busy individuals, who employ magical arts to search into the future. The worship of Artemis in Ephesus was connected with many mysterious ceremonies, by which her priests and worshippers

* Josephus too (Antiq. viii. 2, 5) makes mention of magical charms, which were ascribed to Solomon, and by which the Jewish conjurers attempted to perform cures.

were led to the practice of magical arts, which they cultivated to a great extent. The Ephesian charms and amulets [γράμματα ἀλεξιφάρμακα Ἐφέσια]* were therefore prized above all others.—The estimated value of these books amounted to fifty thousand drachmæ, that is, about six thousand rix dollars.†—Ver. 20. Κατὰ κράτος is to be understood adverbially in the signification of "admodum, vehementer;" not with Θεοῦ supplied in the sense of juvante Deo.)

Vers. 21, 22.—After these occurrences, Paul now determined, as the Gospel appeared quite firmly established in Ephesus, both to revisit the churches in Macedonia and Achaia, and also to go to Rome, the great metropolis of the heathen world. Previously, however, he merely sent away Timothy and Erastus to Macedonia, and for some time longer he exerted his energies in behalf of Asia.—(Ver. 21. The phrase ἔθετο ἐν πνεύματι supposes the previous entrance of the plan into one's mind, and indicates that a decision had been come to in its favour. On the other hand, the words εἰς τὴν Ἀσίαν, in ver. 22, are to be understood as meaning, "for the benefit of Asia."—In Rom. xvi. 23, another Erastus is named, who was resident in Corinth. This travelling companion of Paul appears again in 2 Tim. iv. 20.—Ἐπέχειν scilicet ἑαυτόν, in the sense of "to detain one's self, to sojourn, to tarry," occurs no where else in the New Testament, but frequently in good Greek writers, *e. g.*, Xenophon. Paul's purpose in sending forward his two associates to Macedonia, was no other than this, to make preparations for the collection, which he was desirous of carrying to the poor saints in Jerusalem. Comp. 1 Cor. xvi. 1, etc.)

Vers. 23-27.—But immediately after the dismission of these two assistants, a mighty storm arose against the apostle, which was occasioned by Demetrius, a goldsmith. This man was employed in making little silver images of the celebrated Temple of Artemis, and he found his gains curtailed by the prodigious influence of the apostle in the whole of Asia.‡ Now, as he exercised his trade on a great scale, and many men were dependent upon him, he stirred up against Paul in the hearts of the fanatical multitude the same hatred which burned in his own bosom.—(Ver. 24. It has been

* Hesychius, in his Lexicon under this word, adduces some forms from such magical books; for example, the words ἄσκι, κατάσκι, λίξ, τετράξ, δαμναμενεύς, αἴσιον. He supposes that they were Greek words designedly transposed, but perhaps they were only unmeaning sounds, which have a resemblance quite casually to Greek. Similar sounds in a Latin form are to be found in the magical books of the middle ages.

† In forming a judgment of this great sum (about £1350 stg.), which, according to another calculation, rises much higher still, we must bear in mind, first, the high price of books generally in ancient times, and, secondly, the exaggerated value which the magicians ascribed to their books of magic.

‡ Regarding the rapid spread of Christianity in Asia Minor, see the account given by Pliny in his letters. (x. 97.) This account is printed in my work Monum. hist. eccl. i. 23, etc.

falsely supposed that the silver temples were medals with the impression of the Temple of Diana upon them, but we should rather view them as small images of the building, which travellers and pilgrims purchased for a token of remembrance. Such little temples were called ἀφιδρύματα. Dionys. Hal. ii. 22. And they were made of gold, silver, or wood.—Ver. 25. Εὐπορία, "abundantia, opulence." —Ver. 26. The words ὅτι οὐκ εἰσὶ θεοὶ οἱ διὰ χειρῶν γινόμενοι, refer to the rude popular view which supposed the image to be the God himself. The better educated heathens regarded the image merely as a symbol of the heavenly divinity.—Ver. 27. The word ἀπελεγμός occurs nowhere else in the New Testament: εἰς ἀπελεγμὸν ἐλθεῖν is synonymous with ἀπελέγχεσθαι.)

Vers. 28-34.—The multitude, excited by the covetous Demetrius, raised the cry, "great is Diana of the Ephesians;" and rushed to the theatre, as the place commonly employed for meetings of the people. Two travelling associates of Paul, Gaius and Aristarchus, both from Macedonia, they dragged along with them; Paul himself would have gone forth among the multitude, but he was held back by his distinguished patrons. The unruly crowd, swelled by mere alarmists, who knew not even the cause of the tumult (ver. 32), would not suffer a Jew named Alexander, who wished to speak to the people, to utter a word; and it was only when the town-clerk appeared, that the uproar was hushed.

Ver. 29.—Not to punish the prisoners, as in the persecutions of later times, but only to procure a meeting of the people, the excited multitude betook themselves to the theatre. Aristarchus is more particularly described in chap. xx. 4, as also Gaius. The person named in Rom. xvi. 23, who resided in Corinth, is not to be confounded with him.—Συνέκδημος, fellow-traveller, occurs again in the New Testament in 2 Cor. viii. 19.—Ver. 31 shews how considerable was the influence which Paul had acquired in Ephesus, and with this his declaration in 1 Cor. xvi. 9, quite agrees. The friends of Paul belonged to the Asiarchs, who always required to be the richest and most respectable people of the city. The office of these men, who were changed from year to year, had reference entirely to religious affairs: the Asiarchs had the oversight of the sacred places of the city, and were required to arrange the sacred games at their own expense. Besides Ephesus, the other cities of Asia too appointed Asiarchs, who formed together a college (τὸ κοινόν). The president of this college appears always to have belonged to the metropolis: at least we find that the years were counted by the Asiarch, as by the consuls among the Romans. (See Euseb. Hist. Ecc. iv. 15; Winer's Reallex. under the word Asiarch.)—Ver. 33. Alexander the Jew, who wished to speak, and who doubtless designed to speak against the apostle and his ministry, is perhaps the same person whom Paul describes in 2 Tim. iv. 14, as his furious enemy.* The Jews pushed him forward as their speaker, that their influence too might be employed in turning the tumult to the discredit of Paul; but on this occasion the heathen element had so great a preponderance, that they could make no impression.

Vers. 35–41.—The town-clerk now quieted the uproar; and he both did justice to the zeal of the Ephesians for their goddess, and at the same time referred to the innocence of the accused, and pointed out the hazardous political consequences which such popular commotions might produce. This latter suggestion might probably appear to Demetrius himself a very important one, and he might then employ his influence in appeasing the multitude.—(Ver. 35. The office of the γραμματεύς was a very respectable one in Ephesus, as in the other cities of Asia. The name probably arose from this, that the archives of the state were under his care, and it was his duty to prepare all official writings. The expression corresponds nearly to our secretary of state. [See Hemsen in his life of the apostle Paul, page 232. Note.]—Καταστέλλειν is the usual word for suppressing a popular commotion.—Νεωκόρος means properly sweeping, *i. e.* cleansing the temple, and then in general, careful about the worship of the gods. The word is not unfrequently found on coins as an epithet of several cities.—To Διοπετές supply ἄγαλμα. So were certain idols named, which were supposed to have fallen from heaven. This was long regarded as a mere fable, like the accounts of showers of stones given by the ancients; but it is more probable that real ærolites, whose origin they were unable to explain, were regarded by them as presents from the gods. The stone, which the Romans brought from Asia to Rome as the image of Cybele, was undoubtedly a meteoric stone. The accounts, however, given by the ancient writers of the image of Diana of the Ephesians are very various. [See Plin. H. N. xvi. 79.]—Ver. 36. The town-clerk, as well as the Asiarchs, is manifestly favourably disposed towards Paul; he takes upon himself the defence of him and his attendants.—Προπετής means properly "præceps," "falling forward, then præcipitate, over-hasty, rash." It occurs in the New Testament again in 2 Tim. iii. 4.—Ver. 38, ἀγόραιοι must be carefully distinguished from ἀγοραῖοι in chap. xviii. 5. The latter denotes men who rove or loiter idly about the market-place; the former, with which supply ἡμέραι, means court days, dies judiciales. The plural ἀνθύπατοι does not mean that there were several proconsuls, but only indicates that there was *always* a proconsul among them.—Ver. 40. It was a very skillfully directed warning the town-clerk gave them, that the Ro-

* According to 1 Cor. xvi. 9, however, the apostle had many that withstood him in Ephesus: the Alexander therefore who opposed him towards the end of his life, may have been another individual.

mans might see something of sedition in this tumult; the fear therefore of losing still more in money and goods, than they had lost by the preaching of the apostle, speedily brought them to a state of quietness. Συστροφή here means only an uproar, but as the word also involves the idea of a conspiracy [see Acts xxiii. 12], it was probably designedly chosen to suggest to the meeting, what construction might easily be put upon the commotion.

§ 2. PAUL'S JOURNEY FROM EPHESUS TO JERUSALEM.

(Acts xx. 1—xxi. 16.)

Vers. 1–3.—The departure of Paul from Ephesus took place after a solemn meeting, in which the apostle took leave of the brethren. It stands in connexion certainly with the uproar of Demetrius, but that it was occasioned or hastened thereby, as Eichhorn supposes, is not at all indicated: indeed the words "after the tumult ceased" (μετὰ τὸ παύσασθαι τὸν θόρυβον) are opposed to this idea, for the mention of the ceasing of the tumult shews that the apostle might have remained quietly in Ephesus if he had chosen. We may therefore suppose that the apostle attained his purpose, of waiting in Ephesus till Pentecost, viz., of the year 59, and of seeing Timothy return from his mission (1 Cor. xvi. 8, 11), and therefore the time shortly after the departure of Paul from Ephesus would be a suitable period to which to assign the composition of the first Epistle to Timothy. (See 1 Tim. i. 3.) The apostle, according to what is here narrated, goes first to Macedonia (by Troas, to wit, where he expected Titus, who was to bring him intelligence regarding Corinth, and the impression his first epistle had made on the church there, 2 Cor. ii. 12, 13), and he was also going, according to 1 Tim. i. 3, to Macedonia, having left Timothy behind in Ephesus. Either from Troas, therefore, or from Macedonia, where he wrote the second Epistle to the Corinthians, might Paul have dispatched the letter in question to Timothy. But the internal features of the first Epistle to Timothy are not in accordance with this date, although Hemsen still decides in its favour. The first Epistle to Timothy represents him as presiding over the Ephesian church for a considerable time, while here he reappears immediately in the company of Paul, and again the epistle exhibits an unsettled state of the church, and speaks of the presence of many false teachers, while, according to Acts xx. 29, such teachers are described by the apostle as only to make their appearance afterwards. It is better, therefore, to assign the epistle in question to the last period of the life of Paul.

Regarding the duration of Paul's stay in Troas and Macedonia nothing definite is stated; but, as his stay in Greece, that is in Corinth, is fixed at three months (verse 3), and, as immediately thereafter (verse 6), mention is made of the paschal feast (viz., of the year 60), it is probable that the whole time, from Pentecost to the end of the year, was spent on the journey from Ephesus to Corinth. In this city, where Paul wrote the Epistle to the Romans, the Jews contrived another plot against him, verse 3; and, to escape their snares, he departed from Corinth sooner than he had purposed. As the winter season did not permit him to choose the direct course to Syria by sea, he went back in the first place to Macedonia, that he might thence prosecute his journey.

Vers. 4-6.—In the progress of his journey, the apostle made a stay in Philippi, where Luke (who again uses the first person) meets him, having been formerly left behind (xvi. 40) in Philippi, and having spent perhaps the whole time there. The numerous attendants of Paul went before him to Troas, and waited for him there, and he arrived after Easter, and remained seven days. Many interpreters, to whose views Hemsen in recent times accedes, regard a retinue of seven persons as too large; but it is by no means easy to perceive any thing extraordinary in this. Besides the attendants whom Paul always had beside him, and who were absolutely necessary to him for baptizing and arranging the affairs of the new churches, there are here merely added some believers from the province in which he had been labouring. Of Sopater (Σώπατρος) nothing further is known; perhaps he is the same person with Σωσίπατρος mentioned in Rom. xvi. 21. Aristarchus and Gaius were already mentioned at chap. xix. 29. There, however, the latter is called a Macedonian, while here he seems to be called Δερβαῖος, a man of Derbe. Undoubtedly we might, with Meyer, regard this Gaius as another person: it is well, however, not unnecessarily to increase the number of biblical persons. It has, therefore, already been proposed by Ernesti, Valckenaer, Kuinoel, and Neander, to put a point after Gaius, so that he might be included among the Thessalonians mentioned, and Timothy be described as a native of Derbe. Nor is the position of καί after Δερβαῖος, adverse to this view; for it can be taken in the signification of "even, also," and therefore need not be changed. Secundus is not mentioned elsewhere in the New Testament; the two assistants of the apostle, however, Tychicus and Trophimus, natives of proconsular Asia, are well-known.—Ver. 6. Ἄχρις is used to denote a definite date "till five days," for "on the fifth day." The passages in Rom. viii. 22 and Heb. iii. 13, to which Kuinoel appeals in favour of this idea, are by no means analogous to the one before us; for it is not a point of time which is spoken of in them, but an action continuing and reaching down to a certain term. But it is only by an ellipsis that this passage can be thus explained, to wit, by supplying with ἤλθομεν the idea of the preceding sailing.

Vers. 7-12.—The following account of the meeting in Troas, and of the falling of a young man named Eutychus from the window of the third story, is not of much importance considered in itself, but it is interesting, first, because it presents an example of a meeting by night, and, secondly, because it shews that the observance of Sunday existed as early as the times of the apostles, which is also proved by 1 Cor. xvi. 2. The connexion plainly leads to this conclusion, that the apostle wished to observe Sunday with the church, and to celebrate the Lord's Supper, as also the *agape* with them, before he left Troas. The most natural supposition is, that from the very commencement of the church, believers distinguished the day of our Lord's resurrection, and celebrated it with solemn meetings. Thus the observance of this day spread equally among Christians, both of Jewish and Gentile extraction.

(On the expression μία τῶν σαββάτων, see Comm. at Matth. xxviii. 1.—Ver. 8. The numerous torches served probably not merely to give light, but also for ornament. Sabbaths, it is known, are still celebrated among the Jews with many lights.—Ver. 9. θυρίς, "aperture of a window," occurs again in the New Testament in 2 Cor. xi. 33.—Ver. 10. The declaration of Paul, ἡ ψυχὴ αὐτοῦ ἐν αὐτῷ ἐστιν, *his life is in him*, does not permit us to suppose that this was a case of raising from the dead. The account is quite parallel to the account given by Matthew (ix. 24) of the raising of the daughter of Jairus, and the remarks there made are applicable here also. Calvin expresses himself in the same manner, as so many interpreters do with respect to the perfectly analogous narrative in the Gospels: "non negat Paulus fuisse mortuum juvenum, quia miraculi gloriam hoc modo extinguerit, sed sensus est, vitam illi redditam esse Dei gratia." But it does not become us to increase or to magnify miracles; we should take every thing as the Scripture presents it to us Ver. 11. It is worthy of notice that the apostle does not permit himself to be disturbed by this sad accident: he holds the love-feast which was probably delayed by reason of his long discourse, and enters into affectionate conference with those who were present till the dawn of morning.)

Ver. 13-16.—As Luke himself was now again in the company, he was able to give quite a precise account, and accordingly he specifies with care the stations as far as Miletus. Paul, who seems on this occasion to have had the entire control of the ship, sailed past Ephesus, because he was afraid the multitude of his friends would detain him there too long, as he was desirous of being in Jerusalem at Pentecost. (Ver. 13. Ἄσσος was a city in Troas: Paul went this length on foot, probably that he might enjoy the company of the believers from Troas.*—Ver. 15. Τρωγύλλιον is a promontory of Ionia, opposite the island of Samos.)

Vers. 17-21.—But although the apostle had not himself touched at Ephesus, yet he longed to address the rulers of the church there, that he might give them, as he supposed, his last injunction. He caused the elders of that church, therefore, to be invited to Miletus, and delivered an address to them, which is fully communicated to us by Luke.† This speech is interesting, not simply because it expresses in a very lively manner the heartfelt love of the apostle to his spiritual children and the faithful solicitude of his efforts, but it is also important as opening a prophetic view of the future fortunes of the church. Paul points in it to the threatening dangers which awaited the church from false teachers, and he gives most earnest warnings against them. How much the fears of the great apostle of the Gentiles were unfortunately justified in the sequel, is shewn to us, not simply by the first Epistle of Paul to Timothy, in which he is obliged to instruct his disciple regarding the measures to be taken against the heresy which had broken out, but also from the writings of John. The Gospel and the Epistles of John were composed in Ephesus itself, and they all express, very mildly indeed, but still unmistakably, opposition to the false teachers whom Paul had already assailed. Several learned men of recent times, and even ancient fathers of the church, particularly Irenæus, iii. 14. 2, have supposed that Paul held a formal council in Miletus, there being assembled there, not only rulers of the church at Ephesus, but also of many other neighbouring churches. But the text is not favourable to this view; rather ver. 28, as it speaks of but a single church, is directly opposed to it. Probably this idea arose only from the circumstance that, in ver. 28, several ἐπίσκοποι are named, from which the conclusion was drawn, at the time when the names of presbyters and bishops had become markedly distinguished from one another, that the bishops of several churches must have been convened. But it is now generally acknowledged that in the primitive church the two words were used quite synonymously,‡ as is plain in the New Testament from Acts xx. 17, compared with ver. 28; Phil.

* Hemsen, p. 478, throws out the conjecture that Paul went on foot alone, in order that he might give to his followers an opportunity of meditating and conversing about his last discourses: to me this does not seem probable, for the apostle had chiefly spoken, not for those who were going with him, but for those who remained behind.

† Menken's practical exposition of this speech, in his Blicke in das Leben Pauli, p. 486, etc., is worth reading here. See also Stier's Reden der Apostel, part ii. p. 170, etc. As a farewell speech, this discourse bears a resemblance to Matth. xxiv. As in that passage our Lord himself opens to his disciples views into futurity, so does Paul here to his spiritual children.

‡ See Neander's Church History, vol. i., p. 184, etc.

i. 1; 1 Tim. iii. 2, compared with ver. 8, and Titus i. 17. And even the ecclesiastical father, Theodoret, makes the remark on Phil. i. 1: *ἐπισκόπους τοὺς πρεσβυτέρους καλεῖ, ἀμφότερα γὰρ εἶχον κατ' ἐκεῖνον τον καιρὸν τὰ ὀνόματα, he calls the elders bishops, for they had at that time both names.* The question, however, regarding the *offices* must be carefully distinguished from the question regarding the *names*. With respect to the former it is plain, even from the New Testament (see Comm. on Acts xii. 17, xxi. 18, and on the Epistles to Timothy and Titus) that in the larger churches there was a president of the college of Presbyters, who afterwards received *κατ' ἐξοχήν* the name *ἐπίσκοπος*. Where the number of believers was great, and consequently also that of the presbyters, it would happen in the nature of things that some one possessing the highest qualifications of an external and internal kind, would assume the place of leader of the whole body. But the spirit of brotherly love which reigned in the apostolic church would cause this result to be developed, without that presumption and arrogance which were afterwards unfortunately so much displayed by the bishops towards the subordinate functionaries and members of the church.*

The apostle mentions at the commencement of his address the faithful solicitude with which he had devoted himself to their interests, during the long time he was among them. He could do this without the fear of being regarded as vain and self-sufficient, since it was not himself he praised, but the gift of God in him.—(Ver. 18. The phrase *πάντα τὸν χρόνον μεθ' ὑμῶν ἐγενόμην*, is not to be interpreted with scrupulous exactness, as if the apostle had not left Ephesus for a single day, but certainly it excludes journeys of a month's duration, so that we cannot well suppose him to have made long excursions from Ephesus.—Ver. 19. *Ταπεινοφροσύνη* is frequently found in the epistles of Paul, but elsewhere only in 1 Pet. v. 5. Also the adjective *ταπεινόφρων* occurs in 1 Pet. iii. 8.—Ver. 20. *Ὑποστέλλεσθαι* corresponds to the Latin "se subducere," to withdraw from a thing, to neglect it. Comp. ver. 27.—Ver. 21. The connexion of *μετάνοια* with Θεός, and of *πίστις* with Christ is peculiar. Kuinoel refers the former only to the Gentiles, who were first made acquainted with the true God by the Gospel, the other he refers to Jews and Gentiles. But such a contrast is not here spoken of at all: the explanation rather is that in God the Father

* In Hebrews xiii. 7, 17, 24, the rulers of the church are styled *ἡγούμενοι*, which is equivalent to *ἐπίσκοποι*. This word, like the name *πρεσβύτερος*, is derived from the constitution of the Jewish synagogue, which was presided over by aged persons, זקנים, or by pastors, פרנסים. On the last name, see Buxtorf Lex. Rabb. p. 1821, under the word פרנס, that is, to tend a flock. The constitution of the synagogue, however, did not lead so decidedly to the creation of a president in the college of elders, probably on account of the predominant influence of the Sanhedrim existing in the theocratic centre of the nation.

the idea of strict righteousness is exhibited, to which repentance directs itself, but in Christ the idea of compassion, to which faith looks.) *

Vers. 22–27.—Paul is now led by the dangers he was about to encounter in Jerusalem, which made him apprehend he should see his beloved Ephesians no more, to make mention of his faithful labours in the Gospel among them, and of his consequent freedom from guilt, if any of them still should perish. If we suppose a second captivity of Paul, then certainly he came again into those regions (see 2 Tim. iv. 13–20), but this supposition need occasion no difficulty, because the apostle here expresses merely a private opinion, and by no means intimates that he was led to it by the unerring Spirit of God. He probably saw quite correctly the end of his course, viz., the death of martyrdom, but he did not know the space of time that was yet to intervene in his life.

(Ver. 22.—The words *δεδεμένος τῷ πνεύματι, bound by the Spirit,* refer simply to the journey. To this the apostle felt with himself an inward pressing summons; but, according to his own confession, he knew nothing of what was to befall him. For the Holy Ghost does not teach each one everything, but, according to God's appointment, he teaches each one what is needful for him. His approaching captivity Paul had to learn from other persons, who were endowed with the Spirit of God [see chap. xxi. 12]. Perhaps this arrangement was made by God, for the purpose of testing Paul's obedience to the leadings of the Spirit, even in cases where they appeared to him unsuitable; for certainly it could not but appear to him strange that he who was able every day to gain over thousands to the kingdom of God, should be for years withdrawn from the ministry of the word. The dative *τῷ πνεύματι* further is not to be understood as the dative of association, "bound to the Spirit," but as the dative of instrument, "bound by the Spirit." The Spirit is viewed as a power taking possession inwardly of the will of man, and binding it.—Ver. 25. The words *ἐν οἷς διῆλθον* might be referred to the travels of Paul in different places, and thus it would be made probable, that there were presbyters present from other cities: but the words may be just as well applied to the labours of Paul in the city of Ephesus alone.—Ver. 26.—*Καθαρὸς ἀπὸ αἵματος* = נָקִי מִדָּם. The blood is viewed as the principle of life.)*

Ver. 28.—This verse is in several respects remarkable. We perceive from it, in *the first place,* how very important and influential a position the apostle ascribes to the rulers of the church, which they acquire in nowise *merely* by their own arbitrary power, nor by

* It is not to be overlooked that Paul places first the expression *προσέχετε ἑαυτοῖς,* teaching us that concern for his own soul is the first duty of every individual, and in the case of teachers, an indispensable qualification for their labours.

that of the church that chose them, but from above. The bishops are considered as appointed by the Holy Ghost, and they are admonished not only to take care of their own souls, but also to feed well the flock of God over which they are placed. This representation is not favourable to the view now widely diffused among Protestants,* that the ancient constitution of the church was completely democratical, so that every individual had essentially the same right and the same duty as the rulers of the church. This opinion, too rudely formed in opposition to the principles of the Catholic hierarchy, has still this amount of truth, that every believer, even the humblest, possesses a priestly character, in reference to himself and his household, but not at all in reference to the general body. The Holy Scriptures (James iii. 1) give an express warning against every one setting himself up as a teacher. The idea of *an order of teachers* in the church rests upon the conviction that God imparts his gifts in various measures, and that not only in the case of natural endowments, but particularly also of the gifts of the Holy Ghost. (See Comm. on 1 Cor. xii. 11.) Now those persons, who have received a larger measure of the gifts of the Spirit, ought to possess the guidance of the whole body. In the apostolic church, where the rulers were chosen, either by the apostles, who were filled with the Spirit, or by the congregations among whom the Holy Ghost reigned in his primitive power, these rulers corresponded entirely to this idea. But circumstances were afterwards completly changed : unqualified persons by corrupt practices of all kinds got hold of the government of the church, and qualified persons were excluded from it. This state of matters naturally brought about a reaction, in which men went to another false extreme.

In the *second* place, we see from this verse that the pastoral care of the church (*ποιμαίνειν τὴν ἐκκλησίαν*), which includes alike the government (*κυβέρνησις*) and teaching (*διδασκαλία*) of the church,† by no means concerns itself merely with the statement of true doctrine, but also with refuting the false. The admonition to feed the flock stands in immediate connexion with the prediction that false teachers were to arise, and it is with reference to them that Paul recommends watchfulness. See further on this subject in the pastoral epistles.

Finally, the verse has acquired great importance on account of the concluding words, which, if the usual reading could be regarded as genuine, would not only make Christ bear the name of God, but

* The Reformers were far removed from this view: they rather affirmed most emphatically that a peculiar order of teachers was indispensable in the church. The false extreme indicated above was exhibited in the extremest form among the Anabaptist and Quaker sects.

† On the relation of these *χαρίσματα*, as well as on the distinction between *πρεσβύτεροι διδάσκοντες* and *κυβερνῶντες*, see the particulars at the pastoral epistles.

would also appear to justify the confusion of the qualities of his natures made by the Monophysites.* Its genuineness however cannot be defended consistently with the critical authorities. The reading Θεοῦ occurs in the celebrated Codex B., but it is not the original reading there; it is a subsequent correction, and is found nowhere else save in the Vulgate, the Syriac version, and some of the fathers. But, on the other hand, A.C.D.E., and several other Codices, have the reading *κυρίου*, which all recent critics recognize as the right one. The readings *κυρίου* Θεοῦ and Χριστοῦ are not at all to be taken into account, as they have plainly sprung from the other two. The preponderating critical authorities are also supported by the circumstance, that it may be easily explained how Θεοῦ might be substituted in the room of Κυρίου, but not the reverse. The phrase *ἐκκλησία κυρίου* is nowhere else to be found, while *ἐκκλησία* Θεοῦ is of very frequent occurrence; and therefore it might readily happen that the familiar expression would be chosen instead of the more uncommon one, attention not being paid to the following *αἷμα*. That this connexion of *θεός* and *αἷμα* has no foundation in the style of the apostles, is plain from the fact, that no such forms of expression are found in the New Testament. True, the expression *αἷμα κυρίου*, *blood of the Lord*, is also a singular one, and appears to wear a colouring of Monophysitism, for *κύριος* commonly expresses the Divine nature of Christ. But the connexion with *ἐκκλησία* shews that here it only means in general "leader, governor," and therefore is to be understood in the same manner as in John xiii. 13, 14, 16, and not a few other passages, where *κύριος* stands along with *διδάσκαλος*, and only forms a contrast with *δοῦλος*.

Another various reading in the passage before us is that which Griesbach and other modern critics have received into the text, viz., *αἵματος τοῦ ἰδίου*, instead of the common reading *ἰδίου αἵματος*. This reading is susceptible of meaning, only as we might refer *ὁ ἴδιος* to Christ. (Rom. viii. 32.) But if *κυρίου*, as we have seen, is the right reading, then this explanation cannot be admitted, and *ἴδιος* accordingly must in this case be referred to *αἷμα*. Περιποιεῖσθαι occurs only once again in the New Testament, viz., in 1 Tim. iii. 13, in the signification of "earn, obtain, acquire." But the substantive *περιποίησις* is frequently found. The idea that the Lord has redeemed the church with his own precious blood, and purchased it for a possession, expresses its great value, and thus heightens the obligation of taking the deepest interest in its welfare.

Vers. 29–32.—There is now appended the warning that great dangers threaten the church, to ward off which the apostle demands

* On this point see the ninth excursus appended to the commentary of Heinrichs.

the entire watchfulness of the rulers, after the pattern of his own diligence. The dangers themselves are described as being of two kinds. In the first place, *from without* furious enemies of the church, seeking their own advantage, were to break into her; and, in the second place, even *within* her own bosom false teachers were to spring up. It has been common to understand the parties described in ver. 30 as synonymous with those mentioned in ver. 29, or, like Grotius, to view the wolves as heathen persecutors, and the others as heretics. Both views are certainly wrong. Heathen enemies cannot well be the parties spoken of, because in foretelling them there would have been no need of so solemn an announcement; for, in the nature of things, it was to be expected that the Romans would set themselves against the spread of Christianity. The open enemy too, who insisted upon apostacy, brought far less danger in his train than the apparent friend. Yet the words *καὶ ἐξ ὑμῶν*, and the contrasts between *εἰσελεύσονται* and *ἀναστήσονται*, between *λύκοι βαρεῖς* and *λαλοῦντες διεστραμμένα*, imperatively require that the enemies of the church described in the two verses should be viewed as different. The nature of this difference becomes plain, when, as was intimated above, we view it as grounded on a difference of origin. Hostile men, the apostle means to say, would bring errors into the church from without, but also from amongst themselves, nay from their very instructors, false teachers would arise. Then the concluding words, *τοῦ ἀποσπᾶν τοὺς μαθητὰς ὀπίσω αὐτῶν*, *to draw away disciples after them*, describe the wicked object pursued in common by the two parties, viz., to draw believers away from Christ, and to attach them to their own persons. Here we find exactly described the characteristic distinction of the sectarian, which continues the same in all times and under all circumstances. The upright messengers of the truth forget *themselves* for the sake of the great cause which they are defending: they desire no attachment to their own persons, but only demand obedience to God and his word; but the founder of sects draws men away from the Eternal, and sets up his own paltry self instead; thus he injures both himself and others.—(Ver. 29. Regarding *λύκος*, see Comm. at Matth. vii. 15, x. 16.—*Βαρύς* denotes here "dangerous, terrible." As to ver. 30, comp. 1 Tim. iv. 1.—*Διεστραμμένον* occurs in Matth. xvii. 17.—Ver. 31. Paul's specifying here three years as the time of his stay in Ephesus, which really lasted only two years and three months (see xix. 8, 10), is to be explained on the supposition, that his earlier residence too (xviii. 19) is included, and a round number employed.—Ver. 32. On *παρατίθεμαι*, see Acts xiv. 23.)

Vers. 33-38.—At last, after the apostle had mentioned that he had always supported himself by the labour of his own hands, and had rather given than received, he concludes his discourse, and takes an affecting leave of his friends, who depart from him as if they were to see him no more here below. The reason why Paul adverts here to the manner in which he had supported himself in Ephesus, is doubtless simply to shew that he was not actuated, according to the reproaches of his Jewish enemies, by any outward grounds of self-interest, but solely by love to their souls. (See the remarks at chap. xviii. 3.) The connexion therefore shews that the *ἀσθενοῦντες* of the 35th verse is primarily applied only to those who are literally poor and weak. (On *ἀντιλαμβάνεσθαι*, see Luke i. 54.) But it cannot surely be supposed that the rich meaning of our Lord's words, *μακάριόν ἐστι μᾶλλον διδόναι ἢ λαμβάνειν*, *it is more blessed*, etc., is exhausted by the reference to outward giving and receiving. Rather it holds true of this maxim, as of many others, that it is susceptible of an application to the highest relations as well as to the lowest. It applies in the most absolute sense to the relation of the Creator to the creature, for God is the alone blessed, because he alone gives everything to all. (This maxim finally belongs confessedly to those which were preserved only by tradition. Several of the Redeemer's utterances of this kind are collected in Fabricii. Cod. Apocr. N. T. V. I.)

Chap. xxi. 1–4.—Here follows the continuation of the account of Paul's journey, in the first place, on to Tyre, where he abode one week. It seems an extraordinary statement which is made in ver. 4, that some believers, who were filled with the Spirit, said to Paul that he should not go to Jerusalem. The apostle has already declared (xx. 22) that he was going up under the impulse of the Spirit; it might seem therefore that the Spirit contradicted himself in his communications through different channels. But the apparent contradiction arises solely from the brevity of the narrative, which is supplemented by the more detailed statements of the 11th and 12th verses. Those men possessing the prophetic gift discerned quite correctly by the illumination of the Spirit the approaching captivity of the apostle, and *on this account* they besought him of their own accord, rather not to pursue the journey; but in Paul the Spirit declared, that even though bonds awaited him, he must yet go up.—(Ver. 1. *Πάταρα* was a well-known city of Lycia.—Ver. 3. *Γόμος* signifies wares of every kind, as in Rev. xviii. 11, then particularly the lading of a ship = *φορτίον*, whence *ἀποφορτίζεσθαι*, "to discharge, unload a ship's cargo.")

Vers. 5–9.—At the close of the period specified, the believers in Tyre escorted the apostle, and he came by Ptolemais (now St. Jean d'Acre) to Cæsarea, where he lodged in the house of Philip the deacon.—Ver. 5. *Ἐξαρτίσαι* is explained by Œcumenius as = *πληρῶσαι*. But there is no ground for deviating from the usual signification "to equip, to prepare," for the accusative denotes, as usual, duration of time. The word occurs also in 2 Tim. iii. 17, in the same signification. The fact that children are mentioned along with the rest, cannot be employed as a proof of infant baptism, for not only is there wanting every indication that they were baptized, but it might even be grown children that were meant. As in chap. xx. 6, so here prayer is made upon the knees: the ancient Christians appear always to have prayed in this posture, which symbolizes the deep humiliation of the soul before God; but on Sunday they stood, to indicate that God in Christ had raised men up from the fall.

With respect to Philip, it is plain, from the descriptive clause, ὄντος ἐκ τῶν ἑπτά, *being one of the seven*, that he was not the apostle, but the deacon, of whose labours mention has already been made in chap. viii. When ancient writers call him apostle* (see Euseb. H. E. iii. 31, 39, v. 24), we need not suppose any confounding of the two persons, but the word "apostle" is only used in a wider sense, like εὐαγγελιστής in the signification of "travelling teacher." (On this point, see Acts xiv. 4, 14, where Barnabas too is called apostle.) It seems surprising, however, that this Philip travels and is settled in Cæsarea, when he had a stated ecclesiastical office in Jerusalem. The two things could not be united, and as we afterwards find Philip even in Hierapolis in Phrygia (see the passages above cited from Eusebius), we must suppose that he had resigned his office of deacon. Moreover, as the daughters of Philip possessed the gift of prophecy, so we find something similar even in the Old Testament in the cases of Miriam and Deborah, and in the prophecies Joel iii. express intimation had been given that the gifts of the Spirit were to be imparted also to the female sex. This does not at all stand in contradiction to the law that the woman was not to teach in the church, for we need only suppose that such women made no use of their gift in the public assemblies.

Vers. 10–16.—During Paul's stay in Cæsarea, the prophet Agabus, who has already been mentioned in chap. xi. 28, came thither, and also declared his approaching captivity. But the apostle, following the impulse of the Spirit, expressed his joyful obedience even to death, and departed with a convoy of believers from Cæsarea to Jerusalem, where he took up his abode with an old and well-known disciple named Mnason. (Agabus discloses his prophecy by a symbolical act, as our Lord himself had done in a similar manner to Peter. [See the Comm. on John xxi. 28.] The word ἐντόπιοι is not found elsewhere in the New Testament, but it occurs in the best

* On account of these passages Gieseler (in Ullmann's Studien, year 1829, part i. p. 139, etc.) would, though quite unwarrantably, regard ver. 9 as an interpolation, for he supposed that the four daughters belonged to Philip the apostle, and that a reader had confounded the deacon here mentioned with him. But there is not the least trace in the critical authorities that this verse is not genuine.

Greek authors in the signification of "inhabitants of a place."—Ver. 13. Συνθρύπτω, to break to pieces, applied tropically to deep anguish.—Ver. 15. There are here a multitude of various readings: in place of the usual reading ἀποσκευσάμενοι, we find also ἐπισκευασάμενοι, παρασκευασάμενοι, ἀποταξάμενοι, all words which denote preparing to depart, while ἀποσκευασάμενοι, "sarcinas deponere," is applied to persons arriving. But it is probable that the internal difficulty of the word has occasioned transcribers to make these changes, and this consideration gives strong support to the usual reading. The artifices, however, which have been employed to force a different meaning upon ἀποσκευάζω, are to be altogether rejected; the common meaning is appropriate, if we suppose that Paul left the greatest part of his baggage behind in Cæsarea, that he might the more lightly prosecute the land journey.—Ver. 16. Παρ' ᾧ—Μνάσωνι by attraction for πρὸς Μνάσωνα, παρ' ᾧ κ. τ. λ.)

§ III. THE APPREHENSION OF PAUL IN JERUSALEM.

(Acts xxi. 17—xxiii. 10.)

Vers. 17-26.*—On the appearance of the apostle in Jerusalem, which was the central point of Jewish Christian life, his peculiar position in reference to the law could not but come again immediately into question. On the very day after his arrival he betook himself, with his attendants, to James (without doubt the so-called brother of our Lord, see xv. 13), with whom all the presbyters were assembled. It has already been remarked at chap. xx. 17, that this James plainly appears as primus inter pares, as head of the college of presbyters, that is, as bishop. And if we consider that the whole of Christian antiquity† styles him, and afterwards his brother Simon (see Matth. xiii. 55), bishop of Jerusalem, there is no ground left for doubting that the episcopal dignity is as old as the church itself, although the name was only gradually fixed in this acceptation.‡ As soon, then, as James heard the apostle's account of the progress of the gospel in the heathen world, he drew his attention to the position he occupied with reference to the Jewish Christians, which, on

* A Commentary upon the Acts of the Apostles from this place to the end is furnished in the second part of Böttger's contributions towards an introduction to the Epistles of Paul (Göttingen, 1837), constructed on juridical and archæological principles.

† See the account of his martyrdom taken from the work of Hegesippus in Eusebius (H. E. ii. 23). It is printed in my "monum. hist. eccl. i. 11, etc."

‡ In Jerusalem, where the first great church consisted of thousands, there was also first felt the need of a president of the presbyters. But of course this necessity would first appear when the apostles left the city, for so long as they were present they exercised a controlling influence. (See the remarks at Acts vi. 7, xx. 17.) Therefore probably the episcopal office may have first developed itself in Antioch and Rome.

account of their number, could not but appear a matter of the highest importance. For, granting that the expression πόσαι μυριάδες is not to be taken literally, still it must denote a very considerable number, whom we are not to suppose as belonging to Jerusalem alone, but to the whole of Palestine. (The word θεωρεῖς in verse 20, may refer to the number of presbyters present, which represented, as it were, the number of believers.) The duties of the Gentile Christians had been definitely settled by the apostolic decrees (chap. xv.), but as to the Jewish Christians, the report was now spread abroad that Paul led the Jews, who attached themselves to Christianity in the heathen world, to give up the observance of the law, and this had excited the most furious hatred against the apostle, as one who taught apostacy from the holy law of God. The heads of the church in Jerusalem, therefore, dreaded nothing but an uproar, if Paul's presence in the city should become known. In order, therefore, to appease the multitude, they proposed to the apostle to observe the sacred usages publicly in the Temple, with four men who were paying their vows, and to present an offering for himself (see on this point the remarks at chap. xviii. 18, etc.) a proposal which he willingly adopted.

And here now the question presents itself, was it a just charge, that Paul seduced the Jews to abandon the law when they joined the church? We may easily explain how this charge arose, but it was by no means well-founded. It stood in direct contradiction to the publicly declared principles of Paul, that he would ask no one arbitrarily to renounce the law (see Comm. on Rom. vii. 1, etc., and on Acts xiv. 15): on the contrary it was his practice quietly to let every one decide, according to his spiritual advancement and the instruction of the Spirit, what position he would assume in reference to Old Testament rites; but the connexion of *salvation* with the observance of the law, he energetically resisted as unchristian. Although, therefore, we cannot suppose the Apostle Paul to have made any direct opposition to the ceremonies of the law (see chap. xxviii. 17), yet on the other hand we may readily conceive that his example, and the whole spirit of his ministry, would lead many Jewish Christians to give up with a good conscience the observance of the Mosaic institutions. This was noticed by the strict Jewish Christians, and therefore they ascribed to Paul the positive *design* of supplanting the law, while the event was merely a consequence of the spirit of his doctrine. Without any hypocrisy, therefore, he could observe the law himself, because love prompted him to become a Jew to the Jews. In the same manner the Jews already had experienced, in the ministry of our Lord himself, and also of Stephen, who appears as the forerunner of Paul (Acts vi. 13, 14), that the Gospel occasioned an indifference to the forms prescribed by the law, and therefore they ascribed to them the actual endeavour to overturn the law, although they left the removal of its outward forms to the slow course of inward development, and hence observed the law themselves so long as these forms had existence. (Ver. 26. Ἁγνισμός denotes the abstinence practised during the vow. When the appointed days, which in this case were seven [ver. 27], had expired, Paul made it known [διαγγέλλων] to the priests, for the sake of the offerings which were to be presented.)

Vers. 27-32.—But although the concession of the apostles to the weak brethren proceeded from a good intention, it turned out disastrously. The furious enemies of Paul were only the more exasperated by it, particularly by the circumstance that Trophimus, who was uncircumcised, was found in the company of Paul, and it was supposed that the apostle had taken him with him into the Temple, and had thus defiled it; for Gentiles by birth could only tread the court of the Gentiles, but not that of the Israelites: they were debarred from entering the latter by monitory tablets. (See Joseph. B. J. v. 5, 2.) An uproar was excited in the Temple by Jews from Asia; the apostle was dragged away from the environs of the Temple, and would have been killed, if the Roman garrison had not hastened to his help.

(Ver 30.—They hurried the apostle out of the Temple, that is, out of the courts of it, that they might not stain it with his blood. The watchmen of the Temple also immediately took the precaution of shutting the great gates that led into the courts.—Ver. 31. The Romans, who had a garrison in the castle of Antonia, that lay over against the Temple, viewed this uproar as connected with the attempts of a rebel [ver. 38] and therefore they hastened immediately to the spot, and saved the life of Paul. Φάσις, rumour, occurs nowhere else in the New Testament.—On σπεῖρα, see Matth. xxvii. 27; Acts x. 1.—Regarding χιλίαρχος, see John xviii. 12.)

Vers. 33-40.—After the Roman tribune had rescued the apostle from the tumult, and had learned that he was not the rebel whom he at first supposed him to be, Paul received permission from him to address the excited people, who, when they heard* their beloved mother tongue, listened with quietness to the words of the apostle, who was now beyond their power.—(Ver. 34. Παρεμβολή denotes here the barracks situated in the fortress to which a stone staircase led up, of which the ἀναβαθμοί are the steps.—Ver. 38. With regard to the Egyptian rebel [Αἰγύπτιος], Josephus gives a detailed account of him and his unfortunate attempt against the Romans, which was suppressed by the procurator Felix. [Arch. xx. 8-6. Bell.

* The inference that, according to this passage, it would not have been remarkable if Paul had spoken Greek, leads to the supposition that the Greek tongue even at that time was widely diffused through Palestine.

Jud. ii. 13, 5.] The number of his followers is given by Josephus at a far higher amount than by Luke, viz., 30,000. But there is plainly an error in the number of Josephus, because he mentions that Felix had killed the most of them, and yet in the first of the two passages cited, the number killed is fixed at four hundred. Perhaps, too, the flower of his army ought to be distinguished from the disorderly mass of people who followed it. On this apparent difference, see the remarks of Tholuck in his Glaubwürdigkeit, p. 170, etc., where he supposes that the large number of Josephus must be understood only of the rabble that followed. The name *σικάριος*, sicarius, denotes a class of men that arose amid the terrible distractions of the Jewish state under the rule of the Romans, and abandoned themselves of set purpose to murder and robbery.)

Chap. xxii. 1-21.—Paul hoped to make an impression upon his enemies, by recounting the manner in which God had brought him to the acknowledgment of the Messiahship of Jesus;* but, as soon as he made mention of his Divine calling to go as a teacher among the Gentiles, their rage, hitherto restrained, broke out afresh, and they called upon the tribune to put Paul to death. (On this section, see particulars at chap. ix. 1, etc.)

Vers. 22-29.—When the tribune saw that all was fruitless, he took Paul into custody, and led him into the castle, with the view of scourging him, that he might ascertain, by this kind of torture, in what the transgression he supposed him guilty of, consisted. But the right of Roman citizenship asserted by the apostle, rescued him from this infliction.—(Ver. 23. Throwing dust into the air is a symbolical expression of disquietude and perplexity.—Ver. 24. Ἀνετάζεσθαι, inquirere, refers here to the investigation of the supposed crime.—Ver. 25. Προτείνειν ἱμᾶσι is best understood here in the sense of "hand over," "give up to." And the thongs denote the instrument of punishment, so that the meaning is, "when they gave him over to the scourge." The word cannot well be applied to the binding of the body, and to the stretching of it thus occasioned, because the thongs were not used as instruments of binding. On Paul's right of citizenship, see at chap. xvi. 37.—Ver. 28. Κεφάλαιον is here used in the genuine Greek signification of "sum," "sum of money.")

Chap. xxii. 30—xxiii. 5.—In order however to save himself from being brought to any account, the tribune determined to deliver over the accused to the Jewish tribunals, and Paul was thereupon placed before the Sanhedrim, over which Ananias at that time presided. This violent man commanded his servants to insult Paul,

* In chap. xxii. 3, the apostle himself calls Tarsus his birth-place. The statement of Jerome, therefore (catal. vir. ill. s. v. Paulus), that Paul was born in Giskalis in Judea, and came afterwards to Tarsus, is deserving of no regard.

when he appeared before the Sanhedrim with an open declaration of his consciousness of innocence. Now if the apostle does not here apply the command of our Lord (Matth. v. 39) literally, he is certainly acting quite in the spirit of the precept; as we have seen that the Redeemer himself did not literally follow it with reference to rude men of the world. (John xviii. 22.) But it appears improper for the apostle to use an abusive word,* and the more so, as it was spoken in presence of the court, and to the high priest. The latter circumstance indeed appears to be softened by the consideration, that the apostle declares he knew not it was the high priest: yet again it seems difficult to imagine how he could be ignorant that he was standing before the Sanhedrim, and of course also before the high priest.† This statement of the apostle therefore may seem like an untruth, employed to excuse a word rashly spoken. The matter indeed assumes rather a different aspect, when it is considered that this Ananias, the son of Nebedæus, was a man of criminal life, who was afterwards displaced from his office and dragged to Rome to answer for his conduct, so that the reproach cast upon him by Paul was entirely merited. Besides he was not the legal high priest, for after he was liberated through Agrippa's intercession in Rome, he did not again recover his dignity, though he still arrogated to himself the power of the office. (See Joseph. Arch. xx. 8. 8.) But these circumstances cannot justify the conduct of the apostle, as we must necessarily suppose that he knew before what authority he was standing: if he had wished to notice the fact that Ananias was not the legal high priest, then he should have protested against the investigation altogether, while the course he pursued violated the respect that was due to the supreme tribunal. The supposition propounded by Calvin, and approved by Heinrichs, Meyer, and other modern critics, that the words *οὐκ ᾔδειν* are ironical, and to be understood thus: "I could not at all regard as high priest a man who is so unholy," is plainly forced as to the language, and inappropriate as to the fact. There is nothing left therefore but to say, that the apostle confounded the person of the judge with the office,

* This is the view which Jerome (at Galat. v. 12) takes of the matter, who is by no means distinguished by bold conceptions.

† Suppose Paul did not know it was the high-priest, still he must have known he was standing before a judge, and though it had been the lowest judge, such words would still be improper. According to the view however of *οὐκ ᾔδειν*, which makes it mean, "I did not consider," the precipitation of Paul, of which in any view we must allow the possibility, carries its correction along with it, and thus no harm accrues from supposing its existence. The only way in which the expression can be defended, is to say that the apostle spoke by Divine commission in execution of a Divine judgment, although one sees not how in this case the words *οὐκ ᾔδειν* can be explained. Besides, the apostles could exercise such authority only within the church, as upon Ananias and Sapphira, but not without it; during their earthly life their supreme authority had reference only to the church of Christ.

and hastily vented his feelings against the former, where the latter alone was concerned. And the words *οὐκ ᾔδειν* is this case are best understood as meaning "I considered not." They bear a similar sense in Ephes. vi. 8; Col. iii. 24, agreeably to the analogy of the Hebrew ידע. The remembrance of the words of Scripture in Exod. xxii. 28 leads Paul back to the right position. If we consider* that there is no reference to dogmatical points, and that the apostles nowhere represent themselves as morally perfect, we shall find nothing in this result of the investigation to prejudice the character of the apostle as an infallible teacher of truth: on the contrary, he here teaches by example the maxim so difficult to act upon, that, where undue precipitation has been manifested, it is best immediately to acknowledge it, and bring one's conduct to the word of truth.

(Ver. 3.—The expression *τοῖχε κεκονιαμένε* corresponds to the similar expression *τάφος κεκονιαμένος*, which was explained at Matth. xxiii. 27, and denotes the hypocrisy, which employs outward show and ornament to cover inward abomination.)

Vers. 6–10.—The breach occasioned by this occurrence Paul employed with skilful dexterity, to make the composition of the Sanhedrim subservient to his own views and the holy cause which he represented. The parties of the Pharisees and Sadducees were opposed to one another in the assembly. The high priest himself belonged to the latter party. Against this materializing sect the apostle brought forward the circumstance, that it was really his faith in eternal life and the resurrection of the dead which exposed him to persecution. This manœuvre had a remarkable effect. The two parties fell into strife among themselves, and so the apostle escaped their hands. If we compare this incident with the earlier accounts of the proceedings of the Sanhedrim in reference to Christians, we find indications of a remarkable change of views which had already taken place in the interval. Pharisees and Sadducees were also previously united in the Sanhedrim, but the question about the resurrection of Jesus had never brought them to a contest. Both parties had leagued together against the new church that was springing up. However, we have seen in chap. vi. 7, that at an early period there were priests, mostly Pharisees, who attached themselves to the church; and Gamaliel's counsel (v. 34), points at least to the possibility that Jesus Christ might be the Messiah; and now the party of the Pharisees appear to have turned to the cause of truth so much, that they regarded the difference between them and the Sadducees as more important than their difference with the Christians. And this explains how it was that, according to the accounts of Hegesippus (Euseb. H. E. ii. 23), and also of Josephus (Arch.

* Regarding this point see the similar occurrence mentioned in Acts xv. 36, etc.

xx. 9, 1), James, the brother of our Lord, Christian bishop of Jerusalem, could be so generally honoured and styled the "just." This circumstance shews how near the Jewish people, as a whole, were to the acknowledgment of Jesus as the Messiah, and that perhaps it was only by the influence of a small party of wild zealots that this acknowledgment was prevented.*

(Ver. 6.—In ἐλπίδος καὶ ἀναστάσεως the καὶ is omitted in many Codices, but undoubtedly it is genuine, and the phrase is to be viewed as a Hendiadys.—On the doctrine of the Sadducees, compare the Comm. at Matth. iii. 7 and xxii. 23.—In ver. 9 πνεῦμα, as used by the Pharisees, is plainly to be understood as the apparition of a departed soul, because it is distinguished from ἄγγελος: if hearing something from the Spirit of God were meant, the article could not be dispensed with before πνεῦμα, nor would ἐλάλησε be applied in this manner to the Spirit. The Pharisees, it appears from this, knew the history of the conversion of Paul, and acknowledged something real in it. The additional clause μὴ θεομαχῶμεν is wanting in the MSS. A.B.C.E. and others, as also in the Vulgate and other versions. Perhaps it might creep in from the analogous passage in Acts v. 39, which it was very natural to compare with this. The thought too expressed in these words appears to lead almost too far for Pharisees to have uttered it: it would in fact imply the confession of the Redeemer as risen from the dead, which we cannot assume even in the most favourably disposed members of the Sanhedrim belonging to the Pharisees.—Ver. 10. Εὐλαβεῖσθαι occurs only once more in the New Testament in Heb. xi. 7, in the signification of "apprehending, fearing, dreading." The adjective εὐλαβής we found already in Luke ii. 35.)

§ 4. PAUL'S DEPORTATION TO CÆSAREA AND IMPRISONMENT THERE.

(Acts xxiii. 11—xxvi. 32.)

Vers. 11-15.—On the night after this occurrence, Paul had another vision of the Lord (in an ecstacy, not a dream), to prepare him for his future labours in the capital of a Gentile world, and at the same time to calm his mind in reference to the danger with which he was now assailed. These visions running through the

* The Scriptures themselves permit us to maintain along with the acknowledgment, on the one hand, of *necessity* in the evolution of human affairs, the *possibility*, on the other, of things having been different. Only imagine that the Messiahship of Jesus had been acknowledged by the Sanhedrim themselves, and thus by the whole Jewish nation, and what an effect must this have produced! In John iv. 35, Jesus points to something of the kind.

whole life of Paul, but to be met with in the case of no other apostle, appear to stand connected with the peculiar task to which he was called. Though he had not enjoyed personal intercourse with the Lord, his nevertheless was the high destiny of maintaining not simply in opposition to the enemies of the truth, but even in part against the other apostles, the more enlarged view of the Gospel, as the universal religion, and the spiritual fulfilment of all the prefigurations of the Old Testament. For this calling he required an extraordinary assistance, to make him certain himself that he was in the right way, and this assurance the Lord gave him in the manner which has been indicated.

While in the preceding narrative we must recognize the favourable disposition of a part of the Jewish nation towards Christianity, the following displays in a terrible form the rage of the apostle's enemies. Forty fanatics bound themselves by an oath to kill Paul, and they put themselves in communication with the hostile part of the Sanhedrim, that through their influence they might obtain an opportunity of carrying their wicked plot into execution.—(Ver. 12. On *συστροφή* compare xix. 40.—On *ἀναθεματίζω* see Mark xiv. 71.—Ver. 15. *Ἐμφανίζω* we found in John xiv. 22 in the signification of "shewing;" here it means, "giving information, sending notice." So in chap. xxiv. 1 it denotes judicial information, accusation.)

Vers. 16–22.—With this wicked plot the apostle was made acquainted by his sister's son. Then he caused the centurion who was entrusted with the keeping of him, to conduct the young man to the chief captain, to whom likewise he communicated the whole. (Ver. 16. *Ἐνέδρα*, "concealment, ambuscade, stratagem," occurs again in Acts xxv. 3. The verb *ἐνεδρεύω* has already occurred in Luke xi. 54, and appears again ver. 21. In ver. 21, the clause *προσδεχόμενοι τὴν ἀπὸ σοῦ ἐπαγγελίαν*, *waiting the promise*, etc., intimates that the members of the Sanhedrim had entered into the plot, and that the conspirators were only now waiting for the consent of the tribune.)

Vers. 23–30.—But the faithful Claudius Lysias was far from entering into such a wicked scheme. He immediately commanded two centurions to prepare an escort, and sent down the apostle with them in safety to Cæsarea to the proconsul Felix. Luke gives us the letter containing information regarding Paul, not probably in its original form, but constructed according to his own views of what it would be; for the evangelist might know how such "elogia" (the Roman name for such letters of escort) were wont to be arranged. We are led to this view by the expression *περιέχουσαν τὸν τύπον τοῦτον* in ver. 25, where *τύπος* denotes the sketch or general outline of the epistle. Here then perhaps we have an instance of the formation of single sections by the writer himself, such as are often found in the Roman and Greek historians in the case of speeches, letters, and the like.

(Ver. 23.—The name δεξιολάβος is quite unknown. It is found in no other ancient author. Some manuscripts therefore read δεξιοβόλοι,* that is, slingers, who throw with the right arm; but certainly the common reading is to be preferred on critical grounds. Some have been disposed to understand the word δεξιολάβοι of military lictors, because they held or bound prisoners by the right hand, but the large number of two hundred is not compatible with this idea. Some manuscripts, it is true, read eighty instead, but even this number would be too great for the purpose supposed. The word is best explained either with the Etymologicum Magnum by τοξοβόλος, or with Suidas by παραφύλαξ. The latter explanation is most conformable to etymology, as the name would seem to denote those who guarded the right side of their lord.—In ver. 24 κτήνη, jumenta, sumpter horses. Here too Luke passes over from the direct to the indirect style.—In ver. 25 περιέχω entirely = the Latin contineo. Comp. 1 Pet. ii. 6.—Ver. 26. Nothing further is known of Claudius Lysias, but Antonius Felix was a brother of the well-known Pallas, freedman of the mother of Claudius, and favourite of this Emperor. [Tacit. Hist. v. 9, 6. Annal. xii. 54, 1.] Under the protection of his brother, Felix indulged in the most terrible extortions in his office of proconsul.—On κράτιστος, see Luke i. 3.)

Vers. 31-35.—The whole company conducted the apostle as far as Antipatris, but here the foot soldiers returned, because the greatest danger was past, and the horsemen alone took him all the way to Cæsarea. In the first instance the proconsul enquired only after his place of brith, and then ordered him to be guarded in the prætorium of Herod. (Ἀντιπατρίς, midway between Jerusalem and Cæsarea, was called orignally Καφαρσαλαμᾶ. [1 Macc. vii. 31.] Herod the Great completed the building of the city, and named it after his father.—Ver. 34. Ἐπαρχία, the usual word for provincia.—Ver. 35. On πραιτώριον, consult Comm. at John xviii. 33. Here it simply means palace. Perhaps, however, the proconsul resided in this building, and had chambers fitted up in it for prisoners of the better class.

Chap. xxiv. 1-9.—A few days after the arrival of Paul, the high priest himself came down to Cæsarea with a Roman agent, to accuse the apostle. With base flattering speeches, Tertullus attempted to gain the good will of Felix, while he at the same time attempted to throw suspicion upon Paul as a dangerous stirrer up of strife.

(In ver. 3, several manuscripts read, instead of κατορθωμάτων, the synonymous διορθωμάτων. The word means here improved regula-

* According to Wetstein the word occurs sometimes in the later writers, Theophylact, Simocatta, and Constantine Porphyrogenneta.

tions of government. But to ascribe these to Felix was mere flattery, for he was only concerned about his own advantage, and thought not of the welfare of the country. The improved regulations he had introduced were calculated merely for ostentation.—Ver. 4. Ἐγκόπτω, properly to "cut in or into," *e. g.*, a way; then, to detain, to hinder. Rom. xv. 22, Gal. v. 7.—*Συντόμως*, briefly, concisely; *λεγόντων* may be supplied.—In ver. 5, the participle *εὑρόντες* has no verb after it; the speaker abandoning the intended construction. Λοιμός, properly, plague, then one who brings plague and destruction. The Seventy employ this word to express בְּלִיַּעַל in 1 Sam. ii. 12.—Πρωτοστάτης occurs nowhere else in the New Testament. In the mouth of the orator, it means the same as "head, ringleader." As a name of the Christians employed to express their meanness (chap. ii. 22), Ναζωραῖοι occurs no more in the New Testament. On the form of the name, consult the Comm. at Matth. ii. 23.—In verse 9, the textus receptus reads *συνέθεντο*, *i. e.*, "they concurred." But the best critics have preferred the reading *συνεπέθεντο*, as the more difficult. The word *συνεπιτίθεσθαι* occurs nowhere else in the New Testament: it means "to join in assailing.")

Vers. 10–23.—Having received permission from the proconsul, Paul immediately rose up in his own defence, and gave a true account of the events which had led to his apprehension in Jerusalem. And as here again the Sadducees might be his chief accusers, he brought afresh into view the resurrection of the dead as a principal charge brought against him by his enemies. The proconsul plainly was convinced of his innocence, and therefore granted him much indulgence in his captivity, although he by no means set him immediately at liberty.

(Ver. 10.—Paul could speak with justice of many years during which Felix had governed in Palestine, for although he had now been but six years proconsul, yet he had previously held the chief command in Galilee. [Joseph. Arch. xx. 6, 3, Bell. Jud. i. 2, 12.]—Ver. 11. Among the twelve days here mentioned, are included the five [chap. xxiv. 1] spent by Paul in prison, for he counts the twelve days down to the moment he is speaking. Meyer has shewn from the connexion of the passages touching this matter from chap. xxi. 15, that the number comes out rightly, which furnishes a highly favourable testimony to the accuracy of the account.—Ver. 12. Ἐπισύστασις occurs again in 2 Cor. xi. 28, in the sense of "overflow of business, importunate calls," and the trouble thereby caused. Here it = *συστροφή*, "uproar, tumult."—Ver. 14. Αἵρεσις has here a bad idea associated with it, which is frequently not the case. Comp. Acts v. 17, xv. 5, xxvi. 5.—Ver. 16. Ἐν τούτῳ refers to the foregoing description of his doctrine and views: "according to my principles I make it my endeavour also to walk."—'Απρόσκοπος occurs again only in 1 Cor. x. 32.—Ver. 18. 'Εν οἷς scilicet χρήμασι, amidst these innocent, nay, honourable employments.—Ver. 19. According to the textus receptus, τινές is connected with εὗρον, but Griesbach, on the authority of the Manuscripts A.C.E. and others, has adopted the reading τινὲς δέ, which, as the more difficult, undoubtedly deserves the preference. In this case a verb must be supplied to τινές, and the most suitable is ἦσαν. —Ver. 22. 'Αναβάλλεσθαι means also, in good Greek writers, "to throw back," that is, "to adjourn, to procrastinate, to defer." The phrase ἀκριβέστερον εἰδὼς τὰ περὶ τῆς ὁδοῦ, *knowing more accurately respecting the way*, is not to be interpreted too rigidly, for we cannot suppose this Roman to have possessed an accurate acquaintance with the doctrines of the Gospel; but as there were believers in Cæsarea itself, Felix might have a general knowledge of the sect of the Nazarenes, and [which alone concerned him] of their political inoffensiveness.—Ver. 23. 'Ανεσις denotes here the mildness of his captivity, similar to what Paul, according to Luke's account [Acts xxviii. 30, 31], enjoyed even in Rome.)

Vers. 24-27.—The concluding verses of this narrative furnish evidence both of the spiritual power which displayed itself in the captive apostle, and of the excitable conscience of the Roman, as well as the moral debasement which led him to stifle the impressions he had received. There might be something exciting to him and his wife Drusilla in the appearance of Paul; and therefore they caused him to be brought one day before them. The apostle availed himself of this opportunity to touch their conscience, and with deep knowledge of human nature and skill in teaching, he brought the *law* to bear upon his object. To penitent hearts he preached the crucified Jesus as the Mediator, to these worldly persons he displayed him as the Judge. The sword of God's word pierced deep into the heart of Felix, but for this very reason he suddenly broke off the conference. But his moral baseness betrayed itself strikingly in this, that he could still hold fast his prisoner for the mere purpose of obtaining money for his release, nay, that at his departure from the province, he left him in prison out of complaisance to the Jews.

(Ver. 24.—Felix had two wives of the same name; the first was a grand-daughter of Antony by Cleopatra; the second, who is here referred to, was the daughter of Herod Agrippa, whose death is recorded at chap. xii. 23.* She had been married first to Prince Azizus of Emesa, but deserted him and married the Roman proconsul, Joseph. Arch. xx. 7, 1. Comp. Winer's Reallex. under Drusilla. Drusilla being a Jewess by birth, might particularly

* Heinrichs, in his Commentary (proleg. p. 67) gives a genealogical table of the family of Herod, like that of Raumer in his Geography of Palestine. Regarding the wives of Felix, see Tacit. Histor. v. 9, Sueton. Claud. c. 28.

desire to hear of Jesus, the pretended Messiah, and therefore Felix had Paul brought before him.—Ver. 25. The word ἐγκράτεια refers particularly to abstinence from sexual excesses, of which both of them, Felix as well as Drusilla, had been guilty.—Τὸ νῦν ἔχον scilicet κατά, is a circumlocution for νῦν.—Ver. 26. Διὸ καὶ πυκνότερον κ. τ. λ. Felix wished to let him understand, by the kindness with which he treated him, that he was ready to let him go: perhaps also he designed to put him to the proof, whether he would employ improper means for his rescue.—Ver. 27. Two years appeared now to have been completely lost by the apostle, for in Cæsarea itself he probably had but small opportunity of labouring. But the main design of God in this remarkable procedure might perhaps be to grant the apostle a quiet period for inward recollection and meditation. The continual movement of Paul's life must of course have made difficult for him that self-culture which is the necessary condition of a blessed inward development. Divine grace therefore is able to unite both objects; for while it uses its instruments for the advancement of truth among others, it sometimes puts these instruments themselves to school for their own personal improvement.)

Chap. xxv. 1-5.—The mention of the entrance of Festus upon office is one of the passages of Acts, as has already been remarked in the introduction, which furnish a point of contact with profane history. We know that Nero came to the government in the year 56 after Christ, and that in the seventh year of his reign, and consequently in the year 62 after Christ, Porcius Festus entered upon his office. (Compare Joseph. Arch. xx. 8, 9, and the particulars stated by Hug in his introduction, 2d edition, vol. ii. p. 279, etc.) Immediately after his entrance on office the new proconsul visited Jerusalem, and the fanatical Jews took this opportunity of soliciting him to deliver the apostle again into their hands. But Festus, who had heard of his character and circumstances (compare ver. 10), declined the proposal, because no Roman citizen could be handed over to a foreign tribunal. He announced to them therefore that he would speedily (ἐν τάχει, ver. 4) return to Cæsarea, and be ready there to hear their complaint. (In ver. 4 the expression τηρεῖσθαι τὸν Παῦλον ἐν Καισαρείᾳ is manifestly elliptical. It might refer to the secure keeping of Paul, so that the sense may be: he will not escape you, he is well guarded in Cæsarea. It is better however to suppose, in accordance with the subsequent narrative, ver. 9, etc., that the proconsul designed to intimate that Paul was not subject to their jurisdiction. And thus the Roman authority which had been the means of bringing the Redeemer to the cross, was here to be the instrument of delivering the apostle of the Gentiles.—In ver. 5 δυνατοί denotes the most distinguished members of the supreme council.)

Vers. 6–12.—According to the command of the proconsul, therefore, accusers speedily came from Jerusalem to Cæsarea, whither Festus had returned after a few days. In their fury they brought forward the most unrighteous charges, but charges at the same time altogether incapable of proof, and to them Paul replied with vigour. The proposal, however, of the proconsul, to let the matter be brought to a termination in Jerusalem, was declined by Paul, who appealed to Cæsar.

(Ver. 7.—The impudent accusations brought by the Jews against the apostle appear, from ver. 8, to have been partly of a political character. They probably attempted to make his preaching of Christ appear as if it were the proclamation of a new emperor.—Ver. 9.—The proposal of Festus was perhaps only designed as an act of complaisance to the Jews. Without doubt he knew beforehand, that Paul would not accede to it. The apostle accordingly appeals in his answer to the knowledge which the proconsul had of the state of matters.—Ver. 12. The appeal to the Roman people, or, in later times, to Cæsar, was a right of Roman citizens. Pliny also, Epist. x. 95, mentions that he would send to Rome those Christians who possessed the right of Roman citizenship.—The *συμβούλιον* denotes the counsellors or assistants in the office of the proconsul. They bore the title of consiliarii, or assessores, *πάρεδροι*. Sueton. Tib. c. 33 ; Galba c. 19 ; Ælius Lamprid. in Alex. Severo c. 46.)

Vers. 13–22.—Now after the lapse of a few days, king Agrippa, with his sister Berenice,* arrived in Cæsarea to pay a visit to the new proconsul. Festus availed himself of this opportunity to lay before him the controversy regarding the apostle. From the whole narrative it is apparent that Paul had excited in Festus a lively interest in his favour, nor were Agrippa and Berenice less desirous of beholding the remarkable man. Festus therefore promised to bring Paul before them.

The Agrippa here mentioned is the younger Agrippa, son of the older, who came before us in chap. xii. 20, etc. He enjoyed the favour of Claudius Cæsar, and retained his provinces even after the destruction of Jerusalem, which he outlived. Berenice was his sister, who at first was married to her uncle Herod, prince of Chalcis, and then to king Polemon of Cilicia. She was a woman of distinguished beauty, and captivated even Titus and Vespasian. But her character was very bad, for she lived in incest with her brother. (Comp. Joseph. Arch. xx. 5, 1, and 7, 3. Bell. Jud. i. 2, 21. Sueton. Vit. Tit. c. 7. Tacit. Hist. ii. 81.)

* How accurately informed Luke shews himself here again, how readily he might have confounded this Berenice with other celebrated women of the same name, if he had followed a later uncertain tradition, may be seen by consulting Tholuck's Credibility, p. 168. The name of Berenice, according to Valkenær, has been formed from φερνίκη.

(In ver. 16, many manuscripts supply εἰς ἀπώλειαν to χαρίζεσθαι, but this supplement is unnecessary. The word here bears the signification of "sacrificing, condemning without enquiry at the pleasure of some one." This was contrary to the strict judicial procedure of the Romans, which required a formal investigation. The construction πρὶν ἔχοι, occurs nowhere else in the New Testament: other readings, ἔχῃ or ἔχει, are merely readings made to smooth the difficulty. The optative here may probably be explained on the principle of passing from the oratio directa to the oratio obliqua. [Comp. Winer's Gramm. p. 273.]—Ver. 17. Ἀναβολή "mora, delay," from ἀναβάλλεσθαι, see chap. xxiv. 22.—Ver. 18. Festus had supposed that they would accuse Paul of palpable crimes: religious differences he took not into account.—Ver. 21. Σεβαστός, the standing word for the title of the Emperors, Augustus.—Διάγνωσις occurs only here: the verb we had in chap. xxiii. 15, xxiv. 22.)

Vers. 23-27.—The placing of the apostle before Agrippa and Berenice afforded the first fulfilment of our Lord's prediction: "ye shall be brought before kings and princes for my sake." Matth. x. 18; Mark xiii. 9. With great pomp the royal personages made their appearance, and the most distinguished ones of the city; and thus Paul obtained an opportunity of preaching the power of the risen Redeemer before the elite of a great city, before the king and the proconsul. After the king and his sister had entered, the apostle was introduced in bonds, xxvi. 29, and Festus placed him before Agrippa, briefly stating his case, and declaring that he was desirous of finding out what it was that Paul was really accused of, that he might be able, when he sent him to Rome, to give some information regarding him.

(Ver. 23. Φαντασία occurs nowhere else in the New Testament; it comprehends whatever shines or greatly strikes the eyes. The word ἀκροατήριον denotes the public hall of judgment in the palace of the proconsul.—Ver. 24. Ἐντυγχάνειν τινί means to meet with any one, to go to any one with entreaties.—Ver. 26. Ὁ κύριος is here the emperor Nero. Instead of γράψαι, A. C. and other manuscripts read γράψω. It is probable, however, that this reading took its rise from the preceding γράψαι.)

Chap. xxvi. 1-18.—With the permission of king Agrippa, the apostle delivers a discourse in his bonds before this splendid assemblage. He first of all expresses his joy that he was allowed to defend himself before one, who was acquainted with the manners and customs of the Jewish nation, and then gives a narrative of his life, and, in particular, a detailed account of the important occurrence which had led to his conversion, regarding which compare the particulars stated at chap. ix. 1, etc.

(Ver. 1.—The stretching out of the hand is not to be regarded as designed to produce silence in the meeting ; the presence of the king would at once quell every commotion ; it is rather the gesture appropriate to the commencement of a discourse.—Ver. 3. Γνώστης, "one who accurately knows a thing, a witness, a guarantee," is found nowhere else in the New Testament. It occurs besides in the apocryphal book of Susanna, ver. 42 ; in profane authors the form γνωστήρ is also found. The accusative after the preceding σοῦ is to be explained as an anakoluthon.—Ver. 4. Undoubtedly ἀπ' ἀρχῆς indicates that Paul came at an early period from Tarsus to Jerusalem to the school of Gamaliel.—Ver. 5. Ἄνωθεν is synonymous with the above.—Ver. 6. The ἐπαγγελία of which the apostle speaks, is as is plain from what follows, the promise of the Messiah.—Ver. 7. The substantive δωδεκάφυλον, as denoting the whole people of Israel, is found only here in the New Testament. In James i. 1 the twelve tribes are named to designate the whole people of the Israelites. Ἐν ἐκτενείᾳ = ἐκτενῶς. 1 Pet. i. 22.—Ver. 8. With the hope of the Messiah the resurrection of the dead stands connected, for Jesus the true Messiah was raised from the dead.—On the use of εἰ in direct and indirect questions, compare Winer's Gramm. p. 475, and Passow in his Lex. under this word.)

Vers. 19–23.—In the conclusion of his discourse the apostle appeals to the conscience of the king, whether he could have properly disregarded such a vision, and affirms again that the only ground of charge against him was that he believed the hope of the patriarchs had been accomplished, and the true Messiah had appeared in his suffering state.—(Ver. 20. Ἐπιστρέφειν means, as שוב so often does in the prophets, a spiritual change, conversion. Comp. xi. 21.—Ver. 22. Ἐπικουρία = βοηθεία, occurs nowhere else in the New Testament. According to this passage Paul too recognizes Messianic predictions in the Pentateuch.—Comp. Comm. on Luke xxiv. 27.—Ver. 23 is to be viewed as an indirect question, in which εἰ is used. See at ver. 8. The doctrines regarding the suffering and resurrection of Christ are viewed as presented for examination, and exhibited as proved by the apostle. It has already been remarked in the Comm. on Matth. xxii. 29, that the phrase ἀνάστασις νεκρῶν is also applied to Christ instead of the more usual one ἀνάστασις ἐκ νεκρῶν. See Comm. Col. i. 18.)

Vers. 24–32.—Perhaps the elevated address of the apostle produced not less effect upon the proconsul Festus than Felix had already experienced (chap. xxiv. 25), but he attempted by an unseasonable jest to destroy the impression. Paul however confirmed the substance of his speech by the testimony of Agrippa, who on his part acknowledged that he was mightily affected. If the fear of men and love of the world restrained these persons from doing honour to the truth and joining themselves to the despised company of believers, they were yet obliged to confess the innocence of the apostle. The appeal to Cæsar, however, which already had been made, rendered his journey to Rome still indispensable, because this appeal, according to the principles of Roman law, could not be passed over, or retracted. Böttger, as already cited, page 27, etc.

(In ver. 24 *μαίνεσθαι* means "to be mad, phrenzied, enthusiastic." Festus certainly did not himself believe that the apostle was out of his senses; he only wished jestingly to characterize the elevated state of the apostle's mind. This man of the world, as Pilate had done before him, chose rather to let his head struggle against the impressions his heart had received. Further, he traced the aberration of Paul to his too great love of study, for the apostle had repeatedly referred to the Holy Scriptures.—Ver. 27. Ἐν γωνίᾳ, equivalent to ἐν κρυπτῷ, occurs only in this passage of the New Testament.—Ver. 28. Ἐν ὀλίγῳ, with χρόνῳ supplied, might mean "soon, in a short time," viz. if I should allow you to speak longer. But as in ver. 29, according to A.B. and other authorities, for ὀλίγῳ καὶ πολλῷ we are to read μεγάλῳ, it is on all accounts better to understand the ἐν ὀλίγῳ of the 28th verse as meaning "with a little," that is, with so little exertion, with so few words. This declaration of Agrippa would seem also in jest, but it is probable that he was concealing his inward emotion under the form of pleasantry.)

§ 5. PAUL'S JOURNEY FROM CÆSAREA TO ROME.

(Acts xxvii. 1—xxviii. 15.)

Vers. 1-5.—Under the guidance of a benevolent centurion (ver. 3) named Julius, the apostle proceeded to Rome in pursuance of his appeal to Cæsar, accompanied by Aristarchus and Lucas,* who still narrates in the first person, for, where the third person presents itself here, it is owing simply to the mention of the ship's company. In a ship of Adramyttium, sailing along the coast of Syria and Asia, he came to Lycia. Julius was captain of the σπείρη Σεβαστή, that is, of the cohors Augusta. This name was either derived from the circumstance that in the legion there was a body guard of the emperor, or that the cohort consisted of inhabitants of the city Se-

* The minuteness, so unprecedented, with which this voyage is described, may perhaps be explained from the circumstance of Luke's keeping a diary at the time, and afterwards inserting it unchanged into his work. Regarding the accuracy of the narrative in a geographical and antiquarian point of view, consult here again Tholuck's Credibility, page 385, etc.

haste. To me the former idea appears the more probable, because, on the latter supposition, the phrase used would likely have been σπείρη Σεβαστηνῶν, as Josephus expresses himself in Arch. xx. 6.

(Ver. 2.—The name Ἀδραμυττηνῷ is differently written in the manuscripts. We are not, however, to refer it to Hadrumetum in Africa, but to Adramyttium in Mysia. The adjective formed from the former city is Ἀδρυμήτιος.—Instead of μέλλοντες many manuscripts read μέλλοντι, but the first is to be preferred as the more difficult reading.—Ver. 4. Ὑποπλεῖν denotes to coast along under shelter of the shore before the violence of the winds.—Ver. 5. Instead of Μύρα, Σμύρναν, and even Λύστρα, is an erroneous reading; the former city lay much farther north; the latter was in the interior.)

Vers. 6–12.—In Myra the captain took another ship. An Alexandrian vessel received the apostle and his companions, but the badness of the season made sailing very arduous, and the good advice of Paul to take shelter betimes in winter quarters was disregarded by the Centurion. (In ver. 6, ἐμβιβάζω is a genuine Greek expression for "embarking, putting on board of a ship." Comp. Xenoph. Anab. v. 3, 3.—Ver. 7. Salmone is a promontory of the island of Crete, on the east side of the island.—Ver. 8. Παραλέγω, to sail past: λέγω is applied, quite like the Latin word lego, to "voyaging, sailing."—Καλοὶ λιμένες, fair havens, was the name given to the place mentioned, perhaps because in the one bay there were several good anchorages for ships.—For Λασαία many manuscripts read Ἄλασσα, but on critical grounds we prefer the first reading. Of the place, however, nothing further is known.—Ver. 9. The νηστεία is plainly here a mark of time: it refers to the great feast of atonement on the 10th of Tisri, that is, towards the end of September, when the equinoctial storms blow. Regarding this feast, styled יוֹם הַכִּפֻּרִים, consult Winer's Reallex. under the article Versöhnungstag.—Ver. 10. Ὅτι is connected with the infinitive μέλλειν instead of μέλλει. On this point, compare Winer in his Gram. p. 315.—Ver. 11. Ναύκληρος denotes the proprietor of the ship, the owner who in ancient times was wont to sail in her himself.—Ver. 12. Ἀνεύθετος, "not well situated, inconvenient," occurs nowhere else in the New Testament. The harbour Phœnix, on the south side of the island, was protected against most winds, and they could readily sail into it with a south-west wind [λίψ], and a north-west wind [χῶρος, Latin, corus, caurus],* and therefore the mariners were desirous of wintering in it.)

Vers. 13–20.—But a storm overtook the ship on her way to this harbour, and she was driven ashore on the island of Clauda.—

* Comp. Karl. v. Raumer's treatise on the names of the Greek winds in the Rheinisches Museum, fur Philologie 1837.

(Ver. 13. Ὑποπνέω, "to blow softly," denotes a favourable wind.—Κρατεῖν προθέσεως, to carry a purpose into effect. With ἄραντες supply ἀγκύραν.—For ἆσσον some manuscripts read Ἄσσον, but no name of a city could stand here without a proposition: ἆσσον is the comparative of the adverb ἄγχι, near: it is found chiefly in poetical diction, but it also occurs in good prose. The conjecture θᾶσσον, "rapidly, quickly," is quite unnecessary.—Ver. 14. Τυφωνικός, stormy; the direction of the wind, which was blowing with vehemence, is indicated by the name Εὐρακύλων. This reading I prefer, with Grotius, Mill, Bengel, and others, to the common reading Εὐρυκλύδων or Εὐροκλύδων, words which can only denote the breadth and height of the waves, and consequently indicate the severity of the storm, in which case they form a tautology with τυφωνικός. But Εὐρακύλων denotes the north-east wind, which, according to the direction in which they were going, must have been disastrous to them, because it drove them from land.—Ver. 15. Ἀντοφθαλμεῖν, to look in the face, confront, then, "withstand."—Ver. 16. Κλαύδη, for which Κλαύδα and Καύδη are also found, was a small island beside Crete. Comp. Pliny, H. N. iv. 22.—Σκάφη is the ship's boat, which was put out, and could not be brought on board again without difficulty.—Ver. 17. Ὑποζωννύειν refers to the strengthening of the ship's sides, by beams and cords, that she might withstand the shocks of the waves. Βοήθειαι is then best understood of these material appliances. To lighten the ship still further, they let down the mast. Σκεῦος denotes here either the sail yards with the sails, or the mast. Ver. 40 renders the latter more probable. The ships of the ancients were, after the manner of our river ships, supplied with masts which could be let down. Meyer will have the word to mean the sails: these doubtless, as inseparably connected with the mast, are comprehended, but not exclusively meant.—Besides, they lightened the ship by casting out first bales of goods and other things that did not properly belong to her, and then the proper furniture of the ship, beams, tackling, and so on. Σκευή, found in the New Testament only here, means properly "dress, attire," and applied to a ship, whatever belongs to her equipment.)

Vers. 21–26.—In this dangerous condition of the ship the apostle, full of earnestness and mildness, came into the midst of the desponding crew. He blamed them for having gone further, in opposition to his counsel, but promised, as instructed by a heavenly messenger,* that there should be no loss of human life, though they must be cast away upon an island (δεῖ, according to the Divine ap-

* Here too it is not said that this appearance took place in a dream, nor, in view of the remarks already made on the visions of Paul, is this at all probable. (Comp Comm. on chap. xvi. 10.)

pointment, to God's immutable will.) In these words the only remarkable expression is κεχάρισταί σοι ὁ Θεὸς πάντας κ. τ. λ., *God has granted to you them all*, etc., in ver. 24. We must of course suppose that Paul had wrestled in prayer for the lives of the men, that this prayer had been heard, and that the whole company were in a manner given to him. Such passages as Psalm cxlv. 19 furnish the key to this thought.

Vers. 27–32.—On the fourteenth night the ship's crew suddenly perceived a rapid diminution of the depth of the sea, which indicated approach to land. They threw out the anchor, therefore, that they might not drift upon the shore, and waited for the morning. The seamen, however, persuaded that land was near, attempted to escape by means of the boat. But although the apostle had received assurance from heaven of the deliverance of all on board, yet he omitted no possible precautions, and by his advice the soldiers detained the sailors on board, because they alone were able to supply the proper means of escape.

(Ver. 27.—The Adriatic sea, according to the ancient usage of language, comprehends the whole portion of the Mediterranean lying between Greece, Italy, and Sicily.—Διαφέρεσθαι = φέρεσθαι, to be driven about.—Ver. 28. Βολίζω, from βολίς, the sounding lead. Ὄργυια, from ὀρέγειν, a fathom, the space measured by the arms stretched out.—Ver. 29. Τόποι τραχεῖς, stony places, rocky banks. Four anchors were thrown out, but it must be remembered that the anchors of the ancients were far smaller than ours, for the most part, probably, at this period, heavy stones fastened to chains: no ship now carries four anchors.)

Vers. 33–38.—Although Paul was a prisoner, yet in the general confusion he exercised all the authority of a head, as the rest of the narrative shews. As the ship must be abandoned, he exhorted them all to take food for their refreshment after the long toil which had prevented all regular meals; and when their repast was ended, they threw the provisions overboard to lighten the ship, that she might approach as near as possible to the shore. (Ver. 33. Μηδὲν προσλαβόμενοι is of course to be understood as only intimating that during the period of danger they had sat down to no regular meal, but Paul induced them to do this, that they might be strengthened. This meal was observed by the apostle and the other Christians quite as a love-feast (ver. 35), although it might not be so understood by the unbelievers present.—In ver. 34 the words οὐδενὸς ὑμῶν θρὶξ ἐκ τῆς κεφαλῆς ἀπολεῖται exhibit a manifest allusion to Luke xxi. 18, where the very same words occur.—Ver. 37. The number of men in the ship, two hundred and seventy-six, indicates that her size was considerable.—Ver. 38. Κουφίζω, from κοῦφος, denotes "to lighten, to make light.")

Vers. 39–44.—In the morning the shipwrecked mariners saw the land before them; they lifted the anchors and stranded the vessel upon a favourable part of the shore. To prevent the flight of the prisoners, the soldiers wished to kill them, but Julius the centurion had contracted a love for Paul, and therefore he did not permit this. Agreeably to Paul's predictions, they all reach the land in safety, some on planks and some swimming.

(In ver. 39, instead of *ἐβουλεύσαντο*, several manuscripts read *ἐβουλεύοντο* or *ἐβούλοντο*. The last reading is certainly to be rejected; the two others are equally appropriate to the sense, but critical authorities are decidedly in favour of *ἐβουλεύσαντο*.—Ver. 40. *Εἴων εἰς τὴν θάλασσαν*, they committed themselves to the sea, that is, they let themselves drift.* As the ship was on the verge of being lost, they sacrificed the anchors, cutting them loose. *Περιαιρέω*, chop off, cut away. At ver. 20 we had the word in this sense, but figuratively, as also in Hebrews x. 11.—*Πηδάλιον* means the rudder, of which anciently the larger ships had several. They were managed, as is still the case, with ropes, which were now let go, that the ship might be suffered entirely to drift. [*Ἀνέντες*, from *ἀνίημι*, *remittere*, slacken, let go, abandon.] In order to run the vessel at once quickly and high upon the beach, and facilitate the escape of the crew, they raised up the mast again, and spread out a sail upon it. *Ἀρτέμων* is not the mast but the sail, but as the 17th verse tells us the mast was lowered down, the hoisting of the sail intimates that it was again erected. With *τῇ πνεούσῃ* supply *αὔρᾳ*.—Ver. 41. *Τόπος διθάλασσος*, a projecting headland, which had water on both sides of it. Before this headland there may have been a sand-bank lying, or it may have run out into one, but the phrase *τόπος διθάλασσος* does not by itself mean a shallow, or sand-bank.—*Ἐποκέλλειν*, to drive up, to cause to strike against.—Ver. 44. *Σανίς*, asser, a board or plank. *Τὰ ἀπὸ τοῦ πλοίου* are beams of the ship, that was now broken by the violence of the waves.)

Chap. xxviii. 1–6.—It was when they landed that they first learned that they were driven ashore upon the island of Malta. The inhabitants of the island received the shipwrecked strangers in a friendly manner, and kindled a fire to warm them, stiff as they were with cold. On this occasion Paul experienced the protection of God in a manner which made him appear to the rude islanders endowed with supernatural powers.

(Ver. 1.—There was an island of the name of *Μελίτη*, on the coast of Illyricum, which at the present day is called Meleda. But the subsequent description of their course shews that it can only be Malta beside Sicily which is meant. This island was inhab-

* Doubtful if *εἴων* can be taken thus reflexively. Better (with Hackett, De Wette, etc.) to refer it to *ἀγκύρας*: they let go the anchors into the sea.—[K.

ited by colonists from Phœnicia or Carthage, who are therefore called βάρβαροι.*—Ver. 2. Πυρά, a heap of wood, a pile of wood.—Ἐφεστώς signifies properly adstans, here "oppressive, heavy."—Ver. 3. Φρύγανα, brushwood for keeping up the fire.—Ἔχιδνα, a viper, a poisonous serpent.—Καθάπτω, to fasten to, to affix; here taken, quite unusually, in a middle acceptation. Many manuscripts therefore read καθήψατο. On this point consult the full discussion in Suiceri Thes. sub voce.—The superstitious and fickle multitude are just as ready to record a vote of condemnation as of deification. When it is said, however, for the purpose of evading a miracle, that the serpent may not have been poisonous, we must certainly confess that this is not expressly stated, but just as certainly it is not expressly denied; and the whole tone of the narrative plainly leads to the conclusion, that all who were present regarded the serpent as poisonous. We may therefore in this narrative recognize a fulfilment of the promise contained in Mark xvi. 18.)

Ver. 7-10.—A Roman of distinction named Publius had possessions in Malta. He took a friendly interest in the apostle and his companions, a kindness which Paul was able to requite by healing his father.—(Ver. 7. The Romans had naturally taken this island, lying so near Sicily, into their possession, and a distinguished individual named Publius had even settled in Malta. It is probable that at the same time he exercised the functions of the magistracy; but the word πρῶτος does not necessarily imply this.—Ver. 8. Δυσεντερία, dysentery, diarrhœa with colic or gripes.—Ver. 10. The word τιμαί is to be understood of aids of every kind which were furnished to the apostle, not only during the time of his stay, but also for his departure.)

Vers. 11-15.—After the lapse of three months, when the weather again permitted sailing, the company proceeded on their voyage in a ship of Alexandria, which had wintered in the island. In Syracuse they lay for three days, and then landed in Puteoli. Here there were already believers, and now they proceeded by land to Rome, from which brethren came out to meet them as far as Appii Forum and the Three Taverns.

(In ver. 11, παράσημον denotes the ship's sign, which was usually placed on the prow. For this ship there had been chosen the figures of Castor and Pollux, the guardian deities of seafaring men.—Ver. 13. Ῥήγιον, a city and promontory in Calabria, called at present Reggio.—On δευτεραῖοι, see at John xi. 39.—Ποτίολοι, Pu-

* The mention of Δίκη, that is, of the avenging Nemesis, proves nothing to the contrary; for, in the first place, many barbarians had adopted Grecian elements into their religious views; and again, no nation is without the idea of a retributive justice which displays itself in the government of the world, and Luke may have only employed the familiar Greek term to express this idea. Tradition states, that from this time the island of Malta was entirely freed from serpents.

teoli, was usually called in Greek Δικαιάρχεια. The fact that already there were believers in this city, furnishes an important proof of the rapid spread of Christianity even in Italy. Doubtless the gospel came hither from Rome, with which Puteoli was closely connected, being, as it were, the harbour for the larger ships of the metropolis of the world. Ostium could be visited only by small ships. That Paul received permission to spend seven days with the brethren, is a proof of the good will of Julius. During the centurion's intercourse with Paul he had certainly not remained without movements of heart, and through him Paul might afterwards in various ways be introduced into those military circles where his labours were so effective. [Comp. Phil. i. 13 ; iv. 22.]—Ver. 15. Forum Appii, a town on the via Appia, see Horat. Sat. i. 6, 3. On this road lay the tres tabernæ, six miles from Rome. Comp. Cic. ad Attic. i. 13.)

§ 6. PAUL'S STAY IN ROME.

(Acts xxviii. 16–31.)

Ver. 16.—And now the great apostle of the Gentiles had reached the city which God's providence had appointed to be the queen of the world, not only in the old but also in the new order of things. The most heterogeneous elements were blended together in this huge metropolis. The Lord had a numerous people in it, and there was a flourishing church composed of the excellent individuals that were there; but the world of evil, too, had here its mightiest representative, and, in the very person of the ruling emperor Nero, there had been set up a formal anti-christian power. Before him, the blood-thirsty tyrant, Paul knew that he must appear (xxvii. 24), to defend the gospel of God, and to seal it with his blood. What feelings, then, would agitate the bosom of the apostle, when he trod the city that was first to be drunk with the blood of the saints, and with the blood of the witnesses of Jesus (Rev. xvii. 6–18), and how much he would need brotherly consolation and refreshment in spirit, may be readily understood after these remarks. Here, in the great central point of the heathen world, Paul felt that he had first fulfilled his calling as apostle of the Gentiles in its full extent; hence his desire had long turned hither (Rom. i. 13), but the accomplishment of this desire brought also before his soul the presentiment of the end which was here awaiting him.

(The στρατοπεδάρχης to whom the prisoners were to be delivered, is the præfectus prætorio, the highest military authority in the city. It could hardly be the excellent Burrhus, who was preceptor of Nero, along with Seneca, for he had died so early as the spring of the year 62. The apostle, however, received permission, doubtless on giving security, which the Roman law required in such a case, and which he would readily find among the Christians in Rome, to reside in a private house, with a soldier chained to him, after the Roman custom. (Verses 23, 30, ἐν ἰδίῳ μισθώματι, perhaps with Aquila, who, according to Rom. xvi. 3, had returned to Rome.) But as the soldiers were changed, and Paul was also probably required to appear from time to time before the præfect, he might thus, although residing in a private house, find access to the Emperor's body-guard. Comp. Phil. i. 13.

Vers. 17–22.—A few days after his arrival Paul called together the most influential among the Jews, that he might vindicate himself to them, and prevent them from forming an opposition against him. But they declare that, although they have heard of the sect of the Nazarenes, and of the opposition raised against them, yet they have received no information against the apostle, either by letter or by oral communication. This declaration is very remarkable, when it is considered how zealous the Jews were to send emissaries everywhere after the apostle; and, moreover, as the communication with Rome was so quick, and Paul's journey had lasted so long, we cannot understand how no warning against the apostate should have reached Rome. We cannot conceive there was any concealment of the truth on the part of the Jews, as no ground at all appears which could have led them to be silent on the matter. Böttiger's supposition (work already cited, pages 15, etc., 43, etc.), that the Jews pretend ignorance, as fearing that Paul might put them on their defence, when they felt themselves unable to carry out their charge against him, is quite untenable, because the apostle could institute no process against the Jews of Rome, who had done him no injury, but only against the Jews in Jerusalem. Böttiger represents the matter as if the whole Jewish nation were bound to answer for the wrong, which had proceeded from certain Jews in Jerusalem. Add to this, that if the fear in question might have determined the Jews in Rome to so strange a procedure, certainly it could not be the occasion of their falling out among themselves about the Messiahship of Jesus, according to the account here given by Luke. But we have already noticed, at chap. xviii. 1, what furnishes the key to the difficulty before us. Under Claudius, the Jews, and along with them the Christians, had been expelled from Rome, and thus the connexions which the Jews of Jerusalem had with them were interrupted. And it was only quite slowly and secretly that the Jews returned under the government of Nero, which was very peaceful at its commencement, and at the same time, too, the Christian church was gathered together again. But both Jews and Christians alike maintained a designed separation, and thus gradually lost their acquaintance with one another. But in Palestine they were not so accurately informed with regard to the state of matters in Rome, and thus it happened that no intelligence was sent thither, which certainly would not have been omitted in the case of any other place.

(In ver. 17 the apostle declares most decidedly that he did nothing directly opposed to the customs and usages of the fathers. [See particulars at chap. xxi. 17, seq.]—Ver. 19. Ἀλλά must be supplied to οὐχ ὡς; Paul wishes to intimate that he designs nothing against his nation, but is rather suffering persecution from them.—In ver. 20, ἐλπὶς τοῦ Ἰσραήλ denotes the appearance of the Messiah. Compare Comm. on Luke ii. 25.—Ver. 22. The manner in which the Jews of Rome speak of the opposition given to the Christians, is not such as to render it probable that in Rome itself there had already been such contentions, as arose for example in Galatia. The character of the Epistle to the Romans confirms this supposition, for, according to it, there had only been unimportant collisions there. See the particulars in the introduction to the Epistle to the Romans, and at Rom. xvi. 17, etc.)

Vers. 23-29.—That the Jews in Rome rather speak of the Christians as a sect opposed elsewhere, than as one requiring to be opposed in their own immediate neighbourhood, is plain also from what follows. They are quite in the dark regarding the nature and peculiar doctrines of Christianity, and learn them, as it seems, for the first time from the mouth of Paul. As to the mode of reconciling this with the circumstance that the Epistle to the Romans, which was written before this period, supposes the existence of a considerable Christian church in Rome, read the detailed statement made in the introduction to that Epistle. What is stated in the passage before us, certainly makes the impression, that the Jews in Rome heard the preaching of the gospel of Christ for the first time: there arose, as usual, a controversy among themselves, for some were convinced of the Messiahship of Jesus, others not. This state of matters would be inexplicable, if the church had not, as has been detailed above, been again but recently gathered together. The apostle, however, dismissed the doubting Jews with a reference to the language of rebuke uttered by the prophet Isaiah, and contrasted with their unbelief the faith to be expected from the Gentiles.

(Ver. 23.—As the assemblage in which Paul spoke took place in his own residence, it is not improbable that he staid with Aquila, who always had a place for meetings in his house. See Rom. xvi. 3.—Ver. 26. The passage from Isaiah vi. 9, 10, has already been explained at Matth. xiii. 14, 15.—Ver. 29 is wanting in many Codices, but doubtless improperly. Probably on account of ἀπελύοντο in ver. 25, the words were regarded as superfluous. But there it is the breaking off of the discourse that is meant, here it is the final departure from the house.)

Vers. 30, 31.—Two whole years the apostle remained in this situation, and preached, without hindrance, to all. The specification of the time here made, thus leads us, at the conclusion of the Acts of the Apostles, to the spring of the year 65, as in the spring of 63 Paul arrived in Rome. The supposition of Böttiger (Beitr. Part II. p. 82, etc.), that Paul was only a few days in imprisonment in Rome, as described in chap. xxviii. 16, and that he is here, in verse 30, represented as free from confinement, is quite inadmissible, because the expression ἐν τῷ ἰδίῳ μισθώματι in verse 30 is not different from μένειν καθ' ἑαυτόν in verse 16, but means precisely the same thing. This appears manifest from the circumstance that there is mention made only of the receiving of visits on his part: he was not permitted to go about without restraint, to enter into the synagogue, and the like. The concluding words, therefore, μετὰ πάσης παῤῥησίας ἀκωλύτως refer only to the perfect freedom he enjoyed in his private residence, but not beyond it. That it was not after the lapse of these two years Paul suffered martyrdom, but that he was set free at his first trial before Nero, and then perished in a second imprisonment, will be shewn further in the Commentary on the pastoral epistles. Here the only question is, why Luke concludes his work in the manner he does. Not only is there no particular account of the process against Paul, but we also feel the want of a concluding address to Theophilus, and a review of the whole, in a short formal conclusion of the book. It is certainly a remark of some weight, that this phenomenon may be explained from the circumstance that Luke has detailed the events as far as they had developed themselves at the time, and thus we have a clue to the time of the composition of the work. (Compare in the Comm. B. i. Introd. § vi.) Meyer's remark on the other hand (Comm. on Acts p. 8 and 345), that the sonorous and solemn conclusion marks an absolute completion of the work, is plainly wrong: the sonorousness of the participial conclusion can prove nothing here: the question is about the *substance* of the concluding verses, which leave the commenced account regarding Paul unfinished; the decision of his appeal to the Emperor must have been stated, if it had taken place when Luke concluded. But even suppose that Luke had no additional fact to narrate, or that he supposes everything which has occurred in Rome to be known to Theophilus, still it must always appear to the reader that there was need of a more formal conclusion. The passage xxviii. 31, concludes at most the last narrated event, but it does not form a conclusion to the whole work: we naturally expect a reference to the beginning of the book, and to Theophilus. When we consider the commencement of the treatise (Luke i. 1–4), it seems a natural expectation that Luke would conclude with some such statement as this: "I have now, beloved Theophilus, mentioned everything which I have ascertained: from the point of time which we have now reached, you have a personal knowledge of all that has occurred, and therefore I conclude here." If Luke, then, did not purpose to issue a third treatise, as Heinrichs supposes, undoubtedly the proper formal conclusion of the work is wanting.

If, at the conclusion of this remarkable monument of the ancient church, we look back to the course hitherto taken by the seed of God's word in its growth, we perceive in it three great intermissions or stages, all proceeding from east to west. In the first place, we find the gospel at work among the Jews only, and during this period Jerusalem forms the central point of Christian life; in the next place it advances to the boundaries of the heathen and Jewish world, and Antioch now becomes the centre of activity; and, finally, it gains a firm footing in the greatest city of heathendom, in Rome itself, and thus the victory of the gospel over the Gentile world is declared. As Jerusalem, too, about the same time when Peter and Paul were labouring in Rome, and sealed their ministry with their blood, was destroyed, the universal character of Christianity was then also established in opposition to every particular system. The first two points are completely carried through in the book of Acts; but it merely introduces us to the third point, which is one of great importance. The letters of the apostles, however, which follow, embrace, in substance, its further development; for, like branches into which the one stem of the tree of life is divided, they bring the various tendencies slumbering in its germ to their individual perfection. In this gradual transference, then, of the gospel from the people of Israel to the Gentiles, lies the key to the remarkable fact, which, more than everything else, demonstrates the Divine power of the risen Redeemer, that not only in the book of Acts, but also in the whole extension of the church, and in the writings that constitute the canon of the church, the Twelve who had seen the Lord for three years, and lived with him, give place to a man who hardly had seen Christ, and who had even for a length of time persecuted Christians with a blind fury. The Apostle Paul stands before us as an image of the whole apostate race of man, or at least of Israel, who are long struggling against the Lord, but are at last to become a mighty instrument for the accomplishment of God's designs. After his entire surrender to his Lord and Saviour, his life and spirit became so intimately blended with the being and nature of Christ himself, that in the following treatment of his profound epistles, we cannot be persuaded that we find anything hostile to the gospel, but only its true essential nature, which, mirroring itself in a capacious intellect and a profound sensibility, carries with it, besides its indwelling heavenly nobleness, the magic of living personal experience, and the adornment of profound and richly developed thought. While, therefore, we have had hitherto to do with the greatest and most comprehensive phenomena, with the progress of the Redeemer's life and that of his church, which required the utmost possible expansion of view, we proceed now to inquiries in which individual doctrines and practical relations are brought under the most minute examination; while the concluding book of the New Testament, the Apocalypse, again takes the reader back to the most comprehensive position, uniting the general and the particular in one harmonious whole.

THE

PISTLES OF THE APOSTLE PAUL.

GENERAL INTRODUCTION

TO

THE EPISTLES OF PAUL.

---

§ 1. Of the Life* and Ministry of Paul in General.

Although in the Acts of the Apostles the principal points in the life of the Apostle Paul have already passed before us, yet the connected consideration of his Epistles calls for a summary view of his noble character, as well as of the way in which the Lord of the church prepared this distinguished instrument for the execution of his purposes. For so entirely are Paul's writings the proper growth of his own mind and spirit, living parts, so to speak, of his very self, that it would be most difficult to understand their peculiar nature without a clear perception of these points. Of course, however, the special points, which in Luke's narrative have been thoroughly treated, will here receive no further attention.

Paul was called, for the further spread of the gospel, to form the connecting link between the Græco-Roman and the Jewish world; it was necessary, therefore, that both heathen and Jewish habits of life and thought should bear a part in his education, in order that he might be able to understand and sympathize with both. Born of Jewish parents, and subsequently brought up at the feet of Gamaliel, in the principles of the Pharisees, Jewish views and feelings certainly formed the *ground-work and substance* of his education. But, as his birth-place was Tarsus, where Grecian art and science flourished in a high degree,† this could not fail to exert an imme-

* On the life of Paul, besides the older works of Pearson (Annales Paulini) and Paley (Horæ Paulinæ), there have more recently appeared the writings of Menken, "Blicke in das Leben des Apostels Paulus" (Bremen, 1828), of Hemsen (Göttingen, 1830), of Schrader (Leips. 1830–32, iii. vols.), and of Schott (Jena, 1832). The work of Schrader is rich in new results, which, however, cannot bear the test of an impartial criticism. Very interesting and instructive are the remarks of Tholuck in the "Studien und Kritiken" of 1835. P. ii. p. 364, etc.

† Strabo (Geogr. xiv. p. 991, ed. Almelov.) places Tarsus, in this respect, on a level with Athens and Alexandria.

diate effect upon the *outward form* of his culture; an influence still evident from the quotations made in his writings from Grecian poets. (Acts xvii. 28, 1 Cor. xv. 33, Tit. i. 12.) Again, it is at least more than probable, that, in the later part of his life, when he had escaped from the stern bondage of narrow-minded Pharisaism, the views he had gained in his youth of the nobler aspects of Grecian life, again rose up before his mind, and gave him that just appreciation of Gentile life, which is discernible in his writings.

For, just as Philo and other Jews, who lived entirely amongst Greeks, as well as the earlier Fathers of the Church (*e. g.*, Justin Martyr), regarded the better men amongst the Gentiles as by no means excluded from the blessings of the Divine Logos, the Giver of the heavenly powers of holiness and the knowledge of God; so also did Paul recognize within the heathen world a spiritual Israel; that is, nobler spirits, who thirsted after truth and righteousness (Rom. ii. 14, 15); and whom he sought, through the preaching of the gospel, to lead to the covenant of promise. Even the birth, therefore, of the Apostle, and the elements of culture amidst which he grew up, were so ordered by the providence of God, as best to train him for the teacher of the Gentiles (Galat. i. 15). For though, at first sight, it might appear that his connexion with the sect of the Pharisees would not conduce to that freedom of spirit which he afterwards attained to, yet, on closer consideration, we shall discern in even this, the wisdom of a directing Providence.

In the first place there were found in this sect many elements of truth, more especially moral earnestness and strictness of life, which in *many* only, but by no means in all, became hypocrisy. And, besides this, such a nature as that of Paul needed the full experience of *all* that one system had to offer, before he would become fully conscious of what was erroneous and one-sided in it, and embrace, with complete devotion, and all the powers of his being, the complementary truth which that system obscured or denied. The energy and decision of his will made him carry out his principles as a Pharisee to a fanatical extreme against the Christians; and it was not till he had done this, that he was possessed by that intense longing which this system of life could not satisfy, and which led him to perceive the state into which he had fallen. Hence, although the miraculous vision which was imparted to him, and the startling announcement, that he who was still the raging opposer of the Crucified, was henceforth to be his messenger to the Gentiles, are of course to be considered as the decisive causes of the sudden change in his spiritual state, yet at the same time, we cannot doubt that his sincere striving after righteousness by the mere works of the law had already, though perhaps without his own consciousness, awakened in the depth of his soul the conviction that his own strength could not attain to the fulfilment of righteousness; nay, that it might even lead him, with all his goodness of intention, into the most fearful errors. This conviction brought with it that which, though not the *cause*, was a necessary *condition* of his passing into the new life;—namely, the longing after something higher, and the power of appreciating such moral phenomena, as the ministry and death of Stephen, in which that for which he longed was presented to him in actual life.

Without entering more at length, in this place, into the consideration of that event which transformed Paul into that mighty and honoured instrument in the kingdom of God, which we recognize in him (it having been discussed at that passage in Acts which records it, compare Acts ix. with xxii. and xxvi.), let us notice, first, the position which he obtained with respect to the Twelve and the Seventy, after his conversion. His relation to the Twelve it is of particular importance to determine; for though the Seventy seem to come nearest him, in respect of their ministry, which was also directed to the Gentile world,* yet these so entirely disappear as a body from the history after the resurrection of the Lord, that no trace of them remains. The separate members of it might indeed have been afterwards actively engaged in preaching the gospel, but no rivalry could have arisen between them, as such, and Paul, since no one could doubt that Paul was at least equal to them. But the case was quite different with respect to the Twelve. These formed a strictly defined and limited body; so that, even after the Ascension, the vacancy† which was occasioned in their number by the apostacy of Judas Iscariot was immediately filled up by the express command of the Lord. (Acts i. 15, etc.) This body was, in fact, to contain within itself the pillars and supports of the church, in proof of which we find the twelve apostles spoken of as the spiritual fathers of the spiritual Israel. (Matth. xix. 28; Rev. iv. 10, xxi. 14.) The question, then, is forced upon us:—in what relation did Paul stand, according to the mind of the Lord, to this sacred body of Twelve? Now, regarding this question purely *objectively*, apart from individuals, we cannot deny that the Twelve stand higher than Paul, as those who had been with the Lord throughout his earthly pilgrimage (which Peter considers as requisite in a true apostle, Acts i. 21), and the proper witnesses of the whole progress of the Redeemer's life on earth. They are, and must continue to be, the proper foundations of the New

* See at Luke x. 1.

† It would help us to understand the important position which we find James, the brother of the Lord, afterwards occupying, if we might assume that he was taken into the number of the Twelve in the place of James, who, we learn (from Acts xii. 2), was beheaded. Still, we have no distinct historical evidence on this point; and besides, he does not appear to have left Jerusalem, whilst the apostles were to travel.

Jerusalem (Rev. xxi. 14), the roots, so to speak, of the entire tree, those who received from the Lord the first fruits of the Spirit. Paul might indeed justly call himself a witness of the resurrection,* since he had beheld the crucified Jesus as the risen Lord, and had experienced in his own person his Divine power; but he manifestly had not the privilege of having seen the whole course of the life of Christ, and in this respect he stood, as it were, one step further from that throne of glory which was immediately surrounded by the Twelve. But, turning from the abstract relation to the men themselves as they appear in history, we must confess, on the other hand, that the apostle Paul left all the Twelve far behind him, in that "he (that is, the grace of God in him) laboured more abundantly than they all." (1 Cor. xv. 10; 2 Cor. xi. 23.) And this arose by no means from his personal devotedness alone, but also in a great measure from circumstances. For, since the vineyard of God's kingdom was taken away from the Jews, and opened to the Gentiles, and Paul was called to labour especially among the latter, as the Twelve primarily amongst the former, it was natural that the minstry of Paul should bear much richer fruit, and that all the other apostles should in comparison with him fall into the back-ground. From this we may likewise easily perceive how the relation of the gospel to the outward institutions of the Old Testament, and the admission of the Gentiles into the church without observing these, should have become plain to the Apostle Paul, at an earlier period, and more completely than to any of the other apostles—more especially than to Peter, who was called to labour immediately amongst the Jews, and who was designed to represent, as it were, the element of stability in the church. Under this state of things, therefore, the apostle stood on a level with the Twelve, as entirely independent of them, and occupied a position of his own, as called immediately by the Lord to be the Apostle to the Gentiles. (Acts xxvi. 17.) And this is a point on which Paul often found it necessary to insist in his arguments with his opponents, who wished to impugn his authority as an apostle. (See on Galat. ii. 9.) In doing so he laid particular stress upon the fact, that *he did not in any way receive his knowledge of the gospel from the Twelve, or from any other Christian, but immediately from the Lord himself.* (See on Galat. i. 12.) Now, as regards the purely spiritual part of the gospel, there is no difficulty in conceiving how Paul could have made this his own without any instruction from man. For the Holy Ghost, who was imparted to him, filled his inner man as

* It would indeed appear probable, from 2 Cor. v. 16, that Paul had seen our Lord before his resurrection, on the occasion of his presence at the Passover in Jerusalem; but certainly no nearer connexion had subsisted between him and the Saviour.

an all-pervading light, and made plain to him, through his belief in Jesus as the Messiah, the whole of the Old Testament, in which all the germs of the New were already laid down. In the Spirit, who is absolute truth (1 John v. 6), was given the assured conviction of the truth of the gospel, and insight into its meaning, in details. With regard, however, to the *historical* elements of Christianity, the case appears different; and yet there are points connected apparently altogether with this (as, for example, the institution of the Lord's Supper, 1 Cor. xi. 23, etc.), of which the apostle asserts that he had received them immediately from the Lord. Now, we should undoubtedly be running into an erroneous extreme, if we were to assume that *all* historical particulars in the life of our Lord were imparted to him by revelation. The general outlines of Christ's outward life, the history of his miracles, of his journeys, and what belongs to them, were, no doubt, related to him by Ananias or other Christians. But whatever in that life was necessarily connected with the peculiar doctrines of the gospel, as, for instance, the institution of the Sacraments, the Resurrection, and similar points, came, no doubt, to the apostle in an extraordinary manner, by immediate revelation of the Lord;* so as to accredit him as an independent witness, not only before the world, but also to believers. No one could come forward and say, that what Paul knew of the gospel had been received through him. For it was from no man, but from the highest Teacher himself, that he had received alike the commission to preach, the essential facts of the gospel, and the Holy Spirit who gives light and life to those facts.

By this, however, it is not intended to deny that there was a development in the new life of Paul; though assuredly (as will be shewn more at length in the following paragraphs), no further revolution in doctrinal views could take place in him. But even he, doubtless, advanced gradually from childhood to youth, and then to manhood in Christ. And so, when the apostle came forward as a teacher at Damascus, immediately after his conversion (Acts ix. 19 etc.), it was but the expression of the true feeling of the necessity which lay upon him at once to bear open witness to the change which, through God's grace, had taken place in him. But he himself, no doubt, soon began to perceive that, before he could labour with a blessing, there was needed a deepening and thorough remoulding of the elements of his spiritual life. In consequence of his perception of this truth, he retired into Arabia for three years—a time which, it is probable, he spent chiefly in a thorough study of the Scriptures.† In these studies, probably, the enlightening of the

* According to the account given in the Acts, Paul was more than once graciously honoured with a vision of the Lord. (See Acts xxii. 17, xxiii. 11.)

† See, on this point, the remarks on Acts ix. 20, etc. Paul himself enjoins Timothy

Holy Ghost first revealed to him, as a connected whole, the great purpose of the Lord with respect to the human race; and now inwardly ripened, and firmly established in true principles of doctrine and life, he went forth into the great field of labour which the Lord had appointed him. As the waters of a stream are spread abroad, so did he spread abroad, beyond the narrow depths in which they had hitherto been confined, the quickening powers contained in the new doctrine; and the whole heathen world, which, left to itself, had come nigh to entire corruption, was made fruitful by it with new germs of heavenly life. Now, as an energetic character, as one whose whole work lay out of himself, the apostle was in danger of forgetting himself in his care for others; or, at least, of letting his incessant labours drain and exhaust his inward life. In order to prevent this, we perceive, on the one hand, the grace of God effectually renewing him with the powers of the higher world (2 Cor. xii.), since the mighty labours in which he was engaged had not been undertaken by him on his own impulse, but had been expressly assigned to him by the Lord. And, on the other hand, God so ordered his circumstances as to afford seasons of rest to his spirit; to which belong, particularly, the imprisonments which he had to undergo. In such times of solitary stillness his spiritual life was more fully developed within itself, so that the preacher of the word might not preach to others and be himself a castaway.

The last stage in the Apostle Paul's progress towards perfection was finally to be his martyrdom. That which John experienced inwardly in the spirit, Peter and Paul were to experience also in the body.* It was in the centre of the heathen world, in Rome, during the first great persecution which befel the church of God, that Paul died, beheaded, as a Roman citizen, with the sword. The fact itself of his death is established by so many and ancient witnesses (amongst whom the presbyter Gaius, and the bishop Dionysius of Corinth, are the oldest, see Euseb. H. E. ii. 25.), that it cannot be questioned. There remains, however, an uncertainty as to the year of his death, because in this is involved the doubtful question concerning Paul's second imprisonment at Rome.† The question will subsequently occupy us, and I only here remark, in passing, that I think it necessary to assume a second imprisonment of Paul in Rome, and cannot, therefore, place his death earlier than the last year of the reign of Nero (A.D. 67 or 68).

(1 Tim. iii. 6), that no new convert shall be a bishop. Is it, then, likely that he would have acted in opposition to his own rule? or would his wonderful conversion have exempted him from a rule to which even the Twelve were subject?

* See more on this subject at John xxi. 20, etc.

† Compare, on this point, in Hemsen's Life of Paul, the concluding consideration on his death.

§ 2. The Peculiarities of Paul's Character.*

That Paul was one of those *energetic* characters, of whom, in different ages of the church, the Lord has taken so many into his service, is too evident to escape the observation of any. Whatever may be thought of the sentiments of the apostle, even the sceptic must confess that a powerful and earnest spirit† breathes through his writings, full of the glow of enthusiasm for that which he held as true, and of burning zeal which he was able to communicate to all. But it is of the greatest consequence to obtain a more accurate knowledge of the peculiarities of Paul's mind; because his writings and doctrine will be much more easily comprehended if we keep before our minds a clear image of their author.

Now the simplest way of obtaining an insight into the peculiarities of Paul's character is by comparing him with John the Evangelist. Contemplation (Γνῶσις), in the highest sense of that word, we found to be the peculiar feature of John's life.‡ The whole bent of his mind was introspective and meditative. His soul was entirely receptive, all eye, as it were, to gaze upon the eternal ideas of truth. Thus outward labours were with him less prominent, and the flower and crown of his life was prophecy. The image presented to us by Paul is very different from this. Although, of course, not deficient in a living and *intuitive* knowledge of truth, yet in his mode of treating religion he gives scope to a *dialectical* element unknown to John, an element marked by a predominant intellectual acuteness which loves to work out ideas into abstract conceptions. Through this talent for reasoning Paul became the author of a sharply defined doctrinal language, and the founder of theology, as a science, in the church of Christ. In him is represented the necessity of science for the church, even in the very narrow circle of those on whom the Holy Spirit was first poured forth.§ And the same

* On the subject of the following paragraphs, compare the essay of Neander on the Apostle Paul, in his History of the Apostolic Age (Geschichte des apostolischen Zeitalters, vol. ii. pp. 501, seq.)

† We are easily tempted to picture to ourselves Paul's personal appearance, as very powerful, or even colossal; but, according to 2 Cor. x. 10, just the contrary was the case. In the dialogue Philopatris (which, however, to be sure, was not written earlier than the fourth century), Paul is called, "The Galilean with the bald head, and the hooked nose." (See Tholuck's remarks, noticed at the beginning of this Introduction, in which he describes the temperament of the apostle as the cholerico-melancholic.)

‡ See the Introduction to the Gospel of John.

§ It is in this dialectic character of Paul's discourse that we may find the reason that Longinus places the apostle on a level with the famous Greek orators, if, at least, the famous passage of that rhetorician, in which he makes mention of the apostle, is really genu-

character of mind, which made him express his religious ideas in a scientific form, made him also, in the fruitful labours of his outward life, develop especially the gift of *wisdom* (1 Cor. xii. 8). In addition to the energy which belonged to him as a man of action, we may discern in his activity the peculiar faculty of using the most difficult and complicated worldly relations for the purest and noblest purposes of the kingdom of God, so that we must distinctly recognize in this a distinguishing feature of his character. This is especially clear, if we compare him with Peter; for though in the latter there was no less energy, yet it seems in him to be fettered with a stiffness and want of pliancy which, though quite in keeping with his character as a *rock*, yet contrasts unmistakeably with that of Paul.

This bent of Paul's mind influenced, as we might have expected, his whole apprehension of the gospel. While John received it more, in its abstract character, as an object of contemplation, and so made its revelations of God and Christ the centre of his doctrine, Paul regarded it rather *subjectively*, as bearing upon himself, and so made its relations to humanity and human salvation, the prominent points of his theology. In the experience of his own life he had seen the sinful state of the human heart, as well as man's inability to deliver himself from it, and the consequent need of a Divine remedy such as was realized in Christ; and from this as a living source sprang his whole system of doctrine. The *occidental* character of Paul's mind is seen in this conception of the gospel as clearly as in the bent of those two great kindred spirits of his, Augustine and Luther, in whom indeed his own process of culture was repeated. In John, on the other hand, is shown the *oriental* spirit, which loses itself in the contemplation of that which is presented to it of God, and which, through all the developments of doctrine in later ages, ever dwelt by preference on theology and christology in their more abstract character. So that though there is no specific difference, no actual contradiction between the teaching of Paul and John, yet these two apostles already exhibit in themselves the two chief tendencies of the later development of doctrine. As the grain of corn, though one, opens itself into two halves on the unfolding of the germ, or as the magnet, from one middle point, discharges, at the same time, a positive and a negative power; so the two chief tendencies of the church, the Eastern and Western, which mutually

ine. Besides vigorous powers of reasoning, the might of deep conviction, and the glow of enthusiasm, manifest themselves in Paul's writings, so that Jerome (in his work against Jovinian) declares "quotiescunque Paulum apostolum lego, non verba audire mihi videor, sed tonitrua." (See Flacii clav. S. S. Basil, 1567, p. 387, seq., and the works of Bauer, Philologia Thucydideo-Paulina (Halæ, 1773), Logica Paulina (ib. 1774), Rhetorica Paulina (ib. 1782). Also Tzschirner's treatise in his opusc. acad., edited by Winzer. Leips. 1829. Lastly, Tholuck's Remarks, pp. 387, seq., as noticed at p. 1 of this Introduction.

complete each other, are represented in the earliest ages by the two great apostles, John and Paul.

From the vigorous and decided manner in which the apostle both taught and acted, we might at once conclude that it was not likely that any considerable change would take place in his convictions, after that first great spiritual conversion, by which the fierce opponent of Jesus Christ became his fearless witness. After his admission into the church of Christ, he no doubt early formed for himself a consistent view of Christian truth, and therefore expresses himself, even in his latest epistles, in the same way as in his earliest; from the Epistles to the Thessalonians down to those to Timothy and Titus, we find the same fundamental truths ever recurring. In one single point only can we discern in his later writings a different form of doctrinal statement from that contained in his earlier epistles: that is, in his views concerning the second coming of Christ. In his earliest epistles Paul expresses a hope that he may himself live until the time of the Lord's return (see 1 Thess. iv.; 2 Cor. v.), but in the later he has renounced this hope, and longs to depart and to be with Christ (Phil. i. 23). The modification of his views on this point may, however, be easily explained, from the peculiar nature of the subject. The time of Christ's second coming was, according to our Lord's own teaching, to remain uncertain (see remarks at Matth. xxiv. 1); Paul himself, therefore, neither knew nor could know this time (Acts i. 7). Whilst, therefore, the fervour of his love made him at first regard all things as near, and long after the kingdom of God upon earth as the highest good; at a later period the great crisis of the Advent retreated, in his apprehension, to a greater distance. We cannot therefore say that Paul's convictions on this point of doctrine underwent a change; but only that his own individual position with respect to the object presented in this doctrine was altered. If, however, the above observations show that the *substance* of Paul's doctrine remained unchanged, yet we may certainly observe a constant progress in the merely *formal* development of it; for we cannot fail to perceive, that his theological language is more full, and his conceptions more complete and symmetrical, in the later epistles, especially those to the Philippians and Colossians, than in the earlier.

Paul not only kept aloof from the *gnostical* tendency (the relative truth of which is represented by John), and vigorously combatted the errors into which, as is plain from the Epistles to the Colossians, to Timothy, and Titus, it soon led some of its followers; but also from that *judaico-materialist* tendency, which showed itself in so many of those who had left the sect of the Pharisees to join the Christian church. As a tree torn from its original soil, and transplanted with all its roots and fibres into the other ground, such had been the change effected in Paul at his conversion; he therefore transferred nothing of the one-sidedness and narrowness of the Pharisaic system into his views of Christian doctrine. The attempts made to explain many leading features of his system from his Jewish views of life,* show just as little knowledge of the human heart as those which seek to explain Augustine's doctrine by his former Manichæan errors, and Luther's by his education as a monk. We find, on the contrary, that men of energetic character are generally inclined, after such transitions, to despise too much the systems from which they have escaped, and to reject even what is true in them, rather than to transfer anything belonging to them into their new line of thought and life. But from this error into which Marcion and his disciples fell, Paul was preserved by that fundamental Christian view, wrought livingly in him by the Holy Spirit, which regards the Old Testament as Divine in its nature, and under a typical and prophetical veil, as containing in the germ all the essential truths of Christianity. He merely discarded as erroneous that rigid Pharisaic spirit which regarded the husk of the letter as the substance of the spirit itself. Paul therefore represented the true and just mean between the false spiritualism of the Gnostics, and Jewish materialism, viz., the true scripture doctrine of the reality and proper relations of both spirit and matter; and this in such a manner as fully to maintain his balance, without leaning to either error. In the theology of John while indeed the same correct views of the relation of matter and spirit cannot be mistaken, still in his Gospel and Epistles we find an inclination towards genuine spiritualism, of course without any concession to Gnostic *errors*: it was only in the Apocalypse that John found the opportunity of bringing forward in greater prominence the *material* aspects of the gospel; and therefore any future author who wishes to give a just view of John's doctrine, must consider the ideas of the Apocalypse as complementary of those of his remaining works.

This perfect balance in the character and theology of Paul, is also the reason why the instinct of the church, guided in this matter also into the truth by the Spirit of Christ working in her, has regarded the collection of his epistles in which every thought is expressive of that correct mean which he preserved in his doctrine, as the crown of the canon of the New Testament. Whilst

* We need hardly remark that we do not therefore mean to deny that the history of Jewish doctrine furnishes us with a key to the further understanding of many particular statements in Paul's writings; we only wish to maintain, that the essential points of his system are the results of his own inward experience; the views which he entertained in earlier life at most only affected the form in which he presented the truth.

every separate Gospel found its necessary complement in the other Gospels, and altogether form the roots of the New Testament; whilst the Acts of the Apostles only constitutes, so to speak, the stem, which unites the roots with the crown of the tree—Paul, without laying claim to any independent authority in point of doctrine, stands before us in all the riches of his personal endowments, spreading around on all sides the fruitfulness of his inward life. He was the first, in whom was mirrored in all its various aspects, as far as was possible in *one* man, not indeed the character of the Lord himself, but that Spirit which he had bestowed upon the church; and this universality of character and gifts of grace made him capable, through the powers of the same Spirit, of so unfolding the peculiar nature of the principles of Christianity both in his doctrine and in his life, as to represent it to the Gentile world almost in his sole person. Whatsoever, therefore, appeared in the Gospels as a bud but partially disclosed, and indeed in the synoptical evangelists manifestly engrafted upon Old Testament principles—that the apostle displays before us openly and freely, and in some parts of his writings, for instance, in the Epistles to the Romans and Galatians, in so strictly didactic a form, that it commends itself as much by the cogency of the arguments to the thoughtful, as to the feeling mind by that glow of enthusiasm which breathes throughout his statements. If, however, we compare the collection of the catholic epistles (with which we must also class the Epistle to the Hebrews, as proceeding from the same starting point), with the Epistles of Paul, we shall perceive that the latter are more calculated for the beginning of the spiritual life, whilst the concluding writings of the New Testament tend more directly to the perfection of the fruits of regeneration in holiness and sanctification. Accordingly, if in the epistles of Paul the central ideas, around which he considers everything to move, are *faith* in opposition to the works of the law, *justification* and *atonement*, and we cannot fail to perceive the earnestness with which he labours to impress these deeply on the minds of his hearers and readers; the Epistle to the Hebrews and the catholic epistles, on the other hand, setting out with these doctrines as their admitted foundation, teach from them how man is to perfect himself in *holiness*. The latter epistles, therefore, seem to bear more of a legal character, and on that account found much less access to the mind of the church than those of Paul. They demand, also, for their right comprehension a higher degree of development in the regenerate soul; and because this was often deficient, a correct perception of the difficulties of those writings deterred many expositors from attempting to explain them. The different collections therefore which compose the New Testament canon, proceed each from a different point of view, and on this very account mutually complete each other, furnishing satisfaction for every stage of advancement, and incitement to higher culture. (See Comm. P. I. Introd. § 2.

§ 3. Order of Succession of Paul's Epistles.

From the thoroughly practical character of Paul's life, we might at once expect that his productions as an author would have nothing of an abstract form about them. And in fact we neither possess any treatises by him on religious subjects, nor have we any reason to suppose that he ever wrote any. His letters are all suggested by existing circumstances, and adapted to the most special occasions of actual life. Hence everything in them is individual, marked, traced with strong and definite outlines, and yet, by means of that spiritual principle which animated the apostle, truths the most universal are reflected in those special cases, and give to all his remarks and counsel a meaning and importance for every age. In what manner those epistles of the apostle which have come down to us were formed into one collection, it is now impossible to make out on satisfactory historical grounds. We find, indeed, in the hands of Marcion the Gnostic, a collection of ten epistles of Paul, the three pastoral epistles of Timothy and Titus being wanting, whilst in the Catholic church the collection consisted of thirteen epistles (that to the Hebrews not being included): this might then be regarded as the original nucleus of the collection of epistles, to which the pastoral epistles were added at a later period. And yet on closer consideration, this does not appear probable, and we may therefore suppose that the pastoral epistles were only accidentally omitted from the canon of Marcion. For we find that the order of succession of the epistles, according to Marcion's arrangement, was an entirely different one from that of the collection sanctioned by the Catholic church; but if the latter had only inserted the pastoral epistles of Marcion's collection, the order would have remained unaltered. The discrepancy of the order was, moreover, occasioned by the adoption of an entirely distinct principle of arrangement; the Marcionites arranging the epistles, as we shall soon prove, according to their chronological succession; the Catholics, in the first place, according to the importance of the churches to which they were addressed, and then according to the dignity of the private persons who had received them. This appears most plainly in the case of the Epistle to Philemon; this belongs manifestly to the Epistle to the Colossians, where Marcion has also placed it; but in the collection of the Catholic canon, it followed last of all, as being the shortest epistle directed to a private person. The Marcionite collection was most probably first formed in Asia Minor. In its composition the framers of it either proceeded on the principle of omitting letters to private persons, and only admitting epistles to whole communities (the letter to Philemon finding a place in the collection merely as an appendage to the Epistle to the Colossians), or they were unacquainted with the pastoral epistles. On the other hand, the Catholic collection of Paul's epistles probably had its rise in Rome; and the authors of it followed the order of importance of the communities to which the epistles were addressed, and also admitted such private letters as seemed to be of value for the church at large. The special attention in the Roman church to matters of outward church constitution answers remarkably well to this supposition with respect to the pastoral letters, and therefore also increases the probability that the Catholic canon of Paul's epistles was formed at this place.

In our investigation of the order of succession in Paul's epistles, we shall, however, not only exclude the Epistle to the Hebrews (which does not proceed from the apostle himself, although it was composed under his sanction*), but also the Epistles to Timothy and Titus; for these involve such complicated relations, that they require a distinct consideration. We have, therefore, in the first place, only to do with the order of succession of those ten epistles of Paul, which even Marcion included in his collection. With respect to the *years* to which their composition is assigned, a great discrepancy doubtless exists in the views of the learned, because the chronology of the apostolic history in general, and of Paul's life in particular, is so very uncertain. But our present subject is properly only the order in which the epistles follow upon one another; and in the determination of this point, the views taken are by no means so widely different, as in deciding the years under which every single epistle ought to be arranged, (because this last question must always depend upon the chronological system adopted by the particular investigator), a circumstance by which the correctness of the *general* order of succession assigned to them, is remarkably confirmed. To facilitate our survey of the different views which have been taken on this subject, we give, in the following tabular form, the opinions of three scholars belonging respectively to the earliest, modern, and most recent times.

* See the two critical treatises on the subject of the Epistle to the Hebrews in Olshausen's Opuscula Theologica.—[The author's theory is, that it was written by the clergy of some church in which Paul was sojourning, and that the apostle approved it when finished. Thus he thinks to account at once for the connexion of Paul's name with the epistle, and for the difference from the style of his undoubted compositions. (Opuscula Berol., 1834, pp. 91-122.) The reader may be referred to Dr. Mill's remarks, Prælectio Theologica, Cantabr., 1843, pp. 6, 7, and note p. 32, B.]

*Marcion.**	*Eichhorn.*	*Schrader.*
Galatians.	I. Thessalonians.	I. Corinthians.
I. Corinthians.	II. Thessalonians.	II. Corinthians.
II. Corinthians.	Galatians.	Romans.
Romans.	I. Corinthians.	I. Thessalonians.
I. Thessalonians.	II. Corinthians.	II. Thessalonians.
II. Thessalonians.	Romans.	Ephesians.
Ephesians.	Ephesians.	Colossians.
Colossians.	Colossians	Philemon.
Philemon.	Philemon.	Philippians.
Philippians.	Philippians.	Galatians.

In the first place, from this table, we cannot but perceive that, as we have already mentioned above, Marcion could not have placed the epistles in this order *accidentally;* it corresponds too exactly with the results of the most industrious critical researches, not to have proceeded from the *design* of arranging the epistles according to the date of their composition. The conclusions of the most recent examiner, Schrader, coincide exactly with Marcion's scheme, except with respect to the Epistle to the Galatians. Certainly, with respect to this composition, the discrepancy is so much the greater: for whilst Marcion assigns to it the first place, Schrader places it last. Eichhorn, in this case, agrees rather with Marcion than with Schrader, in that he places the Epistle to the Galatians, in point of time, before those to the Corinthians and Romans; at the same time, he differs from both in respect to the Epistles to the Thessalonians, for whilst they put these letters immediately after the Epistle to the Romans, Eichhorn considers them to have been written first of all. Since more exact information with regard to the dates of the composition of the separate epistles may best be prefixed to the special introduction devoted to each, we will only briefly consider in this place the epistles of which the date is questionable, those to the Thessalonians and Galatians, in respect of the time of their composition, in order to advance a *preliminary* justification of our adoption of the order assigned by Eichhorn, in favour of which Hemsen and the majority of modern scholars have also decided. (Comp. at Acts xviii. 18, seq., xix. 8, seq.)

The peculiarity of Schrader's arrangement of the epistles of Paul, is founded on a theory propounded by this scholar, according to which the apostle made a journey to Jerusalem, after leaving Ephesus (where, according to Acts xix., he passed more than two years). He thinks that this journey took place in the interval between the events recorded in the 20th and 21st verses of this chapter. In consequence of this journey, in which he supposes Paul to have visited Thessalonica, Schrader places the composition of the Epistles to the Thessalonians at a period subsequent to that

* See Epiphanius. *Hær.* xlii., c. 9.

of those to the Romans and Corinthians. Schott has, however, already proved at length,* that nothing can be found in the Epistles to the Thessalonians which favours this later time of composition, but rather that everything indicates that they were written in Corinth, immediately after the first visit of Paul to Thessalonica (Acts xvii.), on the occasion of the first planting of that church. The Epistles to the Thessalonians must, therefore, necessarily be reckoned amongst the earliest, and it is a decided mistake to place them after the Epistle to the Romans, if only for this reason, that Paul did not write the latter until he was at Corinth on his third missionary journey. But Schrader's hypothesis, with respect to the Epistle to the Galatians, is even more capricious. His assumed journey from Ephesus to Jerusalem is in fact supposed to be that mentioned, Galat. ii. 1, from which it would no doubt follow that the composition of the letter belongs to a much later period, since the apostle, in the course of that chapter, mentions many other occurrences in his life. But the very circumstance that Barnabas accompanied the apostle to Jerusalem, in the journey alluded to, Galat. ii. 1, whilst it is certain from the account in Acts xv. 36, etc., that they had parted from one another long before Paul went to Ephesus, is decisive against this wholly unfounded theory; and Schrader's assertion that the difference between Paul and Barnabas had previously been made up, is likewise founded upon mere hypothesis. For though I am very far from accounting for this separation, as Schott appears to do (Erörterung, p. 64, etc.) by supposing a discrepancy in their views, and am much rather inclined to assume merely outward reasons for its continuance, yet the circumstance, that after Acts xv. 26, etc., Barnabas is no more mentioned in connexion with Paul, is decisive against Schrader's assumption.† But the arguments, which Schrader thinks he can adduce from the contents of the Epistle to the Galatians in favour of this hypothesis, are so completely overthrown by Schott in detail (p. 65, etc.), that it is enough in this place to refer to the latter writer's treatise. Schrader thinks especially that he discovers in the passage, Galat. vi. 17, a declaration of the apostle, that he is looking forward to the sentence of death, and, therefore, concludes that the composition of this letter must be referred to quite the end of Paul's life. But how entirely unfounded is such an explana-

* See Schott's Programm, "Isagoge historico-critica in utramque Pauli ad Thessalonicenses epistolam." Jenæ, 1830. And the same author's "Erörterung einiger wichtigen chronolog. Punkte im Leben Pauli" (Jena, 1832), p. 48, etc.

† The passage 1 Cor. ix. 6, is the only one which appears to support a later coming together of Barnabas and Paul; if we are not willing to admit that Barnabas was separated from Paul in Corinth. He must, however, at all events have visited this city, according to the passage above quoted, after the establishment of the Christian community there.

tion of the text will appear hereafter from our commentary upon it. Köhler*, also, has made a similar attempt to refer the composition of the Epistle to the Galatians to a later period; but he does not understand the journey to Jerusalem mentioned in Galat. ii. 1, like Schrader, of a separate journey made from Ephesus, but thinks that he discovers in it the journey recorded in Acts xviii. 22. No doubt, as I have already endeavoured to represent as probable in my commentary on the passage, Paul did visit Jerusalem about that time (which Schott is mistaken in denying, p. 37), but for the assumption that this journey is mentioned in Galat. ii. 1, there is not a shadow of proof; it is certain, rather, that it was that made from Antioch to the council of the apostles, Acts xv. Much less, however, can we assent to Köhler's view, that Paul first preached the gospel in Galatia, on his journey through that province mentioned in Acts xviii. 23, since the words added in that passage, *ἐπιστηρίζων τοὺς μαθητάς*, *establishing the disciples*, plainly express that the apostle wished to confirm in the faith the churches which he had already founded in Galatia. (See Acts xvi. 6.) Since, moreover, this scholar can only give even a shadow of probability to his postponement of the composition of the Epistle to the Galatians to the latest period of Paul's life, by means of a conjecture and hypothesis heaped upon his first assumption, we cannot feel ourselves called upon by his arguments to depart from that order of succession of the epistles of Paul which is now almost universally received. This is connected in the following manner with the principal events of Paul's life, according to the chronology which we have adopted from Hug: in this account, we must, however, as we have already remarked, leave the pastoral epistles again untouched, because they present peculiar difficulties in their adjustment to the history of Paul's life, and hence demand a separate consideration.

After Paul's conversion on the road to Damascus (about the year 36 after the birth of Christ), he went to Arabia, where he remained three years. (Galat. i. 17.) After this he returned to Damascus, but in this city he was persecuted by the Jews, and only escaped to Jerusalem with extreme difficulty (2 Cor. xi. 32. Acts ix. 24, 25). On this visit of Paul to Jerusalem, Barnabas introduced the apostle to Peter and James (Galat. i. 18, 19); he, however, remained there only fourteen days. On leaving Jerusalem, the apostle repaired first to his native city, Tarsus (Acts ix. 25, etc.), from whence Barnabas, who it appears was the first to discover his wonderful gift of teaching, brought him away to Antioch, at which place, in the meantime, Christianity had also begun to spread amongst the heathen. (Acts xi. 19.) This happened about A. D.

* "Über die Abfassungszeit der epistolischen Schriften des Neuen Testament." Leipz. 1830.

42. Paul and Barnabas had been teaching together about a year in Antioch when the great famine made its appearance in Palestine, in consequence of which they were both sent to Jerusalem (Paul for the second time) as the bearers of a contribution to the necessities of the poor brethren at that place. (Acts xi. 30.) Perhaps, however, Paul himself did not go to Jerusalem, for it is not stated in the Acts that he did, and that difficult passage Galat. ii. 1, would render the supposition probable. After the accomplishment of this business, the people of Antioch expressed a wish that the gospel might be preached to the Gentiles in other countries also. The elders of the church thereupon chose Paul and Barnabas as their messengers to the heathen, and they accordingly entered upon their *first missionary journey* (about A. D. 45). They went first by Cyprus through Pamphylia and Pisidia, and then returned to Antioch by sea (Acts xiii. 5; xiv. 26). The time of their return it is as impossible to determine with certainty, as the length of their subsequent stay at Antioch (Acts xiv. 28). At the same time there can be no doubt that the *third* journey of Paul to Jerusalem, occasioned by the disputes concerning the reception of Gentile converts into the church, formed the conclusion of this residence (Galat. ii. 1). The apostles and the presbyters of the church at Jerusalem examined into this question together, and, after hearing the reports of Paul and Barnabas, decided in favour of the milder course, according to which the heathen were not obliged to submit to circumcision, and observe the whole law. This important transaction, the so-called apostolic council (Acts xv.), happened A. D. 52 or 53. Immediately after the return of Paul from Jerusalem to Antioch, about A. D. 53, he entered upon his *second missionary journey*, which he undertook in company with Silas. On this journey he first of all visited again the churches he had already planted, and then proceeded to Galatia, and by Troas to Macedonia (Acts xvi. 9). Philippi was the first city of this country in which Paul taught, but this place he was soon obliged to leave in consequence of a tumult stirred up against him by the employers of a female ventriloquist, and to betake himself to Thessalonica (Acts xvi. 12, etc.) The apostle was able to preach here only a few weeks, yet even in this short time a Christian community was formed there. But a tumult occasioned by the Jews compelled Paul soon to flee from Thessalonica, and to go to Athens by Berea, to which latter place his enemies continued to follow him (Acts xvii. 13). His companions, Silas and Timothy, he had left behind him at Berea, but soon called upon them to follow him to Athens, probably that he might obtain intelligence of the churches in Macedonia (Acts xvii. 15). However, he immediately dispatched Timothy to Thessalonica, in order that he might establish in the faith that young and hardly pressed commu-

nity (1 Thess. iii. 1). In the meantime the apostle, after the dismissal of Timothy, left Athens, where he does not appear to have laboured long, and returned to Corinth (Acts xviii. 1). Here he met with the famous Jewish family of Aquila and Priscilla, which had been expelled from Rome by Claudius; and as Aquila practised the same handicraft which Paul had learned, the latter undertook to work with him, and since his preaching produced great effect, remained there a year and a half. By means of the fact here mentioned, the expulsion of the Jews from Rome by Claudius, we also obtain pretty exact information with respect to the date of Paul's residence at Corinth; it must have been in the years of our Lord 54 and 55. During his stay at Corinth, it would appear that the apostle commenced his labours as a writer, at least nothing remains to us of any letters which he may previously have indited. In fact, when Timothy had returned from his mission to Thessalonica, Paul wrote his *First Epistle to the Thessalonians*, and soon afterwards *the Second*, likewise from Corinth. All his apostolical epistles belong, therefore, to the later and more mature period of his life, a circumstance which is certainly not to be regarded as accidental.

After the lapse of a year and a half Paul left Corinth in the company of Aquila and Priscilla, in order to go up to Jerusalem to keep a vow (Acts xviii. 18). In his voyage he touched at Ephesus, without, however, being able to make any long stay there, as he wished to be at Jerusalem for the feast of Pentecost. At the same time he promised to return thither as soon as possible; and, in accordance with this promise, immediately after a brief sojourn in Jerusalem (his *fourth* visit to that city, see Commentary on Acts xviii. 22) and in Antioch, he set off again to proceed to Ephesus; this forms the commencement of his *third missionary journey* (about A.D. 57). The apostle continued in this important city two years and three months, and wrote from hence in the first place to the Galatians (perhaps as early as A.D. 57, certainly not later than the beginning of 58); he had visited them on his journey to Ephesus, and had perhaps, even on this occasion, remarked sundry errors, or at all events had soon after heard of such. Next the apostle began his correspondence with the Corinthian church, writing likewise from Ephesus, in consequence of the unfavourable accounts which he had received of them also. The First Epistle of Paul to the Corinthians is lost (1 Cor. v. 9), but after it was sent, new reports arrived from Corinth, which caused the apostle to send thither Timothy and Erastus (1 Cor. iv. 17, etc., Acts xix. 22), and immediately afterwards he composed the *first epistle to the Corinthians* which is yet extant. The writing of this letter may be referred to A.D. 59, or the commencement of 60. Scarcely, however, had Paul finished this letter, when the goldsmith Demetrius stirred up a tumult against him in Ephesus, in consequence of which he was obliged to flee. The apostle proceeded by Troas to Macedonia, full of desire to receive more exact information concerning the state of things in Corinth. When he had received this from Timothy and Titus, who came directly from Corinth, he wrote about A.D. 60, the *second epistle to the Corinthians*. Titus conveyed this letter to Corinth; and the apostle himself journeyed after him slowly through Achaia, to the same city. During this his second stay in Corinth, Paul found occasion to write to the Romans, which he must have done as early as in the year 60, shortly before his departure from Corinth, since in Romans xv. 25, 26, he makes mention of the charitable collections made for the Christians in Jerusalem, as well as of the journey he had in prospect. This journey to Jerusalem, his *fifth*, the apostle accomplished by sailing from Philippi in Macedonia to the coasts of Asia Minor, then proceeding to Syria, and from thence visiting Jerusalem (Acts xx. 3, etc.) As early as the tenth day after his arrival there, he was taken into custody, on the occasion of an uproar of the people, and remained (from A.D. 60 to 62) two years in prison at Cæsarea. When, however, Pontius Festus was made Proconsul of Syria in the room of Felix, he sent the apostle to Rome, on his appealing to Cæsar. On his voyage to Rome, Paul was shipwrecked upon the island of Malta, and did not reach Rome, in consequence, until the beginning of the year 63 (Acts xxv–xxvii.) Here he remained two years (from 63 to 65) in a mild imprisonment (Acts xxviii. 30), and composed in this period the Epistles to the Ephesians, Colossians, Philemon, and the Philippians.*

The question concerning the date of the composition of the three pastoral epistles, as well as that concerning the apostle's second imprisonment and the time of his death at Rome,† which is so closely connected with it, we leave here, as already remarked, untouched; inasmuch as the special introduction to these epistles, which form, as it were, a little whole of themselves, will furnish us with a more suitable opportunity for the discussion of these points. We reserve also the more detailed exposition of our reasons for the place which we have assigned to each of the epistles for the special introductory observations on those epistles; and, finally, we explain them in the order followed by the ordinary editions, since the plan of beginning with the Epistle to the Romans

* The view which has quite recently been put forward by several scholars, and especially by Bottger (Beiträge, ii.), that those epistles which have hitherto been attributed to the period of Paul's first captivity at Rome might have been written during his captivity at Cæsarea, we shall consider more at length in our introductions to these epistles, adducing the reasons by which it is supported, and our objections to it.

† Amongst the most recent investigators, Bleek declares himself decidedly for the assumption of a second imprisonment, in his review of Mayerhoff's work, in the Studien, 1836 H. iv. p. 1028.

affords many advantages towards the doctrinal exposition of the rest, and if any one should prefer to study Paul's epistles in their chronological order, nothing would interfere with his subjecting them to a more accurate consideration, according to the assigned order, because every composition, with its commentary, forms a little whole. If any important changes could be pointed out in the course of Paul's spiritual advancement, it would certainly be the preferable plan to expound his epistles in their chronological order; but as this, as we have already seen, is not the case, it appears to us much better to follow the ordinary arrangement. In observing this order, we have, first of all, the opportunity, in the Epistle to the Romans, of considering in their connexion the central ideas of Paul's doctrinal system, presented, so to speak, in a doctrinal compendium. A number of passages in Paul's other epistles thus receive their explanation by anticipation, while it would be difficult to explain them at all if the Epistle to the Romans had not previously been interpreted. On the other hand, in the Epistles to the Corinthians Paul's principles of practice are developed, and the external relations of the apostolical church are discussed with so much accuracy that, by their help, much light is thrown upon many passages in the smaller epistles. Such being the peculiar nature of the larger epistles of Paul, we are persuaded that every connected exposition of the apostolical writings will best begin with them, because only on this plan can the riches of Paul's ideas be properly unfolded in all their different relations, and without repetition.

THE EPISTLE TO THE ROMANS.

INTRODUCTION.*

§ 1. Of the Genuineness and the Integrity of the Epistle.

The authenticity of Paul's Epistle to the Christians of Rome is warranted by such a completeness of evidence, both internal and external, that no one could think of denying, on any system of impartial criticism, its claim to be the composition of the apostle. Nor, indeed, did any one in all antiquity dispute its genuineness ; for, while it is true that the Judaists and all Judaising sects make no use of Paul's Epistle to the Romans (as also of his other epistles), the reason is not that they consider it spurious, but, on the contrary, that they see in it a genuine production of *that* apostle whom they regard as the greatest enemy of Judaism, and an apostate from the truth. Even the searching criticism of later German theology has left this epistle altogether unassailed ; an Englishman of the name of Evanson alone has, in his work against the Gospels, cursorily expressed his doubts as to the genuineness of the Epistle to the Romans also. His grounds, however, are of such a kind that no better testimony *in favour of* its genuineness need be desired than the fact that arguments of this quality are the only ones which can be brought *against* it. The silence of the Acts of the Apostles as to this epistle, the existence of a great Christian community at Rome before an apostle had been there, and the numerous greetings to the church of Rome at a time when Paul had not yet visited it—such are the chief points which appear to Evanson to render the genuineness of the epistle questionable. (Compare Reiche's Comm. p. 20, seq.)

The case is different as to the *integrity* of the epistle ; this has been very often called in question, and especially in modern times. All the more ancient witnesses, however—fathers of the church, versions, and MSS.—regard it as a connected whole ; for Marcion's copies cannot be made to tell on the other side, inasmuch

* For the introduction to the Epistle to the Romans, compare, among earlier writers, J. L. Rambach's Introductio Hist. Theologica in Ep. Pauli ad Romanos. Halæ, 1730. In the most recent times, it has been most fully and learnedly treated by Reiche, in his Commentary, pp. 1–106.

as he treated the Epistles no less capriciously than the Gospels; and Tertullian's quotation of the passage xiv. 10, as contained in the "clausula epistolæ" (Adv. Marcion v. 14) cannot possibly be used as evidence that he was not acquainted with the 15th and 16th chapters, since the expression *clausula* is so general that it need not be strictly limited to the last two chapters. The scholars of later times, consequently, found themselves altogether restricted to the department of what is termed the higher criticism—a department in which it is not often that any very trustworthy results are to be obtained.

Heumann* led the way, by asserting that the Epistle to the Romans properly ends with the chap. xi., and that chap. xii. is the beginning of a new letter, which extends to chap. xv. This letter he supposes to have been likewise addressed to the Romans, but not to have been composed by Paul until after the completion of the first and longer epistle, on occasion of reports which had in the meantime reached him as to the moral laxity of the Romans. In the sixteenth chapter, according to this view, are contained some further postscripts, which had been originally intended to accompany the first letter. These, it is supposed, were written on the same parchment with the two epistles, and thus the various parts came to be united. This hypothesis, however, is so improbable that it has not been able to make any way. Heumann's process of dividing this epistle might, with equal reason, be applied in separating the doctrinal from the ethical part in every other of Paul's writings. In the passage xii. 1, the particle οὖν is evidently a mark of transition from the preceding to the following portion; and so the ἀμήν at the end of chap. xi. is clearly not the termination of the epistle, but merely the doxology with which Paul very appropriately concludes the doctrinal portion.

The integrity of the epistle was attacked in a different way by J. F. Semler, according to whom it is only in chaps. xv. and xvi. that an incongruity with the Epistle to the Romans is to be traced.† The grounds on which he relies, however, are, for the most part, of no greater weight than those which had been advanced by Heumann. Still, there is some plausibility in Semler's manner of turning to account the mention of Aquila and Priscilla's family (xvi. 3, seq.). These persons, it is observed, were still at Ephesus when the first Epistle to the Corinthians was written (1 Cor. xvi. 19); since, then, Paul wrote to the Romans soon after the date of his Epistle to the Corinthians, there cannot, in Semler's opinion, have been time

* Comp. Heumann's Erkl. des N. Test. vol. vii. p. 537, seq.

† Semler de duplici appendice epistolæ Pauli ad Romanos, Halæ, 1767. He supposes chap. xvi. to be a list of persons to be saluted by the bearer of the letter *on his way from Corinth to Rome*, and chap. xv., in like manner, to be a separate production, intended not so much for the Romans as for all brethren who might be met with on the way.

enough for Aquila first to travel to Rome, and afterwards to send accounts of himself to the apostle at Corinth—which he must be supposed to have done, as we find Paul informed that Aquila had again a church in his house. (Rom. xvi. 5.) The case, however, is quite intelligible, if we suppose that Aquila left Ephesus suddenly, and that he sent an early report of his new circumstances in Rome to the apostle at Corinth; for it is impossible to determine exactly by months the dates of the epistles in question, while, even with the slow means of communication which the ancients possessed, a few months would be sufficient for the journey from Ephesus to Rome and back. In any case, a circumstance of this nature cannot be a sufficient argument to justify Semler's theory. But when this learned writer proceeds to make it a difficulty that several places of Christian assembly are mentioned as existing in Rome (xvi. 5, 14, 15), it appears to us that an exactly opposite inference would be more legitimate. In a vast capital, the resort of all the world, such as Rome was, the necessity of places of assembly in various quarters of the city would surely become manifest on the very first formation of a church; and, in like manner, the numerous salutations (xvi.) to a church which Paul had not yet visited, may be easily explained from the character of the city, which was continually receiving visitors from every corner of the world, and in turn sending out travellers into all countries. Hence the apostle may not have been acquainted, except by reputation, with many of the persons who are named; and yet may have sent his greeting to them, because he felt himself most intimately connected with them by the bond of the same faith.

These objections to Semler's hypothesis hold good also against the kindred view of Dr. Paulus,* who is of opinion that chap. xv. is a special epistle to the more enlightened Christians of Rome, and that chap. xvi. is addressed to the governors of the church only. Every letter to a church, he observes, would, as a matter of course, in the first instance, be put into the hands of the presbyters, who read it in public, and delivered the greetings which it contained: it could not be at once given to the whole community. But it does not necessarily follow from this remark that the portion which contains the greetings was addressed to the presbyters *exclusively of the church in general*, and consequently, cannot be regarded as an integral part of the epistle; and while, in like manner, we allow that in chap. xv. the apostle writes *in part* with an especial regard to the more advanced members of the Roman church, still this circumstance by no means obliges us to consider that chapter a letter

* First set forth in a programme (Jena, 1801); afterwards in his Erklärung des Römer- und Galaterbriefs (Heidelberg, 1831).

by itself, inasmuch as the less advanced believers are not excluded from a share in its instruction.

Most recently the genuineness of the last two chapters has been again denied by Baur (Stud. 1836. No. iii.) He supposes that a later writer of Paul's school attempted to effect a compromise between his party and the Judaisers, who were predominant in Rome; and that, with this view, he endeavours, by annexing these two chapters, to soften what was offensive in the epistle. The only evidence offered for the theory is of the internal kind—*e. g.*, that chap. xv. 1–3 contains matter which has already been far better expressed in chap. xii.—xiv. But against this it has already been remarked, by Kling (Stud., 1837. No. ii. p. 309), that, while in chap. xv. 1–13 there is a recurrence of ideas similar to some which had before been treated, they are reproduced with ingenious and spirited modifications, in entire accordance with the apostle's usual practice. It is alleged further, that the phrase *διάκονος τῆς περιτομῆς* (xv. 8), is not in Paul's manner; that, in xv. 14, seq., the *captatio benevolentiæ* seems unworthy of the apostle; and, lastly, that the mention of Illyria and Spain, in xv. 17–24, must be a spurious insertion. These points I have already discussed at length in my essay against Baur (Stud. 1838. No. iv.) and they will be more particularly considered in the commentary on the several passages. I shall only observe further, that the first words of chap. xv. are of themselves sufficient to render Baur's supposition altogether improbable. The expression *ἡμεῖς οἱ δυνατοί*, *we the strong*, characterizes the Gentile Christians as the more liberal and enlightened party; surely a follower of Paul, writing for the purpose of conciliating the Judaisers, could not have made choice of a more inappropriate phrase. Moreover, Baur's idea of a Judaising tendency in the Roman church requires us to assume that the presbyters too were members of the Judaising party; but how can it be supposed that, in such circumstances, a disciple of Paul could add a forged appendage to the apostle's letter? Baur's hypothesis, then, appears to be merely the work of a misdirected acuteness and an unrestrained hyper-criticism, and will, therefore, never be able to establish itself.*

We must notice, finally, the attempts of Eichhorn, Griesbach, and Flatt,† to explain the different positions of the concluding doxology, and its relation to the various forms of conclusion which

* Böttger, in his Beiträge, Supplem. Göttingen, 1838, pp. 17, seq., also declares himself against Baur's theory.

† Eichhorn, Einleit. ins N. T., vol. iii., Griesbach, Curæ in historiam textus Gr. epistolarum Pauli, p. 45. Flatt, in the appendix to his Erklärung des Römerbriefs. Schulz has lately maintained that chap. xvi. does not properly belong to the Epistle to the Romans, but may have been perhaps intended for Ephesus. (Comp. Stud. und Kritiken, for 1829, No. iii. pp. 309, seq.)

occur after xiv. 23. These writers assume, although with various modifications, that Paul ended his epistle on the large parchment at xiv. 23, and that the rest was written on smaller pieces, which were afterwards shifted and arranged in different ways. This hypothesis, it must be allowed—especially as stated by Eichhorn—explains all the critical difficulties which occur in the last chapters. Still, it is not to be denied that it has somewhat of a far-fetched and strained character, and therefore we could wish to dispose of these difficulties by some easier and simpler solution. J. E. Chr. Schmidt (in his Introduction) supposed that this easier explanation was found in assuming the spuriousness of the doxology; and this supposition has lately been stated by Reiche in a manner which in fact renders it very plausible. If, he observes, the circumstances of the case be closely examined, the difficulties of the last chapters are all in reality to be traced to this doxology. But, in the first place, it is altogether wanting in some MSS. (especially in F); while in others, such as D and G, it is struck out by a later hand. Then, it is found in the MSS. in three different places; (1) at the end, in B, C, E, and several other critical authorities; (2) after xiv. 23, in the codex J, and in almost all such MSS. as are written in small letters; and (3), in *both* places, as particularly in the codex A. That such differences are very ancient, is remarked by Origen in his commentary on the epistle; though he does not state that he was acquainted with copies which had the doxology in *both* places. On the other hand, Jerome (on Ephes. iii. 5) knew of copies in which the doxology was altogether wanting. Reiche, then, supposes that the reading of the epistle in the public assemblies of the early Christians probably extended only as far as xiv. 23, since little that is of an edifying kind follows in the after part of the epistle. In order that the conclusion in this place might not be without a benediction, he supposes that the doxology was first added in copies which were used in church; that it was originally moulded after the doxology at the end of Jude's epistle, and was afterwards gradually extended, until at length it was placed, as a full-sounding form, at the conclusion of the whole epistle. To give this view additional support, its learned author endeavours to show that the substance of the doxology itself does not indicate Paul as the writer. He considers it inflated, overladen, obscure as to the connexion of the ideas, and merely made up from Pauline forms. But precisely here seems to me to be the weak side of Reiche's theory. The spuriousness of the doxology would appear to me probable in the highest degree, but for its intrinsic quality. In this opinion concur Schott (Einl. p. 250), Köllner and Fritzsche in their commentaries; the last-named expositor, in particular, may be considered to have settled the question by his excellent defence of the doxology (vol. i. pp. 38

seq.) The very commencement, *τῷ δὲ δυναμένῳ ὑμᾶς στηρίξαι κατὰ τὸ εὐαγγέλιόν μου, κ. τ. λ.*, is enough to make the assumption of its spuriousness exceedingly questionable. If the passage had originated in the way which Reiche points out, we might expect to find it a simple doxology, and in all likelihood a short one ; but here the personal relations of Paul and of his readers are distinctly marked. He addresses them, speaks of himself in the first person, expresses ideas peculiar to himself exactly in the manner usual with him, and yet so that the doxology as a whole appears altogether new, and without a parallel in the Pauline epistles. Such an addition would hardly have been ventured on by one of the clergy who wished merely to supply a good conclusion for the public reading.

I cannot, therefore, regard the doxology as spurious, and am rather disposed to adopt Eichhorn's view,* although not insensible to its partly far-fetched character; it has the merit of solving the difficulties, and hence is to be adhered to until something more deserving of commendation shall be discovered. But at all events, it is established that the various *positions* of the doxology is the only subject to be discussed, and that this subject has no connexion with any question as to the *matter* of the last two chapters. The Epistle to the Romans, consequently, is not only genuine, but it has also descended to us in a state of completeness, without mutilation or addition.

§ 2. Time and Place of the Composition.

The Epistle to the Romans, dictated by Paul to a person named Tertius (xvi. 22), and sent by the hands of the deaconess Phœbe (xvi. 1), contains such decisive indications as to the time and the place of its composition, that there has been little difference of opinion on these points, whether in earlier or more modern times. The only difference which can be properly said to affect the subject, belongs to the general chronology of the apostle's life. Dr. Paulus, of Heidelberg, indeed, has (in the two publications already referred to) proposed the novel opinion, that the epistle must have been written in Illyria, because the writer states xv. 19, that he had travelled from Jerusalem unto Illyricum ; but it is very evident that

* The opinion of Koppe and Gabbler, that the transposition of the concluding doxology is to be traced to the ecclesiastical use of the epistle, would not be undeserving of attention, if a sufficient probability could be made out for the annexation of the doxology to chap. xiv. While chap. xv. has a good termination, it must still be very forced to suppose the final doxology transferred from the end of the epistle, not to chap. xv. but to chap. xiv. If chap. xvi. were omitted, it is most likely that the doxology would also have been given up with it.

the apostle, in that passage, intends to name Illyricum only as the furthest point westward to which he had at the time penetrated, and not as the country in which he was at the moment of writing. An equally extravagant view as to the *time* when the epistle was written has been proposed by Tobler,* who maintains, on the ground of the apostle's extensive acquaintance with the Christians of Rome, that it should probably be referred to a date later than his first imprisonment. But it is at once manifest what a violent construction this supposition would require us to put on such passages as i. 9, and xv. 23, in which the apostle plainly declares that he had not yet been at Rome. The ordinary view, then, which regards the epistle as written from Corinth, during the visit which Paul paid to that city after having been driven from Ephesus, and having travelled through Macedonia—is the only one which has the advantage of accounting easily and naturally for all the passages in which he speaks of himself, his journeys, and his undertakings. Thus, in 1 Cor. xvi. 1, he mentions an intention of going from Corinth to Jerusalem with a collection ; and we find from Rom. xv. 25, that he purposed to set out on this journey immediately after despatching his epistle to Rome. Aquila and Priscilla, who were still at Ephesus when Paul thence wrote his first Epistle to the Corinthians, had, at the date of the present epistle, again arrived at Rome. (1 Cor. xvi. 19 ; Rom. xvi. 8.) We find from Acts xix. 21, that the apostle intended to visit Rome after he should have accomplished his journey to Jerusalem about the business of the collection ; and in Rom. xv. 28, he speaks of the same design, only with the difference, that his plan had been extended to the extreme west (τέρμα τῆς δύσεως), so as to embrace a visit to Spain. If, in addition to these chief grounds, we take into consideration some coincidences in detail with what we know otherwise of Paul's history, *e. g.*, that he sends greetings to the Christians of Rome from Caius (xvi. 23), a person mentioned in 1 Cor. i. 14, as then resident at Corinth ; that Erastus, from whom he in like manner conveys greetings (xvi. 23), and whom he styles οἰκονόμος τῆς πόλεως (*i. e.* of the city in which he was writing) is also mentioned elsewhere as an inhabitant of Corinth (2 Tim. iv. 20); that Phœbe, the bearer of the epistle, was a deaconness of the church at Cenchrea, the port of Corinth—and other circumstances of a like kind—there can be no further doubt that the Epistle of Paul to the Romans was written from Corinth during his second visit to that city. And consequently, according to the system of chronology which we have adopted, the time of its composition is to be referred to about A.D. 59.

The circumstance that the epistle was written in Greece, and in

* Compare Tholuck's Comm. Introd. p. x. Tobler's view is refuted by Flatt in a programme which is inserted in Pott's Sylloge Comment. vol. ii.

an entirely Greek city, would at once render it highly probable that it was composed in Greek; and this idea is confirmed by the universal tradition of the ancient church, and by the style of the composition, which throughout appears to indicate an original. Indeed both earlier and later writers have been almost unanimous in the opinion that it was originally written in Greek, since Paul, as a native of Tarsus, must have had the command of that language, while in Rome it was sufficiently diffused to be generally intelligible. (Comp. Sueton. *Claud.* c. 4. *Dialog. de Orator.* c. 29. Juvenal, *Satir.* iv. 185, seqq.) Bolten, however (whose views have been adopted by Bertholdt), has here, as in other cases, wasted his acuteness, with a view of shewing that Paul probably composed the epistle in Aramean—a notion which is surely, from the nature of the case, the most improbable that could be conceived. We might even rather suppose, with Hardouin, that it was originally written in Latin, and that it is still preserved to us in the ancient form in the Vulgate, if it were not too evident that this supposition is intended merely to enhance the glory of the version received in the Roman Catholic Church. So manifest is this, that the futility of the opinon has been shown even by some more liberal members of the author's own communion.

§ 3. Of the Roman Church.

The circumstances under which the Roman church was formed, and the date of its origin, are involved in a darkness which could only be dissipated by the discovery of ancient documents hitherto unknown—a discovery which we can now hardly venture to hope for. At the time when Paul wrote to the Romans, there already existed in the capital of the world, a church so considerable that it was spoken of throughout the world (i. 8), and required several places of assembly in the various quarters of the city (xvi). The Church of Rome cannot have been founded by an apostle, for in that case Paul would neither have addressed it by letter nor have visited it in person, since it was a general principle with him, as is expressly stated in this very epistle (xv. 20), to avoid interference with the work which had been already begun by another apostle: and when, in addition to this, we find in the Acts no mention of an apostle's having been at Rome, we may fairly reject the assertion, which originated early, and has long been maintained by the Romish Church, that Peter was the *founder* of the Church of Rome.* On the other hand, the presence of Peter in Rome at a later time,

* It is surprising that even some Protestant writers, such as Bertholdt and Mynster, can have acquiesced in this altogether unsupported notion of the *founding* of the Roman Church by Peter.

and his martyrdom there, are facts so well attested by historical evidence that they ought never to have been questioned.* In the first place, Caius, the well-known Roman presbyter, and zealous opponent of the Montanists, states that in his time (towards the end of the second century), the graves of the apostles were pointed out at Rome. When it is considered that he wrote in Rome itself, and that he is particular in mentioning the localities (viz., on the Vatican, and on the road to Ostia), it is inconceivable that there should be a mistake in this statement, since thousands must at once have confuted him. If the apostles died at Rome, and that by public execution, their death, and the place where their bodies rested could not possibly have remained concealed; if they did not die there, it is impossible to account for so early an origin of the tradition that they died there, unless we suppose the whole church to have consisted of mere deceivers; and, moreover, *there must, in that case, have been some other discoverable statement as to the place of Peter's death*, since the most celebrated of the apostles could surely not disappear without leaving some trace. But even allowing Caius to be no valid witness, because he was a Roman presbyter, and might have been desirous to enhance the lustre of his church by the alleged fact, no such exception can be taken to Dionysius, Bishop of Corinth, who lived half a century earlier, and, although interested in like manner for the church of Corinth, yet plainly witnesses that the two great apostles died, not in his own city, but in Rome. (Comp. the passages of the two fathers in Euseb. *Hist. Eccl.* ii. 25.) To these testimonies add those of Irenæus (*adv. Hær.* iii. 1, in Euseb. *Hist. Eccl.* v. 8), Clement of Alexandria (in Euseb. *Hist. Eccl.* ii. 14, 15; vi. 14), and of the critical Origen, who, like others, refers the martyrdom of Peter and Paul to Rome.† (Euseb. *H. E.* iii. 1.)

As, then, the apostles must have died somewhere, and no other city of antiquity claims the honour of their death, there is really no sufficient ground for doubting the account which is thus accredited.

* The question has lately been again raised by Baur, in his essay on the party "of Christ" at Corinth (*Tübing. Zeitschr.* 1831, No. iv.), and even Neander appears to have been shaken by his reasoning, (Apost. Zeitalter, ii. 459, seqq.) To me, however, Baur's grounds seem altogether insufficient, and I consider the death of Peter at Rome a fact not to be denied. In this judgment Bleek agrees (*Stud.* for 1836, No. iv. pp. 1061, seqq.) I have examined the matter more fully in a separate essay against Baur's hypothesis (*Stud.* 1838, No. iv.) Winer, on the other hand (Realllex. new ed. Art. *Petrus*) considers the accounts to be at least doubtful.

† Reiche (*loc. cit.* p. 40), Note 8, doubts whether the account in Eusebius ought to be referred to Origen; but the concluding words of the chapter ταῦτα Ὠριγένει κατὰ λέξιν, κ. τ. λ., evidently apply to the whole relation. We could, at the utmost, only doubt (with Valesius) whether the words from Θωμᾶς μέν, κ. τ. λ., be Origen's; from Πέτρος δέ κ. τ. λ. they are certainly his.

Still, however, we get from this no light as to the *origin* of the Roman church., For even although the Apostle Peter be styled by Caius and Dionysius the *founder* of the church of Rome, the expression refers, obviously, not to the *original* foundation of the community, but to its enlargement *and more complete establishment* by him; and in this sense Paul also is always named with him as joint founder of the church in Rome. We are, therefore, wholly left to conjecture on this point; and perhaps the most likely way of accounting for the formation of this body may be, to suppose that a knowledge of Christianity was early conveyed to the capital by travellers, if not even by the Romans who were present at the feast of Pentecost (Acts ii. 10), and that through the influence of these persons a church was gradually formed there. For if any one decidedly prominent individual had been the only agent in the foundation of the Roman church, it is more than probable that his name would have been preserved. And, again, the lively intercourse which Rome kept up with all parts of the empire, renders it equally inconceivable that Christians should not early have come to the capital from Antioch or Jerusalem; and if they came, their zeal would have also led them to preach the word there.

We have not, however, any certain trace of the existence of a Christian community in Rome *earlier* than the present epistle. For whether (as many have supposed, and as appears to myself *probable*), Aquila and Priscilla were already Christians at the time of their banishment from Rome by the edict of Claudius, is a point incapable of proof, since the passage, Acts xviii. 1–3, does not expressly state it; although, if we consider that otherwise their conversion would surely have been related, it can hardly be well doubted that this family brought its Christian faith from Rome with it.

But, even if it were not so, still it is evident that a community so considerable as that of Rome appears from Paul's epistle to have been, could not have come into existence all at once, but required some time for its formation; and for this reason, if for no other, we must refer the foundation of the church to a period much earlier than the date of the epistle.

There is, however, a difficulty in reconciling this supposition (which the contents of the epistle to the Romans oblige us to adopt), with the narrative of Luke at the end of the Acts, where it is stated that Paul, on arriving in Rome, sent for the elders of the Jews who lived there, and related to them the cause of his being a prisoner, to which they are represented as answering, that they had not received any letters concerning him, but that, as to the sect of the Christians, they begged him to give them some information, since they had only heard that it was everywhere spoken against (Acts xxviii. 17–22). From this it would appear that no church could then have existed in Rome, since otherwise it would seem inconceivable that the Jews should not have been aware of its existence. This conclusion was actually drawn by Tobler (*Theol. Aufs.* Zürich, 1796), who, in consequence of it, referred the composition of the epistle to the latest period of Paul's life—an opinion which is, of course, altogether untenable (as has already been observed), but which has some excuse in the difficulties of this yet unexplained passage, since it certainly removes them. If it be supposed (with Tholuck and Reiche) that the Jews may have concealed their knowledge of the matter, it is impossible to see why they should have done so. A man so dangerous as Paul must have appeared from a Jewish point of view, would surely have been met at once by them with open opposition. But this supposition becomes yet more improbable on a more particular consideration of the sequel, as related in the Acts. For we find that at their next meeting with Paul, the chiefs of the Roman Jews appear really unacquainted with the subject of the gospel; it is evident that they hear it for the first time, and the announcement of it raises, as was usual, a contention among their own number—some assenting to it, and others opposing it; and surely it is impossible to suppose this contention feigned. Hence we might suppose that the church may have been entirely broken up by the persecutions of Claudius (Sueton. Claud. c. 24), and that its subsequent gathering may have been so gradual that the *few Christians* who were at Rome when Paul arrived there were unknown to the Jews of the capital.* I had myself formerly declared in favour of this opinion (Comm. on Acts xxviii. 17, seqq., 1st ed.); but it furnishes no escape from the difficulty, since the date of the Epistle to the Romans falls in the interval between the persecution of the Jews, under Claudius, and Paul's visit to Rome, and the epistle supposes the existence of a *flourishing* church; it is therefore impossible that, at the later period there can have been but a small number of Christians in Rome, as the community was already so numerous at an earlier time.

There is, however, the greater reason for desiring a solution of the difficulty, because thus light would be thrown on the relation of the Jewish and Gentile Christians in Rome—a subject of so great importance for the explanation of the whole epistle. For that there were Christians in Rome when Paul arrived there, appears (if indeed it yet require any proof), from Acts xxviii. 15, where it is related

* There had been an expulsion of the Jews from Rome as early as the reign of Tiberius. (Cf. Sueton Tib. c. 36. Tacit. Ann. ii. 85; Joseph. Arch. xviii. 4, 15.) Perhaps the passage of Suetonius about the expulsion of the Jews in the time of Claudius may indicate also an expulsion of the Christians, who would not at first be sufficiently distinguished from the Jews.

that brethren went as far as Forum Appii and Tres Tabernæ to meet the apostle; nor is there any conceivable reason why the Christians of Rome should have become fewer at the time of Paul's arrival than they were at the date of the epistle, since (in so far as we know) nothing had happened in the meantime to disturb them; and yet it would appear that the chiefs of the Jewish community in Rome knew nothing of the Christians. This indicates a peculiar relation between Gentiles and Jews, Gentile and Jewish Christians, in Rome, and so leads to the important question—*What was the character of the church of Rome, or what may have been the tendencies existing in it* when Paul wrote? a question closely coinciding with the inquiry as to the *occasion and object of the epistle*, since the epistle is the only source from which we can derive our information as to the tendencies which, in the earliest times, were prevalent in that church.

Now in the Epistle to the Romans itself there is no special cause assigned for its being written.* Paul merely mentions (i. 9 seqq.; xv. 15, seqq.) his desire to preach the gospel, as to the Gentiles in general, so especially to the inhabitants of Rome, as being the capital of the heathen world; whence it would simply appear that his object in writing his epistle was of quite a general kind. Notwithstanding this, it has often been attempted to point out particular causes, and thus also particular objects, for the sending of the epistle to the Romans. It has been supposed by many writers, and some of them highly distinguished, that the only, or, at least, the most important object was to mediate between contending parties in Rome, especially the Gentile and the Jewish Christians. Others find in the epistle a controversial design against Jews or Jewish Christians; while others again suppose that Paul wished to guard against the abuse of his doctrine as to grace, or that he meant to oppose the Jewish spirit of insurrection. All these views, however (as to which more particular information may be gathered from Reiche, pp. 75 seqq.), on closer consideration appear untenable; the whole exhibition of doctrine in the epistle is purely objective in its character, nor is there, except in passing, any intentional and conscious regard to anything save the truth of the gospel. But it is, of course, in the very nature of truth that it stands in opposition to all errors, and thus far such opposition appears also in the Epistle to the Romans; and, moreover, it was a part of the apostle's wisdom as a teacher, that he so represents in advance the doctrine of the gospel that the statement itself may be a safeguard against the errors

* Dr. Paulus takes a naif view of the matter, inferring from xv. 19 that the beautiful appearance of Italy from the high coast of Illyria awakened in the apostle's mind a longing for Rome. This æsthetic motive, however, is very problematical, inasmuch as (not to mention other objections) it is well-known that Italy cannot be seen across the Adriatic.

which could not but fall in the way of the Christians; but besides the endeavour to exhibit the gospel to the Christians of Rome in its natural relation to the law, and in its practical results on life, it is quite impossible to discover in the Epistle to the Romans a further design to oppose the Jews, and to keep differences with them in view, such as is clearly expressed in the Epistle to the Galatians.

The idea of differences between the Gentile and the Jewish Christians at Rome, for the appeasing of which it is supposed that the apostle's letter was intended, is, however, so widely prevalent, that it is necessary for us to go into a more particular inquiry as to this point.* This opinion may probably have at first been occasioned by the obvious parallel between the Epistle to the Romans and that to the Galatians; and next by the idea, that on account of the large body of Jews in Rome, there must also have been there a great number of Jewish Christians; and that if so, it is not to be supposed but that the Roman community came in for a share of the all-pervading contentions between Gentile and Jewish Christians. But plausible as this conclusion may appear, it is evident that it ought in the first place to be capable of historical proof; not only, however, is there an utter absence of such proof, but there are very important reasons to the contrary. In the whole Epistle to the Romans *there is not a syllable which mentions disputes as to the relations of the law and the gospel*, such as those which prevailed in Galatia. In xv. 7 seq., there is a faint hint that in the case of the ascetics, towards whom the apostle had recommended a tender course of dealing (ch. xiv.), the difference of Jewish Christians also came into question; and again, in xvi. 17-18, there is a warning against such as *might* cause divisions; but in xvi. 19 the Romans

* It has very recently been again proposed in a peculiar form by Baur (Stud. 1836, No. 3), and Kling (Stud. 1837, No. 2) partly agrees with him. I have more fully considered the treatises of these two writers in an essay (Stud. 1838, No. 4), to which I must here refer the reader, contenting myself with shortly characterizing the views of Baur and Kling. Baur supposes the main part of the epistle to be, not ch. iii.—viii., but the section ch. ix.—xi. This portion, he argues, is intended to assert against the Jewish Christians the universality of the Christian dispensation; and he supposes that ch. iii.—viii. were intended to lead to this conclusion, the object of those chapters being to quench the jealousy of the Jews at the influx of Gentiles into the church, by showing that Jews and Gentiles stand in the same relation with respect to Christianity. Thus it is supposed that a Judaising spirit, opposed to Paul, had prevailed in Rome. Baur had previously endeavoured to prove this in the Tübinger Zeitschrift, 1831, No. 4, and he now attempts to bring further evidence of it from the Acts, which book he supposes to have been composed at Rome, for the purpose of defending Paul's course of operation against the antipauline party; a view of which I have already given my opinion in commenting on the Acts. Kling is inclined to adopt Baur's views, to the extent of recognizing in the epistle a controversial design against Jewish opinions; but finds fault with him for considering the mass of the Roman church as Judaistic, instead of regarding the Judaisers as only one element in it. In the mass, he says (p. 320), the Roman church might rather be considered as animated by a Gentile-Christian tendency.

are plainly described as *yet free* from such errors, so that it is only the *possibility* of a disturbance of their peace that is contemplated. All that could be said, therefore, is this, that, while the apostle's argument is not *openly* directed to the subject of divisions, it is yet so managed as to make us feel through it that he has a covert regard to the two opposite systems.

If, however, the matter be so understood, it must also be allowed that this feeling may very easily deceive, and by so much the more because these possible divisions are not expressly represented as originating from the Judaising party. Where such difference actually existed, as in Galatia, Paul speaks out plainly respecting them; why, then, should he not do so in this case? If he wished, independently of any possible or existing errors, to set forth the nature of the evangelical doctrine of salvation, he could not do so otherwise than by representing the relation of this new element to the two old systems of the Gentile and the Jewish life; both must, of course, give place to the gospel, and hence his mode of conceiving the subject *appears* polemical. But that it is not so, even in a covert, intentionally-concealed manner, is shown by the notice in the Acts of Paul's appearance at Rome, which has not been at all sufficiently brought to bear on the inquiry as to the object of the Epistle to the Romans. If we conceive the state of the church in Rome at the date of the epistle according to the common view, the history of Paul in that capital is utterly incomprehensible. It is supposed that the Roman church was divided into two parties; that the strict Jewish Christians wished still to observe the Law of Moses, even outwardly, with circumcision, keeping of the Sabbath, and the like; that the Gentile Christians, on the other hand, had freed themselves from it. Must we not, on this supposition, necessarily assume that the Roman Jewish Christians adhered to the synagogue in Rome? As the Jewish Christians of Jerusalem remained attached to the Temple, and did not renounce the Jewish policy, so, too, the Jewish Christians of Rome could not have separated themselves from the Synagogue. But now let us read the narrative in Acts xxviii. 17, seq., which represents the Christians as quite unknown to the rulers of the Roman synagogue, and let us ask whether, according to this, the supposition just stated has any appearance whatever of probability? There is in that passage (as has already been remarked) no ground at all for supposing an intentional concealment; and if this cannot be assumed, we are compelled to believe that the chiefs of the Jews really knew nothing of the Christians in Rome. The speech of Paul (Acts xxviii. 17-20) is evidently reported in an abridged form: he had spoken in it of his belief in Christ, as is still indicated by the mention of the hope of Israel (ἐλπὶς τοῦ Ἰσραήλ). On this, then, the

Jews declare that they are aware that this sect is everywhere spoken against (περὶ τῆς αἱρέσεως ταύτης γνωστόν ἐστιν ἡμῖν ὅτι πανταχοῦ ἀντιλέγεται). Do people speak thus of a sect which is before their eyes—on whose struggles and contentions they are looking? This can hardly be made probable. And to this add the discussion which follows with Paul (xxviii. 23, seq.), in which for a whole day he expounds the Scriptures to them, in order to prove the Messiahship of Jesus, whereupon there arises a contention among the Jews themselves:—all which would, according to the common view, have been sheer deception, since by that view the Jews must be supposed to have known of Christ long before, and to have decided against him.* It is only in the towns where there were not as yet any churches that we find the Jews so free from prejudice as they here appear in Rome; where, on the other hand, they were already acquainted with the gospel through the formation of a church, they did not allow any expositions of doctrine by Christians. As, however, there must yet have been a church in Rome, the question is, how we are to explain this remarkable position of the Jews towards it?

The only possible explanation of this phenomenon—and it is one which at the same time indicates the origin of the tendency which we afterwards find in the Roman church—appears to be this.† It must be assumed that the Christians of Rome were induced, by the persecutions directed against the Jews under Claudius in the ninth

* This is decisive against the supposition of Meyer, that the Jews spoke only as officials, and in this capacity shewed an official reserve—that they merely meant to say that nothing had been *officially* announced to them. But—besides that this is an evident transferring of modern circumstances to the ancient world—the disputes which arose among the Jews themselves in consequence of Paul's preaching will not allow us to explain the phenomena before us by the character of the official body of the Roman Jews.

† For the further establishment of this view, and the justification of it against the attacks of Baur, I refer to my essay, already cited above, in the Studien for 1838, No. 4. This only I remark here, that his appeal to Tacitus (Ann. xiv. 44), by way of proof that the Christians were quite well known in Rome, is by no means adapted to decide the question before us, since it is the Jews who are here spoken of as unacquainted with the Christians, while Tacitus speaks of heathens; moreover, it was only by means of the rack that the heathens extorted the names of the members of the Christian community in Rome: which evidently argues their concealed and retired condition. Kling (Stud. 1837, No. 2, p. 307, seq.) refutes, indeed, the capricious fancies of Baur, but himself reverts to the old untenable view, that the Jews of Rome only pretended to know nothing of Christians there, in order to avoid disputes with them. That they wished to hear Paul, is explained by Kling merely from the forward curiosity of Jews, which led them to seek an opportunity of hearing a discourse from a famous rabbi. But it is unnecessary to shew how unsatisfactory this representation is. The Jews of Rome evidently hear of Christ for the first time; they fall into disputes among themselves; this, surely, cannot be pretence! Unless we suppose the Acts of the Apostles to be tinged with fiction (as Baur maintains), there remains no other explanation than that here proposed. Böttger's explanation of the case is also extremely unsatisfactory. He supposes that the difficulties are all of my own creation, and that in reality there are none. (Comp. Beiträge, Supplem. p. 27, seq.)

year of his reign, to make their differences from the Jews clearly and strongly apparent—perhaps in consequence of the influence which even at that early time some disciples of Paul already exercised on the Roman church; exactly as at a later date the Christians of Jerusalem separated themselves from the Jews, that they might not be confounded with them, and might be allowed to live in Ælia. If disciples of Paul early acquired a decisive influence in Rome, we shall also understand how it was that the apostle could regard the Roman church as his own, and could open his correspondence with it without invading another's field of labour. In consequence of this persecution of the Jews, Aquila and Priscilla took refuge at Corinth; and there they were found by the Apostle Paul (Acts xviii. 2), who, without doubt, became even at that time acquainted, by means of these fugitives, with the Roman church and its circumstances. On this knowledge Paul, four or five years later, at the beginning of Nero's reign, on his third missionary journey, wrote from Corinth his epistle to Rome. There is little likelihood that any great number of Jews can have ventured so early to return to Rome; those who returned were obliged to keep themselves in concealment, and it was naturally the interest of the Christian community there to remain as far as possible from them. Even three years later, when Paul himself appeared in Rome, the body of the Jews there may still not have been considerable—in part, too, it may not have been composed of its old members, who had lived there before the persecution by Claudius, but of altogether new settlers, who were unacquainted with the earlier existence of a Christian church. And thus it might come to pass within eight or ten years that the Christian community at Rome appears entirely separated from the body of the Jews in that city; and in such a state of separation we find it, according to the notice at the end of the Acts. As, according to the same narration, the Jews did not receive Paul, so that here also he found himself obliged to turn to the Gentiles, this separation continued, and thus there was gradually developed at Rome a directly anti-Judaic tendency, which caused a prohibition of celebrating the Sabbath, and of everything Jewish.* According, then, to this representation, it is altogether unlikely that there should have been Jewish Christians in Rome from whom contentions with the Gentile Christians could proceed. Christians of the former kind were in the habit of keeping up the connexion with the synagogue, and if

* The latest expositor of the epistle, Dr. Köllner, supposes that Paul, during his imprisonment, sent for the chief of the Jews for the purpose of gaining them, and that Luke did not intend to give an account of his intercourse with the Christians. This, however, is but an evasion of the difficulty; the real point is—how the *behaviour of the Jews* which is in question can be conceivable, if in Rome itself there existed a Christian community, in which there were Judaizing Christians. Köllner has advanced nothing towards the solution of the difficulty.

so, the chief persons of the synagogues could not be unacquainted with the existence of a community which declared him who was crucified to be the Messiah. There might still have been Jews by birth or proselytes among the members of the Roman church, but these would, in that case, have altogether taken up the freer Pauline view of the law, and have detached themselves from the connexion of the synagogue. If, indeed, there were any decided testimony for the fact that in Rome, as in Galatia, there existed within the church itself a party of perverse Jewish Christians, the view which has just been given, and which rests on the evidence of history, might be combated with some appearance of justice; but there is no such testimony whatever. There is, as has been observed, an utter absence of express statements on the subject in the Epistle to the Romans; for (as I have above remarked) xvi. 17, seq., points only to a *possible* danger, and the proper doctrinal body of the epistle (chap. iii.—viii.) treats the relation between law and gospel in a purely objective way, without any reference to differences in the bosom of the church itself. Chapters ix.—xi. are evidently intended for Gentile Christians only, who also are throughout exclusively addressed, and, lastly, chapters xii. and xiii. contain wholly objective admonitions. There remain, consequently, only the earlier and later chapters; and in these very chapters the hints of such contentions have been supposed to be found. In ch. ii., it is said the subject is quite clearly the Jews, who are expressly addressed (ii. 17, 27), so that the epistle must also necessarily be supposed to have been written to Jewish Christians; in iii. 1, seq., the advantages of the Jews are discussed, and, although in ch. xiv. the mistaken freedom of Gentiles is reproved, yet it is in contrast with *Jewish scrupulousness*, which must, therefore, necessarily be also supposed to have had certain representatives in the Roman church. To the observations from the opening chapters, however, it is to be answered, that Paul assuredly did not write to Jews, and yet it is *Jews* and not *Jewish Christians*, who are addressed in the passages ii. 17, 27; the address, therefore, is evidently not to be made a foundation for inferences as to the character of the readers, but is rather to be regarded as merely a rhetorical figure. Paul's object in the first chapters is only to prove of both Gentiles and Jews that they had need of Christ the Saviour; but into these two elements the whole world was divided, when regarded from the theocratic point of view; and thus, so far as Paul had an universal purpose in writing his epistle, in so far was he obliged to contemplate Christianity in its relation to the previously existing stages of religious life and culture, without giving us a ground for thence deducing anything as to the composition of the Roman church. Hence it was requisite that the advantages of the Jews also should be discussed (iii. 1, seq.), inasmuch as it was necessary for the Gentiles, even if they embraced Christianity without any intermediate step, to understand their relation to the Old Testament economy and to the people of Israel; and, consequently, from a discussion on these points nothing can be inferred for the existence in Rome of Jewish Christians in the proper sense of the term—*i. e.*, of persons who not only were of Jewish descent (for in that sense Paul himself would be a Jewish Christian), but who attached an exaggerated value to Jewish views, and adhered to the synagogue and the temple. A more plausible evidence for the existence of such a party at Rome is ch. xiv.—according to which, undoubtedly, there must have been in Rome a class of persons scrupulous as to the law. It is, however, extremely improbable that these were Judaisers of the ordinary kind, such as were found in Galatia; for the latter had no scruple as to the eating of flesh in general, but only the flesh of unclean animals; whereas the Roman ascetics, on the other hand, disapproved of *all use of animal food*, and lived wholly on herbs and fruits (xiv. 2). The whole question as to the character of these persons, therefore, requires a closer examination, which we shall institute in the exposition of the passage; at all events, however, we must not regard ch. xiv. as proving the existence of Judaisers in Rome, since the description is not at all suitable to them.

We regard, consequently, the hypothesis of an intended settlement of dispute between Gentile and Jewish Christians in Rome as wholly untenable; and we find in the Epistle to the Romans *a purely objective statement of the nature of the gospel, grounded only on the general opposition between Jews and Gentiles, and not on the more special opposition existing in the church itself, between Judaising and non-Judaising Christians.*[*]

§ 4. Argument of the Epistle.

With respect to the plan of the Epistle to the Romans, two extremes are to be avoided: *first*, the view which represents the

[*] It were to be desired that the terms *Jewish* and *Gentile* Christians were more carefully distinguished than they usually are from *Judaising* and *non-Judaising Christians*. It is, indeed, certainly to be supposed that most of those who were Jews by birth retained, even as Christians, a great attachment to the Jewish law, and that most of those who were Gentiles by birth remained free from it as Christians; yet, doubtless, there were also many Jews by birth (and consequently Jewish Christians) who, as Christians, did not Judaise; and, in like manner, many of Gentile birth might have already, as proselytes, been so strongly implicated in Judaism, that, even after becoming members of the Christian church, they maintained a Judaising tendency. The names of *Jewish* and *Gentile Christians*, therefore, ought to be used only to signify *descent*, and the erroneous spiritual tendency to be denoted by the epithet *Judaising*.

apostle as having written according to a most exactly elaborated logical scheme ; and, *secondly*, the supposition that, without having any settled design, he merely abandoned himself to his inward impulses. Between the two views, the following appears obviously the true and correct idea—that Paul had undoubtedly designed a general plan for the epistle, but without having carried it into detail. His epistle, consequently, has not the precision of a theological treatise, but preserves the freer form of a letter ; still, there is expressed in it so determined and clear a train of thought that he cannot have written it without any plan, and in mere obedience to the current of his feelings. For how different a shape such an absolutely free and unpremeditated effusion takes, we see, among other instances, in the Epistle to the Ephesians. *One* leading idea, *the relation of Law and Gospel*, is carried out so carefully by the apostle, with the necessary preliminaries for understanding it, and the most important consequences which result, that nothing whatever of essential importance can be pointed out as missing in his statement.*

The whole epistle falls under four divisions. The *first* part contains the *opening* (i. 1-17), in which, after the *salutation* (1-7), is given the *Introduction* to the following discussion (8-17). The last two verses expressly state the theme for the whole epistle, viz., that *the gospel is a power of God, and in it is revealed the righteousness from faith.*

This idea is developed in the *Second Part* (i. 18—xi. 36), which, as being the *doctrinal* portion of the epistle, gives it its great importance. It falls into *five sections*, of which the *first* (i. 18—iii. 20), is a preparation for the deduction properly so called ; being devoted to proving the universal sinfulness of all mankind, in order to manifest the insufficiency of the law, both moral and ceremonial, and the necessity of another way of salvation, the righteousness of faith. First of all, the apostle proves the sinfulness of the Gentile world (i. 18-32); next, he treats of the Jews *more especially* (ii. 1-29) ; lastly, he further considers the relation of the Jews to the Gentiles, and allows to the former great advantages in their calling, but declares that they have forfeited these by their unfaithfulness ; wherefore there is now no difference between Jews and Gentiles in their relation to the gospel (iii. 1-20).

With the *second section* (iii. 21—v. 11), the apostle enters on the doctrinal exposition itself. Since the law, whether ceremonial or moral, was not sufficient to render men righteous and

* The view proposed by Baur (Stud. 1836. No. 3), that the main part of the epistle consists, not of the section ch. iii.—viii., but of ch. ix.—xi., has been already noticed above. The untenable character of this supposition has been shown in my essay, already more than once cited (Stud. 1838. No. 4), to which I now refer the reader.

holy before God, he has opened another way, namely this, that men should become righteous and blessed through faith in Jesus, who is set forth as a mercy-seat* (iii. 21–31). To the germs of this righteousness by faith, Paul points in the Old Testament, as far back as the life of Abraham, who pleased God not by works of the law, but by faith, which was imputed to him for righteousness (iv. 1–25). This holy way, then, by which alone man in his sinful state can attain to peace with God, has through the love of Christ been manifested to all men; for which cause we may not now glory save in Christ only (1–11).

The *third section* indicates the internal necessary connexion of this way of faith with the nature of man. As from Adam the stream of sin poured itself forth over mankind, and hence every one who is descended from him has fallen under sin—so from Christ does righteousness proceed, which he imparts to the faithful in the new birth. The law, therefore, is intended only to make sin powerful, in order that grace may become more powerful (ver. 12–21.) The same, therefore, which took place in Christ, has been accomplished in his people also, seeing that all are in him, as they were in Adam. For this cause, also, must not any one who has been incorporated into Christ any longer serve sin; for he has died in the old man, and, like a woman who has been set free by the death of her husband, he has become married to another husband, even Christ (vi. 1—vii. 6).

After this follows, in the *fourth section*, the description of the course of conversion in man (vii. 7—viii. 39). From the first movements of grace and the quickening of sin, the apostle portrays the progress of the inner life up to the fully developed contest between light and darkness in the soul, which at last is triumphantly ended by experience of the power of the grace of Christ (vii. 7–24). With this is connected the description of the life in grace itself, and in the gradual growth therein, to the completeness and perfection of the entire man in God (vii. 25—viii. 17). Lastly, the apostle passes from the perfection of the individual to that perfection of the whole, which is represented and assured in it; and with this is attained the purpose of the course of the world, since thus all that was corrupted by the fall will be restored to its original purity (viii. 18–39).

In the fifth section (ix. 1—xi. 36), the apostle brings back his readers to the peculiar relation in which the Jews stand towards the Christian system of salvation. It is primarily intended for *them*; and, nevertheless, *they* appear as if expressly shut out from it, and the Gentiles as if called before the Jews. In consequence of this relation, the apostle first unfolds the doctrine of election in general, agreeably to the indications in the Old Testament, and shews that

* Ἱλαστήριον, ver. 25. *Propitiation*, Eng. ver.

the holiness and blessedness of the creature are solely the work of God's gracious election, and that the unholiness and damnation of the creature are no less to be regarded as solely his own work (ix. 1–29). He then shews that it is the unfaithfulness of the Jews which has hindered them from laying hold on the righteousness which is by faith ; they had obstinately clung to the law as the way of salvation, whereas Christ is the end of the law, and in him alone dwelleth peace for Jews and Gentiles (ix. 30—x. 21). And, lastly, Paul opens the prospect, that even for the Jews a conversion to Christ is yet to be expected. He points to the fact that a holy seed has yet remained in the people, which will not be lost ; and then, in bold prophetic glances, he passes on to the end of days, when Israel shall again be engrafted into the olive tree, in whose roots the Gentiles only have at first been set as wild shoots. This contemplation incites the apostle at last to an enthusiastic ascription of praise to God, with which he concludes this second and most important part of the epistle (xi. 1–36).

The *third part*, the hortatory (xii. 1—xv. 33), may be divided into three sections. In the *first* (xii. 1—xiii. 14), Paul gives general admonitions to brotherly love, and to obedience. In the *second section* (xiv. 1.—xv. 13), he treats of the regard to be paid to such as are weak in faith, and suppose themselves obliged to an exact observance of some altogether unessential practices or precepts. The apostle exhorts the stronger members of the church to treat these with a forbearing consideration, and prays them rather, after their Lord's example, to refrain from using their liberty than to offend a brother. In the *third section* (xv. 14–33) Paul communicates notices respecting himself and his intended journeys.

The *fourth* and concluding *part* forms the epilogue, and contains greetings and good wishes for the readers (xvi. 1–27).

According to this summary of the contents, the nine chapters from the third to the eleventh form unquestionably the most essential part of the epistle They furnish a careful doctrinal exposition of the nature of the Christian scheme of salvation,* by no means, as Reiche says (p. 66), merely apologetico-polemical considerations on it. But the peculiar character of the epistle still requires a special consideration, on which we intend to enter in the following paragraphs.

* So, with substantial correctness, Höpfner, De consecutione sententiarum in Pauli epistola ad Romanos ; Lips. 1828. Compare also Fuhrmann's Essay, De Concinnitate in Ep. ad Rom. in Velthusen, etc., *Sylloge*, vol. i. 461, seq.

§ 5. The Value and the Peculiar Character of the Epistle.

Among the epistles of Paul, three classes may be distinguished; first, epistles of *doctrinal* instruction; next, epistles of *practical* instruction; and, lastly, friendly outpourings of the heart. To the last class belong the Epistles to the Ephesians, the Philippians, the Colossians, and Philemon. All these presuppose the common faith as known, and aim only at perfecting believers in it, and confirming them in brotherly love. Those which I have styled epistles of practical instruction are especially occupied with the outward aspects of ecclesiastical life. The Epistles to the Corinthians, to Timothy, and to Titus, are those which, while they touch on individual points of doctrine, set especially before our view the ecclesiastical relations of the apostolic age. But the Epistle to the Romans, with those to the Galatians and Thessalonians, belongs, beyond the possibility of mistake, to the first class—the epistles of doctrinal instruction. In respect of subject, it is most nearly akin to that to the Galatians; both treat of the relations of law and gospel: while, however, as has been shown above, this relation is treated altogether *objectively* in the Epistle to the Romans, the Epistle to the Galatians represents it *polemically*, in opposition to the Judaising Christians. The Epistle to the Galatians, moreover, limits itself exclusively to this relation, and discusses it more briefly than is done in the Epistle to the Romans. In this, on the other hand, the relation of law and gospel is set forth didactically, in the proper sense of the word, nay, scientifically, so that the doctrine of the sinfulness of human nature, which is essential to its foundation, and the doctrine of the Divine decree, which furnishes the key to the passing of the gospel from the people of Israel to the Gentiles, are also set forth in connexion with it.*

Hence we may say that in the Epistle to the Romans is contained, as it were, a system of Pauline doctrine, inasmuch as all the essential points which the apostle was accustomed to bring forward with essential prominence, in treating of the gospel, are here unfolded in detail. It is very appropriate that he, the apostle of the Gentiles, set forth this in an epistle of instruction to the Christians of Rome in particular, since that city represented, as it were, the whole Gentile world, as Jerusalem represented the Jewish.

* That in the Epistle to the Galatians the relation between law and gospel alone is treated, while in that to the Romans the doctrine of election is also considered, may be regarded as the reason why Luther commented on the Galatians only; he wished undoubtedly to avoid declaring himself on predestination.

The Epistle to the Romans is thus far a letter to all Gentiles and Gentile Christians collectively (as the Epistle to the Hebrews is addressed to all Jews and Jewish Christians, with a view of bringing them nearer to the more comprehensive Pauline position);—and in consequence of this significancy, its contents have also, in perfect accordance with the process of the church's development, become the basis of all the doctrinal development of the Western Church. There is in human nature an inclination to deviate ever again and again from the essential character of the gospel, and to sink back into the law. The difficulty of overcoming the law, and of enforcing the gospel truth in its peculiarity, shewed itself, even as early as the founding of the church. Even those who had experienced the power of the gospel, like the Christians of Galatia, might be again led astray, and drawn back to the Old Testament level of the law. Afterwards, during the medieval period, a new legal character was developed in the bosom of the church itself, and the righteousness of faith, without the works of the law, was altogether lost sight of. By the light of the word of God, and especially by the careful, profound, and experimental statement of the doctrine in the Epistle to the Romans, the Reformers again discovered the original doctrine of the righteousness which comes of faith, and so they built the church anew on its eternal, indestructible foundation. Since the middle of the eighteenth century, lastly, the church again sank to the legal position, in the systems of neological rationalism which, from that period, became prevalent; and if a more recent age has been able once more to find the jewel of faith under the ruins of the demolished church, it is mainly indebted for this to the comprehensive, and, to every yearning heart, convincing exhibition of truth in Paul's Epistle to the Romans.* And as the church, collectively, has always been in danger of losing the evangelical truth, and sinking back to the level of the law, the same is to be observed in the development of the life of the individual also. Every awaking of sin, and of striving after deliverance from it, proceeds from the endeavour to fulfil the law of God, whether the inward law of the conscience, or the outwardly given law of revelation. The vanity of the struggle which arises from this striving is the first thing which brings to the conviction that there must be another way which leadeth unto life. From this feeling of the need of salvation, arises by means of the preaching of Christ, faith, and in it regeneration, the transformation of

* That after this the apostle's fundamental suppositions are the only part of the epistle to which Reiche (vol. i. p. 91) is even now able to attach a value, is intelligible from this learned writer's doctrinal position. Köllner (p. 58) considers it necessary to extract the kernel from the husk before we can get at abiding truths in the epistle; he, too, regards its significance as a whole as only temporary.

the whole inward man, and the filling it with the power of Divine life. As, however, the old man, in whom sin dwells, still remains alive in the individual after this has taken place, there remains also for him the danger of relapsing into the law, which becomes all the more threatening, if he is obliged to feel that he has not avoided the opposite extreme, of relaxing in the struggle against sin, and falsely taking comfort from the merits of Christ. And as this danger of relaxing in the struggle threatens the individual, so again does it threaten the collective body also, and to the avoiding of it are directed (as has been already observed) the catholic epistles, with the Epistle to the Hebrews, which, in this respect, form a necessary complement to the body of Paul's epistles in general, and to the Epistle of the Romans in particular.

A treatise of such profound and decisive significancy—which in the course of centuries has been the regulating authority for the church in the most critical moments of her development—which has already been, is, and to the end of time will continue to be, the regulating authority for persons without number, in the training of their individual life—must have had the deepest foundation in the life of its author. It was only from lively experience that the apostle could treat a relation of such unwonted difficulty as is here discussed, in such a manner that his words still, after thousands of years, tell as profoundest truth in the hearts of millions, and in the collective consciousness of great ecclesiastical communities. Indeed the whole substance of the vast experiences through which Paul had passed in his own life may be traced back to the relation between law and gospel. Before his conversion, he knew no other way than that of fulfilment of the law, and with all the ardour of his noble soul he threw himself on the mass of inward and outward precepts which the Mosaic law and the tradition of the Pharisees presented to him, with the intention of fulfilling them all. His zeal was honest, and he advanced far ; he was regarded by those around him as pious and God-fearing. In the depth of his soul, however, the Divine Spirit testified to him the contrary ; the life of the believers, whom in his zeal for the law he persecuted unto blood, shewed him something in which he was lacking. To the stirrings of this inward craving the power of grace attached itself, and the appearance of the Lord near Damascus darted like a ray from a higher world into his darkness. He was now penetrated by a feeling at once of the infinite impotence of man, and of the abounding power of grace. All his exertion in fulfilment of the law had resulted in a fighting against God and his holiest working ; him, the fighter *against* God, grace in a moment changed into an instrument *for* his purposes. Hence the apostle, after this experience, knew not how to preach anything save the grace of God in Christ, whereby man is enabled to accomplish whatever the rigid law can require, and still infinitely more, without becoming high-minded, void of love, or contemptuous towards the weak, inasmuch, namely, as it is grace that works all in him, not he himself by his own might. The words of Augustine—*Da quod jubes, Deus meus, et jube quod vis**—contain, therefore, the whole system of the Apostle Paul.

Such being the nature of the contents of the Epistle to the Romans, it may be understood why it is usually regarded as very difficult. Indeed it may be said that where there is wanting in the reader's own life an experience analogous to that of the apostle, it is utterly unintelligible. Everything in the epistle wears so strongly the impress of the greatest originality, liveliness, and freshness of experience; the apostle casts so sure and clear a glance into the most delicate circumstances of spiritual life in the regenerate; he can with such admirable clearness resolve the particular into the general, that the reader who occupies the low and confined level of natural worldly knowledge, now feels his brain reel as he gazes at those stupendous periods of development in the universe disclosed by Paul, and now finds his vision fail as it contemplates the minute and microscopic processes which Paul unveils in the hidden depth of the soul. Where, however, analogous inward experience, and the spiritual eye sharpened thereby, come to the task, the essential purport of the epistle makes itself clear, even to the simplest mind, as Luther has shewn in the most popular manner in his celebrated preface to the Epistle to the Romans. It is not, however, my intention by this, to deny that, even where experience is presupposed, there still remain considerable difficulties in the general carrying out and mode of statement, as also in particular parts of the epistle—*e. g.*, in the dissertation on election; but these are still only subordinate parts of the epistle, as compared with the leading main ideas respecting law and gospel. It would, however, be a great mistake to suppose from what has been said that it is intended to represent the study of the Epistle to the Romans as useless in cases where the transition from law to gospel has not yet been experienced; rather the thorough and laborious study of its profound contents is very often the means by which a yet defective experience trains itself. My intention is rather to warn against the employment of guides who, without a glimmering of the true sense of the apostolic treatise, can only hinder the beneficial effect of the study of it by their erroneous explanations.

* "Give, O my God, what thou requirest, and require what thou wilt."—[K.

§ 6. Literature.

Hardly any book of the New Testament has been so frequently and fully treated as the Epistle to the Romans—a circumstance sufficiently explained by the significance of its contents. A comprehensive survey of the literature connected with this epistle is furnished by Reiche (pp. 95 seqq.); the following appear to be the principal works.

First, as to the Fathers of the church—we have no commentary from that doctor who would have been qualified, above all others, for a deeply-grounded exposition of the epistle—Augustine. We possess by him only a fragmentary exposition of some passages, under the title, Expositio quarundam propositionum ex Epistola ad Romanos, and the commencement of a work on too extensive a plan, and therefore left incomplete. This embraces only the greeting (i. 1-7), and is entitled Inchoata expositio Epistolæ ad Romanos. On the other hand, a commentary on the Epistle to the Romans by his celebrated opponent Pelagius, is preserved among the works of Jerome, and in the revision of Cassiodorus. The work of Origen on this book we possess only in Rufinus' translation, by which it has lost much of its value for us. Besides these, we have commentaries by Chrysostom and Theodoret, executed in their usual manner. The exposition by the so-called Ambrosiaster is peculiar; but his exposition of Paul's epistles is of more importance with reference to history than to doctrine. In later times Œcumenius and Theophylact employed themselves on the epistles of Paul, and also on the catholic epistles; their commentaries, however, contain but little of their own. But the Greek Fathers altogether have, in consequence of their Pelagianising tendency, been very far from successful in the exposition of the Epistle to the Romans; the whole purport of the epistle was too remote from them to admit of their mastering it.

The middle ages were especially unfitted, by the prevailing tendency to a legal system, for the profitable illustration of the Epistle to the Romans. It was not until the Reformation that a new period for the interpretation of it commenced. Luther, indeed, was in the same case with Augustine; he left no commentary on this epistle. On the other hand, besides Calvin's profound work, the most intimate associate of Luther, Melancthon, has presented us with an exposition in which we clearly trace the spirit of the great reformer. He published in 1522 a shorter exposition, under the title of Annotationes in Epistolam ad Romanos, Viteb. 1522, 4to. A more detailed commentary afterwards appeared under the title of Commentarii in Epist. ad Romanos, 1540, 8vo. Expositions of the

Epistle to the Romans also appeared by Bugenhagen, Zwingli, Œcolampadius, Musculus, Bucer, in all which, however, as is easily accounted for, controversy against the Romish church predominates. In the seventeenth century, and in the earlier half of the eighteenth, many additional commentaries appeared, in which the same polemical reference was prominent. Among the better of the expositors who took this direction is Sebastian Schmidt (Commentarius in Ep. ad Romanos, Hamburg, 1644); Abraham Calovius, in his Biblia Illustrata, combats Grotius, and his often (especially in the exposition of the Epistle to the Romans) very shallow views. Among the Roman Catholics, Cornelius à Lapide wrote in the seventeenth century, a commentary on this, and also on the rest of Paul's epistles, which is still, at this day, not wholly without use. (Antwerp, 1614.)

From the middle of the last century until near its end, special expositions of the Epistle to the Romans were written by Baumgarten (Halle, 1747). Mosheim (whose work was edited by Boysen, 1770), Koppe (first in 1783, the latest edition, under the care of Von Ammon., appeared in 1824), Andr. Cramer (Kiel, 1784), and Morus (edited by Holzapfel, 1794).

After this, for about a quarter of a century, no labour of any importance was bestowed on the epistle, until since 1820, the activity of literary men has again been directed to it. The latest expositions* are by Böckel (Greifswalde, 1821), Tholuck (first edition, 1824 ; third edition, 1830), Flatt (edited by Hoffmann, Tübingen, 1825), Stier, in the second Sammlung der Andeutungen (Leipzig, 1828, pp. 205–451), Klee (Roman Catholic in his view, Mayence, 1830), Rückert (Leipzig, 1831), Benecke (Heidelberg, 1831), Dr. Paulus (Heidelberg, 1831), Reiche (2 vols., Göttingen, 1833–4), Glöckler (Frankfort on the Maine, 1834), Köllner (Göttingen, 1834), and Fritzsche (Halle, 1836, vol. i.) A work very important for the doctrinal part of the exposition is Leonhard Usteri's Entwicklung des Paulinischen Lehrbegriffs (Zürich, 1833, fourth edition). Compare also Dähne's Paulinischer Lehrbegriff (Halle, 1835). Earlier works of this kind, as Meyer's Entwicklung des Paulinischen Lehrbegriffs (Göttingen, 1801), have in the present state of theological science but slight utility.

* Compare Klinge's essay, Der Brief an die Römer und dessen neuere Bearbeitungen, in Klaiber's Stud. vol. iv., No. 2, pp. 59 seqq ; vol. v. No. i., pp. 1 seqq., and his review of Reiche and Köllner in the Stud. for 1836, No. 3.

EXPOSITION OF THE EPISTLE.

PART I.

(I. 1–17.)

THE INTRODUCTION.

The apostle opens the first part of his great doctrinal epistle, according to his practice in all his epistles, with a *salutation* (i. 1–7); but the fulness of the ideas which he brings before his readers even on his first address, such as he seldom (and never in such a degree) thus early presents to them, shows how entirely full his heart was with his subject; he hastens, as it were, even in the salutation, to give a sketch of the whole contents of the composition which is to follow. With the salutation is immediately connected some introductory matter, concluding with the statement of the theme, of which he designs to treat (ver. 8–17). We shall, therefore, consider the first part of the epistle, under these two divisions.

§ 1. The Salutation.

(I. 1–7.)

We find an entirely distinct character impressed upon the forms of salutation in Paul's epistles, in that they contain, instead of the χαίρειν (James i. 1) customary amongst the Greeks, a benediction accompanied by the name, the calling, and the designation of those to whom the letter is addressed. The blessing thus added has the same tenor in all the epistles, except that in those to Timothy, besides χάρις and εἰρήνη, ἔλεος is also mentioned: the same phrase is used in the Second Epistle of John, and a similar in the Epistle of Jude—viz., χάρις, εἰρήνη καὶ ἀγάπη πληθυνθείη, *grace, peace and love be multiplied*, which last word is also found in the two Epistles of Peter. Peculiar, however, to the salutation of the present epistle is the addition of intervening doctrinal statements, by which it is converted into a small self-contained whole; in the Epistles to the Galatians and Titus a similar peculiarity may be observed, but in a very inferior degree. In three parenthetical clauses, which may be distinguished by the usual marks, the apostle directs attention in his Epistle to the Romans—1, To the pre-announcement of the gospel by the prophets; 2, to the dignity of the Redeemer; and 3, to his own calling to the office of apostle: thus he would lead his readers to remark alike the nature of the gospel, its historical connexion with the Old Testament, and the personal relation in which the apostle himself stood to it.

Ver. 1.—Paul generally calls himself at the beginning of his epistles simply ἀπόστολος Ἰησοῦ Χριστοῦ, *an apostle of Jesus Christ*, but in this place and Phil. i. 1, δοῦλος Ἰησοῦ Χριστοῦ, *servant of Jesus Christ*, and in Tit. i. 1, δοῦλος Θεοῦ, *servant of God*. The term δοῦλος designates here the spiritual condition of the apostle in general, whilst ἀπόστολος defines it more exactly. He had been overcome by the Redeemer, conquered and subdued by his higher power (i. 4.) But as one not merely outwardly conquered and still disposed to resist, but inwardly subdued, Paul had at the same time become a willing instrument for executing the purposes of his Lord, as an apostle. Since the article is wanting both to this word and to δοῦλος, we may observe that Paul places himself upon a level with other servants and apostles of Christ, without, however, in this place (as in Galat. i. 1) defending his apostolical dignity with especial emphasis, since it had never been impugned by the Roman Christians. But the epithet κλητός, *called*, designates his office as not chosen by his own will, but one to which he was ordained by the will of God (cf. Acts xxii. 21). Κλητός has not, therefore, here the general meaning (Matth. xxii. 14), under which every member of the Christian church, to whom in any way the Divine *call* has come, is so designated (as in ver. 6 below), but that special meaning which makes it synonymous with ἐκλεκτός, *chosen*. From the general number of the κλητοί, a new and more exclusive κλῆσις (*i. e.*, the ἐκλογή), called Paul to be an apostle. Consequently ἀπόστολος cannot here mean any itinerant teacher of the gospel whatever (as in Acts xiv. 4, 14; Rom. xvi. 7; 1 Cor. xii. 29), but it denotes (as Galat. i. 1, where the apostle himself lays stress upon the word) a teacher chosen by Christ himself, and standing upon a level with the body of the Twelve. Besides Paul, the only one we find in this high position, standing entirely parallel with the Twelve, is James, the brother of the Lord, the Bishop of Jerusalem (cf. at Galat. i. 19, ii. 9), who filled up the vacancy which occurred by the death of James, the son of Zebedee (Acts xii. 1), without, however, having been formally elected, as Matthias. In κλητός, therefore, the same thought is implied, as is expressed, 2 Cor. i. 1, by διὰ θελήματος Θεοῦ, *by the will of God*, or negatively in Galat. i. 1, by οὐκ ἀπ' ἀνθρώπων, *not from men*. The words ἀφωρισμένος εἰς εὐαγγέλιον Θεοῦ, *separated to the gospel of God*, appear therefore tautological if we refer them also, as is commonly done, to Θεός, as the Separator. Besides, if the apostle had meant to say this of God, he would scarcely have added, Θεοῦ to εὐαγγέλιον. It is therefore much better to regard this addition as a nearer definition of ἀπόστολος, and we may then, no doubt, see in them an obvious reference to the account given in Acts xiii. 2, where the *Holy Ghost* says, ἀφορίσατε δή μοι τὸν Βαρνάβαν καὶ τὸν Σαῦλον εἰς τὸ ἔργον, ὃ προσκέκλημαι αὐτούς, *separate for me*, etc. Even Theodoret, amongst the Fathers, appears to have thought of this reference (as later Turretin), in that he bids us remark how, not only the Father and the Son, but also the Holy Ghost, had sent forth the apostle. The reference of ἀφωρισμένος (in Hebrew, פָּרוּשׁ), to the former state of Paul as a Pharisee, must be rejected altogether as a mere play upon words; nor is the element from which Paul was separated to be regarded as the world, but as the Christian church itself, to which he already belonged, when his original calling of God to be an apostle was outwardly confirmed by the choice of the church at Antioch. In the words εὐαγγέλιον Θεοῦ, the genitive does not denote the object, for that is Christ (ver. 3), but the author of the gospel. The words εἰς εὐαγγέλιον, *unto the gospel*, are rightly resolved into εἰς τὸ κήρυγμα εὐαγγελίου, *unto the preaching of the gospel*, for unto the gospel in itself, *i. e.*, to the personal enjoyment and use of the gospel, every Christian is separated, but not every one is commissioned to teach it. (James iii. 1.)

Ver. 2.—The first parenthesis* refers, as already remarked, to the relation of the gospel to the Old Testament Scriptures: being intended to declare that this does not stand disconnected from historical relations, but is, as it were, the blossom which had sprung from the roots of the Old Testament (cf. Acts xxvi. 22). Paul does not, however, subjoin this remark, in order to encounter Jewish opponents, for such did not exist in Rome, but to impress upon his hearers from the very first that truth which he proves at greater length in a subsequent part of his epistle—viz., that the Old and New Testaments are closely connected. It was needful that the relation of the two dispensations should be made no less plain to Gentiles than to Jews; we are not, therefore, from such allusions to the Old Testament, to form any conclusion concerning the position of Jews, and Judaising Christians in Rome. Θεός is to be supplied as the subject of προεπηγγείλατο from the preceding εὐαγγέλιον Θεοῦ. The prophets appear as the instruments of the Divine will, and their

* Fritzche wishes to connect περὶ τοῦ υἱοῦ αὐτοῦ, not with εὐαγγέλιον Θεοῦ, but with προεπηγγείλατο, so as to avoid making ver. 2 a parenthesis, and to consider it quite as part of the principal thought; but the position of περὶ τ. υ. α. does not accord with this view. At the same time, we must allow that the parenthetical nature of the clauses in vers. 3, 5, is much more strongly marked than here.

communications are considered to be contained in the holy Scriptures, whose Divine authority is pre-supposed as a matter of course. The προφῆται are not, however, merely prophets in the more confined sense, but all the sacred writers, inasmuch as they were filled by God's Spirit. All the passages, therefore, which refer to the Messiah are included in these words, from Genes. iii. 15, to Malach. iv. 2; for wherever a prophecy was uttered concerning Christ, it was uttered concerning the gospel, for he is himself the gospel.

(Προεπαγγέλλεσθαι, "to promise or grant anything before-hand [before its appearance]" is found in the New Testament only here. 'Εν γραφαῖς ἁγίαις we must not, with Dr. Paulus, interpret "in passages of the Holy Scripture." The reason of the omission of the article is simply this, that the expression denotes a well-known whole; the words are therefore to be translated, "in the collection of sacred writings with which you are so well acquainted." The Old Testament was naturally introduced at once even into communities consisting of Gentile converts.)

Ver. 3.—The gospel of God treats of *his* Son, it is therefore most nearly connected with himself, and a special object of his care. But the apostle cannot mention the sacred person of the Son of God without entering into a closer definition of his nature; he describes him, therefore, under the two relations of his being, the human and the Divine. To connect περὶ τοῦ υἱοῦ αὐτοῦ, *concerning his Son*, with εὐαγγέλιον Θεοῦ, *Gospel of God*, is no doubt the most natural, since 'Ιησοῦ Χριστοῦ in the 4th verse evidently has regard in the same way to υἱοῦ αὐτοῦ, passing over the second parenthesis. Of this parenthesis, the first half, τοῦ γενομένου ἐκ σπέρματος Δαβὶδ κατὰ σάρκα, *who sprang from the seed*, etc., presents no difficulty. The meaning of κατὰ σάρκα, *as to the flesh*, can hardly be mistaken, if we define it by the help of the contrasted κατὰ πνεῦμα, *as to the spirit*; it will then signify the earthly human element of our Lord's being, that by which he was subject to birth and growth, that by which he appeared to the world. (Γενέσθαι is opposed to εἶναι. See at John i. 1.) Σάρξ is, in fact, employed not merely to denote the substance of the flesh (see at vii. 14), but also the human soul and spirit, that is to say, a complete human nature, which is here designated by the word σάρξ only in order to express more strongly its identity with universal human nature (see at viii. 3). The special reference to the "seed of David" is evidently occasioned by the mention of the prophecies in the preceding verse, which represent the Redeemer as being in his human nature of the family of David.* It might,

* The supposition that Paul here expresses his adoption of the Ebionite view of the generation of Christ by the words ἐκ σπέρματος Δαβὶδ is altogether inadmissible. Christ's descent from David through the Virgin Mary entirely justifies this expression. The apostle's object did not in the least call upon him to specify how Jesus was begotten of

however, at first sight appear that the apostle used the name ὁ υἱὸς τοῦ Θεοῦ, *Son of God*, not only of the Divine, but also of the human nature of Christ, that is of his whole person, since τοῦ γενομένου is immediately connected with υἱοῦ αὐτοῦ. But since, in the very next verse, the fourth, υἱὸς Θεοῦ, *Son of God*, is expressly applied to the Divine nature, we must acknowledge that this connexion of γενομένου with υἱοῦ can be explained only by supposing that reference is made to the *unity of the person* in which the human and Divine natures united in it are not in general expressly separated. That the application of this expression to the God-Man is admissible, is founded upon the fact, that the Lord as man is and may be called the Son of God, no less than as God. When, however, we consciously separate the Divine in him from the human, the term υἱὸς Θεοῦ can *only* be applied to the Divine nature of Christ, to the eternal Logos. (See particulars at Luke i. 35.) Hence there is no tautology in the words of this and the fourth verse, υἱοῦ αὐτοῦ—ὁρισθέντος υἱοῦ Θεοῦ, for the υἱοῦ Θεοῦ (ver. 4), is to be taken in contrast with the υἱοῦ Δαβίδ in ver. 3, or the υἱοῦ ἀνθρώπου which is implied in the first part of verse 4.

Ver. 4.—He did not, therefore, also *become* such; he only *manifested* himself as such in his eternal power. The υἱὸς Θεοῦ, *Son of God*, forms, therefore, in this place, a contrast and climax to the υἱὸς Δαβίδ, *Son of David*. Christ was both at the same time, the Son of God from eternity, the son of David in time. So among recent commentators, Rückert clearly and definitely apprehends the passage. The choice of the word ὁρίζεσθαι, however, has led several ancient and modern commentators to understand the words in an entirely different sense. This word, in the language of the New Testament, means "to fix, determine, choose for some purpose." (Luke xxii. 22, Acts ii. 23, x. 42, xvii. 26.) From this has been derived the translation, "God has chosen, appointed him to be the Son of God," which would at once lead to the Jewish view of Christ's subordinate character, viz., that he was the Son of God not in his essential being, but only by God's election (ἐκλογή). (Justin Martyr. Dial. c. Tryph. Jud., p. 267.) In close connexion with this stands another interpretation, which makes ὁρισθέντος identical in meaning with προορισθέντος, a word which Epiphanius has even admitted into the text. Accordingly the expression is translated *prædestinatus est*, and referred to God's decree with respect to the incarnation. (Iren. adv. hær. iii. 22, 23. August. de prædestin. sanc. c. 15.) But both views, to say nothing of the untenableness of the former

the Virgin Mary. Nothing but that rage for scepticism, which announces itself in the assertion that Christ was not at all descended from David's family, but that this descent was only attributed to him on account of certain passages in the Old Testament, can believe itself warranted in construing this passage as if it denied the generation of Christ by the Holy Spirit.

on doctrinal grounds, must be rejected; because from the connexion it is manifestly not the decree of God, but the *proof* before men of Christ's Divine Sonship, that is here in question. No other course, therefore, remains but to take ὁρίζεσθαι in the sense "to declare, to exhibit as something," as Chrysostom has already rightly done. This explanation of the expression is, in respect to the thought, sufficiently supported by passages such as Acts ii. 22, in which Christ is called "*ἀνὴρ ἀπὸ τοῦ Θεοῦ ἀποδεδειγμένος δυνάμεσι καὶ τέρασι, a man approved of God*, etc." We may therefore render ὁρισθέντος, with Chrysostom, by δειχθέντος, ἀναφανθέντος. There is indeed some difficulty in proving that ὁρίζεσθαι is ever used in this sense. For ὁρίζω means originally "to define the limits," ὁρίζεσθαι, "to determine limits for one's self," *i. e.*, to determine. No passage in which it means directly "declarare, ostendere," is to be found either in the profane or scriptural writers. But still, the notion that Christ was by his resurrection determined to be the Son of God, is so entirely at variance with every doctrinal system, and the whole range of scriptural ideas, as well as with the language of the Bible (for, even supposing that υἱὸς Θεοῦ meant merely "Messiah," yet Christ was not first appointed or made Messiah by his resurrection), that we are compelled to assume that the apostle has here used the word in a rather wider sense, in that the context requires the interpretation "prove, set forth." It can, after all, only be regarded as accidental that a convincing example of this use of the word is wanting; for when a man is defined as to his character by means of some public act, such as the resurrection, he would seem thereby *declared* to be that which he really is. Thus only too can *ἐν δυνάμει, in power*, be fitly connected with ὁρίζεσθαι; the resurrection is in fact considered as an expression of the almighty power of God, as it is also usually represented elsewhere in the New Testament (Acts xvii. 32; Rom. iv. 24; 1 Cor. xv. 3, 17.) But that expression could not be employed of the Divine decree, and any other connexion whatever of ἐν δυνάμει is equally untenable. But if it has been held, as even Tholuck maintains, that the resurrection of Christ was not adapted to prove his higher nature, it is because men have started in this assertion with the supposition that the resurrection of Christ, like the resurrection of Lazarus, was merely the revival of his mortal body; but in our exposition of the history of the resurrection we have proved at length, that the resurrection was the glorification of Christ's humanity, a view which gives to this event an importance such as the New Testament attributes to it. Finally, we have already remarked at Matth. xxii. 29, that this is the only passage in which ἀνάστασις νεκρῶν stands instead of ἐκ νεκρῶν.* But no doubt it is

* The expression ἀνάστασις νεκρῶν has so fixed an usage as signifying the resurrec-

only the preceding ἐκ which has caused the omission of the preposition before νεκρῶν. To understand this formula as having the same signification as ἐξ οὗ ἀνέστη, *since he arose*, and to refer it to the work of the glorified Redeemer by his Spirit in the church, is, so far as respects the thought, unobjectionable. The fact of the resurrection is always presented to us in the New Testament as that from which the ascension and all the influences of the Spirit in the church proceed as simple consequences. But κατὰ πνεῦμα can here, according to the context, be merely contrasted with κατὰ σάρκα, and cannot, therefore, be referred to the operations of the Spirit; and, moreover, if this reference were not admitted, that is to say, if we took ἐξ ἀναστάσεως as merely indicating the time at which the influences of Christ began to manifest themselves, no stress would be laid upon the resurrection as especially declaring him to be the Son of God.

Finally, with respect to the expression κατὰ πνεῦμα ἁγιωσύνης, *according to the spirit of holiness*, the indeterminateness of the word ἁγιωσύνη in the language of the New Testament allows no certain clue to its meaning, and we must therefore be guided entirely by the context. For while ἁγιότης signifies the state of holiness (Hebr. xii. 10; 2 Maccab. xv. 2), and ἁγιασμός denotes the becoming holy (Rom. vi. 19; 1 Thess. iv. 3; 2 Thess. ii. 13), ἁγιωσύνη is sometimes taken as synonymous with ἁγιασμός (2 Cor. vii. 1; 1 Thess. iii. 13), and sometimes equivalent to ἁγιότης. Regarded in itself, therefore, the phrase might be equivalent to πνεῦμα ἅγιον, *Holy Spirit*. But resting on this grammatical possibility, to apply the expression of the text either to those prophecies of the Old Testament, which were given by the Holy Ghost (as if the words stood καθὼς τὸ πνεῦμα ἅγιον προείρηκε), or to that Spirit who was imparted to Christ at his baptism, is, according to the context, which must here alone decide, alike inadmissible. The contrast with κατὰ σάρκα, *as to the flesh*, requires it to refer to the Redeemer himself, and therefore the third Person of the Godhead cannot here be meant, but the Divine nature of Christ. To denote this, πνεῦμα, *Spirit*, is chosen on account of the preceding σάρξ, *flesh*, just as in 1 Pet. iii. 18, compared with Rom. ix. 5. The Divine nature of the Son of God is therefore here very properly said to consist in the Spirit (πνεῦμα), which is the substance of God (John iv. 24), and forms a contrast to the flesh (σάρξ), in which the eternal Word veiled himself (John i. 14). (See also 1 Tim. iii. 16;

tion of the *body*, that we cannot suppose there is in this any reference to that *spiritual* resurrection, which Christ brought into the world; perhaps, however, Paul here chose an expression which does not so emphatically designate the resurrection of Jesus alone, ἀνάστασις ἐκ νεκρῶν, in order to intimate, that with him the saints of the Old Testament had also risen (Matth. xxvii. 53). At the same time this also was but a partial ἀνάστασις, and it was therefore necessary again to distinguish the ἀνάστασις νεκρῶν from the ἀνάστασις τῶν νεκρῶν.

1 John iv. 2; 2 John ver. 7; Heb. ii. 14.) But this Spirit, as the absolute Spirit, is not only in himself the Holy One, but also the sanctifier of collective humanity, *i.e.*, he who communicates his nature to the creatures; this latter quality is however here less prominent, the subject being specially the description of the Lord himself.

Ver. 5.—At the naming of the holy name of Jesus Christ, the common Lord of all believers, the apostle feels himself constrained to enlarge in another parenthesis on that which this bountiful Lord had done for him, who was so undeserving of it. We must not think that any polemical allusion is intended (as in Galat. i. 1), and therefore suppose an implied contrast of *οὐ δι' ἀνθρώπων* with *δι' οὐ*. Paul mentions this grace of the Lord out of a pure feeling of thankfulness for the mercy which had been shewn to him. "Grace and apostleship" (*χάρις καὶ ἀποστολή*) is not to be taken as a hendiadys, but as a designation of general grace (that of calling and forgiveness of sins), and of particular grace (his election to be an apostle). Augustine says justly, "gratiam cum omnibus fidelibus, apostolatum non cum omnibus communem habet." Ἀποστολή, *apostleship*, with the clause defining it, requires *ἐλάβομεν*, *we received*, to be referred solely to the apostle. The whole following clause, *εἰς ὑπακοὴν πίστεως ἐν πᾶσι τοῖς ἔθνεσιν ὑπὲρ τοῦ ὀνόματος αὐτοῦ* is Hebraistic, and answers to the words לְהַשְׁמִיעַ הָאֱמוּנָה בְּכָל הַגּוֹיִם עַל שְׁמוֹ. In pure Greek this must have run, *ἵνα ὑπακούωσι δι' ἐμοῦ πάντα τὰ ἔθνη τῇ πίστει κ. τ. λ.*, *that all nations may obey the faith*, etc. Paul often uses the word *ὑπακοή* (the opposite to *παρακοή*, "neglect of hearing, turning a deaf ear," 2 Cor. x. 6), *e. g.*, Rom. xv. 18, xvi. 19 (also found 1 Pet. i. 2), in the sense of "obedience to the influence of Divine grace," properly the listening to anything, giving earnest heed to it. Πίστις, *faith* (see more at length at Rom. iii. 21) does not mean the doctrines of the faith, but the disposition of faith which necessarily supposes the obedience (*ὑπακοή*). But the ministry of the apostle was to extend to the whole Gentile world, and therefore the Romans could not be excluded from it, since their city was the centre of all Gentile life. (Cf. ver. 11.) Of the words *ὑπὲρ τοῦ ὀνόματος αὐτοῦ* we must certainly regard the most important meaning to be "for the honour and glory of his name" (cf. Acts xv. 26, xxi. 13); *ὄνομα* = שֵׁם, stands for being, the personality itself (cf. Comm. on Matth. xxviii. 19; John xiv. 11–14). Still we must not overlook the fact, that in the language of Paul, as in the discourse of all persons of comprehensive minds, yet not thoroughly trained in style, there often occur expressions which are loosely and indeterminately connected, and therefore allow of manifold applications. Such instances of sublime indefiniteness a considerate expositor will not dare to sweep away; he will take them just as they present themselves. The wide range and bearing of single thoughts gives, in fact, a peculiar charm to the language; it enables us to take a view of the world of the author's ideas, even though it did not permit him, on account of its very riches, to express at once, as he desired, all that filled his mind. Thus, in this very instance, it cannot be denied that the connexion which Tholuck has defended, of these words with ὑπακοὴ πίστεως, so as to give the meaning, "ut obediatur fidei ob ejus nomen," is equally natural with the above ; *all things in all both are and shall be for God and for the accomplishment of his will*, whether it be Paul's apostolical office, the faith of the whole heathen world, or that of every individual member of the church.

Vers. 6, 7.—The Christians in Rome therefore are also members of that great Gentile world which was committed to him ; and in that place the Gentile element from the very beginning assumed a decided prominence in the church. The glory of their calling to be members of the kingdom of God, the apostle represents by several commendatory epithets ; he styles them called, beloved of God, holy. The name ἀγαπητοὶ Θεοῦ, *beloved of God*, is not found elsewhere in the New Testament. It answers to the Hebrew יְדִיד or דּוֹד. This name, as well as the following, ἅγιοι, *saints*, denotes Christians as the spiritual Israel of the new covenant ; for what is called Israel after the flesh in the New Testament also bears the name קְדֹשִׁים Deuter. xxxiii. 3 ; 1 Sam. ii. 9 ; Ps. iv. 3. On ἅγιος, ἁγιάζειν, see the observations on John xvii. 17, and Acts ix. 13. The word, in its *immediate* signification, denotes no degree of moral perfection (the Corinthians, who were in so many respects deserving of blame, are called ἅγιοι, *saints*), but refers to the separation of believers from the great mass of the κόσμος, the Gentile world. Yet it doubtless also implies, that Christians have been made partakers of the principle of a higher moral life, which, as in a course of development, is gradually to pervade the whole man, and produce perfect holiness. Now this principle is the Spirit of Christ, so that Paul's idea, "made us accepted in the beloved" (ἐχαρίτωσεν ἡμᾶς ἐν τῷ ἠγαπημένῳ), is also applied to the conception of ἅγιος. Christians are holy on account of Christ, who lives in them, and who is their true self. The very juxtaposition of κλητοί, *called*, and ἅγιοι, *saints*, which we find here, points to the gradual development of holiness ; for, as Augustine justly observes, " non ideo vocati sunt, quia sancti erant, sed ideo sancti effecti, quia vocati sunt."

The words χάρις ὑμῖν καὶ εἰρήνη, *grace to you and peace*, finally, contain the special form of salutation, Χάρις, *grace*, is no doubt the Latin *salus*, which was also the customary form of greeting in letters ; but in the mouth of the apostle this expression, as well as εἰρήνη, *peace*, which is the oriental form, receives a deeper significance. Grace and peace are related to one another as cause and effect ; grace is the Divine love manifesting itself towards sinful humanity, peace is that state of inward harmony of life which arises in man from the reception of grace. Grace, however, does not merely begin the new life; it also supports it every moment, and is capable of an infinite increase, as a consequence of which peace is also perfected in its turn. The *source* of grace is God, the Father of all men; the *organ* by which it is communicated is the Son, the eternal Word (John i. 1), by whom all things were originally made, and by whom the fallen creature must be again restored. And nothing, finally, speaks more decisively for the divinity of Christ, than these juxtapositions of Christ with the eternal God, which run through the whole language of Scripture, and the derivation of purely Divine influences from him also. The name of no man can be placed beside that of the Almighty. He only, in whom the Word of the Father, who is himself God, became flesh, may be named beside him; for men are commanded to honour him, even as they honour the Father. (John v. 28.)

§ 2. Introduction.

(I. 8-17.)

The apostle begins the letter itself with the expression of his hearty joy for the faith of the Romans, and with the mention of his desire to be permitted to visit them. For, since his commission was directed to all Greeks and barbarians, he naturally entertained the wish to preach the gospel at Rome also. The essence of this gospel Paul immediately points out to be *that righteousness of God by faith* which is revealed in it; he thus propounds the subject, which he intends to treat at length in the epistle itself.

Ver. 8.—Paul opens most of his epistles with giving thanks to God for the faith of his readers; it is only in the second Epistle to the Corinthians, and in that to the Galatians, where he was obliged to find decided fault, that this thanksgiving is wanting. But as in the life of the believer everything is received through his relation to the Redeemer, so also here the apostle thanks God through Jesus Christ. We must not regard this as a mere phrase, but as a true utterance of the apostle's deepest consciousness. Thanksgiving and prayer are only pleasing to God when offered through the Spirit of Christ dwelling in the heart. The object of these thanks is, however, the Roman Christians themselves, not anything in them, for the life of faith is a matter belonging to our essential personality; by means of this life Paul had, as it were, himself gained them, and could therefore return thanks for them as brothers given to him. It followed from the very nature of the case, that the faith of the Roman Christians would be known generally amongst believers, since

Rome, as the capital of the world, had connexions with all parts of it, hence Irenæus (iii. 3) designates the Roman church as that, "in quâ fideles undique conveniunt." In the faith of the capital city, therefore, was contained, in the apostle's view, the pledge that this faith would soon spread itself universally over the Gentile world.

(Paul had in his mind at first a *δεύτερον δέ* to correspond to the preceding *πρῶτον μέν*, but left the second half of the sentence uncompleted.—Instead of *ὑπέρ*, A.B.C.D. read *περί*, which is indeed often interchanged with *ὑπέρ*; at the same time we may here very well prefer *ὑπέρ*, *on behalf of*, as it seems to express the more uncommon thought, that the Romans themselves are the objects of the apostle's thanks.—That no stress is to be laid upon *ἐν ὅλῳ τῷ κόσμῳ*, is self-evident; we must refer it to the countries in which the gospel had already spread itself; beyond the limits of the Christian church little was as yet known of Christianity.)

Ver. 9.—As the reason of the thanks, which he presented to God on their behalf, the apostle appeals to his continual prayers for them, prayers which he no doubt offered up to God, as for the Roman community, so also for all the churches in the world. This calling God to witness is not here intended to remove any distrust on the part of his readers, but only to give more emphasis to the thought. But if Paul here calls himself the servant of God, as he above called himself the servant of Christ, it is plain that he only served God through Christ, and in Christ only served God. The expression *λατρεύω*, however, represents more the spiritual aspect of the relation than *δουλεύω* (see Phil. iii. 3). And therefore in this place (as well as in the passage cited) the worship is referred to the *Spirit*, without, however, any antithesis to the Jewish religion being intended. Against Theodoret's reference of these words to the spiritual gift, charisma, which the apostle enjoyed, it is sufficient to adduce the *μοῦ*; but it is also inadmissible to take *πνεῦμά μου*, *my spirit*, as a mere designation of personality. Both *σῶμα* and *ψυχή* can be put to represent personality, by no means, however, promiscuously, but under such conditions as are supplied by the context. (See on this subject my opusc. theol. p. 156, seqq.) The added clause, *ἐν τῷ εὐαγγελίῳ τοῦ υἱοῦ αὐτοῦ*, *in the gospel of his Son*, refers not merely to Paul's official labours as a teacher, but rather to the element which controlled his own personal religious life, and his worship of God. That strong form of affirmation which has something of the nature of an adjuration, God is my witness (*μάρτυς μου ὁ Θεός*) is often found in Paul. See 2 Cor. i. 23, xi. 31; Phil. i. 8: 1 Thess. ii. 5. The *ὡς* before *ἀδιαλείπτως* is here rightly taken by Fritzsche as equivalent to *ὅτι*; Calvin, Heumann, Flatt, Reiche, take it erroneously for *quam*.—(The form *ἀδιαλείπτως μνείαν ποιοῦ-*

μαι is a favourite expression with Paul, see Ephes. i. 16; Phil. i. 3; Col. i. 3; 1 Thess. i. 2.)

Ver. 10.—As the subject of his prayers, Paul now mentions his wish to reach Rome, by which visit the Romans would receive the surest pledge of his frequent thoughts of them. This desire, on which the apostle enlarges in the following verses, doubtless proceeded from his longing to preach the word of reconciliation in the very heart of the Gentile world. He could not think that he had fulfilled the command which the Lord had laid upon him before he had preached the gospel in Rome, the mistress of the world.

(Εἴπως ἤδη ποτέ must be rendered "whether perchance at length at some time" See on ἤδη in the sense "at length," Hartung's Partikellehre. vol. i. p. 288.—Εὐοδοῦν means strictly "to prepare a favourable way for some one," and then generally "to further, to favour; hence εὐοδοῦσθαι, "to proceed favourably, to succeed." [See 1 Cor. xvi. 2; 3 John ver. 2.] The apostle has learned to place himself and his plans entirely under God's guidance and superintendence.)

Ver. 11.—Entirely possessed with the great object of his calling, Paul longs to communicate to others out of the fulness of his own spiritual life in Rome also, and to strengthen the believers there. "Spiritual gift" (χάρισμα πνευματικόν) we are not, as Reiche justly remarks, to refer to any extraordinary gifts of the Spirit (1 Cor. xii.); for Paul did not estimate these so highly as to consider the communication of them the business of his life; but we are to understand by it the spiritual renewal of faith, and love, and hope, in short, of the Christian life in general. (Χάρισμα = δώρημα, Rom. v. 16, 17.) The apostle, therefore, presupposes that the spark of the Divine life has been kindled in his readers, and only contemplates its increase. (Στηριχθῆναι = βεβαιοῦσθαι, Rom. xvi. 25; 1 Thess. iii. 2, 13; 2 Thess. ii. 17. On εἰς τό with an infinitive following, see Winer's Grammar, p. 304.)

Ver. 12.—Far, however, from wishing to intrude himself upon the Roman Christians as a *teacher*, the humble-minded apostle only places himself upon a level with them as a *brother;* he desires to establish himself together with them in the faith.

(The compound συμπαρακαλεῖσθαι is found only here in the New Testament, in the sense "mutually to strengthen one another in spirit." The infinitive is to be taken as parallel to στηριχθῆναι, not, with Tholuck, to be referred back to ἐπιποθῶ: in fact, it merely explains στηριχθῆναι. The ἐν ἀλλήλοις, *among one another*, denotes, as Reiche well observes, that *reciprocal* feature of the life of faith which has a strengthening and quickening power. In ὑμῶν τε καὶ ἐμοῦ, *both of you and me*, on the other hand, the common *possession* of faith is expressly declared, and brought more distinctly into consciousness.

Ver. 13.—Paul's *wish* to go to Rome had already several times grown into a distinct resolution,* but at the same time he had always been prevented from carrying his resolution into effect. Nothing at all is known of the causes which hindered him; whatever, therefore, may be said on this subject, rests upon mere conjecture. Paul represents, as the object of his journey to Rome, "that he might have some fruit there also," such as he had already gathered among the other Gentiles. That, by this fruit, he meant nothing for himself, but only acquisitions for the kingdom of God, is manifest; which still, under the influence of pure love, he regards as his own gain, according to the principle, "all things are yours."

(Paul frequently uses the formula, οὐ θέλω ὑμᾶς ἀγνοεῖν, see 1 Cor. x. 1, 2 Cor. i. 8. For this very reason, the reading οὐκ οἴμαι, furnished by D.E.G., is perhaps to be preferred, because the alteration of so common a form of expression is scarcely to be expected. In this passage only, in the New Testament, δεῦρο denotes time, elsewhere always place. The reading τινὰ καρπόν is by all means to be preferred, as well on account of its MSS. authority, as of the sense; καρπόν τινα would imply a doubt whether any fruit of his labours would ever be seen, and to doubt this were to doubt the power of Christ. In the term καρπός, *fruit*, the apostle has in mind the image of the sower.)

Ver. 14.—Paul regards his relation to the Gentile world as involving a debt to be discharged. In the gospel an infinite treasure had been committed to him, out of which he considered himself bound to impart *to all Gentiles* without exception. "Greeks and barbarians" (Ἕλλησί τε καὶ βαρβάροις), signify, therefore, merely the universal heathen world; the Jews, whom even Philo (*vit. Mos.* p. 685) reckons amongst the barbarians, are not mentioned at all here, since Paul did not consider himself as their debtor. (See at Galat. ii. 7.) The Romans, however, as partaking of the general civilization of the world at that time, are of course to be reckoned amongst the Greeks, which expression had then lost, to a certain degree, its merely national application, but had obtained this wider meaning, merely because the culture of the old world had proceeded from the Greeks. The second contrast, "wise and unwise" (σοφοῖς τε καὶ ἀνοήτοις), is by no means parallel to the first; amongst the Greeks there were many ἀνόητοι, *unwise*, and amongst the barbarians were individual σοφοί, *wise*. Whilst, therefore, the first contrast is founded upon a general distinction, the second refers to particular,

* According to Acts xxiii. 11, the Apostle Paul had a vision of Christ, in which it was expressly said to him, "Thou must bear witness of me at Rome also." But this vision did not take place until *after* the composition of the Epistle to the Romans.

individual differences; but the gospel is equally adapted to all differences of national and personal character, and therefore Paul regards himself as a debtor to the whole vast Gentile world. The above contrasts, finally, would greatly surprise us in the Epistle to the Romans, if, as Baur supposes, the church in Rome had indulged in a Judaising tendency, and was, therefore, composed for the greater part of Jews. But the supposition, either that Paul was entirely silent about his readers, or (if we consider the Jews included in this expression) reckoned them amongst the barbarians, is certainly irrational.

Ver. 15.—From this, his general spiritual relation, Paul then deduces his readiness to serve the Romans also.

(As to the grammatical connexion of this verse with the preceding, we may best consider *οὕτω* as elicited by a *καθώς*, latent in verse 14. To connect it with the *καθώς* so far back as verse 13, only increases the difficulty. Still the supplying of *καθώς* is not absolutely necessary; the clause may rather be taken merely consecutively according to the analogy of Acts xvii. 33, xxvii. 17, 44; 1 Cor. xi. 28, xiv. 25. "I am debtor to all the Gentiles—so, as such, I am ready to preach to you also." Thus, in profane writers also, *οὕτως* stands directly for *οὗτος*. [See Matthiæ's Gr. Gramm. vol. ii. p. 1235.] The words *τὸ κατ' ἐμὲ πρόθυμον* are best taken in the sense, "my inclination, my readiness." *Πρόθυμον*, as substantive, is found in the best authors, *e. g.*, Eurip. Medea, v. 178; Iphig. Taur. v. 989. And *κατ' ἐμέ* is a circumlocution for *ἐμοῦ*, this form of expression being chosen to point to a contrasted *καθ' ὑμᾶς*.—*Εὐαγγελίζω* and—*εσθαι* = בִּשֵּׂר is construed in the New Testament either with *τινί* or *τινά*.)

Ver. 16.—With a sudden, but, as respects the thought, natural transition, Paul now comes to the nature of the gospel itself. Both the doctrine of Christ crucified, and the circumstances under which it must be preached in Rome, seemed to the eye of man to render a successful result of Paul's preaching there very improbable. In the magnificent capital of the earthly potentate of the world,* in a city where all the schools of Grecian philosophy had their representatives, it might well appear hopeless to the natural man to preach the crucified Son of God, a Master who could only promise his disciples while on earth death and suffering. Nevertheless, under the conviction of that Divine power which resided in the gospel, Paul utters his *οὐκ ἐπαισχύνομαι, I am not ashamed.* This must be considered a Litotes, inasmuch as the preaching of the gospel was to him the subject of his highest glory (1 Tim. i. 8, etc.) To shew plainly how little cause he had to be ashamed of the gospel,

* Alexander Morus says very strikingly on this subject, "audax facinus ad crucem vocare terrarum dominos." See Reiche on this passage.

he terms it "*the power of God*" (*δύναμις Θεοῦ*). The expression combines a reference to the exalted source, and to the almighty power of the gospel, which stand in strange contrast with its insignificant, nay, startling outward appearance, at which both Jews and Gentiles stumbled. (1 Cor. ii. 2, etc.) It is not, however, the *doctrine* in itself which possesses this power, but the doctrine in living unity with the events to which it is related. The gospel is a *Divine act*, which continues to operate through all ages of the world, and that not in the first place outwardly, but inwardly, in the depths of the soul, and for eternal purposes. (*Σωτηρία, salvation*, is the opposite of *ἀπώλεια, perdition.* See Matth. xviii. 11. Because salvation from temporal and eternal ruin is the highest end of Christianity, the gospel itself is called *εὐαγγέλιον τῆς σωτηρίας, gospel of salvation*, and Christ *ἀρχηγὸς τῆς σωτηρίας, Captain or prince of salvation.*) The condition of its operation in man is only *πίστις, faith.* (On the import of *πίστις*, see at Rom. iii. 21.) The medicine only works when it is taken by the patient; and in like manner the gospel is effectual only when received in faith. But this faith is, by God's grace, possible to every one, the time of whose calling has arrived; the Jews have, however, the first claim to this calling. The contrast of Jews and Greeks has nothing in common with that of Greeks and barbarians in ver. 14. There the apostle was speaking of his personal relation to all classes of the Gentile world, here he is speaking of the purely objective relation of the gospel to the human race. Mankind as presented to us in the Divine economy, he considers as forming two divisions, the Jewish and the Gentile world, and ascribes to all the privilege of being called to believe, whilst he recognizes a certain prerogative on the part of the Jews (see also ii. 9, 10). This prerogative was no mere pretension advanced on the part of that people from pride and blindness,* but a Divine ordinance, which had the design of erecting amongst the people of Israel, a hearth and an altar for God,† from which, as a centre, the sacred fire might then be more easily spread over the whole earth. (See at John iv. 22.) How the Jews lost the advantage thus assigned to them, by their unbelief, is mentioned later, in chap. x.

Ver. 17. The apostle again, through *γάρ*, annexes the reason why the gospel could be thus effectual as a Divine power unto eter-

* From the general prevalence of this view arose, no doubt, the omission of *πρῶτον*, observable in some MSS., viz., B.G., which is, however, certainly quite erroneous. No doubt, in the case of the Jews, there was frequently connected with the consciousness of their election, arrogance and contempt of the Gentiles, instead of humility; but the conviction of their election was not, on that account, by any means, itself an error.

† *Πρῶτον* is therefore not merely to be referred, as is done by the Greek Fathers, to the earlier calling, but also to their larger endowment with the gifts and fulness of grace. Theodoret erroneously asserts that *πρῶτον* designates merely *τάξεως τιμήν, οὐ χάριτος πλεονασμόν.*

nal salvation: namely, because in it a new way of salvation is disclosed, "*the righteousness of God, proceeding from faith.*" The explanation of the leading ideas in the theme which the apostle thus proposes, *i. e.*, the "righteousness of God" (δικαιοσύνη Θεοῦ), and "faith" (πίστις), we defer to iii. 21. I merely make the preliminary remark, that the former word does not here signify the Divine attribute of righteousness, or goodness, or faithfulness, as has been supposed, but that the apostle opposes the righteousness of God (δικαιοσύνη Θεοῦ, or ἐκ Θεοῦ, Phil. iii. 9), to legal, or our personal righteousness (δικαιοσύνη ἐκ νόμου, or ἐξ ἀνθρώπου. *i. e.*, ἰδία), and embraces under it the entire peculiar influence of the gospel. The realization of absolute perfection (Matth. v. 18) is the highest end of man's existence; the law could effect nothing of this beyond a mere outward legality; but regeneration produces through grace, in believers, an internal, moral state, *the righteousness of God*, which answers the highest requirements. This new way of salvation was hidden from all eternity (Ephes. iii. 9; 1 Cor. ii. 7); it needed, therefore, to be *revealed* by Christ in his actual accomplishment of the work of redemption; Paul's business was simply to communicate this information. From the connexion with ver. 16, which exalts the gospel as the *power* of God, it is plain, that δικαιοσύνη Θεοῦ, *righteousness of God*, cannot signify the mere declaring a person righteous, but the really making him righteous. This Paul declares, not only of those who were then living, but also of all later generations, because he considers the righteousness of all as absolutely realized in Christ. That which in him was perfected once for all, is gradually transmitted to individual men in proportion to the degree of their renewal, and is received by them in faith, and reckoned to their account. Peculiar in the present passage is the addition of εἰς πίστιν, *to faith.* Doubtless we are not to understand this as denoting an increase of faith, an inward development of faith from a lower degree to a higher, the advance from a more external stage in our personal appropriation of salvation to one more profound and spiritual. There was plainly no occasion whatever here for Paul to allude to the development of faith (in itself by all means to be acknowledged as a fact); on the contrary, this interpretation would leave, in the mention of the righteousness of God, the capital point, namely, that it proceeded (on man's part) *from* faith, entirely untouched. 'Εκ does not, therefore, indicate in this place, as Reiche has justly remarked, the *point of departure* with respect to an *advance*, but the *ground of obtaining* righteousness, the personal appropriation of the Divine benefit, which becomes also particularly clear, if we for a moment leave εἰς πίστιν out of sight. Εἰς πίστιν, therefore, can only be taken as = εἰς πιστεύοντας, since it is only *those who believe* that secure the righteousness of faith, and thus for them alone it is revealed in the gospel.* The entire combination, *ἐκ πίστεως εἰς πίστιν*, seems designed to bring out faith with emphasis, as the essential feature of the New Testament, as works were of the Old.

In the same way that the apostle proves, in a subsequent part of his epistle (chap. iv.), by the example of Abraham, that, even in the case of the pious men who lived before Christ, it was faith which made them righteous; so also here he describes the new way of salvation in its historical connexion. We must not consider this a mere accommodation, and application of Old Testament expressions to entirely different relations; this retrospective use of the Old Testament is rather to be derived from that scriptural fundamental view of it, which supposes that in it all the germs of the New Testament are already really contained, and that, therefore, the New Testament is only the *πλήρωσις*, *fulfilment*, of the Old. (See at Matth. v. 17.) The quotation from Habak. ii. 4, is also made use of in Galat. iii. 11, and Heb. x. 38, in both with reference to faith and the righteousness of the New Testament, and we must acknowledge with justice, since it is but *one* faith at different stages of its development which is represented in both the Old and New Testament. (See Heb. xi. 1, etc.) Eternal life (*ζήσεται* is used in a pregnant sense = *ζωὴν αἰώνιον ἕξει*) is never obtained otherwise than by faith. According to the Hebrew text, צַדִּיק בֶּאֱמוּנָתוֹ יִחְיֶה, *ἐκ πίστεως* cannot be connected with *δίκαιος*, yet in Paul's use it must be thus taken. We frequently meet with such free interpretations of the Old Testament text, and it has already been remarked, that the indeterminateness of Hebrew constructions very much favours such a proceeding.† Applied in a profane spirit, as by the Rabbinical writers, this method perverts the Scripture; but when exercised in the Holy Spirit, this liberty is a means of manifesting the infinite fulness of its contents. (The LXX. must have read בֶּאֱמוּנָתִי, for they translate it *ἐκ πίστεως μου*, and ascribe faith, *i. e.*, faithfulness, to God. But the faithfulness of God is doubtless manifested in sending the Messiah, and in his work, so that this conception of the passage leads us back to the right thought.)

* Better, I think, to take *εἰς πίστιν* as a sort of emphatic and intensifying repetition "from faith into faith," beginning and ending in faith; wholly of faith.—[K.

† See the Comm at Luke iv, 18, 19.

PART II.

(I. 18—XI. 36.)

THE DOCTRINAL EXPOSITION.

SECTION I.

OF THE SINFULNESS OF THE HUMAN RACE.

(I. 18—III. 20.)

THE very nature of the apostle's undertaking required that before portraying the character of the new method of salvation, he should demonstrate its *necessity*. It was further requisite that this necessity should be pointed out in both those great divisions, under which the human race is considered in its relations to the kingdom of God, *i. e.*, alike among Jews and Gentiles or Greeks; that it might plainly appear that such a new and complete way was needed by all in common. Paul, therefore, from chap. i. 18–32, treats exclusively of the condition of the Gentiles; from ii. 1–20, the Jews principally occupy his attention; and lastly, from iii. 1–20, he draws a parallel between the two, in which he considers their different relations to the remedial provisions of Divine mercy. We treat this first section under these three divisions.

§ 3. CONDITION OF THE HEATHEN WORLD.

(I. 18–32.)

In describing the necessity of a new way of salvation for the heathen world, the apostle naturally set out with considering their degraded moral condition.* But it was also required that this state of alienation from God should be traced to its origin. Even the Gentile world was not without some knowledge of God, and in consequence some insight into the Divine law; but the knowledge which was thus within their reach, the Gentiles lost by their own

* See Usteri's Paulinischer Lehrbegriff, 4th ed. p. 15, seq., and the passages there quoted.

fault, and with their theoretical errors, the stream of their practical transgressions rose to a most fearful height. The mere recovery of that general knowledge of God, which they once possessed, could, of course, effect nothing in this evil case, for if it had not been effectual in preventing them from sinking into vice, still less could it raise the mass from the slough of iniquity into which it had fallen; it was therefore necessary that a new element of life, a Divine power (δύναμις Θεοῦ) should be introduced into the world, which should render possible a new beginning for man; such the gospel proved itself to be.

Ver. 18.—The apostle had already used γάρ three times in succession in vers. 16, 17, and uses it yet a fourth time, to connect this verse with the preceding, as (1 Cor. ix. 16, etc.). For with the revelation of God's righteousness in the gospel he contrasts the revelation of his wrath in the law: as the former comes to believers (εἰς πίστιν, *i. e.*, εἰς πάντας πιστεύοντας) so the latter *on all ungodliness* (ἐπὶ πᾶσαν ἀσέβειαν). But the deductive γάρ connects what follows in such a manner with what has gone before, as to direct attention to the life which is by faith. Those only who are just by faith shall live, for God's wrath reveals itself against all unrighteousness (which cannot be avoided by him who lives not by faith). Looking upon γάρ as intended to connect, or explain the clauses of an argument (see Hartung's Partikellehre, i. 363, etc.), we may here translate it by "yea;" it points back to the well-known truth of God's justice in punishing sin, which the life of faith alone can satisfy. In this general idea, therefore, that God punishes sin, on which the apostle Paul grounds his whole argument, he already intimates the contrasts between the two dispensations; since vers. 17, 18, exactly correspond to one another. Sinful man has the most pressing need of the revelation of the righteousness of God, for without this he is subject to the wrath of God (ὀργὴ Θεοῦ). (The endeavours to force another meaning upon γάρ, *e. g.*, "but," are altogether to be rejected. Comp. Winer's Gramm. § 423 etc.) The Divine anger (see at Matth. xviii. 34, 35, John iii. 35, 36), we of course consider as merely signifying the manifestation of God's justice against sin; this is here represented in its two principal forms, as alienation from God (ἀσέβεια), and discord in earthly relations (ἀδικία), and these in all possible cases, greater as well as smaller (πᾶσα). The only further question is this, how are the words ἀποκαλύπτεται ἀπ' οὐρανοῦ, *revealed from heaven*, to be taken? Great stress has been laid upon the expression "from heaven," and some interpret it of some particular judgment of God, *e. g.*, lightning, or refer it to the last judgment. But the general character of the whole passage by no means admits of such special applications. Each and every, outward as well as inward, present as well as future, act of God's punitive justice is here designed; they are for this reason only represented as coming from heaven as they contrast with sin on earth that eternal harmony which reigns in the heavenly and spiritual world, whence alone proceed all pure manifestations of the Divinity—even those of holy and just punishment.

In the contrast lying in the phrase *τῶν τὴν ἀλήθειαν ἐν ἀδικίᾳ κατεχόντων*, *who by unrighteousness repress the truth*, truth, as the principle of all good (comp. in Comm. at John i. 14, viii. 44), is set against falsehood, as the mother of all sin (as well of *ἀσέβεια* as of *ἀδικία*), and is represented as oppressed by it through *ἀδικία*. (We are not to take *ἐν ἀδικίᾳ* as=*ἀδίκως*, or *ἀνόμως*, since the suppression of the truth is, as a matter of course, criminal; the thought is rather this, that unrighteousness = *ἀνομία* departure from the Divine law, stifles the truth, and gives birth to error and lies. *Κατέχειν*, in the sense "to keep under, to restrain the activity of," is found also in 2 Thess. ii. 6, Acts xxvii. 40.) Here, moreover, the suppression of the truth has neither an exclusively external, nor exclusively internal reference; but combines both ideas. This pernicious energy of sin naturally begins, of course, in the heart of the individual man, but extends itself gradually onward, and darkens the conscience of whole nations and ages, rendering it incapable of perceiving the voice of truth and duty. Thus, in the case of the Romans, from the total obscuration of conscience, wickedness reached such a pitch, that the gladiatorial games, one of the most horrible outgrowths of sin which has ever appeared in the history of mankind, were the general custom.* Accordingly there is contained in this passage an assertion, that ever since the fall, and in the state of hereditary sin, there was and is a truth in human nature, which by constant active sin may be kept under and finally stifled. Paul does not represent man as being, in consequence of hereditary sin, in such a state that he can sink no deeper, but rather as having a light in himself; by the extinguishing of which light he may become at length wholly blind.

Ver. 19.—The Gentile world was not, however, excusable in these its errors, from what might be thought the impossibility of its attaining to the knowledge of God—God, on the contrary, revealed himself to it. This thought is expressed in ver. 19, where it is stated that the knowledge of God is founded upon the manifestations of the Divine energy; God, in fact, is spoken of as he who manifests

* It may be said that the practice of causing thousands of their fellow men to be slaughtered merely to feed their eyes with a sight of shows, was almost worse even than that of eating human flesh, which appears to have proceeded at first only out of the unbridled fury of battle. That the gladiatorial games were not only maintained at the time of the highest civilization of the ancient world, but then first attained a definite form, shews how little the education of the head, without the real reformation of the heart humanizes the manners.

himself to men. And it is for this very account that their knowledge of God is so undeniable, viz., because it is conveyed by the beams of the original source of light, God himself. The expression τὸ γνωστὸν τοῦ Θεοῦ, is peculiar to this passage; the word γνωστόν may mean either that which *is* known, or that which *may be* known; according to the first meaning, the phrase would mean the same as γνῶσις τοῦ Θεοῦ; the latter would, on the other hand, distinguish that which may be known of God from that which may not. (1 Tim. vi. 16.) In our choice between the two interpretations, we can be guided only by the whole connexion of the passage, according to which (as will soon be shewn more at length), the absolute incapacity of the heathen for the knowledge of God, is just as strongly denied, as the possibility of their unlimited knowledge of him. The expressions γνῶσις, or ἐπίγνωσις τοῦ Θεοῦ, *knowledge of God*, denote, however, in the language of the New Testament, that absolute knowledge of God which is conveyed to man by means of the manifestation of God in Christ; from which we may assume that the form τὸ γνωστὸν τοῦ Θεοῦ was purposely chosen by the apostle, in order to designate that lower degree of acquaintance with God, which was given to men on the footing of the Gentiles, and which was only gradually obscured by sin.

However, it is plain that the knowledge of God, which is here spoken of, is not to be referred merely to his government of the world, and his works in it, but also particularly to himself.

(Γνωστός in the New Testament generally means recognized, known [Acts i. 19, ii. 14, iv. 10, etc., Luke ii. 44, xxiii. 49], for which in classical Greek the form γνωτός is usual. The sense "which may be known" is supported by no other example in the New Testament; but abundantly by the classics.*—Ἐν αὐτοῖς, *in them*, refers to the internal nature of the knowledge of God; the meaning of the apostle is, that the nature of God is represented in the soul as in a mirror, so as not to be mistaken. It is a misconception of the passage to suppose with some that this expression is used only of the philosophers who lived in the Gentile world, for the apostle is here treating of a universal character of human nature, and what is here said of the heathen, it is needless to say, refers to Jews also.)

Ver. 20.—Once more with a fresh γάρ, *for* (the seventh, which follows without interruption from ver. 16, for διότι, ver. 19, is in meaning exactly the same as γάρ), the apostle annexes a thought in which the agency by which God reveals himself, is described more closely. We can point to no manifestations of Deity, either immediate or by angels, to the Gentile world, such as were vouchsafed to

* See Hermann's note on the Œdip. Rex of Sophocles, v. 362. Even the general analogy of the verbals in τος also supports this interpretation.

the Jews; but God revealed himself to them by his creation from the very beginning.—Ἀπὸ κτίσεως κόσμου, *from the creation of the world*, can only refer to *time*, as Rückert and Reiche justly observe (on which account, also, ἐφανέρωσε stands in the past tense at ver. 19); otherwise ποιήματα immediately afterwards, denoting the created world, is merely tautological.* The determination of the time is besides particularly important here, because it is the apostle's express purpose to prove that at no time, and under no circumstances, was there any excuse for the deep moral depravity of the Gentiles, since the knowledge of God in the works of nature was *always* within their reach. At the same time, *what* God was pleased to reveal concerning himself, is more exactly declared in the words τὰ ἀόρατα αὐτοῦ, *his invisible things*, which expression is explained and limited at the end of the verse by ἥ τε ἀΐδιος αὐτοῦ δύναμις καὶ θειότης, *his eternal power and divinity*. The "eternal power" is very definite and easy to understand. In the contemplation of the creation, the infinite *power*, which this presupposes, first impresses itself upon the spirit (see Wisdom, ch. xiii.); and as compared with the merely temporal evolutions of physical agencies, creative power appears as eternal. On the other hand, the expression θειότης, is both striking and obscure, since Θεοῦ is necessarily supplied. But doubtless the apostle, by this word, as above, by choosing γνωστόν, intended to mark the incompleteness of their knowledge. The divinity of God, *i. e.*, his higher nature in general, the dominion of a mighty power over the elements of the world, and of a condescending benevolence in the care of all the creatures—all this may be recognized in the mere contemplation of nature; but by no means the true θειότης of God, his personal existence as the absolute Spirit, as well as his justice and holiness. Still, the most remarkable part of this passage is the ἀόρατα αὐτοῦ, *his invisible things;* this seems to imply something visible, a ὁρατὸν Θεοῦ. And doubtless this is just the meaning of the apostle. The world is the mirror in which the inward nature and being of God is displayed;† the garment which clothes his very self (Ps. civ. 2). Therefore also, the world, in order to lead man to the knowledge of God, needs to be contemplated with a *spiritual* eye (νοούμενα καθορᾶται = ἐν τῷ νῷ καθορᾶται); as only the spirit can comprehend the spiritual expression of the human countenance, because in like manner, the invisible being of man is mirrored in his visible form, so also nature speaks of God's

* On κτίσις, see the remarks on viii. 19. It denotes properly and primarily the act of creation, κτίσμα, *that which is created*; in the New Testament, on the other hand, κτίσις denotes commonly that which is created.

† Calvin justly observes on this passage, Deus per se invisibilis est, sed quia elucet ejus majestas in operibus et creaturis universis, debuerunt illic homines agnoscere, nam artificem suum perspicue declarant.

might and goodness to him alone, who beholds her with more than the mere bodily eye; the latter finds in her only disorder.

(Κτίσις κόσμου [see at viii. 18] cannot mean the world, that which was created, but only the act of creating. Taken in the former sense, its connexion with καθορᾶται by ἀπό would present a difficulty; in that case, ἐκ would have been chosen, as in an entirely parallel passage in Wisdom xiii. 5. Meyer, to be sure, refers to Matth. vii. 16, where is found ἀπὸ τῶν καρπῶν ἐπιγνώσεσθε [Berl. Jahrb. 1836, N. 113]. But καθορᾶται can scarcely be found constructed with ἀπό.—'Αΐδιος from ἀεί, everlasting, eternal; ἀϊδής, invisible.—Θεότης and θειότης differ, as Θεός, and θεῖος, of which they are the abstract nouns. The fulness of the θειότης resides in the world, the fulness of the θεότης in Christ [Coloss. ii. 9]; in him alone can the Father be *personally* contemplated.)

And now, at this remarkable passage, the question arises, what does Paul wish strictly to intimate by this thought? We might think it implied in the passage, that men *in earlier times*, when they stood nearer to the primeval age, had been able to acquaint themselves with God through nature but by continual unfaithfulness, had all, without exception, lost this knowledge, and become abandoned to idol-worship. But this is plainly not the meaning of the apostle; rather is he speaking here of *human nature as it manifests itself at all times and places*, so that he conceives the knowledge of God may always develop itself afresh from the contemplation of the world, whether by reflection on its phenomena, by immediate impressions on the mind, or the stirrings of conscience. The germ of sin, which existed in all men, would not indeed have been done away with, but certainly, by obedience to that knowledge of God which was thus within their reach, checked in its development. But instead of this, men gave themselves up to the evil desires of their hearts, darkened thereby the knowledge of God which yet remained to them, and thus in turn heightened their animal passions into unnatural and monstrous lusts, and debauched their souls by a still more unnatural and monstrous idolatry. But there were at all times individuals who proved, by leading a nobler life, even in the most debased states of heathenism, that it was at all times possible for man, by the earnest contemplation of nature, to raise himself to a certain knowledge of God. This power given to sinful man of acquainting himself with God in nature, is brought forward by the apostle in other places also, particulary, Acts xiv. 15, etc., xvii. 23, etc. The Redeemer himself assumes such a power in passages like Matth. vi. 22, 28, John viii. 17. (Comp. Usteri's Paul. Lehrb. p. 21.) There is, therefore, nothing in the passage we are now considering that is not found elsewhere. But as this passage is found in the apostle's proof of the sinfulness of human nature, the impression has been produced upon many minds, that the idea expressed in it concerning the capability of man to raise himself to the knowledge of God, limits the greatness of man's depravity. But in this the truth has been overlooked, that moral depravity has not its immediate ground in the *understanding*, but in the *will*, and presupposes the want of real love, on which account even morally evil spirits are said to have the knowledge of God. (James ii. 19.) In fact, the capability of knowing God *heightens* the moral depravity of man; for that they, notwithstanding this knowledge, can go on further and further in sin, supposes a higher degree of aversion of the will from the law than if they had sinned without this knowledge. The Roman Catholic Church, as well as Rationalists, regard altogether erroneously the simple γνωστὸν τοῦ Θεοῦ as involving also true love and obedience. But again, as we have already observed, the apostle restricts that knowledge of God to which man can attain by the mere contemplation of nature, to the knowledge of the might and goodness of God. For the proper nature of God, as the Supreme Spirit, and pure Love, *i. e.*, communication of *self* remained unknown to the heathen, as well as to most of the Jews themselves; on which account Christ is often obliged to tell the Jews that they know not God. Accordingly Paul might, with equal justice, have here brought out the idea (if it had happened to suit his argument), that man, from the mere contemplation of nature, could never arive at the *true* knowledge of God; passages, therefore, such as Ephes. ii. 12, are not in the least inconsistent with the present. Even the best of the heathen, with their weak glimmering of the knowledge of God, remained without hope, because it was able to awaken in their minds only fear, at most a *longing* after the unknown God. But when Schneckenburger says that Paul might have derived this view from the Alexandrian Gnostics, he brings forward a very unnecessary hypothesis; it is much simpler to suppose that it arose independently in his own mind, as it did also in that of the Alexandrians, from the immediate contemplation of the nobler moral phenomena amongst the Gentiles. Granting even that Paul had heard of the doctrine of the Alexandrians, yet he did not adopt it from them, but uttered it only on account of the deep truth which he recognized in it by the light of the Spirit.

Ver 21.—Paul points out the unfaithfulness of the Gentiles to the measure of the knowledge of God which they possessed as the beginning of their errors. (The γνόντες τὸν Θεόν, *knowing* GOD, is not inconsistent with the preceding more general term θειότης, *divinity*, for here he is only speaking historically of that true knowledge of God which existed in men originally, and which they gradually lost.) God, as the absolutely highest Being, claims man entirely, with all his adoration and all his gratitude, and (since God is Spirit and Love, and man, in his true nature, is so likewise), *spiritual* adoration, and *spiritual* gratitude, *i. e.*, the complete surrender of self, and the obedience of the inmost powers of life. *Thus*, as the highest Spirit, and purest Love (ὡς Θεόν) they honoured him *not*, even if they did not fail in outward homage. The consequence of their forsaking the truth was then their sinking into vanity (*ματαιοῦσθαι* = הֶבִלוּ, Jerem. ii. 5); of their forsaking the Light, the sinking into darkness, the element of sin. (The *διαλογισμοί* are the actions of the *νοῦς* [see my *Opusc. Theol.*, p. 157]; hence both *νοῦς* and *καρδία*, the two principal powers of the man, are drawn down deeper into sin. With the *νοῦς* begins also the restoration of the man in the new birth. See at vii. 25.)

Vers. 22, 23.—Gradually the Gentile world became more and more degenerate, till the idea of God was entirely obliterated, so that men, and even beasts of the meanest and most disgusting forms, received divine honours. Amongst modern expositors, Reiche has contested this profound derivation of idol-worship from sin, which is yet undeniably expressed in the Old Testament. (Jerem. ii. 11; Ps. cvi. 20.) His opinion is rather (p. 158), that the deification of the powers of nature, and of individual created things, preceded Monotheism, since all the conditions for the highest development of the religious feeling were wanting. In this Reiche sets out with the quite unscriptural, and altogether untenable view, that the course of human development begins with the completest rudeness, and proceeds to the gradual perfection of our inward as well as outward life. But the doctrine of the apostle is founded on the opposite view of a gradual sinking out of a nobler state into sin, parallel with which degradation appears the restoration of man to his original glory, by a succession of God's gracious manifestations. He means, therefore, to say, that the degradation of the human race did not show itself suddenly in the fearful form of the worship of created powers and images, but presupposed a continual succession of transgressions, and developments of sin.* In consequence of these the higher power of man's life (the *πνεῦμα*) almost entirely disappeared, and only the brutal inclinations and instincts remained, without a ruler. In this way man, of course, fell a prey to the powers of nature, in which he perceived that working on a mighty scale which he felt to be active in himself. It was especially the generative and receptive powers of nature which were recognized by man as the most powerful in himself and in external things, and hence were in all nature-worship honoured with all kinds

* The necessity of a preaching of the name of the Lord (Genes. iv. 26) is the first indication of that falling away from the true God, which it was the object of the preaching of the successive patriarchs to prevent.

of cruel and impure services. Where holy love to the Highest Good was lost, another love must necessarily occupy the heart, for *without* love man cannot exist ; but as is the object of his love such does man himself become, for love implies self-surrender to its object. The speculative reason of man could not free him from this bondage of the powers of nature, for it awakened no higher love, and led at best to a hylozoistic Pantheism. The wisdom of man was foolishness (1 Cor. iii. 9). The law, at the same time, could only awaken the feeling of bondage, and the longing after freedom ; but freedom itself, and the raising of the spirit to communion with God the Spirit, could be wrought only by the imparting of a higher principle of love through Christ ; whence also it is the Son who makes free.

(Ἤλλαξαν δόξαν, κ. τ. λ., answers exactly to Ps. cvi. 20, where the LXX. have ἠλλάξαντο τὴν δόξαν αὐτῶν [*i. e.*, Jehovah], ἐν ὁμοιώματι μόσχου. In ἐν ὁμοιώματι εἰκόνος,* *in the likeness of the image*, is, no doubt, an allusion to Gen. i. 26. Man, according to God's will, is certainly intended to present an image of himself in holiness and righteousness, but this image is not to be abused to purposes of adoration ; since he, as φθαρτός, is separated from the ἄφθαρτος by an infinite chasm. On ὁμοίωμα and ὁμοίωσις, see at Rom. viii. 3. The worship of beasts had developed itself in Egypt in the grossest forms and to the adoption of the most hideous errors, so that even bestiality formed an element of their worship, as in the service of Mendes. The expressions used by the apostle are applicable to the worship of the Ibis, Apis, Crocodile, etc., etc.)

Vers. 24, 25.—God punishes sin by sin, that sin may bring with it those fearful consequences which first tend to lead man to the consciousness of his alienation from God. He, therefore, withdrawing the influences of his grace, now left men in their blindness to their own evil lusts, which shewed themselves especially in the unchecked dominion of the most powerful of their natural instincts, viz., sexual desire, and to the power and Prince of darkness, who is the Lord of sin and all its manifestations. (By ἀτιμάζεσθαι τα σώματα ἐν ἑαυτοῖς, *dishonouring their bodies*, etc., unnatural lust is not yet meant, but simply lust in general, which always in its sinful exercise defiles the body, whilst other sins are without the body. 1 Cor. vi. 18. The opposite is κτᾶσθαι σκεῦος ἐν τιμῇ. 1 Thess. iv. 4.) Such abominations, which were considered not only lawful, but the proper service of their gods, originated in the straying from truth into falsehood.

(Ἀλήθεια, *truth*, and ψεῦδος, *falsehood*, are here to be taken abso-

* The expression κατ' εἰκόνα καὶ καθ' ὁμοίωσιν (Genesis i. 26), which there form a Hendiadys, are here compounded into one expression, ὁμοίωμα εἰκόνος—God will be worshipped only in the perfect image of his Son, not in Adam, and his children.

lutely, not as *logical*, or simply formal, mathematical truth and falsehood, but as essential, real truth. God himself is Essence and Truth [cf. John i. 14]; sin is the absence or perversion of the real, is nothingness and lie. Σεβάζεσθαι = προσκυνεῖν is found in the New Testament only here. Παρὰ τὸν κτίσαντα is best taken as, putting into the back ground, passing over the true God, or being hostile, opposed to him. The doxology is intended to give prominence to the contrast between the heathen's forgetfulness of God, and the honour which was due to him.)

Vers 26, 27.—God let the Gentiles sink to yet lower degradation, in permitting them to fall into unnatural lusts. Here humanity appears degraded below the beasts; in the indulgence of natural passions, man falls under the power of a very strong appetite, and has in that a certain excuse; but sins of unnatural lewdness are the abominations of unmixed wickedness. That they were so much in vogue in the Roman and Grecian world, is a convincing proof of the depravity of the age, notwithstanding all its outward polish of cultivation. (Compare Tholuck's Abhandlung über den sittlichen Zustand der Heidenwelt, at the beginning of Neander's Denkwürdigkeiten, B. I.)

Ver. 28.—The punishment of such abominations was the complete spiritual ruin which accompanied it (ἀντιμισθίαν ἐν ἑαυτοῖς, *i. e.*, ἐν τῷ νῷ ἀπολαμβάνοντες, ver. 27), and which again could not but bring disorder into all political and social relations. God permitted them to fall into this condition, to bring the consequences of their sin completely home to their consciences.

(As the *knowledge* of God is eternal life [John xvii. 3], so Paul rightly finds in the absence of it the source of all sin, and of its results. The ἀδόκιμος νοῦς contains a verbal allusion to οὐκ ἐδοκίμασαν. The fact that they did not consider God, who is the absolute Good, as good, made them reprobates; while they fancied that they were rejecting *him*, he cast away *them*, and they cast away themselves. The reference of the ἀδοκιμία to the νοῦς marks corruption as having penetrated to the deepest spring of life; the νοῦς was intended to govern both body and soul: how great then must be the ruin, if the highest principle, the power by which man receives the Divine element, is itself destroyed. [Matth. vi. 22.] Sexual impurities are set forth as the source of all other vices, because they destroy the most sacred and tender relations of human nature.)

Vers. 29–31.—In the following catalogue of sins (a similar list is found Galat. v. 19, etc.; 2 Tim. iii. 3), by which the mind that is estranged from God discloses its enmity, no perfectly distinct succession can certainly be traced out, and occasionally the apostle is guided in the connexion by similarity of sound in the words; still it is undeniable that, setting out with the more general forms of sin, he passes to its more special manifestations.*

(The reading *πορνείᾳ* is not found in A.B.C. and several other MSS. and critical authorities. Without doubt this reading is not here genuine, as Paul had already treated at length of sins relating to the sexes. Transcribers, who thought that this very sin was here missing, added this expression instead of *πονηρίᾳ*.—Πονηρία and κακία are nearly allied, yet the former renders more prominent the *producing* of evil; πονηρός is rather the corrupting, κακός the corrupted.—Φθόνου and φόνου are connected in the same way on account of the sound in Euripides Troad, v. 768.—Κακοήθεια denotes depravity of mind, inclination to evil, the opposite to εὐήθεια. Ψιθυριστής, a secret calumniator, back-biter; κατάλαλος, every slanderer, even the common, public evil-speaker.—The latest investigations do away the distinction between θεοστύγης, God-hating, and θεοστυγής, God-hated.† The active meaning, contemners of God, is probably to be here preferred, since all evil-doers, as such, are without exception displeasing to God, but sin does not rise in all to the actual contemning of God. The ancients also mention the particular sin of θεοσεχθρία. See Aristoph. Vesp. v. 416.—Ὑβριστής marks the violent and insulting, ὑπερήφανος him who is proud of his personal dignity, etc.—Ἀσυνέτους is wanting in several authorities, but is to be retained as genuine on account of the Paronomasia with ἀσυνθέτους. It is most suitably taken as "foolhardy, rash in wicked enterprises," whilst ἀσύνθετος denotes the covenant-breaker.—Ἀσπόνδους is not found in A.B.D.E.G. and several other critical authorities: still it was probably only omitted by the copyists on account of its similarity in form to the other words, unless it has found its way into this passage from 2 Tim. iii. 3. It differs from the kindred ἀσύνθετος in this, that it marks not the breaking of the covenant, but the refusal to enter into one, and therefore implies implacableness, want of love.)

Ver. 32.—Into this flood of sins the holy God permitted unholy men to sink; not by any special influence tending to make them bad, but according to the necessary law in the moral economy of the world. For where God and his holy character is not, and therefore the vanity of the creature's self is the ruling power, there sin begets sin,

* Glöckler's endeavour only confirms me in my view, that we must not attempt to go further in demonstrating the order of the words in the following catalogue of the manifestations of sin. He regards ἀδικία, κακία, and κακοήθεια as the general expressions, and all that follows upon them, as the special manifestations of these. But against this so much may be urged in almost every particular expression, that it is better to consider the order of succession under a freer aspect.

† The accentuation of the word as an oxytone is to be preferred, in conformity with the rule, that compound adjectives in ης are always oxytones. See Buttmann's Larger Grammar, B. II. p. 317.

and punishes itself by sin. In this law Divine love shews itself as plainly as Divine justice; for the frightful consequences of sin are intended to awaken in the man the germ of those better feelings that slumber there. And if even within the Christian world instances of all these manifold forms of vice present themselves, this is only a proof how carefully the visible church of Christ is to be distinguished from its invisible reality; nay, if even in the heart of the believer traces of some of the sins which are here denounced as heathenish are to be found, this only declares the truth, that in him too the "old man" is living, who, as such, carries with him that alienation from God which is the mother of all sin. But as in the new man, in the case of the individual believer, so also in the invisible church, in the case of that community of Christ on earth to which so much is yet lacking, there is, through the Spirit which fills her, a new principle active, which recognizes the true character of all these abominations, corrects them in itself and others, and contains within itself the power gradually to overcome them. But it is precisely this, viz., *truth existing in the very state of sinfulness, i. e.,* true repentance, which the apostle so painfully feels the lack of in the heathen world. It knows the commandment of God, it knows how deserving of death are its transgressions, and yet it not only practises them itself, but praises others also who practise them.

(*Δικαίωμα* is used here in the sense of *ἐντολή*, חק, ordinance. See on Rom. iii. 21, and on the thought itself on Rom. ii. 14, 15. The MSS. D.E.G. and several versions, contain after *ἐπιγνόντες* the words *οὐκ ἐνόησαν*, or *οὐκ ἔγνωσαν, οὐ συνῆκαν*. These additions have, however, arisen only from a misapprehension of the thought here expressed; the meaning of the apostle is this, that they not only recognized sin, but also punishment as its just desert. *Ἄξιος θανάτου* implies the idea that death is the consequence of sin *as such*, just as life is of righteousness. [See Rom. viii. 13.] The apostle had mentioned many fruits of the sinfulness of the heart, which, considered by themselves, could not be punished with death by the civil power; but in the individual they never appear isolated, and in the sight of God, who knows the inmost disposition of the heart, the lesser outward transgression is considered equally culpable, if committed under aggravating circumstances, with the grosser outward offence committed under circumstances of palliation. A man's own sinful deed commonly disturbs, by the increased force it gives to the lusts, his power of clear judgment; and therefore to take pleasure in the sins of others when one's own evil desires are more subdued, and therefore the voice of conscience is more easily heard, indicates a greater progress in sin than the sinful action itself.)

§ 4. The Condition of the Jews.

(II. 1–29.)

That condition of moral depravity amongst the Gentiles, depicted in the first chapter, made apparent the necessity of a new way of salvation; but previous to describing this way, the apostle directs his attention to the second great division of the human race, as considered from the theocratic point of view, that is, to the Jews. It is, however, only in ver. 11 that Paul begins to treat expressly of the Jews; for in the first verses he is still speaking of Gentiles, of those, namely, who had been preserved from the grosser forms of vice. He represents these as excusing themselves, and declaring the gross sinners to be alone culpable. This denial of the charge of sinfulness lay also in the spirit of the Jewish people, who were accustomed to look down upon the whole Gentile world as sinners compared with themselves; therefore the apostle, in these verses, which form a transition to the other subject, amalgamates this part of the Gentile world with the Jewish world, which must have recognized its share in the rebuke, in order that he might in the first place exhibit the degradation of the latter more plainly, by contrasting it with the excellencies of some really nobler spirits amongst the Gentiles. The apostle, therefore, first proves that the state of sinfulness does not the less exist, even in cases where it produces no such outward evil fruits. The manifestations of sin only assume a less gross and prominent form, without being on that account essentially different. None should therefore judge his neighbour, but rather judge himself, and let the goodness of God lead him to repentance, knowing that the just God punishes without fail all sin, whether refined or coarse, whether outward or inward, and only rewards the good. Now if this principle was applicable to all men, it was so in an especial manner to the Jews, who had received an express law; but on this very account they would but be more strictly punished if they had not observed this holy law, and put to deep shame by many heathens, who had walked according to their inferior knowledge more faithfully than many Jews had followed their deeper acquaintance with God. Even circumcision, the seal of their election to be God's people, had a significance only when recognized as an obligation to a faithful observance of the law. The real character of the Jew was not therefore outward, but inward, and depended on the circumcision of the heart.

Ver. 1.—The view, that the apostle from the very first verse addresses himself to the Jews alone, has been supported by Flatt, Tholuck, Rückert, and Reiche, besides other expositors; this view, however, appears, from the general character of the expressions employed by the apostle, altogether untenable. For instance, *ὦ ἄνθρωπε πᾶς*, *O every man* (in ver. 1) in connexion with *πᾶσα ψυχὴ ἀνθρώπου*, *every soul of man* (ver. 9) is so general, that Jews *alone* cannot well be meant by it.* Besides, *αὐτὰ πράσσεις*, *thou practicest*, etc. (ver. 1) taken according to the usual explanation, as spoken of the outward practice of *all* Jews, bears no proper sense, inasmuch as the Jewish people collectively were actually much more free from gross vices than the Gentile world. At the same time it is quite true that *those* Gentiles, whose condition is depicted in the first chapter, cannot be spoken of in the second (though some older commentators, *e. g.*, Calovius, have supported this view); for the persons who outwardly indulged in all the vices there delineated, certainly would not dare to judge others under the sense of their own innocence. Such persons could only be either hypocrites or idiots, with whom further argument would be useless. The connexion appears then only natural and complete, when we assume that Paul is speaking to Gentiles indeed, but only to such as lived in outward respectability, addicted to no such flagrant vices. These considered themselves better than their degraded fellow-countrymen, and therefore sat in judgment upon their sins. The Jews too stood in a similar position. In general, they were more free from gross viciousness than the Gentiles, and were hence inclined to condemn them; in this manner then, the apostle obtains an easy transition to the consideration of the condition of the Jews, in that he points out how the germ of all those vices is also slumbering in their hearts, as in those of the better Gentiles.† Augustine rightly understood the passage in this manner, and it is only thus that the argument of the apostle receives its full truth. All the Gentiles did not actually live in the commission of the crimes painted in such glaring colours in chapter i., and but few of the Jews especially; nevertheless, they are all, both Jews and Gentiles, sinners without exception, because they all bear within them the germ of all vices. The Gentiles who are commended in chap. ii. 14, 15, receive this commendation only because they assent to this truth. The apostle therefore distinguishes in his description *three classes of men*,‡ who

* Glöckler recognizes the *general* character of these expressions, but supposes still that Paul is merely speaking of the Jews; he does not, however, shew how these two views can co-exist. The first passage ὦ ἄνθρωπε πᾶς might still be construed as is done by Fritzsche, "whosoever thou art, even if thou shouldest belong to the people of God." But ver. 9 is clearly to be taken quite generally.

† Very instructive for the right understanding of this passage is Galat. ii. 15, where it is written, ἡμεῖς φύσει Ἰουδαῖοι, καὶ οὐκ ἐξ ἐθνῶν ἁμαρτωλοί. Here then also the Gentiles are called κατ' ἐξοχὴν the ἁμαρτωλοί, as the most morally sunken, according to which the Jews as a body must be conceived of as the δίκαιοι, *i. e.*, of course as the righteous after the law.

‡ These three classes we meet with again in all places and at all times, and therefore

indeed are all, without exception, sinners, but yet stand in a different relation to sin. The *first* class consists of all those who live unconcerned in flagrant vices; to this class belonged the great mass of the Gentile world, and some few individuals amongst the Jews. The *second* class consists of those who check the grosser outbreaks of sin, but nevertheless bear in their hearts the germ of sinfulness, and with it all its subtler manifestations, but without recognizing their sinful condition, and without longing for something better. To this class belonged the great mass of the Jews and individual Gentiles. Their condition is only apparently better than that of those belonging to the first class, since, while they lacked the latter's coarse sensuality and vice, they suffered from spiritual blindness and want of love, so that their apparent virtues were in fact but "splendida vitia." To the *third* class, lastly, belong those who not only have avoided the grosser outbreaks of sin, but at the same time also recognize, with penitent sorrow, their inward sinfulness, and cherish a longing for a more perfect condition. Of these alone can it be said, that they keep that law (ii. 14, 15, 26, 27) which demands love and truth. They fulfil the law of love in that humility which will not permit them to judge their weak fellow-creatures; they fulfil the truth in that repentance which teaches them to condemn their own sin, even though it does not break out into gross iniquity. A picture of this genuine Gentile piety is presented to us in Cornelius (Acts x.); and Paul can have meant only such, according to his fundamental view in ii. 14, 15, 26, 27.*

Accordingly the person mentioned in ii. 1, as judging others, is a man who has not, indeed, outwardly indulged in the same grosser sins which he condemns in others, but who is, in fact, inwardly living after a subtler form in the same corrupt frame of mind; and it is just precisely this which is expressed by the words "thou doest the same things" (τὰ γὰρ αὐτὰ πράσσεις). According to the usual interpretation, it must be, *e. g.*, a murderer who condemns another for murder, an assumption wholly unnatural, as we have already observed. According to our view, on the other hand, the man who judges the murderer does the same thing if he hates his brother. It is, however, very conceivable, that a man may not recognize the

the apostle's statement has not merely a temporary import, but depicts in an entirely objective manner the nature of the human heart in itself.

* The greater number of modern expositors have misunderstood the apostle's representation in this place. Benecke comes the nearest to the truth, but at the same time he has not accurately and pointedly conceived the character of the pious Gentiles described in ii. 14, 15, inasmuch as he also only understands by these persons men outwardly faithful to the law, without recognizing in them the elements of repentance and faith. The manner in which he approximates to the view taken by us, shews itself especially in his remarks on ver. 23, where he calls attention to the fact, that in the very act of condemning others, that very sin is incurred which in its turn condemns the condemner.

same sin in the hatred as in the murder, and will therefore set himself above his fellow-creature. In the same way, therefore, as our Lord, in the Sermon on the Mount, so here the apostle endeavours to bring to men's consciousness their sin in its radical principle.

(Διό refers to i. 32, where the knowledge of God's law is attributed to sinners. On account of this knowledge, even he who transgresses the law in a less obvious manner, and judges his fellow-man, has no excuse, for the law requires also humility and compassionate love.—Ἐν ᾧ is not to be explained by יַּעַן, but as the following τὰ αὐτά shews, by supplying ἐν τούτῳ. The stress is laid upon the fact that the person judging commits *the same* sin as the person condemned.)

Ver. 2.—The apostle illustrates the foregoing thought from the conception of Divine justice. God's judgment is an absolutely true one, and therefore punishes sin as well in its subtler as in its grosser manifestations, since the law demands its perfect fulfilment. (Κατὰ ἀλήθειαν is to be construed with κρίμα, as designating the nature of the Divine agency in the work of judgment. The verdict of men is often erroneous, God's judgment alone can judge hidden sins in accordance with truth.)

Vers. 3, 4.—In order to awaken the consciousness of sin in these persons, the apostle next points out that the impunity they had hitherto enjoyed in their sinful state was not to be considered as a token of Divine favour towards them, since the only object of God's long-suffering was to lead them to repentance. That, therefore, which the law was specially intended to produce, repentance (μετάνοια), was precisely what was still wanting in them, whilst those who are depicted afterwards (ii. 14, 15) had obtained this blessing.

(In ver. 3 λογίζῃ δὲ τοῦτο is to be understood, "But canst thou suppose or imagine this?"—Ver. 4. The expressions χρηστότης, ἀνοχή, μακροθυμία, *goodness, forbearance, long-suffering,* contain a climax describing the relation of God to this class of sinners, who are often with the most difficulty convinced of their guilt. Χρηστότης, viz., denotes goodness in general, ἀνοχή its exercise in postponing punishment, μακροθυμία, continued ἀνοχή. To all three Paul applies the expression πλοῦτος, which he frequently uses as synonymous with πλήρωμα. [See Rom. ix. 23, xi. 23; Ephes. i. 7, ii. 7, iii. 16; Coloss. i. 27.] Μετάνοια, *repentance,* denotes here, precisely as in the gospels [see on Matth. iii. 2], the painful conviction of sin, accompanied with a longing hope of help from above. Repentance is the mother of compassion, and covers a brother's sin instead of judging him. This expression is not, however, one of those in current use with Paul; it is only found besides in 2 Cor. vii. [illegible] Tim. i. 25.)

Ver. 5.—The abuse of the long-[illegible]d only leaves therefore, in the mind of the impenitent a fearful anticipation, becoming ever more oppressive, of future judgment.

(Σκληρότης denotes that state of spiritual hardness and unsusceptibility by which the influences of Divine grace are rendered ineffectual, and the exercise of repentance prevented. The form ἀμετανόητος is found only here in the New Testament. Κατά is to be taken here, "according to the measure," not, with Koppe, as standing for the *dativus instrumenti*.—The ἡμέρα ὀργῆς is to be understood of the general day of decision, of the judgment of the world, on which the manifestation of the righteousness of God, so long deferred, will infallibly take place. He, then, who despises the goodness of God is increasing his guilt against this day of decision, and therefore increasing that punishment which proceeds from God's punitive justice. In the treasured up *wrath*, therefore, the cause is put for the effect.—The substantive δικαιοκρισία is found only in this passage of the New Testament; it appears elsewhere only in a Greek translation of Hosea vi. 5. Δικαιοκρίτης is found 2 Maccab. xii. 41.—Instead of ἀποκαλύψεως, some MSS. read ἀνταποδόσεως, yet the preponderance of critical authority requires us to retain the common reading. A considerable number of MSS. read καί after ἀποκαλύψεως, and Mill, Wetstein, and Knapp have approved of this reading; yet it has probably been inserted only on account of the three consecutive genitives, and therefore it is better, with Griesbach, to erase it. The passage loses all appearance of harshness, if we consider δικαιοκρισία τοῦ Θεοῦ as one conception, the subject of the ἀποκάλυψις.)

Vers. 6–8.—This passage, which describes so simply the course of retributive justice, has been misunderstood by the Romanists and used as evidence against the Protestant doctrine of justification by faith; it has, in consequence, been interpreted with an excess of caution on the part of Protestants. We cannot, in fact, agree with them in thinking that the apostle intended to speak merely objectively of the judgment of God, and that he wished to assert, not that any one would actually, on account of his works, receive eternal life, but only that *if any one had these to shew*, he would receive it; the fact being that no one has them, because all without exception are sinful, and therefore no one can, on account of his works, obtain everlasting life. There is, indeed, no doubt that this argument is in perfect harmony with Paul's principles; but if he had intended it in this place, surely he would not immediately afterwards have spoken of Gentiles who do the works of the law (ii. 14, 15). The interpretation of the passage turns rather on our determining the import of the true ἔργον ἀγαθόν, *good work* (ii. 7), whence also the phrase ποιεῖν τὰ τοῦ νόμου, *doing the things of the law*, will be rightly apprehended. From the whole tenor of the apostle's argument, it is plain that a good work (ἔργον ἀγαθόν) cannot be understood merely of an outward work done in obedience to an outward law, which work might be combined with self-conceit and pride, but only of works proceeding from a genuine state of penitence, of which state faith always forms an element. As Abraham and other saints, before the coming of Christ, lived a life of faith, so individual pious Gentiles had also those germs of faith in their hearts, without which no good works are possible, because where they are wanting the best outward actions remain ἔργα νεκρά, *dead works*. We may therefore affirm, that God always judges men according to their works, alike those who lived *before* Christ, and those who live *after* him, because, in fact, the inward man must ever be manifested in certain outward appearances, and the latter bear testimony to the character of the former. We may, however, also say, conversely, that as well before as after Christ, men are always judged according to their faith, because it alone is the principle of good works; indeed, we might call faith itself the greatest and most important work (see at John vi. 29), inasmuch as it is the mother of all good works. The faith of men before and after Christ is not, therefore, specifically different, but different only in degree and in object. (See at Rom. iii. 21, etc., Heb. xi. 1, etc.) But as faith in its highest exercise causes men to judge themselves, in so far are believers under the New Covenant not judged at all (John iii. 18), and thus the difficulty of the present passage vanishes when viewed on this side also. The remark, therefore, of Höpfner and Usteri that Paul speaks here from a merely legal point of view, is so far well founded, as that, had the fact been otherwise, Paul would not have so expressed himself.* At the same time, the thought, although proceeding from legal premises, reaches such a universal application, that it has its truth, with regard to God's judicial dealings, for all stages of spiritual development. The distinction between the *blessedness* of heaven and the *degrees* of this blessedness, which latter depend upon the man's works, whilst faith is the condition of the former, is indeed in itself correct and scriptural (see at 1 Cor. iii. 11, etc.), but it has nothing whatever to do with the present passage. Reiche's interpretation of the passage is entirely erroneous. He would distinguish between the strict moral economy of the universe, and its limitation by the grace which is in Christ; here, he thinks, the former is alone spoken of, and the latter left entirely out of sight. But he considers the latter to be merely an amnesty *once* allowed for special circumstances, and which admits

* At the same time we find, even in 1 Sam. xxvi. 23, "The Lord recompenses every man according to his righteousness and his *faith*. On the other hand, in Ps. xxviii. 4; Eccles. xii. 14; Jerem. xvii. 10, as well as in Matth. [illegible] mention is made of works only.

of no further extension so as to embrace the world after Christ. It is manifest, however, that the very nature of Christianity, as a means of salvation, as an institution calculated for all men in all ages, would be entirely destroyed by such an assumption. The grace of God in Christ does not *restrict* the range of the moral economy of the universe, but *establishes* it upon its real principles, and gives it the fullest scope. Finally, this and similar passages (as *e. g.*, iii. 6, xiv. 10, 1 Cor. v. 13), on the subject of the last judgment, are particularly important as coming from Paul, inasmuch as we may conclude from them that Paul did not entertain any discrepant views with respect to the damnation and the resurrection of the wicked. He openly asserts neither of these (except in 2 Thess. i. 9, we find the words "eternal destruction"), and much in his epistles seems to indicate the contrary. (Comp. at Rom. xi. 32, 1 Cor. xv. 24, etc.) But from his description of the day of judgment, it is assuredly probable that, whilst Paul gave but little prominence to this doctrine, he entertained the same fundamental views as the other writers of the New Testament.

(As regards the construction, Reiche has again attempted to connect *ζητοῦσι* with *ζωὴν αἰώνιον*, and, on the other hand, to attach *δόξαν κ. τ. λ.*, to *ἀποδώσει*; but, although this connexion is not absolutely impossible, we prefer, in common with almost all expositors, the connexion of *ζωὴν αἰώνιον* with *ἀποδώσει*, in which case *δόξαν-ζητοῦσι* stands in apposition with *τοῖς μὲν κ. τ. λ.* It is assuredly, beyond denial, a very forced construction to connect *ζητοῦσι ζωὴν αἰώνιον* with *τοῖς μέν*, and throw between the accusatives, governed by *ἀποδώσει*.*—In the conception of the *ἔργον ἀγαθόν*, *good work*, we are to have respect, as has been already observed, not merely to the lawfulness of the deed, but especially to the purity of the motive, which can be nothing but faith, without which it is impossible to please God in any stage whatever of spiritual life; it stands, therefore, opposed, not only to the *ἔργον πονηρόν*, *wicked work*, but also especially to the *ἔργον νεκρόν*, *dead work*.—The addition, *καθ' ὑπομονήν* [see Rom. xv. 4; 1 Thess. i. 3; 2 Cor. i. 6], refers to the continuance of activity in well-doing, and forms the contrast with those transient ebullitions of better feelings in the heart, of which even the wicked are not entirely destitute, but which disappear as quickly as they arise. The expression may be resolved into *πᾶσι τοῖς ὑπομένουσιν ἐν ἔργῳ ἀγαθῷ*, *to all who enduringly continue in good works*. The sense of spiritual need which belongs to

* For *τοῖς δέ* in the Comm. (evidently a mere slip of the pen), I have not hesitated to substitute *τοῖς μέν*. Reiche's construction is, indeed, intolerably harsh. I doubt the precise correctness of Olshausen's. Instead of taking *τοῖς μέν* together, and *ζητοῦσι* in apposition, *i. e.*, "to the one class—seeking," etc., it seems better to take *τοῖς-ζητοῦσι* together, as the subject, giving to *μέν* its usual signification, *i. e.*, "to those on the one hand who seek," etc. So *τοῖς δὲ ἐξ ἐριθείας*, "but to those who are of contention."—[K.

those who receive eternal life is pointed out by the clause in apposition, in which ζητεῖν denotes the hungering and thirsting after righteousness. Δόξα, τιμή, ἀφθαρσία, *glory, honour, immortality*, are to be regarded as forming a climax. The future glory is contrasted with the shame, which is the lot of the humble man here below; the τιμή with that ἀτιμία in which he perceives himself; the ἀφθαρσία with that ματαιότης and φθορά with which he feels himself now burdened. —Ver. 8. Ζωὴν αἰώνιον should have been followed by the accusatives ὀργὴν καὶ θυμόν. The apostle, however, drops that construction, and finishes the sentence as if ἀποδοθήσεται had preceded. Θάνατος, also, should strictly have been opposed to the idea of *life* in the preceding clause; ὀργὴ καὶ θυμός finally denote, as in ver. 5, the cause instead of the effect.—The expression οἱ ἐξ ἐριθείας is founded upon the figure of the being born of a certain element, an idea elsewhere expressed by υἱός or τέκνον. [See Phil. i. 16, 17, 1 John iv. 5.] The word ἐριθεία* is found in the classics only in Aristotle (Polit. v. 2, 3); he uses it in the sense of "faction, party." Its etymology is doubtful; it may come from ἐριθεύω (from ἔριον, "wool") which means "to work in wool," and then "to work" in general, "to work at a person, to seek to bring a person over to one's own side;" or it may come from ἔρις, "strife," and from the verb ἐρίζειν, when it would signify "love of strife." This meaning is best suited to its use in the New Testament. [See 2 Cor. xii. 20; Galat. v. 20; Phil. i. 16, ii. 3; James iii. 14.] Since here ἐριθεία is opposed to ἔργον ἀγαθόν, it can naturally denote only rebellion against God, to which is opposed devotion and praise to God. In this condition the man believes himself to possess all that is necessary for him, and is, therefore, without spiritual desires and aspirations. The apposition καὶ ἀπειθοῦσι κ. τ. λ., gives here a more exact description of the state of the godless, as, above, the ζητοῦσι κ. τ. λ., of the condition of the righteous. The root of their sin is disobedience to the truth. To truth, falsehood should properly be opposed; the apostle, however, puts for it ἀδικία, inasmuch as this, as the opposite to δικαιοσύνη, comprehends falsehood in itself.)

Vers. 9, 10.—The apostle repeats once more the same thought for the sake of greater emphasis, but, in the first place, with that modification which is usually found in the New Testament accounts of the Divine judgments, namely, that the gracious acceptance of believers, and not the just rejection of unbelievers, is mentioned *last*, so as to leave upon the mind the cheerful impression of that redemption which has been accomplished (see on Matth. xxv. 41–46); and, in the second place, with a more distinct reference to the Jews, whose condition alone he considers in fuller detail in what

* With respect to ἐριθεία see the Excursus of Fritzsche, vol. I. p. 143 sqq.

follows. In fact, in the case of the Jews, both blessing and curse must necessarily manifest themselves with increased intensity, since they had much fuller means of becoming acquainted with God, as the following representation illustrates. The Jews, therefore, are so far from being exempt from the general judgment as the chosen people of God, that it visits them the more severely in case of unfaithfulness.

(The opposite to *στενοχωρία*, viz., *εὐρυχωρία*, is not found in the New Testament, though used by classical writers. The word denotes, like *θλίψις*, the *spiritual* punishment of sin, since, in this place, it is not the earthly consequences of wickedness that are spoken of, but the punishments inflicted at the *ἡμέρα ὀργῆς*, *day of wrath* (ver. 5), on which account also it is said *πᾶσα ψυχὴ ἀνθρώπου*, *every soul of man*, which cannot be said of earthly punishments, since many wicked men escape them altogether. In the same way glory, honour, and peace [*δόξα, τιμή, εἰρήνη*] refer here only to life in its inward aspects [see ver. 16]; for, to all outward appearance, the contrary is the case in this world, on which account the natural man, in his false security, supposes that he shall be able to escape the judgment of God (ver. 3). The more special definitions of ver. 7, 8, are here resolved into the abstract terms *κακόν* and *ἀγαθόν*. The verb *ἔρχεται* or *ἔστι* must be supplied.)

Ver. 11.—The higher position of the Jews, *simply* on account of their physical descent from Abraham, a prerogative which they were always so ready to assert against the Gentiles, is denied by the apostle on the grounds of the impartiality of God; the free improvement and application of those means to which each man has access, is that which alone determines his character in the sight of God (see on Matth. xv. 14, etc.) The privileges of the Jews, there fore, only heightened their *responsibility*. The faithful use of them alone enhanced their value. There is, however, here no allusion to converts from Judaism; the apostle is rather treating the subject, as well in regard to Jews as Gentiles, entirely irrespectively of individuals, in order to demonstrate from it the necessity of some other way of salvation than that which the law presented. The substantive *προσωποληψία* is also found in Ephes. vi. 9; Coloss. iii. 25; James ii. 1.)

Vers. 12, 13.—As the cause of the greater responsibility of the Jews, and the lesser responsibility of the Gentiles, the apostle brings forward the law of Moses, which the Gentiles did not possess. But the grace of God always supposes the exercise of free will in man, and therefore wherever this grace is at work, the guilt of man may be increased through the abuse of his freedom.

(*Ἀνόμως*, *without law*, is not intended to express here the absolute absence of all law,* as ver. 15 shews, but only the want of the positive law of Moses. In 1 Cor. ix. 21, ἔννομος is found as the opposite to ἄνομος. The opposite terms διὰ νόμου and ἀνόμως are naturally to be understood as signifying, "with or without reference to the law of Moses." The "perishing without law" (ἀνόμως καὶ ἀπολοῦνται) is startling; we might expect that they would not be judged at all. But as no one is absolutely without law, he shall be judged according to his knowledge. Neither, therefore, can the perdition be considered as absolute. In the same way we find, Luke xii. 48, that he who knew not his Lord's will received *few* stripes, but by no means *none at all*. We shall reserve for Rom. iii. 21, the more exact determination of the meaning of δίκαιοι, and δικαιωθήσονται, and only mark here their general opposition to ἀπολοῦνται and κριθήσονται. In this passage σώζεσθαι, *saved*, might have been substituted for δίκαιος εἶναι or δικαιοῦσθαι, *justified*, since it is only the Divine acknowledgment of the existing δικαιοσύνη which is intended; and of course God, who is eternal truth, cannot recognize anything which does not exist. The ποιηταὶ τοῦ νόμου, *doers of the law*, have therefore, in Paul's opinion, a certain δικαιοσύνη, *righteousness*, at all stages of their spiritual life. But since the performance of the law before regeneration is that which is here spoken of, the δικαιοσύνη which God recognizes in the doers of the law, can of course only be understood of their *own* righteousness (ἰδία δικαιοσύνη). This must, however, be recognized as far as it goes; it is by no means, in consequence of hereditary sin, a matter of indifference, whether a man endeavours to observe the law or not. The righteousness of the law, in its genuine form, that is to say, when the man retains the consciousness of his own need, prepares the way for the reception of that righteousness which is by faith, whilst unfaithfulness renders it more difficult. For that opinion, of which we have already spoken in our observations on ver. 6, which affirms that the apostle is here only speaking *hypothetically* of the performance of the law, since that was altogether beyond the power of sinful man, is plainly inadmissible, since he speaks in the verses immediately following of Gentiles who do perform the works of the law. That this, however, does not deny the truth, that man in his natural state is unable to keep the law, will be shown in the following remarks. De Wette's interpretation of the passage is entirely wrong; for he asserts that ver. 13 refers altogether to the Jews, and that Paul only returns to the mention of the Gentiles in ver. 14. Rather does ver. 13 refer to all who keep the law, whether they be Jews or Gentiles; but since

* In classical writers ἀνόμως is only found in the signification of "contrary to law;" even in Isocrates Panegyr. p. 28, edit. Mori, this meaning is to be retained, although in this passage the other meaning "without law," is also interwoven. (See Alberti observatt. in New Testament, p. 473.)

the possibility of observing the law might seem scarcely conceivable in the case of the Gentiles, it is explained in ver. 14 how far this may be predicated of them also.

Vers. 14, 15.—In order to prove that question of observing the law applies also to the Gentiles, the apostle proceeds to demonstrate, in *the first place*, that a law was in fact also given to the Gentiles. He defines this law as one written in their hearts (νόμος γραπτὸς ἐν ταῖς καρδίαις), which expression forms a contrast with the law of the Old Testament, which was engraven on tables of stone (see 2 Cor. iii. 2, 3), and obviously means by this term the voice of God in the conscience, which makes itself heard, however indistinctly, even in the most degraded state of the heathen world. But with respect to the relation which this inward law bears to the outwardly given law of Moses, we must allow that the latter is not only more clear and definite, and much more exact in its demands, but also that it stands much higher on this account especially, that it claims most expressly to be the law of *God himself*. The want of this distinct reference of the law to God, in the case of the inward law of the heathen, manifests itself most clearly by the struggle of their thoughts; for the language of lust and sin always succeeds in making itself heard in conflict with this better voice, because the latter is not expressly recognized as that which it really is, the voice of the Most High God; at the same time, the more indistinct the inward law appears, the more exalted is the faithfulness of those who yield obedience to its weak and confused admonitions. The difference, therefore, between the law of the heathen, and the clear law of Moses, invested as it is with undoubted Divine authority, is immense, and, in consequence, the advantage of the Jews in the possession of this law was very great also. At the same time, this difference appears somewhat diminished by the fact, that the Mosaic law with all its definiteness, required for any particular case an application determined by the mode in which it was conceived and interpreted; and this naturally depended as much upon the entire state of mind of the individual Jew, as the interpretation of the inward law upon that of the individual Gentile. However, the number of the purely external commandments was so great, that, by means of them, even in those characters amongst the Jews, in which the moral feeling was but little developed, there was continually preserved alive the consciousness of a God, who comes to men with inexorably strict requirements. But still more important than the information, that even the Gentiles were not absolutely without law, is, in the *second place*, the express assertion of the apostle, that they were also in a condition to follow this law, to keep its commandments, and to fulfil it (see vers. 26, 27). It has already been remarked (on ver. 1), that this is not to be understood merely of an external and legal observance of it, in that this would by no means deserve to be called the fulfilment of the law (ἔργον ἀγαθόν, ver. 7), but that the necessary condition of every good work, *faith and love,** which never exist without one another, must also be presupposed in the case of the pious Gentiles. But now the question arises, how is this assertion to be reconciled with the doctrine, that it is only through the grace of Christ that really good works can be produced? Through Christ a pure and holy principle of life has been acquired for man, the Divine seed (σπέρμα τοῦ Θεοῦ), which is absolutely without sin, even as God. The regenerate, in whom this principle dwells, cannot sin (1 John iii. 8); the sins of the regenerate are, in fact, only the utterances of the sinful old man, who at some moments forces back the new; but the essential principle of their life remains untouched by sin. (See further at Rom. vii. 25.) Such an absolutely pure principle wrought neither in the Gentiles, nor in general in the period before Christ; it was first made attainable by men on the completion of the work of Christ. (See on John vii. 39.) Hence, also, the doctrine of the sinfulness of all men without exception, even of those who do the work of the law, retains its full truth; for, in the first place, not only is he under sin who commits it *constantly* or *often*, but also he who commits it only once, or only transgresses the law under a single aspect. (See at Galat. iii. 10.) If, therefore, the devout Gentiles sometimes, or even often, followed their better motions, yet they did not always do so, and therefore they remained sinners. But again, our conception of sin varies widely, according to the degree of our spiritual knowledge. Even the better Gentiles were in this respect but little advanced, and their performance of the law must always, therefore, be but *relative;* he only, who fails not even in a single word, can be reckoned entirely perfect and without sin. (James iii. 2.) The possibility of a *relative* fulfilment of the law is, however, in contradiction neither to the scriptural nor church doctrine of the sinfulness of human nature; both Scripture and the church only deny the possibility of an *absolute* fulfilment of the law.† On this account, also, the *relative* obedience of the Gentiles cannot of course *as such*, be taken as the foundation of their eternal blessedness, this could only be supplied by such an absolute holiness as is possible to no mere man; but in connexion with that whole frame of mind, which even a merely relative fulfilment of the law presupposes in a Gentile, it *can* form such a foundation, inasmuch as it may render him capable

* With respect to the sense in which it may be said of the Gentiles also, that they have faith and love, further remarks will be found in the notes to Matth. xxv. 31, etc., Rom. iii. 21, etc., Heb. xi. 1, etc.

† This manifests itself particularly in the doctrines of the *gratia universalis et actus manuductorii ad conversionem.*

of receiving, in penitent faith, the salvation which is offered in Christ. As, therefore, the true children of Abraham are the children of promise in Christ, so also are the devout Gentiles, because they also are true children of Abraham. (See ii. 28, 29.) This appropriation of the salvation which is in Christ on the part of the Gentile world, is recognized in Scripture as possible in the doctrine of the "descensus Christi ad inferos."

A limitation of the conception of a fulfilment of the law, on the part of the Gentiles, is therefore by all means required; still, with all the necessary restriction, this passage yet contains a most consolatory truth. Even in the wilderness of the heathen world, does the apostle teach us, the λόγος σπερματικός had scattered his precious seed; there were Gentiles, who, by a certain conviction of their sins, had become humble and contrite, who had an earnest desire to be faithful to the light which was vouchsafed them, who cherished longings for a better spiritual state, and therefore possessed the capacity for apprehending Christ, when he presented himself to them, whether in this or a coming state. These elements sufficed, in their position and relations, to constitute a foundation for eternal blessedness; in fact, that which did not accrue to them here, they received in the regions of the dead, after Christ's manifestation there. (See at 1 Pet. iii. 18.) Humble faithfulness then, the apostle would say, to our knowledge, however small, of Divine truth, *in case our ignorance be not self-incurred*, will, whatever be our position and grade of culture, receive its reward. Unfaithfulness, on the other hand, even when accompanied by the greatest privileges, receives at all times its deserved punishment. But the reward of the Gentile world, so far as it was well-pleasing to God, was this, that it was capable of being led to Christ, because it possessed in *repentance* the capacity of apprehending him. It was not, therefore, even in the case of the pious Gentiles, *works as such*, which were the condition of their salvation, but the germ of faith from which they proceeded. That which they retain of undiscovered sin is forgiven them without works, through the merits of Christ, as they inherited this without conscious guilt from Adam. Christ appears, therefore, as the Redeemer of all those who do not positively reject him, and retain the capacity for receiving him into their hearts. (See at Acts x. 34–36.)

(It is wholly erroneous to understand ὅταν ποιῇ of a merely ideal *possibility*; the apostle plainly speaks of an *actual* reality (vers. 26, 27); because there do really exist pious Gentiles, Paul concludes they must have some law or other which they follow. Ὅταν, with a following subjunctive, no doubt denotes a merely possible, but also a frequently recurring relation, with respect to which it is only left indeterminate *where* and *when* it actually occurs. Paul means not to designate any particular persons, but certainly to affirm *that such exist*. [See Matthiæ's Greek Gr. § 251, Winer's Gram. p. 255.] Bengel, followed by Rückert, takes φύσει with ἔχοντα, but both its position and the sense demand its connexion with what follows. It was, in fact, unnecessary to remark that the Gentiles had *not* anything by nature, since the Jews especially already rated their condition low enough; but it was very needful to call attention to the fact, that they could without higher support obey the law in a certain measure. Φύσις, has here a doctrinal significancy. It denotes in the New Testament, 1, the natural constitution of anything, as in Rom. i. 26, xi. 21-24; Galat. iv. 8; or the natural descent after the flesh, as in Galat. ii. 15; 2, the condition of man without the grace of God, as he is flesh born of the flesh. [John iii. 6.] In this sense it is found Rom. ii. 27, and especially in Ephes. ii. 3, 4. Paul, therefore, manifestly supposes that in the fallen nature of man the seeds of something better still remain, which, in individual characters, sometimes attain to a remarkable development, producing a complete susceptibility to gracious influences. So, *e. g.*, in the Canaanitish woman. [See at Matth. xv. 22, etc.] The natural man finds himself indeed burdened with a "proclivitas peccandi," but no "necessitas peccandi," so far at least as *action* is concerned; but for the conquest of evil desires, and an inward conformity to the Divine law, he is wholly inadequate. The words ἑαυτοῖς εἰσι νόμος, *are a law to themselves*, are not intended to deny that God is the author of this inward law also, but merely to intimate that the Gentiles are not *conscious* of this connexion, and, therefore, in so far appear as if they were a law to themselves. The inward law of God, which exists indeed constantly in man, and makes itself known to him unmistakably by the motions of his conscience and the inward conflict of his thoughts, will herafter at length *become manifest to all* in the actual *consequences* of obedience or disobedience to this law [ἐνδείκνυνται ἐν ἡμέρᾳ κ. τ. λ.], in that many will wonder that so many heathens are deemed worthy to sit down with Abraham, and Isaac, and Jacob, in the kingdom of heaven, whilst so many *Jews* are excluded.—Ἔργον τοῦ νόμου, *work of the law*, I cannot consider with Tholuck as pleonastic, nor can I regard it with Reiche as synonymous with the plural τὰ ἔργα, for individual works are not written in the heart of man, since they are elicited by circumstances. The apostle's intention is rather to declare that there is not merely a knowledge of the law in the *minds* of the Gentiles, but also that their *will* has the power to a certain degree of observing this law. On this account the man's thoughts may justly accuse him, because he actually had the power to abstain from the sinful *deed*. And, therefore, ἔργον is to be considered = τὸ ἐργάζεσθαι. Glöckler takes it similarly, as that which the law is intended to produce, viz., righteousness In the same way that Paul speaks of a law written in the heart (*νόμος γραπτὸς ἐν ταῖς καρδίαις*), so also Plutarch [Moral. vol. v. p. 11, edit. Tauchn. ad princ. in erud. c. 3] of a law not written outwardly in books, but dwelling in the soul [*νόμος οὐκ ἐν βιβλίοις ἔξω γεγραμμένος, ἀλλ' ἔμψυχος ὢν ἀνθρώπῳ*]. It is that law of the mind [*νόμος τοῦ νοός*] of which Paul treats, Rom. vii. 23, and of which we shall speak at greater length at that place. But *συνείδησις*, *conscience*, possesses always, in addition to the knowledge of the law, the consciousness in itself of being able and bound somehow or other to observe that law. At the same time, this original law must be accurately distinguished from that which, according to Jerem. xxxi. 33; Heb. ix. 10, is written in the hearts of the regenerate by the Spirit of Christ. This latter is the absolutely perfect law, which communicates at the same time the highest power for its fulfilment, and, therefore, also strengthens the will; the former is a weak glimmer of that light which filled the heart of the first man.*—*Συμμαρτυρεῖσθαι* is only a stronger form of *μαρτυρεῖσθαι*, *i. e.*, to testify, and thereby bring before the consciousness. *Λογισμός* is also found 2 Cor. x. 5. *Διαλογισμός* [i. 21], *διανόημα*, *νόημα*, are more common expressions to denote the operations of the *λόγος* or *νοῦς*. The accusing principle is that of the Divine Spirit, the excusing that of the natural life; this inward heaving and tossing of the thoughts is wanting in those who are wholly dead, but also in those who are perfectly sanctified, whose souls enjoy peace like that of the unruffled mirror of the ocean. This inward conflict, then, as more fully described by Paul in the 7th chapter, is but a melancholy advantage, a consequence of the awakening of the inner life, a witness of our lost original holiness, and yet it is better than death.)

Ver. 16.—With an implied reference to ver. 5, the apostle transfers this manifestation of the state of the Gentile world, of which the Jews in particular would know nothing, to the decisive day of judgment.

(Reiche has defended the old way of connecting ver. 16 with ver. 12, so that vers. 13–15 form a parenthesis. However, this connexion has its difficulties, not so much on account of the length of the parenthesis, as of the contents of vers. 13–15. For the subject of these verses stands in the closest connexion with ver. 12, and forms the foundation of the ideas expressed in the last verse; they cannot, therefore, be regarded as parenthetical. The whole difficulty of the passage disappears if, with Bengel, we lay the emphasis upon

* In the Rabbinical writers the law in the conscience is called דַּת טְבְעִית, or also תּוֹרָה טִבְעִית from טֶבַע, nature. (See Buxtorf. lex. rabb. et talmud. p. 352, and 1349.) The opposite to this is formed by the תּוֹרָה שֶׁבִּכְתָב, lex quæ scripta est scil. in tabellis lapideis.

ἐνδείκνυνται, are manifested, in ver. 15. Conscience and the accusing and excusing thoughts are no doubt always at work in the heart of man, but are not manifested in conjunction with their consequences. This shall take place in the case of all, as well of those who have followed the admonitions of the inner voice, as of those who have neglected them, only at the day of judgment. [See on Matth. xxv. 31, etc.] It is only by this construction too, that ἐνδείκνυνται forms a fitting contrast to τὰ κρυπτά, *the secrects;* those inward transactions which take place in the depths of the soul generally remain quite indiscernible, on which account the apostle deems it necessary in this place to bring them before the consciousness of his readers in general, and of the Jews amongst them in particular. They remain indeed hidden not merely to others, but in their real nature, to the man's own self, in that the *good* consider themselves worse, and the *evil* better than they are. The parable in Matth. xxv. 31, etc., is therefore in this respect an excellent commentary on the present passage. Alike, the acquitting and the condemning voice of conscience in the day of judgment, seem here brought to view. Other explanations of the relation of ver. 16 to what has gone before, such as Heumann's view, that vers. 13–15 might have been written afterwards by the apostle on the margin, or Koppe's opinion, that μεταξύ is to be taken in the sense of μετέπειτα, are altogether untenable. In itself μεταξύ can indeed signify "afterwards" [see at Acts xiii. 42], but here its connexion with ἀλλήλων will not allow of this meaning.—Christ is here, as ever in the New Testament, represented and conceived of as carrying into effect the last judgment of the world. [See on Matth. xxv. 31, etc.; Acts vii. 17, 31.]—The addition κατὰ τὸ εὐαγγέλιόν μου, *according to my gospel,* does not refer, as was erroneously supposed by the ancients, to a written gospel of Paul's, but designates merely the spirit and substance of his evangelical preaching.)

Vers. 17–20.*—Paul now finally directs himself to the Jews *in a definite address,* and in the first place brings forward prominently all those advantages which had been vouchsafed them, in order then to make them perceive how little they had shewn themselves worthy of them, and how therefore they could make no boast of superiority to the Gentiles, amongst whom noble natures were to be found. It has been erroneously concluded, as already remarked in the Introduction, from this address, that there must have been in Rome a party of rank Jewish Christians. Paul however speaks, as already observed in the Introduction, not of Jewish Christians, but entirely objectively of all the Jews and all the Gentiles in the world, and this definite address can therefore be regarded only as a rhetorical figure. If therefore there were even amongst the Roman Christians

* On the passage ii. 17–29, see Augustine, de spir. et litt. c. 8.

as is probable, those who had formerly been Jews, yet these were not affected with a Judaising tendency; but this is the only point of importance in the question respecting the composition of the Roman church.

(The reading of the textus receptus ἰδέ has been rightly rejected by the greater number of modern critics and exegetical commentators; εἰ δέ has not only the most important critical authorities in its favour, especially A.B.D.E. and others, but is also favoured by the connexion. To be sure an anacoluthon is occasioned by it, but it is probably only to the endeavour to get rid of this that ἰδέ owes its origin.—Ἐπονομάζειν, ἐπαναπαύειν are sonorous words chosen on purpose to mark distinctly the excessive self-conceit of the Jews. On the form καυχᾶσαι, see Winer's Gr. p. 72. Ἐν Θεῷ intimates God's special relation to Israel as its covenant God.—Δοκιμάζειν τὰ διαφέροντα is found also Phil. i. 16. Δοκιμάζειν implies not merely examination, but consequent recognition and approval; διαφέρειν marks difference either for the better or worse; in the New Testament only for the better. The objective law of God is taken as the rule of the examination.—In consequence of this position of privilege; the Jews, blind to their own glaring unfaithfulness, arrogated to themselves the most decided spiritual authority over the Gentiles, whom they regarded as altogether blind in comparison of themselves. Ὁδηγὸς τυφλῶν, *guide of the blind*, alludes no doubt to Matth. xv. 14. This tendency in Judaism to overrate their mere outward calling had developed itself most strongly amongst the Pharisees. Ἄφρονες, *foolish*, and νήπιοι, *babes*, have this difference, that the former denotes a low degree of knowledge [in this case of Divine things], the latter a low degree of spiritual development in general.—The description of the law as a μόρφωσις τῆς γνώσεως καὶ ἀληθείας, *form of knowledge and truth*, still indicates an advantage on the side of the Jews; the Gentiles had not even a typical representation of essential truth. At the same time by the choice of the word μόρφωσις it is implied, that in the Old Testament the substance itself was not yet given. Μόρφωσις is used here in the sense of picture, outline [see 2 Tim. i. 13, iii. 5], like the σκιά as contrasted with the σῶμα. [Coloss. ii. 17.] Knowledge [John xvii. 3] and truth [John i. 17] are *essentially* imparted in the New Testament, and not merely typically.)

Vers. 21-24.—In what follows, the unfaithfulness of the Jews is presented in the most glaring contrast with their assumptions. Notwithstanding their possession of the Divine law, the Jews transgress its holy commandments in particular cases outwardly, and the great mass of them inwardly, in cherishing evil desires; and thus, by their openly immoral or arrogant conduct, and that want of real self-knowledge which it betrays even to the pious Gentiles, they injure the cause of truth, instead of promoting it according to God's will by faithfulness and humility. And whilst in such a condition themselves, they wish yet to teach others, in the feeling of their proper vocation to be teachers of the world; but to them may be applied those words of the Psalmist (Ps. l. 16, 17), "What hast thou to do to declare my statutes, or that thou shouldest take my covenant in thy mouth, seeing thou hatest instruction and castest my words behind thee?"

(The answering clause [the apodosis] of the sentence should properly have followed in ver. 21, with perhaps a *διατί, why?* but instead of this, the apostle drops the construction.—I prefer, with Knapp, not to take the following sentences interrogatively; the address becomes more emphatic by the definite declaration, Ye are unfaithful.—In the mere external sense, it is impossible to understand these sins as committed by all the Jews; for as now, so also then, the great mass of the Jews lived in outward morality, especially in respect of sexual intercourse.—*Βδελύσσεσθαι*, to entertain abhorrence, particularly against idolatrous practices; therefore *βδέλυγμα* = שִׁקּוּץ, an idol. [1 Kings xi. 5; Isaiah ii. 8.] With this, however, *ἱεροσυλεῖν* forms no proper contrast, meaning only to plunder or rob the sanctuary. But no doubt covetousness, the national sin of the Jews, was present to the apostle's mind when he made choice of this expression; covetousness he regards as an inward idolatry [Col. iii. 5], so that the contrast thus comes out clearly: "Thou abhorrest idols, and yet, in thy covetousness, thou thyself practicest idolatry."* No doubt *ἱεροσυλεῖν* cannot in itself mean, "to indulge covetousness," but *ἱεροσυλεῖν* as the most daring manifestation of the covetous spirit, may be used to express that which is its motive.† Israel was in God's purpose intended to exhibit to the Gentiles a picture of truly holy national life; its unfaithfulness therefore dishonours God himself; it causes the Gentiles to say, "The God of this nation cannot be the true God!" This fearful effect of Israel's sin [which is repeated in the case of all who are called upon at any period to be the focus of Divine life and by unfaithfulness fall away from their vocation], is already rebuked by the prophets of the Old Testament. See Isaiah lii. 5; Ezek. xxxvi. 20; another parallel is, 2 Sam. xii. 14.)

Ver. 25.—Paul, however, by no means loses sight of the prerogatives of Israel (see iii. 1, etc., where he considers them at greater

* Stier, in his "Andeutungen" (part ii. p. 267), follows Luther, who says on this passage, "Thou art a thief towards God, for honour belongeth unto God, and this all self-righteous persons take from him." The connexion, however, points to actual sin, not to mere self-righteousness.

† An example of such sacrilege is related by Josephus (Arch. xxii. 6, 2), who tells us that the presents of the rich proselyte Fulvia were pilfered by the Jews, to whom they had been entrusted.

length); he only shews that they demand faithfulness to those responsibilities which are connected with them by God, if they are not to turn to their deeper condemnation. The apostle, therefore, pre-supposes, in all stages of spiritual life, the possibility of a certain measure of faithfulness and moral earnestness, corresponding to the degree of knowledge; and the personal condition of the individual is determined by his exercise of this faithfulness.

(Circumcision is here regarded as the seal of the Divine election, so that in it all theocratical privileges are considered as consecrated. The Jews, therefore, with their materializing tendencies, attributed the greatest value to the outwardly performed rite of circumcision. In consequence of this view, it is declared in the Talmudic treatise Shemoth [see Schöttgen on the passage], that in the case of Jews who are damned, the foreskin must first be outwardly restored. The Gentile world is therefore also called at once *ἀκροβυστία* = עָרְלָה, *uncircumcision*, as unclean, lacking the sign of the covenant.* Ἐάν in ver. 25, as in ver. 26, is used not merely conditionally, for Paul does not overlook the transgressions of the Jews, and the faithfulness of many Gentiles; but like ὅταν in ver. 14, of a certain fact which remains uncertain only as to the cases of its actual occurrence.

Vers. 26, 27.—If such a degradation of the Jew to a lower station as to privilege and honour was conceivable to him, from the dreadful threatenings under which the Old Testament demanded obedience (see Deut. xxviii. 15, etc.); yet the reception of the Gentiles to grace was to him inconceivable. And yet the apostle asserts this also, and sets the Gentiles before the eyes of the Jews as rebuking the latter by their good conduct.

(Δικαίωμα = ἐντολή, the particular command of the general νόμος.—In the phrase λογίζεσθαι εἰς περιτομήν there is an evident allusion to the λογίζεσθαι εἰς δικαιοσύνην in iv. 3; that which they have not is imputed to them as if they had it. Now the ground of this imputation is this, that though they have not indeed the sign, they have instead of it the germ of the reality which the sign represents, viz., the covenant with God of a good conscience, which they maintain faithfully, according to the small measure of knowledge which they have of God; and therefore they may not untruly be regarded as having the sign also, ver. 27. Καί is best taken as carrying on the question with οὐχί understood. Κρίνειν of course merely marks the essential rebuke which unrighteousness always receives from righteousness. [Matth. xii. 42; Heb. xi. 7.] The connexion of ἐκ φύσεως is uncertain; at first sight its position seems to necessitate its connexion with ἀκροβυστία, denoting natural in con-

* The form of the word in pure Greek was ἀκροποσθία. See on this point Fritzsche, vol. i., p. 136.

trast with spiritual circumcision. Thus Tholuck, Rückert, and Reiche. Still, plausible as is this construction, I cannot regard it as the right one. For, in the first place, *ἐκ φύσεως* added to *ἀκροβυστία* is wholly superfluous: if Paul had thereby wished to distinguish born Gentiles from Jews with Gentile sentiments, as is the meaning of *ἀκροβυστία* in ver. 25, he must have added *ἐκ φύσεως* to *ἀκροβυστία* at once in ver. 26; but since he twice uses *ἀκροβυστία* in ver. 26 without this addition, it appears out of place in ver. 27. On the other hand, the contrast with *ὁ διὰ γράμματος καὶ περιτομῆς παραβάτης*, imperatively demands that *ἐκ φύσεως* be referred to human nature left to itself, whilst *γράμμα* [= *νόμος*, or *νόμος γραπτός*, 2 Tim. iii. 15, in so far as it is contemplated amongst the Jews as something externally given, and contrasted with the man] and *περιτομή* denote the grace of God, in which the Israelites made their boast. Thus Koppe rightly, but he made the mistake of referring *ἐκ φύσεως* immediately to *τελοῦσα*, a construction conflicting with the order of the words. But the case is otherwise, if we take *ἀκροβυστία τὸν νόμον τελοῦσα* as forming *one* conception: *ἐκ φύσεως* then becomes related to this one collective thought, and the whole idea comes out clearly, while its reference to *ἀκροβυστία* alone introduces some awkwardness. The meaning of the words is then "that Gentile world, which, without special help from above, observed the law, judgeth thee who, in the possession of this special help from above, transgressest the law." Beza's interpretation of *διά* as instrumental, making the sense, "the law and circumcision were to the Jews *occasions* of sin," expresses a thought in itself correct; but it is improbable that Paul should have so far anticipated the course of his argument as to introduce it here; he reserves it to a later stage of the discussion [vii. 14]. Rückert rightly derives the application of *διά* here from its local signification "*through*, hence, with, during, under the circumstances."* See Rom. iv. 11, xiv. 20. The meaning, "notwithstanding, in spite of," which Glöckler supports, is unprecedented. The way in which Meyer endeavours to justify this meaning, "breaking through, as it were, its limits," is in the highest degree forced.)

Vers. 28, 29.—In these verses is contained the key to the whole of the apostle's argument in the first two chapters of the Epistle to the Romans. Paul conceives in a very profound manner the contrast between Jews and Gentiles. It is not bodily physical descent, or the circumcision of the flesh, which constitutes the true son of Abraham, but conformity to Abraham's life of faith (for their ancestor, Abraham, had also sons who were not partakers of the

* That is strictly, *διά*, *through*, either as separative; hence, *between*, *in the midst of*; or as continuative, hence; *during*, *along with*, *attended by*; thus: "those who through, in the midst of, attended by, the letter," etc.—[K.

promise, Rom. ix. 7; Galat. iv. 22), and that circumcision of the heart by which the sinful *προσαρτήματα τῆς ψυχῆς* are removed. In the outward, natural Israel, there exists therefore a heathen world, which God, in that great judgment which visited the Jews at the destruction of Jerusalem, condemned, whilst the few genuine Israelites were either received into the Christian Church, or preserved for later times as the germs of a new generation (Rom. xi.) But in the Gentile world also there is to be discovered an Israel—that is to say, a number of noble souls, truly susceptible to all that is more elevated, for whom the Divine promises are not less intended than for Israel after the flesh, for those at least of it who belong also to the spiritual Israel; still, it is not to be denied that, under like circumstances, the children of Abraham after the flesh had a more comprehensive vocation, so that, for instance, there could not have been Gentiles numbered amongst the Twelve, nor could Christ have been born with the same propriety of a Gentile mother. (See at John iv. 22.) This view is not found merely amongst the later Rabbinical writers,* who might have adopted it from the effects of Christian influence, but also in the Old Testament Scriptures. These not only demand the circumcision of the heart (Deut. x. 16, xxx. 6; Jerem. iv. 4, compared with Coloss. ii. 11; Phil. iii. 2), but also represent the true children of God as scattered throughout all the world, and amongst all nations. Thus especially in Isaiah xliii. 5, etc. Here the Lord commands that his children be brought from the ends of the world, "even every one that is called by his name, and whom he has created for his glory." It is not the dispersion of Israel after the flesh amongst all nations, that is spoken of in this passage; by these, then, can only be meant the nobler souls scattered amongst all nations, those in whose hearts the *λόγος σπερματικός* has deposited its seeds. In the same sense the Redeemer speaks of other sheep, which are not of this fold, *i. e.*, of the community of Israel after the flesh. (See at John x. 16, xi. 52, and, in the Old Testament, Micah ii. 12.) According to this scriptural conception, therefore, the election of God appears in complete harmony with the free self-determination of man. In the case of every man, whether much or little have been entrusted to him, all depends upon the personal faithfulness with which he improves the privileges to which he has been called; and by the faithful employment of that which has been vouchsafed to him the most insignificant may out-

* Compare the remarkable words of Rabbi Lipmann, in the Nizzachon, p. 19. "Irrisit nos Christianus quidam dicendo: mulieres quæ circumcidi non possunt, pro Judæis non sunt habendæ; verum illi nesciunt, quod fides non posita sit in circumcisione, sed in corde. Quicunque vero non credit, illum circumcisio Judæum non facit; qui vero recte credit, is Judæus est, etiam si non circumcisus." Reiche adduces a very striking passage from Plutarch (de Isid. et Osir. p. 352), where, on the principles of the heathen religions, the same is said of the genuine worshippers of the gods.

strip the man to whom the greatest gifts have been entrusted, and who yet shews himself unfaithful. The difficulty returns upon us, however, with increased strength, when, penetrating deeper into the subject, we regard faithfulness itself as a fruit of grace; this, however, will be considered at Rom. ix. The whole passage, finally, is remarkable, as exhibiting the manner in which the apostles and writers of the New Testament explained the Old; *verbally* indeed, but by no means *literally*.

(Ver. 28.—The γάρ is to be explained by the thought implied in ver. 27, "Jews can also be rejected." To this, then, as its reason, is annexed the thought, that the true idea of the Jew as a member of the theocratic nation, and of circumcision as the seal of the theocratic covenant, is not an outward but an inward one. External descent from Abraham, the external rite of circumcision, has no significance without the inward foundation of a right disposition. Κρυπτός, as the opposite of φανερός, used of the moral disposition, is also found 1 Pet. iii. 4.—Ver. 29. Οὐ γράμματι, is difficult from the indefiniteness of the relation of the contrasted ἐν πνεύματι. The contrast of γράμμα and πνεῦμα is not essentially different from that of σάρξ and πνεῦμα. As body is the covering of the spirit, on which the spirit stamps its impress, and without which it does not reveal itself personally on earth—so, in Scripture, the letter is the transparent veil of the spirit, giving it its fixed and determinate form. Thus then we should find expressed in it the contrast of the outward and the inward, the φανερόν and κρυπτόν. But the contrast already expressed in these terms can scarcely be repeated by γράμμα and πνεῦμα without tautology; and hence it is better, doubtless, here, with Beza, Heumann, Morus, and Reiche, to understand γράμμα, as in ver. 27, of the law, but of course of the law conceived in its purely literal aspects. For, regarded in its profounder character, the πνεῦμα was also in the law. Rückert, therefore, is not wrong in understanding πνεῦμα of the New, γράμμα of the Old Testament, for the spirit in the Old Testament is precisely the New in consummation. [Matth. v. 17.] Ver. 29 is therefore to be understood thus: "but the inward Jew and the circumcision of the heart is the *true* circumcision, in that it contains the reality of the thing represented by the outward sign, after the spirit and not after the mere letter." The concluding clause, οὗ ὁ ἔπαινος, κ. τ. λ., refers, of course, to the leading idea, that is, to the true Jew, or perhaps to πνεῦμα, which amounts substantially to the same thing; the judgment of God on man, as the true judgment, is opposed to the false judgment of man, which is determined by outward appearances. Ἐκ is here highly appropriate, for a commendation pronounced *by* man can also be *from* God, if it is a just one.)

§ 5. Comparison of the Jews and Gentiles.

(III. 1–20.)

This spiritual view of the relation between the Jews and the Gentiles might, however, as the apostle, not without reason, feared, be easily misunderstood. Paul, therefore, finds it necessary to call attention to the fact, that this representation of the relation was by no means intended to depreciate in themselves those advantages which the Jews possessed above the Gentile world; on the contrary, he recognizes them as of the greatest importance. But these advantages had annexed to them the *condition of faith*, and this condition had not been fulfilled by the mass of the nation; although, therefore, the promises of God had been accomplished notwithstanding their unbelief, yet the people of Israel, as such, had lost their theocratical prerogative, and the spiritual Israel alone, composed of Jews and Gentiles, had, as the true children of faithful Abraham, received the promise. Under this view of the connexion, the difficulties disappear, which have been supposed to embarrass this portion of the Epistle to the Romans. The apostle does not at all lose the thread of his argument (so that it were necessary to assume, as even Reiche still proposes, that it is resumed only at Rom. ix. 4), but he here, so far as was needful, completely obviates the objection. For that no δεύτερον follows the πρῶτον in ver. 2, is naturally accounted for by the fact, that this *first* which is adduced, includes all else which could still have any claim to be mentioned. The passage iii. 9, stands, however, in no contradiction with ver. 2; for, whilst this passage treats of the original calling of the Jews, the former speaks of the actual state of their relations to God, which had been introduced by their unbelief. All the promises of the Old, as well as the New Testament, are, in fact, conferred upon the *condition* of believing obedience; if this does not exist, they are, *eo ipso*, annulled, nay more, the blessing is converted into its direct opposite, the curse. (See Deut. xxviii. 1, etc., 15, etc.) Paul might, therefore, have expressed himself even more strongly than he does in iii. 9; he might have said, "the Jews have not only no advantages over the Gentiles, but the Gentiles are now preferred to them, they have been grafted into the olive tree in place of those branches which have been hewn off." But, according to Rom. xi. 20, etc., the same condition holds good also of the Gentiles, and they may, through unbelief, just as well forfeit their calling to privileges, as the Jews did before them. Chapters ix.—xi. are therefore a kind of extended commentary upon this passage, but without being a continuation of what is here begun.

Vers. 1, 2.—With a glance back at the foregoing exhibition of the sinfulness of the Jews, the apostle now asks, what then has become of the privileges of the Jews? Their sinfulness had placed them on a level with the Gentiles, for the law had not at all in their case attained its exalted object. The law was intended to produce the ἐπίγνωσις ἁμαρτίας, *knowledge of sin* (iii. 20), that is to say, true repentance, instead of which, on account of their unbelief, and its consequent unfaithfulness, it only produced sin itself, and indeed the very worst form of sin, the exact contrary to repentance, the arrogant opinion that they were without sin, and as the descendants of Abraham after the flesh, were already heirs of the kingdom of heaven. Nevertheless, the Divine promise retained its objective reality; those Jews, who apprehended in faith the salvation offered to them in Christ, received also his full blessing, notwithstanding the great body of the nation forfeited it.

(Τὸ περισσόν stands, like τὸ γνωστόν in i. 19, substantively in the sense of "advantage, prerogative." Here also we are not, as Reiche justly remarks, to regard Paul as disputing with actual personages: the discussion is wholly objective.—The opposite to κατὰ πάντα τρόπον is found in 2 Maccab. xi. 31, κατ' οὐδένα τρόπον.—No doubt πρῶτον μέν points, in its mere *form*, to other advantages, which Paul intended to name. But he felt quite rightly, that all was in *reality* contained in the one which he had adduced. In the interpretation of ἐπιστεύθησαν, Reiche is inclined to the view of Koppe and Cramer, who translate, "the Divine promises were confirmed to them." But its usual meaning "confide," manifestly accords better with the connexion, in which their own faithlessness [ἀπιστία] in keeping the trust is adverted to. The Divine faithfulness [πίστις] is mentioned only in consequence of this ἀπιστία. [On the well-known construction of the passive see Winer's Gram. p. 237.] The λόγια τοῦ Θεοῦ are no doubt primarily the promises [Acts vii. 38; 1 Pet. iv. 11; Heb. v. 12], especially those of the Messiah and the kingdom of God, to which all the others had reference. But inasmuch as these promises constituted the essential part of Holy Scripture, the whole word of God is also indicated by this expression.)

Ver. 3.—It is not altogether easy to follow the course of the apostle's thoughts in this transition; Tholuck has, however, already rightly supplied the links which are wanting. The apostle presupposes the notorious fact of the unbelief of the Jews, just at the time when the promises were being fulfilled, and deduces from thence that even if the blessing was lost to the nation collectively, it yet, according to God's faithfulness, remained even now confirmed to individual believers, and should hereafter also belong to the whole of Israel when God should have led them back by wondrous ways. (Rom. xi. 26.) He forbearingly calls the unbelievers *τινές* in the hope that many in Israel might yet turn to Christ. See ix. 1, etc.

(For *ἠπίστησαν* the MS. A. reads *ἠπείθησαν*, because the *λόγια* were taken as synonymous with the law. It is explained more in accordance with Paul's views by regarding unbelief as the root of disobedience. [See at John xvi. 9.] With regard to *πίστις*, *πιστεύω* and its opposite *ἀπιστέω*, see at Rom. iii. 21. On *καταργεῖν*, which occurs so frequently with Paul, see at Luke xiii. 7, the only place in the New Testament in which it is found except in Paul's writings. In the LXX. also it occurs but four times.)

Ver. 4.—With man's unfaithfulness is now contrasted the unchangeable faithfulness of God, who can form for himself, in spite of sin, the inheritors of his promises. For God's promises cannot be fulfilled without the existence of persons to accept them ; he is, therefore, not only true in giving and keeping his promises for his own part (since, if *all* men were unfaithful, they would surely not remain unfulfilled), but he is also faithful in creating such as are worthy to receive them. In chap. ix. this idea is carried out more at length, and it is only when thus understood that the words, "if we believe not, yet he remaineth faithful, he cannot deny himself," receive their full meaning. The streams of Divine grace, when repelled on the one side, turn themselves to the other, and form for themselves, amongst Jews and Gentiles, organs for the kingdom of God, without, however, operating by constraint, without any prejudice to man's freedom, nay, rather really establishing and completing it.

(Μὴ *γένοιτο* answers to the Hebrew חָלִילָה, which is thus translated by the LXX. [See Gesenius' Lexicon under חָלִיל.] It is also frequently found in Polybius, Arrian, and others ; particularly often with Paul in the New Testament, thus in the Epistle to the Romans iii. 6, 31, vi. 2, 15, vii. 7, etc. To translate *γινέσθω δέ*, "let it be rather so, God is faithful," etc., is forced. Reiche justly observes, the imperative only expresses emphatically the irrefragable nature of the assertion. Πᾶς *ἄνθρωπος ψεύστης*, *every man a liar*, is taken from Ps. cxvi. 11. It has in so far its perfect truth, that man in his separation from, nay, even opposition to God, who has alone essential being and truth, becomes untrue and unfaithful ; so far as he is good and true, it is God in him. Whenever, therefore, this Divine truth takes up its abode in a heart, the man confesses himself to be untrue without God, and with this first truth begins his true life. [See at ver. 10.] For further confirmation, Ps. li. 4 is quoted exactly after the LXX. In this Psalm the struggles by which the soul works its way out of the night of sin are described in an inimitable manner. David wrestles, as it were, and contends with God, who, by the operation of his Spirit, convinces him of his sin ; the con-

fession of David is the victory of the truth in him. On a larger scale the same struggle is going on in this sinful world, and the moment in which any individual emerges into the element of light is that in which he makes the confession here expressed. God is ever the victor when the creature ventures into a controversy with him—a controversy always involved in any distrust of his providences—appearing as just in all his promises.—*Δικαιοῦσθαι* means here "to be recognized as just." See at iii. 21.—The parallelism would certainly lead us to understand *λόγοι* here primarily of law-suits, as in Acts xix. 38, but it stands, in Paul's application of the passage, parallel to *λόγια*, ver. 2. Accordingly, *κρίνεσθαι* in the apostle's use of it can only be taken as passive, although, according to the original text, the active meaning should predominate.)

Ver. 5.—According to the apostle's view, therefore, God is the only good being, the Good in all good, so that even the best man has no merit; sin alone is man's property, and his fault; while yet even this must serve to manifest God's glory and excellence the more brightly. This relation of truth to falsehood, of righteousness to unrighteousness, man, in his estrangement from God, does not recognize; he thinks that God could not punish sin if it produced what was good. But the good belonging to it is the work of God, not of sin; sin still remains, what it is, that, namely, which deserves a curse, and has its punishment in and from itself.

(*Δικαιοσύνη* and *ἀδικία* are here to be taken in the most general sense, see on Rom. iii. 21.—*Συνιστάνειν* signifies here to represent, and by representation to make anything known in its real nature. Rom. v. 8.—The formula *τί ἐροῦμεν* is frequent with Paul, especially in objections. Rom. vi. 1, vii. 7, ix. 14.—The formula *κατὰ ἄνθρωπον λέγω*, *I speak as a man*, is treated happily by Reiche at this passage. He justly observes, that the meaning of this phrase of such multifarious significations is to be determined solely by the context. It may be used either of the way of all men, or of the majority, or of a certain class of men. Here it is most appropriately referred to the natural man as alienated from God, who is without true knowledge of God, and is therefore incapable of forming a judgment of God's dealings. In the passage Rom. vi. 19, *ἀνθρώπινον λέγω* is used instead, for which in profane writers *κατὰ τὸ ἀνθρώπινον*, *ἀνθρωπίνως*, *ἀνθρωπείως λέγω* are found. See the passages cited by Tholuck on vi. 19.)

Vers. 6, 7.—The unreasonableness of the above question is demonstrated by Paul from that truth which all Jews acknowledged, that God would judge the *Gentile world;* this would be impossible, if, the fact that man's unrighteousness exalts the righteousness of God, precluded him from punishing sin. For then the Gentile might also say, "My sin, too, has magnified God's righteousness, how then can I be condemned as a sinner?" Reiche has proved, by convincing arguments, in opposition to Tholuck and Rückert, that ver. 6 is not to be understood of the universal judgment, but only of the judgment of the Gentiles, who from the Jewish point of view were considered as the *world* in its proper sense, as sinners pre-eminently (ἁμαρτωλοὶ κατ' ἐξοχήν, Galat. ii. 16). In fact, it is only in this way of understanding it, that the argument can hold, because we prove that which is uncertain by that which is acknowledged. For it was only with respect to the Gentiles that a Divine judgment was considered certain; regarding *themselves*, the Jews had made it a question (ver. 5). To this may be added, that it is only by this explanation we can gain any distinct notion of the person referred to in κἀγώ, *I also*. "I also," says the Gentile, "might claim exemption from judgment, for of me also the same holds true." The only thing which could be urged against this reference of the passage to the Gentile world with any show of reason, is that this Jewish notion of the judgment which shall visit the Gentile world is false, and that Paul would not argue from an error. But this view of the Jews was not in and of itself false, it only became false in consequence of their supposing that this judgment would concern the Gentiles *only*, and not the Jews also. Now it is precisely this very falsehood in it that the apostle combats, and we need, therefore, surely feel no scruple about assuming his argument to be as stated above.

(As regards the use of κόσμος for "Gentile world," I cannot with Reiche so explain it in Rom. iii. 19; 1 Cor. xi. 32,* but no doubt the context imperatively demands it in Rom. xi. 12; 1 Cor. i. 21. This meaning may be unhesitatingly assigned to the word, since its general idea, "that of the creature in its alienation from God," may be restricted to the Gentile world, as representing the corruption of the creature in its most glaring colours. —Ψεῦσμα is not found elsewhere in the New Testament. In opposition to ἀλήθεια it denotes that entire state of falsehood, *i. e.*, alienation from God, from which all the particular utterances of sin proceed. The Divine δόξα is here the knowledge of God's sublime attributes, which are brought out more distinctly by the contrast of man's sin)

Ver. 8.—As at all times, so even in the apostle's day, the gospel was reproached as tending to *promote* sin,† and teaching men to

* In his explanation of Rom. iii. 19, this scholar rightly understands the whole human race to be meant by κόσμος. His adducing the passage as above, can therefore only be an oversight.

† Of such hypocritical slanderers Luther says, "God grant us grace that we may be pious sinners (that is, poor in spirit, humble), and not *holy slanderers* (that is outwardly

do evil that good might come; yet this did not deter him from declaring God's faithfulness amidst our unfaithfulness. Paul therefore finds himself obliged (vi. 1 etc.) to refute this error with greater care, and to expose it in all its absurdity. The man who can make such an assertion as this pronounces his own condemnation, by showing that the nature of Divine grace, and of that love which it kindles in the heart, is wholly unknown to him. Doubtless, it was men such as the Judaisers, whom Paul had to oppose in Galatia, who circulated such blasphemies.

(With respect to the construction καὶ μή is to be taken as an anacoluthon; the apostle intended at first to proceed with ποιήσωμεν but afterwards connected the principal thought by means of ὅτι immediately with λέγειν in the parenthesis. The conjecture ἔτι is therefore as inadmissible as the omission of ὅτι.—Ἔνδικος, that which is founded ἐν τῇ δίκῃ, is only found besides in the New Testament at Heb. ii. 3.)

Ver. 9.—After obviating these misunderstandings of that important truth, that the unfaithfulness of men does not annul the faithfulness of God, the apostle could bring forward the concluding thought of the whole argument contained in the first two chapters, and assert, *that all Jews as well as Gentiles are under sin.* He in no way contradicted by this assertion his previous declaration as to the great advantages of the Jews (iii. 1), for to every Jew who acknowledged his sinfulness, in whom, therefore, the law had accomplished its purpose, in stopping his mouth (ver. 19), and awakening him to a knowledge of his own sin and need of redemption (ver. 20), these privileges were still available in their fullest extent. But to those τινές (ver. 3), who formed the mass of the nation, these advantages were no doubt lost, for in them the truth had so far yielded to falsehood, that they no longer even retained the fundamental truth of confessing their own sinfulness, but boasted of external things as of essential privileges. Hence only the true inward Jews, amongst Israelites and Greeks, the poor in spirit, the humble, hungering and thirsting after salvation, these only, received the promise. But since it was in every one's power to become such an one, in that he only needed to give up his active resistance to the Spirit of truth, which bore witness to him of his sin, no one could complaim; God appeared just, as in his promises, so also in their fulfilment.

(Τί οὖν; is best taken as a separate sentence. It is found complete Acts xxi. 22. Προέχω is found no where else in the New Testament; in the active it means "to have advantage over," *præstare.*

observers of the law, apparently holy, but really proud). For the Christian is in the state of becoming such, not in the state of having become so; whosoever therefore *is* a Christian, is no Christian, that is, whosoever thinks that he is already a Christian, whilst he is only becoming one, is nought."

But in this case the passive form springs from the meaning "to prefer," a usage completely established also in classical Greek; "are we then preferred by God?"* The meaning "to advance as a pretext," hence, "have we anything to urge in palliation?" which Meyer and Fritzsche have lately defended after Ernesti, Morus, Koppe, etc., is allowed indeed by the word, but unsuited to the context. For the question is not, whether the Jew has anything to defend himself with, to allege in his defence, but whether or not he has any advantage over the Gentiles. In *οὐ πάντως*, the negative particle could no doubt limit the meaning of *πάντως*, = "not in every respect;" but the context demands that *πάντως* be taken as giving emphasis to the negation, *nequaquam*. If persons have demurred about giving to *πάντες* its full signification, and have wished to explain it by *πολλοί*, although the *οὐδὲ εἷς* which follows leaves no doubt as to the apostle's meaning, this has arisen from a misapprehension of the proper nature of the *ἀκροβυστία νόμον τελοῦσα* [ii. 27], to which assuredly we must naturally suppose a *περιτομὴ νόμον τελοῦσα* [xi. 4] to correspond in every age of history. This misapprehension has presented a considerable obstacle to a well defined conception of this section in the case of the greater number even of modern expositors. A more detailed explanation of this subject will immediately follow in the notes upon verses 10-18.—*Προαιτιάομαι* is found nowhere else in the New Testament.—In the words *ὑφ' ἁμαρτίαν εἶναι* sin is represented as a tyrannical power from which a *λύτρωσις* is needed. [See on Rom. vii. 1, etc., and vii. 14. *Πεπραμένος ὑπὸ τὴν ἁμαρτίαν*.] The two parallel passages, Rom. xi. 32; Galat. iii. 22, throw a striking light upon this passage. See the exposition of them.)

Vers. 10-18.—Since nothing is more intolerable to the high-spirited natural man than the confession of his sinfulness, *i. e.*, not only of individual sinful actions, but of sinful corruption in general, and the inability to do anything good of himself, the apostle justly applies all his power to the proof of this point. By a long succession of passages from the Old Testament, he proves that the word of God corroborates his doctrine, in that it denies to *every man, without exception*, a true righteousness. The question now arises, how are the assertions of the apostle, ii. 14, 26, 27, to be reconciled with the present text. For there individual Gentiles were spoken of who observed the law, and we must of course assume, that this could be said of multitudes of pious men among the Jews. (See Luke i. 6.) The usual assumptions that the apostle is speaking only of his contemporaries, or secondly, that the observance of the law is only to be understood of an external observance, and not of that in-

* Better, I think, to regard *προεχόμεθα* as Mid. in Act. sense: "do we have ourselves above?"—"do we surpass?" "are we superior?"—[K.

ward law as more strictly defined by Christ in his Sermon on the Mount, or lastly, that the words of the apostle refer only to the mass, and may yet admit particular exceptions, are (without denying the truth contained in the second remark) still mere ways of escaping from the difficulty, rather than of satisfactorily solving it. The last view is especially erroneous, namely, that particular exceptions are to be admitted to the general rule of man's sinfulness, for the apostle's whole demonstration of the necessity for a new way of salvation for all men without exception, rests upon the fact that all, without exception, are sinful. As already indicated above, but *one* interpretation of the passage is possible, and by this all Paul's ideas preserve their full harmony. The apostle, namely, understands by the faithful men who observe the law, such as unite with earnest endeavours to walk in conformity with their knowledge, an humble insight into their spiritual poverty, and real need of redemption, men of whom the centurion Cornelius (Acts x.) furnishes us with an example. These faithful persons are then so far from being excluded from the universal sinfulness, that they confess themselves in the most decided manner to be sinners, and acknowledge the justice of the charge which the Word of God brings against them.* Those, in whose minds the earnest endeavour to keep the law is not united with humility, have but a mere apparent righteousness, inasmuch as that law, all whose commandments may be reduced to love and truth, they grossly violate in its innermost substance by their want of love, and denial of their alienation from God. To them, therefore, apply the apostle's words in Rom. ii. 1. All men, therefore, without exception, are sinners; the only difference between them is this, that some give honour to the truth, and acknowledge themselves as such, and in their case the law has accomplished its purpose and they are ripe for the gospel; whilst others are either in a complete state of death, and serve sin without any rebuke from conscience, or if impelled by conscience to a certain legal striving they thus only accumulate to themselves fresh sin, viz., proud self-complacency, and contempt of others.

(In the Codex Alexandrinus the collection of texts which Paul here adduces are adopted into Psalm xiv., doubtless only from this passage.—Vers. 10–12 are cited freely from Ps. xiv. 1–3.—*Συνιῶν* = מַשְׂכִּיל.—'Εκκλίνω = סָר.—'*Αχρειόω* is not found elsewhere in the New Testament, but frequently in Polybius.—Ver. 13 is from Ps. v. 9. The image is probably derived from beasts of prey.—'Εδολιοῦσαν is a Bœotian form for *ἐδολιοῦν*. The words *ἰὸς ἀσπίδων ὑπὸ τὰ χείλη αὐτῶν* are from Ps. cxl. 3.—Ver. 14 is after Ps. x. 7. The Hebrew text has מִרְמוֹת which does not mean *πικρία* but deceit. Probably the

* This confession is the first work in them, which is wrought in God, whence they do not shrink back from coming to the light. (See notes on John iii. 20, 21.)

LXX. had another reading.—Vers. 16, 17 are taken from Isaiah lix. 7, 8.—*Σύντριμμα καὶ ταλαιπωρία* answer to שֹׁד וָשֶׁבֶר.—Ver. 18 is from Ps. xxxvi. 1, *Ἀπέναντι τῶν ὀφθαλμῶν αὐτῶν* = לְנֶגֶד עֵינָיו. These passages of the Old Testament refer indeed undeniably in their primary connexion to more special relations, but these the apostle recognizes as types of the universal; and justly. For every germ of sin contains within it the possibility of all the different forms which it can assume, and no one is without this germ. The more entirely, therefore, the inward eye is opened, the more ready is man to recognize in his heart the source of every error whatever. Even the least leaven leavens the whole lump; and man is in God's sight only either *entirely* holy, or *entirely* a sinner.)

Ver. 19.—The delineation of sinfulness in the above-cited passages has so objective a character, that it applies not only to the Jews, but equally well to the Gentiles. The law of nature also forbids such manifestations of sin not less than the written law of Moses. Therefore the apostle, in conclusion, considers the position of men with respect to the law quite universally, and declares that the law condemns every one who has such sinful motions in himself, and that as none can entirely acquit himself from these, every one, without exception, falls under the curse of the law. The connexion requires that *νόμος* be taken in the same sense in vers. 19 and 20; but as the conclusions which Paul derives from the substance of the first two chapters are entirely general, therefore *νόμος* must also in this place signify in the most general sense the law as such, as well the Mosaic law (and that especially in its moral requirements) as the law written in the heart (ii. 15). No *formal* reference therefore is here intended to the passages above cited, but only to the substantial thought which they express. *Every* law forbids such sins to those who are subject to it. Reiche most inconsistently understands by *νόμος* the law of the Jews only, and yet proceeds to refer *πᾶς ὁ κόσμος*, *all the world*, to all men. The context indeed imperatively demands the latter reference, but on this very account *νόμος* must also be taken in the most comprehensive sense.*

(The expressions *λέγειν* and *λαλεῖν* are here accurately distinguished; the former denotes rather speech in its intellectual char-

* I believe that Reiche is right; that ver. 19 does refer directly and formally to the above-cited passages from the Old Testament; and that *ὁ νόμος* refers (as the article clearly indicates) specifically to the Jewish law. The passage is cited to meet the inquiry whether the Jews have any *essential* superiority to the Gentiles; and after quoting from the Old Testament a passage which affirms universal sinfulness, the apostle adds most naturally, that such a declaration made by the law of course applies to those who are its immediate subjects. This becomes perfectly consistent with the application of *πᾶς ὁ κόσμος* to all men, by merely assuming a very slight and natural ellipsis: "it saith to those who are under the law in order that (thus by bringing down the Jew to the level of the Gentile) *every* mouth," etc. Thus then we take *ὁ νόμος* (ver. 19) of the revealed Jewish law; *οἱ ἐν τῷ νόμῳ* of Jews; and *νόμος* (ver. 20) of law in general.—[K.

acter, in its production of thoughts and words ; the latter, the mere outward utterance of our conceptions. The dative λαλεῖ τοῖς ἐν τῷ νόμῳ is of course to be taken thus, "this it declares for those living under the law," *i. e.*, in order that they may fulfil it. By the expression οἱ ἐν τῷ νόμῳ we are led, indeed, to think, in the first place, of ii. 12, where it denotes the Jews ; but the context in the present passage is too distinctly general to allow us to retain this meaning here. We must, therefore, understand the thought as including all those who are subject to the sphere of the law, without its having particular respect to the wider or narrower sphere of law, amongst Jews and Gentiles.—Στόμα φράσσειν is a strong expression for "to reduce to silence," in this case by convincing of unrighteousness. Ὑπόδικος, fallen under δίκη, is not found elsewhere in the New Testament. Most interpreters, even Tholuck and Reiche, erroneously understand ἵνα in this place as denoting result, and not purpose. The strong delineations of man's sinfulness, in Scripture, have the *object* of excluding every excuse. Calvin rightly said, long ago, "ut præcidatur omnis tergiversatio, et excusandi facultas.")

Ver. 20.—As the great and decisive result of his whole argument concerning the nature of sin, the apostle therefore, with a retrospective glance at Rom. i. 16, 17, sets forth this truth, that man in his natural condition cannot attain to true δικαιοσύνη, *righteousness*,* by means of the works of the law, because the law produces only the conviction of sin. And therefore the revelation of a new way of salvation was needed, in accordance with which δικαιοσύνη should be revealed and communicated *without law;* and this way both Jews and Gentiles had to follow in order to obtain salvation. (Ver. 21, etc.) The impossibility of attaining to δικαιοσύνη by ἔργα νόμου, *works of law*, is founded, in fact, upon the absolute character of the law, in consequence of which the *smallest* transgression, and that only *once committed*,† constitutes a transgression of the *whole* law, and that *for ever.* (Galat. iii. 10.) Human weakness (σάρξ) cannot, without the help of the Divine Spirit (πνεῦμα), satisfy these absolute requirements. It is, moreover, by no means the purpose of the law to realize in man true righteousness (Galat. iii. 19, 21), but only to present moral perfection as the object of his endeavours, to produce thereby a sense of sin (ἐπίγνωσις ἁμαρτίας) and thus pave the way for the reception of the gospel. (Galat. iii. 25.) This ἐπίγνωσις ἁμαρτίας is, however, by no means to be regarded as a mere un-

* The first half of this verse, like the parallel passage in the concluding words of Galat. ii. 16, appears to be a reminiscence of Ps. cxliii. 2.

† The popular feeling has embodied this truth in a proverb: He who has once stolen is, and ever remains, a thief; [Once a thief always a thief] even if he never steals anything again, yet he remains for ever one who has stolen. Thus the transgressor in the smallest matter retains also for ever the character of a sinner in the sight of the holy God, until the ἄφεσις τῆς ἁμαρτίας and δικαίωσις have erased this *character indelibilis.*

concerned *knowledge about sin;* (this may be possessed by one who is entirely unawakened, and in whom the law has not at all done its work ;) but as a true knowledge of its nature and reality. This can only be conceived as existing in connexion with deep sorrow on account of it, and a lively, longing desire to be delivered from it. The ἐπίγνωσις ἁμαρτίας is, therefore, synonymous with that μετάνοια, *repentance*, unto which, as the proper fruit of the Old Testament economy, John the Baptist baptized those who came to him. (See on Matth. iii. 1.) It relates not merely to *particular* unlawful actions and their unpleasant *consequences*, but to *sin itself*, to that sin which affects the whole man, and thus to the *habitus peccandi.** But sin in its true nature is always *unbelief* (John xvi. 9), from which, as their source, all other sinful outbreaks proceed. We may, therefore, affirm, that the ἐπίγνωσις ἁμαρτίας, as the λύπη κατὰ Θεόν, *sorrow after a godly sort* (2 Cor. vii. 10), has necessarily the germ of faith already existing in it. It is only truth which can discover falsehood in its true character, only πίστις, *faith*, which can fathom ἀπιστία, *unbelief*. Although, therefore, the law brings down the *curse* (Galat. iii. 10), and man, under the consciousness of sin, bitterly experiences this curse, yet this feeling again always contains within itself a *blessing;* the deepest repentance is, on this very account, the farthest from *despair*, because the humble and contrite heart, as an already believing heart, is well pleasing to God (Ps. li. 19), and because it is only out of that which he has already reduced to *nothing* that the Lord creates *something*, that is to say, the new man created in Christ Jesus unto good works. (Ephes. ii. 10.)

SECTION II.

(III. 21—V. 11.)

EXHIBITION OF THE NEW WAY OF SALVATION IN CHRIST.

Having thus laid the foundation for his superstructure of doctrine, by proving the *necessity* of a new way of salvation, the apostle proceeds to describe this way itself. In this everything assumes a different aspect from that which it wore under the Old Testament ; instead of the demands of the law we hear the voice of grace ; instead of works faith is presupposed ; and yet the law is not abolished but

* Stier distinguishes in a very striking manner (Andeut. P. ii. p. 269) between the ἐπίγνωσις ἁμαρτίας and the mere ἐπίγνωσις τοῦ δικαιώματος τοῦ Θεοῦ (i. 32, ii. 2), which alike the depraved and the apparently reformed may bear in their conscience.

rather confirmed (iii. 21–31). Of this way of salvation, says Paul, even the Old Testament itself gave intimations, *especially* in that Abraham, the great progenitor of Israel, was justified by faith and not by works, and only received circumcision as a sign and seal of that faith which he had whilst yet uncircumcised. Faith in Christ, therefore, was indeed a *new* way of salvation, and yet, after all, the ancient way, which all the saints had trodden (iv. 1–25). This is therefore the only way which leads to the desired end, and even the sorrows, which are connected with walking in this way, must minister to man's perfection. For, instead of the spirit of fear, the spirit of love will be thereby shed abroad in his heart—of love enkindled by the exceeding abundant love of Christ (v. 1–11).

§ 6. THE DOCTRINE OF FREE GRACE IN CHRIST.

(III. 21—31.)

Before we enter upon the explanation of this important passage, the citadel of the Christian faith, we must explain the leading terms, which Paul employs in communicating his ideas, and throw light upon the *various points of view* from which they have been considered. To the leading conceptions with which we have to do in apprehending Paul's doctrine, belongs, primarily, δικαιοσύνη [righteousness], by which word is denoted the common object as well of the Old as of the New Testament dispensation. In the definition of this term, the common mistake has been, either to enumerate too many meanings of it, deduced from a mere superficial view of particular passages (thus Schleusner gives it not less than fourteen significations), or, as Bretschneider and Wahl, whilst assuming fewer meanings, to neglect to develope them from the fundamental meaning. Notwithstanding several separate treatises on this term, as those of Storr (in his opusc. acad., vol. i.), of Koppe in his fourth Excursus to the Epistle to the Galatians, of Tittmann (de synonymis N. T. i. p. 19, seq.), and of Zimmerman, we are yet in want of a thorough development of this important term from its radical meaning. I therefore propose the following essay to the consideration of scholars.

The root of δίκαιος, δικαιοσύνη, and all expressions connected with it, is δίκη, whose fundamental meaning is "manner and way, right relation," as Timæus explains in his Platonic Lexicon, ὁ τρόπος καὶ ἡ ὁμοιότης. This term came to be principally applied in common language to the relations of law, and δίκη therefore denoted the right relation between guilt and punishment, between merit and reward. As applied to earthly affairs, the terms thus used in accordance with their fundamental signification, present no difficulty; but when transferred to spiritual matters the manifold character of the relations creates obscurity. We best distinguish here two relations, first that of God to men, and secondly that of men to God; from this distinction arises the following difference of meanings. Since in God, as the absolute Being, all qualities are absolute, we must conceive of the *δικαιοσύνη* in him as absolute, so that he orders all relations with absolute justice. God's inherent righteousness (*justitia Dei, quâ justus est*) manifests itself therefore differently according to the different characters of men; towards the *wicked* as *punishing*, towards the *good* as *rewarding*. Hence *δικαιοσύνη*, applied to God and his relation to men, has not merely the signification of *punitive justice*, but also that of *goodness, grace*. That צְדָקָה, in the language of the Old Testament, as well as of the Rabbinical writers, is also used in the same manner, has lately been proved at length by Tholuck. (Exposition of the Sermon on the Mount, p. 347, etc.) (Comp. Ps. xxiv. 5; Prov. xxi. 21; with Matth. i. 19, vi. 1; 2 Cor. ix. 10.) But as regards, in the second place, the position of man with respect to God, this is, first of all, in his present condition, a disturbed relation to God, *ἀδικία*. The right relation, the *δικαιοσύνη*, must be sought after by him. But this endeavour can only gradually attain its object. Man, in his alienation from God, commences, namely, with considering that law of God which meets him from without as something *external*, and by sincere endeavours, corresponding to his knowledge, to observe this as an *outward* law, he enters into a relation to God which is relatively true. On this account there is ascribed* to him a righteousness of the law (*δικαιοσύνη τοῦ νόμου*, or *ἐκ νόμου*), a righteousness of *his own* (*δικαιοσύνη ἰδία*, Rom. x. 3; Phil. iii. 9), because the man renders this obedience with, so to speak, his *own* powers, those moral powers which remain to him after the fall, without the operation of grace. But if we consider the matter more deeply, we must of course regard these powers also as of God, and man's own righteousness also as incapable of being produced without God and his co-operation; though grace in its proper and special sense does not yet appear operative in this case. But man is not to stop with this relatively true condition, rather must he arrive at an absolutely right relation; not merely his outward act, but his inward disposition and inclinations must be conformed to the Divine law. But this, as presupposing an inward transformation, man cannot of himself, and by his own strength, accomplish; hence it is called *δικαιοσύνη Θεοῦ*, or *ἐκ πίστεως* = *διὰ πίστεως* (Galat. ii. 16), because God gives it, and man receives it in *faith*. In this case it is God himself in man, Christ in us, who

* Paul also uses, as equivalent to this, the words *δικαιοῦσθαι ἐξ ἔργων νόμου*, or *ἐν νόμῳ*, *διὰ νόμου*, see Galat. ii. 16, 21, iii. 11.

satisfies that which God demands of him,* and, therefore, that which on the side of evil exhibits itself not as substance, but as a mere relation, has on the side of good in its completion passed into *substantiality;* for nothing is really good but God himself and his influences ; but where he works there he also *is*. From these considerations we very easily explain the use of the expressions derived from *δίκαιος*. Δικαιόω = הִצְדִּיק, denotes the Divine agency in calling into existence *δικαιοσύνη*, which of course involves the recognition of it as such. Δικαιοῦσθαι = צָדַק, denotes, on the other hand, the condition of the *δίκαιος εἶναι*, and of being recognized as such. In both expressions, at one time, the notion of making righteous, or of being made righteous, at another, that of accounting or declaring righteous, or being accounted or declared righteous, comes forward the more prominently, but always in such a way that the latter presupposes the former. Nothing can be reckoned or declared righteous by God which is not so. Δικαίωμα = *τὸ δίκαιον* signifies that which is right in any particular relation, so that it may be taken as synonymous with *ἐντολή*, מִצְוָה, חֹק. Δικαίωσις, on the other hand, denotes the act of *δικαιοῦν* taken abstractly, the making righteous (Rom. iv. 25, v. 18). In two passages, Rom. v. 16, 18, the signification of *δικαίωμα* passes over into that of *δικαίωσις* ; which cases are, however, accounted for by the peculiarity of the context, as will be shewn in the exposition of the passage.

From this explanation it is plain that the common rendering of *δικαιοσύνη*, by "virtue, uprightness," proceeds from the Pelagian and Rationalistic view of the subject, and is, therefore, at most, only admissible for the *δικαιοσύνη τοῦ νόμου*. For the righteousness which is by faith it is wholly unsuited ; we shall therefore best translate *δικαιοσύνη* by "righteousness," and, indeed, "the righteousness of God,"† since the expressions "justification," or "righteousness which avails in the sight of God," so far as they are considered as synonymous with "recognition as righteous," do not, at all events, express the immediate and original meaning of the word, as the phrase *γίνεσθαι δικαιοσύνη Θεοῦ ἐν Χριστῷ, become the righteousness of God in Christ*, 2 Cor. v. 21, evidently proves.

To the common goal of *δικαιοσύνη*, therefore, two ways lead ; first, that by the *νόμος*, *law*, secondly, that by *χάρις*, *grace*. With both of these, on the part of man, are connected certain corresponding acts, with the law, *works* (*ἔργα*), with grace, faith (*πίστις*). These terms now equally need a closer definition. With respect, first, to

* Therefore it is termed in Paul's writings *δικαιοσύνη ἐκ Θεοῦ* (Phil. iii. 9), which is equivalent to *δικαιωθῆναι ἐν Χριστῷ* (Gal. ii. 17), because union with Christ by faith (*εὑρεθῆναι ἐν Χριστῷ*, Phil. iii. 9) is the means of obtaining it.

† See Augustine (de spir. et litt. c. 9), who observes with great justice : "justitia Dei, non quâ justus est, sed quâ induit hominem, cum justificat impium."

the term *νόμος*, *law*, this designates, in its widest sense, the Divine will, so far as it meets man with certain *requirements*. The particular expressions of the law, in concrete cases, are termed *ἐντολαί* *commands*, or *δικαιώματα*, *judgments*, *ordinances*. But the Divine law manifests itself as well among the heathen, by the inward voice of conscience (Rom. ii. 25), as in the Old Testament by means of the Mosaic institutions (in which, besides moral, ceremonial and political injunctions also are found), and finally, as in the New Testament, where Christ, especially in his sermon on the mount, establishes the law in its completeness (*πλήρωσις*). The essence of this *πλήρωσις* does not consist in imparting altogether new laws, different from that of conscience and that of Moses ; but in revealing the nature of these very laws in their inmost depths. It is, therefore, merely a development of that one principle, " Be ye perfect even as God is perfect" (Matth. v. 48) which is the same thing as, *Love God above all things*, for it is, in fact, by means of love that the Perfect One communicates himself, and produces what is perfect. It is, then, entirely erroneous, in exhibiting Paul's view of the way of salvation, to confine our conception of the law to any *one* of these forms of its manifestation, and especially with Pelagian and Rationalistic interpreters to refer it merely to the *ceremonial* part of the Old Testament law. The apostle speaks of *all* men, Jews as well as Gentiles, and therefore the law is also to be taken in its widest sense, so that the meaning of *χωρὶς νόμου*, *without law*, is, " in no form can the law produce a true spiritual righteousness : only an apparent and external righteousness is attainable by the mere votary of law." Further, if we consider more closely the relation of man to the law, * *i. e.*, the *ἔργα*, *works*, which the law requires or forbids, we find that *three classes* of them may be distinguished. *First*, *ἔργα πονηρά* or *κακά*, *wicked works* (Rom. xiii. 8), *i. e.*, open transgressions of the commandments, *ἔργα σκότους*, *of darkness* (Rom. xiii. 12), or *σαρκός*, *of flesh* (Galat. v. 19), also called *ἁμαρτήματα*, *sins*, *παραπτώματα*, *trespasses*, *παραβάσεις*, *transgressions*, in short, the utterances of *ἁμαρτία*, of the sinful nature of man. *Secondly*, *ἔργα νεκρά*, *dead works* (Heb. vi. 1, ix. 14), or *νόμου*, *of law*, *i. e.*, works, which outwardly correspond with the commandments, but do not proceed from an absolutely pure disposition ; these, therefore, in their extension over the whole life, constitute the condition of *δικαιοσύνη ἰδία*, a higher state, no doubt, than that of open disobedience to the law, but yet only in case it is accompanied by a consciousness of distance from the goal, by true repentance. Unless it include this, it becomes Pharisaic self-right-

* The general character of the legal position is the prominence of *activity* (the [illegible]), whilst that of the New Testament is marked by the predominance of *passivity*, that is, an openness to receive the Divine powers of life, by which, however, certainly a new and higher activity is generated.

eousness, which is no less displeasing to God than gross transgression of the law; for it is in fact itself a gross, nay, the grossest transgression of the law, being a violation of that fundamental principle of all the commandments, love, which is self-renunciation, whilst the former state implies self-exaltation. (See at Rom. ii. 1, etc.) The *third* class of works, lastly, are the ἔργα ἀγαθά, *good works*, or πίστεως, *of faith*, also called ἔργα καλά (Tit. ii. 7, 14; Colos. i. 10); ἔργα τοῦ θεοῦ (John vi. 28); in them is realized not merely an outward, but also an inward conformity to the law. They are, therefore, possible only through that faith which receives the powers of grace; for good works are fruits (καρποί), *i. e.*, the organic productions of the inward life, and it is, of course, only the tree which has been made generous that can bear generous fruit; this can, however, never be conceived as without fruit, because the powers of its inward life necessarily produce them. When, therefore, Paul declares of the works of the law, that they are incapable of leading to δικαιοσύνη, he means especially those of the second class; but he does not say the contrary even of those of the third class, because he would rather lay stress upon the *principle*, πίστις, than upon the effects; James speaks differently (ii. 24).

Now, with respect to the *second* way, that of *grace*, this is found also in the Old Testament, as also the law is recognized in the New; but grace forms the predominant feature of the new covenant, and manifests itself there in its full power, while before Christ it only appeared indistinctly revealed. For in its most comprehensive signification *grace* is the will of God, as it exhibits itself in communicating, and not in demanding.* Since now justice and grace are the eternal forms of God's revelation of himself, he worked also under the form of grace amongst Jews and heathen. Grace, however, in these phases of spiritual life could only manifest itself in *consolations* and *promises;* it was not until after the accomplishment of Christ's work that grace appeared in the New Testament, imparting itself as a positive and *creative* power. All the former operations of Divine grace were, therefore, so to speak, but a breathing of the Spirit upon humanity, it was only in the Redeemer that the streams to grace were poured forth. (See on John i. 14.) To Christ, therefore, *grace* is pre-eminently ascribed, whilst *love*, *i. e.*, the source of grace, resides in the Father. (See on 2 Cor. xiii. 13.) But we are by no means to regard grace as the mere heightening of the natural powers of the man from within, but as the commu-

* In relation to the *creature*, therefore, χάρις conveys the idea of that which is undeserved, see Rom. iii. 23, iv. 4. The communication of the life of the Father to the *Son* is not called χάρις, but ἀγάπη. But, inasmuch as the creature is at the same time regarded as *miserable*, ἔλεος, σπλάγχνα are substituted for χάρις. (Comp. the principal passage, 2 Cor. xiii. 13.)

nication of a higher, absolutely pure, and perfect principle, that is to say, of the πνεῦμα ἅγιον, to which the human πνεῦμα stands in the same relation as the ψυχή to the πνεῦμα in man. (See on Rom. viii. 16.)

Finally, with respect to faith, by which man is brought into relation to grace, we have, indeed, spoken already several times concerning this term, in our observations on Matthew viii. 2, xiii. 58; Mark ix. 20–27; Matth. xxi. 17; but its importance demands here a fresh and more comprehensive consideration. We start in the first place with the assertion, that this term also has in all the writers of the New Testament but *one* radical meaning, though modified by its respective relations. Holy Scripture itself gives us this radical meaning in a formal definition, inasmuch as it designates faith, as ἐλπιζομένων ὑπόστασις, πραγμάτων ἔλεγχος οὐ βλεπομένων, *substance of things hoped*, etc. (Heb. xi. 1.) Faith, therefore, taken in its most general meaning, forms the opposite to that knowledge of the visible which appears to the natural man to be the most certain of all, as well as to that *beholding* of invisable things which belongs to a higher state, and which Paul denotes by the expression περιπατεῖν διὰ εἴδους (2 Cor. v. 7, compared with 1 Cor. xiii. 12). Now man's relation to that which is invisible and eternal may be regarded as *threefold;* it is either entirely founded upon the *thinking* faculty, or it is entirely based upon the *will* and the affections, or lastly, it rests uniformly upon *all* the powers of man. In the first of these significations, Scripture ascribes πίστις even to the devils (Jas. ii. 19), and supposes the possibility that faith may exist in men,* without a corresponding life (Jas. ii. 17, 20; 1 Cor. xiii. 2). Such a dead *head-faith*, merely literal faith, is not only of no use to men, but even makes them more deeply responsible.† In the *second* relation, it appears as the *faith of the heart, i. e.*, as a living susceptibility to the powers of the higher world, the soul absorbing, so to speak, the streams of the Spirit as a thirsty land. It was this kind of faith, which, as we showed, in the above quoted passages of our Commentary, was exhibited by those who came to Christ to be healed, as recorded in the Gospels. In these persons we could only assume a very imperfect and indistinct knowledge of Divine things, but they manifested a heart glowing with love, and were therefore capable of receiving χάρις. We, in consequence, also designated faith as identical with *receiving love*, whilst grace is *imparting love*. Since now

* Petrus Lombardus makes the following just distinction between "credere Deum, *i. e.*, credere quod Deus sit, quod etiam mali faciunt," and "credere in Deum, *i. e.*, credendo amare Deum, credendo ei adhærere." The belief *in* God is a dedication, a consecration of ourselves to him.

† The case of the man who is burdened with such a dead faith is doubtless worse than if he did not believe at all; yet not for those around him. The word which is spoken even by one who is dead, may be the means of awakening others to life.

from the heart proceeds life (Prov. iv. 23), such faith is ever a living, though still often an imperfect faith. For it only shews itself as a complete faith when, in the *third* place, it takes possession of the whole man, when, therefore, it combines a living susceptibility with clear and comprehensive knowledge. Meanwhile, we find that New Testament usage applies to that true knowledge of the Divine which springs from its *essential* communication, the term γνῶσις, *knowledge*, so that πίστις and γνῶσις are complementary to one another, as expressing respectively the intellectual and the emotional elements of our spiritual life. But if in the passage in John xvii. 3, γνῶσις presupposes πίστις, so, conversely, in many passages, πίστις presupposes γνῶσις. Neither can be conceived absolutely without the other, so long as both retain their true nature; though, for their equal and harmonious cultivation, particular circumstances are required. Such equal culture is not necessary to salvation, though faith, as an element of the *heart*, is absolutely so; for without this, the reception into our own nature of the principle of Divine life is utterly impossible. But if faith is modified in this way by the *extent* to which it reigns in man, its character depends equally upon the *object* to which it refers. In fact, faith is the universal foundation of religion at all stages of spiritual development, so that not only in the New, but also in the Old Testament (see the whole 11th chapter of the Epistle to the Hebrews), nay, even amongst the Gentiles, the existence of faith must be recognized. "Without faith it is impossible to please God." (Heb. xi. 6.) Those faithful Gentiles, therefore, whom God regards as the circumcision (Rom. ii. 14, 26, 27), must have been well-pleasing to God from their faith, in the same way as the true Israelites. It also appears from the gospel history, that there existed in many Gentiles (the centurion of Capernaum, the Canaanitish woman, and others),* a very powerful faith, a lively susceptibility to the powers of the Divine life. What, then, is the difference between these degrees of faith? From the point occupied by the *noble Gentiles* the object of faith was *Divinity* as an abstract, indefinite conception, whence, in their case, it could only manifest itself as a *longing*, testifying of the remains of the Divine likeness in man. This longing is not, properly speaking, faith, until the moment when the desired object presents itself, and is embraced by it, in the same way that the eye does not see until the sun discovers itself. We might, therefore, ascribe to the noble-minded Gentiles faith *potentially*, *i. e.*, the completely developed capacity for believing, which presents itself *actually* only on the revelation of Divinity to them, either in doctrine or in life. The condition of ἀπιστία, *unbelief*, may, on the other hand, be considered as the undevel-

* Worthy of special remark are the passages with respect to Rahab, to whom, as a Gentile woman, faith and the works of faith are attributed, Heb. xi. 31; Jas. ii. 25.

oped, or even suppressed, capacity for believing, according as the term is taken merely in the negative, or also in the privative sense. Even, therefore, when this *Gentile* faith, so to speak, was exercised towards Christ himself, as, for example, in the case of the centurion of Capernaum, etc. (Matth. viii. 1, etc.), it was still incapable of *recognizing* in him more than a general manifestation of Divinity, although the thirst of the spirit found itself truly quenched in coming to him, as the eye of the child rejoices in the sun, without *knowing* what it is. *Genuine Judaism,* on the other hand, held a position which enabled it to recognize, consciously, in its object of faith, the personal Godhead. But the faith of the Jew still conceives this personal manifestation of God as merely *future,* to be realized in the Messiah, and as something *external.* It is only *Christian faith* that is able to raise itself to the conception of the Divine Personality, that had appeared in Christ, as *present* and *internal.* Christ, in his work and character, will not merely shine upon men from without; but he will dwell and work in them inwardly, in order that man may become what *he* is. (1 John iv. 17.) As humanity in general, has, therefore, to pass through these different stages of faith, so also the individual. In childhood, when even human personality is as yet but imperfectly unfolded, he believes only in the Divine: with advancing age he beholds in Christ the Divine Personality, but first only as an outward fact, whose full influence upon his heart is yet future: at last he experiences its operation as something present and inward, and then only is his faith completed: it becomes a devotion of himself to God, an espousal of his soul to the heavenly bridegroom, whereby he becomes one with Christ, and Christ's whole work and Being become his own. (Hosea ii. 20.)* In this form, therefore, faith is identical with *regeneration,* because, whilst faith thus manifests its power, the whole disposition becomes a new creature; the man of earth is transformed into a man of heaven and of God. (2 Tim. iii. 17.) The lower degrees of faith, on the other hand, are as yet without regeneration. (See at John i. 17.) In all stages of development, the essence of faith remains the same, the susceptibility of the inward life to Divine influence. But, as divinity reveals itself variously, under the successive aspects of Father, Son, and Spirit, hence this *one* faith presents itself in several forms. Finally, it was only in its *subjective* character (fides quâ creditur) that πίστις required a minute investigation; of its *objective* use (fides quæ creditur) as denoting

* When faith is represented as a χάρισμα (1 Cor. xii. 7, xiii. 3), it denotes the capacity for appropriating the Divine power, so as to perform miracles by means of it. Faith, indeed, is requisite for the reception of all gifts of the Spirit (see Matth. xvii. 19, 20), but it appears in a particularly heightened and concentrated form as a special gift of grace in the passages above cited.

the subject-matter of faith, we need only make mention. When used of God (Rom. iii. 3; 2 Cor. i. 18; 2 Tim. ii. 13, several times), it denotes the faithfulness of God in the fulfilment of his promises.

From this unfolding of the import of terms, we proceed to consider the contents of the passage itself, Rom. iii. 21. In the first place, *νυνί*, *now* (=*ἐν τῷ νῦν καιρῷ*, Galat. iv. 4, and below, in ver. 26), is evidently to be referred to the time since the accomplishment of the work of the Lord, so that the ages before Christ appear as the mighty past.* In these, indeed, redemption, as a future blessing, was announced beforehand, and confirmed by witnesses, in the Law (Gen. xlix. 10; Ex. xxxiv. 6; Deut. xviii. 15) and in the prophets (Jer. xxiii. 6, xxxiii. 16; Is. xlv. 17, liii. 1, etc.); but in these, and in the symbols of the sacrificial worship, it was hidden under a veil, on which account the saints of the Old Testament itself had only an indistinct presentiment of the mode of redemption (1 Pet. i. 10, 11); it was not until the death and resurrection of the Redeemer, that the mystery was *revealed*. (Rom. i. 18, xvi. 25, 26.)† Now the subject of this revelation is this: the high goal of humanity, the righteousness of God (*δικαιοσύνη Θεοῦ*), is to be obtained *without law*, through faith in Christ. The *χωρὶς νόμου*, *without law*, however, as is self-evident, is not intended to express a renunciation of the law, for the law is holy and good (vii. 12), and necessary for all phases of life, but to designate an altered position of man in relation to it. By nature, man stands *under* the law, and is impelled by the law to righteousness; this relation is to cease; man can, indeed, never be *above* the law, but can certainly live *in* the law, and bear the law essentially in himself. Accordingly, in 1 Tim. i. 9, it is said, *δικαίῳ νόμος οὐ κεῖται*, *the law is not made for the righteous*, on which passage consult Augustine's excellent remarks (de spir. et. lit. cap. 10). This condition, in which man is thoroughly *one* with the law, even as our Lord tells us God himself is (Matth. v. 48), constitutes

* Fritzsche takes *νυνὶ δέ* as a mere form of transition, and it is no doubt correct to suppose that no determination of time is indicated in the relation of ver. 21 to ver. 20. But the subsequent mention of the law and the prophets renders it necessary to assert for *νυνί* the sense of time. [I think not. The reference to the law and the prophets is equally pertinent and forcible, if we give to *νυνί* the meaning, not of *now*, in contrast with a former time, but of *now, as the case stands*, in contrast with the other case stated or supposed. Such a use of *νῦν* (more rarely *νυνί*) is abundant in the Greek classics, and frequent in the New Testament (Luke xix. 42; 1 Cor. xv. 20). It is therefore very natural, in contrasting the *existing* fact of a righteousness without law, with that legal state in which righteousness is impossible, to add that it is "attested *by* the law," "the prophets" being then added as a mere after-thought, to complete the idea. While, therefore, I reject Olshausen's interpretation of *νυνί* as that of mere *time*, I regard Fritzsche's as equally unsatisfactory, which makes it a mere particle of transition.]—[K.

† Paul does not merely say: The *way* to attain to the righteousness of God is manifested, but *this latter is itself* revealed, for it is personally in Christ, and appears in men only as Christ in us; man has no righteousness of God besides Christ, whatsoever of this righteousness the regenerate man possesses is entirely of Christ.

exactly that righteousness of God to which faith brings us, because through faith man receives the being of God into the depths of his soul. In this passage, therefore, χωρὶς νόμου, *without law*, is exactly parallel to χωρὶς ἔργων νόμου, *without works of law* (Galat. ii. 16), by which it is not denied that good *works* exist in the life of faith, but only that these works form the *foundation* of that right relation to God which is restored under the new covenant, they being, in fact, merely the *consequences* of this relation. This *foundation* lies positively in the work of Christ, negatively in faith, from which works both outwardly and inwardly conformable to the law necessarily proceed. *Dead* works, in *the sight of God*, do not even constitute a δικαιοσύνη νόμου—these, therefore, cannot at all be meant. The profound meaning of this verse will unfold itself before our eyes most plainly in detail, if we review the false interpretations to which it has been exposed. Of these, the coarse view of Pelagian Rationalism refutes itself. According to this, νόμος is to be understood simply of the ceremonial law, πίστις of the assent of the understanding to the *doctrine* of Christ, and δικαιοσύνη of morality; so that the sense would be, "outward religious exercises avail nothing, but only virtue according to the pure moral precepts of Christ." In this entirely external view, however, one slight circumstance is overlooked, that, according to the apostle's doctrine, it is impossible for sinful man to exhibit this pure morality (viii. 3); the question, therefore is, whence does the man obtain strength for this work? The new features of the gospel do not consist in a more excellent system of morality, but in its *opening a new source of strength*, by which true morality is attainable. Much subtler is the error of the Roman Catholic Church in its doctrine of δικαιοσύνη. The point of difference, with respect to this doctrine, between her and the Protestant Church is this, that the latter considers δικαιοσύνη as a judicial *act of God* (actus forensis), a recognition as righteous (declaratio pro justo),* whilst the former regards it as a *condition of soul called forth in the man* (habitus infusus), in accordance with which "justificatio" has its degrees; so that the Protestant view regards it mainly in its *objective*, and the Roman Catholic in its *subjective* aspect. The Protestant Church by no means denies the truth contained in the Roman Catholic view; she places the *subjective* element under the name of *sanctification*, immediately along side of *justification*, making it spring from justification as its necessary

* It is quite false to suppose, that the Protestant Church regards justification as something merely outward, because she sees in it a declaration of God, as Möhler misrepresents us in his Symbolik. Justification contains, according to Luther's system of doctrine, not merely *remissio peccatorum*, but also *imputatio meriti Christi*, and the *adoptio in filios Dei*. The Divine declaration is consequently to be regarded as an inward *operation* in the consciousness of the man, as is, indeed, necessarily implied in the idea: what God declares *is* so by his very word.

consequence. The Roman Catholic church, however, denies the truth contained in the Protestant doctrine, and here lies the error of her doctrine. Looking at the strict meaning of the word, *δικαιοῦσθαι* is no doubt more properly interpreted "rendered righteous," than, according to the Protestant church "declared righteous;" but since nothing can be *declared* by God to be righteous which *is* not so in fact, it follows that the translation of *δικαιοσύνη* by "the righteousness which avails before God," is not false, but only secondary; *δικαιοσύνη* Θεοῦ, means, primarily, the righteousness which is *wrought* by God: but that which God produces answers to his idea, and must therefore avail before him.* The Roman Catholic church, therefore, gains by this mere verbal advantage absolutely nothing; on the other hand she has not only *lost sight* of an important element of the truth, but also, when this was pointed out to her, *opposed* it; an element which the Protestant church has established with more grammatical strictness upon the formula *λογίζεσθαι εἰς δικαιοσύνην, to impute as righteousness,* than upon the expression *δικαιοσύνη* Θεοῦ, *righteousness of God.* This important point is, in fact, *the purely objective nature of justification,* which the expression *actus forensis* is intended to affirm, so that justification does not depend upon the degree of sanctification, but entirely upon the purpose of God in Christ Jesus; by the passive and active obedience of Christ the sin of all has been expiated, and the obedience of all fulfilled in him. God, then, regards no more men in Adam, but in Christ, from whom, in the work of conversion, the germ of the new man is transmitted to the individual. Thus only does the gospel become, in truth, good news, since thus the salvation of man does not depend upon his own unstable conduct (on which supposition, as the Roman Catholic church believes and requires, a constant *uncertainty* must remain in the man's mind here below whether or not he be in a state of grace), but on the contrary, by the unchangeable purpose of God, which man apprehends in faith, the instability of his own character is corrected. "If, therefore, man believes not, yet God abideth faithful, he cannot deny himself" (2 Tim. ii. 13), and the unfaithfulness of man is not removed by the fact that he strives to be faithful (for this very endeavour is unfaithful, and at best but discloses presumptuous pride), but simply and alone by believing in the faithfulness of God in Christ, through which faith he becomes partaker of a higher power. As, therefore, the *mother of all sins* is the *not* believing in him whom God hath sent,

* Benecke's opinion, that *δικαιοσύνη* Θεοῦ in this passage, as well as in vers. 25, 26, means the *justitia Dei quâ justus est,* is equally untenable in the connexion, with his view, that *πίστις Ἰησοῦ* denotes the *faithfulness* which Jesus exercises. Faith stands here evidently in opposition to the *ἔργοις* implied in the words *χωρὶς νόμου.* That, however, the grace and faithfulness of Christ produce faith also in men, is maintained by him with perfect justice.

so to believe in him is *the mother of all virtues* (John xvi. 9); *beside* faith, there can exist no virtue, but all that is true and real in man proceeds *from* it. The Roman Catholic church erroneously understands by faith, fides formata, *i. e.*, faith *with* other virtues, from its always regarding faith as a dead assent of the understanding to mere historic truth, while, according to the Protestant view, harmonizing also with that of Scripture, it is life and blessedness. The doctrine of a meritum congrui, and meritum condigni, has arisen entirely out of the Pelagianizing views of the Roman Catholic church, which make man, in the fall, to have lost merely a *donum supernaturale*, but still to possess all his natural faculties, and, consequently, the capability of loving God, and keeping his commandments. According to my view, the transition from the state under the law to the state under the gospel (of which we shall treat more at length at ch. vii.), must be conceived of somewhat after this manner: In his state under the law, man is able, by his natural powers, which, however, can never be considered as wholly separated from the influences of the Logos, to perform certain *opera civilia*. But the more powerfully the light of truth works in his mind, the more plainly will he perceive that all his endeavours to establish a perfect righteousness are vain, and that his best works, on account of the selfishness which cleaves to them, are, as Augustine says—severely, indeed, yet truly—but *splendida vitia*, the wild fruit of a degenerate tree. With this recognition of sin (ἐπίγνωσις τῆς ἁμαρτίας, iii. 20) is connected the longing for deliverance (vii. 24), and if the preaching of the gospel brings to his view the true Redeemer, faith apprehends this Saviour, and appropriates both him and his work. On man's side, no merit, no righteousness, is pre-supposed, but simply a living faith in the merits and righteousness of Christ; these faith takes up into itself, and thus everything which is Christ's becomes man's. This transfer to the sinful man of the being of Christ is denoted by the expression "righteousness is imputed to him." The work which was objectively accomplished upon the cross, is thus subjectively applied to the individual believer; the germ of the new man which exists in Christ is grafted into and born in the old man. This act of transfer is, therefore, a mysterious process in the depths of the soul, a new creation, which none can effect by his own power, a pure gift of the Spirit, who breatheth where he will. Since, however, in every regenerate man, the old man still lives, and, therefore, sinful motions must still exist, the question arises, how can God, the Omniscient, the Holy, the Just One, regard the imperfectly sanctified man as entirely righteous? The answer is: Because God judges the man not according to that which is realized in him, but according to that which is in Christ. As all men have fallen in Adam, so in Christ have they all been raised; God therefore recognizes all as righteous in him, even generations yet to come. If this Divine declaration is actually made to man, and he receives it in faith, it produces in him the new life: but inasmuch as this life is derived from another, and can, therefore, also be lost, it does not constitute the decisive point in the Divine judgment as to the state of grace. And therefore, also, the believer, in his own judgment, must not found his hopes of salvation upon his inward condition, but upon the merits of Christ. Still, as an evidence of being in a state of grace, the inward condition is important, because a justifying faith cannot be conceived to exist without an inward transformation, and powers received from above, which enable the regenerate man to do that which under the law he could not do. (See at Rom. vii. 24, viii. 3.)

Vers. 22, 23.—This way of salvation by faith is now equally necessary for all, because the law could conduct none to the righteousness of God, in that *all without exception have sinned*, even if not actually, in such gross forms as those mentioned in ch. i. and ii. yet inwardly, since the germ of all sins lies in every one.

(The εἰς πάντας καὶ ἐπὶ πάντας constitutes not merely an accumulation of synonyms, but a climax; the image of a flood of grace seems to be at the foundation of this expression, a flood which penetrates *to* all, and even streams *over* all.—The words δικαιοσύνη Θεοῦ [scil. ἔρχεται] εἰς πάντας, *the righteousness of God for all*, are, however, only to be understood of the Divine purpose, "it is intended for all," without any intimation of the actual restoration of all.—Πίστις Ἰησοῦ, *faith of Jesus*, stands for πίστις εἰς Ἰησοῦν, *faith in Jesus*, as elsewhere πίστις Θεοῦ for εἰς Θεόν. [Mark xi. 22; Acts iii. 16; Galat. ii. 20.]—Πάντες ἥμαρτον, *all have sinned*, refers not merely to actual sin, the consequence of hereditary sin, but especially to the latter. Even where no actual sins have been committed, as, *e. g.*, in the case of unconscious children, the power of redemption is still needed. [See at vii. 12.]—To understand ὑστεροῦσθαι τῆς δόξης τοῦ Θεοῦ, *to come short of the glory of God*, of the approval of God, as Winer, Fritzsche, and Reiche still hold, or of boasting before God, for which καύχημα commonly stands, as Rosenmüller and Tholuck explain it, is plainly feeble. Rückert has decided in favour of the old interpretation, which refers it to the image of God in which man was created; and this appears to me also to be alone admissible. There is no difficulty in giving this meaning to the expression δόξα τοῦ Θεοῦ, according to the analogy of כְּבוֹד יְהוָֹה [see on John i. 1], even though it does not happen to occur elsewhere in the New Testament. Finally, the comparison of these words of Paul in ver. 22, δικαιοσύνη Θεοῦ διὰ πίστεως, *righteousness of God through faith*, with the parallel, Galat. v. 5, ἐκ πίστεως ἐλπίδα δικαιοσύνης ἀπεκδεχόμεθα, *we await the hope of righteousness from faith*, is instructive. The words in the present passage are uttered from a point of view entirely *objective;* in Christ the righteousness of God exists for believers absolutely complete; but the *subjective* mode of contemplating it has also its truth, although occurring less frequently in Paul's writings. From this point of view *righteousness* is an object of hope, because in this world it can only be imperfectly realized in man. See the Comm. on Galat. v. 5.)

Vers. 24, 25.—Since, then, they cannot become righteous by merit, they are made righteous gratuitously, *i. e.*, without previous works and proper deserts, out of pure grace *through* the redemption of Christ. (Grace is the operative cause, redemption the means by which it works.) We arrive now at another very important point, namely, How has Christ produced the possibility of the δικαιοσύνη Θεοῦ through faith in himself? The apostle answers this question by laying stress, not upon the communication of a higher spirit through Christ and upon his Divine glory, but, on the contrary, upon his deepest humiliation, his sufferings and his death, by which he declares that *redemption* was accomplished. Now, in the *first place*, with respect to the language of the Bible on this point, we meet with *three* expressions, by which the redemptive agency of Christ is designated. 1. The term ἀπολύτρωσις, *redemption*, of which we have already treated at Matth. xx. 28. Paul generally employs this form (Ephes. i. 7, 14, iv. 30; 1 Cor. i. 30), since the ἀπό expresses the idea of making free more strongly than the simple λύτρωσις. At the foundation of this word lies the figure of *slavery*,* from which man must be redeemed by a ransom (whence ἐξαγοράζω is used, Galat. iii. 13, iv. 5), in order to attain to freedom, as with σωτηρία, *salvation* (Rom. v. 9, 10), the figure is that of *great danger or distress* (ἀπώλεια), from which he is to be delivered. The ransom (λύτρον) is the blood of Christ, which constitutes the offering made by love to justice, which objective transaction in God, alone renders possible the real forgiveness of sins and its appropriation in the individual case. 2. We find the expression καταλλαγή, *reconciliation* (Rom. v. 10, ix. 15; 2 Cor. v. 18, 19), at the root of which lies the idea of an *enmity* which is done away. The choice of this particular word to express this thought is, however, in the highest degree significant. Καταλλάσσω, in fact, means, primarily, "to exchange, interchange," and hence "to reconcile." (Rom. v. 10; 2 Cor. v. 18, 19.) In reconciliation, harshly opposing contraries make, as it were, mutual exchanges, and form again an harmonious unity. So Christ takes upon himself our misery, and imparts to us his glory, in order to reconcile us to God. The distinction which Tittmann

* No doubt, therefore, redemption and atonement are *symbolical* expressions, but symbols full of *essential truth*, which cannot find any substitute whatsoever in human language, and are therefore necessary.

assumes between *διαλλάσσω*, to remove a *reciprocal* enmity, and *καταλλάσσω*, an enmity existing on one side only, has been proved by Tholuck to be utterly unfounded. (Bergpred. p. 192, etc.)* We find, 3, and lastly, *ἱλασμός*, *propitiation* (1 John ii. 2, iv. 10; *ἱλάσκεσθαι*, Heb. ii. 17), the proper term, even in Old Testament language, for expressing the idea of expiation by sacrifice.† Christ is therefore himself called the *θυσία*, *sacrifice*, or *προσφορά*, *offering* (Ephes. v. 2; Heb. x. 12; and *πάσχα*, *passover*, 1 Cor. v. 7), or *ἀμνός*, *lamb* (John i. 29, 36; 1 Pet. i. 19), *ἀρνίον* (Rev. v. 6, 8, 12, 13, vi. 1, etc.) With respect to the relation of these expressions to one another, we may finally remark, that *καταλλαγή* and *ἱλασμός* always denote the *beginning* of Christ's work, whilst *ἀπολύτρωσις* includes not only the beginning, but the *end* also (see Rom. viii. 23; 1 Cor. i. 30) so that this is the most comprehensive term, comprising even *ἁγιασμός*, *sanctification*, itself (it stands = *ἄφεσις τῶν ἁμαρτιῶν*, *remission of sins*, Ephes. i. 7; Col. i. 14, whilst equivalent to *καταλλάσσων*, we find *μὴ λογιζόμενος αὐτοῖς τὰ παραπτώματα αὐτῶν*, *not imputing to them their offences*, 2 Cor. v. 19).

But in the second place, the *ideas* themselves designated by these terms belong to the most difficult in Holy Scripture. Still, the last few years have brought to light such profound views on these subjects, that, in fact, very much has been done towards their solution. In particular, we may not only consider that rationalistic view to be set aside, which, in reducing the work of Christ to doctrine and example, wholly misunderstands the essence of Christianity, but also the infinitely deeper mode of representation of Schleiermacher (Glaubenslehre P. ii. p. 252).‡ The latter theologian, namely, considers the work of Christ as the Redeemer to precede his work of reconciliation, and considers both only from his own *subjective* point of view. With him, therefore, *redemption* is the communication to believers of the sinlessness and perfection of Christ, and *reconciliation* the adoption into that blessed fellowship

* In Heb. ii. 15, we find *ἀπαλλάττειν*, but = *ἐλευθεροῦν*.

† Nitzsch, in his "System of Christian Doctrine," distinguishes between "Versöhnung" and "Versühnung," *i. e.*, "reconciliation" and "propitiation." This distinction is very serviceable for maintaining the distinction between *καταλλαγή* and *ἱλασμός*. That a separation of these two expressions has not long ago been established, may be explained from the fact, that the profound meaning embraced in the idea of *propitiation* had entirely escaped our entire age. It was not, in fact, merely in theology that the significance of this idea was overlooked, but also in the science of law; punishment was degraded into a mere human invention *for deterring men from crime*, instead of being ennobled and hallowed by that *propitiation of justice* which it manifests. In the recovery of this idea, an essential advance has been made towards deeper views of the whole work of Christ.

‡ Usteri, in the fourth edition of his "Paulinischer Lehrbegriff" (p. 86, etc.), still adheres to Schleiermacher's view of this doctrine. Amongst the most recent exegetical commentators, Rückert has, in particular, taken a correct exegetical view of Paul's doctrine, without, however, having been able to adopt the idea of an atonement, not merely on man's part, but also on God's.

with Christ, which follows, as a necessary consequence, from that communication. This is an entirely arbitrary definition of the terms. Besides, this view leaves out of sight a most essential point, namely, *the blotting out of the guilt of sin*, which Schleiermacher was obliged in consistency to omit, because he had denied the reality of evil, and was thus obliged to rest content with a mere replenishment of man's emptiness. This one point, therefore, it only remains for us to discuss—how the death of Christ is related to the forgiveness of sins, and whether this death has reference merely to men, or also to the Divine Being himself. And here, in the first place, I feel myself constrained to remark, that the views I expressed at Matth. xx. 28, implying that reconciliation was an act on man's side *alone*, have been modified by recent profound researches, as I have also intimated at John iii. 16 (vol. ii. p. 362, note). For the profoundest investigation of this subject we are indebted to a man who has rendered great service to Theology and Philosophy, as well as to Law, Karl Friedrich Göschel.* In fact, we may say, if reconciliation were an act taking place in man only, we could speak of no "ministry of reconciliation" (2 Cor. v. 18); for then to preach reconciliation would not be to announce an act of *God*, but only an act of *men*, and indeed only of a *few* men, for how many are there who will not be reconciled unto God! Even if, therefore, in the New Testament, the expression, "God is reconciled," does not occur (see the note to John iii. 16), because he appears throughout it as the Author and Founder of this reconciliation, yet there is contained in the very idea of sacrifice and expiation (as the Old Testament plainly shews) a necessary reference to an altered relation of God himself. Every sacrifice is intended to *expiate* the guilt of men, and *propitiate* the anger of God, consequently the sacrifice of sacrifices, in which alone all the rest have their truth, must *effect* that which the others only *foreshadow*. Since now the view of the Scotists (gratuita acceptatio) disproves itself, inasmuch as God can never regard an object as that which it is not, and the view of Grotius (acceptilatio) is erroneous, in which law and righteousness are considered as detached from the Divine Being and Nature; there remains but the highly acute theory of Anselm (satisfactio vicaria) a theory, when rightly understood, equally consonant with the doctrine of Scripture and the demands of philosophy. The elements of which it is composed are, on the one side, the enormity of sin itself, and the guilt and

* See Göschel's "Zerstreute Blätter aus den Hand und Hülfsacten eines Juristen." Erfurt, 1832. See besides the Essays in Tholuck's lit. Anz. 1833. Num. 8–14. An essay of the same in the Evang. Kirch. Zeit. 1834, January No. Very well worth reading are also the treatises of Stier, which appeared earlier (Andeut. P. i. p. 379, seq., more accurately defined in the Andeut. P. ii. p. 24, seq.), of Meyer (in the "Blätter für höhere Wahrheit," vol. vi. 384 etc., xi. 206 etc.), and Tholuck ("Von der Sünde, und vom Versöhner," p. 92, ff.).

liability to punishment which proceeds from it; and, on the other, the impossibility of conceiving in God *one* attribute as active *without* the other, as, *e. g.*, love without righteousness, on which account God *cannot* forgive sin on mere repentance, as can a man who is himself a debtor; and between these two elements comes the Person of the God-Man, who is not *a* man, amongst and by the side of many others, but *the* man, the second spiritual Adam of the whole race,* who is connected alike with sinners by his true though most holy humanity, and with the Lord of the world by his Divine nature, in that in him love is manifested as brightly as righteousness in the Father, while again love in the Father shines as purely as righteousness in the Son. That, therefore, which cannot be conceived as united in any human act (as man can ever only exercise *either* grace *or* justice), the highest act of grace, the absolution of a whole sinful race, and the perfectly righteous punishment of sinners in the death of him who bore the whole race in himself (as the centre embraces the collective radii of the circumference), is harmoniously blended in the death of Christ; and therefore the giving up of the Son by the Father, and the free sacrifice of the Son, constitute the *highest act of God*, worthy to form the subject of preaching to the whole human race, because it has power to breathe life into the dead bones, and truly to impart that peace which flows from the forgiveness of sins. It is to this objective act of God, according to Protestant doctrine, that faith attaches itself, and by the powerful glow of its flame all those half or wholly Pelagian views must be dissipated, which would have the Divine life of love to derive assistance from the exertion of man's natural powers. For where life is not awakened by gazing on that serpent which is lifted up (an effect just the contrary to that produced by beholding the head of Medusa), the most decided commands, and the most ascetic exertions and acts of self-denial, can only produce a bare respectability, or ridiculous conceit. In this fountain thus opened alone flows the water of life; on this altar alone can heavenly fire be obtained; here righteousness and grace melt into an ineffable unity, as they are one in God himself; for the forgiveness of sins on account of the death of Christ is *οὐδὲ κατὰ νόμον, οὐδὲ κατὰ νόμον, ἀλλὰ ὑπὲρ νόμον καὶ ὑπὲρ νόμον*, *i. e.*, not *according to* the law, for by that man was to bear his own sin, and yet not *against* the law, since in the sufferings of Christ satisfaction was rendered to its demands, but *above* the law, because grace is mightier than righteousness, and *for* the law, because law is itself established thereby. (See Tholuck "von der Sünde," p. 108, 3d ed.)

* On the vicarious character of Christ see details at Rom. v. 2, seq. [illegible] immediately concerned only with the idea of *satisfaction*, which is [illegible] though the *expression* is not found in Scripture.

It is only as thus apprehended that the representation of the apostle admits also an exact verbal interpretation. He calls Christ *ἱλαστήριον*, a word which is not, however, to be taken = *ἱλασμός*, or to be explained with the addition of *θῦμα* of the sin-offering, but with *ἐπίθεμα* supplied, of the *covering* of the *Ark of the Covenant*, in which expression, at all events, the idea of *expiation* is most distinctly enunicated, even according to the etymology of the word. This covering, in fact, made of fine gold, 2½ cubits long and 1½ broad, at whose ends the two cherubim stood overshadowing the ark with their wings, was the throne of the Shechinah, symbol of the presence of God; on this account it is called, Heb. iv. 16, *θρόνος χάριτος*, *throne of grace*. (See Exod. xxv. 17, etc.) On this mercy-seat the High Priest sprinkled once every year, on the great day of atonement, the blood of a bullock seven times, and the blood of a goat seven times, to make atonement for the sin of the people. (Levit. xvi. 18, etc.) This lid is called in the Old Testament כַּפֹּרֶת, from כָּפַר, "to cover," i. e., according to the Old Testament view, "to forgive," because sin in this dispensation could not yet be entirely removed, but only remained suspended through the long-suffering of God, until the completion of that true sacrifice which was able to take it away. The LXX. translate it *ἱλαστήριον*. As now the whole form of Old Testament worship was symbolical, so this institution also represented figuratively the essential truth. As the mercy-seat of the tabernacle presented itself to the spirits of the people as the place from which the forgiveness of their sins proceeded; so also is the Redeemer solemnly presented, in the Holy of Holies of the universe, as in the true Temple of God, to the believing gaze of the whole of that spiritual Israel, which is gathered out of all nations, in order that they may receive forgiveness of sins through his blood. As he is therefore the sacrifice, so is he also the mercy-seat itself, because all opposites are harmonized in him: "God was in Christ reconciling the world unto himself." (2 Cor. v. 19.) So God himself was enthroned between the cherubim, above the sacred covering of the Ark of the Covenant, and accepted the offering made for the forgiveness of the sins of the people. (Lev. xvi. 2; Heb. ix. 7, etc.)

On the side of man *faith* alone is required (*διὰ πίστεως* is not to be connected with *δικαιούμενοι δωρεάν* so as to stand parallel with *διὰ τῆς ἀπολυτρώσεως*, but with *ἱλαστήριον*, though we are not to consider this latter as dependent upon *πίστις*, but must supply as follows, "which must be received through faith in his blood"); but this faith is not by any means to be regarded as a human work, but as the gift of God, and is indeed *πίστις ἐν τῷ αὐτοῦ αἵματι*, *faith in his blood*. (*Πίστις ἐν αἵματι*, after the analogy of *πίστις ἐν Χριστῷ*, Galat. iii. 26; Ephes. i. 15, is repeatedly found, in which phrases no interchange of prepositions is to be assumed, for the indwelling of believers in Christ, and of Christ in them, and their abiding with him and his blood is indicated by them.) But the usual assertion, that *αἷμα*, *blood*, denotes the bloody death of Christ, and that this represents his collective sufferings, is not indeed untrue, but still does not exhaust the meaning. We *never* find a faith in Christ's *death* (*πίστις εἰς θάνατον*) spoken of,* it is the *blood* of Christ which is constantly mentioned. (Acts xx. 28; Rom. v. 9; Ephes. i. 7, ii. 13; Col. i. 14, 20; 1 Pet. i. 18, 19; 1 John i. 7; Heb. ix. 12, 14, x. 19, xiii. 12; Rev. i. 5, v. 9, vii. 14, xii. 11.) The invariable use of this language must be founded upon some internal reason, and this we find plainly at Heb. ix. 22, "without shedding of blood there is no remission of sins." (See Levit. xvii. 11.) For, as we find it expressed in this latter passage, "the life of the body is in the blood." The phrase *πίστις εἰς θάνατον*, *faith in death*, would therefore be much less appropriate, as not conveying the idea of the forgiveness of sins and of the expiatory sacrifice, and, again, *θάνατος* denotes only death as such, the mere dying. But the death of Christ, who is life itself (John i. 3), is the effusion or pouring forth of his holy life, *i. e.*, of his blood, which he also communicates constantly to his people in faith, and in the sacrament of the Lord's Supper. (John vi. 47, 54.)

The formula *πίστις ἐν τῷ αἵματι*, *faith in his blood*, is therefore in the highest degree significant, in that it declares, that the shedding of the blood and the death of him, who was called the Life itself, is the expiation of the sin of the world, and is not something dead, but essentially and pre-eminently living, so that in his death, death itself appears swallowed up of life. As therefore the vial of balsam, if it is to refresh all those who are in the house by the odour of its contents, must be opened and poured forth, so also did the Redeemer breathe out into the dead world that fulness of life which was contained in him, by pouring forth his holy blood, the supporter of his life,† and this voluntarily, since none could take his

* We find in Rom. v. 10, "we are reconciled to God by the *death* of his Son," only because the opposition with *ζωή* required this expression. In Col. i. 22, *θάνατος* is more exactly defined in ver. 20.

† No doubt a true and deep idea lies at the foundation of Ackerman's ingenious treatise "On the chemical feature in the Christian conception of sanctification" (in Fichte's Zeitschrift für Philosophie and speculative Theologie. Bonn, 1837. 1 vol. 2d part, pp. 232 seq.); this namely, that in the influence of Christ and his blood (*i. e.*, of his life) upon the sinful race of man there exists an analogy with chemical agents and reagents; that thus God has formed Christ by the development of his human life into a special source of healing and principle of attraction. But this idea, when carried out into detail, easily gives rise to dangerous errors, and tends to lower the whole process of restoration revealed in Christianity into a mere physical one.

[The note proceeds to cite from Ackermann, in terms of decided condemnation, passages which illustrate the influence of the Saviour's death and blood by the action of chemical agents. The English translator has omitted this portion of the note, and the American editor has not thought it worth while to add it.]

life from him. (John x. 18.) Thus did he, through the Holy Spirit, offer himself as the most precious sacrifice to God, that he might purge our consciences by the sprinkling of his blood, to serve the living God. (Heb. ix. 14.)

In the concluding words of ver. 25, δικαιοσύνη, in εἰς ἔνδειξιν τῆς δικαιοσύνης αὐτοῦ, *for the manifestation of his righteousness*, might, in itself, be understood of the *goodness* of God, which, in the sacrifice of Christ, manifests itself as plainly as his *rigour;* but the added clause, "for the remission," etc. (διὰ τὴν πάρεσιν, κ. τ. λ.), and ver. 31, demand here specially the adoption of the latter signification. Those sins of the world before Christ, which had hitherto been, as it were, overlooked (Ps. lxxviii. 38), rendered necessary the final manifestation of God's righteousness, and were punished by the righteous God in Christ, the representative of the whole race, who voluntarily gave himself up for all. At the same time, as is proved by the πρὸς ἔνδειξιν, κ. τ. λ., in ver. 26 (which is by no means a simple repetition of εἰς ἔνδειξιν), there is a constant allusion to that *grace* which manifests itself in the work of redemption, and is particularly expressed in the δικαιοῦντα, κ. τ. λ., *even while justifying*, etc.; and, in fact, both these attributes, justice and mercy, like the Divine and human natures of Christ, can, in the work of redemption, properly be considered separate only *in abstracto*, inasmuch as it *actually* exhibits them blended into a perfect unity.

(Πάρεσις occurs nowhere else in the Bible; had Paul intended it then as = ἄφεσις [as the term itself would allow], he would doubtless have chosen, in preference, the latter well-known word. Exod. xxxii. 34, in connexion with Acts xvii. 30, is a sufficient explanation of this passage; ὑπεριδεῖν = עָבַר there signifies "the overlooking," or "letting go."* The ἁμαρτήματα προγεγονότα, *sins that are past*, can, however, according to the following ἐν τῷ νῦν καιρῷ, *at the present time*, only mean the sins of the world before Christ's coming, in connexion, of course, with that original sin of Adam which was the source of all subsequent transgressions. In the Old Testament there was no *real*, but only a symbolical forgiveness of sins;† the former could not then exist [Heb. ix. 12, 18], because it was only

* Com. Ver.: "For the remission of sins that are past." Olshausen: "On account of God's overlooking (πάρεσιν) sins previously committed," i. e., leaving them unpunished, whence they *now* need expiation and forgiveness.—[K.

† The expression ἡ ἄφεσις τῶν ἁμαρτιῶν or παραπτωμάτων, *remission of sins* (Ephes. i. 7), must not be confounded with ἄφεσις ἁμαρτήματος, *remission of a sin*. The theocratical forgiveness of any *particular* sin was possible even under the Old Testament, but the forgiveness of *all* sins, actual sins as well as hereditary sin, can only proceed from Christ, and is a Divine act. It presupposes, namely, nothing less than the creation of a new and holy man, and the slaying of the old man, inasmuch as it is regeneration itself, on which account the forgiveness *of sins* is at the same time life and salvation. This happens, therefore, also only *once or twice*, and is only *confirmed* from time to time to the believer, as in the Eucharist; the former, however, is frequently repeated. (1 John ii. 1; Job xxxiii. 23.)

through their relation to Christ that the sacrifices of the Old Testament received their power of forgiveness.)

Finally, nothing can be more erroneous than, as Rückert and Reiche have recently proposed, to confine the redeeming and forgiving power of Christ to those sins only which were committed in the time of *ignorance*, and to deny the possibility of any forgiveness in the case of believers. This view, consistently carried out, would entirely destroy the very essence of the gospel, and convert it into glad tidings for the unbelieving only, but for believers a new and even more hopeless law. The utter fallacy of this opinion will, however, be further demonstrated at vii. 14, etc. Rather may we regard the time of ignorance as belonging not only to the whole race, and to whole nations, but also to *every individual*, and it must ever be regarded as a state which only gradually disappears. We must, if I may thus express myself, conceive of humanity as divided, not merely in its breadth, but also in its length; and every individual passes through, in his own case, the same stages of development as the race. To connect *ἐν τῇ ἀνοχῇ τοῦ Θεοῦ*, *in the forbearance of God*, with what follows, is entirely unnatural: it should be construed with *πάρεσις*, *overlooking, passing by*, of which it discloses the inward ground.

Ver. 26.—As the apostle had first exhibited the element of severity, he now also brings forward that of grace, which no less displays itself in the work of redemption. That to designate this, he likewise uses the expression *δικαιοσύνη*, arises no doubt from his desire to accumulate expressions of the same kind. As *δικαιοσύνη*, *righteousness*, itself proceeds from Christ, as he produces nothing but *δικαίους*, *righteous*, so also his work, in every form of its manifestation, has the Divine *δικαιοσύνη* as its foundation.

(Πρὸς ἔνδειξιν is scarcely a mere repetition of the foregoing *εἰς ἔνδειξιν*; true, *ἐν τῷ νῦν καιρῷ* might seem to favour it; but *δικαιοῦντα*, *κ. τ. λ.*, is too decidedly against it. In *εἰς τὸ εἶναι αὐτὸν δίκαιον*, *that he may be just*, is implied at the same time his being recognized as such by men.—*Δικαιοῦν* can only be understood as a manifestation of grace.)

Vers. 27-29.—After this explanation of the nature of the new way of salvation, Paul returns to that question which he had been treating in iii. 1, etc., whether there was any advantage in the case of the Jews,* and answers, no! (Ἐκκλείω, see Galat. iv. 17, "to exclude, *i. e.*, to make unavailing, inadmissible.") For, since here the question is not concerning such works as the law could alone produce, but concerning faith, Gentiles as well as Jews had access

* In the conception of *καύχησις*, *glorying*, *boasting*, is implied that which belongs to self, as opposed to grace; this iv. 2 shews with especial clearness. To *ἐξεκλείσθη* we must supply *ὑπὸ τοῦ Θεοῦ*.

to this grace, in case they believed. If the Jews had lived in true love, they would have rejoiced at this fact, but instead of this they were offended because God was so gracious.

(Νόμος, *law*,* has here the more extensive signification of "Divine ordinance or institution." The gospel may therefore be called the νόμος πίστεως, *law of faith*, in so far as it is that Divine ordinance which requires of men faith. And indeed faith *alone*, [as Luther rightly translates this passage in the sense of the apostle], for *in* it is contained everything, as the collective fruit of the tree in its germ; *beyond* and *besides* it there is nothing which belongs to the same spiritual position. Since, however, Gentiles as well as Jews are here spoken of, the ἔργα νόμου, *works of law*, can only mean the works of the moral law, which are derived from the will of God, demanding man's obedience.† These, in the most favourable case, are but the products of the man's own life, and are therefore transitory, like this life itself, but the works of faith partake of the eternal nature of that principle from which they proceed.)

Vers. 30, 31.—The one God stands in the same relation to all his children, and his different modes of dealing do not contradict one another,‡ but afford to one another mutual support.

('Επείπερ, *quandoquidem*, *siquidem*, is found nowhere else in the New Testament. On this account, also, it is not probable that the reading εἴπερ, which Lachman has admitted into his text from A.C. and other critical authorities, is the original one.—'Εκ and διὰ πίστεως do not stand *parallel* to one another, as designations of the source and cause, as Reiche still supposes; in this case, ἐκ τῆς πίστεως must also have been written. Διὰ τῆς πίστεως alone refers to the principal thought; ἐκ πίστεως has a special reference to the Jews [see iv. 12], who supposed that they were partakers of Divine grace, not as believers, but simply as the children of Abraham after the flesh.—The gospel establishes the law because it is the most sublime manifestation of the holiness and strictness of God. Sin

* The *meaning* of νόμος here may, perhaps, be what Olshausen assigns to it: the *ground* of its use, however, seems purely rhetorical. As the apostle is dwelling on *law* and its inability to justify, he naturally employs the same term in describing its opposite. Just as a man would say, "I know no law but the law of love." So at ch. viii. 2, "the law of the spirit of life." It seems, therefore, hardly worth while to attempt to fix the exact signification of a term which is used simply by way of rhetorical contrast.—[K.

† Glöckler is quite mistaken in his view that χωρὶς ἔργων νόμου is to be translated, "without the law of works," as the very collocation of the words shews. The law, according to Paul, is only to be abolished in its old form, in which it appears as making requirements upon the man from without; in the economy of grace it presents itself again as an inwardly operative law. (See on Galat. ii. 16, 18.)

‡ Calvin has this apt remark on the passage: "Ubi lex fidei opponitur, ex eo statim quondam repugnantiæ suspicionem caro arripit, ac si alterum alteri adversaretur. Præsertim vero facile obtinet falsa hæc imaginatio inter eos, qui præposterâ legis intelligentiâ imbuti nihil aliud in eâ quærunt quàm operum justitiam, promissionibus omissis."

never appears more fearful than at Golgotha, where, on account of it, God spared not his own Son.)

§ 7. ABRAHAM JUSTIFIED BY FAITH.

(IV. 1–25.)

In order to demonstrate more exactly the connexion between the New Testament and the law, and to vindicate the gospel from every charge of introducing any foreign element into religion, the apostle next proceeds to shew that even the saints of the Old Testament, amongst whom he mentions Abraham and David, had walked in the path of righteousness by faith. In order rightly to comprehend this whole argument, we must further remark, as was already observed on Matth. xi. 11, that the position of all the pious men in the Old Testament was by no means similar. There were some amongst them whose piety wore a purely legal expression, *e. g.*, Elijah; others in whom the legal form was thrown into the background, and the life of faith was predominant. To these last belong, in an especial degree, Abraham and David, the development of whose spiritual life bears, in fact, considerable resemblance to that of believing Christians. At the same time, with all this similarity, we must not lose sight of the difference between them, for by so doing we should rob the gospel of its specific character (John i. 17). The faith of Abraham and David had indeed, as well as the Christian's, the person of the Redeemer for its object, but then it was directed to him that *should come*, not to him who *had appeared;* it was only after the appearance of Christ, and the accomplishment of his work, that real power could proceed from him. (John vii. 29.) The very regeneration of the Old Testament, if we are disposed to assume its existence (see on Matth. xi. 11), can therefore only be regarded as *symbolical*, a character which the apostle himself seems to ascribe to it in ver. 23.

Vers. 1, 2.—Paul proves, from the Old Testament itself, that the righteousness of Abraham had not proceeded from his works.* He names Abraham, as being the natural progenitor of the Jewish race, as one whose spiritual character formed the illustrious example to which all Israelites looked.

(*Τί οὖν ἐροῦμεν* is not here constructed as an independent formula; for *τί* must be connected with *εὑρηκέναι*. Were we to take *τί ἐροῦμεν* in the usual way, we should still be obliged to supply *τί* to *εὑρηκέναι*. [See Æschyl. Eumenid. v. 154.] Strictly, Paul does not wish to ask,

* That it is possible to take another view of the history of Abraham is shewn by the epistle of James, ch. ii.

what has Abraham found or obtained, but *how* has he received that righteousness which we allow him to have? This thought is, however, intimated in the turn, what has he obtained *κατὰ σάρκα, according to the flesh?* The answer, therefore, is also not completely carried out, but only negatively; ver. 3 contains, on the other hand, the *positive* side, though indirectly. The *οὖν, then*, in ver. 1, connects this chapter with *ἀλλὰ νόμον ἱστῶμεν, we establish law*, in the last; "If, then, we establish the law by faith, so that the two cannot contradict one another, what can Abraham have obtained by works?"—We must connect *κατὰ σάρκα* with *εὑρηκέναι* [*i. e.*, hath found according to the flesh], and not with *πατέρα*. In its sense it = *ἐξ ἔργων*, *from works*, ver. 2. We may best understand *flesh*, here, of the outward in general [Galat. iii. 3], as contrasted with the *πνεῦμα, spirit*, the inward and life-giving. [See on Jas. ii. 26.]—*Δικαιοῦσθαι ἐξ ἔργων* = *ἔχειν δικαιοσύνην ἐκ νόμου*.—*Καύχημα* denotes the act of boasting and its object, *materia gloriandi*.—The fourth verse discloses plainly the ideas which lie at the foundation of this whole argument. Works give merit, merit justifies demands or boasting; grace, therefore, is incompatible with works; its only relation is that of debt. But God can never stand in the relation of a debtor to any creature, therefore Paul says *ἀλλ' οὐ πρὸς τὸν Θεόν*. For even where a *δικαιοσύνη τοῦ νόμου, righteousness of the law*, is in question, it is only by a gracious condescension on God's part that this becomes possible; it is, in fact, always only a righteousness in the sight of men. In ver. 2, *εἰ ἐδικαιώθη—ἔχει καύχημα* is to be construed, "if he, namely [as is in fact the case], is justified by works, he has indeed glory, but not before God, only before men." Paul then says here the same as James ii. 21. [On *εἰ* with the indicative, see Winer's Gram. p. 267.] If it meant, "if he had become righteous he would have glory," we should have *εἶχεν ἄν*.)

Vers. 3–5.—The apostle then proves from Gen. xv. 6, a passage which he quotes from the LXX., that it was not by his works that Abraham became righteous, but that his faith was reckoned to him for righteousness. *Works* might have brought him into the relation of a debtor or creditor, but *faith* brought him into the relation of grace, since it referred to a promise flowing entirely from the Divine mercy. This line of argument, taken in connexion with chapter vii., where we shall return to it, is admirably calculated to give us a clear conception of Paul's doctrine of justification. For it is not *δικαιοῦσθαι, justified*, itself, but *λογίζεσθαι εἰς δικαιοσύνην, counted for righteousness*, which corresponds to the Hebrew וַיַּחְשְׁבֶהָ לּוֹ צְדָקָה, and which forms the centre of the apostle's statement in this chapter. The two are, however, by no means synonymous, but stand exactly in the same relation to one another as the Roman Catholic (so far at least as it contains truth) and Protestant doctrines of justification, inasmuch as the former is implied in the δικαιοῦσθαι (to be *made* a righteous person), the latter in the λογίζεσθαι (to be *accounted* as such). Whatsoever is reckoned or imputed to a person, that the person cannot himself possess (see Rom. ii. 26, ἀκροβυστία εἰς περιτομὴν λογίζεται, *uncircumcision is counted*, etc.), but he is looked upon and treated as if he had it. This, now, is not predicated in the present passage of Abraham only, who lived 2000 years before the reconciliation effected in Christ, without which the δικαιοσύνην τοῦ Θεοῦ, *righteousness of God*, cannot be conceived as existing, but also of *those who lived* according to his example *after* Christ (vers. 11–24), so that the formula λογίζεσθαι εἰς δικαιοσύνην, *counted for righteousness*, appears as a general designation of justification in addition to δικαιοῦσθαι, *made righteous, justified*. In order duly to understand the meaning of these expressions, and to perceive their bearing upon the subject before us, we must consider yet more closely than was done at iii. 21, the *transition* from the legal position to that of grace, a matter which it is particularly difficult to represent. When the law has accomplished its purpose on the man, *i. e.*, when the recognition of sin (ἐπίγνωσις τῆς ἁμαρτίας, iii. 20) or true repentance is produced in him, he regards righteousness (which he recognizes as a reality, and in recognizing which he becomes aware of the contrast of his own condition) as something completely *external* to himself. But in the announcement of the Messiah the promise is made to him, that this righteousness shall, through His work, become an *inward* reality to himself; this announcement he embraces in *faith*, and, although still sinful, and far from δικαιοσύνη, yet his faith in that which is outward and future is reckoned to him as righteousness, *i. e.*, he is treated as a righteous person, and therefore as standing in a state of grace.* Now, the difficulty in this view lies especially in the circumstance that God, in his truthfulness, cannot regard a person as that which he is not; if the man is sinful, it would seem that the True One must look upon him and treat him as a sinner, until he ceases to be such; and if he actually ceases to be such, he can then again only be regarded as a righteous person, and no longer as a sinner at all. On this argument rests the opposition of the Roman Catholic church to the Protestant view, an argument which it seems at first sight impossible to refute; yet on closer examination it proves false, and calculated to lead men entirely astray with respect to the way of salvation. In fact, according to the Romish view, it is not the objective purpose of God which forms the irre-

* Redemption makes man, in the process of sanctification, free *from* sin; *with* sin no one can become blessed, as is, indeed, self-evident, for sin itself is the only source whatsoever of misery. But it is quite true that redemption begins *in* sin, that is to say, the man must begin as a sinner, must look upon himself in faith as righteous *for Christ's sake*, not on account of the somewhat improved condition of his own soul.

fragable foundation of man's faith, but the shifting condition of his own heart. If man thinks that he can discover this condition of righteousness wrought in him, he assures himself of his state of grace, but if, in times of temptation, he cannot discover it in himself, he doubts or despairs of it The purged eye of the regenerate man can detect, even in his best condition, much in himself that still needs to be cast out. (See at vii. 14.) The Romish church consequently maintains, and in perfect consistency with her principles, that man, in his earthly life, can never be *certain* of his being in a state of grace, but must remain in constant uncertainty; whilst the Protestant church teaches the exact contrary. The truth of the Protestant conception of this subject is seen most distinctly when we look more closely at that principle on which the Catholic doctrine is founded, namely, that God cannot regard any one as different from what he is. Take this sentiment literally, and since without the work of Christ no forgiveness of sins and no sanctification is conceivable, it will follow that *before* the accomplishment of Christ's atoning sacrifice no holy man could have lived, which contradicts the whole doctrine of Scripture. The notion must therefore be modified, in the first place, in accordance with that principle which teaches, that in every action of God all his attributes co-operate. God can therefore assuredly account a man to be something which he is not at present, whilst he looks to his own purpose which shall render the man that which he as yet is not. As unalterable, therefore, as is this determination, so true, also, is God's contemplation of that which *is* not yet as already existing (ver. 17). But besides this, it belongs to the very nature of faith, as a living state, and not a mere historical assent, *that it already contains within itself the essence of the object of belief;* it is an act of man appropriating the Divine, which of course presupposes that his inmost nature is akin to the Divine. At the time of Abraham, indeed, Christ himself and his whole work were as yet future; of Abraham, therefore, it can only be said, that God counted to him his faith for righteousness, inasmuch as in that omniscience to which all things are present, he regarded this future work as already accomplished. But in the case of all those who believe after the coming of Christ, faith contains already in itself the substance of this righteousness, in that the Redeemer has once for all accomplished the work of justification, as well, indeed, as of sanctification and glorification for all men (Rom. viii. 30). But if faith turns itself away from its proper object, the *Christ without* us and God's objective purpose of redemption, and directs itself to the *Christ within* us as the ground, not the consequence, of redemption, and we regard ourselves as objects of Divine favour only because and so long as we discover him within us—then faith altogether loses its proper nature, and we fall again under the law, as did once the Galatians. For man, therefore, so long as he is in this world, the imputing of righteousness (λογίζεσθαι εἰς δικαιοσύνην) must ever remain the way to true δικαιοσύνη itself; and if he thinks that he no longer needs the *former* because he already possesses the *latter*, he has fallen from faith.* As, therefore, the forgiveness of sins (that *first single* remission, by which man is translated into the state of grace, as well as subsequent *daily* forgiveness) is not imparted to the *old* man, who must die, nor to the *new* man, who cannot sin (1 John iii. 9), but to the inmost personality itself, which is conscious alike of the old man and of the new, as *belonging to it*, and which in the progress of regeneration must be gradually altogether transformed into the new man; so, also, with the imputation (λογίζεσθαι). Righteousness is not imputed to the old man but to the true personality, which perceives the essence of the old man *as its own*, but with deep repentance, and with a lively longing to be delivered from it. The substance of this true personality is, however, nothing else than that *scintilla* of the Divine likeness which has remained in man since the fall, and without which sin would form the very substance of the human being. Faith attaches itself to this spark, and then, deriving nourishment from the higher world, elicits again from this spark the flame of the Divine life.

(Ἐργάζεσθαι = ἔργα ποιεῖν, and that moreover as a means of attaining to δικαιοσύνη. According to the Divine *jus talionis*, man is treated according to the position which he assumes; the man who has recourse to justice alone, is treated according to its stern law, "Cursed is every one who continueth not in *all* that is written in the law" (Galat. iii. 10); but whosoever, on the other hand, clings in faith to grace, is regarded according to its overruling law. Χάρις, *grace*, as the opposite to ὀφείλημα, *debt*, has here accordingly the sense of, "what is undeserved," "what depends on no merit."—In ver. 5 the epithet applied to God, δικαιῶν τὸν ἀσεβῆ, *justifying the ungodly*, does not refer to Abraham *alone*, as Reiche still asserts, nor yet to other men *without* him; rather is it a general designation of God's relation to mankind. For to suppose that allusion is here made to some particular sin of Abraham's, for instance to his participation in the idolatry of his father Terah, as many commentators have been disposed to assume, is quite inadmissible; the question regards entirely universal sinfulness. And then we have in this way of understanding the passage an important proof, that

* We must not, therefore, frame the antithesis in this manner, *either* the man is a sinner, *or* he is a regenerate and holy man; the latter, also, is still a sinner, inasmuch as he retains the old man until death. But in his case God does not look to the old man, but to his own purpose of grace in Christ, and regards him, for Christ's sake, as altogether righteous.

Paul does not consider any one as excluded from the general sinfulness of the race; even Abraham himself, that venerable and holy patriarch, is an ἀσεβής, *ungodly*. *All* men in respect of God are in a state of *ungodliness*, and unable by their own powers to raise themselves into any other condition.* God *alone*, therefore, is the author of δικαιοσύνη, and proves himself to be such to those who come forward to meet him in faith; the endeavour to establish one's own righteousness is the surest method of shutting one's self out from the δικαιοσύνη Θεοῦ, *righteousness of God*. See Rom. x. 3.)

Vers. 6–8.—Paul then corroborates the truth he has advanced by the example of David, from Ps. xxxii. 1, 2, a passage which is likewise quoted according to the LXX. If we find here expressly added χωρὶς ἔργων, *without works*, it is yet plainly not the meaning of the apostle that works should be *wanting;* on the contrary, these possess in faith, and in that imputation of righteousness of which it is the means, their most plentiful source (Galat. v. 6); but however richly and purely works may proceed from this source, the *foundation* of final blessedness does not exist in *them*, but in that *principle* by which alone they become possible, *i. e.*, not in man, but in God. As, therefore, it is to God *alone* that thanks are due for the existence and creation of man, so also to him *alone* for man's *goodness:* it is not as if there entered into the latter *two* creative energies, first that of God, and then that of man (such a dualism makes all true goodness impossible, for this *consists especially in the deliverance from all that belongs to self*); there is assuredly but *one*, namely, of God, because all pure, good, true action on man's part, *is the act of God*, the only true Good, *in him*, so that man has and can regard nothing as *his own*, but sin, unfaithfulness and unbelief. (See at ix. 1.)

In the passage, however, adduced by the apostle, the question appears not at all to regard the *positive* imputation of righteousness, but only the *negative* non-imputation of sin, while at the same time nothing is expressed about faith. We might therefore regard the passage as inapplicable: but *forgiveness of sins* is surely not a human fancy, or a human action, in which man says to himself, "I have forgiveness of my sins," but a Divine act, a living *word of God*

* The *degrees* of sinfulness are not to be considered in regard of the life of faith, in and for themselves, but only the *effect* which is thereby produced upon the inmost condition of the soul. A person in a deeply sunken state may stand quite near to the kingdom of God, if sin has made him of a broken and contrite spirit (Matth. xxi. 31; Luke xv. 30), and a strict observer of the law outwardly may be far from this kingdom, if he has become, through his striving, hard-hearted, loveless and arrogant. The most desirable condition is, of course, one of earnest striving and freedom from gross transgressions, combined with humility, a sense of need, and faith. But every one who desires to come to Christ, must altogether, and in everything, recognize himself as a sinner.

uttered into the heart, which faith alone can appropriate. But the word and act of God is the most positive thing we can conceive, it is *being* itself; on which account Luther most rightly terms the forgiveness of sins, "life and blessedness," since it contains within itself the imputation of the righteousness of God.

('Αφιέναι and ἐπικαλύπτειν = נָשָׂא and כִּסָּה. The first expression indicates rather the New Testament aspect of the forgiveness of sins, as the real, even though but gradual, *taking away* of sin; the second, on the other hand, as well as the ἁμαρτίαν οὐ λογίζεσθαι, *not imputing sin*, rather the Old Testament view, according to which sin *remains* under the forbearance of God [Rom. iii. 25], until the completion of the work of Christ, in connexion with which the actual forgiveness of sins was first imparted to those who lived before Christ. Comp. Matth. xxvii. 53; 1 Pet. iii. 18.)

Vers. 9, 10.—Hereupon the apostle returns to consider the relation between Jews and Gentiles, and proves that this way of salvation by faith was designed, not merely for the Jews, but *also* for the Gentiles, since the occurrence in Gen. xv. 6 took place *before* circumcision was instituted, at a time, therefore, when Abraham stood on a level with the Gentiles.

(In ver. 9, supply ἔρχεται.—It were better to connect λέγομεν γάρ, κ. τ. λ., *for we say*, etc., with ver. 10, for the sense is, "from the passage concerning David it is not so distinctly to be gathered, whether or not the Gentiles are to be included amongst those to whom faith is counted for righteousness, but from that concerning Abraham, for," etc.—In ver. 10 πῶς means "under what circumstances.")

Vers. 11, 12.—Circumcision was not, therefore, the *means* of his justification, but only the *sign* of that justification which had preceded it; just as, also, baptism does not beget faith, but presupposes it. On this account also his name, "the Father of the Faithful," relates not merely to those who are physically circumcised, but to all those, whether Jews or Gentiles, who, like him, believe.

(A. C. and other critical authorities read περιτομήν instead of περιτομῆς; the genitive is, however, to be preferred as well on external as internal grounds.—Σημεῖον = אוֹת, that which points back to something else; σφραγίς the impression of a seal, by which something is confirmed [1 Cor. ix. 2; 2 Tim. ii. 19]. So in Heb. חוֹתָם.—Δικαιοσύνη πίστεως [ver. 18], the righteousness imputed, is treated as a *true* righteousness.—Εἰς τὸ εἶναι is not, with Tholuck, to be understood merely of consequence, but of intention, as ver. 16 proves. Abraham received the seal of circumcision first, *in order that* he might be presented as the general *Father* of believers. The conception of Father turns here on the community of character in father and child; believers are his true children [for the outward circumcision is the unessential part, ii. 28, 29], and these alone receive also the righteousness which he received.—In πιστεύοντες δι' ἀκροβυστίας, διά is not to be understood *causaliter*, but as in ii. 27, "during, under such circumstances."—The transition from the genitive to the dative (τοῖς) was perhaps occasioned by his looking back to λογισθῆναι.—Στοιχέω = περιπατέω, comp. Galat. v. 25, vi. 16; Phil. iii. 16. To refer στοιχοῦντες again to the Gentiles, is inadmissible, and requires the harsh inversion of explaining τοῖς οὐκ by οὐ τοῖς.)

Ver. 13.—This leads to the more explicit statement, that in Abraham's case *legal* relations had nothing whatever to do, but, as in the case of every promise, *grace* alone. It is remarkable, that it is here not merely said, the promise did *not* come by the law, for of course all that follows upon this must be regarded as reward, but that there is added, it came through the righteousness of faith. We should have expected that it would be said through grace, for it seems natural that the promise should precede, and then faith apprehend it as an object. But this difficulty vanishes, if we consider that the promises of God to Abraham form a climax, and that in this, whilst the first promise preceded his faith, the higher ones followed it. Here then, as Tholuck rightly remarks, reference is made to that promise which succeeded Abraham's greatest trial of faith (Gen. xxii. 16), and therefore his *heirship of the world* (κληρονομία κόσμου) does not mean the mere possession of Canaan, either literally or spiritually, but the incorporation into himself of the whole race, so far as it is believing, and the consequent spiritual control of the world by his influence. At the same time the idea reaches yet further, as even the Rabbinical writers indicate in that saying "possidet Abraham pater noster (et nos cum illo) mundum hunc et futurum." In its deepest sense it points to Christ's dominion over the world, which his believing people shall share with him (Rom. viii. 17; Rev. iii. 21), and in which spiritual elements shall manifest their energy outwardly. On this account, also, τῷ σπέρματι αὐτοῦ, *to his seed*, is added,* by which expression, according to Galat. iii. 16, Paul considers Christ to be designated, and further, in Christ, as the second Adam, the collective body of believers. (Galat. iii. 28, 29.) A similar thought is found in so many words in no passage of the Old Testament, but substantially in Gen. xv. 7 (where Canaan is promised) and Gen. xxii. 16.

Vers. 14, 15.—If accordingly they who are of the law were heirs, the promise would be annihilated, for they would be able to demand

* We must not overlook ἢ τῷ σπέρματι, for which only inconsiderable MSS. read καὶ τῷ σπέρματι. The ἢ introduces a more exact definition, "or rather," for it was in Christ that Abraham first became truly heir and lord of the world, and in Christ the human race.

all as *reward*. But since none can so keep the law as to be able to found any demands upon it, since it rather kindles God's anger against them, the entire assumption is inadmissible. (In ver. 14, οἱ ἐκ νόμου are opposed to οἱ ἐκ πίστεως, see Galat. iii. 9, 10.—Κενοῦσθαι, to be made κενόν, empty, powerless.—Between ver. 14 and ver. 15, we must supply the thought, "But it is in the very nature of the law impossible that it should make men heirs of the world, for so far from conferring merit, it only awakens indignation."—Ver. 15, ὀργὴν κατεργάζεται, *worketh wrath*, not by its nature, for that is holy and good, but through its power in bringing to light the depths of sin. [See more at vii. 10, etc.] "For where there is no law," etc. [οὐ γὰρ οὐκ, κ. τ. λ.], is merely a clause suggesting the ground of the ὀργὴν κατεργάζεσθαι; it is the law only that involves men in wretchedness, how then should it be able to make them the heirs of the world?)

Ver. 16.—The promise, then, could only come through faith, inasmuch as it thus only proved a *true* promise, *i. e.*, a merely gracious assurance; thus only, indeed, could it appear assured to *all*, inasmuch as if dependent upon the law its fulfilment would have been left to the will of unfaithful man, who in fact is only *by* the law exhibited as exceeding sinful. The contrast therefore, between "him who is of the law" (τῷ ἐκ τοῦ νόμου) and "him who is of faith" (τῷ ἐκ πίστεως), is not between Jews and Gentiles, but only between the legally righteous and believers, whether Jews or Gentiles. The member of the theocracy has not, merely as such, a share in the promise, unless he is at the same time a believer. But in these words the expression εἰς τὸ εἶναι βεβαίαν, *that the promise may be sure*, introduces to us a thought which is very important for the understanding of Paul's ideas in their entire connexion. Everything which depends upon the decision, faithfulness, and constancy of such an irresolute and wavering being as man, is, in Paul's view, extremely uncertain; but that which depends upon God, the unchangeable and eternal, is firmly established. On this account, the Divine promises afford an irrefragable certainty, because nothing can annul them; as God gives the promise, so also does he raise up men to believe it, and thus accomplishes all his works. But so great is the perversity of man, that he will not recognize this most certain foundation of salvation; he wishes to have God's unalterable promises and prophecies considered as *dependent* upon him for their execution, though in this way the fulfilment of a prophecy would tend to the merit of man, and not to the glory of God, which were plainly a blasphemous assertion. According to Paul's mode of representation, the blessedness of man is certain only because God has promised it and firmly intends it, and he only who believes in this decided will of God, has this salvation also wrought in him. (On the harmony of this with human freedom, nay, on its being the only true basis of that freedom, see at chap. ix 1, etc.)

Ver. 17.—The citation of Gen. xvii. 5 (which passage is also quoted exactly according to the LXX.), is intended to prove still more decidedly Abraham's right to the title of Father of the Faithful, as a relation extending beyond the limits of Israel, and embracing all nations. (*Τιθέναι* = the Hebrew נָתַן.) But with respect to the latter half of the verse, which presents many difficulties, in the first place the reading *ἐπίστευσας*, which is given by F. G. and the Syriac version, by which the following words are connected with the quotation, must be rejected as inadmissible, from the preponderance of critical evidence in favour of the usual reading. The construction *κατέναντι οὗ ἐπίστευσε Θεοῦ* must be explained as an attraction of an unusual character certainly, since in this case a dative is affected by it. (See the treatise of Schmidt on this verse in the tübinger Zeitschrift, 1831, part ii.; Bernhardy's Syntax, p. 299, etc.; and Winer's Gram. p. 155.) But the sense of the words it must be allowed that it is difficult to determine, on account of the *κατέναντι*, whose usual signification, "against, over against," seems here unfitting. We may, however, take it most simply as = לִפְנֵי or בְּעֵינֵי, in the following sense; "Abraham is, in the eye of God, *i. e.*, of his omniscience, the father of us all, even before we existed."* To this sense the subsequent description of God, the object of Abraham's faith, as the Creator, answers very well. The *ζωοποιεῖν τοὺς νεκρούς*, *quickening the dead*, and *καλεῖν τὰ μὴ ὄντα ὡς ὄντα*, *calling the things which are not as though they were*, refer, primarily, as the context shews, to the begetting of Isaac (ver. 19, 20) by his parents, Abraham and Sarah, when their bodies were "dead." The whole history of Abraham is, however, here as also elsewhere (Gal. iv.) *treated as a type*, and thus Isaac, who was born through the power of God, is considered as an image of the entire spiritual Israel, and consequently *ζωοποιεῖν*, *quickening*, and *καλεῖν*, *calling*, as designations of spiritual awakening and regeneration. (vi. 13.) Thus taken, the "calling the non-existent as existent" (*καλεῖν τὰ μὴ ὄντα ὡς ὄντα*) becomes particularly significant. The non-existent (*τὰ μὴ ὄντα*) is by no means to be understood of that which is absolutely nothing (nihilum negativum), of which it can only be said that it *is not;* but only of that existence which is not yet fashioned into a concrete form, as it is also to be taken in the language of Plato and Philo.

* Amongst the many explanations from different sources to be found in Tholuck and Reiche, that of the ancient Fathers, Chrysostom, Theodoret, and others, deserves attention. They take *κατέναντι* after Genes. ii. 18 — *καθ' ὁμοίωμα*, so as to get the sense, "Abraham is the image of God, an image of the true Father of all paternity." The meaning is beautiful, but does not agree with the context, because the following description of the creative agency of God, if this interpretation were admitted, must then bear an application to Abraham, which is not the case.

(See Philo de vitâ Mosis, p. 693, de creat. p. 728.) Thus, not only may whole nations, in so far as they have not yet entered into existence, be called *μὴ ὄντα*, although they already exist in God's sight, and already live potentially in their progenitors, but the natural, unregenerate man, may also be called a *μὴ ὢν*, *non-existent*, inasmuch as in him the true idea of man, the *ἄνθρωπος Θεοῦ*, is not yet realized, which is realized only by his regeneration.

(Καλεῖν = קָרָא, is the creative call of the Almighty, by which he, according to the analogy of the first act of creation [Gen. i. 3], calls forth concrete formations from the general stream of life. Ὡς is to be taken simply as a particle of comparison, "vocat ea, quæ [non nondum] sunt, tamquam [jam] adsint." What a powerful description of that God who beholds all the future as essentially present!)

Ver. 18.—The example of Abraham was of too much importance to the apostle for him to break off his contemplation of it so soon. Every thing, in fact, which is related of him, is a type of the life of faith under the new economy (vers. 23, 24). As, therefore, Abraham, *against* all hope, was obliged to believe in hope, and, consequently, to wrestle in order to hold fast his faith and hope against all the contradictions of the senses and of nature ; so also does the conflict of faith manifest itself in every child of God.*

Harder and more deeply reaching than all legal struggles, is the struggle of faith against unbelief, which would rather have the tender conscience believe anything than its own salvation. It was only in appearance that Abraham's fight of faith referred to anything else than his salvation ; for, in fact, Abraham's blessedness depended just as much upon the birth of his promised son, from whom the Messiah was to descend, as the blessedness of every believer upon the birth of the new man in him. But faith itself is already this new man coming to the birth, and, therefore, all depends upon its maintenance and increase.

(Chrysostom very justly observes, in explanation of the Oxymoron, *ἐπ' ἐλπίδι τῇ τοῦ Θεοῦ, παρ' ἐλπίδα τὴν ἀνθρωπίνην*, *in hope*, viz., *in God*, *against hope*, viz., *human hope*.—Εἰς τὸ γενέσθαι must again be understood of *purpose* : the exercises of Abraham's faith were appointed not only with the design of perfecting him, but also of depositing in him the germs of perfection for future believers ; his life was not merely a foreshadowing, but, if I may be allowed the expression, the

* We might accordingly say, that the further faith stands from the objects of its longing, or hope from its fulfilment, the more intense and powerful it must be, if it asserts itself at all. Abraham's faith may therefore appear to be greater than that of believing Christians, for they have their exercise of it rendered easier, by beholding the effects of that which they believe. At the same time, in considering the degree of faith and its character, we must especially take into account its real substance, and in this respect the New Testament stands far above the Old.

fore-*reality*, *i. e.*, the true germ of what was to come. De Wette supposes that this interpretation would ascribe to Abraham a distinct intention in his believing. But we surely need not assume that the patriarch was conscious of the purpose of these dispensations; the words refer only to the purpose of God.—The new quotation is from Gen. xv. 5, where *οὔτως*, *so*, refers to the stars, with whose multitude God compares Abraham's descendants.)

Vers. 19-22.—As the object on which Abraham's faith was especially exercised, the apostle now names the birth of Isaac. If we regard this event merely as securing to Abraham legitimate issue, there appears in fact an essential difference between Abraham's faith and that of the New Testament; but this mode of understanding it is entirely opposed to the view of Paul. From Galat. iv. 22, etc., it appears that the significance of Isaac was no less than this, that he was a *type of Christ*, who was to proceed from his descendants. Paul, therefore (Galat. iii. 16), treats of the seed of Abraham, *i. e.*, primarily, Isaac, as Christ, and in Christ again, as the second Adam, beholds all his believing people.

(Ver. 19.—The usual reading *οὐ κατενόησε* is indeed preferable to the *ὡς*, which perhaps sprang from *οὐ* by a mistake of the copyists, but must yield, as Reiche justly remarks, to the simple *κατενόησε*. For this brings out the thought that Abraham was well acquainted with all the unfavourable outward circumstances, and yet believed. A. C. 67, as well as the Syriac and Coptic versions, support *κατενόησε*, but it is difficult to understand how *οὐ* can have crept into the text. Yet it is only with the reading *κατένοησε* that the following *δέ* [ver. 20] has its proper force.—The words *νεκροῦσθαι* and *νέκρωσις* refer here to the deadness of the powers of generation. [Heb. xi. 12.] Concerning Abraham's and Sarah's age, see Gen. xvii. 17.—Πον without accent means, in the case of numbers, "about;" so in the New Testament only here; in Heb. ii. 6, iv. 4, it means "somewhere."—*Διακρίνεσθαι*, properly "to be divided, separated," and thereby "to lose one's position, to waver, stagger." So repeatedly of unbelief, as spiritual unsteadiness [Matth. xxi. 21; Mark xi. 23; James i. 6; Rom. xiv. 23]. With this is contrasted, in *ἐνδυναμοῦσθαι*, moral firmness and strength.—As opposed to *πληροφορεῖσθαι*, unbelief might also have been designated by *κένωσις*; for this verb, as well as the substantive *πληροφορία*, represents faith as the replenishment of the inward man with spiritual life [Rom. xiv. 5; Col. ii. 2; 1 Thess. i. 5; 2 Tim. iv. 17].—"Giving glory to God' [*δοὺς δόξαν τῷ Θεῷ*] is the practical recognition of the Divine omnipotence, which accomplishes that which it promises.)

Vers. 23, 24.—After this detailed consideration of the life of faith as manifested in Abraham, Paul declares the *principle* which justifies such a consideration. Abraham's history he regards not as something dead and past, but as the living history of believers in every age. This passage, along with 1 Cor. ix. 10, x. 6; Galat. iv. 24, etc., belongs to those most significantly instructive as to the mode of treating the Old Testament according to the doctrine of the apostles. Its value lies not in the externals of its history, but in *the spirit which pervades them*, and in this it has under the new economy, also, its abiding truth. To attribute the whole mode of treatment, which Paul here as elsewhere applies to the Old Testament, to Jewish habits of thought, a view which Reiche in particular has again defended, destroys not only the apostolical character of Paul, but also the very essence of the Old Testament, which, as the eternal word of God, is, according to our Lord's own words (Matth. v. 18), to abide when heaven and earth have passed away.

(The μέλλει λογίζεσθαι, *is to be reckoned*, must be regarded from the position occupied by Abraham and his generation. But if in this place not faith in Jesus, but in the Father who raised him up, is brought forward, it is accounted for by a reference to the "quickening" [ζωοποιεῖν] in ver. 17, which manifested itself most gloriously in the resurrection of Christ. For the physical and spiritual interpenetrate each other in the conception of ζωοποιεῖν, as in that of ζωή. [John vi.] God is the awakener of life in every form of its manifestation. Besides, the ἐγείρειν, *raising*, presupposes a preceding θνήσκειν, *dying*, so that a reference to the death of Christ is implied in this verse, as well as distinctly expressed in that immediately following.)

Ver. 25.—But while in iii. 25 δικαιοσύνη is connected simply with the blood-shedding of Christ, δικαίωσις is here connected with the resurrection. The older commentators have found great difficulty in this mode of representation, but understood according to the tenor of v. 10, vi. 4, the thought expressed in the passage is quite simple. For as resurrection necessarily presupposes the preceding death, so also upon the death of Christ, who is the life, necessarily follows the resurrection, *i. e.*, the victory over death. These therefore in the life of our Lord stand related to each other as two necessary complementary halves, which it is altogether impossible to conceive as existing without each other. It is not the death of Christ in itself which has significance, but only that death which is done away by the resurrection. But as the death and resurrection of Christ form an intimate unity, so also in man the death of the old and the rising up of the new; neither can be conceived apart from the other. It is impossible, that in any person sins can really be forgiven, and the old man be crucified without the new man arising; and when the new man begins to live, the death of the old man must take place at the same time. In consequence, therefore, of the necessary connexion between these two events, only one at a time is commonly mentioned, *either negatively* the forgiveness of sins, *or positively* the communication of the new life. But in some cases both are united, as here, and in v. 10, and then the *negative* feature, the putting away of the old, is connected with the death, and the *positive*, the communication of the new, is annexed to and founded upon the resurrection of the Redeemer. In the term *δικαίωσις* in this passage, therefore, we must recognize the act, which makes righteous and creates the new man, an act expressed in ver. 10, by *σώζεσθαι*, *saved;* while the expression *διὰ τὰ παραπτώματα ἡμῶν*, *for our offences*, answers to the *καταλλαγή*, *reconciliation*, in v. 11. For the *παραπτώματα* are the sins which separate man from God, and which need first of all a remission, a reconciliation (*ἄφεσις*, *καταλλαγή*), on account of which the Son of God was delivered up to death. In these two mutually complementary halves the whole work of God in the soul of man is complete, and neither can be wanting where this work has truly begun, although no doubt at different crises of the spiritual life, now one, now the other element may predominate.

(On *παραδιδόναι*, scil. *εἰς θάνατον*, see Acts iii. 13; Rom. viii. 32; Isaiah liii. 12. In Ephes. v. 2, it is said, *παρέδωκεν ἑαυτὸν προσφορὰν καὶ θυσίαν*, *he delivered himself an offering and sacrifice.* —In the life and work of Christ all was done *for us*, *nothing for himself;* for he already possessed all things with his Father, before he became man [2 Cor. viii. 9].—*Δικαίωσις* is not here = *δικαιοσύνη*; for as *διὰ τὰ παραπτώματα ἡμῶν* must be understood "in order that our transgressions might be pardoned," so *διὰ τὴν δικαίωσιν ἡμῶν* must be explained "in order that righteousness may be wrought in us." *Δικαίωσις*, therefore, denotes the Divine act of making righteous, as *διὰ τὰ παραπτώματα*, the Divine act of forgiveness.)

§ 8. Of the Fruits of Faith.

(V. 1–11.)

To this complete exposition of the doctrine of the new way of salvation itself, according to its scriptural foundation, the apostle now annexes some intimation of the *effects* of the life of faith, by which its pre-eminent excellence is first fully brought to light. True, Paul could here only cursorily allude to them, because their full development needed to be preceded by some preliminary topics which are discussed in the next chapters. It is not until the eighth chapter that we find a full portraiture of the infinite consequences of redemption, alike to the individual and to the whole creation.

Ver. 1.—Paul includes under one expression the whole fulness of those blessings which accrue to the man who is justified *through* faith (as the receptive cause), *by* grace (as the creative cause), viz., εἰρήνη πρὸς τὸν Θεόν, *peace with God.* The conception of εἰρήνη = שָׁלוֹם is here distinguished by the addition of πρὸς τὸν Θεόν, not merely from false peace, the εἰρήνη πρὸς τὸν κόσμον, *peace with the world*, which is destroyed by the influence of Christ (John xvi. 33), which calls forth a struggle against sin (ver. 3, etc.); but also from that higher degree of peace, that inward peace of soul, the εἰρήνη πρὸς σεαυτόν, which Paul also calls εἰρήνη Θεοῦ, *peace of God* (Phil. iv. 7 ; Col. iii. 15), and Christ in John's gospel εἰρήνη ἐμή, *my peace.* (John xiv. 27.) The two stand, in fact, in the same relation to one another as justification and sanctification ; justification (the λογίζεσθαι εἰς δικαιοσύνην) gives at once *reconciliation*, and with it *peace toward God*, the consciousness of being in a state of grace, the contrary to which is enmity toward God (ἔχθρα εἰς Θεόν. See viii. 7). No doubt this state contains within itself sanctification in the germ, but only in the germ ; because the old man still lives, inward harmony of life is at first only partially restored. The completeness of this harmony is only a *fruit* of life in the Spirit (Rom. viii. 6 ; Galat. v. 22), whilst the life of faith *begins* with εἰρήνη πρὸς τὸν Θεόν, as flowing at once from the first act of grace. As an author of peace in every form, God himself is moreover called ὁ Θεὸς τῆς εἰρήνης, *the God of peace* (Rom. xv. 33 ; 2 Cor. xiii. 11 ; 1 Thess. v. 23 ; 2 Thess. iii. 16. The reading ἔχωμεν, which Lachmann and Scholz have adopted from A.C.D.I., must, from internal considerations, yield to the reading ἔχομεν ; for it is scarcely pertinent to call upon men to have peace with God ; peace with God is the gift of his grace.)

Ver. 2.—As the second blessed consequence of justification, the apostle, after a parenthesis, presents to us the exultation felt in the hope of future glory. For the words " through whom," etc., cannot be understood to mean, that the access (προσαγωγή) is another result of the justification by faith (δικαιοῦσθαι ἐκ πίστεως), for then in the first place the construction would have been continued with καί, and then Paul would have avoided the introduction of the words εἰς τὴν χάριν, *into the grace*, which necessarily suggest quite another thought. Tholuck, indeed, has proposed to place a stop after ἐσχήκαμεν, but this the reading τῇ πίστει will not permit. These words are indeed wanting in B.D.F.G. and other critical authorities, but were manifestly omitted only to avoid the connexion of προσαγωγή with what follows. Besides, even if τῇ πίστει were away, the placing a stop after ἐσχήκαμεν leaves to εἰς τὴν χάριν ταύτην no proper connexion with what follows. And further, that Paul elsewhere (Ephes. ii. 18, iii. 12, the verb is found 1 Pet. iii. 18) uses this word of that access to God which is opened for the soul, can be no reason for giving it this sense in the present passage, since here it is defined more exactly by the addition of *εἰς τὴν χάριν ταύτην*. The whole clause, *δι' οὗ—ἐστήκαμεν*, *through whom—we stand*, must therefore be placed in a parenthesis, expressive of the fact that the power of the Redeemer not only produces peace at the same time *with* justification, but even introduces the soul into the *antecedent* state of grace so that "this grace" (*ἡ χάρις αὕτη*) is the very *righteousness of faith* itself, to which not our own power, but Christ's grace alone can conduct us.

(The allusion to a *προσαγωγεύς* who, so to speak, introduces the soul to God, is, by the above remarks, proved to be inappropriate; nor has it otherwise any scriptural foundation.—The perfect, *ἐσχήκαμεν*, *we have had*, forms an opposition to the preceding present *ἔχομεν*. Paul wishes to refer *all* to Christ, to make him appear as the Author and Finisher of our renewal. The *καί* is, therefore, to be taken emphatically, "by whom *also already* we have received access."—Τῇ *πίστει* may also be connected with *εἰς τὴν χάριν*, yet it is better to take *εἰς* = *πρός*, to connect it with *προσαγωγή*, and to regard *τῇ πίστει* = *πιστεύοντες*.—'Εστήκαμεν does not denote the mere standing in a certain relation; but intimates the firmness and security of the state of grace, as opposed to all wavering.—The *δόξα Θεοῦ*, *glory of God*, Reiche refers to the Divine image in man; this does not, however, suit the context, because *ἐπ' ἐλπίδι*, *in hope*, is added; for the Divine likeness is not merely restored to the regenerate man in hope, but in reality. The expression rather denotes the heavenly existence of God, participation in which constitutes the highest blessedness of the creature. And in the connexion of *καυχᾶσθαι* with *ἐλπίς* is implied the irrefragable certainty of being partaker of the glory of God.)

Vers. 3, 4.—Parallel with this survey of *the glory of the future*, the apostle, by a bold contrast, places the *sufferings of the present*, which proceed just as necessarily from the *righteousness of faith*, as does the *peace with God*. (2 Tim. iii. 12.) For there resides in the believer a principle which rebukes the sin which is in the world, and by so doing excites it against him, which allows no indecision, but everywhere either attracts or repels. In these very sufferings of the present, therefore, is contained a source of exaltation* for the Christian, in that they are not punish-

* Rückert very pointedly remarks on this passage: "We must not detract anything from the conception contained in *καυχᾶσθαι*, unless we wish, at the same time, to detract from the powerful character of the apostle; he is not only undaunted, not only of good courage, but really joyful, really lifted up in mind, nay, he reckons it *as an honour to himself*, that tribulation befals him, for this is to him a pledge of future glory." But what an advance manifests itself here when compared with the Old Testament! In the book of Job the doubts of the sufferer, on account of his sufferings, wrestle anxiously

ments to him, but the means of his perfection. (James i. 2, etc.) The three stages of ὑπομονή, δοκιμή, and ἐλπίς, *endurance, approval*, and *hope*, are considered as proceeding from the sufferings; whilst the former denotes the state of moral earnestness and of faithful endurance, δοκιμή relates to that state of *approval as genuine* which thence results, and bears within it *hope* as its blossom.*

(Δοκιμή is the act of testing, but also that state of approval as genuine which proceeds from trial. So δοκίμιον unites in itself both significations. [See James i. 3; 1 Pet. i. 7.] Καταισχύνω is to be taken actively, "hope puts not to shame," not intransitively, "hope is not ashamed," *i. e.*, is well-founded.)

Ver. 5.—This hope, thus born in conflict, contains, however, within itself, the assurance of obtaining *future* glory; for, as an earnest of it, we have already *here below* the love of God shed abroad in our hearts. The "love of God" is thus conceived, therefore, to be only, so to speak, the *secret* presence of God himself in our souls, whilst in eternal blessedness God gives himself to his saints as the manifested One. Accordingly the love of God is not the inward life of man in a state of exaltation, the life of feeling heightened in intensity, but it is a higher principle which has been grafted into the man, the Πνεῦμα ἅγιον, *the Holy Spirit*. These words express the *substantial* cause, *love* the *actual* effect: but essentially they are identical, for the love of God cannot be regarded as separate from the essential being of God in its highest *manifestation, i. e.*, the Holy Ghost. God's love is there only where he himself is, for he *is* love, and does not *have* love as something in or beside himself.

(Καταισχύνω = בּוֹשׁ "to make ashamed, to disappoint by want of success." Rom. ix. 33, x. 11.—In ἡ δὲ ἐλπίς the article is not to be taken = αὕτη, for there is but one true hope; rather is this clause to be taken as the fourth member, denoting, "but hope works fulfilment, or has in itself fulfilment," so that the colon must be placed after καταισχύνει. The words ὅτι, κ. τ. λ., ver. 5, are not in fact to be connected with καταισχύνει alone, but with καυχώμεθα [ver. 3,] and indeed the whole passage in vers. 3, 4.—According to that Pelagian and Rationalistic view which is opposed to the doctrine of the communication of the Spirit, ἀγάπη Θεοῦ, *love of God*, means the love of man to God; in the apostle's meaning it is the love of God to man, which however awakens in him reciprocal love [1 John iv. 19], not indeed proceeding from his own mere natural powers, but from the higher powers of the Divine Spirit. Only when thus taken can

with his still weak faith; here the believer rejoices boldly in all affliction, and exults in it.

* On the import of ἐλπίς see more at Rom. viii. 24.

it be properly said of love, that it is shed abroad, for it is identical with the element of the Spirit, and only contained in his manifestation. The *ἐκκέχυται*, *shed forth*, is founded upon the figure of a spiritual stream which spreads itself out over men; a figure, indeed, but in which there is this reality, that a higher power takes possession of man's being. [See John vii. 38, 39; Acts ii. 16, seq.; Is. xxxii. 15; Ezek. xxxvi. 25; Joel ii. 28.] The movement, by which the Spirit is shed abroad, is conceived as connected with his *remaining* in the inner man; therefore we find *ἐν* not *εἰς*.—The *καρδία*, *heart*, is regarded as the receptacle of the Spirit, as the centre of the disposition and of the inclinations; for instance, *νοῦς* could not be used here. [See my opus. theol. p. 156 seq.]—The added clause *τοῦ δοθέντος ἡμῖν*, *who is* [*was*] *given to us*, is not pleonastic beside *ἐκκέχυται*; the relation of the two expressions is this: the Spirit was given at the day of Pentecost once for all to mankind as a whole, but it is not therefore *shed forth* in every individual heart; this requires the personal appropriation of the work of Christ. The addition of *τοῦ δοθέντος ἡμῖν* is not therefore unnecessary, but expresses the *possibility*, which is provided for every one, of receiving the Holy Spirit poured forth into his heart. See John vii. 39, xvi. 7.)

Ver. 6.—The nature of Divine love is then exhibited by the apostle, in the most illustrious proof which it could give of its power, in the sacrifice of the Son of God. It manifests itself, therefore, in the same self-sacrificing character in the hearts of believers also, to whom it is imparted by that Holy Spirit which Christ obtained for men by his death. (John vii. 39.) The leading thought in this verse presents no difficulty, after what has been said on iii. 25, but the different readings of the text demand a more exact consideration. The *ἔτι* at the commencement of the verse has probably occasioned all the variations with which it abounds.* In the first place, for *ἔτι* several MSS. read *εἴγε*, others *εἰ γάρ*, or *εἰ τι*. Semler, followed by Usteri, concludes, therefore, that *εἰ* is the right reading, and supposes, in the original letter of the apostle, an anacoluthon, to avoid which some transcribers wrote *ἔτι*. This hypothesis seems, in fact, at first sight, decidedly plausible; yet the unwonted position of *ἔτι* affords a sufficient explanation of the origin of the different readings, while on carefully weighing the passage, we find its pre-

* Compare, on this point, the critical essay of Professor Franz Ritter, of Bonn, in the "Zeitschrift für Philosophie und kathol. Theologie," Heft 19 (Cologne, 1836), p. 46, etc., who reckons this passage among the few in the New Testament to which conjectural criticism must be applied. In fact, according to Ritter, we should here read *ἔτι γὰρ ὄντων ἡμῶν ἀσθενῶν κατὰ καιρὸν Χριστὸς ὑπὲρ ἀσεβῶν ἀπέθανε*, according to the analogy of ver. 8, in which the same collocation is found. But the exercise of conjecture, where so many critical appliances present themselves, appears justly to most modern critics altogether inadmissible.

fixture accounted for on grounds of *emphasis*, which led the ardent soul of the apostle to its premature utterance. Yet, besides this, several weighty authorities, A.B.C.D.F.G. and others, repeat ἔτι after ἀσθενῶν. Griesbach has even admitted this reading into the text; but it was rejected at once by Knapp, and, in fact, it appears only to have been adopted by those MSS. which had erased ἔτι at the beginning of the verse, and were determined by the parallel in ver. 8. If we retain the double ἔτι, we must explain the repetition by the strong feeling under which Paul wrote, just as in vii. 21. No doubt the whole stress of the thought (as in iv. 5) is laid upon the fact, that men did not amend themselves *before*, and do not now receive the blessings of Christ, as it were, for a reward, but that he died for them, even whilst they were *yet* godless and estranged from God, so that this highest act of love was the very *means* of their transformation. The objection, viz., that God, in his holiness, cannot love the ungodly so long as they remain what they are, is obviated by the consideration that in no man does evil manifest itself *absolutely*, but always in such a way as to attach itself to the remains of the image of God in him. Inasmuch, therefore, as God loves the proper substance of man, his true, though now darkened and repressed self, he hates that element of sin in or about man which impedes his free development. (On the transposition of ἔτι, see Winer's Gram. p. 509.—Ἀσθενῶν, *weak*, is explained not merely by ἀσεβῶν, *ungodly*, but also in ver. 8, by ἁμαρτωλῶν, *sinners*, and in ver. 10 by ἐχθροί, *enemies*. At the same time it is not personal trangressions which are referred to, which are only derived from something deeper, nor a *few* particularly sinful men only (iv. 5), but the *condition* of moral weakness belonging to *all* men, without exception. [See Galat. iv. 9, 13; Heb. iv. 15, v. 2.]—Κατὰ καιρόν = εὐκαιρῶς, at the time appointed by God. [Galat. iv. 4; 1 Pet. i. 20; Heb. ix. 26.]—On the signification of ὑπέρ, in its reference to the vicarious death of Christ, see Rom. v. 15.)

Vers. 7, 8.—In order to display in the fullest light the excellency of the Divine love, it is compared with the noblest workings of natural human love, which, however, remain far below it. But in the communication of the love of God to men through the Holy Spirit (ver. 5), is also given the possibility of imitating Christ in the point of loving our enemies (Matth. v. 44, 45; 1 Pet. ii. 21). Special difficulties have been discovered, strange to say, in ver. 7, though, as Reiche justly remarks, the passage is quite simple. Semler even regarded vers. 7, 8, as interpolated; Grotius would read ἀδίκου for δικαίου, and others have asked, whether δικαίου and ἀγαθοῦ were substantives or adjectives, masculines or neuters. Since the whole question is about persons, in the first place both expressions must, of course, be also referred to persons. And further, as regards the terms δίκαιος, *righteous*, and ἀγαθός, *good*, the context plainly leads us to assume that δίκαιος designates the character of the righteous man, who performs whatever can be *required* of him, ἀγαθός the character of the benevolent man, who does *more* than others venture to ask.* The former we may esteem and respect, the latter, on the other hand, we can love; and even earthly love can lay down its life for the object of its affections, but Divine love died for its enemies.

(Ver. 7.—The first γάρ is explained by an ellipsis, "but this is something noble, something unheard of!"—Τάχα = ἴσως is found again in the New Testament, only at Philem. ver. 15.—Τολμᾶν marks the highest degree of self-sacrifice.—Συνιστάναι, "to prove, make known." See iii. 5.)

Vers. 9, 10.—As in iv. 25, Paul now again places alongside of the *first effect wrought by Christ*, viz., the justification (δικαίωσις) procured by his death, *the other* part of his work which is here designated as *salvation* (σωτηρία), and ascribed to his *life*. The two, as already remarked at the former passage, are by no means to be *separated*, but, at the same time, in their connexion they must also not be *confounded*. The *first* is always absolute; for although the first forgiveness of sins, by which man enters into a state of grace, is daily repeated, on account of continual transgressions (1 John ii. 1), yet it is always vouchsafed *total and entire*, for a *partial* forgiveness is none at all; the *second*, on the other hand, is the subject of a gradual *development*, and is complete only with REDEMPTION (ἀπολύτρωσις, 1 Cor. i. 30; Rom. viii. 23), in the more limited sense of the word. On this very account, therefore, as has already been remarked, the state of grace cannot have its foundation in the new life in man, because this is always but relative, and therefore can never give peace (ver. 1); where this is, notwithstanding, done, as in the doctrine of the Romish church, its consequence is continual insecurity (*i. e.*, an uncertainty as to one's being in a state of grace), a condition which the doctrine of truth rejects, because no effort can be successful which does not proceed from a heart altogether reconciled, and living *at peace with God*. In this essential difference between forgiveness of sins and sanctification, lies the apostle's justification for representing them *as standing in mutual relation*, and drawing from one a conclusion with respect to the other.

(Δικαιοῦσθαι, *justified*, and καταλλάσσεσθαι, *reconciled*, are here used as entirely synonymous; the proper substance of both is *the remission of sins*, the negative element of salvation, the removal of the old, the barrier. [On καταλλαγή, see at Rom. iii. 24, 25.] This

* The same relation subsists in Latin between *justus* and *bonus*. See Cicero de offic. iii. 15. "Si vir bonus is est, qui prodest quibus potest, nocet nemini, recte *justum* virum, *bonum* non facile reperiemus."

transaction, *an act of God*, occurs while man is yet in the condition of an enemy to God; since, then, by this act, he becomes a friend [φίλος Θεοῦ, ἠγαπημένος, Ephes. i. 6], how much more easy is it to be assured that the work he has begun will be consummated in salvation, [σωτηρία]? Neither is this last, however, according to the apostle, *a work of man*, as if God began, indeed, the new life in him, but the man himself is to continue and complete it [see at ix. 1]; he who is the Author is himself also the Finisher of our faith [Heb. xii. 2], and that indeed by his ζωή, his glorified life at the right hand of God. And it is precisely this climax, indicated by the πολλῷ μᾶλλον, *much more* [which is expressly repeated in ver. 10] that constitutes the peculiarity of the present passage as compared with iv. 25. The thought is not to be understood *objectively*, as implying that Christ, when exalted, had more power than in his humiliation, but only *subjectively*, as it is apprehended by man. The power of Christ is equal in all stages of his life, but in his state of humiliation he withheld the manifestation of his power, and hence, after his resurrection, it presents itself to our human apprehension as a positively *increasing* power. We may explain the thought, therefore, thus: he whom God has regenerated, he will, we may trust, maintain and perfect in his regenerate state, and the conceivableness of apostacy gradually diminishes till it reaches a minimum. Σωτηρία, *salvation*, here, as well as ἀπολύτρωσις, *redemption*, in 1 Cor. i. 30, is to be taken in the narrower sense; in its wider signification it includes, also, that justification (δικαιοῦσθαι) in which lies the pledge of the further development of spiritual life. Σωτηρία, finally, stands commonly alone, as the mere contrary to ἀπώλεια, *perdition*, but in this passage it appears in a connexion which we should never have expected, and this shews us with what care and judgment we should supply ellipses in Scripture. Had not ἀπὸ τῆς ὀργῆς, *from wrath*, stood here, certainly no one would have supplied this phrase, but perhaps ἀπὸ τῆς ἁμαρτίας, *from sin*. For it would seem that justification had already relieved us from wrath, and that therefore in the further development of the life the only question could be about our entire deliverance from the old man of sin. But however true this may be, it is not less true that every, even the least sin, has the Divine wrath [ὀργή] for its necessary accompaniment. We may therefore say of him who is justified [δικαιωθείς] or reconciled [καταλλαγείς], on the one hand, that he, as such, is already delivered from wrath, inasmuch as in the substance of his character he is saved [John iii. 36], but, on the other hand, that he remains yet under "wrath," inasmuch as the totality of his being is not yet sanctified, and he needs continual forgiveness; the latter mode of representation is that here chosen, while the former is the more usual.)

Ver. 11.—Yet with this *salvation*, whose attainment is still *future*, the apostle once more contrasts, as in ver. 2, that joy already *present*, which is to believers the earnest of the Divine glory (viii. 24). The present blessing of reconciliation here below, with which is connected the gift of the Spirit (ver. 5), is to them so sure a pledge of their future inheritance, that they feel as if they possessed it already.

(To σωθησόμεθα is opposed καυχώμενοι sc. ἐσμεν [for which later MSS. read καυχώμεθα and καυχῶμεν].—The climax οὐ μόνον—ἀλλὰ καί raises καυχᾶσθαι above the preceding σωθησόμεθα; the latter contains, in fact, only the mere conception of ἐλπίς, whilst καύχησις goes far beyond this. There is no reference here to a new and higher *object*. Fritzsche and Winer retain the strict participial construction of καυχώμενοι, and co-ordinate it with καταλλαγέντες, making both depend upon σωθησόμεθα, with the following sense: "not only reconciled, but also glorying, exulting in God, we shall be saved." But the thought "we shall be saved exulting," is scarcely accordant either with itself, or with the previous "we shall be saved, being reconciled." We therefore prefer to take the participle as = Ind. making an advancement from the subject of redemption to the new subject of καύχησις.)

SECTION III.

(V. 12—VII. 6.)

Of the Vicarious Office of Christ.

After this exhibition of the nature of the new way of salvation, and its effects, Paul might at once have proceeded to set forth how the individual man is developed in it, which at chap. vii. 7, etc., he does, but that an intermediate thought, which then presented, as it does now, especial difficulties to men, *the vicarious office of Christ*, required a further treatment for the establishment of the doctrine itself. Without the idea of his vicarious office the whole work of the Saviour would remain isolated, a splendid act of individual sacrifice, with none of that real power for the mass which alone made it a proper object of proclamation to the world, and the turning-point of the world's history. The apostle proves, therefore, this important point most carefully, and does so *first*, by bringing Christ, as the second Adam, into parallel with the first, and shewing that, as from the first, *sin*, so from the second, *grace* issues, like streams from different well-springs (v. 12–21). *Secondly*, Paul sets forth how, accordingly, all that took place in Christ was accomplished also in believers, who are in him as they were in Adam (vi. 1–11). And, *lastly*, he infers, that no one, consequently, who is in Christ can serve sin, for that, by his very being in Christ, he has died to sin and become free, in order to his entering a higher relation (vi. 12, vii. 6).

§ 9. PARALLEL BETWEEN ADAM AND CHRIST.*

(V. 12–21.)

According to the general tenor of the epistle, the apostle's primary object here was only to set forth Christ as the representative of the whole race, and as the author of righteousness for all. In order, however, to make this relation perceptible, he sets out from the relation of Adam to the human race, which he presumes as acknowledged, and so gains occasion to trace the *fact* of universal sinfulness, developed in chapters i. and ii. in its *ultimate* principle. Accordingly, the following weighty section forms the foundation for two doctrines of truth equally important, and mutually supporting each other ; for the *doctrine of original sin*, that is, the *proclivitas peccandi*, which diffuses itself over the race, in the way of generation from Adam, independently of the proper *personal* sin of men, and for the doctrine of *the vicarious office of Christ*. As Paul's exposition sets out from the former as a thing presumed, we also take it first into consideration that the latter may follow upon it. Meanwhile both rest upon a *common basis*, to which, therefore, we must previously make reference. For a discussion like that in which we are now engaged, it is quite impossible to arrive at any satisfactory result if we are divided in fundamental views. The hope of uniting all expositors in the view of this passage must be entirely abandoned, for the reason that there is no prevailing unity in their principles. No one with the best intention, can make any other exposition, than such as shall apprehend the ideas of the sacred writer (with which he himself wishes to agree), in a complete harmony that is, in accordance with *his* principles ; a process certainly far from producing a uniformity of result. Of the truth of this assertion with regard to this passage, every one may be convinced by the treatise of Reiche (Comm. ad loc. p. 409–446). This learned man treats the difficult and important passage with great industry,

* Compare, upon this important section of the epistle, Rothe's Monographie (Leipzig, 1836), and the Essays of Finkh (Tübing. Zeitschrift, 1830, H. 1.), and Schmid (Ibid. H. 4).

and certainly with impartiality: yet he arrives at results which are in direct contradiction to the express words of the apostle, and the collective doctrine of Scripture; and this, for the single reason that he sets out from an entirely different basis from that occupied by Paul. From this, his different point of view, all the expressions of the apostle present themselves to him in a false light; so that his entire conception is necessarily erroneous. The controversy, therefore, regarding the mode of interpreting individual passages, is endless, and hence utterly unsatisfactory and useless. Yet from a conference in regard to the *common basis* something may surely be hoped—to this, therefore, we mainly apply ourselves; as to particulars, touching, according to our plan, only upon what is most important.

Antiquity knew but two different points of view from which to consider this passage, which though under altered names and forms, with shades of distinction and modification, have yet continued to the present essentially unchanged, since their first clear and sharp utterance, viz., the *Augustinian* and the *Pelagian*. The difference between these two, when carefully considered, is not in *some*, but in *all* points, and they vary specifically upon the great collective problems; reconciliation, therefore, between them is out of the question: they run like parallel lines, constantly beside, without getting nearer to each other. For our purpose, these two systems suggest the following observations upon the interpretation of this passage. The Pelagian (whether a *partial*, or a *complete* one, makes no difference here) can never conceive of mankind otherwise than as an aggregate of independent, free, intelligent individuals; in virtue, as in sin, every person stands and falls by himself.* The Augusti-

* Whether the fall of individuals be said to occur in this world, or, according to Origen, in a former, is in the main all one; each individual ever stands or falls by himself according to this theory. See thereon the admirable exposition in the Phil. des Rechts by my honoured colleague, Prof. Stahl, vol. 2, part i. (Heidelberg 1833), p. 99, etc., where he says, "Adam is the *original matter* of humanity, Christ is its *original idea* in God, both personally living. Mankind is one in them, therefore Adam's sin became the sin of all, Christ's sacrifice the atonement for all. Every leaf of a tree may be green or wither by itself, but each suffers by the disease of the *root*, and recovers only by its healing. The shallower the man so much the more isolated will everything appear to him, for upon the surface all lies apart. He will see in mankind, in the nation, nay, even in the family, mere individuals, where the act of the one has no connexion with that of the other. The profounder the man, the more do these inward relations of unity, proceeding from the very centre, force themselves upon him. Yea, the love of our neighbour is itself nothing but the deep feeling of this unity, for we love him only with whom we feel and acknowledge ourselves to be one. What the Christian love of our neighbour is for the heart, that unity of race is for the understanding. If sin through one, and redemption through one is not possible, the command to love our neighbour is also unintelligible. Christian ethics and Christian faith are therefore in truth indissolubly united. Christianity effects in history an advance like that from the animal kingdom to man, by its revealing the essential unity of men, the consciousness of which in the ancient

nian just as necessarily conceives of mankind as a collective, self-completed body, in which the separate individuals are by no means disengaged and independent wholes, but integrating parts of the totality. The interpreter who makes the former system his starting-point, has only the choice between two ways; *either* to take the words of the apostle, in this place, to mean, that the effect of Adam's sin and the effect of Christ's righteousness are to be understood merely as the operation of doctrine and example, but in no respect as really inwrought, which indeed, according to his principles, they cannot be, *or* to say, that Paul proposes indeed a different view, but that this view is false. He, on the other hand, who interprets the words from the *second* point of view, finds himself in their most obvious, and simplest meaning, in perfect harmony, alike with the Apostle Paul, and the whole Scripture. That the *advantage*, therefore, is on this side, needs no proof; yet that alone certainly cannot determine one to incline to it; but independently of this, the deeper truth lies in the contemplation of mankind as a completed unity, since the independence and separateness of individuals is but a very relative one, and being thus relative is comprised in that unity, just as the relative independence of the members of a body is embraced by the absolute vital unity of the entire animal organism. (Comp. further at xi. 1.) This is, of course, not the place to enter more particularly into this extensive inquiry; suffice it here to notice, that the Scripture itself accords with this conception by the images of the body (1 Cor. xii. 20), of the vine (John xv. 1, etc.), and olive tree (Rom. xi. 17, etc.), whereby it marks the vital unity of our collective humanity. But in these images, consecrated by spiritual use, the idea is expressed in a singularly illustrative manner. For, as in a tree not every little branch is of essential importance to its whole growth, but as many may be broken off, without causing damage to the entire tree, so also in the human race. But at two points the destruction even of the smallest twig utterly annihilates the tree. First, at the sprouting of the seed, secondly, at the grafting of the tree. By breaking off the apparently insignificant sprout, or the feeble graft, the whole tree is destroyed. Even so, mankind has *two critical periods* in its development, on which turns its entire destiny. *First*, Adam, the germ from which the whole race was developed; his death immediately after his creation would have annihilated mankind; the injury he suffered damaged the whole race that sprang from him, as a mutilated germ makes the whole tree grow scant and crooked. *Secondly*, Christ, whose relation to the race de-

world had vanished when the nations were separated." Even so; man comes not truly to himself until he comes to God in Christ; without Christ he remains in the element of animal life.

rived from Adam, is like that of the noble graft to the wild tree [Jer. ii. 21];* were it conceivable that Christ had been taken away before the completion of his work, mankind would then have remained in their natural rudeness, as a tree whose graft was destroyed, and which now puts forth mere water-shoots. But if the noble graft abide, it ennobles the whole tree; all juices, which are conducted through it, change their nature, and are no more wild. Men are wont to say that parables prove nothing; nevertheless, comparisons in their depth of meaning often teach infinitely more and better than all abstract arguments, seeing they are derived from nature, the mirror of the glory of the unseen God, living demonstrations, as it were, of the Most High God himself. Finally, it follows of course, that these fundamentally different views, must essentially modify our opinions (which here come naturally under consideration) respecting the *origin of souls.*† The Pelagian can only consistently follow *Creatianism*, or what leads to the same isolating of men, *Præ-existentianism*, for which Benecke has again attempted to plead. The Augustinian principle leads to *Traducianism*, which alone accords with Scripture and experience, and, *kept clear of Materialism*, is able to satisfy all requisitions of the Christian consciousness. The consequence, therefore, is, that, as the *existence* of this passage, with its definite declarations, has only compelled the Pelagians of all centuries to endeavour by subtleties to evade its import so hostile to their system; so even were it *wanting*, the Augustinian principle would stand equally firm, since it rests by no means merely on these words, but upon the coherent doctrine of Scripture and its inward necessity.

An entirely different position, however, regarding the questions discussed in this passage, from that occupied by antiquity, has been assumed by recent theologians,‡ from which point of view also,

* As to how far it can be said that Christ represents also the sinful tendency in humanity, see the observations at Rom. viii. 3.

† The discussion of this subject at large we defer to Heb. vii. 9, etc. I have only now to remark, that it would not be very difficult to get rid of the objections, lately made by Tholuck (lit. Anz. Jahrg. 1834, Num. 23), against the traducian view, from the experience of bad children being often begotten of good parents, and *vice versa*; since the old man still lives even in the best, and germs of nobler life are resting in the worst; and in individual cases we cannot trace, without prejudicing in some degree the main view, by what law the one element or the other gains predominance in the moment of generation. The assertion, however, that every traducian view is materialistic, is decidedly false, and will meet its refutation at the passage referred to.

‡ The interpretation of the passage proposed by Benecke needs but a brief notice, since it proves itself at once to be untenable. He supposes, with Origen, that every man has sinned by himself, not, however, in this world, but in a state of *pre-existence*. The Scripture, however, does not acknowledge any personal pre-existence, it teaches rather merely a pre-existent state of being in the Divine mind, since God beholds the future as present. (Comp. thereon Ephes. i. 4.) The further defence of pre-existence by Benecke in a letter to Lücke (Stud. 1832, No. 3, p. 616, etc.), brings forward no new matter.

Usteri (Paul. Lehrbegr., 4th edit. p. 24, etc.) gives his exposition. This recent school discards that *mechanical* view of the world on which rests the Pelagian scheme of isolation; on the contrary, in respect to the relation of the individual to the whole, it adopts entirely the *dynamical* system which forms the basis of the Augustinian theory. But it deviates none the less, in the result, because it sets out from a different view in regard to *evil*. As Schleiermacher's doctrine of predestination could not but be quite different from the Augustinian, since he openly avowed the restoration; so also the doctrine of original sin could not but take a different form, if evil, as he and the Hegelians assert, is held as *mere negation*. Adam's fall could be no loss to him, for he had nothing to lose, but only the manifestation of that deficiency which clave to him as a creature; the sinfulness of the race could not proceed from Adam's act, because all bear in themselves the same deficiency which made Adam's fall necessary, and they just as much as Adam must have been brought into that opposition, of which it is no advantage not to know; Christ, accordingly, worked only so far in redeeming and atoning, as by his Divine fulness of life he made up the created deficiency in the creature. Infinitely more full of spirit and depth of meaning, however, as is this doctrine of modern theology than the shallow Pelagian rationalism, we feel ourselves nevertheless unable to adopt it, since evil, according to the Scripture, is by no means represented as a *mere* negation. It is not, indeed, like good in its complete manifestation, *substance*, as Manichæism holds, yet surely something *real* and *positive;* it has, that is, without substantial being, its positive reality in *actually disturbed* relations. As such positive discord in the relations ordained by God, Holy Scripture transfers evil in its origin and its operative power into the spiritual world; from hence it works, ever propagating its disorganizing nature, until it finds its barrier in the element of good. Therefore is the fall of Adam set forth in the Bible as *the opening of a gate* to the spirit world, so that it is not his act, outward and isolated, which is efficient, but that act in connexion with the fearful element to which it allowed entrance. Thus, as a spark thrown into inflammable matter can enkindle a fire to consume the greatest wood, or one stone taken from a protecting dam cause a whole stream to pour away; so Adam's apparently inconsiderable sin. Spark and stone, without touch-wood and stream, could do no essential harm; so without the existence of a kingdom of darkness Adam's sin could not have caused such injury. In relation to this kingdom Adam stood like the porter, while he also held in his hand the keys of the kingdom of light; he opened *that* door and the lot was cast for ages. In the same position we behold the Saviour. According to the history of the temptation, the key to the kingdom of the prince of this world was offered also to him, but he refused it and opened for mankind Paradise instead, whereby the stream of light which broke in had power to chase away the shadows which had been gathering through the night of centuries. It is only as thus apprehended, that Adam and Christ appear in their full representative and central significance, as portrayed in Scripture. They are the hinges round which the doors of the powers of the universe move; the poles from which life and death, light and darkness stream, which reveal themselves in world-controlling power alike in the mass and in the individual. The life of the great collective body, which we call mankind, oscillates between Adam and Christ, nay, the life of the whole universe, for Adam's fall and Christ's resurrection are turning-points of universal development. (Comp. at Rom. viii. 19, etc.) And even so the being touched by the life-stream of Christ is for individuals greater or less, for nations and men, the turning-point of their existence. If, therefore, our recent theology and philosophy are to attain to a complete appropriation of the substance of the gospel which they are striving for as the noblest object, a revision and more profound establishment of the doctrine of evil will be of urgent necessity. (Comp. the observations at Matth. viii. 28.)

Ver. 12.—The apostle now clearly, as he passes with a *διὰ τοῦτο*, *for this reason*, from the foregoing exposition of the efficacy both of the death and life of Christ, presumes, by the particle of comparison *ὥσπερ*, *just as*, the relation of Adam to the sinfulness of the whole race as acknowledged. The question, however, is, how far Paul could do this? For we certainly do not find among the Rabbins any agreement upon the doctrine of the origin of sin. They term the general sinfulness קִלְקוּל, that is, "confusion, desolation," or as inherited sin יֵצֶר הָרָע, that is, "framing, thinking evil." (Comp. Buxtorf. lex. talm. pag. 973 and 2041.) At one time, however, they refer the origin of sin in man to Adam's fall, at another they represent it as created with man by God.* Meanwhile Tholuck observes justly,

* Compare Schöttgen and Wetstein ad loc. Tholuck and Reiche also have given copious extracts in their commentaries; the views of Biblical Dogmatists may be seen in Usteri, Paul. Lehrbegr. s. 25, note. Among the passages which refer sin to the fall of Adam, besides the interpretations of later Rabbins, to which certainly we are to attach less importance, and the Targums on Eccles. vii. 29; Ruth iv. 22.—Jalkut Rubeni, fol. 18, 1, is particularly important, where it is said: "nisi Adam peccaset, fuisset nudus et coitum exercuisset et concupiscentia prava neminem induxisset; postquam vero peccavit et concupiscentia prava יֵצֶר הָרָע adest, nemo nudus incedere potest." The יֵצֶר הָרָע on the contrary, appears as created by God in Succa fol. 52, 2. "Quatuor sunt, quorum pœnitet Deum, quod ille *creaverit*, nimirum captivitatem, Chaldæos, Ismaelitas et concupiscentiam pravam." It may be questioned notwithstanding, whether *creare* here, like *plantare* in Aben Ezra *ad Psalm*. li. 7, ought not to be otherwise interpreted, namely, to be understood of the negative operation of God, permission. Nothing evinces more a correct apprehension of the doctrine by the Rabbins than the circumstance that they had

that the latter of these conceptions could proceed only from the theory of cabbalistic emanation, which makes evil appear as mere negation. Since then no trace is to be found among the Jews of the properly Pelagian view, that every one is himself the originator of his own sinfulness by personal abuse of free will, we may all the more consider the doctrine of Adam's sin as the *causa efficiens* of the sinfulness of his race to have been the prevailing Jewish doctrine; for the cabbala was always confined within a narrow circle, and the Apocryphal writings clearly shew how fully the doctrine of original sin was matured at the time of their composition. (Comp. Wisd. Sol. ii. 23, xii. 10, xiii. 1; Sirach xxv. 24.) Most decisive, however, is the collective import of the Old Testament with its doctrine of the Messiah and his sacrifice, which, as the Epistle to the Hebrews proves at large, necessarily presupposes the sinfulness of the entire race through Adam. For were all men born with the same moral powers as were created in Adam, and did they all sin by the mere abuse of their own free will, neither regular expiatory sacrifices could have been *beforehand* ordained for all, since at any moment some one might have proved himself entirely pure, and at all events children who died in infancy must have been excepted (whom nevertheless the law held as equally unclean with the *dead*); nor could so all-pervading an influence have been derived from the appearing of *One Person*, as is connected with the Messiah. Passages like Ezek. xviii. 1, etc., are but apparently contradictory, for the doctrine of original sin in no way excludes responsibility for particular sins, nor a faithful use of the proffered means of salvation spoken of in that passage. The doctrine of original sin does not say, that one *must* steal, commit adultery, or such like; on the contrary man possesses even after the fall, according to the doctrine alike of Scripture and the systems of faith, power enough to perform *opera civilia*, and to abstain from positive transgressions of the law. It only teaches, that man is unable by his own power to get rid of the *prava concupiscentia*,* the evil desire that swells up in the heart, and the *bias to sin*, into which the mere *possibility of sinning* created by God in the first man passed, when by the first sin he yielded to the influence of darkness.

also conceived correctly the parallel between Adam and the Messiah as his antitype. So in Neve Schalom, fol. 160, 2. "Quemadmodum homo primus (Adam) fuit יחיד בחטא (that is, the first, or rather only one, in sin, the representative of the whole sinning race of man) sic Messias erit ultimus ad auferendum peccatum penitus." The doctrine of the Messiah alone, in the complete form in which the Jews already had it, could not, indeed, consistently followed out, lead to any other view upon the origin of the sinfulness of the race, than that the whole must have fallen *in* Adam and *through* him.

* Luther: "Original sin is not *done* like all other sins, but it is, it liveth and *doeth* all other sins."—And in another place: "Thou canst do nothing but sin, do as thou willest; all which thou settest about is sin, and abideth sin, let it show as fine as it may; beginning, furthering, and perfecting [righteousness] is all of God."

Now, how the apostle could have expressed in more decided and explicit terms the doctrine of the sin of Adam originating the sinfulness of his race, than by saying: "through one man sin entered into the world" (δι' ἑνὸς ἀνθρώπου ἡ ἁμαρτία εἰς τὸν κόσμον εἰσῆλθε), cannot certainly be conceived: and yet upon these simple words have been lavished all the arts of subtle criticism. One mode of evasion is by taking ἁμαρτία, *sin*, as denoting independently sinful actions (*peccata actualia*), while it in fact designates the *sinful habit* (*habitus peccandi*), whose particular manifestations are termed ἁμάρτημα, παράπτωμα, παράβασις. So far as these separate acts necessarily *presuppose* the sinful habit, ἁμαρτία also *may* certainly denote the sinful act, but the following exposition of the apostle shews, that where a sinful act is to be expressly mentioned, he makes use of one of those words. Granting, finally, that ἁμαρτία might be so taken here, the δι' ἑνὸς ἀνθρώπου (which thus occurs again 1 Cor. xv. 21), would be sufficient to forbid that the passage should be interpreted: "Adam opened the series of sinful acts," whereby alone it can be brought near to the Pelagian view. But the modern theory of sin being created in man is contradicted not only by the διά, *through*, but the εἰσῆλθε, *entered*, Sin, on that theory, existed already *with* and *in* Adam, it did not *come* first *by* him. According to that Paul must have written "as sin in the first man first also manifested itself."—The εἷς ἄνθρωπος, *one man*, is moreover, as ver. 14 shews, *Adam*. If it is said, 1 Tim. ii. 14, of *Eve*, that she, not Adam, was deceived, this form of exposition refers merely to the relation of woman and man, the former being certainly more accessible to sin. But where mention is made of the race collectively, and the relation of man and woman is not brought forward, Adam is named, as the head of the first human pair, which is to be regarded as unity.—As consequence of sin, *death* only is made prominent, in which, as the sum of all evil, every other form of it is comprised. Here indeed θάνατος signifies principally the death of the *body*, as also Gen. iii. 3, 4, but this had not been possible without the spiritual death, which entered with sin itself.* For it is the nature of death to disturb and separate that which belongs together; in the first state, indeed, man was no more exempted from the *possibility of dying*, than from the *possibility of sinning;* both these possibilities he possessed, and they passed by sin into the *necessity of dying;* and the *proclivitas peccandi*. Thus, while *bodily* death is the separation of the *soul* from the

* Comp. Augustine's treatise hereon, in the first chapter of the thirteenth book, *de civitate Dei;* particularly in cap. 5, upon the question: "Quod sicut iniqui male utuntur lege, quæ bona est, ita et justi bene utuntur morte, quæ mala est." Adam's life after his fall was, as it were, a slow dying, that reached its completion in his physical death: Christ's ζωοποίησις, *quickening*, of mankind is also gradual, the culminating point of which is the glorification of the body

body, *spiritual* death appears as the separation of the *spirit* from the *soul*. This latter, however, was not a *total* separation, as sin did not develope itself, as with the fallen angels, in man himself, but was brought to him from without, as in the temptation of Christ. The *necessity of sinning* appears therefore only as the *second* death (θάνατος δεύτερος), as the highest point of sinful development. The reciprocal influence of spiritual and physical elements, which here finds expression, is not, however, limited according to the Pauline doctrine merely to man; its disturbance reacts also upon the creation (κτίσις) generally, as at Rom. viii. 17, etc., will be further shewn.* But if to Adam's sin was applied only the expression εἰς κόσμον εἰσῆλθε, *it came into the world* (where κόσμος signifies not the universe, for sin was already in the spiritual world, but the world of man), yet this sin, in death as its bitter fruit, appears as a principle penetrating through (διῆλθεν) the entire race, and which is true of all development, advancing in ever heightened forms toward perfection. (The οὕτως must be understood therefore "in the connexion of sin and death.") Although therefore Adam's act was not the act of an isolated individual, but the act of the race, since he is not to be considered as *a* man by the side of and among many others, but as man,† yet the continued progress of sin by the sin of his posterity, so far from being thus set aside, is most decidedly established. But sin itself is ever to be considered as punishment of sin, so that the sinning of posterity became the very saddest consequence and punishment of the first sin. Had it been possible for the immediate descendants of Adam, for instance Abel, or Seth, by perfect righteousness to stop the stream of corruption that came breaking in, to stand in the gap (Ezek. xxii. 30), Adam's act would have had no greater significance than any other sin, and it would then have been not merely fitting for the apostle to mention any other, by way of antitypical comparison with Christ's act, but it would have answered even better: for instance, Cain's *killing* would apparently have formed a far stronger contrast with Christ's *being killed*. But every one feels that such a course would have been utterly inconsistent with the views of the apostle. To him Adam's sin is the *mother of all the rest*, and therefore, however insignificant in outward seeming, yet in its essence the sin of all sins; because the greatness of the sin depends on the position which the sinner

* Glöckler (p. 84) says very strikingly: "Sin has the power of reproducing itself in our immediate descendant, and that to the full extent, with all its consequences, unless it be subdued by that descendant's mightier spiritual power (derived from Christ). Especially must this be the case with *that* offspring who owes his whole existence to a living organism which is penetrated throughout by the power of sin. Here, conception is already a conception in sins, even the first germ of life receives the whole form of sin."

† Rightly says Augustine: "In Adamo omnes tunc peccaverunt, quando in ejus natura adhuc omnes ille unus fuerunt." (De pecc. mer. et rem. iii. 7.)

occupies, and no sinner ever yet stood where eternal love had placed Adam.

After these observations, it is clear what ought to be thought of the ordinary Pelagian-rationalistic view, that the clause *ἐφ' ᾧ πάντες ἥμαρτον*, *in that all sinned*, signifies that the sinfulness of men is not caused by *Adam's* act, but by their *own* sins. For it is evident that the apostle regards that universal sinning as the *consequence* of Adam's sin, and adds this clause merely to shew that if any one could have been supposed who sinned not, as was afterwards the case with Christ, then indeed a limit had been thereby set to death, provided that he occupied as central a position as Adam and Christ. Aside from this, we could only say that the apostle intends to intimate that the unfaithfulness of men, in not resisting sin even *to the extent* that with the moral powers still left to them they might have done, diffused the common sinfulness more *quickly* and *generally* than otherwise it would have been. Although, therefore, *ἐφ' ᾧ* is doubtless not to be translated with the Vulgate *in quo, in whom*,* and so forms no *proof* in favour of the representation of the race by Adam, still it furnishes no weapon against this doctrine itself, which, in the *connexion* of the whole argument, is sufficiently established. Gramatically, *ἐφ' ᾧ* can only be taken as conjunctive, as absolutely no antecedent can be traced, to which the relative could be naturally applied.† Thus, *ἐφ' ᾧ* answers to our "in that" (indem) = אֲשֶׁר, and denotes the being connected with and dependent upon another.‡ As to *ἥμαρτον*, many are of opinion that Paul refers in the word to actual sins which proceed from the *proclivitas peccandi*. But if the *πάντες*, *all*, as the tenor of the whole chapter requires, is to be understood in its most proper sense of the entire mass, and so

* How little *ἐν ᾧ* would be contrary to Paul's meaning, is shewn by 1 Cor. xv. 22, where it is said: *ὥσπερ ἐν τῷ 'Αδὰμ πάντες ἀποθνήσκουσιν, οὕτω καὶ ἐν τῷ Χριστῷ πάντες ζωοποιηθήσονται.*

† Glöckler and Schmid (ad loc. p. 191, etc.) would refer *ἐφ' ᾧ* to *θάνατος*, "unto which all sinned," making death the *end* (*τέλος*.) of sin; but this is extremely forced.

‡ In passages like 2 Cor. v. 4; Phil. iii. 12, *ἐφ' ᾧ* is also conjunctive, not merely *ἐπί* with the relative, as also it cannot possibly be here. According to Rothe's explanation, who takes *ἐφ' ᾧ* = *ἐπὶ τούτῳ ὥστε*, the sense would also be: "in such wise that, under the certainty that." But he assumes that all sinned *themselves*. Now this was not so; death struck many without their having themselves sinned, *e. g*, all infant children. But it is precisely on *πάντες*, *all*, that all the emphasis in the argument is laid. According to the apostle's meaning, therefore, *ἐν αὐτῷ* is doubtless to be supplied, and the passage to be taken thus: since they had all (collectively) sinned, namely in Adam. This sense, too, alone agrees with what follows, where even the difference of the sinning, of those, for instance, who lived before the Mosaic law, from Adam's sinning, is set forth. Adam acted as a person, and transgressed a positive command of God, the collective body sinned only in him; yet the punishment of death fell upon all together, as a proof, that even the participation in the general sin is of itself sin before God, although certainly in another sense than purely personal sin. (Upon the classical usage of *ἐφ' ᾧ* in the signification *ἐπὶ τούτῳ ὥστε*, comp. Matthiæ's Gr. § 472, p. 1063; Bernhardy's Syntax, p. 268; Fritzsche ad loc. p. 299, etc.—Upon the use of the synonymous *ἐν ᾧ*, comp. at Rom. viii. 3.)

to include children dying in unconsciousness, this view becomes involved in extreme perplexity, and is driven to the assertion that Paul speaks only of individuals capable of sin; an assertion, however, which assuredly draws on the difficult argument, where the capability of sin begins.* How entirely untenable this view is, appears by this its own principal support in the most glaring light! Augustine's theory, on the contrary, although his translation of ἐφ' ᾧ by *in quo* is wrong, is here in thought impregnable. For the ἥμαρτον signifies "*being* sinful," together with "*committing* sin," and it is only accidental in individual cases that the latter does not issue from the former, the *being* sinful remaining nevertheless. The sense of the words therefore is: "in that (in Adam) all (without exception) sinned, and with the greater number as consequence thereof the original sin expressed itself besides in further sinful acts, therefore did death also, the wages of sin, penetrate through to all." Taken so, the *imputatio in pœnam et reatum* of the sin of Adam has its truth; taken so, the efficiency of Christ, in whom all in fact rose again just as they had in fact fallen in Adam, forms with that truth a true parallel. The question how in Adam all who were not yet in existence could sin with him is difficult only while we hold the isolation of individuals. Relinquish this, and all takes a simple form, and in Adam every one of his descendants must have sinned with him, just as in the act of one man all his members and every drop of blood co-operate; and in an army not the general only conquers or is defeated, but every warrior of the host conquers or is conquered with him.†

(As concerns the structure of the whole sentence, ὥσπερ has no apodosis. To consider vers. 13–17 as parenthetic digression, in favour of which Reiche, after Grotius, Wetstein, and Flatt, has again pronounced, is harsh, because in this digression the substantial thought of the apodosis is already anticipated. It is better therefore to suppose an anacoluthon here also, and to consider ver. 18 as a recapitulating resumption of the discourse in ver. 12. So Rothe explains it, with Winer, Rückert, and others. Besides this conception of the passage as anacoluthon, De Wette's view is the only one which can claim any attention, that the second member is introduced

* The manner in which Meyer (in his comm. ad loc.) tries to solve the difficulty, why children should die in infancy, if death is the consequence of actual sins only, is too meagre; he supposes (p. 120): "Paul entirely forgot this necessary exception (!)" Elsewhere, surely, the memory of the great apostle in no respect fails him.

† Rückert's explanation of ver. 12 is quite correct. He says, p. 218, "According to this verse, therefore, Adam is the *originator* of human sinfulness, and so far the first cause of death; but men have *withal* by their own sinning deserved it." But the last part of the sentence is not quite strictly expressed, for Paul does not intend to allege *two* causes, the sinning of men rather is itself founded in Adam's sin; their unfaithfulness has only enhanced sin.

with ὥσπερ, and the first presupposed from what has been said before, as ὥσπερ occurs Matth. xxv. 14. But it is against this interpretation, that this preceding member has not previously been sufficiently expressed to be immediately understood with the words: διὰ τοῦτο ὥσπερ. Moreover, with this construction the leading thought of the apostle would be the connexion of sinful man with Adam; while his chief purpose, on the contrary, is to set forth the connexion of believers with Christ. Hence this principal idea must also be considered as resting upon the incidental subordinate thought, which he assumes as acknowledged, viz., the sinfulness of men since Adam, and hence the ὥσπερ be followed by an οὕτως. But as Paul wished to shew the difference as well as the similarity between Adam and Christ, and further to exhibit the relation of the law to these two critical stages in the life of humanity, while the parallel obviously suggested itself from the line of argument, he neglected the formal apodosis, and at ver. 18 returned to the leading thought.—In the Codd. D.E.F.G., and other critical authorities, ὁ θάνατος is omitted before διῆλθεν. There are grounds for the omission alike critical and exegetical; for θάνατος being but subordinate,* it would *seem* more fitting to refer διῆλθε to the principal idea, ἁμαρτία, out of which the presence of θάνατος follows of course. But the γάρ connecting ver. 13 with the preceding, favors the reading ὁ θάνατος διῆλθεν, since *thus* the mention of ἁμαρτία implies an immediately preceding θάνατος, which, as mere consequence, presupposes the *cause*, and as crown and consummation, is put for *all* consequences.)

Vers. 13, 14.—This general dominion of death, even in the time before the promulgation of the positive Law of Moses, when therefore men *could* not by *personal* transgression of the law incur guilt as Adam did (vii. 7), proves the presence of sin in humanity, through the influence of original sin, for the righteous God cannot suffer *punishment* (*i. e.*, here, θάνατος) to come where there is no guilt. These two verses are commonly considered as a passing observation; but according to the train of thought above indicated, such is not the case. The apostle uses them rather, immediately to corroborate the principal thought in ver. 12. That sin was in the world *after* the law he presumes as a matter of course, but even *before* it, he says, sin was there, as *death* proves, although it might have been supposed there was then no sin, because there was no commandment to transgress. Paul therefore clearly infers from the imputation of punishment (*imputatio pœnæ*), the imputation of the guilt of Adam's sin (*imputatio reatus peccati Adamitici*).

* Rothe (p. 36) protests against θάνατος being subordinate, but the διὰ τῆς ἁμαρτίας ὁ θάνατος, *death by sin*, clearly enough makes death to be conditioned by sin; it is subordinate, therefore, although it becomes especially prominent afterwards.

As regards the supposition of many of the most distinguished expositors and dogmatists, as Origen, Augustine, Thomas Aquinas, Melancthon, Beza, that the sinfulness of *children* is intended here, this view, in itself inadmissible, has somewhat of truth, in that the period from Adam to Moses is in fact the time of the *childhood of humanity*. Adam himself *before* the fall occupied indeed a higher level of consciousness, but *after* it he sunk with his descendants to a childish unconsciousness, in which a law could not even be given to men. Every individual has a similar period in his own life, during the twilight consciousness of childhood (comp. at vii. 9, etc.); nevertheless man, like the race in general, nay the very child in the cradle, is even during this period in sin, and suffers the punishment for sin, even death; so that here it is perfectly clear that the apostle means by *ἁμαρτία* not sinful independent actions, but the *state* of *inward* discord from which springs that *outward* discord whose consummation is death. This disorganized condition is found also in the beast, nay in the physical creation (Rom. viii. 17, etc.), but it is called *ἁμαρτία*, *sin*, only in connexion with the *possibility* of conscious development, elsewhere only *φθορά*, *corruption*.

(Ver. 18.—Paul does not mean to assert an *absolute* absence of law, as Rom. ii. 14, 15, shews; but where there is no outward law, it is only by very indistinct warnings that the inward law gives indication of itself, especially in the dawning life of childhood. Personal *imputation* [*ἐλλογεῖσθαι*] of personal acts [the unconscious one shares only the guilt of the mass], is therefore out of the question during such a state.* Yet a *βασιλεία θανάτου*, *kingdom of death*, found place [the opposite of the kingdom established by Christ, the *βασιλεία ζωῆς*, *kingdom of life*], *even* [*καί*] over those who had not, like Adam, transgressed a positive command; death therefore has of course no less dominion over those who, arrived at a state of consciousness, have by their *own* guilt increased the sin which they *inherited*.—The *μή* before *ἁμαρτήσαντας* is omitted in some of the Fathers. But as all MSS. have it, and the context properly understood requires it, the omission can proceed only from misinterpretation.—The *ἐπὶ τῷ ὁμοιώματι* answers to בִּדְמוּת Daniel x. 16). With an entirely new thought: *ὅς ἐστι τύπος τοῦ μέλλοντος*, *who is the*

* The acceptation of *ἐλλογεῖσθαι* proposed by Usteri (fourth edit. of the Paul. Lehrbegr. p. 42) and Glöckler (p. 82), instead of the explanation given here, and correctly put forth by Rückert also, is *quite inadmissible*. They would understand it not of the imputation of God, but of the self-imputation of men, so that the sense should be: "Without law, man does not impute sin to himself, that is, he is not conscious of it as such, heeds it not, therefore, and does not take it truly to heart." This is opposed to the train of thought, because it is not the subjective judgment of man which is here treated of, but the judgment of God. God allows to death, indeed, admission to all men, because it is the consequence of the collective guilt contracted through Adam, but the individual guilt of men is not yet punished, as is shewn by the instance of Cain and Lamech, the law being wanting (Comp. upon the *πάρεσις* at Rom. iii. 25.)

type of the future, sc. Adam, Paul now passes to that statement to which the representation of the efficacy of Adam's sin is intended merely to be a foil. Christ and Adam bear the relation of antitype to type, or as a Rabbin says : ס״ד אָדָם הוּא ס״ד הַמָּשִׁיחַ—that is : "the mystery of Adam is the mystery of the Messiah." The elements of forgotten typology are becoming more and more recognized, and cannot, consistently with truly historical exposition, be overlooked in the New Testament. The Old Testament is to all the writers of the New Testament an adumbration of truth [*μόρφωσις τῆς ἀληθείας*], and according to this principle Christ must naturally appear as the *second* Adam (1 Cor. xv. 45), the whole race being represented by him after a spiritual, as by Adam after an outward manner. Now the point of comparison between Adam and Christ here is manifestly the *passing over* of sin and of righteousness from them upon all. Accordingly this passage must present great obstacles to Benecke's doctrine of pre-existence ; he is obliged therefore to have recourse to the forced interpretation of *μέλλοντος* as neuter, scil. *γένους*, so that Adam is called a type of the race to come, because all sinned like him. The arbitrariness of this construction is evident.*

Ver. 15.—Yet the relation between the effects wrought by Adam and by Christ, with all its analogies, still involves great diversity ; the power revealed in Christ is incomparably more mighty. But this preponderance is not, with Grotius and Fritzsche, to be referred to a mere logical superiority of possibility and certainty, but to the intensive power of grace. *First* (ver. 15) it shews itself stronger, in that in Adam's sin the principle of righteousness merely is manifested, but in Christ the overflowing element of Divine grace. *Next* (ver. 16) Adam wrought but negatively, Christ positively, forgiving the many sins by his sacrifice. Nay, not by forgiveness merely does he operate, but also (ver. 17) by communicating a new and higher life. Then follows, in vers. 18, 19, an antithetic repetition of the whole thought. Here accordingly Paul asserts the idea of the *vicarious office* of Christ, with which the doctrine of satisfaction, expressed Rom. iii. 24, 25, is so closely united. For were Christ *one* man beside and among many others, it were indeed inconceivable how his doing and suffering could have any essential influence upon collective humanity ; he could have worked only by doctrine and example ; but he is, besides his Divine nature, to be conceived of as *the* man, that is, as realizing the absolute idea of humanity, and therefore potentially bearing mankind in himself *spiritually*, just as

* The whole exposition given here may be used in favour of the doctrine of the restoration. Since namely Adam's sin came in fact to all, its power would appear greater than the power of Christ, if the wicked could resist the latter, and it penetrated all. That would, however, lead to the *gratia irresistibilis*, which Paul does not teach, as will be shown at ch. ix. ; we must, therefore, with regard to the greater power of grace, lay stress only on those points which are brought forward.

Adam did *corporeally*. This character of the human nature of Christ dogmatic theology designates by the term *impersonalitas*, and Philo, anticipating the profound idea, described the Logos as *τὸν κατ' ἀλήθειαν ἄνθρωπον*, that is, as the idea of man, the human ideal. Under this his universal character, the Redeemer becomes in a twofold respect *vicarious*;* first, in that standing in the stead of sinful men, by his own suffering he takes their suffering on himself, as a sacrifice for the sins of the world; then, in that he perfected in himself absolute righteousness and holiness, so that the believer does not generate them afresh, but receives their germ along with the Spirit of Christ. The former is the *obedientia passiva*, the latter the *obedientia activa*. The latter will be further treated of at ver. 19; of the former it is to be remarked with reference to vers. 6, 7, 8, that it is commonly said of Christ in the language of the New Testament: *ὑ π ὲ ρ ἡμῶν ἀπέθανε, he died* ON BEHALF OF *us*. Meanwhile it has been already noticed at Matth. xx. 28, that also *περί*, *διά*, and even *ἀντί* are used. The two former of these prepositions certainly can signify no more than "for, in behalf of," but in *ἀντί* the signification "in the place of, instead," is clearly prominent, which, according to ver. 7, and 2 Cor. v. 20, *ὑπέρ* also undoubtedly bears. But according to the contrast here carried through of Adam and Christ, it becomes perfectly evident that the apostle conceives the life and death of our Lord as *vicarious*, so that what took place in him, virtually occurred in all (2 Cor. v. 15.)—But again the term *χάρισμα* is here (ver. 15) contrasted with *παράπτωμα* (the sin of Adam), as also at ver. 16 placed parallel with *δώρημα*, that in Christ's act of love the circumstance of its having been done *once for all* may contrast with the sin committed once for all by Adam (this being indicated by the termination *μα*).† Moments, not extended periods, decide the destinies of the race; so also in the life of individuals and nations there are sharply-defined moments on which is staked the determination to better or worse for long periods; alternative courses, the choice of which at the outset may control ages of development.

(Οἱ πολλοί, *the many* (with the article) is equivalent to *πάντες*, *all*, above, ver. 12. As Augustine, cont. Jul., vi. 12, says: omnes revera sunt multi. Without the article, indeed, a part only of the race could be meant,‡ but *with* it the expression has regard to the

* In both relations the power of Christ, in its passing over into humanity, is to be compared with a movement proceeding from a centre, concentrically diffusing itself. Christ brings his *death* and *resurrection* to every individual, the former for the old, the latter for the new man.

† Compare Buttman's large Gramm. B. ii. p. 314. The syllable *μος* denotes the abstract, *μα* the concrete, *μη* fluctuates between both. This with reference to Rothe's opinion, who thinks this conception of *χάρισμα* and *δώρημα* capricious.

‡ Glöckler is wrong in saying that *πάντες* could not be used, because the one is taken

preceding *πάντες*.—*Χάρις*, *grace*, is general, the love of God in its utterance toward sinners, *δωρεά*, *gift*, its special expression in the mission and the work of Christ. *Περισσεύω* is not to be taken transitively, as Paul certainly uses the word [2 Cor. ix. 8 ; Ephes. i. 8 ; 1 Thess. iii. 12], but as usual, intransitively. The aorist is put, that grace in its historical manifestation in the work of Christ may be set in the balance against *ἀπέθανον*, the effect of justice.)

Vers. 16, 17.—But there is a further distinction between Christ's efficacy and that of Adam, in that it operates not merely *negatively*, but *positively*, justifying mankind from the infinitely many transgressions, nay even imparting to them a new and higher life.

(Ver. 16.—The reading *ἁμαρτήματος* is found instead of *ἁμαρτήσαντος*, arising doubtless merely from the seeming incompleteness of the antithetic member. The complete construction would require *δι' ἑνὸς δικαίου* to be added to *δώρημα*.—*Κρίμα*, *judgment*, is the act of Divine justice objectively considered, which after Adam's, the first man's sin, could shew itself only as *κατάκριμα*, *condemnation*. The antithesis *ἐκ πολλῶν παραπτωμάτων*, indicates *παραπτώματος* to be supplied with *ἐξ ἑνός*. In *ἐκ πολλῶν παραπτωμάτων*, *πολλῶν* is not masculine ; the *many* sins rather are opposed to Adam's *one*. The preposition, however, is in neither case explained as "proceeding from," but "on account of, in consequence of ;" so that the sense is : "in consequence of one sin God's judicial agency passed into condemnation, in consequence of the many sins among mankind God's gracious agency passed into justification."*—The use of *δικαίωμα* here and ver. 18 is peculiar, as was observed at Rom. iii. 21. Commonly it signifies that which in a particular case is *δίκαιον*, therefore "statute, ordinance, *ἐντολή*." But here it is used, as *δικαίωσις ζωῆς* in ver. 18 shews, like *δικαίωσις* = *τὸ δικαιοῦν*, הַצְדִּיק, *justification*. This deviation from the common use in the passage before us has its ground in the structure of the entire sentence. The apostle's point was, to contrast the *act* of Christ's efficacy with the *act* of the fall ; and *δικαίωμα* expressed the momentary better than *δικαίωσις*.—Ver. 17. The dative *παραπτώματι* denotes the *causa efficiens* of death, *διὰ τοῦ ἑνός*, *through the one*, designates Adam as the organ, through whom the cause became operative. So was God also through Christ the *causa efficiens* of his work (2 Cor. v. 19).—The *δικαιοσύνη* is that which is worked in man by the *δικαίωσις* = *δικαίωμα* of Christ.—By an easy turn of the parallel, instead of putting

out. For it is the same at ver. 18, and yet *πάντες* is used there. Besides, the one continues to belong to the whole, nay he *is* the whole.

* If *ἐξ ἑνός* and *ἐκ πολλῶν* are to form an antithesis, it might be supposed whether the many sins did not designate those merely which brought Christ to the cross ; certainly ; but this was done not merely by the sins of those who lived at the time, but of all men of all times ; so that it comes to the same thing. The emphasis in this verse, moreover is laid on *δικαίωμα* ; God did not only forgive the sins, but he made the sinners righteous

ζωή, *life*, itself as the reigning power in opposition to the reigning *θάνατος*, *death*, the living [*ζῶντες*] are represented with Christ as those who reign *ἐν τῇ βασιλείᾳ τοῦ Θεοῦ*, *in the kingdom of God*.)

Vers. 18, 19.—Finally, the apostle once more comprises in these verses this great contrast between Adam and Christ, and in so doing not only lays stress on the fact that their respective influences are *universal*,* but indicates also, that the *δικαιοσύνη* and *ζωή*, which he had just before treated abstractly, as separate points, in the concrete blend with each other, yet with this distinction—that the *δικαίωσις*, *justification*, always appears as absolute, no degrees being conceivable in the forgiveness of sins, the *ζωή*, *life*, on the contrary, perfects itself gradually.—In ver. 19, the fundamental idea of the whole passage is expressed in altered terms, and with a distinctness which sheds light on Paul's real meaning beyond all he has said before.† Not the personal transgressions of individual men, but the *disobedience* of Adam was the sole ground of all being sinners; and so conversely, the personal strivings of individuals could not make them righteous (for the very best efforts of man's own powers remain powerless and defiled without Christ's support), but the *obedience* of Christ is the only effectual cause of the righteousness of all. No expression can be imagined by which Paul could have himself more distinctly defined vers. 12 and 15, and protected his meaning from erroneous conceptions. If he has still not succeeded in preventing them, the ultimate cause of the failure must be found in the heart's resistance to this doctrine, bringing, as it does, to nothing, all man's self-sufficiency, a resistance which even unconsciously asserts itself in the interpretation of such passages.—The expression *ὑπακοή*, *obedience*, applied to Christ, deserves a closer consideration here, as it involves the question of the *obedientia activa* and *passiva*. (Comp. Phil. ii. 8.) Now we must certainly allow, that the doctrine of active obedience cannot be proved from this passage, for *ὑπακοή* in contrast to *παρακοή* (Adam's eating of the fruit), must denote primarily the obedient surrender of Christ to death, as the single, unrepeated act of love, to which Phil. ii. 8 also has reference. Still, the doctrine of active obedience has foundation in the Scripture, though it must rest on other passages, particularly Rom. viii. 30.

* As *οἱ πολλοί* is said as well of Christ as of Adam, i. e., *πάντες*, it must be said, to evade the restoration, that mention is here made of the Divine *purpose* in the work of the redemption, and not its *result*. (Comp. upon the restoration more particularly at ix. 1, and xi. 25.)

† Yet Usteri says (p. 27) even of this passage, that it means no more than: "that in the sinfulness of Adam, which first made itself known as actual conscious sin in the transgression of a positive command, the sinfulness of the whole human nature was brought *to light*. How the words *διὰ τῆς παρακοῆς τοῦ ἑνός*, *by the disobedience of the one*, could be chosen to express such a thought as this, the foundation of which is the false assumption that sinfulness belongs to the character of the creature, is inconceivable.

The whole life of Christ, as such, is his work, and even his death, as its consummation, receives its significance only from its connexion with his perfect life. As death and resurrection, so in this his collective life, Christ's active and passive obedience stand related; while again we must remember that there is here no *absolute* distinction, as the passive and active elements mutually pass into and complete each other.

(Ver. 18.—Ἄρα οὖν, in Scripture, contrary to classical usage, commences a clause. [Comp. Rothe ad loc. p. 136.] In ver. 18 also, κρίμα and χάρισμα ἔρχεται are to be supplied from ver. 16. As to κατασταθήσονται in ver. 19, καθίστασθαι certainly signifies "to be set forth as something, and by the setting forth to be declared something," so that the expression is parallel with λογίζεσθαι εἰς δικαιοσύνην, *imputed for righteousness*. But as the discourse relates to Divine acts, it must be borne in mind that God cannot pronounce any one to be what he is not; so far καθίστασθαι, like καλεῖσθαι, ὀνομάζεσθαι, coincides with εἶναι.)

Ver. 20.—The apostle's readers must naturally, after this exposition, have felt it requisite to ascertain in what relation then the law, which is assuredly a Divine institution, stood to the great critical points of the world's history.* Paul therefore here briefly touches upon this question, although in chap. vii. he discusses it at large. His view is briefly this: the import of the law lies in its being a *preparatory stage* to the life of faith; it comes in between Adam and Christ, to awaken the consciousness of sin, and thereby to sharpen the longing for redemption; (comp. at iii. 30, and vii. 24, 25.) The chief object, therefore, in its being given, is not that it may be fulfilled—for no one exists who could keep it in its spirituality, as set forth in the Sermon on the Mount; and a half or imperfectly fulfilled law is, before God, a law not kept at all (Gal. iii. 10); although, in respect to man, the prevention of *gross* sins is not unimportant (Gal. iii. 19)—it is rather to be the παιδαγωγὸς εἰς Χριστόν (Gal. iii. 24). Yet, as Divine and eternal in its nature (vii. 12), it continues, even to believers, the absolute law and rule for all the conduct of life.

(The παρεισῆλθεν indicates not only its coming in between, but also its subordinate and not strictly indispensable character, the law being essentially comprised in the ministry of Christ; its antecedent promulgation by Moses was only to facilitate man's attaining to Christ.—The παράπτωμα, *trespass, offence*, is remarkable; for the law was to enhance, indeed, internal sin, but to check [Gal. iii. 19] rather than augment its *open outbreaks;* yet παράπτωμα cannot signify the

* The treatise, Gal. iii. 19, etc., is quite a parallel to this; the commentary upon it may be compared here.

sinful state.* Doubtless, therefore, the expression here must be taken thus: the law, indeed, is not purposely to multiply the outbreaks of sin, but they are, notwithstanding, its inevitable consequences [vii. 8]; inasmuch, then, as the consciousness of sin is awakened by it, the transgression itself may be also regarded as an object of the law. It is inappropriate to take ἵνα merely ἐκβατικῶς; to regard it as mere consequence, is in evident contradiction to the sentiment of the apostle, as chap. vii. 8, etc., will further shew. He regards the law as a beneficent medicine, which forces outwards a disease which is raging undiscerned amidst the nobler elements within.† On account of the aorists, οὗ is better taken, with Grotius and De Wette, in the signification "as, when," instead of "where:" the apostle is speaking of the Divine arrangements altogether objectively, in their *results;* their subjective aspect in the Divine purpose is here left out of the account. The aorist ἐπλεόνασε refers, therefore, to the fact of the killing of the Son of God, in which sin actually reached its summit, but at the same time grace appeared in still higher measure, in that the highest sin gained and made sure the salvation of the world. Rothe endeavours to explain the aorists from the circumstance that the clause, in his opinion parenthetical [οὗ — χάρις], contains a thought expressed as an axiom or proverb. But this is opposed by the peculiar character of the thought, so entirely harmonizing with the system of Paul, and bearing not the slightest proverbial character.—Ὑπερπερισσεύω is to be taken like πλεονάζω, intransitively, in the signification of "superabounds." In the passages 2 Cor. vii. 4; 1 Tim. i. 14, the parallel ὑπερπλεονάζω occurs.)

Ver. 21.—The absolute reign of grace, therefore, to eternal life (vi. 22, 23), is the final aim of redemption through Christ, while till then sin reigned to death.

(The strict antithesis would have required εἰς θάνατον or ἐν ζωῇ, but as discriminated, ἐν denotes that sin itself is spiritual death, εἰς points rather to the end. The δικαιοσύνη is conceived as the means by which grace exercises her dominion. But beyond this Christ him-

* Rothe's supposition must be considered faulty, which explains παράπτωμα of Adam's παράπτωμα more and more developing itself, and diffusing itself according to its effects. In treating of the operation of the law upon the sinful state, the actual sins of single individuals only, but not the entire collective act of Adam, can be intended.

† Augustine correctly expresses himself upon the relation of the law: "Data est lex ad ostendendum, quantis quamque arctis vinculis peccatorum constricti tenerentur, qui de suis viribus ad implendam justitiam præsumebant." Equally so, Calvin: "Erant quidem homines naufragi ante legem, quia tamen in suo interitu sibi videbantur natare, in profundum demersi sunt, quo illustrior fieret liberatio, quum inde præter humanum sensum emergant. Neque vero absurdum fuit, legem hac partim de causa ferri, ut homines semel damnatos bis damnet; quia nihil justius est, quam modis omnibus adduci homines, imo convictos trahi, ut mala sua sentiant."

self is considered as the holy Instrument, through which the reign of life is realized; an instrument, viz., inasmuch as the Father, who sends the Son into the flesh, is thus conceived as the ultimate ground and author of the plan of grace.

§ 10. The Believer is Dead to Sin.

(VI. 1—VII. 6.)

The incidental mention of the law, and its relation to grace (v. 20, 21), can hardly have induced the apostle, in what follows, to proceed to refute the error, that we might continue in sin that grace should abound. It answers far better to connect (with Rothe, p. 49) the subsequent words with the leading thought of chap. v. in this manner: "What shall we say, then, in this state of things? That is, since justification through faith in the redemption by Christ, in its specific operation is essentially the sanctification of believers. Shall we, therefore, yet think of continuing in sin?" The apostle then prosecutes the refutation of this error in such a manner, that the principal idea of the section, *the vicarious relation of Christ* to the collective body, always continues in the foreground, and forms the substance of the argument. Although, however, according to the general scope and tenor of the epistle, the following discussion forms but a subordinate part of it, it is, notwithstanding, of the highest importance for the *practical application* of the apostle's doctrine of justification by faith, without the works of the law; and this indeed not merely at that time, but in every time, and especially in the present. For, *first*, there are never wanting persons who, in fact, *misunderstand* this holy doctrine, and through misunderstanding *abuse* it. Whether from stupidity, or which is perhaps more common, from depravity, more or less unconscious, many construe the doctrine of justification as allowing them to live on quietly in sin, as if Christ would make a man blessed *with* sin, which yet is itself unblessedness, and not *from* sin. No one has ever consciously taught such doctrine, because it is in fact too absurd for the lowest grade of spiritual attainment not to acknowledge its perverseness; but depravity of heart beclouds the consciences of many, and in such a state they apply the doctrine falsely, and turn grace to wantonness. (Jude ver. 4.) But, *secondly*, this discussion is no less important for the reason that the opponents of the doctrine of justification regard this abuse of it as legitimate, and essentially founded in it, and think themselves obliged, therefore, to combat the doctrine as an extremely dangerous one. In this error are found not merely all the grossly rationalistic-pelagian theologians, but others, also, who, with no living experience of the nature of faith and of justification, are animated by a kind of legal jealousy, and flatter themselves that by their own efforts they can soon attain, if they do not already exhibit the type of absolute perfection. With every one, however, who is willing to see, the apostolic doctrine, as illustrated by this section, will find a ready justification; on the other hand, indeed, against impurity of heart, or against the conceit of self-righteousness, there is no remedy to be found, unless grace itself reveals to the heart its secret sins; at least the statement of the apostle has not itself been able to prevent the errors either of the former or of the latter. Meanwhile the Scripture fulfils, even by this inability, one of its purposes, that, namely, of becoming, like Christ himself, the *fall* of many (Luke ii. 34), not to destroy them, but by revealing to them their most secret sins of impurity, or of conceited self-confidence, to save them.

Vers. 1, 2.—Without noticing any particular party—such as Jews or Jewish Christians only—the apostle proposes the question quite generally, as one proceeding from impurity of heart in general—whether, according to what had been said, the meaning be, that sin could be continued in, in order to let grace have its full power? He answers this question most decidedly in the negative, by designating believers as those who are dead with respect to sin, who cannot therefore live in it any more.* This idea of believers being dead, Paul carries through to ver. 11, and that in such a manner as to regard the death of Christ not merely as a symbol of the death of believers, but as a *real event* in them of which, through faith, they are partakers, as also of his resurrection. Here, then, is manifest, how sharply, and with what thorough decisiveness Paul conceives and applies the vicarious office of Christ. *He* is mankind; what occurred in him, occurred virtually in all; in him *are* all dead, have all suffered death for sin; in him *are* all risen again, and have received the new life. The history of Jesus, therefore, is a living, abiding history, since it is livingly repeated in every one. (1 Pet. ii. 24.) According to the Pelagian interpretation, this passage is understood only of the *resolution* or the *vow* of abstaining from sin, which was entered into at baptism. But Paul, by such a sentiment, would clearly contradict himself, for down to iii. 20 he had shewn at large that man is incapable, by mere resolve, of renouncing sin. According to such an acceptation, moreover, even the δοξάζειν, *glorifying*, in the passage Rom. viii. 30, could not be conceived as a thing already past, which nevertheless, like all the other several

* So Calvin, when he justly observes: "Plusquam igitur præpostera esset operis Dei inversio, si occasione gratiæ, quæ nobis in Christo offertur, peccatum vires colligeret. Neque enim medicina morbi, quem extinguit, fomentum est." Yet man can hardly believe in the power of Christ without law; hence Luther says well: "The multitude will have a Moses with horns;" that is, the law, with its terrifying power.

points, is put in the aorist. The Pauline idea doubtless is, that our Lord, in those words upon the cross, "it is finished," declared the work of atonement and redemption to be accomplished not merely for himself, but also for all believers of all times, so that whoever believes in him as surely died with him,* and with him rose again. The very idea of substitution renders such a postulate not merely, perchance, *admissible*, but *necessary;* as in Adam all fell, so must all die and rise again in Christ, for *he* was *themselves*.

(Griesbach is right in putting the reading ἐπιμένωμεν into the text; as also Lachmann; while other codd. read ἐπιμείνωμεν, ἐπιμένομεν, ἐπιμενοῦμεν. The last is the reading of the *text. rec.*, and has distinguished critical authorities also in its favour; yet it must yield to the first. Ἀποθνήσκειν τινί, *dying to one*, like ζῆν τινι, *living to one* (ver. 10) is also in profane authors the usual figurative expression for "maintaining or breaking off connexion with any one." But the following discussion shews that Paul does not use the language merely as figurative, but employs it spiritually indeed, yet in its strictly proper sense. Αὐτῇ alone might have stood for ἐν αὐτῇ.)

Vers. 3, 4.—In proof of the above affirmation, Paul appeals to the consciousness of his readers with regard to their own experience. They had gone through, he says, *in baptism*, the death, nay, the burial of Christ with him, as also the awakening to a new life.† In this passage, also, we are by no means to refer the baptism merely to their own resolutions, or see in it merely a figure, in which the one half of the ancient baptismal rite, the *submersion*, *merely* prefigures the death and the burial of the old man—the second half, the *emersion*, the resurrection of the new man—we are rather to take baptism in its interior and spiritual character, as a process in the soul. That which was already *objectively* fulfilled on and in the person of Jesus, the same is through him in faith appropriated *subjectively* to man; he experiences the *power* as well of the sufferings and of the death, as of the resurrection of the Lord (Phil. iii. 10). Accordingly this efficacy can only be ascribed to the baptism of grown persons, and in their case it coincides with regeneration; in the baptism of infants a spiritual influence certainly is already wrought upon the child; but the personal *appropriation* of the power of Christ does not take place before that later awakening and conversion, the necessity of which is prefigured by confirmation.

* The old man is not to be gradually sanctified, but must die as a sinner, as Luther aptly says: "Flesh and blood abideth ever and ever unclean, until they fetch shovel strokes upon it;" that is, until it is dead and buried. And in another place: "We must scourge the old man and strike him on the face, pain him with thorns, and pierce him through with nails, until he boweth his head and giveth up the ghost."

† Rückert's observation ad loc. is quite just; that the apostle is not saying here what Christians have done at their baptism, but what has *been done* to them in baptism.

(The *συνετάφημεν*, *buried with*, is only a stronger expression for *θάνατος*, *death*. Burial withdraws the dead person entirely from view, and is equivalent to annihilation. [Comp. Rom. viii. 17 ; Col. iii. 1 ; 2 Tim. ii. 11.] The *βαπτισθῆναι εἰς Χριστόν*, *being baptized into Christ** [comp. at Matth. xxviii. 19], is only more fully defined by the *βαπτισθῆναι εἰς τὸν θάνατον αὐτοῦ*, *being baptized into his death*, as by the *συνταφῆναι αὐτῷ εἰς τὸν θάνατον*, *being buried with him into death*. The baptized person vows himself to the *whole* Christ, and Christ himself wholly to him, consequently death and resurrection become equally man's. The *εἰς θάνατον*, is not to be understood, therefore, = *εἰς πίστιν θανάτου*, *into the faith of his death*, but of death itself, the participation of which indeed is secured by faith. For the awakening power we are pointed to "the glory of the Father" [*δόξα τοῦ πατρός*], that is, the whole fulness and majesty of his being ; for even in the creation of the world the Divine attributes beam not with such splendour, as in the redemption and the resurrection of Christ. Περιπατεῖν, *walking*, means abiding continuance and living in that newness of life [*καινότης ζωῆς*, 2 Cor. v. 17 ; Galat. vi. 15 ; Ephes. ii. 15, iv. 23] which forms the contrast with the *old*, sinful state, which is in itself properly a death, so that in the regeneration, death, which has in itself a positive power, is, in truth, itself killed, that is, the life of pure spirit is born.)

Ver. 5.—Upon the necessary connexion of the one with the other, the apostle then grounds the proof, that where the death of Christ shews itself effective, his awakening life must be also powerful (comp. 2 Cor. iv. 14) ; for it is life only that kills the old man.

(Σύμφυτος is found in the New Testament only in this passage ; in profane authors it occurs, like *συμφυής*, very often in the signification, "grown to, grown together, hence, united, bound together." This sense is perfectly applicable here ; believers are considered as grown together with Christ to one unity.† Instead of Christ himself, first *ὁμοιώματι θανάτου*, *with the likeness of his death* only [that is, *ὁμοίως*, or *ὅμοιοι θανάτου*], and afterwards *ἀναστάσεως*, *of his resurrection*, is used, because the two combined represent his entire work. It is inappropriate to take the dative as *instrumental* here, and to found *σύμφυτοι γεγόναμεν* upon it. Tholuck asserts, that according to the acceptation proposed here the *ἀνάστασις* must then be applied not merely to the spiritual, but also to the bodily resurrection. But we need not hesitate at that [comp. at Rom. viii. 11], since the

* Against Bindseil's observations upon this formula (Stud. 1832, p. 410, etc.), comp. the striking refutation of Fritzsche ad h. l. p. 359, not.

† Calvin observes rightly on the passage : "insitio non exempli tantum conformitatem designat, sed arcanam conjunctionem, perquam cum ipso coaluimus, ita ut nos spiritu suo vegetans ejus virtutem in nos transfundat. Ergo ut surculus communem habet vitæ et mortis conditionem cum arbore, in quam insertus est, ita vitæ Christi non minus, quam et mortis participes nos esse consentaneum est."

bodily resurrection is but the ultimate and crowning exhibition of the life of Christ in man [comp. at John vi. 39]. Ἀλλὰ καί is not to be taken as merely inferential, as Rückert and Reiche correctly observe, but to be explained rather from a latent οὐ μόνον in the first clause, since the resurrection, as life, is more powerful than death [comp. at v. 10, 11.] The reading ἅμα καί has arisen merely from a correction.)

Vers. 6, 7.—But at all events the service of sin must be out of the question with one who is dead; for death, the sum of all punishment, necessarily frees every one from the sin on account of which it is suffered.

(Τοῦτο γινώσκοντες = οὐκ ἀγνοοῦντες, "since we know *certainly*."—Συνεσταυρώθη, *was crucified with*, a stronger expression than θάνατος, which is partly chosen to point to the death of Christ, partly to describe the death of the old man, as a painful and ignominious one. The παλαιὸς ἄνθρωπος, *old man*, forms the contrast with the καινός, *new* [Ephes. iv. 24], answering to the בְּרִיָּה חֲדָשָׁה, by which proselytes were designated. In consequence of the doctrine of regeneration this name was assigned in a higher signification to believers. In the passage Rom. vii. 21, etc., the relation of the two will be treated more at large. I only observe here, that this contrast is by no means identical with "the outward, and the inward man" [ὁ ἔξω, ὁ ἔσω ἄνθρωπος, Rom. vii. 22], for this latter contrast has place also in the *natural* man, but the first only in the *regenerate*.—Καταργεῖσθαι = συνταφῆναι, to be entirely done away, annulled in its efficacy.—The opinion, that *here* the σῶμα τῆς ἁμαρτίας, *body of sin*, denotes the body as in and by itself the seat of sin, which De Wette has again adopted, is sufficiently refuted by Reiche.* After the συνεσταυρώθη the καταργηθῇ cannot have any weaker meaning; according to De Wette it is merely "to make inactive." Yet in the stronger and strict acceptation, the thought is untrue, for the body subject to sin is not to be annihilated in the process of regeneration, but glorified. It were a forced explanation to say, that in its very glorification the sinful body is actually annihilated and absorbed by the spiritual body. Here, therefore, we might perhaps compare the Hebrew usage of עֶצֶם or גּוּף, by which the reality and substance of a thing is denoted. Still it is simpler to interpret σῶμα from the complete carrying out of the image of the crucifixion of sin, sin itself being considered as embodied. Thus Theodoret, later Koppe, Flatt, Benecke, Reiche.—Ver. 16, etc., the service of sin is described at length as δουλεία, *bondage*.†—The whole of ver. 7 is wanting in

* We shall declare ourselves more at large at the close of the 7th chapter, on the relation which, according to the Pauline conception, the bodily substance bears to sin.

† At the words τοῦ μηκέτι δουλεύειν Calvin observes: "unde sequitur, nos, quamdiu sumus Adae filii ac nihil quam homines, peccato sic esse mancipatos, ut nihil possimus

some of the Fathers, but it is without doubt genuine, and omitted only as being merely explanatory; as such it cannot refer immediately to spiritual, but to physical death; though conceived indeed in its analogy with spiritual death. In physical death, however, we are not so much pointed to the fact that the sinner is free from sin, that is, that he cannot sin any more [for δεδικαίωται, *is justified*, has a character too decidedly judicial], as rather to a *sentence of punishment* to which Christ's death also points; he who died in consequence of this sentence, even although he returned to life is acquitted from the sin on account of which he was condemned,* for he has expiated it. [Guilt before men only, is spoken of in this sentence, and satisfaction to civil justice; not Divine eternal justice.] So is man also dead in Christ, and as dead, incapable of serving sin. Thus, justification stands in no contradiction with the law. According to the law the sinner must die, and even so he dies who is justified through Christ; but in the dying of the old man the new gets life. Upon δικαιοῦσθαι ἀπό comp. Acts xiii. 39.)

Vers. 8, 9.—In the certainty, therefore, of death with Christ lies the certainty also of life with him, that is, of his life in us, for in him dwelleth the fulness of infinite, immortal life. Entirely the same train of thought is found 2 Cor. v. 14, etc., from which repetition may be perceived what deep root it had in the apostle's mind. (While the believer has in his immediate consciousness the certainty of his death with Christ, yet his *living with Him* [συζῆν], although likewise present in him in the germ, is still in so far future, as it reaches its complete development only in the ζωὴ αἰώνιος, *eternal life*. But this faith has its firm ground in the unconquerable life of Christ, which he dispenses without ceasing to his people.—The οὐκέτι κυριεύει, *hath dominion no longer*, intimates that death certainly had dominion over Christ,† in that he really died, but not by the necessity of nature, but by freely giving up himself in love [John x. 18; Phil. ii. 7]. Yet even in death life could not be holden of death.)

Ver. 10.—The relation which Christ, the life (John i. 4), bore to death, on which our hope of life rests, is yet more nearly defined, namely, that *His* death, suffered once for all, occurred only for our sins; but in that he liveth, he liveth to God. There is no diffi-

aliud, quam peccare; Christo vero insitos a misera hac necessitate liberari; non quod statim desinamus in totum peccare, sed ut simus tandem in pugna superiores."

* In entirely the same sense the Talmud says: postquam mortuus est homo, cessat a preceptis. Shabb. fol. 151. 2 (comp. Meuschen, N. T. e Talmude, illustr. pag. 170).

† If theologians of the Reformation believed that death had dominion over Jesus until the resurrecton, their opinion rests upon a false conception of the descent to hell and its import. (Comp. at 1 Pet. iii. 18.) Our Lord appeared among the dead as already conqueror over death; God is not a God of the dead, but of the living, may also be said of him.

culty in the first half of the verse; the idea of κυριεύειν (ver. 9) leads the apostle to a closer description of the death of Christ. He died not for himself, but *for* men, that is, for the doing away of their sins, not often and for ever, but once. (Hebr. ix. 12, 26, etc., x. 10.) The greatness of his sacrifice outweighed by his dying once mankind's eternal death. In the second half, however, the ζῇ τῷ Θεῷ, *liveth to God*, causes a difficulty, some antithesis being looked for to ἐφάπαξ, *once for all*, or at least to ἁμαρτία, *sin*, but neither is found in the ζῇ τῷ Θεῷ. The antithesis to ἐφάπαξ, *once for all*, may lie in the present tense by its expression of continuity. The τῷ Θεῷ is more difficult. For if the words are to be construed: "He liveth *for* God, with regard to God," this did Jesus even on earth, and in his heavenly Being he lives again not less for men than on earth. The whole thought, then, appears somewhat irrevelant; δικαιοσύνη might, it would seem, have been better opposed to ἁμαρτία. The only tenable acceptation of the passage seems to many to be that of the Fathers. Chrysostom, and after him Theophylact, take τῷ Θεῷ as ἐν τῇ δυνάμει τοῦ Θεοῦ, that is, *through* God; taken so, the idea certainly of eternal and imperishable life, which the context requires, comes clearly into view, since it is God who only hath immortality (1 Tim. vi. 16). But even so, there arises no antithesis to ἁμαρτία, and then too we have no fitting sense for ver. 11, where "living to God" is said of men, and where yet it can have no other sense than ver. 10. Accordingly we can only say, that to live to God is the same as "to live to righteousness," namely, for the purpose of furthering it among men; thus this sense results: Christ died once for sin, that is, to extirpate it, and lives eternally for God, that is, to further righteousness. Death is then as at v. 10, 11, understood as working forgiveness, and the resurrection, righteousness. And in ver. 11, the idea is brought down to the human level, and understood as a dying from sin and a living for God.

(The ὅ is best taken as accusative of the object, in the sense, "in as far as, in respect that," so that in the first member the σάρξ, in the other the πνεῦμα, is to be understood. Thus the passage becomes entirely parallel to 1 Pet. iii. 18, θανατωθεὶς μὲν σαρκί, ζωοποιηθεὶς δὲ πνεύματι, *put to death indeed in the flesh*, etc. [comp., too, the parallel 2 Cor. xiii. 4]. Reiche take it so only in the second member, but the antithesis requires it equally in the first. To complete the antithesis, some would construe τῇ ἁμαρτίᾳ also: "*through* sin" [comp. upon the ablative use of the dative Winer's Gram. p. 194]. But the parallel νεκροὶ ἁμαρτίᾳ, ver. 11, forbids this, as we observed upon ζῇν Θεῷ, which cannot mean to live *through* God.)

Ver. 11.—Hitherto Paul had conceived and set forth the relation of believers to sin entirely *abstractly*, and accordingly said that what came to pass in Christ, came to pass virtually in all believers. As

Christ died and rose again, so are also all, who are incorporate in him through the washing of regeneration, really dead in the old man, can therefore, as being dead, serve sin no more, and live really in the new man. But the relation does not so purely shew itself in the *concrete case.* As doubtless the kingdom of God, which has peace, righteousness, and happiness in its train, exists on earth, yet peace, righteousness, and happiness have not yet *dominion* upon earth ; so may also the new man, Christ in us, truly live in an individual man, without having as yet *absolute* dominion. Rather does the process alike of the dying of the old man, and of the growing life of the new (which mutually condition each other) extend over our *whole* earthly life, while to the *future* life is reserved their consummation, which without the glorification of the body (Rom. viii. 11), is impossible. Therefore the life of the believer exhibits itself as an oscillating between two opposite extremes ; its result, the final perfection of the new man, as well as the complete death of the old, reaches beyond this present life. To this relation, as it appears in the concrete, the apostle passes with the *λογίζεσθε ἑαυτοὺς νεκρούς, reckon yourselves dead.* For as iii. 21, etc., he had represented abstract righteousness, and then iv. 1, etc., in the imputation of righteousness (*λογίζεσθαι εἰς δικαιοσύνην*), considered its concrete *production* in man, he draws here a like distinction. This passage is therefore pre-eminently important to the apprehension of Paul's doctrine of the old and new man, a doctrine specially treated at vii. 8, etc., in the portraiture of the process by which the new man is developed. The common view already touched at vi. 2, that the apostle is treating here merely of purposes and vows to forsake sin, and practise righteousness, as assumed at baptism, has an apparent support in the imperative form given to the subsequent discourse. Paul *exhorts* to forsake sin and serve righteousness (vers. 13, 18, 19); he presumes consequently, it is said, that this has been, as yet, by no means done, but merely promised in good resolutions. Thence it is inferred that no *real* vicarious power is ascribed to the dying and rising again of Christ, but that it has only the weight of an influential *example.* But the conception of the true relation between the old and the new man gives a perfect insight into Paul's mode of expression. Where by regeneration a new man is born, there the man is certainly no more *sub lege* (ver. 14), but still as yet by no means *in lege*, since even the new man needs for this a full development, in which alone he gets absolute dominion ; he must rather walk constantly *cum lege*, and by no means arbitrarily break loose from the law, for against this, vii. 1, etc., he is warned, as against a spiritual adultery. Just as little, however, may he fall back again into a legal state (which the apostle censures in the Galatians), since then fear rules him instead of love, and his works are not the outgushing of grateful love, but the *means* of purchasing salvation. Yet the spectacle of the old man still mighty in him tempts him continually to such relapse into the state *under* the law; therefore the apostle gives here the wise precept, preventing alike both forms of deviation, so in faith always to *regard* himself as absolutely dead to sin, that is, in other words, constantly in faith to appropriate Christ, as him who slays sin and quickens the new man. By this continual action of faith the new man is constantly nourished by powers from above, and the *man*—the essential *self*—is engaged in a continual Exodus from the Babel of sin. *This considering ourselves dead to sin*, however, is no comforting self-deceit, but it is a spiritual operation entirely genuine, perfectly corresponding to the purpose of Christ, without which in general no real sanctification, the gaining, above all, of thorough humility and divesture of selfishness, is possible. For it has its truth in this—that the germ of the man created in regeneration in fact is absolutely pure (1 John iii. 9), and *salvation* is not to be considered as depending on its development, but the *degree of glorification* only. (Comp. particularly thereon at 1 Cor. iii. 11, etc.) Therefore may the believer, although he knows that he is capable of a greater development of the new man, look towards death without anxiety for his salvation, because this depends not upon the degree of individual development, but upon the faithful laying hold of God's objective decree of grace, which can neither be increased nor diminished, but abides unchangeable, as God himself. This "reckon yourselves dead unto sin, but alive unto God," is finally so much the more an urgent admonition for all, as even in the life of the maturest believers times of heavy conflict frequently set in, in which their new life in God is quite hidden from themselves, and they seem abandoned to sin. In such times of sternest ordeal, it behooves them, through the faith that sees not, that against hope believes in hope (iv. 18), to maintain themselves, and secure the victory.

(The addition *τῷ κυρίῳ ἡμῶν* is wanting in the oldest and best Codd. Perhaps the words have found way into the passage from liturgical use. Whether the stop be placed after *ὑμεῖς* or after *ἑαυτούς* makes no difference to the thought; after *ὑμεῖς* is the more simple as to grammar.)

Vers. 12–14.*—Sin, therefore (with a glance back to ver. 1), is no more to have *dominion* over him who does not live under the law, but under grace, than death over Christ (ver. 9); he has access to those resources of spiritual life in Christ, which are stronger than sin (v. 15). But the apostle purposely chooses the words *βασιλεύειν*,

* From ver. 12 the principal ideas of sin, unrighteousness and righteousness, have assumed almost personal forms; in order that this personification may be distinguished, Fritzsche has had them not unsuitably printed with capital initial letters

κυριεύειν here, to signify the relation of the believer to sin. For while the *law* is able to check gross outward transgressions (ἔργα πονηρά), and in it a man, even without grace, can perform *opera externa* and *civilia;* yet even under grace he may not entirely avoid and check more subtle workings of sin, inconsiderate words and deeds, sinful desires and impulses, since the old man at times represses the new, and restricts his action. Hence there is need of the constant cleansing and ever renewed intercession of Christ (1 John ii. 1), of daily repentance and forgiveness, as expressed in the Lord's Prayer, and symbolically represented by the washing of the feet. (Comp. at John xiii. 11, etc.) From this state, however, the *dominion* of sin must be distinguished, that is, its free, unresisted sway in the life of man; this in the regenerate is utterly inconceivable. (Comp. at vii. 25.) The whole representation finally in this passage (as in the following 16-21) is so managed that the man never appears *absolutely independent*, as the natural man is disposed to consider his state, but as constantly *governed by an element.* As one who is swimming in a powerful stream, notwithstanding his self-willed movements, finds himself compelled to follow the course of the current; such is the condition of the unregenerate man in this world's sinful stream; he receives his course from the prince of this world (ἄρχων τοῦ κόσμου τούτου), and is incapable of freeing himself from this stream, however he may be able, by applying his powers in true practice of law (which affords him the attainment of a *justitia civilis*), to avoid sinking yet deeper into the mire. But if the higher and redeeming power of Christ has drawn him from this sinful stream (vii. 24), he stands not even then absolutely isolate and independent. A new stream receives him, yet a holy, blessed stream of Divine light, by which to let himself be governed and determined is the highest freedom. *In service, therefore, man is always;* and there is no middle state between the service of sin and the service of God. Man has either *justification*, or forgiveness of sins (and with it life and salvation), *entirely*, or he has it *not at all.** *Sanctification*, which springs from living faith, as the fruit of love returned, has its *degrees*, and may be pursued more earnestly or more lukewarmly; but this does not determine, as was observed before, the state of grace, salvation, but only the *degree* of glory in salvation (1 Cor. iii. 12-15.) This is the apostolic and evangelical doctrine, which no force and no prudence can protect from *misunderstanding* (whether it come undesignedly from ignorance, or designedly from depravity of heart), but which nevertheless remains

* Rightly says Luther: "Where this article is gone, the church is gone, and no error can be withstood. If we stand to it, we have the true, heavenly sun, but if we let it go, we have nothing but hellish darkness."

the way which *alone* leads to God, and upon which the sincere and humble cannot err. The erring of the insincere upon it, as well as the offence which the proud take at this way of God, is most properly, as was observed before, one among the Divine purposes in having this word of reconciliation preached (2 Cor. v. 18, etc.), for Christ is to be as well the rock on which the proud are shattered, as on which the humble stay themselves. The key, however, to this mystery, that the doctrine of reconciliation without exacting works, begets in the mind the purest works, lies here; that love awakens answering love and strong desire for holiness. Thereby man's striving ceases to be a heavy, bitter task-work; he no more struggles *that* he may be saved and please God; but *because* he is become, without deserving, saved, and acceptable to God in the Beloved (Ephes. i. 6), he works for love as in his own cause. So there are but *two states* of man (ver. 14); he is either under *law*, or under *grace*. Under the scourge of the law he deals in works, and serves for hire (iv. 4), but according to strict principles of retribution, he fares by it but badly; if he is tempted he falls, and sin *has rule*, even though the better elements occasionally conquer. On the other hand, under grace, man is indeed also tempted, but he *conquers*, even though sin, at intervals, still reasserts her power.

(As regards the expression ἐν τῷ θνητῷ ὑμῶν σώματι, *in your mortal body*, θνητὸν σῶμα, *mortal body*, is used entirely = σάρξ, *flesh* [vii. 18], or τὰ μέλη, *members* [vii. 23-25]. But this by no means implies that, in Paul's view, sin is to be sought for in the body, and its sensual impulses *alone;* it would seem rather merely to signify that it commonly makes itself known in the body by excited sensuality. [Comp. more particularly thereon at Rom. vii. 17.] But in the "body," its attribute of *mortality* is made prominent, in order to contrast the sinful body, and, as sinful, especially exposed to all temptations, with the sanctified organ of the glorified one [viii. 11]. The words "let not sin reign in your body," must not therefore be regarded as distinguishing the body as the place where it should not reign, for in vii. 25 the body is described as still subjected to sin, even in the regenerate; but they are to be connected thus: "let not the sin revealing itself in your mortal body reign, so that ye yield to it, but oppose strong resistance to it from the spirit." With ἐν τῷ θνητῷ ὑμῶν σώματι, we may, therefore, supply οὖσα, *being*, or οἰκοῦσα, *dwelling*.—At the close of ver. 12, the Codd. vary much. Some have only αὐτῇ, others only ταῖς ἐπιθυμίαις αὐτοῦ, others both together. *One* dative only can be received, for the blending of the two in the *text. rec.* by an additional ἐν is certainly inadmissible. Göschen has declared for the reception of ταῖς ἐπιθυμίαις αὐτοῦ; notwithstanding, the addition of the dative might be more easy of explanation than its omission, as the mere infinitive seems somewhat bare.—Παριστάναι, to present, that is, to give up or offer for disposal. The word ὅπλα is suggested by the figure of a contest, which lay at the foundation of the apostle's conception. [Comp. Ephes. vi. 12, etc.] The addition ὡς ἐκ νεκρῶν ζῶντας, *as alive from the dead*, intimates that the service of sin is possible only in spiritual death; where life is, there is its longing for the fountain of life.)

Vers. 15, 16.—After this statement, the apostle expressly resumes the question from ver. 1, only with this modification, that he considers more definitely the Christian's relation to the law, his being under law and under grace. For as the purpose of God in Christ is so hard to be comprehended, not merely by the Jew, but by man generally, that he slowly abandons the dream that righteousness and salvation must be *his* work, not God's act; so also he is exposed to the opposite Antinomian error, that, if man is not saved by the law, but by grace, sin is a thing indifferent, and the law useless. To this error the apostle, in what follows, opposes the reasoning, that if the man be no more *under* law, he on no account lives *without* the law, or *above* the law, but *in* and *with* it. Man's state is *under* the law, when, as a foreign element, it meets him from without, and by its rigid commandment, checks and confines the resisting life; this is not in itself a false, though a subordinate state, which is to bring on the higher one of the life *in* and *with* the law. For in this state, the law establishes itself as the inward principle of life itself; it appears as written on the tables of the heart, and as one with the will of man. *Without* law, or altogether *above* the law, man can never be, for the law is the expression of the Divine essence itself. Upon this deeper conception of the nature of the law, Paul also founds his argument, in which, although he does not use the terms ἐν νόμῳ, σὺν νόμῳ, he, in fact, expresses the idea which they denote. He refutes, namely, the question, whether we shall sin, because we are not under the law, but under grace? by saying, we are in the very state of grace made free from sin, and become servants to God (δουλωθέντες Θεῷ, ver. 22), and therefore can serve it no more. This thought of the *service of God*, or, which is the same thing, of righteousness, must not, however, be again understood as an *outward* and servile relation towards God, as under the dominion of the law; for this is just what grace has overcome (viii. 15); but as an *inward* one. The soul of him who is living in the state of grace serves God, inasmuch as he makes abode in it by his Spirit, which is his own being (John xiv. 23; Rom. v. 5), and so becomes the determining principle of its life. Now, as the Divine nature has the law not *in* itself or *beside* itself, but being Divine, is itself the law, so also the regenerate man, in the indwelling of the

Divine Spirit, as the moving, governing power within him, has the law itself essentially within him (Rom. viii. 14), and cannot, *as such*, act otherwise than perfectly (1 John iii. 9). True, this state appears absolutely, in no one here on earth; for as in every regenerate man the old man still lives, so also moments occur in the life of every one in which it gets the better of the new (1 John ii. 1). The service of God in Christ still appears to the old man as a yoke (Matth. xi. 30), because he feels that it leads him unto death; while on the other hand, in his exemption from the yoke of the law, he feels himself entirely without restriction. Thus understood, the entire following passage is in strictest consistency with itself, and with what precedes it; to the false *ἐλευθερία*, *liberty* (Galat. v. 13; 1 Pet. ii. 16) is opposed the true, which is indeed dependence upon God himself.

(The reading *ἁμαρτήσωμεν* has certainly weighty authorities; particularly the Codd. A.C.D.E., etc. Still it is probably only a correction of *ἁμαρτήσομεν*, because the future seemed unusually applied here. But it is to be understood here as the possibility or admissibleness of disregarding the law. The conjunctive of the future, besides, is not found in the New Testament, except in various readings.* (Comp. Winer's Gr. p. 70, e.) The first half of ver. 16 seems pleonastic, but the *actual* bondage [*δοῦλοί ἐστε ᾧ ὑπακούετε*] is to be understood as the *consequence* of the *yielding* one's self [*παριστάναι*], so that the sense is: "to whom ye yield yourselves to obey, to him ye *must* then pay obedience." Thus the dependence of man as creature is held to view; he serves always, if not God, then sin and its prince. [John viii. 44.] He cannot, however, at any moment he would, release himself from his service to whom he once yielded himself; but the power of that element to which he surrendered himself, either of good or evil, binds him. As the sinner feels the heavy yoke of sin, he would often be quit of it; but as he hates only the evil consequences, and not sin itself, he continues bound, and sin becomes the punishment of sin. As the Christian feels the bitterness of the Cross, and the world's contempt, which befalls him, the wish may at the same time rise within him, Couldst thou be again as thou wast before! but the power of grace holds him to his good, and so becomes its own reward.—Ver. 16. "Sin and obedience" [*ἁμαρτία*, *ὑπακοή*], and "death and righteousness" [*θάνατος*, *δικαιοσύνη*] do not form sharply defined antitheses. However, as it is clear, according to v. 19, that the very nature of *sin*, is disobedience [*παρακοή*, comp. 1 Sam. xv. 23. Rebellion is as the sin of witchcraft], its contrast may be *ὑπακοή*, *obedience*. And to *θάνατος*, as spiritual and bodily death, as consummated fruit of sin (ver.

* But *ἁμαρτήσωμεν* is *not* a Conj. Future, but Aorist, the 1 Aor. from ἡμάρτησα being used in the New Testament. So Win. Gr. 6 ed. p. 76.

21), not less aptly is opposed δικαιοσύνη = δίκαιος εἶναι, the essential internal state of righteousness, as in germ identical with *eternal life* [ver. 22], which is not merely to be hoped for hereafter, but begins already here.—The omission of εἰς θάνατον in D.E. and other authorities, may doubtless be accounted for by θάνατος not appearing to the copyists to form an antithesis to δικαιοσύνη.—The ἤτοι is = ἤ, the earlier writers usually put ἤτοι once only, the later also repeat it.

Ver. 17.—This salutary turn then, Paul continues, has, thanks be to God (vii. 24), taken place with his readers; they have abandoned the service of sin, and become obedient to the truth. The same holds good of all the truly converted; the old is passed away, and a new life has begun. In the passage vii. 24, 25, this transition will be more particularly represented in its peculiar character.

(In the ἦτε δοῦλοι the preterite has its full force, so that the former state is conceived as past by; for, though sin in the believer is not entirely removed, yet it does not *control* the man, but is *controlled* by him. The ὑπακούειν is = δοῦλος εἶναι τοῦ Θεοῦ; in order, however, to distinguish it from a mere show of life in faith, the apostle adds ἐκ καρδίας, *from the heart* [= בְּכָל לְבָב, Deut. vi. 5], which marks the entrance of the whole being, with the very seat of personality, into the gospel.—The expression τύπος διδαχῆς, *form of doctrine*, for εὐαγγέλιον, is remarkable. The idea of "form, type," scarcely harmonizes with the verb ὑπακούειν; it should have been said, seemingly: "Ye have *shaped* yourselves to the form of doctrine." But in the ὑπακούειν this idea is, in fact, latent, for as the servant of sin admits its image in himself, so he who obeys the truth receives her form within him. Commonly, indeed, the Old Testament is called τύπος, as type of the New [1 Cor. x. 6; Heb. viii. 5], but the New Testament itself may also be called τύπος, as the model for the life of believers.—As to the construction, ὑπακούειν is never construed in the New Testament with εἰς, but always with the dative; it is more appropriate, therefore, to connect εἰς with παρεδόθητε, = ὃς παρεδόθη εἰς ὑμᾶς or ὑμῖν; so that παραδιδόναι denotes the guidance of Divine grace, which leads men to the gospel. This certainly unaccustomed use of παραδίδοσθαι has induced Van Hengel, after the analogy of Rom. i. 24, 26, 28, to refer it to a deliverance to errors, which, however, τύπος διδαχῆς cannot possibly denote. The accusative τύπον stands according to the proposed resolution of the construction by attraction for τύπῳ.)

Vers. 18-20.—To the *false* freedom, which the natural man is wont to find without the restraint of the law, the apostle opposes the *true*, which consists in deliverance from the yoke of sin, and in the service of God and of righteousness, which his Spirit creates in man. This conception of righteousness as a new bondage (δουλεία),

Paul justifies as a necessary condescension to the level of his readers. The notion of freedom (John viii. 36) might have been conceived by them as absolute and unbounded licentiousness, therefore he describes it as a new and nobler bondage, as the Redeemer also himself (Matth. xi. 29, 30) represented it as the assuming of a yoke, a burden. The earthly life of the believer, since true freedom never appears perfected, is represented with perfect truth as the going under a yoke or burden (ζυγός, φορτίον), though easier than that of the Old Testament. For although God's commandments are not grievous to the *new* man who lives in love (1 John v. 3), yet this new man, the real *self*, still continues united with the old man, and so far is sensible of a servitude of righteousness. Not until in the *impossibility* of sin comes absolute perfection, and God in Man is become all in all, does the ἐλευθερία τῆς δόξης τῶν τέκνων, τ. Θ., *glorious freedom of the sons of God* (Rom. viii. 21) appear. Yet even in the earthly life of the believer we observe a specific difference from the natural state. In the latter, although with some good, the man expressly and unresistingly served sin ; in the state of grace, although he sometimes fall, he as expressly* serves righteousness unto perfection.

(The parenthesis: ἀνθρώπινον λέγω κ. τ. λ., has reference, not barely to the figure generally, but also to the nature of the figure, as Rückert rightly observes. The ἀνθρώπινον therefore can only be = κατ' ἄνθρωπον [comp. iii. 5], but on no account signify, as Origen, Chrysostom, Wetstein, Semler, propose, "what is to be performed by man, possible for man ;" for Paul requires, what no man can perform, absolute righteousness.—The ἀσθένεια τῆς σαρκός, *weakness of the flesh*, however, cannot be understood, with Reiche, of mere weakness of intellect, which we have no warrant whatever for attributing to the Christians of Rome ; there is intelligence, indeed, treated of here, but the relations to which it refers are such that the comprehending of them is hard even to men of *strong* intellect, if wanting in the inward experience, and easy to those of *weak* intellect, if they possess it. Σάρξ, *flesh*, therefore, is the whole sinful nature of man, whereon more particularly at vii. 18.—Paul again calls the μέλη as ver. 12, the σῶμα, in order to denote the coming of the evil desire into act, in which sin, when it is finished, bringeth forth death (James i. 15).—'Ακαθαρσία, *uncleanness*, and ἀνομία, *lawlessness, iniquity*, regard sin respectively in its more passive and more active elements, that of enjoyment, and that of violence. In εἰς τὴν

* Excellent are the words of Anselm, ad loc., which Tholuck quotes: "Sicut ad peccandum vos nullus cogebat timor, sed ipsius libido voluptasque peccati, sic ad juste vivendum non vos supplicii metus urgeat, sed ducat delectatio justitiæ. Sicut ergo ille iniquissimus, quem ne pœnæ quidem temporales deterrent ab immundis operibus, ita justissimus ille, quem ne pœnarum quidem temporalium timore revocatur a sanctis operibus."

ἀνομίαν the idea of *ἀνομία* is extended, so as to become the entire opposite to *ἁγιασμός*, thus designating the nature of sin as opposition to law. But the apostle with profound perception makes this to spring, like a blossom, from sin itself; *for sin continually brings forth sin;* only that she produces forms ever more and more fearful from her teeming womb. Even so also, righteousness successively reproduces herself in nobler forms, until she becomes sanctification [*ἁγιασμός*. Comp. upon *ἁγιάζειν* at John xiii. 31, 32]. This expression denotes here, as in 1 Thess. iv. 3, 4, 7, the state of *being* holy, which arises in the holy God's communication of his holiness to man [1 Pet. i. 16]; but so far as the being holy proceeds from a gradual development of the new man, *ἁγιασμός* is used also for *becoming* holy [2 Thess. ii. 13; 1 Cor. i. 30; 1 Pet. i. 2].—Δοῦλος occurs as an adjective in the New Testament only here.)

Vers. 21, 22.—To discriminate still more sharply between the two conceptions of law and of grace respectively, the apostle points, in conclusion, to the final result of their development. He designates it as *fruit*, according to that uniform Scripture image which compares man, in his moral constitution, with good or bad trees. (Ps. i. 3; Is. lxi. 2; Matth. xii. 33; John xv. 1, etc.; Rom. xi. 16, etc.; Jude ver. 12.) This image is eminently significant in its decisive antagonism to the Pelagian spirit, so convenient to fallen human nature. The natural man, without knowledge of himself, of God, and of sin, fancies that he will, by his own power and adequate endeavour, produce a virtue which shall be able to stand before God's judgment; he knows not, that necessarily and naturally he *can* bear no other than evil fruit, as the wild tree can only bring forth uncultured, bitter fruits. For, granting his virtuous striving to be completely successful, it brings in its train a hard unloving spirit, and conceited presumption, and thus as inevitably has death for its reward as if the life were defiled by fleshly transgressions. The beginning of truth—whose fruit, holiness, is no less conformable to nature, and the product of that moral necessity which is identical with true freedom—is for man ever the confession that the principle of death rules in him, and that life must be conveyed to him from without (vii. 24).

(Τότε and *ὅτε*, ver. 20, answer to the *ὑπὸ νόμον*, as *νῦν* does to the *ὑπὸ χάριν εἶναι*.—Paul does not name the fruit of sin itself, as no expression parallel to *ἁγιασμός* presented itself to him; hence arises the inexact connexion by *ἐφ' οἷς*, which refers back to *καρπός*, taken collectively, and thus refers to those evil works [*ἔργα πονηρά*], the consciousness of which fills the better part in man with shame.*

* From deep experience Calvin says: "Sola est lux Domini, quæ potest oculos nostros aperire, ut prospicere queant latentem in carne nostra fœditatem. Ille igitur demum

The note of interrogation, therefore, is without doubt better placed after τότε, than after ἐπαισχύνεσθε.—Τέλος is by no means to be taken = καρπός, but as denoting the final use made of the fruit in accordance with its essential nature. *Death* therefore signifies here the being rejected as of no use and worthless; *eternal life*, the being acknowledged as useful, essentially answering its end. This, of course, does not imply that θάνατος and ζωὴ αἰώνιος have here other than their ordinary signification; but that the *figure* from which they properly spring gives to them a modified relation. To explain καρπός as "advantage, gain," is, as Reiche has well proved, here less natural, especially as vii. 4, 5, speaks of bearing fruit unto *death* [καρποφορῆσαι τῷ θανάτῳ]. In the ἔχειν καρπὸν εἰς ἁγιασμόν, *having fruit unto holiness*, holiness again is conceived, as at vi. 19, as the gradually developed result of the life of faith.)

Ver. 23.—In the closing verse there is not so much a new thought expressed, as that stated in vers. 21, 22, more closely defined. Although, namely, both courses of life bring their fruit, whose different quality decides the final event, yet their respective relations are by no means identical. Sin is altogether man's; death, therefore, the wages of it, must also devolve upon him, according to the law of strict justice; but righteousness and holiness are absolutely not of man, but the work of God in him (Ephes. ii. 8-10). He cannot, therefore, as holy, demand, and, according to the law, receive, anything; but the mercy of God adds to the gracious gift of forgiveness of sins and sanctification, the new gift of eternal life beside. Thus the lost one must confess, that through himself he has lost *all*, the saved one that through himself he has gained *nothing*, to the glory of the justice and grace of the Lord. Thus did Augustine rightly apprehend the passage (Epist. 105), while he writes: "adversus elationis pestem vigilantissime militans, *stipendium*, inquit, peccati mors. Recte stipendium quia debetur, quia digne retribuitur, quia meritum redditur; deinde, ne justitia de humano se extolleret bono merito, sicut humanum malum non dubitatur esse peccatum, *gratia*, nquit, Dei vita æterna."

('Οψώνιον properly signifies provisions, then pay of soldiers [Luke iii. 14; 1 Cor. ix. 7; 1 Macc. iii. 28, xiv. 32], finally, merited, earned wages [2 Cor. xi. 8]. So here = μισθός, contrast to χάρισμα, comp. iv. 4. How Reiche in such passages as 2 Cor. iv. 17, v. 10; 2 Tim. i. 12, iv. 8, 18 [Phil. iv. 5 is wrongly cited], can find the contrary, namely that eternal life is a merited reward, not the gift of grace, is to me inconceivable.)

Chap. vii. 1-3.—Now although the question proposed at vi. 1, as to the relation which one living under the gospel sustained

Christianæ philosophiæ primordiis imbutus est, qui sibi serio displiceri ac suæ miseriæ verecundia bene confundi didicerit."

to sin, might appear sufficiently elucidated by the previous discussion, yet the apostle, in order to leave no uncertainty in regard to this important and difficult point, deems it proper once more summarily to exhibit his idea by a fresh similitude. This comparison is taken from *marriage*, by the laws of which the wife is bound to the husband until he dies. His death allows her the freedom to form another connexion, without being therefore considered as an adultress. This relation of the wife to the husband belongs to the race universally; any predominant reference, therefore, to Jews or proselytes, is here inadmissible. Even with the nations, among whom polygamy prevails, the *wife* is the property of the husband, and is not free of him until he dies. Rückert, therefore, is right in observing that neither the address ἀδελφοί, *brethren*, relates to Jewish Christians, nor the clause "for I speak to persons who know law" (γινώσκουσι γὰρ νόμον λαλῶ). Baur, therefore, seeks here in vain a support for his opinion, that the Christians of Rome had a Judaising tendency. For as the article is used neither with γινώσκουσι nor with νόμον, no contrast can be found here, to others, who do *not* know the law (and such indeed could hardly be supposed);* but the clause is to be taken like the ἀνθρώπινον λέγω, vi. 19. Νόμος signifies here the regulation existing among all nations, that the wife is bound to the husband, not the Mosaic law. The apostle reasons from premises common to mankind; in writing, therefore, to his immediate readers, he writes for all intelligent men without exception. The way of *applying* this parable, however, to the relation of man to sin has its difficulties. The figure of marriage as significant of the relation of the soul to God is certainly not unusual either in the Old (Is. liv. 5; Hos. ii. 16, etc.) or in the New Testament (John iii. 29; Ephes. v. 22, etc.); but here a *second* marriage is spoken of, which is entered into, the first being considered as dissolved by the death of the husband. Now unless it be said that we are not to press the dying of the husband, which of course cannot be admitted, inasmuch as it is on this very point that the whole argument turns, the question then is, who is to be considered as the dying husband? Rückert, indeed, asserts that we have here no *comparison*, but a mere *example*; that the apostle could find no instance, in which the *subject* party should die, and, therefore, notwithstanding the want of strict consistency, chose this one of marriage, in which the *ruling* party dies; and that Paul might have merely reversed the same similitude, and said that by the death of the wife the husband is free of her, if that had served his purpose better. But taken so he could make no possible use of the comparison of

* Glöckler would have those understood who *will* not know the law, that is, the unruly; however, if this contrast had been intended, another expression would probably have been chosen for γινώσκειν.

marriage for the illustration of his thoughts. De Wette dispenses entirely with the solution of the difficulty by asserting, that the apostle has not chosen his example accurately, and in this, instead of bringing in the death of the party bound to the law (ver. 1), has brought in the death of the one to whom the law binds, and has continued this confusion in the application (ver. 4). As we may safely assume that Paul knew how to choose his instances with exactness and precision, we must ascertain with more carefulness who the dying husband is. Two opinions prevail upon this; according to *one*, which Origen, Chrysostom, Ambrose, and Hilary proposed, and afterwards Calvin and Bucer defended, as lately Tholuck also has done, the *law* is the dying husband. But first of all, it is manifestly unfit to consider the law, holy, just, and good (vii. 12), as abolished; it is in fact not abolished for the believer (Matth. v. 17), but only assumes a different relation towards him; he is no more *under* the law, but lives *in* it. In the next place, according to this view, we pass suddenly at ver. 4 into another comparison, for there it is said, "ye are dead;" yet such a change is at all events extremely awkward, and should be assumed only in extreme necessity.*

The *other* opinion is proposed by Augustine, and afterwards especially defended by Beza. According to this, the lust of sin is at first the husband, and the old man, the wife; but in the second marriage, the new man is the wife, and Christ, the principle of righteousness, the husband. Against this there is less weight in Tholuck's objection—"that in what follows (ver. 7, etc.) it is not the relation to lust, but to the moral law, that is treated of;" for the law excites (according to ver. 11) lust (vii. 8, etc.)—than in its assuming a second wife, while according to the comparison, the wife continues the same. This difficulty will be radically removed only by the following conception of the passage. As in Christ himself, without prejudice

* There seems no objection to supposing a slight inexactness in the *form* of the apostle's figure. He illustrates the Christian's emancipation from the law by that of the wife from her obligations to her husband. In both cases the relation is broken up by the *death* of one of the parties; in the case of the wife, by the death of her husband; in that of the Christian, by the seeming paradox of his own death. In both, therefore, the emancipation is complete, and turns upon the same general fact, viz., death. The comparison then is pertinent and forcible, the two cases having a substantial resemblance, and their difference being but subordinate and incidental. The great fact is brought out, that *death* has come in to dissolve a pre-existing relation. The more obvious explanation of the comparison seems therefore preferable to the somewhat fanciful one adopted by Olshausen. There would, indeed, be no objection to regarding believers as emancipated by the death of the *law*. For if it be urged (as by Olshausen) that the law is *not* dead to the Christian, since he still lives in it, we may answer that it is not of the law as a rule of life that the apostle is speaking, but as a *ground of justification*. In this sense, therefore, as he is said (ver. 6) to be dead to the law, the law may, with equal propriety, be said to be dead to him. Still it seems more accordant with the apostle's purpose and language to represent the change as taking place rather in the person than in the law.—[K.

to the unity of his personality, the mortal is distinguished from the immortal Christ (comp. ver. 4, with 1 Pet. iii. 18), so in man also the old man is distinguished from the new, without prejudice to the unity of his personality, which Paul subsequently (ver. 20) designates by ἐγώ. This true personality, the proper self of man, is the wife, who, in the natural state, appears in marriage with the old man, and, in intercourse with him, generates sins, the end of which is death (vi. 21, 22). But in the death of the mortal Christ, this old man is dead with him; and as the individual man is grafted by faith into Christ, his old man dies, by whose life he was holden under the law. As, however, with the death of Christ, the immortal Saviour of the world also arose, even so with the death of the old man, the new man becomes living; and with this, the Christ in us, the proper self (the ἐγώ) enters upon a new marriage, from which the fruits of the Spirit are born. But here it might be asked, whether such a distinction of the self, the "I," from the old and new man has warrant from other passages of Scripture? I refer with regard to this question, besides the explanation already given at Matth. x. 40, to the following illustration of Rom. vii. 7, etc., for the distinction lies at the foundation of this passage throughout; and I have only to refer further to the forgiveness of sins, the nature of which necessarily leads to this difference; for sin cannot be forgiven to the old man, that must die; not to the new, for this is sinless; but to the *personal self*, who is the bearer, as well of the old as of the new man, and through whom the man can speak of *his* old and *his* new man. In the reference, however, to the νόμος, *law*, there is still a seeming inexactness in the apostle's statement; but this is inseparable from the use of similitudes, since the thing compared can never entirely resemble the object to which it refers. In vers. 2 and 3, which contain the similitude itself (ver. 1 expressing the thought which forms its general basis), the νόμος is only the marriage law, or the precept, that the woman may only be the wife of one man, to whom she belongs. But in the three following verses (vers. 4-6), νόμος is the law generally, and in fact not merely the ceremonial law, but the law in every expression of it, and thus particularly the moral law; wherefore Paul's statement holds good for all times and every state of things, because the moral law is given with the very essence of man.

(Ver. 1. comp. upon ἢ ἀγνοεῖτε, *or are ye ignorant*, the passage vi. 3.—The ὁ νόμος κυριεύει τοῦ ἀνθρώπου expresses the general thought, from which is deduced, ver. 2, the special case of marriage with the precepts relating to it. The thought exactly answers to the passage vi. 7. Hence ἄνθρωπος need not be explained of the wife, for the same thing is true of the husband, as it is also of the slave. Death makes every one free from every law.—Ver. 2. Ὕπανδρος signifies subject to the power of the husband, according to Numb. v. 29. אִשָּׁה תַּחַת אִישָׁהּ [comp. Sirach ix. 9, xli. 21].—The construction *κατήργηται ἀπὸ νόμου* is peculiar. The verb *καταργεῖσθαι* commonly refers to *things*, especially to law, but not to persons. Besides this passage it is found vii. 6, and Galat. v. 4, used in the same way = *ἐλευθεροῦσθαι*. The Chald. בַּטֵּל מִן, Ezra iv. 21, 23, v. 5, vi. 8, is used in exactly the same manner, for which the LXX. have always *καταργεῖν*, though without the following *ἀπό*.—Νόμος *ἀνδρός* not the law, which the husband gives, the *imperium domesticum*, but which protects the husband in his right over the wife, and determines it.—Upon *χρηματίζω* in the meaning "to be, to be called," comp. at Acts xi. 26.—*Γίνεσθαι ἀνδρὶ ἑτέρῳ* = הָיְתָה לְאִישׁ אַחֵר, Deut. xxiv. 2.)

Ver. 4.—The apostle now applies this comparison by representing believers themselves as dead in their old man, and thereby freed from the yoke of the law (Acts xv. 20), so that freedom is acquired for them to devote themselves to another husband, even Christ (2 Cor. xi. 2). But the death of the faithful in the old man is again, as vi. 2, 4, 6, connected with the death of the Redeemer, so that *his* death was *their* death, and did not merely prefigure it; for no one by his own power or resolution can die in the old man, because no one can generate the new man, by whose birth the death of the old is conditioned. Christ is therefore the living type both of the old and new man; of the old, by that *ἀσθένεια τῆς σαρκός, weakness of the flesh* (2 Cor. xiii. 4; 1 Pet. iii. 18), which was in him, and because he bore the sin of the world; of the new, by the power of the Eternal Spirit, which filled him. From this spiritual union, then, spring spiritual fruits (Galat. v. 22), begotten to the honour of God. According to this representation, it is clear that the liberation from the law must not be an act of *self-will*. As little as the wife may wantonly separate from her husband, since his death is requisite for her liberation; so little may the *ἐγώ* free himself from the law, as long as the old man is living. If this is done, therefore, as is always the case where a mere seeming faith prevails, it is a spiritual adultery, the lust after false freedom, that is, licentiousness, lawlessness. The liberation from the law rightly takes place only where the new man has arisen in the stead of the old, where, therefore, Christ is truly living in the man. There is no licentiousness, for Christ brings with him the strictest law, wherever he works; but the *yoke* of the law is removed by that love, which is shed forth into the hearts. This love impels to do more than the law requires, and to fulfil every act with purer intention than the most threatening law can demand. For Love is insatiable, she never satisfies herself and the Beloved; she burns on, till with her fire she glows through the whole heart and being, and has sacrified her all to the Beloved. In this manner works the gospel *all* in man without law

(iii. 21) although it exacts *nothing* from him, but only promises and gives to him. But because it gives all of grace, and even loves and blesses enemies, it wins the inmost self of man, and with this all his powers. As on the one side, however, there is danger lest a man liberate himself from the law, and persuade himself that he has faith and is regenerate, a way that seduces to false freedom; so, on the other side, there threatens a danger equally great, which leads into a new, and indeed still more galling slavery, than the former.* A false zeal for sanctification, proceeding from vanity, and striving only to see itself speedily perfected in an image of its own design, often fancies that the slow but certain way of sanctifying grace in Christ does not lead quick enough to the goal, and so when the life in grace has scarce begun, draws back again under the law. What God in man has begun, the man himself (in contradiction to Phil. i. 6; Heb. xii. 2) would complete; he will not become blessed *through* Christ, but with and beside him through himself, and so destroys the delicate work of the new man in him. This then, is not merely to wake up the old dead man again, but even to despise the new true husband, to rate lightly his power, nay, to count the blood of the covenant unholy, and to do despite to the Spirit of Grace. (Heb. x. 29.) Hence it is, that Paul so emphatically warns the Galatians, who had entered on it, from this dangerous byway. (Galat. ii. 16, etc, iii. 3, etc.) And yet so strong is the temptation, for precisely the more earnest, zealous men, to fall into this error, that even the Apostle Peter, Barnabas, and others, could be for a moment seduced from the way of grace! (Galat. ii. 12, etc.) Nay, the history of sects shows that most of their founders made use of a self-willed striving after sanctification as their motive-power in collecting their followers, and, in their guidance of that striving, exercised often a frightful spiritual tyranny. Therefore the Apostle Paul teaches the true middle way, which in the conduct of this striving equally forbids a man arbitrarily to loose himself from the law, and again to subject himself to it, since Christ continues to him alike the Beginner and Finisher of Faith. (Heb. xii. 2.)† This completion, however, Christ, of course, does not perfect *out of* and *without* the man, but *in* the very depth of his own self, since he takes in full possession the noblest thing man possesses, even his

* Of this Luther says, coarsely but strikingly, "Where law and reason unite, i. e., where sophistry seeks to prove that there is salvation only in the law, faith has there lost her virgin purity."—(Leipz. Ed. vol. xi. p. 83.)

† Of the contrast between true and false righteousness, Luther speaks profoundly in his exposition of the 38th Psalm: "It is a wondrous thing; whoso hath no sin (because of faith) he feeleth and hath it (in true penitence and humility); and whoso hath sin, he feeleth it not, and hath none" (after the conceited blindness of his heart). And at the 143d Psalm: "Satan is such a dexterous master that he can make even the very best works (by admixture of conceit) the very greatest sins."

love, and fills it with the powers of his higher love, which makes him mighty enough for all, even the weightiest requirement. If he sees, therefore, that the old man still is stirring, he draws in faith unceasingly fresh power from Christ's fountain, and so is more than conqueror in him who loved us.

(Ὥστε is here a particle of inference, "accordingly;" comp. Winer's Gr. p. 271. The expression διὰ τοῦ σώματος τοῦ Χριστοῦ, *through the body of Christ*, can, of course, only form the antithesis to the ἐγερθεὶς ἐκ νεκρῶν, *risen from the dead.* Hence prominence is here given to the σῶμα, as at 1 Pet. iii. 18, to σάρξ, in order to signify the mortal portion of the Redeemer, to which is opposed the immortal, the spirit [πνεῦμα] of the risen Christ.)

Vers. 5, 6.—That he may once more render clear to his readers the difference between the two states, Paul places them alongside of each other in their fundamental features. In the legal state, the sinful *impulses* (τὰ παθήματα τῶν ἁμαρτιῶν, the individual movements of the spiritual members of the old man), work with absolute sway in man's entire nature, even to the utmost limits of physical life, so that they become act. In the state of grace the old man dies with all his individual impulses, and man can then, free from the fetter of the law, which could only bind the old man, serve God in spirit and in truth. The dying of the old, and the rising of the new man, however, are, of course, not perfected in him all at once, but through his earthly life they maintain themselves side by side in the believer (comp. more particularly at vii. 25), although the former is to be constantly decreasing, the latter ever growing. Therefore the problem is, because the old man still continues to exist, and may become strong again, never to be *secure*, and yet on account of the ever efficacious and accessible grace, never to despond, but to fight most zealously against all doubts of God's grace and power against sin.*

(Σάρξ can here signify only the old man, as viii. 8, 9; it forms

* The observation of Melancthon, ad loc., is very pertinent: "Hic locus diligenter observandus est ut *discamus dubitationes de gratia Dei esse peccatum*, ut repugnemus et erigamus nos evangelio et sciamus, *esse cultum Dei in illis terroribus repugnare dubitationi et diffidentiæ.* Surely the beloved man of God says right, that it is not permitted only, but a duty, ay, *holiest service of God*, to contend to the utmost *against all doubts of God and of his grace*, for those never spring from a good source. Yet, on the contrary, it is very wrong to smother *the doubts of himself and his own virtue*, which God's Spirit of grace calls forth, in order to convert the man; it is to contend against God and hinder regeneration. The Romish church, however, with which all sects that proceed from Pelagain principles agree, deters from the certainty of the state of grace, and demands uncertainty towards God. Such uncertainty of *hearts* is then a convenient means to keep men in the leading-strings of the priesthood or ambitious founders of sects; for since they are not allowed to have any certainty themselves respecting their relation to God, they can only rest upon the judgments of their leaders about it, who thus rule souls with absolute dominion; the true evangelic doctrine makes free from such slavery to man.

indeed the antithesis to the νυνί, κ. τ. λ. (ver. 6). Theodoret, Grotius, and others, would understand it of the Old Testament, which in and by itself might certainly be admissible, but still only where the contrast of the πνεῦμα clearly stands out. With τὰ διὰ τοῦ νόμου only κινούμενα can, according to ver. 11, be supplied; it would seem to be intimated that the law is the inducing, provoking cause of sin.—To take ἐνηργεῖτο passively, leads entirely to error; for the μέλη = σῶμα appear then to be the proper seat of sin, whereas it really manifests itself outwardly from within. Doubtless indeed its crowning development is thus made in the outward life, for a restraining power of spirit is implied in any hindrance of its outward eruptions.—Θάνατος appears again as the τέλος [vi. 23], inasmuch as the sins collectively work, as it were, for it and its kingdom.—In ver. 6, a variety of readings are found. For the ἀποθανόντος of the *text. rec.*, A.C., and many other Codd., as also the Greek Fathers, have ἀποθανόντες, while D.E.F.G. and the Latin Fathers read τοῦ θανάτου. This latter reading, however, looks very like a correction of the copyists, from their not understanding how the apostle could speak of a dissolution of the law itself. The genitive singular again proceeded from that conception of the passage, which regards the law as the dying husband; but to this ἐθανατώθητε, ver. 4, is opposed. Ἀποθανόντες, therefore, is certainly the only correct reading, for which Lachmann also has decided.—Κατέχεσθαι, *to be held*, marks the binding, compulsory power of the law. The ἐν ᾧ refers to νόμος, and is on no account to be taken, "in as far, in as much as."—Καινότης πνεύματος, *newness of spirit*, is = καινότης ζωῆς, *newness of life*, in vi. 4. The πνεῦμα is considered as the principle from which the new life issues. The old, therefore, is a spiritless, merely physical life (1 Cor. ii. 14).—The substantive παλαιότης is found in the New Testament only here. But γράμμα forms here, as in ii. 29, an antithesis with πνεῦμα, as σάρξ elsewhere, to denote the exterior as the form in which the life manifests itself. The choice of this particular expression is founded in this passage upon the reference to the law, which, in its most complete form, the law of Moses, appears to be embraced in the letter, but in this form is for sinful man a heavy, death-producing yoke. 2 Cor. iii. 6, 7.)

END OF VOL. III.